UNDERSTANDING
IMMIGRATION LAW

UNDERSTANDING IMMIGRATION LAW

Kevin R. Johnson
*Dean and Mabie-Apallas Professor of Public Interest Law
and Chicana/o Studies
University of California, Davis*

Raquel Aldana
*Professor of Law and Director of the Inter-American Program
University of the Pacific
McGeorge School of Law*

Bill Ong Hing
*Professor of Law
University of California, Davis*

Leticia Saucedo
*Professor of Law
Boyd School of Law
University of Nevada, Las Vegas*

Enid F. Trucios-Haynes
*Professor of Law
Brandeis School of Law, Louisville*

Library of Congress Cataloging-in-Publication Data

Understanding immigration law /Kevin Johnson... [et al.]. -- 1st ed.
p. cm.
Includes index.
ISBN 978-1-4224-1179-7 (soft cover)
1. Emigration and immigration law--United States. 2. United States--Emigration and immigration--Government policy.
I. Johnson, Kevin.
KF4819.U53 2009
342.7308'2--dc22

2009016883

This publication is designed to provide accurate and authoritative information in regard to the subject matter covered. It is sold with the understanding that the publisher is not engaged in rendering legal, accounting, or other professional services. If legal advice or other expert assistance is required, the services of a competent professional should be sought.

NOTE TO USERS
To ensure that you are using the latest materials available in this area, please be sure to periodically check the LexisNexis Law School web site for downloadable updates and supplements at www.lexisnexis.com/lawschool.

Editorial Offices
744 Broad Street, Newark, NJ 07102 (973) 820-2000
201 Mission St., San Francisco, CA 94105-1831 (415) 908-3200
www.lexisnexis.com

MATTHEW◆BENDER

(Pub. 3240)

Preface

"illegal" is not entirely accurate. Restrictionists frequently decry "illegal aliens" and call for their mass deportation. The use of the very term "illegal aliens" ordinarily betrays a restrictionist bias in the speaker and we do not employ it in this book. Similarly, the very term "alien," although literally the DNA of the INA, has negative connotations. *See* Kevin R. Johnson, *"Aliens" and the U.S. Immigration Laws: The Social and Legal Construction of Nonpersons*, 28 U. MIAMI INTER-AM. L. REV. 263 (1996-97). However, because the term "aliens" is effectively the organizing term of the entire statute, we must employ it, although we strive to do so carefully and sensitively in the pages that follow.

Despite the many challenges, *Understanding Immigration Law* lays out the basics of U.S. immigration law in an accessible way to newcomers to the field. We first offer some background about the intellectual, historical, and constitutional foundations of U.S. immigration law. The book also identifies the factors that have historically fueled migration to the United States, including the economic "pull" of jobs and family in the United States and the "push" of economic hardship, political instability, and other facts of life in the sending country. In the middle chapters, we provide a capsule summary of the law concerning the admissions and removal procedures under the Immigration and Nationality Act and implementing regulations. We end the book with a chapter speculating about the future of U.S. immigration law and the challenges and opportunities facing the nation.

This book provides a comprehensive overview of U.S. immigration law. It has been designed to supplement the most-widely adopted immigration law casebooks, including STEPHEN H. LEGOMSKY, IMMIGRATION AND REFUGEE LAW AND POLICY (4th ed. 2005) and THOMAS ALEXANDER ALEINIKOFF, DAVID A. MARTIN, HIROSHI MOTOMURA, AND MARYELLEN FULLERTON, IMMIGRATION AND CITIZENSHIP: PROCESS AND POLICY (6th ed. 2008). The background of some of the leading Supreme Court decisions discussed in this volume can be found in IMMIGRATION STORIES (David A. Martin & Peter H. Schuck eds., 2005).

Immigration is the topic of many websites and blogs. For up-to-date immigration law news and analysis, visit the Immigration Prof blog,), which is edited by the authors of *Understanding Immigration Law*. Bender's Immigration Bulletin (http://www.bibdaily.com/) also provides comprehensive immigration news, court decisions, and other immigration materials. The Mexican American Legal Defense and Educational Fund maintains a website, Truth in Immigration (http://www.truthinimmigration.org/), which attempts to refute some of the inaccuracies floating around about immigration and immigrants in the United States.

Kevin R. Johnson
Raquel Aldana
Bill Ong Hing
Leticia Saucedo
Enid F. Trucios Haynes

Preface

In writing *Understanding Immigration Law*, we faced a formidable set of challenges. First, this book is analyzes one of the most pressing public policy issues facing the United States in the new millennium. Immigration law has long perplexed the best and the brightest of legal minds. The heated debate over immigration at the dawn of the twenty-first century suggests the complex policy choices at stake. Immigration law and policy responds to a number of competing demands and interests that touch on delicate — and often hotly disputed — issues of national identity.

Nor is immigration law known for its particular accessibility to students and lawyers. To the contrary, U.S. immigration law is notorious for its complexity. Only the much-maligned Internal Revenue Code rivals the intricate, lengthy, and frequently obtuse Immigration & Nationality Act of 1952, which is the centerpiece of American immigration law. *See* Castro-O'Ryan v. INS, 847 F.2d 1307, 1312 (9th Cir. 1988) ("With only a small degree of hyperbole, the immigration laws have been termed 'second only to the Internal Revenue Code in complexity.' ") (citation omitted); *see also* Lok v. INS, 548 F.2d 37, 38 (2d Cir. 1977) (stating that U.S. immigration laws resemble "King Minos's labyrinth in ancient Crete").

The balance between simplifying while not dumbing down the fundamentals of U.S. immigration law in one volume proved to be an extraordinary challenge. We have striven throughout to provide the reader with the essentials of immigration law without getting lost — buried might be a better word — in the minutiae. Seeing the forest through the trees often proves most difficult for both the newcomer to, as well as the expert in, immigration law.

To add to the enormous complexity of the law, Congress amends the Immigration & Nationality Act just about every year, with the changes slowly making the law lengthier and more complex, if not clearer and easier to understand. The immigration bureaucracy (*see* Chapter 5) regularly promulgates complicated new regulations, and amends existing ones, which often obfuscate rather than elucidate matters. Just keeping up with the changes in this highly technical body of law proves to be a formidable endeavor. Ensuring that the text is current proved challenging and undoubtedly will be challenging in the future.

Change in the law — indeed, perhaps even a wholesale restructuring of the law — in the near-future is a distinct possibility. Discussion of immigration reform has constantly been in the air for many years, almost since the last major reforms of 2005. One must be prepared for massive changes in the law with little more than a moment's notice. In 1990, for example, to the surprise of most informed observers, Congress overhauled the immigration laws and expanded lawful immigration in many ways, including by creating a new-fangled — and arguably not carefully conceived — "diversity" visa program. In 1996, Congress passed far-reaching, stringent reforms that one informed observer characterized as "the most radical reform of immigration law in decades — or perhaps ever." PETER H. SCHUCK, CITIZENS, STRANGERS, AND IN-BETWEENS 143 (1998). Within months of the tragic events of September 11, 2001, Congress passed the USA PATRIOT Act, which added tough new immigration provisions ostensibly designed to combat terrorism. In 2005, Congress passed the REAL ID Act, which tightened the immigration laws in a number of important respects, including further restricting judicial review.

Preface

In the last few years, rumblings in Congress of "comprehensive" immigration reform have come and gone in fits and starts. Although much-debated, immigration reform has failed to come to fruition. In December 2005, the U.S. House of Representatives passed an enforcement-oriented reform proposal — known as the Sensenbrenner bill after its sponsor, Representative James Sensenbrenner — that many immigrant rights activists claimed to be punitive. In spring 2006, major pro-immigrant protests occurred in cities across the United States. In 2006-07, major immigration reform, which, as proposed, would have included major changes to legal immigration, created new legalization and guestworker programs, and increased enforcement measures, appeared to be on the horizon. In the summer of 2007, so-called "comprehensive" immigration reform died in the U.S. Senate.

The inability of Congress to enact immigration reform legislation had ripple effects, with a number of state and local governments passing laws designed to address immigration. Chapter 4 reviews the constitutionality of such efforts, and whether they intrude on the federal power to regulate immigration.

Besides the sheer complexity and frequent change in the law, U.S. immigration law deviates in many important respects from mainstream public law. "Aliens" as noncitizens of the United States may lawfully be treated in ways that U.S. citizens could never be. In the words of the Supreme Court, "[i]n the exercise of its broad power over naturalization and immigration, Congress regularly makes rules that would be unacceptable if applied to citizens." Mathews v. Diaz, 426 U.S. 67, 79–80 (1976); *see also* Harisiades v. Shaughnessy, 342 U.S. 580, 596–97 (1952) (Frankfurter, J., concurring) ("[W]hether immigration laws have been crude and cruel, whether they may have reflected xenophobia in general or anti-Semitism or anti-Catholicism, the responsibility belongs to Congress."). Immigrants lack many rights that U.S. citizens have and are subject to measures that citizens cannot be — most notably, noncitizens can be deported and citizens cannot be. Such deviation from mainstream public law — what might be termed a sort of immigration exceptionalism — frequently requires explanation.

Specifically, the role of the judiciary in reviewing the constitutionality of immigration laws remains in dispute. For example, the Supreme Court has never overruled its foundational decision upholding racial exclusions in the immigration law, *see* Chae Chan Ping v. United States (*The Chinese Exclusion Case*, 130 U.S. 581 (1889), and holding that the courts lack the power to review the constitutionality of the substantive immigration admissions criteria adopted by Congress. *See* Gabriel J. Chin, *Segregation's Last Stronghold: Race Discrimination and the Constitutional Law of Immigration*, 46 UCLA L. REV. 1 (1998). Indeed, it remains uncertain today whether (and, if so, how) the U.S. Constitution applies to the review of the immigration laws and how much of it applies to the law's treatment of noncitizens physically present in the United States. Since September 11, the Bush administration has regularly invoked the "plenary power" doctrine, which posits that the political branches of government possess "plenary power" over immigration, doctrine to justify the harsh treatment of noncitizens in the so-called "war on terror," with courts generally reluctant to intervene.

A terminological note is in order at the outset. Although not found in the Immigration & Nationality Act, the emotion-laden phrase "illegal aliens" figures prominently in the public debate over immigration. *See generally* MAE M. NGAI, IMPOSSIBLE SUBJECTS: ILLEGAL ALIENS AND THE MAKING OF MODERN AMERICA (2004). Because the lawfulness of the status of some immigrants is not always clear, characterizing them as

Table of Contents

Table of Contents

Chapter 7   IMMIGRANT VISAS 225

Table of Contents

Table of Contents

Table of Contents

Table of Contents

Table of Contents

Table of Contents

Carens found Walzer's justification for broader admissions restrictions unpersuasive. Because such restrictions are inconsistent with rights to free movement, the law generally does not allow local communities to limit entry into their jurisdictions to foster community self-determination, even though we generally value self-determination. Consequently, Walzer has suggested that moral limits exist on the admissions criteria adopted by any community, with racial restrictions being invidious and impermissible.[11] Once the concession is made that *some* limits are necessary, however, the question becomes where the limits on community self-determination end and the rights of the individual, or other moral limits on immigration restrictions, begin.

In the end, liberal theory is difficult to reconcile with a system of closed borders. However, the United States' legal system is devoted to both — individual rights and limited admissions under the immigration laws. A tension between these two strands of thought plays out throughout U.S. immigration law, with great ambivalence toward the rights of immigrants in a system of laws that restrict their rights.[12]

Apart from philosophical arguments, strong moral claims for more liberal admissions continue to be made by immigrant rights advocates.[13] In recent years, religious-based arguments have been made with increasing frequency for more liberal immigration admissions and more generous treatment of immigrants.[14] For example, one law professor called for comprehensive immigration reform — including calling for employment enforcement, a guest worker program, legalization, and foreign development — based on Catholic social thought.[15]

---

[11] *See* WALZER, *supra* note 9, at 40.

[12] *See generally* LINDA BOSNIAK, THE CITIZEN AND THE ALIEN: DISCUSSIONS OF CONTEMPORARY MEMBERSHIP (2006) (analyzing ambiguous status of U.S. Immigrants in Society).

[13] *See, e.g.*, Saby Ghosray, *Is There a Human-Rights Dimension to Immigration? Seeking Clarity Through the Prism of Morality and Human Survival*, 84 DENV. U.L. REV. 1151 (2007).

[14] *See* Marah Carter Stith, *Is Immigration Control: A Catholic Dilemma?*, 84 U. DET. MERCY L. REV. 73 (2007); Rebecca van Uitert, *Undocumented Immigrants in the United States: A Discussion of Catholic Social Thought and "Mormon Social Thought" Principles*, 46 J. CATH. LEG. STUD. 277 (2007); Michael Scaperlanda, *Immigration and Evil: The Religious Challenge*, 83 U. DET. MERCY L. REV. 835 (2006); Stephen H. Legomsky, *Emigration, Obligation, and Evil: A Response to Michael Scaperlanda's Keynote Address at Fordham University School of Law Delivered Feb. 25, 2005*, 83 U. DET. MERCY L. REV. 849 (2006); Michael Churgin, *Lobbying by Jewish Organizations Concerning Immigration: A Historical Study*, 83 U. DET. MERCY L. REV. 947 (2006); *see also* MICHELE R. PISTONE & JOHN J. HOEFFNER, STEPPING OUT OF THE BRAIN DRAIN: CATHOLIC SOCIAL TEACHING IN A NEW ERA OF MIGRATION (2007) (analyzing the moral impacts of migration of skilled workers on sending and receiving countries); Gastón Espinosa, *"Today We Act; Tomorrow We Vote": Latino Religions, Politics, and Activism in Contemporary U.S. Civil Society*, ANNALS 612, July 2007 (considering impact of religion on Latina/o political activism).

[15] *See* Michael A. Scaperlanda, *Reflections on Immigration Reform, the Workplace and the Family*, 4 U. ST. THOMAS L.J. 508, 518–28 (2007); *see also* James Parry Eyster, *Pope John Paul II and Immigration Law and Policy*, 6 AVE MARIA L. REV. 85 (2007) (analyzing Catholic social doctrine as foundation for Catholic approach to migration).

overwhelmed by hordes of immigrants of different races, cultures, and creeds.[5]

In modern times, we have witnessed the globalization of the international economy, with increased migration accompanying the integration of national economies. It has been contended that, in light of the economic disparities between nations, migration to the United States from Latin America today is nothing less than inevitable.[6] Chapter 16 discusses some future possibilities for changes in the U.S. immigration laws to comport with some of the realities of global integration and increase movement of people the world over.

A.　THE MORALITY OF IMMIGRATION RESTRICTIONS

Liberal theory, with its devotion to individual rights against government encroachment, serves as the bedrock of the U.S. legal structure. The U.S. Constitution, especially the Bill of Rights, stands as nothing less than a monument to individual rights.

Liberal theory militates in favor of a system with more open admissions then the United States has today. By demonstrating how radically different contemporary approaches to political theory all generally militate in favor of open borders, political theorist Joseph Carens in a famous article advocates free migration across national boundaries.[7] To that end, Carens's open border system would allow for narrow restrictions that are consistent with liberal theories of rights.

Recognizing the need for restrictions to take steps against a clear "threat to the public order," Carens would relax border controls but would bar mass migration that would threaten chaos and the end of liberal society.[8]

In contrast, Michael Walzer, in *Spheres of Justice*[9], offered a communitarian defense to immigration restrictions, which views such restrictions as a means of community self-definition. In defending closed borders, Walzer contended that the community should be able to adopt criteria that limit the admission of outsiders in order both to preserve community self-definition and to allow the community to make decisions that reflect shared community values. "The heart of Walzer's argument is that admissions decisions are the legitimate and essential prerogative of the current members of any particular national community."[10]

---

[5] *See id.* at 26–31. The experience in the European Union, which has permitted migration within its member nations, further suggests that fears of mass migration are overstated. *See id.* at 28–30.

[6] *See* Ryan D. Frei, Comment, *Reforming U.S. Immigration Policy in an Era of Latin American Immigration: The Logic Inherent in Accommodating the Inevitable*, 39 U. Rich. L. Rev. 1255 (2005).

[7] *See* Joseph H. Carens, *Aliens and Citizens: The Case for Open Borders*, 49 Rev. Pol. 251, 251. For analysis of ethical and moral issues in regulating migration, *see* Bruce Ackerman, Social Justice in the Liberal State 93–95 (1980); Timothy King, *Immigration From Developing Countries: Some Philosophical Issues*, Ethics, Apr. 1983, at 525–31.

[8] Carens, *supra* note 7, at 259.

[9] Michael Walzer, Spheres of Justice (1983).

[10] Linda S. Bosniak, *Membership, Equality, and the Difference That Alienage Makes*, 69 N.Y.U. L. Rev. 1047, 1072 (1994).

and their enforcement. This chapter outlines the morality of immigration restrictions and the devotion of the nation-state to the exercise of sovereign power over its borders. It proceeds to offer a basic understanding of the factors contributing to the modern flow of immigrants to the United States.

The fundamental truth is that immigrants are people who are influenced by the myriad of factors that make people want to leave all that they call home to uproot themselves (and, at times, family) to move somewhere new and different.[1] Some of those reasons are rather mundane, like migration for economic opportunity or to rejoin family members in the United States. Other reasons are more dramatic, such as the migration decisions of persons who flee persecution on account of their political views, religion, or war, or because of a natural disaster, such as hurricane, earthquake, or famine.

Importantly, most people if for nothing else other than inertia, live and die in their nation of birth.[2] Nevertheless, fears run rampant among the public in many Western nations that the reduction of border controls will open the "floodgates[3] and that millions of immigrants from around the world would overwhelm the United States. This deep-seated fear indelibly influences the formulation and enforcement of U.S. immigration law. Related to this concern is the perception that relaxing the borders in any way would mean nothing less than an abandonment of national sovereignty. Such conceptions betray the view that people the world over could not resist coming to the best of all countries on earth (the United States) if the opportunity existed and that national sovereignty requires closed borders.

Wealth disparities between the United States and sending nations increase fears that this nation will be overrun with migrants if it let its guard down. However, contrary to popular intuition, free movement *within* the United States generally has not led to mass migrations, although significant economic, political, and social disparities exist between the various states, such as between Mississippi and California, or between New York and North Dakota. Migration from Puerto Rico, a U.S. territory, is stable despite the fact that all Puerto Ricans as U.S. citizens can migrate to the mainland of the United States. Most Puerto Ricans remain in Puerto Rico despite the economic disparities between the island and the mainland.[4] Most Mississippians remain in Mississippi despite the superior economic opportunities in states such as California, Texas, and New York. Despite the reality of human inertia as well as the general affinity for family and homeland, any debate about immigration — from relatively minor reform efforts to broader ones — almost invariably confronts the fear that the country risks being

---

[1] *See* Oscar Handlin, The Uprooted (2d ed. 1973).

[2] *See* Migration Policy Institute, Migration Information Source, http://www.migrationinformation.org/Feature/display.cfm?ID=361#1 (quoting Professor Rubén Rumbaut on the fact that 98% of world population lives in country of birth); Alan Dowty, Closed Borders: The Contemporary Assault on Freedom of Movement 223 (1987) (offering similar insights).

[3] This deep-seated fear is the inspiration for the title of Kevin R. Johnson, Opening the Floodgates: Why America Needs to Rethink Its Borders and Immigration Law (2007). For analysis of the "floodgates" fear, *see id.* at 26–31. Parts of this chapter have been adapted from Johnson, *supra*.

[4] *See id.* at 26–31.

Chapter 1

UNDERSTANDING AND EVALUATING U.S. IMMIGRATION LAW AND POLICY

SYNOPSIS

Migration is an incredibly complex series of processes affected by innumerable variables. This chapter offers background that affect these processes and immigration generally that helps one better appreciate the U.S. immigration laws

Table of Contents

Table of Contents

Table of Contents

Table of Contents

B.   NATIONAL SOVEREIGNTY AND NATIONAL BORDERS

There is an almost natural presumption that nations have unfettered sovereign power to maintain closed borders. U.S. immigration law — and the U.S. Supreme Court — is founded on this presumption. *See* Chapter 3. Federal law — and, before that, the law of some states[16] — regulates migration. However, despite the assumed dominance of national sovereign power over borders, a growing body of international law limits the sovereign powers of nation-states to restrict migration into their territories.

1.   Expansive Notions of Sovereignty

In *Chae Chan Ping v. United States* (The Chinese Exclusion Case)[17] the Supreme Court upheld an infamous late nineteenth century law — one in a series of laws known as the "Chinese exclusion laws" — prohibiting virtually all immigration from China. In so doing, the Court emphasized that "[t]he power of exclusion of foreigners [is] an *incident of sovereignty* belonging to the government of the United States, as part of [its] *sovereign powers delegated by the Constitution.*"[18] The Court emphasized that

> the United States, in their relation to foreign countries and their subjects or citizens are one nation, invested with powers which belong to independent nations, the exercise of which can be invoked for the absolute independence and security throughout its entire territory. . . . *To preserve its independence, and give security against foreign aggression and encroachment, is the highest duty of every nation, and to attain these ends nearly all other considerations are to be subordinated. It matters not in what form such aggression and encroachment come, whether from the foreign nation acting in its national character or from vast hordes of its people crowding in upon us.*[19]

Courts, political leaders, and commentators continue to invoke notions of sovereignty in attempts to justify the many exclusions in the U.S. immigration laws. *See* Chapters 6, 9. However, international law today restricts the sovereign powers of nations to limit entry. Commentators have forcefully argued that there are numerous limits under international law on the sovereign power of nations to exclude outsiders.[20] For example, the United Nations Protocol Relating to the Status of Refugees[21] restricts the powers of nation-states to bar certain noncitizens fearing persecution. The Convention Against Torture and Other Cruel, Inhuman or

---

[16] *See generally* Gerald L. Neuman, *The Lost Century of American Immigration Law (1776–1875)*, 93 Colum. L. Rev. 1833 (1993).

[17] 130 U.S. 581 (1889); *see also* Fong Yue Ting v. United States, 149 U.S. 698, 707 (1893) ("The right of a nation to expel or deport foreigners . . . is as absolute and unqualified as the right to prohibit and prevent their entrance into the country.").

[18] *Chinese Exclusion Case*, 130 U.S. at 609 (emphasis added).

[19] *Id.* at 604, 606 (emphasis added).

[20] *See* James A.R. Nafziger, *The General Admission of Aliens Under International Law*, 77 Am. J. Int'l L. 804 (1983).

[21] 19 U.S.T. 6223, 606 U.N.T.S. 267 (1967).

Degrading Treatment or Punishment[22] also limits a nation's ability to return a noncitizen likely to suffer torture to his or her native country.

Despite the many changes in international law in intervening years, the United States remains firmly committed to closed borders and often trumpets its unfettered power over border security. The U.S. government greatly fortified its borders after September 11, 2001. *See* Chapter 16. We see echoes of sovereignty discourse from critics who view global trade agreements and the creation of international institutions as surrendering national sovereignty. *See* Chapter 16. Immigration often is viewed by the nation-state as a wholly domestic matter, albeit one that touches on foreign nations, their citizens, and foreign relations.

2.   Borders and Border Controls

Generally speaking, nation-states are organized with borders between nations. Those borders often, although not always, are accompanied by border enforcement. Border enforcement is especially strong in the developed nations of the West, which often fear being overrun by foreigners. Beginning in the 1990s, the United States has unquestionably fortified its borders. *See* Chapter 2. The European Union has fortified its borders at the outer perimeter of the common market so much that it is often referred to disparagingly as the "Fortress Europe." *See* Chapter 16. Border controls often are thought of as being part and parcel of national sovereignty.

Even assuming that nation-states possess sovereign power to establish border controls, that does not mean that nation-states *must* have border controls or ones that greatly restrict entry. Nations can as a sovereign power decide that less restrictive immigration laws and policies are the most sensible for the country and its residents. For some possibilities, *see* Chapter 16. That is precisely what immigration laws do — delineate who the nation will admit, exclude, and deport.

3.   The Social Contract and Community Membership

The nation unquestionably has sovereign power over all residents — immigrants and citizens — within its jurisdiction. The social contract, generally speaking, binds the residents of a nation-state.

Throughout its history, the United States has been deeply ambivalent about the rights to accord noncitizens.[23] It therefore has been ambivalent over the social contract with immigrants. Legal immigrants unquestionably have more rights than undocumented immigrants. In some ways, legal immigrants in the United States hold similar bundles of rights as citizens. In important instances they do not, however. Noncitizens generally cannot vote or serve on juries, for example. Undocumented immigrants in some ways hold few rights. However, in other ways, they hold similar rights, such as access to a public elementary and secondary

---

[22] 1465 U.N.T.S. 85 (1984).

[23] *See generally* BOSNIAK, *supra* note 12 (analyzing ambiguous status of immigrants in U.S. society).

education, as U.S. citizens and lawful immigrants.[24] For a discussion of the constitutional rights possessed by noncitizens, *see* Chapter 3.

C. HUMANITARIAN AND HUMAN RIGHTS PRINCIPLES

A rather large body of international law deals with a problem that existed with the old Soviet Union and a number of other nations — bars on emigration outside the country.[25] This, of course, was a large problem in the old days of the Cold War, with communist nations often limiting the ability of its citizens to leave the country.[26] A more limited body of law deals with immigration and the ability of states to close the borders to outsiders. A growing body of international human rights law, such as the United Nations Protocol Relating to the Status of Refugee[27] and Convention Against Torture and Other Cruel, Inhuman or Degrading Treatment or Punishment[28] restricts the power of nations to limit migration into their territory. Similarly, scholars have emphasized the increasing importance of human rights principles in immigration law.[29]

1.   The Rights of Immigrants

There are limited rights under international law to migrate into a nation. However, there are some basic limitations on how immigrants within a jurisdiction can be treated.

---

[24] *See* Plyler v. Doe, 457 U.S. 202 (1982) (invalidating Texas law effectively barring many undocumented children from public elementary and secondary school education). For analysis of *Plyer*, see Michael A. Olivas, Plyler v. Doe, *The Education of Undocumented Children, and the Polity, in* IMMIGRATION STORIES 197 (Davis A. Martin & Peter H. Schuck eds., 2005).

[25] *See* Thomas Kleven, *Why International Law Favors Emigration Over Immigration*, 33 U. MIAMI INTER-AM. L. REV. 70 (2002); *see* Joy M. Purcell, Note, *A Right to Leave, But Nowhere To Go: Reconciling an Emigrant's Right to Leave with the Sovereign's Right to Exclude*, 39 U. MIAMI INTER-AM. L. REV. 177, 178 (2007) ("[W]hile most nations are quick to criticize other nations for restrictive emigration policies, there has never been widespread international recognition of a corresponding right to immigrate."). Increasing attention has been paid to emigration, and the emigrant's ties with his or her native country, in recent scholarship. *See, e.g.*, Kim Barry, *Home and Away: The Construction of Citizenship in an Emigration Context*, 81 N.Y.U. L. REV. 11 (2006); Anupam Chander, *Disapora Bonds*, 76 N.Y.U. L. REV. 1005 (2001); Michael J. Trebilcock & Matthew Sudak, *The Political Economy of Emigration and Immigration*, 81 N.Y.U. L. REV. 234 (2006); Symposium, *A Tribute to the Work of Kim Barry: The Construction of Citizenship in an Emigration Context*, 81 N.Y.U. L. REV. 1 (2006).

[26] *See e.g.*, Rodriguez-Roman v. INS, 98 F.3d 416 (9th Cir. 1996) (deciding asylum case of person barred from leaving Cuba).

[27] 19 U.S.T. 6223, 606 U.N.T.S. 267 (1967).

[28] 1465 U.N.T.S. 85 (1984).

[29] *See, e.g.*, Elizabeth M. Bruch, *Open or Closed: Balancing Border Policy with Human Rights*, 96 KY L.J. 197 (2007/08); Jaya Ramji-Nogoles, *A Global Approach to Secret Evidence: How Human Rights Law Can Reform Our Immigration System*, 39 COLUM. HUM. RTS. L. REV. 287 (2008); Lesley Wexler, *Human Rights Impact Statements: An Immigration Case Study*, 22 GEO. IMMIGR. L.J. 285 (2008); Lesley Wexler, *The Non-Legal Role of International Human Rights Law in Addressing Immigration*, 2007 U. CHI. LEGAL F. 359 (2007); *see also* Sonja Starr & Lea Brilmayer, *Family Separation as a Violation of International Law*, 21 BERKELEY J. INT'L L. 213 (2003) (analyzing involuntary family separation as violation of international law).

a.   A Right to Migrate?

There is not really any general right to migrate under international law, although actual or potential victims of persecution or torture enjoy certain protections under international law.[30] As mentioned above, the focus of much international law has been on restricting national limits on emigration.[31]

b.   Visitors, Residents, and Community Members: The "Stake" Doctrine — A Sliding Scale of Rights for Noncitizens

International law has focused increasingly on protecting the rights of undocumented immigrants, but the available protections have not caught on in the United States.[32] Under U.S. law, the rights of noncitizens generally grow with one's "stake" in U.S. society. "Some scholars have argued that the interests of immigrants, including undocumented immigrants, should be of increasing concern to Americans as the immigrants' 'stake' in the country increases. By 'stake' they mean particular attachments and commitments and expectations that develop over time through relationship."[33]

Under the law, there is a rough hierarchy of aliens with different rights, all roughly correlated with their roots in the United States. Undocumented immigrants have few rights. Temporary visitors have more. And lawful permanent residents possess the most, but not quite as many as citizens. *See* Chapter 3.

The U.S. courts have not expressly embraced anything resembling the stake theory to justify its reasoning in the cases. However, it is a helpful shorthand for rationalizing the results of the cases. The sliding scale of rights can be used to explain and rationalize some of the Supreme Court's jurisprudence on the rights of noncitizens. *See* Chapter 3. As you read through this book, consider how the stake theory helps explain (or not) a court decision addressing the rights of immigrants.

2.   Protecting Refugees and Displaced Peoples

The protection of refugees and displaced peoples is at the core of international human rights law. The nation and international community often talks of obligations of nations to admit persons who have fled political, racial, religious, and related forms of persecution.

---

[30] *See supra* text accompanying notes 21–22.

[31] *See* Kleven, *supra* note 25.

[32] *See* Linda S. Bosniak, *Human Rights, State Sovereignty and the Protection of Undocumented Migrants Under the International Migrant Workers Convention*, 25 INT'L MIGRATION REV. 737 (1991); Beth Lyon, *Tipping the Balance: Why Courts Should Look to International and Foreign Law on Unauthorized Immigrant Worker Rights*, 29 U. PA. J. INTL'L L. 169 (2007); Sandesh Sivakumaran, *The Rights of Migrant Workers One Year On: Transformation or Consolidation?*, 36 GEO J. INT'L L. 113 (2004).

[33] Linda S. Bosniak, *Opposing Prop. 187: Undocumented Immigrants and The National Imagination*, 28 CONN. L. REV. 555, 619 n.99 (1996) (citing David A. Martin, *Due Process and Membership in the National Community: Political Asylum and Beyond*, 44 U. PITT. L. REV. 165 (1983)); *see also Developments in the Law: Policy and the Rights of Aliens*, 96 HARV. L. REV. 1286, 1289–90 (1983).

The United Nations Protocol Relating to the Status of Refugees and the Refugee Act of 1980[34] demonstrates a firm commitment to humanitarian principles in the treatment of refugees.[35] Similarly, the Torture Convention does as well.[36] Chapters 7, 9, and 11 discusses the law's treatment of persons who fear persecution or have been tortured.

D.   PUSH AND PULL FACTORS OF MIGRATION

Separate and apart from legal and moral considerations, immigration to the United States has traditionally been analyzed and explained through "push factors" and "pull factors." Many immigrants move to pursue economic opportunity and to rejoin family.[37] Political and other freedoms in the United States attract some immigrants. These "pull" factors attract migrants. In addition, the lack of economic opportunity or the lack of political freedoms in one's native country, for example, are "push" factors that can serve as incentives for people to leave their native countries. Importantly, traditional push/pull analysis has limits in explaining national and individual migration decisions.[38] Family and social networks contribute significantly to migration patterns.[39]

In many respects, modern immigration to the United States amounts to labor migration — the movement of workers across national boundaries for employment.[40] Labor migration, due to improvements in travel and technology, is different today than it was in the past. The information age has meant that information can move quickly around the world. Workers in India, for example, can easily learn of job opportunities in the Silicon Valley of California. Today's immigrants have more access to jobs and knowledge about U.S. society.

Recent years have seen repeated attempts at major immigration reform in the United States. *See* Chapter 16. For reform efforts to be truly successful, the law will need to address and consider both the push and pull factors contributing to immigration, as well as how family and social networks, world events, and natural disasters fuel migration.

---

[34]   19 U.S.T. 6223, 606 U.N.T.S. 267 (1967).

[35]   Refugee Act of 1980, Pub. L. No. 96-212, 94 Stat. 102 (1980). *See generally* Deborah E. Anker & Michel H. Posner, *The Forty Year Crisis: A Legislative History of the Refugee Act of 1980*, 19 SAN DIEGO L. REV. 9 (1981).

[36]   1465 U.N.T.S. 85 (1984).

[37]   *See generally* WAYNE A. CORNELIUS, MEXICAN MIGRATION TO THE UNITED STATES: THE LIMITS OF GOVERNMENTAL INTERVENTION, WORKING PAPERS IN U.S.-MEXICAN STUDIES (1981).

[38]   *See* Alejandro Portes & József Böröcz, *Contemporary Immigration: Theoretical Perspectives on its Determinants and Modes of Incorporation*, 23 INTERNATIONAL MIGRATION REVIEW 606, 607–14 (1989).

[39]   *See* Douglas Massey, *The Social and Economic Origins of Immigration*, 510 ANNALS 60, 68–70 (1990).

[40]   *See* JOHNSON, *supra* note 3, at 131–37; Jagdeep S. Bhandari, *International Migration and Trade: A Multi-Disciplinary Synthesis*, 6 RICH. J. GLOBAL L. & BUS. 113 (2006) (analyzing relationship between international trade and labor migration); Trebilock & Sudak, *supra* note 25 (studying economic impacts of immigration and emigration of labor).

1.   Economics

a.   Push: Poverty and Limited Economic Opportunity in the Developing World

Poverty in the developing world has contributed to migration pressures. As mentioned above, lack of economic opportunity tends to "push" people from a country to places where they will have greater economic opportunities.

b.   Pull: The Demand for Labor in the United States

This factor is not entirely separate from the first. The availability of jobs in the United States — including for undocumented workers — has served as a powerful magnet pulling immigrants to the United States for many generations. The pursuit of economic opportunity can be seen both in the legal immigrants who come on immigration visas, as well as many immigrants who also come to rejoin family.

Calls often have been to make U.S. immigration law more consistent with the nation's labor needs.[41] Billionaire Bill Gates of Microsoft regularly testifies before Congress on the need for more liberal admissions of skilled labor to the United States.[42] Many undocumented immigrants also come for employment available in the United States.

3.   Push: Migration Pressures Resulting from U.S. Foreign Policy

With the globalization of the economy, increasing attention has been paid to the relationship between migration and international trade.[44] The North American Free Trade Agreement, World Trade Organization, European Union, and other multilateral arrangements, and related "market adjustments" have an impact on immigration. *See* Chapter 16. Some observers claim that trade agreements exacerbate economic inequality and hurt workers. U.S. international economic polices have been charged with increasing poverty and wealth disparities in other nations, which in turn have contributed to migration pressures. In North America, the North America Free Trade Agreement, which did not squarely address

---

[41] *See, e.g.*, Susan Martin & B. Lindsay Lowell, *Competing for Skills: U.S. Immigration Policy Since 1990*, 11 L. & Bus. Rev. Am. 387 (2005); Jonathan G. Goodrich, Comment, *Help Wanted: Looking for a Visa System that Promotes the U.S. Economy and National Security*, 42 U. Rich. L. Rev. 975 (2008); Devon M. Collins, Note, *Toward a More Federalist Employment-Based Immigration System*, 25 Yale L. & Pol'y Rev. 349 (2007).

[42] *See* Robert Pear, *High-Tech Titans Strike Out on Immigration Bill*, N.Y. Times, Jun. 25, 2007, at A1; Kim Hart, *Gates Calls on Congress for Science Education, Visas*, Wash. Post, Mar. 13, 2008 at D3; Chris Nuttall, *Intel Chief Calls for Easing of Visa Curbs*, Fin. Times, Feb. 8, 2006, at 6; S. Mitra Kalita, *For Green Card Applicants, Waiting is the Hardest Part*, Wash. Post, July 23, 2005, at D1. *See generally* Ayelet Shachar, *The Race for Talent: Highly Skilled Migrants and Competitive Immigrant Regimes*, 81 N.Y.U. L. Rev. 148 (2006).

[44] *See* Patricia Fernandez-Kelly, *Introduction: NAFTA and Beyond: Alternative Perspectives in the Study of Global Trade and Development*, 610 Annals 6 (2007); Jagdeep S. Bhandari, *International Migration and Trade: A Multi-Disciplinary Synthesis*, 6 Rich. J. Global L. & Bus. 113 (2006); Jagdeep S. Bhandari, *Migration and Trade Policies: Symmetry or Paradox?*, 6 J. Int'l Bus. & L. 17 (2007).

migration,[45] *see* Chapter 16, caused some economic dislocation in Mexico, that according to some observers, contributed to migration pressures.[46]

Similarly, the foreign policy measures of the U.S. government to promote democracy have at times contributed to civil war and violence. Civil wars in El Salvador and Guatemala in the 1980s resulted in the migration of hundreds of thousands of people fleeing those countries, many making their way to the United States.[47] Some commentators contend that support for authoritarian regimes by the United States in Central America in the 1970s and 1980s contributed to civil strife in that region.[48] The same has been said of Haiti in the 1980s and 1990s.[49]

Military conflicts unquestionably result in migration flows. War in Iraq after September 11, 2001 led to massive flows of refugees out of the country.[50] This is nothing new but was evident in the aftermath of the Vietnam conflict.[51] Persecution and violence in the Sudan, Kenya, and other African nations have resulted in population displacements.[52]

---

[45] *See* Kevin R. Johnson, *Free Trade and Closed Borders: NAFTA and Mexican Immigration to the United States*, 27 U.C. DAVIS L. REV. 937, 954–59 (1994).

[46] *See* Teresa A. Miller, A *New Neo-Liberal Economic Policies and the Criminalization of Undocumented Migration*, 61 SMU L. REV. 171, 178–80 (2008). *See generally* Ranko Shiraki Olivier, *In the Twelve Years of NAFTA, the Treaty Gave to Me . . . What Exactly?: An Assessment of Economic, Social, and Political Developments in Mexico Since 1994 and Their Impact on Mexican Immigration into the United States*, 10 HARV. LATINO L. REV. 53 (2007) (reviewing data suggesting that NAFTA had negative economic impacts on Mexico).

[47] *See generally* Eli Coffino, Note, *A Long Road to Residency: The Legal History of Salvadoran & Guatemalan Immigration to the United States with a Focus on NACARA*, 14 CARDOZO J. INT'L & COMP. L. 177, 178 (2006).

[48] *See supra* note 47 (citing authority).

[49] *See, e.g.*, Sale v. Haitian Centers Council, Inc., 509 U.S. 155 (1993) (upholding interdiction and repatriation program in which persons fleeing Haiti were returned there). For commentary on the case, *see* Harold H. Koh, *The "Haiti Paradigm" in United States Human Rights Policy*, 103 YALE L.J. 2391, 2391 (1994); Harold H. Koh, *Reflections on Refoulment and Haitian Centers Council*, 35 HARV. INT'L L.J. 1 (1994).

[50] *See* Neil MacFarquhar, *Leaving Home Behind to Escape a Nightmare*, N.Y. TIMES, June 22, 2008, at A15; Dawna Friesen, *Iraqi Refugees Weighing Down Syria*, NBC NEWS, Sept. 21, 2007, *available at* http://worldblog.msnbc.msn.com/archive/2007; Lorraine Ali, *When Home Becomes Hell*, NEWSWEEK, Mar. 19, 2007, at 44; Scott Wilson, *Iraqi Refugees Overwhelm Syria*, Wash. Post, Feb. 3, 2005, at A18; *see also* UNITED NATIONS REFUGEE AGENCY, 2007 GLOBAL TRENDS: REFUGEES, ASYLUM-SEEKERS RETURNEES, INTERNALLY DISPLACED AND STATELESS PERSONS (June 2008), *available at* http://www.unhcr.org/statistics/STATISTICS/4852366f2.pdf (offering a statistical picture of current state of refugees).

[51] *See* Harvey Gee, Book Review, *Some Thought and Truths About Immigration Myths: The "Huddled Masses" Myth: Immigration and Civil Rights*, 39 VAL. U. L. REV. 939, 946–951 (2005) (book review); Harvey Gee, *The Refugee Burden: A Closer Look at the Refugee Act of 1980*, 26 N.C. J. INT'L L. & COM. REG. 559 (2001) (book review) (discussing nativist reaction in the United States to Vietnamese refugees that contributed to passage of the Refugee Act of 1980).

[52] *See* M. Rafiqul Islam, *The Sudanese Darfur Crisis and Internally Displaced Persons in International Law: The Least Protection for the Most Vulnerable*, 18 INT'L J. REFUGEE L. 354 (2006); Zachary A. Lomo. *The Struggle for Protection of the Rights of Refugees and IDPS in Africa: Making the Existing International Legal Regime Work*, 18 BERKELEY J. INT'L L. 268 (2000); Charles Mwalimu, *The Legal Framework on Admission and Resettlement of African Refugees with an Emphasis on Kenya, Tanzania, and Uganda*, 18 EMORY INT'L L. REV. 455 (2004).

Environmental disasters also can result in migration flows.[53] Severe economic circumstances can as well.[54] There is a long history of such migration, with the Irish potato famine of the 1800s a memorable example.[55]

E. THE IMPACTS OF IMMIGRATION ON THE UNITED STATES

The impacts on immigration to the United States are often hotly contested but, at the same time, greatly influence the public dialogue over immigration. The following pages sketch the contours of the debate.

1. Economic Impacts

Restrictionists and immigrant rights advocates often engage in high-pitched debates over whether immigrants hurt or help the U.S. economy.[56] From an economic perspective, labor and capital are fungible factors of production in a market economy. Migration to the United States directly affects the labor supply in this country and thus directly impacts the domestic economy.[57] An increase to a factor of production ordinarily would be viewed as a net positive to the economy. Matters are complicated when it comes to immigration, however.

Advocates for immigration come from the mainstream business community, as well as from immigrant rights activists. It is not exclusively low-skilled labor that employers demand. As mentioned previously, Bill Gates, billionaire founder of Microsoft, often complains that immigration restrictions hamper employers from securing skilled workers from other countries.[58]

Economists marshal arguments favoring liberal migration between nations and the ready mobility of labor. The labor market benefits of immigrant workers to the United States are undeniable. Nonetheless, as one policy analyst put it,

> U.S. immigration policy is based on denial. Most lawmakers in the United States have largely embraced the process of economic "globaliza-tion," yet stubbornly refuse to acknowledge that increased migration, especially from developing nations, is an integral and inevitable part of this

---

[53] *See* Brooke Havard, Comment, *Seeking Protection: Recognition of Environmentally Displaced Persons Under International Human Rights Law*, 18 VILL. ENVIRONMENT'L L.J.. 65 (2007).

[54] *See* Francis Gabor & John B. Rosenquest IV, *The Unsettled Status of Economic Refugees from the American and International Legal Perspectives — A Proposal for Recognition Under Existing International Law*, 41 TEX. INT'L L.J. 275 (2006).

[55] *See* OSCAR HANDLIN, BOSTON'S IMMIGRANTS: A STUDY IN ACCULTURATION 50–51 (1959) (discussing Irish immigration to United States during this period); STEPHEN THERNSTROM, POVERTY AND PROGRESS: SOCIAL MOBILITY IN A NINETEENTH CENTURY CITY 17–21, 25–26 (1977) (same); Lolita Buckner Innis, *Dutch Uncle Sam: Immigration Reform and Notions of Family*, 36 BRANDEIS J. FAM. L. 177, 185–86 (1997/98).

[56] *See* JOHNSON, *supra* note 3, at 131–67; BILL ONG HING, TO BE AN AMERICAN: CULTURAL PLURALISM AND THE RHETORIC OF ASSIMILATION 76–145 (2000).

[57] For a discussion of the role of immigrants in the U.S. labor market, *see* CONGRESSIONAL BUDGET OFFICE, THE ROLE OF IMMIGRANTS IN THE U.S. LABOR MARKET (Nov. 2005).

[58] *See supra* note 42 (citing authorities).

process. Instead, they continue in an impossible quest that began shortly after World War II: the creation of a transnational market in goods and services without a corresponding transnational market for the workers who make those goods and provide those services. *In defiance of economic logic, U.S. lawmakers formulate immigration policies to regulate the entry of foreign workers into the country that are largely unrelated to the economic policies they formulate to regulate international commerce.* Even in the case of Mexico . . . , the U.S. government tries to impose the same arbitrary limits on immigration as it does on a country as remote as Mongolia. Moreover, while the global trade of goods, services, and capital is regulated through multilateral institutions and agreements, U.S. policy-makers persist in viewing immigration as primarily a matter of domestic law enforcement. . . . Lawmakers must devise a realistic solution to this dilemma. *Perpetuating the status quo by pouring ever larger amounts of money into the enforcement of immigration policies that are in conflict with economic reality will do nothing to address the underlying problem.*[59]

In a similar vein, the Immigration Policy Center contends that "current U.S. immigration policies remain largely unresponsive to the labor needs of the U.S. economy by imposing arbitrary and static limits on employment-based immigration that have merely diverted labor migration to the undocumented channels or further clogged the family-based immigration system."[60]

As many economists have observed, the domestic economy benefits from an expanding labor force that allows steady economic growth with a minimum of inflation. Economists have credited the influx of immigrant labor with helping to spark the economic boom times of the 1990s, one of the more sustained periods of economic growth in U.S. history.[61] The much-revered former chair of the Federal Reserve Board, Alan Greenspan, opined that immigrants contributed more than their fair share to the economy.[62] Many immigrants assume low-wage jobs that are not particularly easy for employers in many parts of the country to fill at the wage level they want to pay.[63]

The global economy has become increasingly competitive. Some U.S. employers bank — figuratively and literally — on undocumented labor in order to compete in the global marketplace. Low-cost immigrant labor increases a business's capacity to

---

[59] Walter A. Ewing, *From Denial to Acceptance: Effectively Regulating Immigration to the United States*, 16 STAN. L. & POL'Y REV. 445, 445–46 (2005) (emphasis added).

[60] IMMIGRATION POLICY CENTER, ECONOMIC GROWTH & IMMIGRATION: BRIDGING THE DEMOGRAPHIC DIVIDE (Nov. 2005).

[61] *See* AMERICAN IMMIGRATION LAW FOUNDATION, MEXICAN IMMIGRANT WORKERS AND THE U.S. ECONOMY: AN INCREASINGLY VITAL ROLE (2002); ANDREW SUM ET AL., IMMIGRANT WORKERS AND THE GREAT AMERICAN JOB MACHINE: THE CONTRIBUTIONS OF NEW FOREIGN IMMIGRATION TO NATIONAL AND REGIONAL LABOR FORCE GROWTH IN THE 1990s (National Business Roundtable, 2002).

[62] *See* Richard W. Stevenson, *Greenspan Holds Forth Before a Friendly Panel*, N.Y. TIMES, Jan. 27, 2000, at C1; *Alan Greenspan is Embraced as a Champion of the Huddled Masses*, WALL ST. J., Mar. 14, 2000.

[63] *See* RAKESH KOCHHAR, LATINO LABOR REPORT, 2004: MORE JOBS BUT AT LOWER WAGES 1–2 (Pew Hispanic Center, May 2005), *available at* http://pewhispanic.org/files/reports/45.pdf (last visited Aug. 24, 2008).

compete and benefits employers and the U.S. economy as a whole. Consumers benefit from lower prices for many commodities, including fruit and vegetables, meat and poultry, and for services, such as domestic service work, and in hotels and restaurants, as well as in the construction industry. In addition, the money spent by immigrants — including undocumented immigrants — on goods and services spurs further economic activity. Immigrant expenditures have postive ripple effects throughout the entire U.S. economy.[64]

Large employers in certain industries in the United States rely heavily on undocumented immigrants. Entire industries, such as agriculture, meat and poultry processing, construction, and hotels and restaurants, for example, often employ undocumented labor. This dependence on undocumented labor has led to resistance to federal immigration enforcement efforts, especially workplace enforcement. For example, when the federal government began an operation to enforce the laws barring the employment of undocumented immigrants in meat packing plants in Nebraska in 1999, state and local politicians protested because of the impacts on the state economy.[65] An American Farm Bureau Federation study concluded that, "*if agriculture's access to migrant labor were cut off, as much as $5–9 billion in annual production of . . . commodities . . . would be lost in the short term. Over the longer term, this annual loss would increase to $6.5–12 billion as the shock worked its way through the sector.*"[66]

At times, the U.S. government has stepped-up workplace enforcement. The last few years have seen increased numbers of workplace raids.[67] For example, in May 2008, in Postville, Iowa, the U.S. government engaged in the largest raid on undocumented workers at a single site in U.S. history.[68] Helicopters, buses, vans encircled the western edge of town in a massive law enforcement operation; nearly 900 agents surrounded the Agriprocessors plant, the nation's largest kosher

---

[64] *See* JOHNSON, *supra* note 3, at 139–41.

[65] *See* David Bacon, *And the Winner Is . . .* , AM. PROSPECT, Nov. 2005, at A12.

[66] *See* AMERICAN FARM BUREAU FEDERATION, IMPACT OF MIGRANT LABOR RESTRICTIONS ON THE AGRICULTURAL SECTOR 1 (Feb. 2006) (emphasis added).

[67] *See, e.g.*, Raquel Aldana, *Of Katz and "Aliens": Privacy Expectations and the Immigration Raids*, 41 U.C. DAVIS L. REV. 1081, 1092–96 (2008) (discussing raids of meatpacking plants in December 2006); Anil Kalhan, *The Fourth Amendment and Privacy Implications of Interior Immigration Enforcement*, 41 U.C. DAVIS L. REV. 1137 (2008) (analyzing legal impacts of raids and other forms of interior immigration enforcement); David B. Thronson, *Immigration Raids and the Destabilization of Immigrant Families*, 43 WAKE FOREST L. REV. 391 (2008) (identifying negative impacts on families of immigration raids); *see also* Huyen Pham, *The Private Enforcement of the Immigration Laws*, 96 GEO. L.J. 777 (2008) (studying various modes of private enforcement of the immigration laws); Shoba Sivaprasad Wadhia, *Under Arrest: Immigrants' Rights and the Rule of Law*, 38 U. MEMP. L. REV. 853, 862–88 (2008).

The U.S. government has conducted immigration raids at worksites across the United States. *See, e.g.*, William Wan, *Authorities Detain 45 in Immigration Raid of Painting Company*, WASH. POST, July 1, 2008, at B2 (Maryland); Anna Gorman, *U.S.-Born Children Feel Effect of Raids*, L.A. TIMES, June 8, 2008, at B1 (California); Libby Sander, *Immigration Raid Yields 62 Arrests in Illinois*, N.Y. TIMES, Apr. 5, 2007, at A12 (Illinois); Pam Belluck, *Lawyers Say U.S. Acted in Bad Faith After Immigrant Raid in Massachusetts*, N.Y. TIMES, Mar. 22, 2007, at A1 (Massachusetts); Julia Preston, *Immigration Raid Draws Protest From Labor Officials*, N.Y. TIMES, Jan. 26, 2007, at A7 (North Carolina).

[68] Spencer S. Hsu, *Immigration Raid Jars a Small Town*, WASH. POST, May 18, 2008, at A1.

slaughterhouse and meat-packing plant.[69] In mass proceedings, many of the workers pled guilt to criminal immigration charges. Many observers protested.[70]

Do such enforcement measures make economic sense? The answer is far from clear. John Kenneth Galbraith, perhaps the leading economist of his generation, has emphasized that

> [w]ere all the illegals in the United States suddenly to return home, the effect on the United States economy would . . . be little less than disastrous. . . . A large amount of useful, if often tedious, work . . . would go unperformed. Fruits and vegetables in Florida, Texas, and California would go unharvested. Food prices would rise spectacularly. Mexicans wish to come to the United States; they are wanted; they add visibly to our well-being. . . . Without them, the American economy would suffer. . . .[71]

Despite the tangible economic benefits bestowed on the nation by immigrants, U.S. immigration law has been deeply ambivalent, if not downright schizophrenic, about immigration and immigrant workers. Overall, the law has done a poor job of balancing the economic interests at stake. The U.S. government often fails to consider basic labor economics in formulating immigration law and policy. As a result, the nation has created a system in which undocumented workers are integral to the national economy but, at the very same time, find themselves exploited, marginalized, and abused. *See* Chapter 16. To make matters worse, because the labor pool depends on the vagaries of immigration enforcement, employers may face fluctuating supplies of labor, which necessarily affects productivity.

While the political clamor for immigration enforcement continues unabated, attention to the aggregate economic consequences of immigration has been minimal. Globalization of the world economy has been steadily proceeding over the post-World War II period. By the end of the twentieth century, economic integration of national economies had been achieved to a level never previously attained. For better or worse, multinational corporations have come to dominate the economies of many nations all over the world.

Despite globalization, and despite the increasingly interlinked economies between nations, the increasing prominence of borders, border guards, and border enforcement serve to limit the movement of people into the United States. Oddly enough, the United States continues to treat labor and goods and services differently. It embraces comprehensive immigration restrictions as it simultaneously opens its borders to trade and flows of capital, goods, and services. As Kitty Calavita has aptly observed, "the irony is that in this period of globalization marked by its free movement of capital and goods, the movement of labor is subject to greater restrictions than at the dawn of the Industrial Revolution."[72]

---

[69] *See id.*

[70] *See, e.g.*, Erik Camayd-Freixas, *Interpreting After the Largest Ice Raid in U.S. History: A Personal Account*, N.Y. TIMES, July 14, 2008; *The Shame of Postville*, N.Y. TIMES, July 13, 2008, at WK11.

[71] JOHN KENNETH, GALBRAITH, THE NATURE OF MASS POVERTY 134 (1979).

[72] KITTY CALAVITA, U.S. IMMIGRATION LAW AND THE CONTROL OF LABOR, 1820–1924, at 152 (1984).

There is one critically important — and rather obvious — difference between goods and people: Workers are human beings. New people bring families, cultures, languages, and change to the nation. What they bring therefore is qualitatively different than that brought by an influx of foreign capital or goods. As Max Frisch wrote in discussing guest workers in Germany, "[w]e wanted workers, but humans came.[73] This fact, as a political matter, seriously complicates the debate over immigration. People fear the cultural and other change brought by new people[74] which is discussed later in this Chapter. That fear, in part, animates the nativism that has arisen time and again in U.S. history. *See* Chapter 2. Such fears at various times have been allowed to trump economic imperatives.

It is true that immigrants transform the societies they join. But this transformation has occurred time and time again in world, and U.S., history. In many respects, change in societies is natural, expected, and essential to survival. Immigrants therefore should be viewed as the economic, social, and cultural lifeblood of U.S. society, rather than as a threat to be feared and punished.

2.   The Economic Benefits of Immigration

The 2005 Economic Report of the President analyzes in detail the positive effects of immigration on the economy. The Report unequivocally concludes that "[a] *comprehensive accounting of the benefits and costs of immigration shows that the benefits of immigration exceed the costs.*"[75]

The federal government is not alone in this conclusion. Long an unabashed supporter of easy labor migration, the *Wall Street Journal* proclaimed in 1984 that "[i]f Washington still wants to 'do something' about immigration, we propose a five-word [constitutional] amendment: There shall be open borders."[76] This sentiment is far from a humanitarian gesture. As discussed above, employers and business gain handsomely from the ready availability of relatively inexpensive labor, which is particularly advantageous in highly competitive industries. Put bluntly, employers generally support more open immigration policies because of the profits that they hope to reap through the employment of immigrant labor.

At various times in U.S. history, business interests have vigorously supported less restrictive immigration laws.[77] Driven by the profit motive, employers may be expected to support policies, including guest worker programs and lax enforcement of the laws barring businesses from employing undocumented

---

[73] Max Frisch, *Uberfremdung I, in* Schweiz Als Heimat? 219 (1990).

[74] *See, e.g.,* Samuel P. Huntington, Who Are We?: The Challenges to National Identity (2004); Victor Davis Hanson, Mexifornia: A State of Becoming (2003); Peter Brimelow, Alien Nation: Common Sense About America's Immigration Disaster (1995).

[75] Economic Report of the President 93 (2005) (emphasis added).

[76] *In Praise of Huddled Masses,* Wall St. J., July 3, 1984, at 24; *see The Simpson Curtain,* Wall St. J., Feb. 1, 1990, at A8 ("Our view is, borders should be open.").

[77] *See* Calavita, *supra* note 72, at 151–57 (analyzing business efforts to loosen immigration restrictions in the 1920s); Julian Samora, Los Mojados: The Wetback Story 33–57 (1971) (contending that the Border Patrol's enforcement efforts were closely related to the needs of growers); John A. Scanlan, *Immigration Law and the Illusion of Numerical Control,* 36 U. Miami L. Rev. 819, 836 (1982) (recognizing business goals to ease restrictive immigration policies).

immigrants, which allow them ready access to relatively inexpensive immigrant labor. Employers resist and aggressively fight efforts at meaningful enforcement of the immigration laws. Even with congressional passage of the Immigration Control Act of 1986[78] which for the first time made employers subject to sanctions for the employment of undocumented immigrants, *see* Chapter 13, many employers have continued to employ undocumented immigrants. In addition, business has strong economic incentives to advocate law and policies that ensure continued — and hopefully expanded access to immigrant labor.

The employer interest in cheap labor helps explain the somewhat unique domestic politics surrounding immigration law and policy. Conservative business interests generally favor more immigration and fewer immigration restrictions for this reason. One wing of the Republican party — exemplified by the *Wall Street Journal* — supports more liberal immigration admissions. The somewhat peculiar politics surrounding immigration greatly complicate reform efforts. *See* Chapter 16.

Of course, employers are not the only economic actors to benefit from immigrants. Upon migrating to the United States, immigrants often see tangible economic benefits in the form of increased wages. Indeed, economic opportunity is unquestionably one of the primary motivators behind many migrants' difficult decisions to leave their homeland and come to this country. Not surprisingly, the immigrants most likely to migrate to the United States come from the developing world, where wages and economic opportunities are less than those in this country.

Many, perhaps most, immigrants come to this country for jobs that pay more than those in their homeland. Earnings that are low by U.S. standards represent real improvements over what many migrants would be able to earn at home. Working conditions, while substandard by American lights, may well be worth the wage gains to the migrant worker from the developing world. Indeed, they may be comparable to, or perhaps better than, those available in the migrant' s homeland.

However, undocumented immigrants bring other economic gains. Undocumented immigrants living in this country are not just workers. They also are consumers who purchase goods and services. As the undocumented immigrant population has grown in this country, so has its purchasing power, and thus its importance to economic activity at the national, state, and local levels. Not surprisingly, businesses seeing the future have responded aggressively to this new, and growing, market.

In order to tap into new and lucrative markets, increasing numbers of banks, health insurers, savings and loans, and home mortgage companies have begun to accept foreign identification cards, rather than requiring official U.S. identification cards. For obvious reasons, businesses are eager to pursue new and expanding opportunities and are not overly concerned with the immigration status of paying customers.[79]

---

[78] Pub. L. No 99–603, 100 Stat. 3359 (1986).

[79] For a discussion of competition for the immigrant market for financial services, *see* Laura Sonderup, *The Business of Immigrant Markets: Providing Access to Financial Services*, 60 CONSUMER FIN. L.Q. REP. 503 (2006); *see also* Tisha R. Tallman, *Liberty, Justice, and Equality: An Examination*

Not surprisingly, immigrants have helped to economically revitalize run down urban centers. Bringing ambition and energy, migrants and their families have helped turn around abandoned urban centers across the United States. New York and Los Angeles are two well-known examples of cities that have seen urban decay transformed into renewal due to immigration.[80] Immigrants come to these urban areas in search of economic opportunity. High immigration areas often tend to be areas of high economic growth and great economic activity. That makes perfect economic sense. Migrants have no incentive to migrate to places where jobs and opportunities are not available.

In a regime of limited immigration opportunities, like that which exists under current U.S. immigration law, undocumented immigration provides concrete economic benefits that encourage economic actors to violate the law. As one economist aptly put it:

> It is not easy to fashion a convincing economic argument against an open door toward temporary workers with employer sponsorship, and thus illegal immigration may be in large part the result of economically unsound U.S. policies. Furthermore, because illegal aliens participate only minimally in entitlement programs, do not vote, and usually pay taxes like other workers, it is by no means clear that their presence should be viewed as a "problem." Without an appropriate policy regarding the admission of temporary workers, illegal immigration may be a "second-best" response to the resulting economic inefficiencies.[81]

The economic arguments in favor of more open immigration policies resemble those employed by international trade advocates for the free trade of goods and services across national boundaries.[82] The proliferation of trade agreements, including regional arrangements such as the European Union and the North American Free Trade Agreement, and global institutions, like the World Trade Organization, show the current popularity of free trade. See Chapter 16. Leaders of many nations have promoted eliminating the barriers to the exchange of capital, goods, and services. They have recognized that opening the borders benefits their own nation, as well as the world community.

Relying on international trade economics, Howard Chang has argued that liberalizing immigration policies would likely increase national and global economic welfare. In his estimation, freer migration policies would permit a more efficient use

---

of Past, Present, and Proposed Immigration Policy Reform Legislation, 30 N.C. J. INT'L L. & COM. REG. 869, 881–82 (2005) (referring to studies of contributions of undocumented immigrants to job market and consumer expenditures).

[80] See HING, supra note 56, at 54–56.

[81] Alan O. Sykes, The Welfare Economics of Immigration Law: A Theoretical Survey With an Analysis of U.S. Policy, in JUSTICE IN IMMIGRATION 158, 159 (Warren A. Schwartz, ed., 1995).

[82] See Howard F. Chang, The Economics of International Labor Migration and the Case for Global Distributive Justice in Liberal Political Theory, 41 CORNELL INT'L L.J. 1, 1 (2008) ("Economists . . . recommend liberalized trade as a policy that is likely to produce gains for each national economy. Economists recognize that the same theory that applies to goods also applies to international trade in other markets. Nations can gain from not only the free movement of goods across national boundaries but also free movement of labor across national boundaries.") (footnote omitted).

of the untapped source of relatively low-wage labor in countries across the world.[83] One influential econometric study found that "[a]lthough highly speculative, the calculations reported here clearly suggest large potential worldwide efficiency gains from moving toward a worldwide labor market free of immigration controls."[84]

Moreover, immigration arguably contributes to the greater global good. One of the most influential economists of the twentieth century, John Kenneth Galbraith, observed that: "[m]igration . . . is the oldest action against poverty. It selects those who most want help. *It is good for the country to which they go; it helps to break the equilibrium of poverty in the country from which they come.*[85]

The economic benefits of immigration, however, are not all easy to quantify, or to identify concretely. It is difficult, for example, to estimate precisely the impact of the ready availability of immigrant labor on consumer prices. The costs of immigration to the nation — such as the costs of providing a public education and emergency services by state and local governments — far easier to identify numerically and are ably documented by advocates of immigration restrictions. For this and other reasons, the costs of immigration tend to dominate discussion of the economics of immigration. Because the benefits are ignored, the economic impacts of immigration are often presented in a one-sided fashion — a cost/benefit analysis without a good estimate of the benefit.

3.   The Economic Costs of Immigration

Studies attempting to measure the overall economic impacts of immigration have not been entirely consistent. Some studies conclude that the costs of immigration outweigh any benefits.[86] Other observers, including as we have seen the U.S. government,[87] contend that the alleged economic costs of immigration are overstated and are greatly outweighed by the benefits.[88] The most comprehensive empirical studies conclude that, in the larger scheme of things, any negative

---

[83] *See* Howard F. Chang, *Liberalized Immigration as Free Trade: Economic Welfare and the Optimal Immigration Policy*, 145 U. Pa. L. Rev. 1147 (1997); Howard F. Chang, *Migration as International Trade: The Economic Gains From the Liberalized Movement of Labor*, 3 UCLA J. Int'l L. & Foreign Aff. 371 (1999) [hereinafter Chang, *Migration as International Trade*]; *see also* Larry J. Obhof, *The Irrationality of Enforcement? An Economic Analysis of U.S. Immigration Law*, 12 Kan. J.L. & Pub. Pol'y 163 (2002) (analyzing the adverse economic impact of current U.S. immigration law). *But see* Julian L. Simon, The Economic Consequences of Immigration 365–66 (2d ed. 1999) (disputing that international trade and immigration are equivalent economically).

[84] Bob Hamilton & John Whalley, *Efficiency and Distributional Implications of Global Restrictions on Labor Mobility*, 14 J. Dev. Econ. 61, 74 (1984).

[85] *See* Galbraith, *supra* note 71, at 136 (emphasis added).

[86] *See, e.g.,* Roy Beck, The Case Against Immigration: The Moral, Economic, Social, And Environmental Reasons For Reducing U.S. Immigration Back to Traditional Levels (1996); George J. Borjas, Heaven's Door: Immigration Policy And The American Economy (1999); Brimelow, *supra* note 72, at 137–77.

[87] *See supra* text accompany note & note 75.

[88] *See, e.g.,* Simon, *supra* note 83; *see also* Michael A. Olivas, *Immigration Law Teaching and Scholarship in the Ivory Tower: A Response to Race Matters*, 2000 U. Ill. L. Rev. 613, 632–35 (reviewing studies on the economic costs and benefits of immigration).

economic impacts of immigration on some segments of the U.S. labor market are relatively small and outweighed by the overall benefits to the economy.[89]

Even assuming that the costs of immigration on some segments of the U.S. economy do somewhat outweigh its benefits, more liberal admission policies might still offer net welfare gains. In contrast to the current immigration laws' emphasis on family-based immigration[90] greatly enhanced labor mobility might increase employment-based migration. Many economists, including some who criticize current U.S. immigration policy, advocate this strategy.[91] In order to reap the greatest economic benefit from liberal admissions, the United States might even want to institutionalize systems that recruit the best and the brightest to come to work in this country.

Because of the United States's position as a global economic leader, thousands of skilled workers migrate here annually.[92] However, there are many obstacles. The employment visa process "has been widely criticized as a broken system that is, at best grossly inefficient and, at worst, irrational."[93] Skilled workers must navigate a complex set of time-consuming and costly requirements that require the assistance of skilled attorneys. Employers frequently complain about the labor certification process (see Chapters 7, 8) for legally bringing skilled workers into the United States because of the time and expense. The law unquestionably inhibits the migration of skilled workers. More liberal admissions would eliminate many of the obstacles associated with the immigration of skilled workers and allow employers, and the nation, to more readily benefit from this labor source.

Another economic impact of immigration should be considered. According to some observers, globalization has led to increased economic inequality, with capital gaining at the expense of labor.[94] Adherents to this view vocally condemn the

---

[89] See NATIONAL RESEARCH COUNCIL, THE IMMIGRATION DEBATE: STUDIES ON THE ECONOMIC, DEMOGRAPHIC, AND FISCAL EFFECTS OF IMMIGRATION (1998); see also BILL ONG HING, TO BE AN AMERICAN 76–106 (1997) (summarizing various studies on the economic consequences of immigration); LEGOMSKY, supra note 43, at 61–75 (same); Peter H. Schuck, Alien Rumination, 105 YALE L.J. 1963, 1981–87 (1996) (book review) (analyzing various economic studies on immigration, and concluding that any adverse economic impacts were small compared to the overall size the U.S. economy).

[90] See LEGOMSKY, supra note 43, at 250 ("Since [1952], one central value that United States immigration laws have long promoted, albeit to varying degrees, is family unity.") (footnote omitted).

[91] See, e.g., BORJAS, supra note 86; SIMON, supra note 83; Gary S. Becker, Give Us Your Skilled Masses, WALL ST. J., Nov. 30, 2005, at A18.

[92] Immigrants tend to be over-represented in the highest — and lowest skilled jobs in the United States. See JEFFREY S. PASSEL, BACKGROUND BRIEFING PREPARED FOR TASK FORCE ON IMMIGRATION AND AMERICA'S FUTURE 24 (Pew Hispanic Center June 2005) ("Some have characterized the educational distribution of immigrants as an 'hourglass' because immigrants tend to be over-represented at both extremes [of education] relative to natives. . . . ").

[93] Enid Trucios-Haynes, Temporary Workers and Future Immigration Policy Conflicts: Protecting U.S. Workers and Satisfying the Demand for Global Human Capital, 40 BRANDEIS L.J. 967, 986 (2002) (footnote omitted).

[94] See, e.g., Fran Ansley, Inclusive Boundaries and Other (Im)possible Paths Toward Community Development in a Global World, 150 U. PA. L. REV. 353 (2001); Gil Gott, Critical Race Globalism? Global Political Economy, and the Intersections of Race, Nation, and Class, 33 U.C. DAVIS L. REV. 1503 (2000); Chantal Thomas, Globalization and the Reproduction of Hierarchy, 33 U.C. DAVIS L. REV. 1451 (2000); Sylvia R. Lazos Vargas, Globalization or Global Subordination? How LatCrit Links the Local to Global

economic impacts of globalization. Perceived growing economic inequality resulting from globalization has generated controversy and, at times, protest. Strong opposition to free trade, as exemplified by the, at times, violent protests in the 1990s against the World Trade Organization,[95] has been voiced at various times in recent years.

Like global economic integration, any proposal to allow more liberal migration can expect vociferous opposition. (Watch CNN's Lou Dobbs on virtually any evening for an example.) Immigration restrictionists often make forceful economic arguments for the maintenance of a limited entry immigration system.[96] One major concern is that, although employers stand to benefit from an open borders system, the concomitant costs would be imposed on poor and working people. Fears of greater economic inequality in the United States due to liberal immigration policies — with businesses getting wealthier while workers' wages decline with the influx of low wage labor — often contribute to the populist, and often tumultuous, nature of anti-immigrant movements.

Along these lines, immigrants often are blamed for placing downward pressure on wages. The fear stems from the idea that immigrants will work for lower wages than U.S. citizens are willing to accept and that employers will consequently become unwilling to pay more than immigrants are willing to take. Employers and immigrant advocates, however, counter by claiming that immigrants are willing to perform labor that Americans simply will not do. Others argue that Americans would in fact take these jobs if they paid a higher wage. On the basis of this argument, some commentators have embraced immigration restrictions as a way of improving the wages and working conditions of unskilled workers in certain industries.[97]

Similarly, the claim that immigrant labor adversely affects *minority* citizens in low wage jobs often finds its way into the immigration debate in the United States.[98] The argument has been voiced by liberal as well as conservative commentators. For well over a century, immigration's impact on unskilled workers, especially African American workers, has been a frequently-voiced concern. Some

---

and the Global to the Local, 33 U.C. DAVIS L. REV. 1429, 1436–50 (2000).

[95] *See* Ibrahim J. Gassama, *Confronting Globalization: Lessons from the Banana Wars and the Seattle Protests*, 81 OR. L. REV. 707, 730 (2002); Clyde Summers, *The Battle in Seattle: Free Trade, Labor Rights, and Societal Values*, 22 U. PA. J. INT'L ECON. L. 61 (2001); Susan Tiefenbrun, *Free Trade and Protectionism: The Semiotics of Seattle*, 17 ARIZ. J. INT'L & COMP. L. 257 (2000); Aaron Perrine, Notes and Comments, *The First Amendment Versus the World Trade Organization: Emergency Powers and the Battle in Seattle*, 76 WASH. L. REV. 635, 635–41 (2001); *see also* Adam Warden, *A Brief History of the Anti-Globalization Movement*, 12 U. MIAMI INT'L & COMP. L. REV. 237 (2004) (offering brief summary of movement against globalization).

[96] *See* CONTEMPORARY DEBATES IN APPLIED ETHICS 211–14 (Andrew I. Cohen & Christopher Heath Wellman eds., 2005).

[97] *See, e.g.*, PHILIP L. MARTIN & DAVID A. MARTIN, THE ENDLESS QUEST: HELPING AMERICA'S FARM WORKERS (1994).

[98] *See, e.g.*, VERNON M. BRIGGS, JR., MASS IMMIGRATION AND THE NATIONAL INTEREST 211–15 (1992); MICHAEL LIND, THE NEXT AMERICAN NATION: THE NEW NATIONALISM AND THE FOURTH AMERICAN REVOLUTION 181–216 (1996).

observers forcefully contend that, in recent years, immigration has adversely affected the economic fortunes of African Americans.[99]

Traditionally, workers in the United States have feared labor competition, and the downward pressure on wages, from immigrant labor. Labor unions historically have supported restrictionist immigration laws and policies, such as employer sanctions in 1986 immigration reform. *See* Chapter 13. Organized labor's unequivocal support for the Chinese exclusion laws in the nineteenth century, discussed in Chapters 2, 3, and 6, is a striking example. As will be discussed later in this Chapter, organized labor's position on immigration, however, has changed significantly in recent years.

An inextricably related economic fear is that easy migration increases wealth inequality. This line of reasoning, which finds some support empirically, sees cheap labor allowing business to reap greater profits, accumulate more wealth, and gain at the expense of labor. As the old saying goes, the rich get richer, the poor get poorer. This, however, may well be an enduring characteristic of a market economy rather than the result of immigration and liberal admissions policies. Even if such fears were real ones, it may not be possible through border enforcement measures to halt highly motivated immigrants from entering the United States. Other policies might better address wealth distribution concerns — including those involving the tax system.[100]

There is some evidence that low-wage immigrant workers in the United States have palpable effects on the wage scale of the lowest paid workers in the United States. Low-skilled workers currently immigrate to the United States in substantial numbers.[101] Because these immigrants are willing to work for relatively lower wages compared to domestic workers, employers may offer to pay less. Unskilled U.S. citizens in urban, high-immigration areas are the most directly affected. One much-cited 2005 study by Harvard economists George Borjas and Lawrence Katz attributed wage reductions for low skilled workers to undocumented immigration from Mexico.[102] Other empirical studies, however,

---

[99] *See, e.g.*, BRIGGS, *supra* note 98, at 213–15; Steven Schulman & Robert C. Smith, *Immigration and African Americans, in* AFRICAN AMERICANS IN THE U.S. ECONOMY 199 (Cecilia A. Conrad, John Whitehead, Patrick Mason, & James Stewart eds., 2005); MICHAEL LIND, NEXT AMERICAN NATION: THE NEW NATIONALISM AND THE FOURTH AMERICAN REVOLUTION 139–216 (1996); HELP OR HINDRANCE? THE ECONOMIC IMPLICATIONS OF IMMIGRATION FOR AFRICAN AMERICANS (Daniel S. Hamermesh & Frank D. Bean, eds., 1998); STRANGERS AT THE GATES: NEW IMMIGRANTS IN URBAN AMERICA (Roger Waldinger ed., 2001); ROGER WALDINGER, STILL THE PROMISED CITY? AFRICAN-AMERICANS AND NEW IMMIGRANTS IN POST INDUSTRIAL NEW YORK (1996); *see also* Lawrence H. Fuchs, *The Reactions of Black Americans to Immigration, in* IMMIGRATION RECONSIDERED: HISTORY, SOCIOLOGY, AND POLITICS 293 (Virginia Yans-McLaughlin ed., 1990) (analyzing public opinion polls showing that African Americans historically have supported immigration restrictions); Marion Crain & Ken Matheny, *Labor's Identity Crisis*, 89 CAL. L. REV. 1767, 1826–27 (2001) (noting the conflict between African American and Latina/o immigrant workers); *see also* Jennifer Gordon & R.A. Lenhardt, *Rethinking Work and Citizenship*, 55 UCLA L. REV. 1161 (2008) (evaluating status of Latina/o and African American workers through different labor market and citizenship experiences).

[100] *See* Chang, *Migration as International Trade, supra* note 83, at 409–10.

[101] *See, e.g.*, BORJAS, *supra* note 86; BRIGGS, *supra* note 98.

[102] *See* GEORGE J. BORJAS & LAWRENCE F. KATZ, THE EVOLUTION OF THE MEXICAN BORN WORKFORCE IN THE UNITED STATES (2005).

undermine this claim.[103] In fact, growing wage disparities may be attributable to factors other than undocumented immigration, such as globalization (and increasing worldwide competition) and decreasing labor unionization in the United States.[104]

Even if the overall effects of immigration on unskilled citizens are relatively small, the impacts on discrete parts of the labor force are tangible and help generate tension between citizens and immigrants.[105] Immigration unquestionably has transformed — and continues to transform — certain labor markets. Over the last few decades, for example, jobs in the poultry and beef industries in the Midwest and Southeast and the janitorial industry in Los Angeles have shifted from citizens to immigrants. In some circumstances, jobs have moved from being held predominantly by African Americans to mostly Latina/o immigrants.[106]

Especially in major urban areas, immigrants — many of them Latina/o — may find themselves in competition with African American workers for low wage jobs.[107] In addition, migration may not only affect the labor markets in high immigration areas, where wages may be depressed, but also may lead to migration of citizens outside of those areas, which in turn has economic ripple effects throughout the United States.[108]

Despite these costs, economists have identified many oft-ignored economic benefits from the migration of unskilled labor. Unskilled labor tends to increase demand for middle and higher skilled immigrants who are needed in order to efficiently utilize that unskilled labor. Complementarity of skills must be considered in evaluating the net benefit of immigrants on the labor market.[109] As one economist has noted,

---

[103] *See* Chang, *Migration as International Trade, supra* note 83, at 408–09 (citing and summarizing studies).

[104] *See* Eduardo Porter, *Cost of Illegal Immigration May Be Less Than Meets the Eye*, N.Y. TIMES, Apr. 16, 2006, at § 3, p. 3. One study shows that immigration generally increases the wage level and constitutes only a small fraction of the increase in the wage gap between college educated students and high-school dropouts from 1990 to 2004. *See* GIANMARCO I.P. OTTAVIANO & GIOVANNI PERI, RETHINKING THE EFFECTS OF IMMIGRATION ON WAGES (July 2006); *see also* GIANMARCO I.P. OTTAVIANO & GIOVANNI PERI, IMMIGRATION AND NATIONAL WAGES: CLARFYING THE THEORY AND THE EMPIRICS (July 2008).

[105] *See* ROGER WALDINGER & MICHAEL I. LICHTER, HOW THE OTHER HALF WORKS: IMMIGRATION AND THE SOCIAL ORGANIZATION OF LABOR (2003); ETHNIC LOS ANGELES (Roger Waldinger & Mehdi Bozorgmehr eds., 1996); ROGER WALDINGER, STILL THE PROMISED CITY? AFRICAN AMERICANS AND NEW IMMIGRANTS IN POSTINDUSTRIAL NEW YORK (1996).

[106] *See* Leticia Saucedo, *The Browning of the American Workplace: Protecting Workers in Increasingly Latino-ized Occupations*, 80 NOTRE DAME L. REV. 303 (2004); Leticia Saucedo, *The Employer Preference for the Subservient Worker and the Making of the Brown Collar Workplace*, 67 OHIO ST. L.J. 961 (2006); Leticia M. Saucedo, *Addressing Segregation in the Brown Collar Workplace: Toward a Solution for the Inexorable 100%*, 41 U. MICH. J.L. REFORM 447 (2008).

[107] *See* Roger Waldinger, *Black/Immigrant Competition Re-Assessed: New Evidence From Los Angeles*, 40 SOC. PERSPECTIVES 365 (1997).

[108] *See* RONALD G. EHRENBERG & ROBERT S. SMITH, MODERN LABOR ECONOMICS: THEORY AND PUBLIC POLICY 353 (5th ed. 1994).

[109] *See* Lawrence F. Katz & Kevin M. Murphy, *Changes in Relative Wages, 1963–1987: Supply and Demand Factors*, 107 Q. J. OF ECON. 35 (1992).

[f]oreign-born workers do not substitute perfectly for, and therefore do not compete with, most native-born workers. Rather the complementary nature of the skills, occupations, and abilities of foreign-born increases the productivity of natives, stimulates investment, and enhances the choices available to consumers. *As a result, immigration increases the average wages of all native-born workers, except those who do not have a high-school diploma.* Even for the small and shrinking number of native born workers without a high-school diploma, the decline in wages from immigration is much smaller than some have estimated.[110]

In fact, the relative decline in domestic wages due to immigration has been estimated at about 1 percent, quite small in the larger scheme of things.

Moreover, as discussed previously, immigrants may contribute to overall gains to the economy, which ultimately translates into an overall increase in average wages for *all* workers.[111] The labor added by migrants may add to the overall economic growth of the United States as a whole.

Despite the overall benefits of immigrants to the economy, organized labor has often taken restrictionist positions in the sporadic national debates on immigration. Traditionally, organized labor has greatly feared downward pressures on the wage scale resulting from an influx of immigrant workers. The impact of immigrants on the job market is a bread-and-butter concern that has contributed greatly to periodic xenophobic outbursts. These have, at times, dramatically affected the political process, culminating in patently restrictionist and punitive immigration laws. Historically, labor unions have supported restrictionist measures, including the infamous Chinese exclusion laws of the late nineteenth century.[112]

In recent years, organized labor has moved away from its restrictionist past. Unions in the United States have dramatically shifted their position on immigration and are now exploring ways of organizing immigrant labor[113] and unionizing across national boundaries.[114] At the dawn of the new millennium, the AFL-CIO called for an end to employer sanctions and a new amnesty for undocumented workers.[115] Forced by reduced unionization rates to reconsider its position, the AFL-CIO announced its change after evidently coming to the realization that border controls

---

[110] GIOVANNI PERRI, IMMIGRANTS, SKILLS, AND WAGES: REASSESSING THE ECONOMIC GAINS FROM IMMIGRATION (Immigration Policy Center, 2006) (emphasis added); *see* DAVID CARD, IS THE NEW IMMIGRATION REALLY SO BAD? (Nat'l Bureau of Econ. Research Working Paper, Aug. 2005).

[111] *See* GIANMARCO I.P. OTTAVIANO, RETHINKING GAINS FROM IMMIGRATION: THEORY AND EVIDENCE FROM THE U.S. (Nat'l Bureau of Econ. Research Working Paper, Sept. 2005).

[112] *See* 3 PHILIP S. FONER, HISTORY OF THE LABOR MOVEMENT IN THE UNITED STATES 256–81 (1964) (describing the traditionally restrictionist positions of the American Federation of Labor).

[113] *See* Crain & Matheny, *supra* note 99, at 1828–30.

[114] *See* Frederick M. Abbott, *Foundation-Building for Western Hemispheric Integration*, 17 NW. J. INT'L L. & BUS. 900, 922 (1996–97). *See generally* DALE HATHAWAY, ALLIES ACROSS THE BORDER: MEXICO'S "AUTHENTIC LABOR FRONT" AND GLOBAL SOLIDARITY (2000) (analyzing efforts by Mexican labor unions to organize workers across borders).

[115] *See* AFL-CIO, Immigration, Feb. 16, 2000. For a report on the success of the AFL-CIO's new emphasis, *see* Rosanna M. Kreychman & Heather H. Volik, *The Immigrant Workers Project of the AFL-CIO*, 50 N.Y.L. SCH. L. REV. 561 (2005/06).

and aggressive border enforcement have not prevented immigrant labor from entering the country and are unlikely to do so in the foreseeable future.[116]

Importantly, not all immigrants are poor and unskilled.[117] "[M]igration, in general, and the flow coming to the United States, in particular, do not originate mostly in the poorest countries on most destitute regions . . . . This explains why the average and educational skill credentials of the immigrant population of the United States at present are not much inferior to those of the native-born.[118]

4.   Immigrants and Public Benefits

Restrictionists historically have prevailed in convincing Congress to limit the immigration of poor and working noncitizens to the United States because of the widespread fear that they would empty the public coffers and fill the poor houses.[119] Such fears animate various provisions of the U.S. immigration laws, such as the exclusion of immigrants likely to become "public charges." *See* Chapter 9. Based in no small part on popular stereotypes about immigrants of color from the developing world, the deep fear is that poor and working noncitizens who come to this country will consume public benefits, drain the economy of resources, and thus constitute a net drag on the national economy.[120] Few issues in the United States touch off the firestorm of controversy that is triggered by the perception that immigrants are consuming public benefits for which they are undeserving.

California's Proposition 187, which voters passed by a 2-1 margin in 1994, exemplifies the heated public reaction to the belief that undocumented immigrants are excessively using public benefits.[121] If it has been implemented, this measure would have denied undocumented students access to the public schools (contrary to Supreme Court precedent)[122] and would have rendered them ineligible for virtually every public benefit. The campaign that culminated in the passage of Proposition 187 was marred by deeply anti-immigrant, and often anti-Mexican, rhetoric. Over a decade later, Arizona voters, after a similarly heated political

---

[116] *See* Linda Bosniak, *Citizenship and Work*, 27 N.C. J. Int'l L. & Com. Reg. 497, 503–05 (2002).

[117] *See* Alejandro Portes & Rubén G. Rumbaut, Immigrant America: A Portrait 15–16 (3d ed. 2006).

[118] *Id.* at 15.

[119] *See generally* Kevin R. Johnson, *Public Benefits and Immigration: The Intersection of Immigration Status, Ethnicity, Gender, and Class*, 42 UCLA L. Rev. 1509 (1995).

[120] *See* Howard F. Chang, *The Immigration Paradox: Poverty, Distributive Justice, and Liberal Egalitarianism*, 52 DePaul L. Rev. 759 (2003) (analyzing complexities caused by the fact that many citizens are unwilling to bear fiscal costs associated with immigration).

[121] *See generally* Bosniak, *supra* note 33 (analyzing nature of opposition to Proposition 187); Johnson, *supra* note 119 (analyzing the impacts of Proposition 187 in light of the history of concern with immigrant public benefit consumption); Kevin R. Johnson, *An Essay on Immigration Politics, Popular Democracy, and California's Proposition 187: The Political Relevance and Legal Irrelevance of Race*, 70 Wash. L. Rev. 629 (1995) (analyzing the anti-Mexican sentiment at the core of the initiative campaign); Gerald L. Neuman, *Aliens as Outlaws: Government Services, Proposition 187, and the Structure of Equal Protection Doctrine*, 42 UCLA L. Rev. 1425 (1995); Ruben J. Garcia, Comment, *Critical Race Theory and Proposition 187: The Racial Politics of Immigration Law*, 17 Chicano Latino L. Rev. 118 (1995) (same).

[122] *See supra* text accompanying note 24.

campaign marred by a racially-polarized vote, passed a similar law.[123] Although a federal court barred most of Proposition 187 from going into effect because the state law intruded on the federal power to regulate immigration,[124] its passage demonstrates how fears of public benefit receipt by immigrants may translate into anti-immigrant laws. Proposition 187 ultimately led to federal welfare reform in 1996 that eliminated eligibility of many legal immigrants for federal benefit programs. [125] See Chapter 4 for further discussion.

The available data suggests that immigrants benefit the U.S. economy more than they cost it.[126] Nevertheless, the fear of immigrant welfare abusers deeply influences the public discussion of immigration. Stereotypes of fertile Mexican women sneaking into the United States to give birth to U.S. citizen children only adds fuel to the fire, just as images of the Black welfare "queen"[127] deeply influence the public policy debates over welfare.[128] The public benefits issue arises sporadically and often influences any controversy involving the rights of immigrants. For example, undocumented immigrant eligibility for a driver's license — an important public safety concern — has been challenged by opponents contending that undocumented immigrants are seeking some kind of public benefit to which they are not entitled.[129]

In evaluating immigrant benefit consumption, it is important to note that immigrants are not eligible for the most costly federal public benefits programs. In 1996, Congress enacted welfare reform that made both *lawful* and undocumented immigrants ineligible for Temporary Assistance to Needy Families and Food Stamps, the two major federal public welfare programs.[130] Previously, lawful

---

[123] *See* Raquel Aldana, *On Rights, Federal Citizenship and the "Alien?* 46 WASHBURN L.J. 263, 275–76 (2007) (stating that Arizona's Proposition 200 "provoked even grater anti-immigrant feelings . . . during which the undocumented became the scapegoat for many of the state's problems."). The Arizona measure survived a court challenge. *See* Friendly House v. Napolitano, 419 F.3d 930 (9th Cir. 2005); Hector O. Villagra, *Arizona's Proposition 200 and the Supremacy of Federal Law: Elements of Law, Politics, and Faith*, 2 STAN. J. CIV. RTS. & CIV. LIB. 295 (2006).

[124] *See* League of United Latin Am. Citizens v. Wilson, 908 F. Supp. 755 (C.D. Cal. 1995).

[125] *See* Personal Responsibility and Work Opportunity Reconciliation Act of 1996, Pub. L. No. 104-193, 110 Stat. 2105.

[126] *See* EHRENBERG & SMITH, *supra* note 108, at 355.

[127] *See* Catherine R. Albiston & Laura B. Nielsen, *Welfare Queens and Other Fairy Tales: Welfare Reform and Unconstitutional Reproductive Controls*, 38 HOW. L.J. 473, 476–88 (1995); Angela Onwuachi-Willig, *The Return of the Ring: Welfare Reform's Marriage Cure As the Revival of Post-Bellum Control*, 93 CAL. L. REV. 1647, 1665–73 (2005).

[128] *See generally* STEVEN W. BENDER, GREASERS AND GRINGOS: LATINOS, LAW, AND THE AMERICAN IMAGINATION (2003) (analyzing stereotypes about Latina/os in American culture); LEO R. CHAVEZ, THE LATINO THREAT: CONSTRUCTING IMMIGRANTS, CITIZENS, AND THE NATION (2008) (studying negative stereotypes of Latina/o immigrants).

[129] *See* Kevin R. Johnson, *Driver's Licenses and Undocumented Immigrants: The Future of Civil Rights Law?*, 5 NEV. L.J. 213 (2004); María Pabón Lopez, *More Than A License to Drive: State Restrictions on the Use of Driver's Licenses by Noncitizens*, 29 S. ILL. U. L.J. 91 (2004/05); *see also* Sylvia R. Lazos Vargas, *Missouri, the "War on Terrorism," and Immigrants: Legal Challenges Post 9/11*, 67 MO. L. REV. 775, 798–807 (2002) (analyzing controversy in Missouri over driver's license eligibility for undocumented immigrants).

[130] *See* Responsibility and Work Opportunity Reconciliation Act of 1996, Pub. L. No. 104-193, § 402,

immigrants had been eligible for these benefits. Importantly, *undocumented* immigrants have *never* been eligible for the major — and most costly — public benefits programs.

Immigrants pay taxes, a fact often ignored in the debate over immigrant receipt of public benefits. Indeed, "each year undocumented immigrants add billions of dollars in sales, excise, property, income and payroll taxes, including Social Security, Medicare and unemployment taxes, to federal, state and local coffers. Hundreds of thousands of undocumented immigrants go out of their way to file annual federal and state income tax returns."[131] Despite not having a Social Security number, undocumented immigrants can and do pay federal taxes by securing a Taxpayer Identification Number. Undocumented immigrants are often counseled to pay taxes in order to improve their chances of regularizing their immigration status at a later date. Nonetheless, ineligible for major public benefit programs, undocumented immigrants see few direct benefits from their tax payments. In addition, hundreds of thousands of undocumented immigrants work under assumed names and false Social Security numbers. Undocumented immigrants thus contribute billions of dollars to help keep afloat the financially-strapped Social Security system. They contribute to the system without ever collecting benefits.[132]

One of the major sources of tension between state and federal governments is the current allocation of costs and benefits of immigration between the state and federal governments. Many of the economic benefits stemming from immigration accrue to the federal government through the collection of tax revenues and employers through increased profitability (which translates into higher federal tax collections). State and local governments, on the other hand, do not receive the bulk of the tax benefits, but are obliged to pay for some expensive public services, such as a public education and emergency health care and services, consumed by immigrants living in these jurisdictions. This fiscal disconnect is often at the crux of the dispute over the costs of immigration and the proliferation of state and local laws seeking to regulate immigration and immigrants. *See* Chapter 4.

A few high-immigration states have aggressively pursued federal funds to help pay for the costs of immigration incurred at the state and local levels. Arizona, California, Florida, New Jersey, New York, and Texas all have sued the U.S. government for compensation for the costs of immigration.[133] In 2005, Arizona and New Mexico experimented with a new ploy to offset the costs of immigration by declaring immigration states of emergency, thus becoming eligible for federal

---

110 Stat. 2105, 2260. Congress later restored certain benefits to legal immigrants. *See* Noncitizen Benefit Clarification and Other Technical Amendments of 1998, Pub. L. No. 105-306, 112 Stat. 2926 (1998).

[131] Francine J. Lipman, *Taxing Undocumented Immigrants: Separate, Unequal and Without Representation*, 59 TAX. LAW. 813, 818, 9 HARV. LATINO L. REV. 1, 5 (2006) (footnotes omitted).

[132] *See* Eduardo Porter, *Illegal Immigrants Are Bolstering Social Security With Billions*, N.Y. TIMES, Apr. 5, 2005, at 1.

[133] *See* Arizona v. United States, 104 F.3d 1095 (9th Cir.), *cert. denied*, 522 U.S. 806 (1997); Texas v. United States, 106 F.3d 661 (5th Cir. 1997); California v. United States, 104 F.3d 1086 (9th Cir. 1997); New Jersey v. United States, 91 F.3d 463 (3d Cir. 1996); Padavan v. United States, 82 F.3d 23 (2d Cir. 1996); Chiles v. United States, 69 F.3d 1094 (11th Cir. 1995), *cert. denied*, 517 U.S. 1188 (1996).

emergency funding.[134] The federal government at various times has provided funds to several states experiencing high rates of immigration in order to help offset the associated costs.[135]

5. Social and Cultural (Including Crime, Language, and National Identity) Impacts of Immigration

The effects of immigration on the fabric of U.S. society is hotly debated. The United States has a checkered history of its response to perceived high rates of immigration. At times, the nation has experienced nativist outbursts to immigrants.[136] U.S. immigration law is famous for its cyclical, and ambivalent, nature. *See* Chapter 2.

At times, the nation has embraced some of the most liberal immigration admissions laws and policies in the world. The nation 's immigration laws, in these times, have been truer to the ideal of offering open arms to the "huddled masses," as inscribed on the Statue of Liberty, than they are today. Despite the law's current restrictions on immigration, U.S. law remains more open in terms of admissions and access to citizenship than the laws of many developed nations.

At other times in U.S. history, the nation has capitulated to the nativist impulse and embraced immigration laws and policies that, in retrospect, make us cringe with regret. Time and time again, fear and social stress have sparked fiery attacks on the nation's most vulnerable outsiders. *See* Chapter 2. Punitive immigration laws and tough enforcement, as well as harsh treatment of immigrants and minorities who shared similar characteristics in the United States, followed.

The cyclical nature of immigration politics — and thus immigration law and policy — often have been directly linked to the overall state of the U.S. economy and the perceived social evils of the day. A wide divergence in popular opinion about immigration and immigrants has contributed to the wild fluctuations in U.S. policy. War, political and economic turmoil, and other tensions affect the nation's collective attitude toward immigration. Social stresses, like the fear of terrorism after the horrible events of September 11, 2001 demonstrate, find a ready and unimpeded outlet in immigration law and its enforcement. Immigration law, unlike the vicissitudes of the economy or the whims of terrorists, can be controlled (even if enforcement might not work, *see* Chapter 16).

Immigrants become easy targets for harsh treatment because they often have a distinctively negative image in popular culture. Although not officially found in the omnibus immigration law, the Immigration & Nationality Act of 1952, the emotion laden phrase "illegal aliens" figures prominently in popular debate over

---

[134] *See* JOHNSON, *supra* note 3, at 153–54.

[135] *See* Hiroshi Motomura, *Federalism, International Human Rights, and Immigration Exceptionalism*, 70 U. COLO. L. REV. 1361, 1366–68 (1999); Jay T. Jorgensen, Comment, *The Practical Power of State and Local Governments to Enforce Federal Immigration Laws*, 1997 BYU L. REV. 899, 937–39.

[136] *See generally* JOHN HIGHAM, STRANGERS TO THE LAND: PATTERNS OF AMERICAN NATIVISM 1860–1925 (3d ed. 1994); BILL ONG HING, DEFINING AMERICA THROUGH IMMIGRATION POLICY (2004); KEVIN R. JOHNSON, THE "HUDDLED MASSES" MYTH: IMMIGRATION AND CIVIL RIGHTS (2004); LUCY E. SALYER, LAWS HARSH AS TIGERS: CHINESE IMMIGRANTS AND THE SHAPING OF MODERN IMMIGRATION LAW (1995).

immigration.[137] "Illegal aliens," as their moniker strongly implies, are law-breakers, abusers, and intruders, undesirables we want excluded from U.S. society. The very use of the term "illegal aliens" ordinarily betrays a restrictionist bias in the speaker. By stripping real people of their very humanity, the terminology helps rationalize the harsh treatment of undocumented immigrants under the immigration laws.

Immigration regulation has led to some of the most regrettable chapters in all of U.S. history. Intolerance, particularly in the form of racism and nativism, has deeply and indelibly influenced U.S. immigration law and policy. *See* Chapters 2, 3, and 6. To make matters worse, the courts have rarely intervened to halt the excesses of the political process. *See* Chapter 6. Consequently, periodic waves of harsh exclusions and deportation campaigns dominate the history of immigration law and its enforcement. *See* Chapter 2. Restrictionist measures, such as the Chinese exclusion laws, anti-Semitic national origins quota system, and sporadic deportation campaigns that targeted Mexican nationals, are monuments to times when anti-immigrant sentiment dominated the political process and carried the day. *See* Chapter 2. These sordid chapters in U.S. immigration history are exceedingly difficult to square with the nation's commitment to equality under the law.

As summarized in Chapter 2, the United States has historically excluded disfavored groups from it shores. In the early days of the Republic, political dissidents were punished with impunity through the Alien and Sedition Acts. During the Red Scare after World War I and the McCarthy era of the 1950s, any communist sympathy of the loosest variety could result in the deportation of a hapless noncitizen, even a long term resident. In one such case, a long term lawful permanent resident faced the prospect of indefinite detention on Ellis Island because he was found subject to deportation because of his allegedly communist sympathies and his native land refused to allow him to return. The flimsy evidence relied on by the U.S. government was never revealed to him; as it turned out, the Board of Immigration Appeals concluded that there was insufficient evidence supporting the government's claim that the noncitizen was a danger to society.[138]

There is nothing more inconsistent with the nation's oft repeated commitment to the "huddled masses" of the world than to bar poor and working immigrants from coming to the United States. But poor and working class immigrants have been excluded in large numbers from this country for much of U.S. history. *See* Chapter

---

[137] *See* MAE M. NGAI, IMPOSSIBLE SUBJECTS: ILLEGAL ALIENS AND THE MAKING OF MODERN AMERICA (2004). For analysis of the negative connotations of the term "alien," which is the centerpiece of the comprehensive federal immigration law, the Immigration & Nationality Act, *see* Kevin R. Johnson, *"Aliens" and the U.S. Immigration Laws: The Social and Legal Construction of Nonpersons*, 28 U. MIAMI INTER-AM. L. REV. 263 (1996–97).

[138] *See* Shaughnessy v. United States *ex rel.* Mezei, 345 U.S. 206 (1953) (finding the U.S. government could indefinitely detain a long-term lawful permanent resident based on secret evidence that he was a danger to the national security); *see also* United States *ex rel.* Knauff v. Shaughnessy, 338 U.S. 537 (1950) (declining to disturb U.S. government's refusal to allow alien to come to United States to be with U.S. citizen spouse based on secret evidence that she was a danger to national security). *See generally* Charles D. Weisselberg, *The Exclusion and Detention of Aliens: Lessons From the Lives of Ellen Knauff and Ignatz Mezei*, 143 U. PA. L. REV. 933 (1995).

2. The driving force behind their exclusion has been the idea that poor people would contribute little to the U.S. economy and might use precious public benefits. The nation therefore simply has no use for them.

The immigration laws have also sought to keep out immigrants who shared characteristics with groups unpopular in the United States. The historical exclusion of women, gay men and lesbians, the disabled, and many other groups have reflected biases in U.S. society generally.[139] Indeed, until 1990, the immigration laws classified homosexuals as "psychopathic personalities" who could be lawfully barred from coming to the United States.[140]

In restricting the admission of undesirable noncitizens, immigration law has been used to systematically maintain the racial demographics of the United States. For much of U.S. history, race has been expressly incorporated into the immigration laws and their enforcement. Laws like the Chinese exclusion laws, which later were extended to most of Asia, the national origins quota system, which preferred immigration from northern Europe[141] and the requirement that an immigrant be "white" to naturalize that was the law of the land from 1790 until 1952[142] exemplify this express racial bias. Before 1952, immigrants from Asia somehow able to enter the United States still were barred from citizenship, refused full membership in U.S. society, and denied the right to vote. National identity was a primary justification for those measures, as the nation attempted to preserve its predominantly white Anglo Saxon Protestant roots. *See* Chapter 2.

The civil rights movement in the United States of the 1950s and 1960s led to the revisiting of the racial exclusions in the U.S. immigration laws. The triumph of that movement, and its embrace of the antidiscrimination principle and accompanying demise of Jim Crow, led Congress to remove expressly race-based exclusions from the immigration laws. The Immigration Act of 1965[143] eliminated the discriminatory national origins quota system and embraced color-blindness in immigrant admissions.

Since 1965, without racial exclusions, many more immigrants from Asia have come to the United States than previously was the case. This "mass migration" of people of color from the developing world has worried those restrictionists concerned about maintaining the American way of life — now generally coded in terms of national identity — as well as those concerned about immigration's impact on labor markets and wages.

---

[139] *See generally* JOHNSON, *supra* note 136.

[140] *See* JOHNSON, *supra* note 136, at 140–51; *see, e.g.*, Boutilier v. INS, 387 U.S. 118 (1967) (holding that Congress intended to include homosexuals as "psychopathic personalities" subject to exclusion from the United States).

[141] *See supra* note 136 (citing authorities).

[142] *See generally* IAN HANEY LOPEZ, WHITE BY LAW: THE LEGAL CONSTRUCTION OF RACE (10th commemorative ed. 2006) (analyzing the requirement that an immigrant be white to naturalize).

[143] Pub. L. No. 89-236, 79 Stat. 911 (1965); *see* Gabriel J. Chin, *The Civil Rights Revolution comes to Immigration Law: A New Look at the Immigration and Nationality Act of 1965*, 76 N.C. L. REV 273 (1996).

In modern times, the United States continues to use its immigration law and policy to respond to the perceived social problems of the day. Today, many people in the United States view Mexican migration as a serious social problem.[144] Many Americans express the belief that the United States has "lost control" of its borders and that too many immigrants are coming to this country. Similar fears exist in the post-September 11, 2001 world with respect to terrorists.

The 1990s saw nothing less than a monumental shift toward aggressive immigration enforcement in the United States. Border enforcement became one of the nation's highest priorities and received great increases in funding. *See* Chapter 2. Greater immigration enforcement was consistent with Democratic President Bill Clinton's tough on crime stance, which included congressional passage of a comprehensive crime bill that, among other things, authorized the imposition under federal law of the death penalty for certain crimes.[145]

In 1996, Congress enthusiastically joined the fray. Bent on curbing undocumented immigration, deporting criminal aliens, protecting the nation from terrorists, and guarding the public fisc, Congress passed a series of "get tough on immigrant" laws.[146] Detention of many aliens became mandatory, with the number of immigrants detained increasing dramatically in local jails, federal penitentiaries, and privately run detention facilities. Discussed in greater detail later in this Chapter, "criminal aliens" — with the vast majority from Mexico and Central America — have been detained and deported in record numbers since 1996. The U.S. government vigorously enforced the 1996 reforms with little regard for the rights of immigrants.

Congress also in 1996 greatly expanded the definition of "terrorist activity" that could subject a noncitizen to deportation and other negative immigration consequences. An apparatus, including a procedure for holding secret evidence hearings, was established for the ostensible goal of combating terrorism. The definition of "terrorist activity" was fortified and expanded by the U.S. Congress in the form of the USA PATRIOT (Uniting and Strengthening America by Providing Appropriate Tools Required to Intercept and Obstruct Terrorism) Act[147] increased funding, and other laws and regulations affording the Executive Branch even greater authority to act in the name of national security. Many of the immigrants adversely affected in the "war on terror" were people of color, which all too often has been the case by immigration responses to the perceived crisis. *See* Chapter 2.

The anti-terrorism policies after September 11, 2001 dramatically — and negatively — affected the civil rights of immigrants in the United States. Muslims and Arab communities in particular have been under siege. *See* Chapters 2, 16.

---

[144] For a distinctively Mexican perspective on immigration from Mexico to the United States from the former foreign minister of Mexico, *see* JORGE G. CASTAÑEDA, EX MEX: FROM MIGRANTS TO IMMIGRANTS (2007).

[145] *See* Violent Crime Control and Law Enforcement Act, Pub. L. No. 103-322, 108 STAT. 1796 (1994).

[146] *See* Illegal Immigration Reform and Immigrant Responsibility Act, Pub. L. No. 104-208, 110 Stat. 3009 (1996); Antiterrorism and Effective Death Penalty Act, Pub. L. No. 104-132, 110 Stat. 1214 (1996); Personal Responsibility and Work Opportunity Act, Pub. L. No. 104-193, 110 Stat. 2105 (1996).

[147] Pub. L. No. 107-56, 115 Stat. 272 (2001). In 2006, Congress extended, as modified, the Act but narrowed in response to certain criticisms. *See* Pub. L. No. 109-177, 120 Stat. 192 (2006).

They have been targeted for, among other things, arrest, detention, and interrogation. They face an entire array of onerous immigration requirements that target individuals based on racial and religious profiles rather than any specific suspicion of wrongdoing by the individual. As government effectively labeled them terror suspects, and thus enemies of the United States in the wake of the government's frequently proclaimed "war on terror," hate crimes against Arabs, Muslims, and others, followed.[148]

With the events of September 11, 2001, public fears over immigration escalated dramatically. Immigration law is known for the remarkably vast powers delegated to the Executive Branch and Congress. *See* Chapter 6. It became the focal point of the nation's domestic war on terror. In light of the fact that noncitizens were responsible for the horrible death and destruction of September 11, this to a certain extent is understandable. Many observers, however, believe that the federal government went overboard in its response, sacrificing the civil rights of many Arab and Muslim noncitizens, as well as many others, with minimal, if any, gains to national security. *See* Chapters 2, 6, 16.

Other immigrant groups have also suffered the ripple effects of the "war on terror." Immigrants generally were adversely affected. The deportation of Mexican and Central American immigrants, which had increased to record levels after the 1996 immigration reform measures kicked in, escalated dramatically in the days after September 11, 2001.[149]

Even though the law is color blind on its face, the modern U.S. immigration laws continue to have discriminatory impacts.[150] People of color from the developing world, especially those from nations that send relatively large numbers of immigrants to the United States, are the most disadvantaged of all groups — especially those of a select few high immigration nations. They suffer disproportionately from tighter entry requirements and heightened immigration enforcement. For example, under certain visa categories, many noncitizens from India, the Philippines, and Mexico face much longer waits for entry into the United States than similarly situated noncitizens from other nations.[151] Consequently,

---

[148] *See* Muneer I. Ahmad, *A Rage Shared by Law: Post-September 11 Racial Violence as Crimes of Passion*, 92 CAL. L. REV. 1259 (2004); Bill Ong Hing, *Vigilante Racism: The De-Americanization of Immigrant America*, 7 MICH. J. RACE & L. 1441 (2002).

[149] *See* Kevin R. Johnson, *September 11 and Mexican Immigrants: Collateral Damage Comes Home*, 52 DEPAUL L. REV. 849 (2003).

[150] *See* Kevin R. Johnson, *The Immigration Laws, and Domestic Race Relations: A "Magic Mirror" into the Heart of Darkness*, 73 IND. L.J. 1111 (1998).

[151] *See* Bernard Trujillo, *Immigrant Visa Distribution: The Case of Mexico*, 2000 WIS. L. REV. 713 (showing how annual ceilings on certain immigrant admissions from a single country apply to all nations but have a disproportionate impact on prospective immigrants from Mexico, and noncitizens from several other developing nations, because demand for immigration from there for reasons of proximity, jobs, and family ties, greatly exceeds the ceiling); Jennifer M. Chacón, Loving *Across Borders: Immigration Law and the Limits of* Loving, 2007 WIS. L. REV. 345, 359–60 (same); Stephen H. Legomsky, *Immigration Equality and Diversity*, 31 COLUM. J. TRANSNAT'L L. 319, 321 (1993) (commenting on disparate racial impacts of per country ceilings); Jan C. Ting, *"Other Than a Chinaman": How U.S. Immigration Law Resulted From and Still Reflects a Policy of Excluding and Restricting Asian Immigration*, 4 TEMPLE POL. & CIV. RTS. L. REV. 301, 309 (1995) (same).

although there are no express racial limits on immigration to the United States, disparate racial impacts remain in the operation of the law. The disparate impacts of the immigration laws are no surprise to the people affected, or to many of the restrictionists who press for immigration reform. *See* Chapter 2.

Throughout U.S. history, restrictionists have regularly made calls to drastically reduce immigration to the United States, claiming that, if the nation did not, it would suffer horrible consequences. Today, anti-immigrant positions grab the headlines, add sensational flare to Fox News and CNN (Lou Dobbs in particular), and sell tremendously well in book stores.

Alarmist books about the evils of immigration have a long, if not illustrious, history. Early in the twentieth century, Madison Grant, *The Passing of the Great Race, or The Racial Basis of European History* (1916) and Lothrop Stoddard, *The Rising Tide of Color Against White World Supremacy* (1920), both with titles that betray their appeal to claims of white racial superiority, antipathy for immigration and immigrants, and "crisis," helped define the national immigration debate. The restrictionist, fervently anti-immigrant reasoning offered by Grant and Stoddard offered intellectual justification for the discriminatory national origins quota system enacted by Congress in 1924. *See* Chapter 2. These laws, which favored immigrants from northern Europe over all others, were unquestionably based on racially discriminatory views and the fervent belief that it was necessary and proper to curtail immigration to ensure white supremacy.

Concerns with the racial composition of the United States is a link between the restrictionists of yesterday and today. The last decade has seen a proliferation of best-selling books advocating the need to drastically reduce the current levels of immigration to the United States. Recent bestsellers in the restrictionist genre include Victor Davis Hanson, *Mexifornia: A State of Becoming* (2003), Patrick J. Buchanan, *Death of the West: How Dying Populations and Immigrant Invasions Imperil Our Country and Civilization* (2002), Michelle Malkin, *Invasion: How America Still Welcomes Terrorists, Criminals, and Other Foreign Menaces to Our Shores* (2002), and Peter Brimelow, *Alien Nation: Common Sense About America's Immigration Disaster* (1995). The titles alone suggest the depth of the antipathy for immigration and immigrants and the ominous "crisis" posed to the United States by those twin evils.

Importantly, commentators of many different political persuasions advocate restrictionist positions. Indeed, mainstream Harvard professor Samuel Huntington recently expressed fears of the "Hispanization" of immigration.[152] Some progressives embrace restrictionism in the name of protecting poor, minority, and working U.S. citizens. In this vein, Todd Gitlin, *The Twilight of Common Dreams: Why America Is Wracked by Culture Wars* (1995), Michael Lind, *Next American Nation: The New Nationalism and the Fourth American Revolution* (1996), and Roy Beck, *The Case Against Immigration: The Moral, Economic, Social, and Environmental Reasons for Reducing U.S. Immigration Back to Traditional*

---

[152] *See* HUNTINGTON, *supra* note 74, at 221–56.

Levels (1996) all contend that immigrants undercut the wage scale and that domestic racial minorities, and working people generally, would benefit from dramatic reductions in immigration.

Throughout the 1990s, many observers expressed concern with the changes that had swept the nation due to immigration and the emergence of a truly multiracial, multicultural nation. Such concerns are deeply intertwined with domestic unhappiness with the "excesses" of the civil rights movement, such as affirmative action, identity politics, and a growing racial consciousness among the nation's minorities.

In his provocative book *Who Are We?: The Challenges to National Identity*.[153] Samuel Huntington expresses his fear that the increasingly multicultural United States could disintegrate into the type of ethnic strife that destroyed the former Yugoslavia in the 1990s, or, in less dramatic fashion, divided Quebec for much of the twentieth century.[154] Forming a cohesive national identity with a heterogeneous population is a formidable task and critically important to the future of the United States.

A most controversial part of Samuel Huntington's book is his treatment of immigration and immigrants from Mexico, the focal point of the modern public debate over immigration. He unequivocally proclaims that immigration from Mexico is a threat to the national identity and national unity. Huntington views Mexican immigration as particularly dangerous because of the unique relationship between Mexican immigrants and the United States. He further asserts that they are different from other immigrant groups because of the proximity of Mexico to the United States, the number of immigrants — legal and undocumented — from Mexico, the regional concentration of Mexican immigrants in the Southwest, the persistence of high levels of immigration from Mexico, and the historical claim of persons from Mexico to U.S. territory.[155]

At various times, the U.S. government has attempted to coerce immigrants and people of color to assimilate into the mainstream and adopt "American" ways. Coerced assimilation of noncitizens was particularly popular early in the twentieth century. *See* Chapter 2. In a time when U.S. society openly suppressed domestic minorities and racial segregation was the norm, such measures were much easier to put into place. The national rise of a civil rights consciousness, and a public commitment to respect and tolerance for different cultures and peoples, changed everything. Today, it is much more difficult to adopt coercive measures that mandate assimilation or to criticize as somehow inferior the culture of people of Mexican ancestry.

---

[153] *See* HUNTINGTON, *supra* note 74.

[154] *See also* ARTHUR M. SCHLESINGER, JR., THE DISUNITING OF AMERICA: REFLECTIONS ON A MULTICULTURAL SOCIETY (1991).

[155] For a response, *see* Kevin R. Johnson & Bill Ong Hing, *National Identity in a Multicultural Nation: The Challenge of Immigration Law and Immigrants*, 103 MICH. L.REV. 1347, 1364–68 (2005); *see also* George A. Martnez, *Immigration: Deportation and the Psuedo Science of Unassimilable Peoples*, 61 SMU L. REV. 7, 10–11 (2008) (questioning claim of Huntington, and others, that modern immigrants fail to assimilate).

The forced assimilation of immigrants is inconsistent with the nation's modern sensibilities and commitment to multiculturalism.[156] Nonetheless, demands for immigrant assimilation, and complaints about the failure of today's immigrants to assimilate, reappear in the public debate with remarkable consistency. Such demands, however, tend to be more refined than in the past. Relatively few claims are made — at least in polite company — that the racial inferiority of today's immigrants makes their assimilation next to impossible.

## 6.	Costs of Immigrant Crime

A number of recent studies suggest that immigrants are less prone to crime than the native-born.[157] Nonetheless, the U.S. government has focused enforcement efforts on the deportation of criminal aliens[158] including but not limited to so-called gang members.[159] Immigration crimes, such as illegal reentry into the country, have seen record rates of prosecution and clog the federal courts in the U.S./Mexico border region.[160]

Like some U.S. citizens, some noncitizens in the United States commit crimes and are incarcerated. State and local governments prosecute many of these crimes, and pay for the incarceration of many convicted criminals. Such costs may be substantial in high-immigration states. California, for example, pays millions of dollars annually for the incarceration of undocumented immigrants.[161] As a result of the "war on drugs," and the ever increasing rates of incarceration of young men, costs have swelled over the last few decades.

Like immigrant benefit recipient, the "criminal alien" generates great fear in the general public and often provokes political reaction. Criminals have few

---

[156] See George A. Martinez, Latinos, Assimilation and the Law: A Philosophical Perspective, 20 Chicano-Latino L. Rev. 1, 13–18 (1999) (analyzing relationship between multiculturalism and assimilation).

[157] See Kristin E. Butcher & Anne Morrison Piehl, Crime, Corrections, and California (Public Policy Institute of California 2008); Rubén G. Rumbaut & Walter Ewing, The Myth of Immigrant Criminality and the Paradox of Assimilation: Incarceration Rates Among Native and Foreign-Born Men (Spring 2007); Robert J. Sampson, Rethinking Crime and Immigration, Contexts, Winter 2008, at 29. One policy group announced in July 2008 that "[r]ecent data from New Jersey and California once again confirms what researchers have found repeatedly over the past 100 years; immigrants are less likely than the native-born to be in prison, and high rates of immigration are not associated with higher rates of crime." Immigration Policy Center, New State-Level Research Debunks the Myth of Immigrant Criminality (July 17, 2008) (emphasis in original).

[158] See Jennifer M. Chacón, Unsecured Borders: Immigration Restrictions, Crime Control and National Security, 39 Conn. L. Rev. 1827 (2007); Stephen H. Legomsky, The New Path of Immigration law: Asymmetric Incorporation of Criminal Justice Norms, 64 Wash. & Lee L. Rev. 469 (2007); Teresa Miller, Blurring the Boundaries Between Immigration and Crime Control After September 11, 25 B.C. Third World L.J. 81 (2005); Juliet Stumpf, The Crimmigration Crisis: Immigrants, Crime, and Sovereign Power, 56 Am. U. L. Rev. 367 (2006).

[159] See Jennifer M. Chacón, Whose Community Shield?: Examining the Removal of the "Criminal Street Gang Member", 2007 U. Chi. Leg. F. 317.

[160] See Chacón, supra note 158, at 1846–48.

[161] See Richard Sybert, Population, Immigration and Growth in California, 31 San Diego L. Rev. 945, 982–84 (1994).

defenders in the political process.[162] "Criminal aliens" have even fewer political allies. Due to a lack of political power, fears of criminal aliens have resulted in stringent provisions in the immigration laws, with the immigration reforms of 1996 especially onerous.[163]

The 1996 immigration reforms made deportation of criminal aliens a top priority and dramatically expanded the criminal removal grounds. More crimes subjected noncitizens to removals. A crime classified as an "aggravated felony" under the immigration laws was transformed to include crimes that now are not always particularly "aggravated" or a "felony" under the criminal law. See Chapter 11. The 1996 reforms also made detention of criminals awaiting deportation much more common, even mandatory in certain cases. See Chapter 11. Following the passage of the reforms, the federal government aggressively pursued criminal deportations. Consequently, removals of criminal aliens have occurred at record levels over the last decade.[164]

However, despite popular stereotypes about the criminal alien, there is no evidence that the crime rate among immigrants in the United States is any higher than that among the general population. As Peter Schuck stated in a comprehensive review of the data a few years ago,

> [a]lthough the systematic data on point are somewhat dated, legal immigrants do not appear to commit any more crime than demographically similar Americans; they may even commit less, and that crime may be less serious. Nor does today's immigrant crime appear to be worse than in earlier eras. The immigrants who flooded American cities around the turn of the century (the ancestors of many of today's Americans) were also excoriated as congenitally vicious and usually crime prone, not only by the public opinion of the day, but also by the Dillingham Commission, which Congress established to report on the need for immigration restrictions. The evidence suggests that those claims were false then, and similar claims appear to be false now.[165]

The evidence suggests that immigrants come to the United States to work, not to collect welfare or commit crime. A November 2005 study titled "Why Are Immigrants' Incarceration Rates So Low? Evidence of Selective Immigration, Deterrence, and Punishment," found that "[o]ver the 1990s, . . . immigrants who chose to come to the United States *were less likely to be involved in criminal*

---

[162] *See* Chacón, *supra* note 159, at 321–27; Chacón, *supra* note 158, at 1836–50.

[163] *See, e.g.*, Chacón, *supra* note 159, at 321–27; Chacón, *supra* note 158, at 1836–50; Daniel Kanstroom, *Deportation, Social Control, and Punishment: Some Thoughts About Why Hard Laws Make Bad Cases*, 113 HARV. L. REV. 1890 (2000); Nancy Morawetz, *Understanding the Impact of the 1996 Deportation Laws and the Limited Scope of Proposed Reforms*, 113 HARV. L. REV. 1936 (2000); Teresa A. Miller, *Citizenship & Severity: Recent Immigration Reforms and the New Penology*, 17 GEO. IMMIGR. L.J. 611, 616–20 (2003).

[164] *See* JOHNSON, *supra* note 136, at 853–55.

[165] Schuck, *supra* note 89, at 1988–89 (emphasis added); *see* Chacón, *supra* note 158, at 1879 ("In spite of the persistent belief that immigrant groups are more likely to commit crime than the native-born, the available evidence suggests that the belief is unfounded.").

activity than earlier immigrants and the native born.[166] One 2006 commentary published in the *Wall Street Journal* speculated that the recent drop in crime rates may be attributable to increased immigration.[167]

Nonetheless, concerns with criminal aliens remain politically popular and the United States has focused much time and effort deporting them.[168] Increasingly, the federal government has coordinated with state and local governments to facilitate their removal.[169] *See* Chapter 4.

7.   Environmental Concerns

Concerns frequently have been raised about the environmental consequences of immigration. Restrictionists argue that hundreds of thousands of immigrants coming to the United States have resulted in overpopulation. The argument effectively amounts to an economic concerns with the allocation of a perceived scarce resource, in this case access to this country. To those who fear over-population of the United States, limits on immigration promise to keep a lid on population growth. Concerns with the world population, as well as the global environment, are secondary to those who adopt this type of "America first" attitude.

For one of the nation's most influential environmental groups, the Sierra Club, immigration has been a dividing line. Although the group has not formally taken a stance on the issue of immigration,[170] there have been numerous internal debates about the issue.[171] Members in favor of stricter immigration policies contend that limiting immigration in this country is crucial to decreasing sprawl and pollution.[172] Other members oppose restrictionist measures. In 2004, the executive director of the Sierra Club stated that supporters of stricter immigration policies were "in bed

---

[166] Kristin F. Butcher & A.M. Piehl, Why Are Immigrants' Incarceration Rates So Low? Evidence of Selective Immigration, Deterrence, and Punishment 2 (Federal Reserve Bank of Chicago, Nov. 2005) (emphasis added).

[167] *See* Robert J. Sampson, *Open Doors Don't Invite Criminals*, Wall Street J., March 11, 2006, at A27.

[168] *See* Robert A. Mikos, *Enforcing State Law in Congress's Shadow*, 90 Cornell L. Rev. 1411, 1444–56 (2005).

[169] *See* Peter H. Schuck & John Williams, *Removing Criminal Aliens: The Pitfalls and Promises of Federalism*, 22 Harv. J.L. & Pub. Pol'y 367 (1999); U.S. Senator Jeff Sessions & Cynthia Hayden, *Immigration in the Twenty-First Century: The Growing Role for State & Local Law Enforcement in the Realm of Immigration Law*, 16 Stan. L. & Pol'y Rev. 323 (2005). For criticism, *see* Huyen Pham, *The Inherent Flaws in the Inherent Authority Position: Why Inviting Local Enforcement of Immigration Laws Violates the Constitution*, 31 Fla. St. U. L. Rev. 965 (2004); Michael J. Wishnie, *Civil Liberties in a New America: State and Local Police Enforcement of Immigration Laws*, 6 U. Pa. J. Const. L. 1084 (2004).

[170] The Sierra Club, *Immigration*, (last adopted Nov. 17, 2007), *available at* http://www.sierraclub.org/policy/conservation/immigration.pdf.

[171] *See* Eric K. Yamamoto & Jen-L W. Lyman, *Racializing Environmental Justice*, 72 U. Colo. L. Rev. 311, 349–51 (2001).

[172] *See* Traci Watson, *Sierra Club Could Add Immigration to Green Agenda*, USA Today, Mar. 8, 2004, at 3A.

with racists."[173] Some Sierra Club members feared adopting restrictionist positions would lose allies.[174] In 1998, the Sierra Club membership voted on taking a position on immigration; 60 percent of club members voted that the club should not take a position on immigration while 40 percent voted in support of an immigration policy only allowing less than one million immigrants into the United States.[175]

Environmental concerns continue to be raised in the debate over immigration.[176]

---

[173] *See* Felicity Barringer, *Bitter Division of Sierra Club on Immigration*, N.Y. TIMES, Mar. 16, 2004, at A1.

[174] *See* Watson, *supra* note 172.

[175] *Id.*

[176] *See* Dan Blankenau, *Ecosystem Protection Versus Immigration: The Coming Conflict*, 12 GREAT PLAINS NAT. RESOURCES J. 1 (2007); Richard D. Lamm, *Immigration: The Ultimate Environmental Issue*, 84 DENV. U.L. REV. 1003 (2007).

Chapter 2

THE EVOLUTION OF U.S. IMMIGRATION LAW AND POLICY

A. COLONIAL IMMIGRATION

Prior to Columbus's arrival to the islands off our southeastern shores, perhaps 18 million Native Americans resided in what is now the United States and Canada. Although the first people to colonize the New World were the Spanish and French, the European explorers who followed Christopher Columbus to North America in the sixteenth century had no notion of founding a new nation. Neither did the first European settlers who populated the thirteen colonies on the eastern shores of the continent in the seventeenth and eighteenth centuries. They regarded America as but the western rim of a transatlantic European world.

Life in the New World made the colonists different from their European cousins, and eventually, during the American Revolution, these new Americans came to embrace a vision of their country as an independent nation. They had much in common to begin with. The colonies had been *British* colonies. Most came determined to create an agricultural society modeled on English customs. Conditions in the New World deepened their common bonds. Most learned to live lives unfettered by the tyrannies of royal authority, official religion, and social hierarchies that they had left behind. They grew to cherish ideals that became synonymous with American life — reverence for individual liberty, self-government, religious tolerance, and economic opportunity. The original colonists and their progeny became the "founders" of a new nation, and as such they have come to be regarded as the original Americans. By accepting this notion, we have come to accept the idea that an "American" is someone attached to the United States of America; thus the founders of the United States were the original, new Americans. Almost immediately, the original Americans displayed a willingness to exclude certain others from the concept of a true American. They displayed a willingness to subjugate outsiders — first Indians, who were nearly annihilated through war and disease, and then Africans, who were brought in chains to serve as slave labor, especially on the tobacco, rice, and indigo plantations of the southern colonies.

But if the settlement experience gave people a common stock of values, both good and bad, it also divided them. The thirteen colonies were quite different from one another. Puritans carved right, pious, and relatively democratic communities of small family farms out of rocky-soiled New England. Theirs was a homogeneous world in comparison to most of the southern colonies, where large landholders, mostly Anglicans, built plantations along the coast from which they lorded over a labor force of black slaves and looked down upon the poor white farmers who settled the backcountry. Different still were the middle colonies stretching from New York to Delaware. There, diversity reigned. Well-to-do merchants put their stamp on New York City, as Quakers did on Pennsylvania, while out in the countryside sprawling estates were interspersed with modest homesteads. Within individual colonies, conflicts festered over economic interests, ethnic rivalries, and religious practices. All those clashes made it difficult for colonists to imagine that they were a single people with a common identity much less that they ought to break free from Britain. British tyranny unified the colonies, and a new nation was born, peopled by those who were openly welcomed, those who withstood discouraging sentiment, and slaves.

During the early Colonial Period, some individual colonies attempted to regulate immigration, but essentially there was no integrated immigration policy. The first settlers were French and Spanish. Prior to 1680, most newcomers were English Protestants. A combination of religious, political, and economic motives brought these settlers to the New World. However, when English emigration began to decline in the 1680s, colonies — particularly Pennsylvania and North Carolina — began to promote the immigration of certain other nationalities and ethnic groups while attempting to exclude undesirables. This produced an influx of French Huguenots, Irish Quakers, and German Pietists. Newcomers from Scotland, Portugal, Spain, Switzerland, the Netherlands, and the Rhineland followed. About 450,000 immigrants — representing a dozen nationalities — arrived during the eighteenth century.

These new immigrants came for a myriad of reasons. German Pietist sects, including the Mennonites and Moravians, also fled persecution in search of religious freedom, many in response to the sympathetic Quaker teachings of William Penn. A later German group, the Hessians, came to fight as mercenaries with the British in the American Revolution, and five thousand stayed to become immigrants. Dutch and Swedes came for political freedom and economic opportunity, and the Scotch-Irish came throughout the eighteenth century for economic, religious, and political motives. European migration was not limited to the original thirteen colonies. Spain wanted to expand the Spanish Empire and sent immigrants to California, Florida, and Mexico to search for gold, to trade with Native Americans, and to convert them to Christianity. French settlers came to Louisiana and Canada to seek land and business opportunities, convert the Native Americans, and to protect French trading interests. The French Hueguenots immigrated to flee religious persecution after the revocation of the Edict of Nantes in 1685.

Even during this "open" era of immigration, the original colonies attempted to define their new America by promoting immigration only to select groups. When the first census was taken in 1790, the total population was recorded at 3,227,000. English, Scots, and Scotch-Irish accounted for 75 percent; Germans made up 8 percent; and other nationalities with substantial numbers included the Dutch, French, Swedes, and Spanish. In addition, the 1790 census recorded a population of 750,000 blacks, a result of the involuntary migration of the 350,000 African slaves into the colonies. By the census of 1810, the white population had increased to approximately 6 million, and the black population to approximately 1,378,000.

B. EARLY STATE AND FEDERAL IMMIGRATION LAW AND POLICY

As the new nation emerged, "immigration policies" continued to be handled by individual states with little federal intervention. As in the Colonial Period, these policies were aimed at the exclusion of certain undesirables, as individual states begin to delineate who should become part of their community. Yet beyond those who were not wanted, the doors were open in unlimited numbers to able-bodied souls who made the trek to the new nation. In fact, one of the complaints the authors of the Declaration of Independence made against King George III was that his policies sharply restricted immigration. King George saw burgeoning population as a threat to his hold on the colonies and tried to strangle further influx. Thus, in the Declaration of Independence, King George was castigated as having " . . . endeavored to prevent the population of these States; for that purpose obstructing the laws for naturalization of foreigners, refusing to pass others to encourage their migrations hither, and raising the conditions of new appropriations of lands."

Prior to 1875, state immigration provisions, that often applied to interstate as well as to foreign migrants, regulated at least four groups: criminals, paupers, slaves or free blacks, and certain religions. A fifth category involved those espousing unorthodox or unpopular views, although state colonial screening on the basis of political belief was implemented on a limited basis. This early sentiment — seeking only those who would become patriotic loyalists — represents an early version of a viewpoint (manifested in anti-communist, anti-anarchist, and anti-terrorist screening) that has remained an important part of the immigration policy debate throughout the nation's history. While the migration of a sixth group of individuals — those suspected of carrying contagious diseases — raised concerns among the colonists, regulation through quarantine was not immigrant-specific.

1. Criminals

The early colonies opposed the immigration of persons convicted of crimes. Under modern immigration laws, individuals with certain criminal backgrounds are barred from entering the country. Thus for example, an individual who might fall into an immigration category reserved for relatives of U.S. citizens or for those with special job skills, can still be excluded if immigration officials discover that the applicant has been convicted of a narcotics offense or a crime involving moral turpitude. In the seventeenth and eighteenth centuries, however, British attempts to transport criminals to the U.S. concerned the colonists. English judges could sentence felons to the colonies as punishment, and felons could also be shipped to the colonies as indentured servants. Several colonies enacted restrictions on the entry of such individuals, only to be overruled by the British government. The British lost this veto authority after the war of independence, but even after 1783, the British continued to send convicts as indentured servants. In 1788, the Congress of the Confederation adopted a resolution recommending that states "pass proper laws for preventing the transportation of convicted malefactors from foreign countries into the U.S." Within a year, several states responded. Massachusetts, Pennsylvania, South Carolina, and Virginia prohibited the importation of person who had ever been convicted of a crime. In later years, after the federal Constitution had taken effect, further states enacted similar legislation: Maine, Maryland, New Jersey, New York, and Rhode Island.

2.   Paupers

The Statue of Liberty's "give us your tired, your poor" refrain [written by political dissenter Emma Lazarus in 1883] was definitely not the philosophy of the colonies, nor is it today's philosophy as modern laws exclude those immigrants who are "likely to become a public charge." The colonists were comfortable with the notion of members of the lower class fleeing the overcrowded, rigid social structure of Europe, as long as they were hard-working and honest. But the colonists feared that Europe was using the new world as a dumping ground for the lazy and disabled. After all, English judges could also banish vagrants along with felons to the colonies. Thus, after independence, a number of states instituted legislation aimed at the poor from abroad as well as those from other states. In Massachusetts, the 1794 poor laws imposed a penalty on any person who knowingly brought a pauper or indigent person into any town in the Commonwealth and left him there. This applied to intrastate, interstate, and international transporting of the poor. Beginning in 1820, Massachusetts returned to the colonial system of demanding security from masters of vessels when their passengers seemed likely to become paupers. In New York, a 1788 statute authorized the justice of the peace to order a newcomer removed if it was determined that the person would likely become a public charge within the first year of residence. Until 1813, paupers who returned after removal were subject to severe corporal punishment as well as retransportation. The 1788 poor law required masters of vessels arriving in the New York City harbor to report within 24 hours the names and occupations of all passengers; if any passenger appeared likely to become a charge, the vessel was required to either return the passenger or post a bond.

3.   Blacks

Prior to the Civil War, Southern slave states adopted legislation prohibiting the migration of free blacks and urged free Northern states to do the same. Since many white inhabitants of the North were prejudiced against blacks, several free states obliged. They did so by either blocking the movement of blacks into the state, or requiring good behavior and assurances that blacks would not become public charges. Slave states also subjected their free black residents to more stringent regulations and criminal laws than whites. The sentiment behind some of these laws was related to immigration from abroad. Many states did not welcome fleeing French slaveowners who brought slaves that may have been influenced by the ideals of freedom. These fears were not entirely unfounded. A successful slave revolt in Saint Dominique ultimately produced the nation of Haiti. In 1803, Southern states succeeded in pushing for federal legislation prohibiting the importation of foreign blacks into states whose laws prohibited their entry. Relatedly, in the early 1800s, Southern states regulated free black sailors aboard vessels arriving in Southern ports. States such as South Carolina did not want black sailors wandering its streets, even temporarily. As such, South Carolina and other states required black seamen to be held in jail or quarantined on the ship, barring communication with local blacks.

In addition to legislation adopted by the states, blacks were also attacked through early federal immigration policy. In the First Congress, on Mar. 26, 1790 a provision was made, pursuant to constitutional power (Art. 1, § 8, clause 4), to establish a uniform rule of naturalization, for aliens who were "free white males" who had two years residence. This provision excluded indentured servants, slaves, and most women, all of whom were considered dependents and thus incapable of casting an independent vote. The person had to be of good moral character, a requirement that remains today.

4.   Religious Views

Religious belief often limited one's choice of domicile in the New World. In the spirit of the time, colonial charters frequently denied admission to Catholics. Virginia is an example of one such state that denied admission on the basis of religious belief. The first settlers to Virginia were emigrants from England who were of the English church, at a point in time when the church was flushed with complete victory over the religions of all other persuasions. Yet the settlers showed intolerance with their Presbyterian brethren, who had emigrated to the northern colonies. Furthermore, Virginia passed several laws aimed at Quakers, who had fled from persecution in England and cast their eyes on the New World as an asylum of civil and religious freedom. Sadly, the Quakers found the New World free only from the reigning sect. Several acts of the Virginia assembly of 1659, 1662, and 1693 aimed at Quakers espoused Virginia's strong religious beliefs. These laws made it a crime for parents to refuse to have their children baptized, prohibited the unlawful assembling of Quakers, and penalized any master of a vessel bringing a Quaker into the state. The laws further ordered Quakers already present in Virginia and Quakers that attempted to enter the state to be imprisoned until they left the country, providing a mild punishment for their first and second return, and death for the third. In addition, the laws inhibited all persons from holding Quaker meetings in or near their homes, entertaining Quakers individually, or disposing of books that supported Quaker tenets. Statutory oppressions of religion were wiped away in 1776.

In contrast to Virginia's stringent anti-Quaker laws, Pennsylvania espoused a broader religious philosophy. King Charles II granted the charter for Pennsylvania to William Penn in 1681. Penn, a Quaker, was driven by two principal motives in founding the colony, "the desire to found a free commonwealth on liberal and humane principles, and the desire to provide a safe home for persecuted Friends." English Quakers were the dominant element, although many English settlers were Anglican.

Penn was far in advance of his time in his views of mankind's capacity for democratic government, and equally so in his broad-minded tolerance of different religious beliefs. The 1701 declaration of his final charter of privileges was not:

> Intended as the fundamental law of the Province and declaration of religious liberty on the broadest character and about which there could be no doubt of uncertainty. It [was] a declaration not of toleration but of religious equality and brought within its protection all who professed one Almighty God, — Roman Catholics, and Protestants, Unitarians, Trinitar-

ians, Christians, Jews, and Mohammedans, and excluded only Atheists and Polytheists.

His toleration of other forms of religious belief was in no way half-hearted and imbued the Society of Friends with feelings of kindness toward Catholics, or at least accentuated those feelings in them. In the 1720s, a Catholic chapel was erected in Pennslyvania, which was thought to be contrary to the laws of Parliament. The chapel was not suppressed pending a decision of the British Government upon the question of whether immunity granted by the Pennsylvania law did not protect Catholics. When, after Braddock's defeat during the French War, hostility to France led to an attack upon the Pennsylvania Catholics by a mob, the Quakers protected them. It has been said of Pennsylvania that no other American colony had "such a mixture of languages, nationalities and religions. Dutch, Swedes, English, Germans, Scotch-Irish and Welsh; Quakers, Presbyterians, Episcopalians, Lutherans, Reformed, Mennonites, Tunkers and Moravians all had a share in creating it." Although the Constitution of Pennsylvania protected religious freedom, it was held that Christianity is part of the common law of Pennsylvania; not Christianity founded on any particular tenets, but Christianity with liberty of conscience to all men.

Another example of religious tolerance was New York, a colony that accommodated Quakers in its constitutional convention. In its provision related to requirements of voters, the convention provided, "[t]hat every elector, before he is admitted to vote, shall, if required by the returning-officer or either of the inspectors, take an oath, or, if of the people called Quakers, an affirmation, of allegiance to the State." In fact, although the convention affirmed that the "common law of England" would continue to be the law of the state, any "such parts of the said common law . . . as may be construed to establish or maintain any particular denomination of Christians or their ministers . . . are abrogated and rejected."

Anti-Catholicism in some quarters persisted after the American Revolution. Several states enacted legislation against the Catholic religion. The Carolinas had a law preventing a Catholic from holding office, and New Hampshire had a similar provision in its constitution. Anti-Catholic violence occurred in 1834, when the Ursuline Convent in Charleston was burned. In Philadelphia in 1844, anti-Catholicism led to riots that lasted three days.

5.   Unorthodox Views

Some colonies attempted to exclude or screen would-be immigrants on the basis of political belief or affiliation. For example, a 1727 Pennsylvania act required immigrants "to take an oath of allegiance to the king and fidelity to the proprietors and the provincial constitution." Banishment — the probable antecedent of deportation as an instrument of immigration policy — was sometimes used during the colonial era to punish persons espousing unorthodox or unpopular views.

Several of the nation's most prominent people spoke out about foreign influence during this time period. Benjamin Franklin's 1755 expression against further German migration to Pennsylvania was not simply about language:

[W]hy should the Palatine [German] boors be suffered to swarm in our settlements and, by herding together, establish their language and *manners* to the exclusion of ours? Why should Pennsylvania, founded by the English, become a colony of *aliens*, who will shortly be so numerous as to *germanize* us instead of our anglifying them? [emphasis added]

Franklin continued these expressions during the Continental Congress, warning of the increasing German influence in American society. Similarly, in 1788 John Jay (a year later appointed to be the first chief justice of the Supreme Court by George Washington) noted in The Federalist Number 2:

Providence has been pleased to give this one connected country to one united people-a people descended from the same ancestors, speaking the same language, professing the same religion, *attached to the same principles of government, very similar in their manners and customs*, and who, by their joint counsels, arms, and efforts, fighting side by side throughout a long and bloody war, have nobly established general liberty and independence. [emphasis added]

And in the same vein, Thomas Jefferson stated:

[I]t is impossible not to look forward to distant times, when our rapid multiplication will expand itself . . . [and] cover the whole northern, if not the southern continent, with a people speaking the same language, governed in similar forms, [and] by similar laws; nor can we contemplate with satisfaction either *blot or mixture on that surface.* [emphasis added]

In addition to Franklin and Jefferson, John Adams, a Federalist and the nation's second president, was also wary of foreign influence. In his inaugural address, March 4, 1797, he warned that the nation should never "lose sight of the danger to our liberties if anything partial or extraneous should infect the purity of our free, fair, virtuous, and independent elections. . . . If that solitary suffrage can be obtained by foreign nations by flattery or menaces, by fraud or violence, by terror, intrigue, or venality, the Government may not be the choice of the American people, but of foreign nations. . . . [It is] the pestilence of foreign influence, which is the angel of destruction to elective governments . . . ."

Fears of foreign influence led to an early attempt at federal immigration control. The 1798 Alien and Sedition Laws, a series of four laws passed by the Federalist-controlled U.S. Congress and signed by President Adams, purportedly was enacted not only in response to hostile actions of the French Revolutionary government on the seas, but also designed to quell political opposition from the Democratic-Republican Party, led by Thomas Jefferson and James Madison. The first of the laws was the Naturalization Act, passed by Congress on June 18. This act required that aliens be residents for fourteen years instead of five before they became eligible for U.S. citizenship. This adversely affected Jefferson's party that depended on recent arrivals from Europe for much of its voting strength. Congress then passed the Alien Friends Act on June 25, authorizing the President to deport aliens "dangerous to the peace and safety of the United States" during peacetime. The naturalization and alien acts were aimed largely at Irish immigrants and French refugees who had participated in political activities critical of the Adams administration. The third law, the Alien Enemies Act, was enacted by Congress on July 6. This act allowed the wartime arrest, imprisonment and deportation of any alien subject to an enemy power. President Adams made no use of the alien acts. The last of the laws, the Sedition Act, passed on July 14, declared that any treasonable activity, including the publication of "any false, scandalous and malicious writing," was a high misdemeanor, punishable by fine and imprisonment. Under this legislation, twenty-five men, most of them editors of Democratic-Republican newspapers, were arrested and the newspapers were forced to shut down. One of the men arrested was Benjamin Franklin's grandson, Benjamin Franklin Bache, editor of the Philadelphia Democrat-Republican Aurora. Charged with libeling President Adams, Bache's arrest erupted in a public outcry against all of the Alien and Sedition Acts. Resolutions against the acts became part of the Democratic-Republican platform in the 1800 presidential election, and were partly responsible for the election of Jefferson to the presidency. Once in office, Jefferson pardoned all those convicted under the Sedition Act, and Congress restored all fines paid with interest. The Alien Friends Act and the Sedition Act expired by 1801; Congress repealed the Naturalization Act in 1802 (restoring the residency requirement to five years), and the Alien Enemies Act was amended.

The impetus behind the Alien and Sedition Acts was fear of foreign influence. For example, in the Sedition Act, the United States government was in effect declaring war upon the ideas of the French Revolution. To protect the American way — as interpreted by the Federalists — the people were to be safeguarded against the dangerous opinions spreading over the world. According to this theory, the only way to preserve the health of the body politic was to impose a "quarantine upon ideas." Federalists believed that many Republicans, being more French than American at heart, would join a French army of invasion should it land on American shores. The Federalists craved security from the threat of Bonaparte's army, revolutions and subversive ideas. As upholders of the implied and inherent powers of the national government, the Federalists found support for the Alien Act in the right of Congress to defend the country against foreign aggression. To them, self-preservation was the higher law — a power with which every government was endowed. Every morning Secretary of State Timothy Pickering methodically pored over the Republican newspapers in search of seditious material. He demanded all U.S. District Attorneys to closely scrutinize Republican newspapers published in their districts, insisting on prosecution of both author and publisher.

In spite of these early colonial, state, and federal expressions of exclusion, until Chinese were excluded in 1882, no limits on the numbers of immigrants or refugees to what has become the United States existed. Immigration was limited or discouraged principally by the cost of travel, diseases, conflict with indigenous inhabitants, or racial, religious, or political discrimination by prior immigrant groups.

As long as they were the *right kind* of immigrants, the new nation wanted them. In 1791, Alexander Hamilton warned Congress that if the United States were to develop into an industrial power, immigration would have to be encouraged so as to offset the "scarcity of hands" and the "dearness of labor." The nineteenth century witnessed recruitment efforts by the U.S. government and the states, as well as private employers, who saturated Europe with promotional campaigns to stir up emigration to the United States. Substantial European immigration, especially from Germany, occurred in the two decades prior to the Civil War. As Andrew Carnegie explained it, "The value to the country of the annual foreign influx is very great indeed. . . . These adults are surely worth $1500 each — for in former days an efficient slave sold for that sum." To Carnegie, immigration was a "golden steam which flows into the country each year." Policy makers throughout the nineteenth century extolled the economic benefits of abundant immigration and fashioned U.S. immigration policies to maximize the flow.

The Republican party platform of 1864, that Abraham Lincoln helped to draft, fostered the same philosophy:

> Foreign immigration which in the past has added so much to the wealth, resources, and increase of power to this nation — the asylum of the oppressed of all nations — should be fostered and encouraged by a liberal and just policy.

Months earlier, on December 8, 1863, President Lincoln strongly recommended legislation to the 37th Congress that would encourage immigration:

> I again submit to your consideration the expediency of establishing a system for the encouragement of immigration. Although this source of national wealth and strength is again flowing with greater freedom than for several years before the insurrection occurred, there is still a great deficiency of laborers in every field of industry, especially in agriculture and in our mines, as well of iron and coal as of the precious metals. While the demand for labor is thus increased here, tens of thousands of persons destitute of remunerative occupation are thronging our foreign consulates and offering to emigrate to the United States if essential but very cheap assistance can be afforded them. It is very easy to see that under the sharp discipline of civil war the Nation is beginning a new life. This noble effort demands the aid and ought to receive the attention and support of the Government.

Not surprisingly, the first comprehensive federal immigration law, passed in 1864, was an Act to Encourage Immigration. This law established the first U.S. Immigration Bureau, whose primary function was to increase immigration so that American industries would have an adequate supply of workers to meet production needs during the Civil War. In addition, in an effort to reduce the number of immigrants who left industry for homesteading or army enlistment, the law made pre-emigration contracts binding. Although the law was repealed in 1868, it spawned the host of private labor recruitment agencies that for many years continued to be a significant force behind European emigration.

Of course immigration was not without its critics. During the decades preceding the Civil War, when the massive wave of immigrants, mostly from Ireland and Germany, came to America, prejudice or nativism reached new heights. The Irish were Catholic, a fact that fed Protestant fears that the papacy intended to take over the U.S. government. Even though the immigrants were vital to the industrial and economic expansion of the nation, many natives attacked them as foes of the Republic. Some joined nativist groups to combat the "alien menace." Others pressured the Whigs and Democrats to pass anti-immigrant legislation, such as laws lengthening the time it took to become a citizen. Several such groups combined to form the Order of the Star-Spangled Banner, that adopted a pledge of secrecy; if people asked them about their program, they responded "I know nothing." The organization became the most powerful nativist organization of the era. The basic tenets that defined the order's ideology included a belief that Protestantism sustained and preserved the Republic because it emphasized individualism, democracy, and equality, while Roman Catholicism threatened the Republic because it emphasized authoritarianism, opposed freedom of thought, dictated how Catholics should vote and insisted that priests act as intercessors between God and the faithful. This culminated with the birth of the American or Know-Nothing Party in the 1850s. In 1856, the American Party nominated ex-President Millard Fillmore as their presidential candidate, who attracted almost 900,000 votes. The American Party platform included the following planks:

> III. *Americans must rule America;* and to this end, *native*-born citizens should be selected for all state, federal, or municipal offices of government employment, in preference to naturalized citizens. . . .

> IX. A change in the laws of naturalization, making continued residence of twenty-one years, of all not heretofore provided for, an indispensable requisite for citizenship hereafter. . . .

Yet, mostly pro-immigration sentiment prevailed through the 1800s.

The mass migration of the nineteenth century was the result of a near perfect match between the needs of a new country and overcrowded Europe. Europe at this time was undergoing drastic social change and economic reorganization, severely compounded by overpopulation. An extraordinary increase in population coincided with the breakup of the old agricultural order which had been in place since medieval times throughout much of Europe. Commonly held lands were broken up into individual owned farms, resulting in landless status for peasants from Ireland to Russia. At approximately the same time, the industrial revolution was underway, moving from Great Britain to Western Europe, and then to Southern and Eastern Europe. For Germany, Sweden, Russia, and Japan, the highest points of emigrants coincided with the beginnings of industrialization and the ensuing general disruption of employment patterns. The artisans joined the peasants evicted from their land as immigrants to the United States. Population pressure and related economic problems, sometimes in the extreme form of famine, were the major causes of the mass migration of this long period, followed by religious persecution and the desire for political freedom.

America, on the other hand, had a boundless need for people to push back the frontier, to build the railways, to defend unstable boundaries, and to populate new States. The belief in America as a land of asylum for the oppressed was reinforced by the commitment to the philosophy of manifest destiny. Immigration was required for settlement, defense, and economic well-being.

C. THE RISE OF COMPREHENSIVE FEDERAL REGULATION: THE CHINESE EXCLUSION ERA AND BEYOND

The discovery of gold, a rice shortage, and the recruitment of Asian labor led to the initiation of noticeable Asian migration in the nineteenth century, in turn triggering a backlash against that migration. Examining the impetus and development of exclusion laws directed first at Chinese and eventually at all Asian immigrants reveals a sordid tale of racism and xenophobia. The antipathy demonstrated toward Asians paralleled the repugnance that America showed to African slaves. The attack on Asian immigrants represented the first comprehensive federal regulation of immigration that would later serve as the model for exclusion of eastern and southern Europeans.

Early on, the Chinese were officially welcomed in the United States. The simultaneous opening of both China and the American West, along with the discovery of gold in 1848, led to a growing demand for and a ready supply of Chinese labor. Chinese were actively recruited to fill needs in railroad construction, laundries, and domestic service. In 1852, the governor of California even recommended a system of land grants to induce the immigration and settlement of Chinese. A decade later, a select committee of the California legislature advocated continued support of Chinese immigration. It reported that the 50,000 Chinese in the state paid almost $14 million annually in taxes, licenses, duties, freights, and other charges, that their cheap labor would be of great value in developing the new industries of the state, and that trade with China should be fostered. After the Civil War, some Southern plantation owners seriously considered replacing their former slaves with Chinese laborers. By 1882, about 300,000 Chinese had entered and worked on the West Coast.

Favorable sentiment was certainly not universal. In 1857 at the Oregon constitutional convention, a nativist amendment was introduced to exclude Chinese. It failed principally because most in attendance felt that Chinese made "good washers, good cooks, and good servants."[1] Despite official encouragement of importing Chinese labor by some, the Chinese who arrived encountered fierce racial animosity by the 1840s, as did miners from Mexico, South America, Hawaii, and even France. Irish Roman Catholics in California, replicating the prejudice they had suffered on the East Coast, rallied against the brown, black, and yellow foreigners in the mines. This racial prejudice, exacerbated by fear of competition from aliens, prompted calls for restrictive federal immigration laws.

For a time this sentiment gained powerful political backing from the newly formed Know-Nothing party. Organized in the 1850s, this secretive political organization was formed to push for the exclusion of all foreign-born citizens from office, to discourage immigration, and to "keep America pure." The organization also demanded a twenty-one year naturalization period. On the East Coast it fought against Irish Catholic immigration, while on the West Coast the target was usually the Chinese. Members fostered the attitude that these immigrants were subversive influences, and induced the federal government to pass restrictive regulations

---

[1] MARY R. COOLIDGE, CHINESE IMMIGRATION 21 (1909).

governing the entry of foreign workers. If asked about the members or program of the party, which eventually adopted the name American Party, its members were instructed to answer, "I know nothing about it." A division within the party over the question of slavery, and the voluntary enlistment of thousands of immigrants (principally on the East Coast) into the Union armies during the Civil War, led to the demise of the Know-Nothings in the 1860s.

The demise of the Know-Nothing party notwithstanding, by the late 1860s, the Chinese question became a major issue in California and Oregon politics. Many white workers felt threatened by the competition they perceived from the Chinese, while many employers continued to seek them as inexpensive laborers and subservient domestics. Employment of Chinese by the Central Pacific Railroad was by this time at its peak. Anti-coolie clubs increased in number, and mob attacks against Chinese became frequent. Seldom outdone in such matters, many newly organized labor unions were by then demanding legislation against Chinese immigration. Chinese were at once admired and resented for their resourcefulness in turning a profit on abandoned mines and for their reputed frugality. Much of this resentment was transformed into or sustained by a need to preserve "racial purity" and "Western civilization."[2]

Eventually, Sinophobic sentiment prevailed. First, Chinese immigrants were judged unworthy of citizenship. In amending the Nationality Act of 1790, that had limited citizenship through naturalization to "free white persons" (specifically excluding African Americans and Native Americans), Congress in 1870 extended the right to naturalize to aliens of African descent. But it deliberately denied Chinese that right because of their "undesirable qualities."[3] Then, responding to law-enforcement claims that Chinese women were being imported for prostitution, Congress in 1875 passed legislation prohibiting their importation for immoral purposes. The overzealous enforcement of the statute, commonly referred to as the Page Law, effectively barred Chinese women and further worsened an already imbalanced sex ratio among Chinese.

The exclusion of prostitutes marked the beginning of direct federal regulation of immigration, though it did little to stem nationwide pressure for further significant curbs on Chinese immigration. During the 1881 session of Congress, 25 anti-Chinese petitions were presented by a number of civic groups, like the Methodist Church and the New York Union League Corps, and from many states, including Alabama, Ohio, West Virginia, and Wisconsin. The California legislature declared a legal holiday to facilitate anti-Chinese public rallies that attracted thousands of demonstrators.

Responding to this national clamor, the 47th Congress enacted the Chinese Exclusion Act of May 6, 1882. The law excluded laborers for ten years, and effectively slammed the door on all Chinese immigration. It did permit the entry of teachers, students, and merchants, but their quota was quite small.

---

[2] ROGER DANIELS, THE POLITICS OF PREJUDICE: THE ANTI-JAPANESE MOVEMENT IN CALIFORNIA AND THE STRUGGLE FOR JAPANESE EXCLUSION 19 (1962).

[3] EDWARD HUTCHINSON, LEGISLATIVE HISTORY OF AMERICAN IMMIGRATION POLICY 5–6 (1981).

The act crippled the development of the Chinese American community because Chinese women were defined as laborers. Chinese laborers who had already immigrated therefore had no way to bring wives and families left behind. Chinese pleas for a different statutory interpretation were to no avail. Initially men could leave and return, but they could not bring their spouses with them. As a result, the only women permitted to enter were the wives of American-born Chinese and of a few merchants. The ban on laborers' spouses effectively halted the immigration of Chinese women, thereby exacerbating the restraints imposed by the exclusion of women through expanded enforcement of the Page Law and preventing family formation for Chinese immigrants.

Leaders of the anti-Chinese movement, however, were not satisfied. They pressed for something beyond the ten-year exclusion period. They succeeded, over the next dozen years, through a series of treaties and new laws that led to an indefinite ban on Chinese immigration in 1904. The 1904 legislation extending Chinese exclusion indefinitely marked the culmination of a thirty-five-year series of laws that, beginning with the 1870 naturalization act specifically barring Chinese, limited and then excluded Chinese immigrants. Not until the alliance with China during World War II would Congress reconsider any aspect of those barriers to membership; Chinese simply were not viewed as worthy of being American. And not until 1965 would Congress substantially alter nearly a century of laws aimed at keeping the Chinese marginalized.

1.   The Gentlemen's Agreement with Japan

Not coincidentally, the first appreciable number of Japanese immigrants entered at the height of the Chinese exclusion movement. Agricultural labor demands, particularly in Hawaii and California, led to increased efforts to attract Japanese workers after the exclusion of the Chinese. In 1884, two years after the Chinese Exclusion Act, the Japanese government yielded to internal pressures to permit laborers to emigrate to work on Hawaiian sugar plantations. The next year, in the midst of Meiji Japan's new-found interest in foreign lands, the Japanese Diet passed the country's first modern emigration law, allowing government-sponsored contract laborers to travel to Hawaii.

Like the initial wave of Chinese immigrants, Japanese laborers were at first warmly received by employers. These young and healthy men were needed to perform the strenuous work on Hawaiian sugar plantations. So many of them came that the Japanese became the largest group of foreigners on the islands. Few came to the mainland, so little effective political pressure was incited to exclude them. In San Francisco in 1869, the new immigrants were described as "gentlemen of refinement and culture . . . [who] have brought their wives, children, and . . . new industries among us."[4] By 1894, as Chinese exclusion was being extended, Japan and the United States reaffirmed their commitment to open travel, each promising the other's citizens liberty to enter, travel, and reside in the receiving country.

---

[4] Peter Irons, Justice at War 9 (1983).

By the turn of the century, unfavorable sentiment toward the Japanese laborers grew as they began to migrate to the western United States. After Hawaii was annexed in 1898, the Japanese were able to use it as a stepping stone to the mainland, where the majority engaged in agricultural work. Economic competition with white farm workers soon erupted.

By the 1890s, when economic xenophobia was gaining greater acceptance on the East Coast, nativists — many motivated by racial dislike for Asians — with the backing of organized labor in California formed the Japanese and Korean Exclusion League (later renamed the Asiatic Exclusion League). The league joined forces (and membership often overlapped) with smaller organizations such as the Anti-Jap Laundry League and the Anti-Japanese League of Alameda County. Exclusion once again became a major political issue, only this time the Japanese were the target.

After Japan's crushing victories over China in 1895 and Russia in 1905, policymakers viewed exclusion as a means of controlling a potential enemy. Many Americans had regarded Japan as an eager student at the knee of the United States. But the Japanese Navy defeated its Russian counterpart, signaling a turning point in relations between the United States and Japan.

In the wake of the 1906 San Francisco earthquake, fierce anti-Japanese rioting resulted in countless incidents of physical violence. Japanese students in San Francisco were ordered to segregated schools — an act that incensed Japan and later proved a major stumbling block in negotiations over restrictions on Japanese laborers. Demands for limits on Japanese immigration resonated.

Japanese laborers were eventually restricted but not in conventional legislative fashion. Japan's emergence as a major world power meant that the United States could not restrict Japanese immigration in the heavy-handed, self-serving fashion with which it had curtailed Chinese immigration. To do so would have offended an increasingly assertive Japan when the United States was concerned about keeping an open door to Japanese markets. To minimize potential disharmony between the two nations while retaining the initiative to control immigration, President Roosevelt negotiated an informal agreement with Japan. Under the terms of the so-called Gentlemen's Agreement reached in 1907 and 1908, the Japanese government refrained from issuing travel documents to laborers destined for the United States. In exchange for this severe but voluntary limitation, Japanese wives and children could be reunited with their husbands and fathers in the United States, and the San Francisco school board would be pressured into rescinding its segregation order. The ability for Japanese immigrants to have and form families ensured the community of natural growth, distinguishing it from the more bachelor-oriented Chinese immigrant community whose population began to decline after the Chinese exclusion laws.

Japanese immigrants attempted to attack their preclusion from citizenship through naturalization without success. In *Takao Ozawa v. United States* (1922), one Japanese immigrant took his claim to the Supreme Court, arguing that he should be regarded a "free white person" under the naturalization laws. The Court disagreed, simply concluding:

[T]o adopt the color test alone would result in a confused overlapping of races and a gradual merging of one into the other, without any practical line of separation. . . . [T]he federal and state courts, in an almost unbroken line, have held that the words "white person" were meant to indicate only a person of what is *popularly known* as the Caucasian race. . . . With the conclusion reached in these several decisions we see no reason to differ. [emphasis added]

2.   Filipinos and Asian Indians

At the turn of the century, the United States was beginning its relationship with the Philippines as it was changing its view toward Japan. After the U.S. victory over Spain in the 1898 Spanish-American War, President McKinley concluded that the people of the Philippines, then a Spanish colony, were "unfit for self-government" and that "there was nothing left for [the United States] to do but to take them all, and to educate the Filipinos, and uplift and civilize and Christianize them.[5] The sentiment was a clear expression that the President did not view The U.S. takeover met with violent resistance from many Filipinos who had struggled for independence from colonial domination.

Ironically, the fact that the Philippines became U.S. colony meant that Filipinos automatically became noncitizen nationals of the United States. They could travel in and out of the United States without regard to immigration laws, they were not subject to exclusion or deportation, and requirements for obtaining full citizenship were relaxed. When appreciable numbers of Filipinos came in after World War I (when Chinese and Japanese workers could not longer be recruited) exclusionary efforts against them began.

The advent of the twentieth century witnessed the entry of other Asians, such as Asian Indians, but in small numbers. Even though those seeking trade were among some of the earliest migrants to the United States, Indians had insignificant contacts with this country during the nineteenth century. The poorer workers among them found labor opportunities in British colonies. The few thousand who did come, most of them men, settled primarily in California, and most of them found agricultural jobs.[6] Their families remained in India while husbands and fathers worked to earn money to send for them or to return. A small number of more educated Indians also entered.

Even small numbers of Asian Indians managed to agitate the Asiatic Exclusion League, which had sprung up in response to Japanese and Korean immigration. Racial and economic nativism was again at the core of the agitation. Asian Indians competed for agricultural jobs and were willing to work for lower wages in other jobs, so nativists used violence to force them out of local jobs. Not satisfied with making life in the United States miserable and even dangerous, exclusionists also persuaded federal immigration authorities to block their entry. The California commissioner of state labor statistics concluded that the "Hindu is the most

---

[5] JAMES PATTERSON, AMERICA IN THE TWENTIETH CENTURY 94 (1983).

[6] Many Asian Indians who migrated to the Western Hemisphere settled in Canada first, because of the British Commonwealth connection.

undesirable immigrant in the state. His lack of personal cleanliness, his low morals and his blind adherence to theories and teachings, so entirely repugnant to American principles, make him unfit for association with American people."[7] Although about two thousand Asian Indians immigrated from 1911 to 1917, more than seventeen hundred were denied entry during the same period, mostly on the grounds that they would need public assistance.

Like the Chinese and Japanese before them, many Asian Indians fought for acceptance. Some sought to have laws discriminating against them overturned by the courts. Lower federal courts had granted them the right to naturalize on the grounds that they were Caucasians and thus eligible "white persons" under the citizenship laws of 1790 and 1870. But in *United States v. Bhagat Singh Thind* (1923), the Supreme Court reversed this racial stance, deciding that Indians, like Japanese, would no longer be considered white persons, and were therefore ineligible to become naturalized citizens.

But barring Asian Indian and other Asian immigrants from naturalization was not enough to keep them from exclusion from the definition of American if immigration bars were not erected. Strict control of Chinese and Japanese immigration had done little to satisfy the demands of American nativists who maintained a closed view of the American society. They insisted that all Asians were racially inferior to whites and should be completely barred.

Congress responded to this anti-Asian clamor and a renewed xenophobia aroused by the influx of southern and eastern Europeans by passing the Act of February 5, 1917. The constant flow of Italians, Russians, and Hungarians, that peaked in the first decade of the century, fueled racial nativism and anti-Catholicism, culminating in a controversial requirement that excluded aliens "who cannot read and understand some language or dialect. But the act also created the "Asiatic barred zone" by extending the Chinese exclusion laws to all other Asians. The zone covered South Asia from Arabia to Indochina, as well as the adjacent islands. It included India, Burma, Thailand, the Malay States, the East Indian Islands, Asiatic Russia, the Polynesian Islands, and parts of Arabia and Afghanistan. China and Japan did not have to be included because of the Chinese exclusion laws and the Gentlemen's Agreement. But together these provisions declared inadmissible all Asians except teachers, merchants, and students. Only Filipinos and Guamanians, under U.S. jurisdiction at the time, were not included.

The reactionary, isolationist political climate that followed World War I, manifested in the Red Scare of 1919–20, led to even greater exclusionist demands. The landmark Immigration Act of 1924, opposed by only six senators, once again took direct aim at southern and eastern Europeans, whom the Protestant majority in the United States viewed with dogmatic disapproval. The arguments advanced in support of the bill stressed recurring themes: the racial superiority of Anglo-Saxons, the fact that immigrants would cause the lowering of wages, and the unassimilability of foreigners, while citing the usual threats to the nation's social unity and order posed by immigration.

---

[7] California Board of Control, *California and the Oriental: Japanese, Chinese, and Hindus* 101–2 (Sacramento: State Printing Office 1920).

The act restructured criteria for admission to respond to nativist demands and represented a general selection policy that remained in place until 1952. The scheme provided that immigrants of any particular country be limited to 2 percent of their nationality in 1890. The law struck most deeply at Jews, Italians, Slavs, and Greeks who had immigrated in great numbers after 1890, and who would be most disfavored by such a quota system.

Though sponsors of the act were primarily concerned with limiting immigration from southern and eastern Europe, they simultaneously eliminated the few remaining categories for Asians. The act provided for the permanent exclusion of any "alien ineligible to citizenship." Since Asians were barred from naturalization under the 1790 and 1870 laws, the possibility of their entry was cut off indefinitely. Asians were not allowed even under the two percent quota rule. The primary target were the Japanese, who, while subject to the Gentlemen's Agreement, had never been totally barred by federal immigration law until then.

The only Asians not affected by the 1924 Act were Filipinos, who remained exempt as nationals and who by then had settled into a familiar pattern of immigration. Before 1920, a few resided mostly in Hawaii; their presence on the islands helped establish conditions later conducive to a more substantial labor migration. They became a convenient source of cheap labor after Japanese immigration was restricted in 1908. Just as the Chinese exclusion law had encouraged employers to look to Japan, so the limitations on Japanese immigrants led to an intense recruitment, especially by the Hawaiian Sugar Planters' Association, of Filipino laborers because of their open travel status as noncitizen nationals.

By the late 1920s, Filipino laborers began to look beyond Hawaii, where the demand for their labor was shrinking, to the mainland where the need for cheap labor, especially in agriculture, was growing. Many left Hawaii partly in response to employers' recruitment efforts. Most Filipinos who had come to the mainland previously had been students. But in the late 1920s, laborers came to California predominantly to work on citrus and vegetable farms.

Because of their special immigration status, Filipinos considered themselves American in important respects. Still, on their arrival familiar cycles of rejection quickly surfaced, much to their consternation. They were met with acceptance by eager employers and then, almost immediately, resentment from white workers, particularly as their numbers increased on the mainland in the late 1920s.

To white workers in California, the privileged immigration status of Filipinos did not change the fact that they were an economic threat who had the physical characteristics of Asiatics. They were just another undesirable Asian race who had a disturbing attitude, because they knew something of American culture, could speak English, and in some cases lived with white women. They also seemed to be taking over white jobs and lowering standards for white wages and working conditions. As it had toward Chinese and Japanese, white resentment of Filipinos soon boiled over into violence, and numerous anti-Filipino outbursts erupted in California between 1929 and 1934. Their strong concentration in agriculture made them visible and competitive (of the 45,000 reported on the mainland in 1930, about 82 percent were farm laborers) especially during the severe unemployment of the

Great Depression. Since Filipinos were often on the bottom of the economic ladder, the depression struck them particularly hard. Exclusionists suggested that the United States ought to repatriate unemployed Filipino workers, for their own benefit as well as for that of the United States.

Calls for the exclusion of Filipino workers were warmly received in Congress, which welcomed any seemingly uncomplicated proposal that promised relief for the depression's high unemployment. For policymakers, however, dealing with anti-Filipino agitation was not as simple as responding to earlier anti-Chinese, anti-Asian Indian, and even anti-Japanese campaigns. They could travel in and out of the country without constraint, so until the Philippines was granted independence, Congress could not exclude Filipinos.

An unlikely coalition of exclusionists, anti-colonialists, and Filipino nationalists managed to band together to promote the passage of the Tydings-McDuffie Act in 1934. Many of the exclusionists had initially wished to keep the Philippines, but they soon realized that to exclude Filipino laborers they had to support Filipino nationalists and anti-colonialists and grant the nation its freedom. Independence and exclusion became so intertwined that the former was often used as a motive for the latter.

Tydings-McDuffie was everything exclusionists could hope for. When their nation would become independent on July 4, 1946, Filipinos would lose their status as nationals of the United States, regardless of where they lived. Those in the United States would be deported unless they became immigrants. Between 1934 and 1946, however, any Filipino who desired to immigrate became subject to the immigration acts of 1917 and 1924, and the Philippines was considered a separate country with an annual quota of only 50 visas!

The passage of Tydings-McDuffie, the last congressional act excluding immigration from Asia, signaled the formal end of an era. The refusal to extend Asians the right to naturalize, the laws against the Chinese, the Gentlemen's Agreement with Japan, the 1917 and 1924 immigration acts, and Tydings-McDuffie were the legacy of the schizophrenic attempt by Congress to satisfy economic ambitions, some egalitarian views of the world, and nativist prejudice. These exclusion laws remained in full force throughout the 1930s and much of the 1940s, symbolizing a peak in anti-immigrant power.

D.   THE NATIONAL ORIGINS QUOTA SYSTEM

Manifested in the Red Scare of 1919–20, the reactionary, isolationist political climate that followed World War I led to even greater exclusionist demands. To many Americans, the ghost of Bolshevism seemed to haunt the land in the specter of immigrant radicals, especially after the 1919 wave of industrial unrest in immigrant-dominated workforces of the coal, steel, meatpacking, and transportation industries. In reaction to the isolationist political climate, Congress passed a variety of laws placing numerical restrictions on immigration.

The reactionary exclusionist sentiment of the time was combined with the ethnic. The 1917 literacy law was inadequate for restrictionists who remained concerned about the continuing entry of southern and eastern Europeans. Southern and eastern European immigrants numbered 4.5 million in 1910, and by 1920 the figure surged again to 5.67 million. The 100 percent American campaign was alarmed that one fifth of the California population was Italian American by then.

In addition to the menace of leftist political influence emanating from parts of Europe, public and congressional arguments in support of more restrictive legislation stressed recurring themes: the racial superiority of Anglo-Saxons, the fact that immigrants would cause the lowering of wages, the unassimilability of foreigners, and the usual threats to the nation's social unity and order posed by immigration. Popular biological theories of the period alleging the superiority of certain races also were influential.

The result of the continued assault on southern and eastern European immigrants was the Quota Law of 1921, enacted as a temporary measure. This legislation introduced for the first time numerical limitations on immigration. With certain exceptions, the law allocated quotas to each nationality totaling 3 percent of the foreign-born persons of that nationality residing in the United States in 1910, for an annual total of approximately 350,000. Since most of those living in the United States in 1910 were northern or western European, the quota for southern and eastern Europeans was smaller (about 45,000 less). The latter groups filled their quotas easily, but northern and western European countries did not fill their quotas under this law.[8] This law was scheduled to expire in 1922, but was extended to June 30, 1924.

A permanent policy of numerical restrictions was was enacted in 1924. One problem with the 1910 model for the 1921 law was that the period between 1900 to 1910 witnessed a large influx of southern and eastern Europeans. So a 1910 population model would include a higher proportion of southern and eastern Europeans than earlier years. So the landmark Immigration Act of 1924, opposed by only six senators, took an even greater malicious aim at southern and eastern Europeans, whom the Protestant majority in the U.S. viewed with dogmatic disapproval.

The 1924 legislation adopted a national origins formula that eventually based the quota for each nationality on the number of foreign-born persons of their national origin in the United States in 1890 — prior to the major wave of southern and eastern Europeans. The law provided that immigrants of any particular country be reduced from 3 percent under the 1921 law to 2 percent of the group's population under the new law. And instead of 1910 as the population model year for determining how many could enter, the 2 percent was based on a particular nationality's population in 1890, when even fewer immigrants from southern and eastern Europe lived in the United States. The quota formula was hailed as the "most far reaching change that occurred in America during the course of this quarter century," enabling a halt to "the tendency toward a change in the fundamental composition of the American stock."

---

[8] There was a non-quota exception of which some southern and eastern Europeans took advantage. The law permitted a person to be admitted to the United States as an immigrant if the individual had resided in the Western Hemisphere for one year (later changed to five years). So by temporarily living in a Western Hemisphere country, the quota could be avoided.

This formula resulted in a sharp curtailment of immigrants from southern and eastern Europe, and struck most deeply at Jews, Italians, Slavs, and Greeks. Quota immigrants were limited to approximately 165,000 per year, with the proportion and number even smaller for southern and eastern Europeans than before. However, natives of the Western Hemisphere countries could enter without numerical restriction. Other nonquota groups included wives and children of U.S. citizens and return lawful residents. Those who entered in violation of visa and quota requirements were deportable without time limitation. Another provision, aimed at Asians, barred all aliens ineligible to citizenship, thus completely barring Japanese (as well as all other Asians), some of whom had continued to enter under the 1907 Gentlemen's Agreement.

The impact of the national origins quota system on the southern and eastern European population in the United States is evident from census information on the foreign-born population of the country. They numbered about 1.67 million in 1900. After the big immigrant wave of the first decade of the twentieth century, the figure almost tripled to 4.5 million in 1910. The population surged again in the next decade to 5.67 million in 1920. However, after the quota systems of 1921 and 1924 took effect, the number of immigrants from those regions of Europe declined. The population increased to only 5.92 million by 1930. The figures for immigrants from specific countries are also telling. The population of Italian immigrants increased only 11.18 percent between 1920 and 1930, after experiencing a 176 percent jump in the first decade of the century. The number of Polish immigrants in the United States increased only 11.4 percent during the 1920s, and the number of Hungarians in the country actually declined from 397,283 to 274,450.

E.   THE IMMIGRATION AND NATIONALITY ACT OF 1952

Influenced by the cold war atmosphere and anti-communist fervor of the post-World War II era and the onset of the Korean War, the McCarran-Walter Act of 1952 was enacted, overhauling the country's immigration laws in major ways. While the quota system of the 1920s was influenced by the Red Scare of 1919–1920, the limitation on southern and eastern Europeans was not an explicit limitation on the entry of communists and subversives. The 1952 law was more direct and reminiscent of the alien and sedition laws of early America: individuals who held certain political viewpoints were not welcome; certain viewpoints were un-American. Moreover, the 1952 law lay the groundwork to exclude another social group that was un-American: homosexuals.

The fear of communism and other "non-democratic" ideas played an important part of the national psyche leading up to the law. The Smith Act of 1940, that made it illegal to advocate the overthrow of the government by force or to belong to an organization advocating such a position, was used by the Truman administration to jail leaders of the American Communist Party. In response to criticism, particularly from the House Committee on Un-American Activities, that his administration was "soft on communism," Truman established the Loyalty Review Board in 1947 to review government employees. In 1950, Senator Pat McCarran of Nevada (the co-author of the 1952 legislation) sponsored the Internal Security Act that required communist-front organizations to register with the attorney general and barred their members from defense work and travel abroad. The same year, Alger Hiss, a former State Department official who had become president of the Carnegie Endowment for International Peace, was convicted of perjury, following allegations that he was a communist who had supplied classified documents to the Soviet Union. Also in 1950, Julius and Ethel Rosenberg, as well as Harry Gold, were charged with and convicted of giving atomic secrets to the Soviet Union, and eventually the Rosenbergs were executed. Earlier in 1950, Senator Joseph R. McCarthy embarked on his infamous hunt for subversives, stating that he had a list of known communists who were working in the State Department; later his attacks expanded to include diplomats, scholars, and filmmakers.

With this backdrop, little wonder that the 1952 Act contained several provisions relating to the exclusion and deportation of subversives and communists. For example, the law provided these exclusion provisions that, in large part, have endured:

> Aliens who are, or at any time have been, members of any of the following classes:
>
> (A)   Aliens who are anarchists;
> (B)   Aliens who advocate or teach, or who are members of or affiliated with any organization that advocates or teaches, opposition to all organized government;
> (C)   Aliens who are members or affiliated with (i) the Communist Party of the United States, (ii) any other totalitarian party of the United States, (iii) the Communist Political Association, (iv) the Communist or any other totalitarian party of any State of the United States, of any foreign state, or of any political or geographical subdivision of any foreign state . . . *Provided*, that nothing in this paragraph, or in any other provision of this Act, shall be construed as declaring that the Communist Party does not advocate the overthrow of the Government of the United States by force, violence, or other unconstitutional means;
> (D)   Aliens . . . who advocate the economic, international, and governmental doctrines of world communism or the establishment in the United States of a totalitarian dictatorship, or who are members of or affiliated with any organization that advocates the economic, or international, and governmental doctrines of world communism . . .
> (G)   Aliens who write or publish, or cause to be written or published, or who knowingly circulate, distribute, print, or display . . . any written or printed matter, advocating or teaching opposition to all organized government, or advocating or teaching . . . the overthrow by force, violence, or other unconstitutional means of the Government of the United States or of all forms of law. . . . [9]

The act also called for grounds for exclusion, that contained detailed provisions relating to health, criminal, moral, economic, and subversive criteria. Expulsion was

---

[9]   8 U.S.C. § 1182(a)(28) (1952).

authorized without time limitation of aliens who enter unlawfully, nonimmigrants who overstay their allotted time, and those who are guilty of certain misconduct such as criminals, narcotics violators, prostitutes, and of course subversives.

In spite of his sensitivity to being called "soft on communism," President Truman opposed the enactment of the 1952 Act. His veto, which was easily overridden by Congress, was not based on opposition to the subversion and anti-communism provisions nor the new entry or deportation sections. In fact, he was certainly not averse to jailing or throwing communists out of the country. The act continued the national origins quota selection system of the 1920s, perpetuating the policy that immigrants from one part of the world were better than others. This continuation of the racialized quota system triggered Truman's adamant opposition to the legislation. But on June 27, 1952. Congress passed the bill over Truman's veto.[10]

In addition to continuing the national origins quota system for the Eastern Hemisphere, the 1952 Act also established a four-category selection system. Fifty percent of each national quota was allocated for first preference distribution to aliens with high education or exceptional abilities, and the remaining three preferences were divided among specified relatives of U.S. citizens and lawful permanent resident aliens. This four-point selection system was the antecedent of the current preference system that places higher priority on family reunification than on needed skills. However, under the 1952 law national origins remained the determining factor in immigrant admissions, and Northern and Western Europe were heavily favored. As in the past, the Western Hemisphere was not subject to numerical limitations. Although the Asian exclusion laws were finally deleted, in its place a new "Asia-Pacific Triangle" was established with a trivial 2,000 annual quota, continuing the blatant form of racial and ethnic discrimination that epitomized the retained quota laws.

The ostracism that gays and lesbians endure in American life also has immigration-related underpinnings partially rooted in the 1952 law. The immigration laws of the nation, especially provisions related to who can enter, who cannot enter, and who can be removed, represent the judgment of our elected leaders as to whom we would allow or not allow to enter and become an American. For decades, the immigration laws contained provisions that were intended to keep immigrant homosexuals out of the country, thereby institutionalizing the sentiment that homosexuals should not be Americans. Homosexuals were first statutorily excluded from entry by the Immigration Act of 1917, which prohibited the admission of "persons of constitutional psychopathic inferiority" certified by a physician to be "mentally. . . . defective."[11] In 1950, the Senate subcommittee that eventually recommended the overhaul to the Immigration and Nationality Act reported that the "purpose of [an existing] provision against 'persons with constitutional psychopathic inferiority' will be more adequately served by changing that term to 'persons afflicted with psychopathic personality,' and that the classes of mentally defectives should be enlarged to include homosexuals and other sex

---

[10] Public Law 414, 82d Congress (66 Stat. 163).

[11] Ch. 29, § 3, 39 Stat. 874 (1917) (repealed 1952).

perverts."[12] Thus, among the major changes to the immigration laws that resulted in 1952, Congress included in the list of individuals to be excluded those "afflicted with psychopathic personality."[13]

In 1962, the federal Ninth Circuit Court of Appeals, in *Fleuti v. Rosenberg*,[14] allowed a homosexual man to reenter the country, ruling that the term "psychopathic personality" was too vague to encompass homosexuals under certain circumstances. In response, in 1965 Congress amended the law to include the words "sexual deviation" in order to "serve the purpose of resolving any doubt on this point."[15] Now the law excluded "aliens afflicted with psychopathic personality, sexual deviation, or a mental defect."[16]

The constitutionality of the exclusion of homosexuals was resolved by the Supreme Court a few years later in *Boutlier v. INS* (1967),[17] a deportation case. The Supreme Court held that the legislative history of the provision indicated "beyond a shadow of a doubt" that Congress intended to exclude immigrants who were homosexuals via the "psychopathic personality" provision. As a result, the Court upheld Boutilier's deportation, because prior to his entry in the United States when he was 21 years old, he had engaged in homosexual activity on a regular basis. Since he was excludable at the time of his immigration, he could now be deported.

In spite of Congress' clear intent to exclude homosexuals and the Supreme Court's finding of constitutionality to do so, the ability of INS to enforce the homosexual exclusion provision continued to be tested. After years of intense debate over the exclusion of homosexuals, the Immigration Act of 1990 removed the psychopathic personality and sexual deviation language from the exclusion provisions along with all language referring to mental retardation, insanity, and mental defects.

F.   THE IMMIGRATION REFORM AND CONTROL ACT OF 1986 (IRCA)

Concerns over the number of undocumented workers (predominantly Mexican) in the United States deepened in the 1970s and early 1980s. While no one knew the exact number, some of the more hysterical estimates ranged from eight to twelve million. In spite of increased authority and resources for Border Patrol efforts, INS efforts were perceived as ineffectual. Proposals were made to address the situation from a different perspective — by penalizing employers who were hiring undocumented workers, through what was called "employer sanctions." By 1986, employer sanctions became part of the nation's immigration laws. The passage of the

---

[12] S. Rep. No. 1515, 81st Cong, 2d Sess, p. 345.

[13] 8 U.S.C. § 1182(a)(4) (1952).

[14] 302 F.2d 652 (9th Cir. 1962), *vacated on other grounds*, 374 U.S. 449, 83 S. Ct. 1804, 10 L. Ed. 2d 1000 (1963).

[15] S. Rep. No. 748, 89th Cong., 1st Sess. 19, reprinted in 1965 U.S. Code Cong. & Ad. News 3328, 3337; H.R. Rep. No. 745, 89th Cong., 1st Sess. 16 (1965).

[16] 8 U.S.C. § 1182(a)(4) (1976).

[17] 387 U.S. 118 (1967).

Immigration Reform and Control Act (IRCA) represented the culmination of years of social, political and congressional debate about the perceived lack of control over our southern border. The belief that something had to be done about the large numbers of undocumented workers who had entered the U.S. from Mexico in the 1970s was reinforced by the flood of Central Americans that began arriving in the early 1980s. While the political turmoil of civil war in El Salvador, Guatemala, and Nicaragua drove many Central Americans from their homeland, they, along with the Mexicans who continued to arrive, were generally labeled economic migrants by the Reagan Administration, the INS, and the courts.

Employer sanctions had earlier iterations. In 1952 — when the immigration laws were overhauled to clamp down on subversives and communists, the notion of punishing employers got nowhere. As a provision outlawing willful importation, transportation or harboring of undocumented aliens was debated, an amendment was proposed imposing criminal penalties for the employment of undocumented aliens if the employer had "reasonable grounds to believe a worker was not legally in the United States." The amendment was soundly defeated, but beginning in 1971, legislative proposals featuring employer sanctions as a centerpiece reappeared and were touted as the tool needed to resolve the undocumented alien problem. By the end of the Carter Administration in 1980, the Select Commission on Immigration and Refugee Policy portrayed legalization as a necessary balance to sanctions. However, the story of congressional support for IRCA is complicated. Although some broader-mined members of Congress may have wanted legalization to be implemented generously once enacted, Congress' support for legalization itself was decidedly underwhelming.

So within thirty years of the 1952 rejection of employer sanctions, things had changed. Most Americans were convinced that a crisis over undocumented immigration — especially undocumented *Mexican* migration — existed and that something had to be done. The desire to rid the country of the unwanted was too strong. The power of employers to resist sanctions collapsed, and by 1986 federal employer sanctions were enacted as the major feature of reform. By a bare swing vote of only four members of the House of Representatives, legalization (amnesty) provisions (one part for those who entered prior to 1982, and another for certain agricultural workers) were also made part of the package to address the undocumented immigrant issue. Although on paper the appearance of a deal of employer sanctions for amnesty was struck, there was no political tradeoff; IRCA would have gone forward if legalization were dropped by the House, and its effective implementation in the hands of an inept Immigration and Naturalization Service was seriously in doubt.

1.   Reasons Given for Legalization

The major justifications advanced by legislative supporters of a legalization program were varied.

a.   No Alternative to Legalization

How could Congress deal with the huge number of undocumented aliens living in the United States? Members of Congress only had a handful of alternatives: first, legalize some or all of the aliens; second, find and deport some or all of them; or third, do nothing. The second alternative would have required a huge effort to "round up" aliens, would probably have violated many civil rights and therefore engendered a horde of lawsuits, would have cost a fortune, and simply would never have worked. The third alternative was not possible since Congress was under pressure to do something about the perceived undocumented problem. Legalization was the only alternative.

Thus, in a real sense, this argument boiled down to a logistically realistic response to the "problem of undocumented aliens." Existing enforcement was failing and massive deportations would certainly never have worked. Thus, one could argue that the program had to be generous if the goal was to rid the country of undocumented aliens. Yet the cutoff date adopted for legalization was not generous, and the "no alternatives" argument was not the only reasoning offered to support legalization.

b.   Spread INS Resources

A different justification for legalizing undocumented residents was that this would allow the INS to stop concentrating its enforcement resources on locating and apprehending longtime residents and concentrate instead on enforcement of the border against newly arriving, undocumented aliens.

c.   Elimination of the Underclass

For some, legalization was the mechanism to address the fact that many undocumented aliens lived in what some described as an "underclass" in poverty without the protection of labor or health laws. The Select Commission had complained of the existence of a "second class" society. And many members of Congress hoped that legalization would eliminate the underclass.[18] A spokesman for the Mexican American Legal Defense and Education Fund (MALDEF) was typical of supporters who contended that "[l]egalization is the only realistic and meaningful way to bring the undocumented population 'out of the shadows' and into the mainstream of American life with the minimum of disruption and expense."[19] And on signing the legislation, even President Reagan, who was more interested in the employer sanctions provisions of the law, expressed hope that the legalization program would remove people from "the shadows."[20]

---

[18] *See, e.g.,* 132 Cong. Rec. 30,064 (1986) (statement of Rep. Bill Richardson).

[19] Housing Hearing 28 at 128 (statement of Richard Fajardo, MALDEF).

[20] Statement on Signing the Immigration Reform and Control Act of 1986, 1986 Pub. Papers 1522.

d.   Equity, Fairness, Dignity, Compassion, and Reality

Many lawmakers supported the legalization program because of the contributions that undocumented workers had already made to the country, and charged the nation with a responsibility to account for those contributions. This view was used to respond to complaints that legalization was not fair to prospective immigrants waiting in line abroad or that it might be a "magnet" for further unlawful entrants thinking they could cheat their way into the program. Indeed, the House Report argued that legalization was "equitable" to the undocumented aliens working in the United States, and in President Reagan's words, "fair to the countless thousands of people throughout the world who seek legally to come to America."[21]

For others, it demonstrated "compassion" for those now part of American society, giving "dignity" and "honor" to those working without permission in America; in short, it was "necessary," "humanitarian," and the "American way."[22] Even the INS Commissioner touted legalization as a compromise between a "humanitarian recognition of illegals who have significant equities in the U.S." and "fair and reasonable screening requirements that do not reward proven criminals."[23]

2.   Intent of the Special Agricultural Worker Program

Evidence of the scope and intent behind the Special Agricultural Worker (SAW) legalization program is sketchy. The program made its way to inclusion in IRCA virtually without congressional debate and without any attempts to change it. Naturally, the program had its supporters and detractors. But few made statements revealing the intended scope of the program or the reasoning behind its structure. Several legislators viewed the SAW program as a compromise between growers and workers. No one seemed to think the SAW program was primarily for the benefit of laborers, although the legislative history makes it apparent that Congress was mindful not to reenact elements of the Bracero guestworker program from the 1950s.

3.   What Legalization Entailed

IRCA contained two major amnesty or legalization provisions that had the potential of benefiting millions of undocumented aliens. The first provided permanent residence status to aliens who had resided in the United States since before January 1, 1982. The other afforded permanent residence status to farm workers or Special Agriculture Workers (SAWS) who had performed agricultural work for at least ninety days between May 1, 1985 and May 1, 1986."

Those who commonly fell under the first program either entered by crossing the border without inspection prior to January 1, 1982, or entered on a visitor or student visa and worked without permission or overstayed the permitted length of

---

[21] H.R. Rep. No. 682-1, at 71; Statement on Signing of IRCA, at 1522.

[22] Statements of Representative H. Fish and Senator D. Moynihan.

[23] House Hearing 28, at 203 (statement of Alan Nelson, Commissioner, INS).

stay prior to that date. About seventy percent who ultimately applied under the pre 1982 program were Mexican; the next largest groups were Salvadoran (8.1 percent) and Guatemalan (3 percent). However, the percentages may simply reflect the results of publicity priorities of the INS and community based organizations (CBOs). Demographers who scrutinized the 1980 census data prior to IRCA concluded that only fifty five percent of the undocumented population was Mexican in origin.

Those qualifying under the farm worker program were also mostly Mexican. They predominated with 81.6 percent of the SAW applications. Haitians received 3.4 percent, El Salvadorans 2 percent, and Guatemalans and Asian Indians 1.4 percent each.

Ultimately, 1.7 million applicants filed under the pre-1982 program and 1.2 million applied as SAWs. The number for the pre-1982 program was far below most estimates, while the figure for agricultural workers was higher than expected.

4.   Employer Sanctions

Under IRCA, for the first time Congress prohibited employers from hiring workers who are not authorized to work in the United States, imposing civil and criminal penalties on violators. IRCA was the product of years of debate regarding the impact of undocumented immigrant workers on the United States. Employer sanctions was the centerpiece of the legislation, but employers also became subject to penalties for new employment discrimination laws.

In response to intense lobbying by civil rights advocates and concerned members of Congress who feared that employer sanctions would cause employment discrimination, protections were included in the law intended to safeguard against discrimination. IRCA contained provisions that attempted to insure that employers would not use the new employer sanctions law as a pretext for discriminating against immigrant workers. Prior to IRCA, private employers could require employees to be U.S. citizens, but after IRCA, employers had to hire a qualified immigrant job applicant, unless a citizen was equally qualified applied for the job. Employers could be fined for such discriminatory hiring practices, as well as for requiring new immigrant employees to come up with more proof than necessary to establish eligibility to work.

IRCA mandated the General Accounting Office (GAO), the investigative arm of Congress, to conduct three annual studies from 1987 to 1989 to determine whether employer sanctions had resulted in "widespread discrimination." A "sunset" provision further stipulated that employer sanctions could be repealed if the GAO concluded that compliance caused employers to discriminate.

The first two status reports on employer sanctions by the GAO found that "one in every six employers in GAO's survey who were aware of the law may have begun or increased the practice of (1) asking only foreign-looking persons for work authorization documents or (2) hiring only U.S. citizens." In spite of the fact that almost 17 percent of employers admitted to practices that violated the discrimination provisions of IRCA, GAO concluded that the findings did not establish a pattern of "widespread discrimination," citing lack of conclusive evidence that the employer sanctions requirements were the cause of discrimination.

In 1989, a number of groups across the country began to compile information that they had received from individuals of mostly Asian, Latino, and Middle Eastern descent regarding discriminatory treatment they had experienced while seeking new employment or working in the current positions. Several civil rights organizations issued reports of the anecdotal evidence collected. While the reports documented disturbing accounts of discrimination, proponents of employer sanctions dismissed the data collected by advocacy groups as unreliable.

Eventually, some of the independent research could not be ignored by the GAO. A methodological survey of 416 San Francisco employers was conducted in San Francisco, revealing that an overwhelming 97 percent of the firms regularly engaged in at least one employment practice that could be discriminatory under IRCA or other anti-discrimination laws. Another 53 percent reported that they engaged in three or more such practices. The research was submitted to the GAO in September 1989, and influenced the GAO's third report.[24]

Despite the GAO's findings of "widespread" IRCA-related employment discrimination and similar evidence by independent researchers in its final two reports, Congress did not repeal employer sanctions. The findings were routinely dismissed by anti-immigrant groups, Senator Alan Simpson (a co-sponsor of IRCA), and the AFL-CIO as insignificant or unreliable. Several bills to repeal employer sanctions were introduced in Congress in 1990 and 1991, but none reached the floor of Congress (in spite of bi-partisan support from Senators Kennedy and Hatch).

Although employer sanctions were not repealed, the Immigration Act of 1990 did strengthen IRCA's anti-discrimination provisions. The law increased employer and employee education, added Special Agricultural Workers to the category of protected workers, changed the penalties for discrimination to conform with those for employer sanctions penalties, made document abuse an unfair immigration-related employment practice, prohibited retaliation against those who file charges, made it easier to prosecute for document abuse by adding civil, as well as criminal penalties, and eliminated the requirement that a non-citizen who makes a discrimination charge must have filed an official "declaration of intent" to become a citizen.

By the early 1990s, many members of Congress, most notably Senator Simpson, contended that no further employer education was necessary to decrease employment discrimination. In fact, Simpson argued at a 1992 Senate Judiciary Committee hearing that the employer sanctions provisions, both the documentation requirements and the anti-discrimination protections, were as familiar to employers as were the requirements to pay taxes.

---

[24] Lina M. Avidan, *Employment and Hiring Practices Under the Immigration Reform and Control Act of 1986; A Survey of San Francisco Businesses*, Coalition for Immigrant and Refugee Rights and Services, 1989.

Only a fraction of U.S. employers and workers have received education from the Office of Special Counsel, which spent approximately $14 million on educational outreach between 1990 and 1996. OSC's education program did not begin in earnest until 1990, when it initiated a grants program, contracting with local groups to conduct educational campaigns. The OSC is located in Washington, D.C., with no branch offices. Between 1987 and 1996, the OSC received 4,868 charges of discrimination from workers, but only 145 formal complaints were filed by the OSC against employers, 83 of whom were fined for IRCA-related unfair employment practices. Distribution of INS' *Handbook for Employers* that explains the regulations and has pictures of acceptable documents has also been inadequate. Only two nationwide distributions of the handbook took place by 1996: one in 1987 and again in 1991.

Although employer sanctions remain part of the immigration laws, by 2001, the concept had lost one of its ardent supporters. As organized labor, including the AFL-CIO, realized that its future viability rested solidly on the shoulders of immigrant workers, unions called for the repeal of employer sanctions and for the legalization of undocumented workers.

G. THE 1965 AMENDMENTS AND THE IMMIGRATION ACT OF 1990

1. The 1965 Framework for Selection

Since the 1952 Act changed little in the immigration selection system, the question over which immigrants to admit to the United States remained a battlefront. The survival of the national origins quota system of the 1920s through the 1952 Act continued the Western European dominance over immigration to the United States. The law continued to exasperate many observers, including President Truman, who vetoed the 1952 legislation largely due to its failure to repudiate the quota system. Congress, however, overrode Truman's veto, and critics were resigned to cite the law as an embarrassment that was inconsistent with our stature as leader of the free world.

Truman and others did not relent. Soon after the enactment of the 1952 law, he appointed a special Commission on Immigration and Naturalization to study the system. A 319-page report issued in 1953 strongly urged the abolition of the national origins system and recommended quotas without regard to national origin, race, creed, or color. President Eisenhower embraced the findings, but his push for corrective legislation failed. Despite repeated attempts at new legislation, no major action was taken on any of the commission's recommendations until more than ten years later.

Entering office in January 1961, President Kennedy submitted a comprehensive program that provided the impetus for ultimate reform. His proposals reflected his long-standing interest in immigration reform. Kennedy called for the repeal of the discriminatory national origins quota system and the racial exclusion from the Asia-Pacific triangle, while assailing the nativism that led to the infamous Chinese exclusion laws. He envisioned a system governed by the skills of the immigrant and family reunification. For him, his proposed changes meant both an increase in fairness to applicants and in benefits to the United States.

President Kennedy's hopes for abolishing the quota system were realized when the 1965 amendments were enacted. The Asia-Pacific Triangle geographic restrictions were also eliminated (although the ceiling of 2000 visas for that area had already been deleted in 1961). But his egalitarian vision of visas on a first-come, first-served basis gave way to a narrower and more historically parochial framework that provided few, if any, obvious advantages for prospective Asian immigrants. The new law allowed twenty thousand immigrant visas annually for every country not in the Western Hemisphere. The allotment was made regardless of size of a country, so that mainland China had the same quota as Tunisia. Of the 170,000 visas set aside for the Eastern Hemisphere, 75 percent were for specified "preference" relatives of citizens and lawful permanent residents, and an unlimited number was available to immediate relatives (parents of adults, minor unmarried children, and spouses) of U.S. citizens. First preference was for the adult, unmarried sons and daughters of U.S. citizens, second preference for the spouses and unmarried children of lawful permanent resident aliens, fourth preference for married sons and daughters of U.S. citizens, and fifth preference for the siblings of U.S. citizens. Two occupational categories and a nonpreference category were also established. The occupational categories helped professionals and other aliens who filled jobs for which qualified U.S. workers were not available; although, for the first time, aliens seeking entry as skilled and unskilled labor were required to have approval of the Secretary of Labor. Under the nonpreference category, an alien who invested $40,000 in a business could qualify for immigration to the United States. A seventh preference was a refugee-like category for conditional entrants who were fleeing communist-dominated countries or the Middle East.

2.   Restraints on Mexican Immigration in the 1970s

Although the 1952 Act did not place a numerical limit on immigration from these areas, Congress included the Western Hemisphere quota of 120,000 in the 1965 amendments as a compromise for abolishing the national origins system. Concern was raised over the fact that immigration was on the increase from countries of the Western Hemisphere, particularly from Mexico.

Thus, while the rest of the world enjoyed an expansion of numerical limitations and a definite preference system after 1965, Mexico and the Western Hemisphere were suddenly faced with numerical restrictions for the first time. The Western Hemisphere was allotted a total of 120,000 immigrant visas each year, and while the first-come, first-served basis for immigration sounded fair, applicants had to meet strict labor certification requirements and demonstrate that they would not be displacing U.S. workers. Waivers of the labor certification requirement were available, however, for certain applicants, e.g., parents of U.S. citizen children. As one might expect given the new numerical limitations, by 1976 the procedure resulted in a severe backlog of approximately three years and a waiting list with nearly 300,000 names.[25]

---

[25] *See* CHARLES GORDON & STANLEY MAILMAN, IMMIGRATION LAW AND PROCEDURE § 1.4c (1993); Memo-

As the immigration of Mexicans became the focus of more debate, Congress enacted legislation in 1976, curtailing Mexican migration even more. The law imposed the preference system on Mexico and the Western Hemisphere along with a 20,000 visa per country numerical limitation. Thus Mexico's annual visa usage rate (which had been about 40,000) was virtually cut in half overnight, and thousands were left stranded on the old system's waiting list.[26] In 1978, the 120,000 Western Hemisphere and 170,000 Eastern Hemisphere quotas were merged into a single 290,000 worldwide numerical limit on immigration.

An 11-year misallocation of visas to Cuba eventually led to the permanent injunction and a "recapturing" of the wrongfully issued visas in lawsuit *Silva v. Bell*.[27] Finally, people who would have been able to immigrate years earlier, but for the mistake in taking away visas from the Western Hemisphere allocation, were able to now lawfully immigrate. However, Mexicans again received the short end of the stick when the State Department's formula for reallocation, which failed to provide sufficient visas for thousands of Mexicans on the *Silva* waiting list, was upheld. As a result, in February 1982, INS authorities began to round up those *Silva* class members who had not been accorded immigrant visa, advising them that they were now deportable and that work permission was terminated. The recipients were further informed that unless provisions of the existing immigration law qualified them to remain in the United States, they would have thirty days for voluntary departure. Although INS delayed enforcement for awhile, by February 1, 1983, the Enforcement Branch of the INS resumed the roundup of *Silva* class members.[28]

To make matters worse, in the first year of the new Western Hemisphere preference system and 20,000 limit on countries in the region, Mexico lost 14,000 visas due to a congressional mistake. The enactment date of the new law was January 1, 1977. However since the government's fiscal year runs from October 1 to September 30, the amendments did not become effective until after one full quarter of fiscal year 1977 had expired. During that first quarter, 14,203 visas were issued to Mexicans pursuant to the immigration system that prevailed in the Western Hemisphere before the new law became effective. The State Department nevertheless charged those visas against the newly-imposed national quota of 20,000, leaving only 5,797 visas available for Mexican immigrants between January 1 and September 30, 1977. In *De Avila v. Civiletti*,[29] the Seventh Circuit Court of Appeals sustained the State Department's approach even though it was "obvious

---

randum for the Associate Attorney General, Re: Allocation of Visas under *Silva v. Levi*, Deputy Assistant Attorney General, Office of Legal Counsel, Department of Justice, 3 (May 15, 1978).

[26] Act of Oct. 20, 1976, Pub.L. No. 94-571, 90 Stat. 2703 (1976); Silva v. Bell, 605 F.2d at 980–982.

[27] Silva v. Bell, No. 76C 4268 (N.D. Ill. Oct. 10, 1978) (order granting permanent injunction); *See also* No. 76C 1456 (N.D. Ill. June 21, 1977) (final judgment order-visas recaptured).

[28] Telegraphic Message of Hugh J. Brian, Asst. Commr. Detention and Deportation, Central Office Immigration and Naturalization Service, CO 242.4-P (Aug. 20, 1982); Memorandum from E. B. Duarte, Jr, Director, Outreach Program, Central Office Immigration and Naturalization Service, To Outreach Centers, Subject: Silva Update (February 3, 1983).

[29] 643 F.2d 471, 476 (7th Cir. 1981).

that Congress . . . through inadvertence failed to inform the State Department how to administer during a fraction of the fiscal year a statute designed to apply on a full fiscal year basis."

3.   Affirmative Action for Western Europeans: "Diversity" in the 1980s and 1990s

By the end of the 1970s and through the 1980s, immigrant visa demands from Mexico remained high, and demand from certain Asian countries surged. By 1990, immigrants from Mexico, the Philippines, India, Korea, and Chinese from China, Taiwan, and Hong Kong dominated legal immigration categories. Given the per-country numerical limitations, Mexico and Asian countries shared (and continue to share) the largest backlogs in family reunification categories. This was especially true for preference categories reserved for siblings of U.S. citizens and relatives of lawful permanent resident aliens. Yet, in 1982, as part of a major legislative package, Republican Senator Alan Simpson of Wyoming initiated a crusade to eliminate the immigration category allowing U.S. citizens to be reunited with siblings and persisted in his efforts to abolish the category until his retirement in 1996.

In 1986, Congress responded to the rising domination of Asian and Latinos in immigration totals in a different manner. Although the country's population was still overwhelmingly white and of European descent, Congress added a little publicized provision in the Immigration Reform and Control Act to help thirty-six countries that had been "adversely affected" by the 1965 changes. To be considered "adversely affected," a country must have been issued fewer visas after 1965 than before. Thus, the list included such countries as Great Britain, Germany, and France, but no countries from Africa who sent few immigrants prior to 1965. So the so-called "diversity" program was not about diversifying the country, which of course remained overwhelmingly white. It also was not about helping immigrants from countries that had little ability to voluntarily immigrate to the United States historically, e.g., African nations. The "diversity" program was actually an affirmative action program for natives of countries who already made up the vast ethnic background of the country, such as Western European countries.

The new allocations were significant. The 1986 law provided an extra 5000 such visas a year for 1987 and 1988, but the number increased to 15,000 per year for 1989 and 1990 through additional legislation. These visas were above and beyond the 20,000 visas that were already available for immigrants from each of the "diversity" countries under the preference system. But in order to qualify for the diversity visas, applicants did not have to have close relatives already in the United States or special job skills that would benefit the country. The program was a "first-come-first-served" worldwide mail registration program, benefiting the earliest-registered applicants and their immediate families, requiring them only to meet the nationality, health, and morals qualifications of immigration laws.

Part of the impetus for the "diversity" program was the fact that many Irish nationals who came to the United States were unable to fit into the regular immigration categories. They did not have close relatives who could petition for them, and many did not have special job skills. In the 1980s, a severe economic downturn in Ireland motivated many of its young professionals to look for work abroad. Ireland's gross domestic product (GDP) grew an average of only 1.8 percent each year from 1980 to 1985. Its national debt rivaled that of many Third World countries; in 1986, the debt stood at 134 percent of the GNP.[30] Ireland's foreign debt, in per capita terms, was one of the highest in the world — three times as high as Mexico's. One out of every five Irish workers was out of a job by 1987, and the unemployment rate was worse in major cities such as Dublin.[31]

Discouraged by the economy in Ireland, many of its young residents traveled to the United States, usually on temporary visas such as for tourism. Eventually they overstayed their visas. By 1989, the Irish government estimated that perhaps 50,000 Irish nationals resided in the United States in undocumented status.

So in 1988, Congress set aside an extra 20,000 visas to increase immigration diversity over a period of another two years. This time, the "OP-1" lottery for the visas was available to nationals of countries that were "underrepresented," namely a foreign state that used less than twenty-five percent of its 20,000 preference visas in 1988. As a result, all but thirteen countries in the world were eligible. Mexico, the Philippines, China, Korea, and India were among the countries that were not eligible. Over 3.2 million applicants were received for the 20,000 visas.

Legislation in 1990 extended the diversity visa concept even more. Until October 1, 1994, a transition diversity program would provide 40,000 visas per year for countries "adversely affected" by the 1965 amendments, except that forty percent of the visas were effectively designated for Irish nationals. True, displaced Tibetans residing in India or Nepal were also given extra numbers, but the overwhelming diversity beneficiaries would be white. After October 1, 1994, 55,000 diversity visas would be available annually in a lottery-type program to natives of countries from which immigration was lower than 50,000 over the preceding five years — certainly not Mexico, China, South Korea, the Philippines, or India. Under a complicated formula that weighs countries and regions of the world and uses relative populations, the State Department determines the distribution of lottery visas. A single state can never get more than seven percent (3,850) of the total diversity visas available each year. In one early projection of the formula, the first year's regional distribution looked like this: Africa 20,900, Asia 6,380, North America 0, Europe 24,310, Latin America 2,530, and Oceania 880.

In order to take part in the lottery program in 1988, an applicant needed only to submit a letter with family and other biographical data. Under the 1990 diversity program, however, the applicant must have a high school education, or within five years of application, the applicant must have at least two years of work experience in an occupation that requires at least two years of training or experience. That left out most Africans who wanted to immigrate.

---

[30] Karen DeYoung, *Irish Again Look Abroad for Economic Opportunities; Emigraion Rates Have Risen Sharply*, THE WASHINGTON POST, Dec. 6, 1986, at A1.

[31] Ray Moseley, *In Ireland, An Election, A Dilemma*, CHICAGO TRIB., Feb. 8, 1987, at C12; *Poorest of the Rich*, THE ECONOMIST, Jan. 16, 1988, at 10.

The justification for special treatment for Irish nationals at various junctures of the diversity program was the recognition that under the primarily family-based immigration system, a special seed or pipeline category needed to be established. Only then could a significant number of people immigrate who could then take advantage of the family reunification categories by becoming U.S. citizens or filing under the category reserved for relatives of lawful permanent resident aliens.

4.   Debating Foreign Professional Workers

The historical tensions between employers and the native work force over strategies of filling jobs with foreign workers (seen vividly in the agricultural industry) was highlighted in the battle over visas for skilled and professional workers in the 1980s and 1990s.

The battle also coincided with parallel attacks on the family immigration system — which had been the foundation of the immigration laws since the 1965 amendments. Prior to 1990, 80 percent of the worldwide preference system quota of 270,000 was reserved for kinship provisions, and the category of immediate relatives of the United States citizens was numerically unlimited. The effect of this priority was demonstrated vividly in the subsequent flow of Asian immigration, even though nations such as those in Africa and Asia, with low rates of immigration prior to 1965, were handicapped. In other words, the nations with large numbers of descendents in the United States were expected to benefit from a kinship-based system, and in 1965, less than a million Asian Americans resided in the country. Although the kinship priority meant that Asians were beginning on an unequal footing, at least Asians were on par numerically, in terms of the per country quotas. Gradually, by using the family categories to the extent they could be used and the labor employment route, Asians built a family base from which to use the kinship categories more and more. By the late 1980s, well over 90 percent of all Asian immigration to the United States was through the kinship categories, as with virtually all immigration to the United States.

The genesis for the legislation that ultimately became the Immigration Act of 1990 came in the form of Senate bill S. 358, whose primary sponsor was Republican Senator Alan Simpson, and House bill H.R. 4300, led by Democratic Congressman Bruce Morrison. Simpson had been a member of the Select Commission on Immigration and Refugee Policy that issued a report in 1981 calling for major changes in the immigration laws. After IRCA was enacted in 1986 to address issue of undocumented migration through employer sanctions and legalization, Simpson turned his attention to legal immigration categories. At the time, although 20 percent of preference categories were available to labor employment immigrants (54,000), when the unrestricted immediate relative immigration categories were added to the total number of immigrants each year, less than 10 percent of immigrants who were entering each year were doing so on the basis of job skills.

At a time when legal immigration continued to be dominated by Asians and Latinos even after "diversity programs" were being implemented to aid non-Asian and non-Mexican immigrants, Simpson wanted the family immigration numbers reduced or at least managed. S. 358 was approved by the Senate in July 1989, which would establish a ceiling of 630,000 legal immigrants for three years. Of the total, 480,000 would be reserved for all types of family immigration and 150,000 would be set aside for immigrants without family connections but with skills or job related assets. Yet after numerous markups and hearings, the House of Representative passed Morrison's H.R. 4300, a rather different bill, on Oct. 3, 1990. The bill actually would reduce family immigration more dramatically — thereby reducing the number of Asian and Latino family immigrants, providing 185,000 family-based visas and 95,000 employment-based visas annually.

As originally introduced, H.R. 4300 revamped most immigrant and nonimmigrant work visa categories. It created four categories, which would have priority within the 95,000 total visas for employer sponsored immigrants. These aliens would also be exempt from the labor certification requirement which had demanded that employers demonstrate the unavailability of U.S. workers. The bill would also allow up to 1,000 foreign investors to obtain a two-year conditional resident status by investing at least $1million and creating 10 new jobs for unrelated U.S. citizens or other workers. Critics noted that this would essentially allow foreign investors to buy citizenship. Employers could also sponsor other aliens provided they prove a shortage of U.S. workers.

As passed, H.R. 4300 would increase the number of legal immigrants to 775,000 a year from the prior 540,000. It would also speed the process of uniting families, attract more skilled workers and create a new diversity category for immigrants from countries whose nationals have largely been excluded in the past. After passing the bill, the House changed the bill number to S. 358 to enable it to go to a joint House-Senate conference. However, many were opposed to the more liberal House bill and negotiated to cap legal immigration and place new measures to control illegal immigration, including tougher provisions against criminal aliens.

Enacted on Oct. 26, 1990, the compromise bill would allow 700,000 immigrants from 1992–94 and 675,000 annually in subsequent years.[32] For the time being, proposals to cut back on family immigration were defeated, and the Immigration Act of 1990 had responded to lobbying efforts by American businesses. The Act was a significant, and to some a revolutionary, revision of the focus of U.S. immigration law. After passage of the Act, although the main thrust of immigration law continued to be family immigration, highly-skilled immigrations would be deliberately encouraged to resettle in the United States more than ever before. In the long run, the number of employment based visas would nearly triple from 54,000 to 140,000 per year. Predictably, the bill met with a great deal of resistance from labor organizations. They were mollified, however, by the fact that the labor certification requirements remained essentially the same as they were prior to passage of the Act, and were not streamlined even though an earlier House version of the bill had called for that.

---

[32] The compromise included portions of S. 3055 sponsored by Simpson, which would speed deportations of criminal aliens. Section 501 expanded the definition of "aggravated felony" to include illicit trafficking in any controlled substance, money laundering, and any crime of violence with a 5 year imprisonment imposed. The bill also included both federal and state crimes. Aliens convicted of aggravated felonies would have expedited deportation hearings and would not be released from custody while in deportation proceedings. 67 IR 1229–31.

Under the new law, that remains part of today's system, occupational visas were divided into five categories: (1) 40,000 visas for priority workers who possess extraordinary ability in the arts, sciences, education, business, or athletics, or outstanding professors and researchers, and certain multinational executives; (2) 40,000 visas for professionals holding advanced degrees or aliens of exceptional ability; (3) 40,000 visas for skilled workers, professionals with baccalaureate degrees, and unskilled workers for jobs for which qualified American workers are not available (only 10,000 visas can be issued for unskilled workers); (4) 10,000 visas for special immigrants, and (5) 10,000 visas for employment creation immigrants, specifically investors of $500,000 to $3 million whose investments create at least ten new jobs.

Most of the available immigrant visas are still reserved for relatives of U.S. citizens and lawful permanent resident aliens. However, the near tripling of occupational visas from 54,000 to 140,000 in the 1990 legislation signaled the beginning of a shift in the focus of U.S. immigration law from concern with family reunification toward a policy of importing skilled workers. In fact, before 1990, up to one-half of the 54,000 occupational visas could be used for unskilled workers who were not displacing American workers; but the figure for unskilled workers was reduced to 10,000 by the 1990 law.

The creation of the investor or employment-creation visa was also noteworthy. This new category was designed for immigrants seeking to engage n a new commercial enterprise. The law requires that the investment be at least $1 million, but the amount is reduced to $500,000 if the enterprise is located in a targeted employment area, such as a rural area or any area that has experienced high unemployment of at least 150 percent of the national average rate. No fewer than 3,000 of the 10,000 visas are reserved for applicants whose enterprises will be located in targeted employment areas.

5.   More Visas for Temporary Workers: the H-1B Category

The Immigration Act of 1990 also implemented at new H-1B program that has proven to be quite popular with U.S. businesses, but also opposed by some who think businesses should hire available U.S. workers and groups that have seen the program used mostly by professionals from India and China.

Prior to 1990, an unlimited number of nonimmigrant H-1 work visas were available to individuals of "distinguished merit and ability."[33] This requirement was easily satisfied by professional-level employees. The law did not require the person to have an advanced degree or to be renowned in the field. In essence, all that was required was that the alien have at least a baccalaureate degree or its equivalent in a given field, and that the knowledge required for a particular job be a realistic prerequisite to entry into a particular field of endeavor.[34] As a result, tens of thousands of nonimmigrants entered annually in this H-1 professional category.

---

[33] 8 C.F.R. 214.2(h) (1989).

[34] Matter of Shin, 11 I.&N. Dec. 686 (Dist. Dir. 1966).

In 1990, the old H-1 program was replaced with the H-1B program for nonimmigrants entering "in a specialty occupation."[35] Like its predecessor, this provision provides a convenient way for professional workers to enter for temporary employment purposes. Again, the main requirement is that the occupation requires at least a bachelor's degree in the particular specialty. But an important new requirement was added; the employer must submit a Labor Condition Application (LCA) to the Department of Labor, attesting that the foreign worker's employment does not adversely impact similarly-employed U.S. workers. In other words, H-1B workers cannot be exploited and must be paid at least the prevailing wage in the industry, and working conditions must be the same as similarly-employed workers in the same area of employment.

A critical difference, however, between the former H-1 program and the newer H-1B program has to do with numbers. The 1990 law imposed a 65,000 limit on the number of aliens who could be given H-1B status each year. This number proved highly controversial and subject to much political struggle, as the quotas were easily reached in the late 1990s at the height of the high-tech boom. More than half of the visas were issued to nonimmigrants (mostly engineers) from India, and another 10 percent were issued to nationals of the Republic of China. Also, some 60 percent of the visas were issued for computer and systems analyst positions.

Led by the high technology industry in the late 1990s, businesses lobbied Congress to increase the H-1B visa numbers. In spite of critics who argued unconvincingly that U.S. workers were available to fill these positions, in October 2000 Congress cleared the backlog of pending H-1B cases and increased the annual allotment to 195,000 for 2001, 2002, and 2003. Much of these efforts proved unnecessary as hundreds of high-tech industries went belly-up in 2001 and 2002, and the need for H-1B workers went dry.

H. IMMIGRATION REFORM IN 1996

1.   Antiterrorism and Effective Death Penalty Act of 1996

Although the primary focus of the Immigration Act of 1990 was on the debate over the number of visas for kinship categories versus employment categories, Senator Alan Simpson insisted on stronger provisions to deal with aliens convicted of crimes as well. The compromise included portions of S. 3055 sponsored by Simpson, which would speed deportations of criminal aliens. Section 501 expanded the definition of "aggravated felony" to include illicit trafficking in any controlled substance, money laundering, and any crime of violence with a 5 year imprisonment imposed. Aliens convicted of aggravated felonies would have expedited deportation hearings and would not be released from custody while in deportation proceedings.[36]

---

[35] 8 U.S.C. § 1101(a)(15)(H)(i)(b).

[36] 67 IR 1229–31.

The 1990 enforcement provisions stemmed from Congress' belief that aliens in deportation proceedings and those convicted of crimes had too many rights.[37] Congress also presumed that aliens and their attorneys unnecessarily delayed deportation proceedings through frivolous motions and appeals. After the passage of the Immigration Act of 1990, other acts of Congress further limited the rights of aliens convicted of aggravated felonies through the Immigration and Technical Corrections Act of 1994, the Illegal Immigration Reform and Immigration Responsibility Act of 1996, and the Antiterrorism and Effective Death Penalty Act of 1996 (AEDPA).

On April 24, 1996 President Clinton signed AEDPA into law. The act was passed with broad bipartisan support by Congress (91-8-1 in the United States Senate, 293-133-7 in the House of Representatives) the Antiterrorism and Effective Death Penalty Act of 1996 (AEDPA). The law expanded the government's ability to take antiterrorism measures, increased circumstances under which victims of crime can receive restitution from defendants, and narrowed habeas jurisdiction, and eased standards required to deport immigrants.

AEDA included very significant changes to the immigration laws relating to exclusion, criminal aliens, and special removal proceedings for alien terrorists. Special removal procedures for alien terrorists set forth the establishment of a new removal court composed of five federal district court judges appointed by the chief justice of the U.S. Supreme Court. The court could hear a case whenever the attorney general certified that an alien terrorist physically present in the United States would pose a risk to national security if removed by normal deportation procedures. A judge could then grant the application for removal, ordering the alien detained pending removal. If an alien removed attempted to reenter without authorization, he or she would be subject to imprisonment for ten years. The bill denied other forms of relief for terrorists, including asylum and voluntary departure. Habeas corpus was also foreclosed.

AEDPA's provisions affecting the treatment of criminal aliens included several immigration offenses to be predicate offenses for Racketeer Influenced and Corrupt Organization (RICO) convictions. The new RICO-predicate offenses included document fraud and trafficking in aliens. Other criminal alien provisions included long-distance relocation plans for any criminal alien who had attempted illegal entry into the United States at least three times. AEDPA also provided for deportation of criminals before their entire prison sentence is served. If such an alien were to later illegally enter the United States, that alien would have to serve the remainder of the prison sentence at that time.

AEDPA added crimes to the list of aggravated felonies for which a criminal alien would be subject to expedited removal. These offenses include: forgery of a passport or other document for entry into the United States and running a gambling business. It also modified the expedited procedures, including extreme limits on any challenge to the removal order and limitations on discretionary review of a removal order.

---

[37] 68 IR 197.

2.   Welfare Reform

On the eve of the 1996 Democratic National Convention, President Clinton signed into law a sweeping reform bill, the Personal Responsibility and Work Opportunity Reconciliation Act of 1996 (the "Act").[38] By eliminating a federal commitment to provide even a minimal level of assistance to America's poorest, the legislation carried harsh consequences for a range of economically vulnerable individuals and families. Since the Act specifically targeted immigrants for major cuts, its effects were felt quickly and severely by non-citizen immigrants in economic need.

The Act made legal immigrants ineligible to receive a number of federally-funded public benefits. It similarly authorized state and local governments to deny locally-funded benefits to legal immigrants, transgressing the long-held constitutional requirement that states treat citizens and legal immigrants alike in terms of public benefits eligibility. The legislation also tightened restrictions affecting undocumented immigrants, further marginalizing a group that was already ineligible for most benefits and services.

Social welfare laws commonly distinguish between the eligibility of *undocumented* immigrants and *documented* immigrants (which includes refugees). The 1996 Act originally barred both groups of immigrants from participating in two federal benefits programs: Supplemental Security Income (SSI) and food stamps. Until the 1997 budget compromise reached by Congress and President Clinton restored benefits to documented immigrants who were in the country as of August 26, 1996, data from the Social Security Administration indicated that approximately half a million immigrants would lose SSI as a result of the new law; a million were likely to lose food stamps.

Certain classes of legal immigrants were exempt from these restrictions: (1) refugees, asylees, and individuals granted withholding of deportation, but only for the first five years after being granted that status; (2) active duty service members, veterans, and their direct family members; and (3) permanent residents who can prove that they have worked at least forty qualifying quarters, or ten years, for social security purposes. All *future* immigrants would be barred for a period of five years after "entry" from any federal means-tested program, again certain classes of legal immigrants were exempt. In addition to barring future immigrants from receiving SSI and Food stamps, the Act authorized states to pass legislation denying legal immigrants access to a range of state-administered federal programs. As the costs of social welfare programs shifted to the states, they were increasingly tempted to deny legal immigrants assistance under these programs.

While the Act directly excluded legal immigrants from receiving some benefits and enables states to restrict eligibility for others, the Act also made changes that affect immigrant eligibility indirectly. In particular, the legislation toughened standards for immigrants whose eligibility depended on a sponsor. Applicants for family-based immigrant visas had to demonstrate that they were not likely to become a public charge. In making this demonstration, petitioning relatives of visa

---

[38] Pub. L. No. 104-193, 110 Stat. 2105 (1996).

applicants were now required to submit a legally binding affidavit, agreeing to provide financial support to the applicant. Some programs included the sponsor's income in calculating eligibility, a practice called "sponsor-deeming."

The Act was also harsh to immigrants in unprecedented semantic ways. Immigrants who did not meet the Act's definition of "qualified" immigrants were considered "unqualified," including immigrants who were residing in the United States legally or with the permission of immigration authorities. The legislation barred unqualified immigrants from receiving any "federal public benefit," including any of the major federal public benefit programs: Temporary Assistance for Needy Families (TANF, which replaced Aid To Families with Dependent Children), Food stamps, Medicaid, SSI, unemployment compensation, school loans and grants, and subsidized housing. Many of these programs historically were closed to undocumented immigrants. Under prior law, however, immigrants were eligible to receive Medicaid, SSI, and AFDC if they were "permanently residing in the United States under color of law" (PRUCOL), a category eliminated by the Act's blanket exclusion of unqualified immigrants. All immigrants could qualify for social security benefits and unemployment insurance compensation if they had employment authorization and a valid social security number. These programs were now completely closed to those considered "unqualified."

In the wake of the 1996 Act, many legal immigrants began the process of naturalization, since citizens would still be eligible for benefits, albeit subject to many new restrictions. Welfare reform thus contributed to record-setting naturalization applications during much of 1997. Some who failed or who were not eligible for naturalization may have had access to local cash assistance programs such as General Assistance. Others who were frightened by the prospect of losing benefits committed or contemplated committing suicide. The financial outlook for these groups was very grim.

By August 5, 1997, a year after the passage of the welfare reform legislation, the Clinton administration and congressional leaders compromised and restored most disability and health benefits to immigrants who were in the country and covered before the initial legislation. Reached as part of a budget agreement, this re-reform allowed legal immigrants to remain eligible for SSI and Medicaid if they were receiving such benefits on August 22, 1996, when the 1996 welfare reform law was enacted. Lawful immigrants who were not yet receiving benefits, but were residing in the United States as of the enactment date, were eligible for SSI and Medicaid if they became disabled. The exemption from SSI and Medicaid restrictions for refugees was extended from five to seven years. However, restrictions on most programs other than SSI including the bar on food stamps, deeming provisions, and binding affidavits of support were retained.

3. Illegal Immigration Reform and Immigrant Responsibility Act

The Illegal Immigration Reform and Immigrant Responsibility Act of 1996 (IIRIRA)[39] made vast changed the immigration laws. One major change eliminated basic relief from deportation for long term lawful permanent residents who have been convicted of an aggravated felony. Prior to IIRIRA, such individuals could seek a discretionary waiver of deportation if they could demonstrate rehabilitation, remorse, and important family and community ties. However, the 1996 law renders aggravated felons ineligible for such discretionary relief.[40] An aggravated felony is defined in 8 U.S.C. 1227(a)(2)(A) as murder, rape, sexual abuse of a minor, any illicit trafficking in any controlled substance (including drugs, firearms, or destructive materials), money laundering, or any crime of violence (except for purely political offenses) for which the term of imprisonment imposed is at least one year. The definition also includes offenses of theft, if the term of imprisonment imposed is at least one year.

IIRIRA also affected asylum seekers. The law created procedures to remove aliens appearing at the border without documentation and required that anyone desiring asylum must file within one year of entering the country. The expedited procedures were designed to remove aliens who arrived in the United States without proper travel documents or who were suspected of carrying documents procured by fraud. A single immigration officer at an airport or other port of entry screens individuals to determine whether they intend to apply for asylum or fear persecution. If the officer thinks that the person does not fear persecution, the officer can order the person summarily removed from the country and bar the person from reentering the country for five years, without any further hearing or judicial review.

Those persons arriving who do express fear or want to apply for asylum immediately are transferred to a detention center. They may be placed in handcuffs, even shackles, at the airport, then transported to detention centers or jails. Although they are not charged with any crimes, they remain locked up at least until asylum officers can conduct extensive interviews to determine whether the applicants have a "credible fear" of persecution. If the asylum officer determines that the person does not have a credible fear of persecution, then the person must affirmatively request a review by an immigration judge. There is no right to judicial review. The review before an immigration judge is expedited and limited. The review must be concluded no later than seven days after the credible fear determination and need not even be conducted in person; it can be conducted by telephone or video connection. Counsel cannot be present, no evidence can be submitted, and no witness can be called.

---

[39] Pub.L. 104-208, 110 Stat. 3009.

[40] 8 U.S.C. 1229(a).

I.   NATIONAL SECURITY AND POST — 9/11 MEASURES

Since 9/11 Congress and the President have screened immigration policy proposals and enforcement procedures through the lens of national security. For anti-immigrant forces in the United States, 9/11 provided a once-in-a-lifetime opportunity to use the tragic events to draw linkages with virtually every aspect of their nativist agenda. But this is a neo-nativist agenda born of old hate cloaked in suggestions of international intrigue.

The Bush White House helped fuel the neo-nativist agenda in its legislative proposals that led to the USA PATRIOT Act, authorizing broad sweeps and scare tactics. The Bush White House epitomized its philosophy by words such as these in its July 2002 National Strategy for Homeland Security:

> Our great power leaves these enemies with few conventional options for doing us harm. One such option is to take advantage of our freedom and openness by *secretly inserting terrorists into our country* to attack our homeland. Homeland security seeks to deny this avenue of attack to our enemies and thus to provide a secure foundation for America's ongoing global engagement.[41]

A restrictionist organization like the Center for Immigration Studies (CIS) takes these words and argues that in the Department of Homeland Security's

> expansive portfolio, immigration is central. The reason is elementary: no matter the weapon or delivery system — hijacked airliners, shipping containers, suitcase nukes, anthrax spores — operatives are required to carry out the attacks. Those operatives have to enter and work in the United States. . . . Thus keeping the terrorists out or apprehending them after they get in is indispensable to victory.[42]

Thus, CIS used the opportunity presented by 9/11 to argue against issuing driver's licenses to undocumented people and to advocate for sweeps and apprehensions. Apparently, the idea is to make it hard for potential terrorists (i.e., foreigners) to move around or make a living, so they will become discouraged and leave. And who can argue against keeping terrorists out or apprehending them after they arrive?

Congress and the Bush administration heeded the appeals to implement harsh immigration policies. The events of 9/11 and the ensuing call to action from many quarters — including the anti-immigrant lobby — resulted in far-reaching legislative and enforcement actions. These enforcement actions had implications not only for suspected terrorists but also for immigrants already in the United States and noncitizens trying to enter as immigrants or with nonimmigrant visas.

---

[41] President Releases National Strategy for Homeland Security, July 16, 2002, *available at* http://www.whitehouse.gov/news/releases/2002/07/20020716-2.html (emphasis added).

[42] Mark Krikorian, *Keeping Terror Out — Immigration Policy and Asymmetric Warfare*, THE NATIONAL INTEREST (Spring 2004).

The USA PATRIOT Act is the most notable enactment.[43] The Act passed Congress with near unanimous support, and the President signed it into law a mere six weeks after 9/11. The vast powers embodied in the law provide expanded authority to search, monitor, and detain citizens and noncitizens alike, but its implementation since passage has preyed most heavily on noncitizen Arabs, Muslims, and Sikhs. Authority to detain, deport, or file criminal charges against noncitizens is specifically broadened. Consider the following noncitizen-related provisions in the law:

- Noncitizens are denied admission if they "endorse or espouse terrorist activity," or "persuade others to support terrorist activity or a terrorist organization," in ways that the State Department determines impede U.S. efforts to combat terrorism.
- The Act defines "terrorist activity" expansively to include support of otherwise lawful and nonviolent activities of almost any group that used violence.
- Noncitizens are deportable for wholly innocent associational activity, excludable for pure speech, and subject to incarceration without a finding that they pose a danger or flight risk.
- Foreign nationals can be detained for up to seven days while the government decides whether or not to file criminal or immigration charges.
- The Attorney General has broad preventive detention authority to incarcerate noncitizens by certifying there are "reasonable grounds to believe" that a person is "described in" the antiterrorism provisions of the immigration law, and the individual is then subject to potentially indefinite detention.
- The Attorney General can detain noncitizens indefinitely even after prevailing in a removal proceeding "until the Attorney General determines that the noncitizen is no longer a noncitizen who may be certified [as a suspected terrorist.]"
- Wiretaps and searches are authorized without a showing of probable criminal conduct if the target is an "agent of a foreign power," including any officer or employee of a foreign-based political organization.

To further emphasize how future visa issuance and immigration enforcement must be screened through the lens of national security, the Immigration and Naturalization Service (INS) was subsumed into the Department of Homeland Security (DHS) on November 25, 2002. Previously, the INS was under the control of the Attorney General's Justice Department — an enforcement-minded institution, but now the Administration has institutionalized the clamping down on noncitizens in the name of national security. The new Cabinet-level department merged all or parts of 22 federal agencies, with a combined budget of $40 billion and 170,000 workers, representing the biggest government reorganization in 50 years. DHS placed INS functions into two divisions: US Citizenship and Immigration Services (USCIS) which handles immigrant visa petitions, naturalization, and

---

[43] The clumsy, complete title is the Uniting and Strengthening America by Providing Appropriate Tools Required to Intercept and Obstruct Terrorism Act, *voila* the USA PATRIOT Act (Pub. L. No. 107-56).

asylum and refugee applications and the Under Secretary for Border and Trans-portation Security, which includes the Bureau of Customs and Border Protection along with Immigration and Customs Enforcement units, for handling enforcement matters.

Before and after DHS' creation, and presumably using pre-existing authority and new-found power under the PATRIOT Act, the administration implemented a number of policies and actions aimed at noncitizens in the name of national security:

- Amending its own regulations on September 17, 2001, INS authorizes the detention of any alien for 48 hours without charge with the possibility of extending the detention for an additional "reasonable period of time" in the even of an "emergency or other extraordinary circumstance."
- On September 21, 2001, the chief immigration judge orders new procedures requiring all immigration judges to hold "secure" hearings separately from all other cases, to close the hearings to the public, and to avoid discussing the case or disclosing any information about the case to anyone outside the immigration court.[44]
- On October 31, 2001, Attorney General John Ashcroft asks the Secretary of State to designate 46 new groups as terrorist organizations pursuant to the PATRIOT Act.
- On November 9, 2001, Attorney General Ashcroft calls for the "voluntary" interviews of up to 5,000 aliens from countries suspected of harboring relatively large numbers of terrorists; interviewees may be jailed without bond the Attorney General finds they are violating immigration laws.
- On November 9, 2001, the State Department slows the process for granting visas for men, ages 16 to 45, from certain Arab and Muslim countries by about 20 days.
- On November 13, President Bush issues an executive order authorizing the creation of military tribunals to try noncitizens on charges of terrorism.
- On December 4, 2001, U.S. Senator Russ Feingold holds hearings on the status of detainees. Attorney General Ashcroft suggests that those who question his policies are "aiding and abetting terrorism."
- On December 6, 2001, INS Commissioner James Ziglar announces that the INS will send the names of more than 300,000 aliens who remain in the United States, despite prior deportation or removal orders, to the FBI for inclusion in the National Crime Information Center database. This becomes known as the Alien Absconder Initiative.
- On January 8, 2002, the Department of Justice adds to the FBI's National Crime Information Center database the names of about 6,000 men from countries believed to be harboring al-Qaeda members who have ignored deportation or removal orders.
- On January 25, 2002, the Deputy Attorney General issues instructions for the Alien Absconder Initiative to locate 314,000 people who have a final

---

[44] A subsequent proposal by the National Association of Immigration Judges (NAIJ) is noteworthy. On January 2002, NAIJ proposed the creation of a separate executive branch agency to house the trial-level immigration courts and Board of Immigration Appeals, citing "disturbing encroachments on judicial independence" taken by the Present, the Attorney General and the Department of Justice in the aftermath of 9/11.

- deportation order, but who have failed to surrender for removal. The Deputy Attorney General designates several thousand men from "countries in which there has been al-Qaeda terrorist presence or activity" as "priority absconders" and enters them first into the National Crime Information Center database.

- On March 19, 2002, the Department of Justice announces interviews with 3,000 more Arabs and Muslims present in the United States as visitors or students.

- In June 2002, the INS proposes broadening special registration requirements for nonimmigrants from certain designated countries.

- On July 15, 2002, the Department of Justice announces a surveillance pilot program whereby U.S. citizens, including truckers, bus drivers, and others, can act as informants to report "suspicious activity." The program is to be called Operation TIPS (Terrorism Information and Prevention System).

- On July 24, 2002, the Department of Justice authorizes any state or local law enforcement officer — with the consent of those who cover the jurisdiction where the law enforcement officer is serving — to perform certain functions of INS officers during the period of a declared "mass influx of aliens."

- On August 21, 2002, the INS deports approximately 100 Pakistanis arrested on immigration violations.

- On September 16, 2002, Attorney General Ashcroft orders the INS to launch a "prompt review" of political asylum cases to identify any immigrants who have admitted to accusations of terrorist activity or being members of any terrorist organizations.

- On November 6, 2002, INS expands the special registration or National Security Entry-Exit Registration System (NSEERS) by requiring certain male nationals and citizens of Iran, Iraq, Libya, Sudan and Syria admitted to the United States prior to September 10, 2002 to register with INS. Failure to report to an INS office for fingerprinting, a photo, and an interview will result in deportation. On December 16, 2002, nonimmigrant males 16 years or older from Saudi Arabia and Pakistan are added to this list. On January 16, 2003, five more countries — Bangladesh, Egypt, Indonesia, Jordan, and Kuwait — are added to the list of 20 whose male citizens must register with INS.

- On November 18, 2002, the Foreign Intelligence Surveillance Act (FISA) Court of Review rules that the USA PATRIOT Act gives the Department of Justice broad authority to conduct wiretaps and other surveillance on terrorism suspects in the United States.

- On March 17, 2003, the Bush administration launches Operation Liberty Shield to "increase security and readiness in the United States." As part of this effort, DHS implements a temporary policy of detaining asylum seekers from 3 countries where al-Qaeda is known to have operated.

- On March 20, 2003, the Attorney General reveals that since December 18, 2002, FBI agents and U.S. marshals have detained foreign nationals for alleged immigration violations in cases where there is not enough evidence to hold them on criminal charges.

- In late 2005, President Bush confirmed that the U.S. had engaged in secret wiretapping of telephone calls of U.S. citizens with others from abroad without going to the FISA court for authorization.

In 2002, Congress created the National Commission on Terrorist Attacks Upon the United States (better known as the 9/11 Commission) that Congress charged with investigating the circumstances surrounding the 9/11 terrorist attacks and recommending responses. It released its final report and recommendations in July 2004. Soon after the Commission's report, Congress drafted legislation to implement its recommendations. During debates on the legislation, several members of Congress, most notably Representative James Sensenbrenner (R-Wis), the Chair of the House Judiciary Committee, argued for the inclusion of a number of contentious immigration measures. These measures went beyond the Commission's specific recommendations, nearly preventing the legislation's passage. The immigration-related proposals would have expanded the government's authority to arrest, detain, and deport immigrants, restricted judicial review and oversight, and reduced the number of documents immigrants may use to establish their identity. Sensenbrenner wanted to include a provision barring states issuing driver's licenses to undocumented aliens. But Commission members and 9/11 victims' relatives spoke out against these provisions, arguing that the debate was delaying legislation and would not make any significant contribution to public safety and security. Congress removed Sensenbrenner's proposal and the other anti-immigrant measures from the final version of the legislation, and Congress passed the Intelligence Reform and Terrorism Prevention Act of 2004.

In early 2005 Representative Sensenbrenner quickly reintroduced the controversial provisions (dubbed the REAL ID Act) he had removed, and on February 10, the House of Representatives passed Sensenbrenner's full package. One month later, the same legislation was attached to a huge emergency appropriations bill — a must-sign piece of legislation — to fund U.S. military efforts in Iraq and Afghanistan. The House passed this massive funding bill without any public debate or hearings. When the debate shifted to the Senate, the legislation did not include the REAL ID Act. But when the bill went to the Conference Committee, House supporters pushed strongly for the provisions to be included. During debates legislators removed a few of the most unsavory proposals, including one that would have created private bounty hunters to enforce immigration law. But the REAL ID Act provisions remained, and the Act was part of the package signed into law.[45]

J. THE PUSH FOR IMMIGRATION REFORM

The furor over illegal immigration is palpable. Rightly or wrongly, segments of the United States media, policy leaders, and populace continues to be obsessed with the issue of undocumented immigration to the United States. With an estimated 12 to 15 million undocumented aliens in the United States, advocates for immigration reform have become louder and more visible. Over the past few years, immigrant

---

[45] The REAL ID Act affects everyone in the United States. Beginning in 2008, anyone living or working in the United States must have a federally approved ID card to travel on an airplane, open a bank account, collect Social Security payments, or take advantage of nearly any government service. Practically speaking, every drivers license likely will have to be reissued to meet federal standards. The REAL ID Act hands the Department of Homeland Security the power to set these standards and determine whether state drivers' licenses and other ID cards pass muster.

rights advocates have called for a broad legalization program, while restrictionists unrealistically demand that the entire undocumented population be rounded up and deported and that the border somehow be secured.

President Bush re-ignited a discussion beyond a let's-round-up-and-deport-them approach with a proposal for a large-scale guestworker plan. In many respects, his plan reflected smart politics as well as a method to address the undocumented challenge. Under Bush's plan, first presented on January 7, 2004, and reiterated shortly after his re-election, each year 300,000 undocumented immigrants and workers from abroad would be able to apply for a three-year work permit; the permit could be extended once for a total of six years. Workers would be allowed to switch jobs and to move from one type of work to another. Those coming from abroad would be able to bring family members.[46] The shrewdness of the proposal begins with the fact that no automatic path toward citizenship is provided to the workers, addressing concerns of some anti-immigrant groups. But by providing an opportunity to work for up to six years, many undocumented workers would step forward and reveal themselves, while a large pool of low-wage workers would make the business community extremely happy. In fact, providing a perpetual pool of low-wage workers would revolutionize the labor market.

The debate over the guestworker solution does not divide along neat partisan lines. Democratic U.S. Senator Dianne Feinstein, the AFL-CIO, and immigrant rights organizations who recall the abuses of the Bracero program have opposed guestworker programs. Republican Congressmen Lamar Smith and Tom Tancredo as well as the restrictionist Federation for American Immigration Reform are also quite vocal in their opposition. Yet in 2005 and 2006, President Bush, Senators John McCain and Ted Kennedy, Republican Congressmen Jeff Flake and Jim Kolbe, businesses and even some farmworker organizations came to embrace guestworker proposals. The later group came to embrace a legalization plan as well in the summer of 2006.

By the time 2007 rolled around, the presidential race began in earnest and all bets were off. In order to appease the far right of the Republican Party, John McCain withdrew his support from his 2006 McCain-Kennedy legislation, and comprehensive legislation took a far turn to the right. The theme was that the border had to be secured before any steps toward legalization could be taken, and from left field a provision eliminating family immigration categories became part of a compromise package that would install an elitist point system for immigration categories instead.

By the end of 2007, any possibility of comprehensive immigration reform was derailed by those who viewed guestworkers and even a burdensome legalization plan as amnesty. Even the immigrant rights community was splintered by then — some arguing that getting something would be better than nothing, while others maintaining that eliminating family categories and accepting a burdensome legalization plan was not worth the price. Congress dropped any serious work on comprehensive reform during the 2008 presidential campaign, as both parties appeared hesitant to take on the political hot potato of immigration reform.

---

[46] Ricardo Alonso-Zaldivar, *Bush Would Open U.S. to Guest Workers*, L.A. Times, Jan. 8, 2004, at A1.

President Barack Obama has pledged to renew efforts to pass comprehensive immigration reform. Great pressure has been placed on his administration and Congress by the Congressional Hispanic Caucus to engage in reform. The question is whether the challenges of the economic downturn and anti-immigrant forces will derail those efforts.

Chapter 3

THE FEDERAL IMMIGRATION POWERS

This Chapter considers the power of the federal government to regulate immigration. Today, the regulation of admission to the United States is primarily a function of federal law enacted by Congress, with enforcement largely in the hands of the Executive Branch. Chapter 5 offers a summary of the various federal agencies that regulate immigration as well as their respective functions.

Change perhaps is in the winds. State and local governments in recent years have increasingly attempted to intervene in the regulation of immigration and immigrants. Public debate continues to be heated over the proper role, if any, of state and local governments in immigration matters. Despite the controversy, the federal government undisputedly remains the primary source of immigration law and its enforcement. The only real question concerns whether any — and how much — residual authority to regulate immigration and immigrants resides with the state and local governments. Chapter 4 discusses state and local involvement in immigration matters.

The basic distribution of the power over the regulation of immigration to the United States is relatively straight-forward. As the Supreme Court has interpreted the Constitution, the federal government possess primary — near exclusive — responsibility for regulating immigration to the United States.[1] Congress passes the immigration laws and courts ordinarily defer to the substantive immigration judgments of Congress, such as to which categories of immigrants to admit to, and deport from, the country. To the extent it intervenes in immigration matters, the Supreme Court generally focuses on ensuing adherence to proper procedures for noncitizens — specifically compliance with Due Process — facing removal from the United States as well as the proper interpretation of the omnibus immigration statute, the Immigration and Nationality Act.[2]

A. THE CONSTITUTIONAL POWER TO REGULATE IMMIGRATION

No provision in the U.S. Constitution unequivocally authorizes the federal government to regulate immigration and immigrants in the way that we see in modern times in the United States. Indeed, not much in the Constitution pertains to immigration and immigrants. Immigration apparently was not a pressing concern at the time of the framing of the U.S. Constitution; establishing a national government that would attract settlement of the U.S. territories unquestionably was a greater concern. As one commentator observed, however,

> [t]here is also little reason to believe that the Framers contemplated creating a federal immigration power. One of the grievances directed against the Crown in the Declaration of Independence was that the King had obstructed free immigration to the colonies. And at the time of the framing, the United States generally encouraged free immigration, while various states maintained laws authorizing the expulsion of aliens deemed undesirable. In 1788, after the Constitutional Convention, the Congress of the Confederation recommended that the several states "pass proper laws for preventing the transportation of convicted malefactors from foreign counties into the United States." The action was later viewed by some as confirming the states' primacy in regulating the entry and exit of aliens.[3]

---

[1] For a skeptical look at the conventional wisdom, *see* Clare Huntington, *The Constitutional Dimension of Immigration Federalism*, 61 VAND. L. REV. 787 (2008) and sources cited in note 80.

[2] Pub. L. No. 82-414, 66 Stat. 163 (1952) (codified as amended in scattered sections of 8, 18, & 22 U.S.C.).

[3] Sarah H. Cleveland, *Powers Inherent in Sovereignty: Indians, Aliens, Territories, and the Nineteenth Century Origins of Plenary Power Over Foreign Affairs*, 81 TEX. L. REV. 1, 81 (2002) (footnotes omitted).

Despite this omission, the conventional wisdom today is that the federal government possesses the constitutional power to regulate immigration, with state and local governments having limited authority in the field.[4]

Several provisions of the Constitution do in fact touch on immigration and nationality matters. Most importantly, Article I, § 8, Clause 14 of the Constitution authorizes Congress "[t]o establish a uniform Rule of Naturalization." From the nation's early days, Congress has exercised this power and created a mechanism for lawful immigrants to naturalize and become citizens. Chapter 15 summarizes the law of citizenship, including the process as well as the basic requirements for naturalization.

Two particular provisions of the Constitution dealing with immigration and nationality have been in the news in recent years. Article II, Section I, Clause 5 provides that "[n]o Person except a natural born Citizen, or a Citizen of the United States, at the time of the Adoption of this Constitution, shall be eligible to the Office of the President."[5] This is the only constitutionally compelled "natural born" citizenship requirement for a U.S. government post. Not even a Justice of the U.S. Supreme Court must be a "natural born Citizen." The requirement became an issue of controversy in the 2008 presidential election, with the eligibility of Senator John McCain, who was born in the Panama Canal Zone where his father served in the military, to be President placed in question.[6] Some opponents of Senator Barack

---

[4] For a thoughtful look at the development of the federal immigration power, *see* Cleveland, *supra* note 3, at 81–163.

[5] Charles Gordon, *Who Can Be President of the United States: The Unresolved Enigma*, 28 MD. L. REV. 1 (1968) is the classic analyses of this question. One much-publicized article, by Gabriel J. Chin, *Why Senator McCain Cannot Be President: Eleven Months and a Hundred Yards Short of Citizenship*, 107 MICH. L. REV. FIRST IMPRESSIONS 1 (2008), concluded that Senator McCain was ineligible for the Presidency. The U.S. Senate passed a resolution declaring Senator McCain to be a "natural born Citizen" of the United States. *See* S. Res. No. 511, 110th Cong., 2d Sess (Apr. 30, 2008). Nonetheless, at least two unsuccessful lawsuits challenged McCain's eligibility for the Presidency. *See* Inland Empire Voters v. United States, 1st Amended Complaint for Declaratory Relief, Civil Action ED CV 08-00304 SGL (Opx) (C.D. Cal. Filed Mar. 31, 2008); Hollander v. McCain, First Amended Complaint, Civil Action No. 1:08-cv-99-JL (D. N.H. Apr. 3, 2008).

Other analyses of the issue — some of which were influenced by talk of the ineligibility for the United State Presidency of California Governor Arnold Schwarzenegger, an Austrian immigrant — can be found in J. Rebekka S. Bonner, *Constitutional Reinterpretation of Article II's "Natural Born" Presidential Eligibility Clause*, available at SSRN.com; Sarah Helene Duggin & Mary Beth Collins, *"Natural Born" in the USA: The Striking Unfairness and Dangerous Ambiguity of the Constitution's Presidential Qualifications Clause and Why We Need to Fix It*, 85 B.U. L. REV. 53 (2005); Lawrence Friedman, *An Idea Whose Time Has Come–The Curious History, Uncertain Effect, and the Need for Amendment of the "Natural Born Citizen" Requirement for the Presidency*, 52 ST. LOUIS U. L.J. 137 (2007); Christina S. Lohman, *Presidential Eligibility: The Meaning of the Natural-Born Citizen Requirement: Globalization as the Impetus and the Obstacle*, 81 CHI.-KENT L. REV. 275 (2006); Andrew D. Miller, Note, *Terminating the "Just Not American Enough" Idea: Saying "Hasta La Vista" to the Natural-Born-Citizen Requirement of Presidential Eligibility*, 57 SYRACUSE L. REV. 97 (2006).

Robert Post identifies "the natural born citizen" requirement as the "worst" provision of the Constitution. *See* Robert Post, *What is the Constitution's Worst Provision?*, 12 CONST. COMMENT. 191 (1995).

[6] *See* Michael Dobbs, *McCain's Birth Abroad Stirs Legal Debate*, WASH. POST, May 2, 2008, at A06; Carl Hulse, *McCain's Canal Zone Birth Prompts Queries About Whether That Rules Him Out*, N.Y. TIMES, Feb. 28, 2008; Pete Williams, *McCain's Citizenship Called into Question*, NBC NEWS, Feb.

Obama's candidacy claimed, with little supporting evidence, that he was not in fact born in Hawaii and thus was ineligible for the Presidency.

Another provision of the U.S. Constitution that deals with citizenship grew out of one of the constitutional amendments that ended slavery in the United States. Section 1 of the Fourteenth Amendment provides that "[a]ll persons born or naturalized in the United States, and subject to the jurisdiction thereof, are citizens of the United States and of the state wherein they reside." This provision, which ensures full national citizenship of the United States for *all* citizens — both those born in the United States as well as those who have naturalized — was designed to eliminate the denial of citizenship to freed slaves under *Dred Scott v. Sandford*,[7] a decision that contributed to the American Civil War. The traditional rule, which has come under attack (as discussed in Chapter 15), has been that any person born in the United States — whatever the immigration status of the parents — is a U.S. citizen.[8] The rule means that children of undocumented immigrants born in the United States are citizens under the Fourteenth Amendment.

With these exceptions, the U.S. Constitution makes no direct reference to immigration or immigrants. Scholars have struggled in search of a constitutional justification for the general exercise of federal power over immigration.[9] Nonetheless, since the late nineteenth century when Congress enacted immigration laws excluding, among others, most Chinese immigrants to the United States, comprehensive federal regulation of immigration has been the rule.

1.   Enumerated Powers

A fundamental principle of U.S. constitutional law is that the federal government is one of "enumerated powers."[10] As a result, the federal government generally cannot exercise powers not expressly authorized by the U.S. Constitution, which reserves most powers to the states. The enumerated powers doctrine poses difficulties in attempting to find a constitutional justification for the federal government's authority to regulate immigration. Because immigration implicated the movement of slaves, and thus the very institution of slavery, the framers were reluctant to address the topic.[11] Thus, we are left largely with constitutional silence.

29, 2008, *available at* http://www.msnbc.msn.com/id/23415028/.

   [7] *See* Dred Scott v. Sandford, 60 U.S. (19 How.) 393 (1856).

   [8] *See* United States v. Wong Kim Ark, 169 U.S. 649 (1898). For a short summary of the ongoing dispute over birthright citizenship, see James C. Ho, *"American": Birthright Citizenship and the Original Understanding of the 14th Amendment*, 9 GREEN BAG 2d 367 (2006). *Compare* John C. Eastman, *Born in the U.S.A.? Rethinking Birthright Citizenship in the Wake of 9/11*, 42 U. RICH. L. REV. 955 (2008) (calling for rethinking of interpretation of 14th amendment's birthright citizenship clause), *with* James C. Ho, *Birthright Citizenship, The Fourteenth Amendment, and State Authority*, 42 U. RICH. L. REV. 969 (2008) (defending birthright citizenship).

   [9] *See* Huntington, *supra* note 1, at 812–13 (questioning whether constitutional text grants sole authority to federal government to regulate immigration).

   [10] *See, e.g.*, THE FEDERALIST No. 45, at 292 (James Madison) (Clinton Rossiter ed., 1961) ("The powers delegated by the proposed Constitution to the federal government are few and defined. Those which are to remain in the State governments are numerous and indefinite.").

   [11] *See* ARISTIDE R. ZOLBERG, A NATION OF DESIGN: IMMIGRATION POLICY IN THE FASHIONING OF AMERICA 78

a.   The Naturalization Power

Article I, § 8 clause 4, of the U.S. Constitution specifically grants Congress the power "[t]o establish a uniform Rule of Naturalization." Before ratification of the Constitution, states had greatly differing rules for granting citizenship. Some states immediately granted citizenship to those who landed on their shores while other states established a waiting period.[12] This power was expressly delegated to Congress to prevent the confusion that might arise from individual state laws bestowing citizenship on foreigners.[13] The result has been a single national set of naturalization rules.

As it has evolved, the Executive Branch for the most part has administered the naturalization rules established by Congress. Since early in this nation's history, Congress has exercised the naturalization power. Chapter 15 reviews the process and criteria for naturalization. Importantly, the U.S. naturalization laws are generous in certain respects, such as, for example, the five-year residency requirement for naturalization that generally has been the rule over the last 200-plus years. The rules, however, have not always been laudable. From 1790–1952, for example, the requirement in the naturalization law was that a person be "white" to naturalize.[14]

Article I's naturalization power does not expressly bestow federal power over immigration. The power to establish a process and requirements for becoming a citizen does not necessarily confer the power to establish admissions criteria and deportation grounds. However, the rationale for a uniform system of naturalization would seem to apply to immigration generally. As a practical matter, it is difficult to see how the nation could cope with a hodge-podge of varying state immigration laws regulating admission and removal. A "uniform" set of laws appears to be most sensible. Although Congress did not comprehensively occupy the field of immigration until late in the 1800s,[15] those times lacked the magnitude, or ease, of migration that exists today. The federalization of the immigration laws occurred when immigration to the United States increased and generated national concern. Today, although some might dispute this contention,[16] the impracticalities of state regulation of admissions and removal of immigration are even greater than in the past.

(2006); Cleveland, *supra* note 3, at 98; Gerald L. Neuman, A *Lost Century of American Immigration Law (1776–1875)*, 93 COLUM. L. REV 1833, 1866–67 (1993).

[12] *See* Ricardo Gonzalez Cedillo, *A Constitutional Analysis of the English Literacy Requirement of the Naturalization Act*, 14 ST. MARY'S L.J. 899, 912–14 (1983).

[13] *See* JAMES H. KETTNER, THE DEVELOPMENT OF AMERICAN CITIZENSHIP, 1608–1870, at 224–25 (1978).

[14] *See* IAN HANEY-LÓPEZ, WHITE BY LAW (10th anniversary ed. 2006) (analyzing caselaw interpreting the requirement in place from 1790 to 1952 that an immigrant be "white" to naturalize); *see, e.g.,* Ozawa v. United States, 260 U.S. 178 (1922) (holding that immigrant from Japan was not "white" and thus ineligible for naturalization); United States v. Thind, 261 U.S. 204 (1923) (ruling to the same effect with respect to immigrant from India).

[15] *See* Neuman, *supra* note 11.

[16] *See infra* note 80–81 (citing authorities).

b.   The Commerce Power

Article I, § 8, clause 3, of the Constitution provides Congress with the power "[t]o regulate Commerce with foreign Nations, and among the several States, and with the Indian Tribes . . . ." In the earliest immigration cases, the Supreme Court viewed the federal government's power to regulate immigration as based on the power to regulate commerce. The Court invalidated a number of state statutes that sought to regulate immigration through the imposition of taxes or other regulations on carriers.[17]

For example, in the *Passenger Cases*,[18] the Court in 1849 relied upon the Commerce Clause to bar the imposition of fees by a state on immigrants disembarking at ports. Similarly, in *People v. Compagnie Generale Transalantique*,[19] the Court struck down a New York statute that imposed a one-dollar tax on each foreign passenger arriving at the Port of New York. The Court emphasized that "[i]t has been so repeatedly decided by this court that such a tax as this is a regulation of commerce with foreign nations, confided by the constitution to the exclusive to the exclusive control of congress."[20]

In the *Head Money Cases*,[21] the Court in 1884 relied on the commerce power to uphold a federal fee on immigrants and emphasized that "Congress [has] the power to uphold a federal fee on immigrants and emphasized that "Congress [has] the power to pass a law regulating immigration as *a part of commerce of this country with foreign nations.*" A few years later, in *Nishimura Ekiu v. United States*,[22] the Court listed the Commerce Clause as one of a litany of constitutional provisions that afforded the federal government to regulate immigration.

Professor Mary Sarah Bilder has summarized the Commerce Clause caselaw as follows:

> People are articles of commerce, or so the United States Supreme Court held in 1941, emphasizing that the issue was "settled beyond question." [citing *Edwards v. California*, 314 U.S. 160, 172 (1941) (invalidating a law criminalizing bringing poor people into state).] At the time, Justice Jackson expressed some discomfort with the theory that "the migrations of a human being . . . are commerce." [*Id.* at 182 (Jackson, J., concurring).] . . . For the first hundred years, the Court debated the question of immigration power under the Commerce Clause. The consequences of the unsettled

---

[17] *See e.g.*, Chy Lung v. Freeman, 92 U.S. 275 (1876) (declaring unconstitutional a state law requiring noncitizens to secure bond or face exclusion); Henderson v. New York, 92 U.S. 259 (1876) (striking down New York requirement that ship masters pay $1.50 tax per passenger brought to New York or provide $300 bond to indemnify city for relief expenses for four years); Smith v. Turner *(The Passenger Cases)*, 48 U.S. (7 How.) 283 (1849) (invalidating Massachusetts and New York taxes on immigrants).

[18] 48 U.S. (7 How.) 283, 306–07 (1849). Justice Daniel in dissent disagreed that the Commerce Power justified federal regulation of immigration. *See The Passenger Cases*, 48 U.S. 283, 477, 500–05 (1949) (Daniel, J., dissenting).

[19] 107 U.S. 59, 60 (1883).

[20] *Id.*

[21] 112 U.S. 580, 600, Treas. Dec. 6714, Treas. Dec. 6714 (1884) (emphasis added).

[22] 142 U.S. 651, 658 (1891).

jurisprudence reappear in every constitutional law casebook; the classic line of commerce cases stretching from *Gibbons* [*v. Ogden*, 22 U.S. (9 Wheat) 1 (1824),] through [*Mayor of New York v. Miln*, 36 U.S. (11 Pet.) 102 (1837),] to *The Passenger Cases* [Smith v. Turner, Norris v. Boston, 36 U.S. (11 Pet. 102 (1837)]. In 1876, the Court finally unanimously decided to link immigration to the exclusive federal commerce power based on the perception that immigrants were "articles of commerce." [*Henderson v. Mayor of New York*, 92 U.S. 259 (1875)].[23]

As mentioned above, the Supreme Court in *Edwards v. California*[24] in 1941 struck down a California law that made it a crime to bring an indigent person into the state on the ground that it interfered with the power of Congress to regulate interstate commerce. The Court stated that "it is settled beyond question that the transportation of persons is 'commerce,' "[25] adding that "[i]t is immaterial whether or not the transportation is commercial in character."[26] In a concurring opinion, Justice Jackson expressed his belief that, although the California statute violated the Privileges or Immunities clause of the Fourteenth Amendment, human beings "do not fit easily into my notions of what is commerce. To hold that the measure of his rights is the commerce clause is likely to result eventually either in distorting the commercial law or in a denaturing human rights."[27]

The Commerce Clause is an attractive constitutional justification for the federal power to regulate immigration. Migration and commerce, international and domestic, are obviously linked. Immigration often is attributable to the movement of labor, which as discussed in Chapter 1 has distinct economic impacts on the labor, consumer, and other markets. From an economic perspective, labor and capital are fungible factors of production. Perceived economic benefits of immigration often are employed to justify tighter or looser immigration laws.[28]

At the same time, as Justice Jackson alluded to in *Edwards v. California*, it may seem insensitive to commodify immigrants as "articles" of commerce. We understandably are skittish over classifying people as anything less than human or treating them as nameless "factors of production."[29] But whatever the qualms, immigration unquestionably has an impact on both interstate and international commerce. The Commerce Clause thus offers a sensible justification for the federal regulation of immigration.

---

[23] *See* Mary Sarah Bilder, *The Struggle Over Immigration: Indentured Servants, Slaves, and Articles of Commerce*, 61 Mo. L. Rev. 743, 745–46 (1996) (reviewing different views of the meaning of the Commerce Clause at the time of its adoption).

[24] 314 U.S. 160 (1941).

[25] *Id.* at 172.

[26] *Id.* at 172 n.1.

[27] *Id.* at 182 (Jackson, J., concurring).

[28] *See* Kevin R. Johnson, Opening the Floodgates: Why America Needs to Rethink Its Borders and Immigration Laws 131–67 (2007) (summarizing literature on economic impacts on immigration).

[29] *See generally* Rethinking Commodification: Cases and Readings in Law and Culture (Martha M. Ertman & Joan C. Williams eds., 2005).

c.   Migration and Importation Clause

Article I, § 9, clause 1, of the Constitution provides that "[t]he Migration or Importation of such Persons as any of the States now existing shall think proper to admit, shall not be prohibited by the Congress prior to the year one thousand eight hundred and eight but a Tax or duty on such importation, not to exceed ten dollars each Person." Although the framers consciously avoided expressly referring to slavery in the Constitution, this clause has generally been interpreted as prohibiting congressional attempts to end the slave trade before 1808, a critical compromise in the constitutional framing. Congress banned the importation of slaves effective January 1, 1808.[30]

Considerable debate about the meaning of the Migration and Importation Clause ensued at the time of the clause's adoption.[31] Because slaves were considered as articles of commerce, it was widely agreed that slaves were considered "imports" and thus subject to taxation.[32] The main disagreement arose from whether this clause allowed for the taxation of free immigrants. Some delegates, such as James Madison from Virginia, believed that this clause only governed the importation of slaves.[33] In contrast, Luther Martin stated that, even if it had only been intended for slaves, the scope of this clause would allow for the taxation of all immigrants.[34]

Robert Whitehill also believed that " 'importation' " included the " 'migration of Europeans.' "[35]

Linked as it is to slavery, the Migration and Importation Clause is difficult to employ as a general constitutional justification for the federal regulation of immigration. It was established as a sunset clause on a particular type of forced migration and involuntary servitude. It thus is a stretch to claim that this provision provides the express authority to the federal government to regulate immigration.

One might argue that the sunset on Congressional limits on regulating the "Migration or Importation" of persons implicitly authorizes the power to regulate the migration or importation of persons after 1808. That seems something of a stretch, however. The framers almost certainly intended the Migration and Importation Clause to limit congressional power to end the importation of slaves, not to provide a general power to regulate migration.

---

[30] *See* Act of March 2, 1807, ch. 22, 2 Stat. 425. *See generally* DAVID B. DAVIS, THE PROBLEM OF SLAVERY IN THE AGE OF REVOLUTION, 1770–1823, at 119–31 (1975); Walter Berns, *The Constitution and the Migration of Slaves*, 78 YALE L.J. 198 (1968).

[31] Bilder, *supra* note 23, at 787 (reviewing different views of the meaning of the clause at the time of its adoption).

[32] *See id.* at 784.

[33] *See id.* at 785.

[34] See *id.* at 787. Gouverneur Morris feared that the clause would be interpreted in this way. *See id.*

[35] *See id.* at 787 (footnote citing THE DEBATE ON THE CONSTITUTION: FEDERALIST AND ANTIFEDERALIST SPEECHES, ARTICLES, AND LETTERS DURING THE STRUGGLE OVER RATIFICATION 831 (Dec. 3, 1787) (Bernard Bailyn ed., 1993)).

d.   War Power

Under Article I, § 8, clause 11, Congress possesses the authority "[t]o declare War." The Supreme Court has held that the War Power authorizes laws providing for the exclusion and expulsion of so-called "enemy aliens," including the infamous Alien and Sedition Acts of the 1790s discussed in Chapter 2.[36] The Supreme Court has upheld the constitutionality of such provisions.[37]

Justice Daniel, dissenting in the *Passenger Cases*,[38] conceded that the War Power provision authorizes Congress to regulate "alien *enemies*" –i.e., nationals of countries with which the United States is at war, but doubted whether it could justify the general regulation of immigration. There are obvious limits on the War Power as a general justification for immigration regulation by the federal government. It fortunately is relatively rare for war and conflict to be implicated by the admission and removal of a specific immigrant. As a practical matter, only a small number of a nation's admissions and deportations will truly implicate war or foreign relations.

The flip side of the War Power, which has been raised relatively recently in the immigration debate, is the federal government's duty to the states under Article IV § 4 of the Constitution: "The United States shall . . . protect each [State] against Invasion . . . ." In response to, among other things, concerns over the costs of immigration in recent years, several states have sought to invoke the Invasion Clause in actions against the federal government for allegedly failing to effectively enforce the immigration laws. California, for example, unsuccessfully sued the federal government to recover billions in emergency medical care, incarceration and parole supervision, and education imposed as the result of an "invasion" of undocumented immigrants in violation of Article IV.[39] Other states have unsuccessfully sued the federal government on similar grounds.[40]

---

[36] *See* Kevin R. Johnson, *The Antiterrorism Act, the Immigration Reform Act, and Ideological Regulation in the Immigration Laws: Important Lessons for Citizens and Noncitizens*, 28 St. Mary's L.J. 833, 865–69 (1997); *see also* Gregory Fehlings, *Storm on the Constitution: The First Deportation Law*, 10 Tulsa J. Comp. & Int'l L. 63, 63–70 (2002) (discussing reasons why Congress passed Alien and Sedition Acts); Jules Lobel, *The War on Terrorism and Civil Liberties*, 63 U. Pitt. L. Rev. 767, 767–70 (2002) (stating that Alien and Sedition Acts was first law that allowed Presidents to exercise the deportation power); Robert R. Reinstein, *Foreword: Balancing Security and Liberty in the New Century*, 14 Temp. Pol. & Civ. Rts. L. 329, 33 (2005) (discussing that Congress passed the Alien and Sedition Acts because the Federalists feared that aliens were disloyal). *See generally* John C. Miller, Crisis in Freedom: The Alien and Sedition Laws (1951); James Morton Smith, Freedom's Fetters: The Alien and Sedition Laws and American Civil Liberties (1956).

[37] Ludecke v. Watkins, 335 U.S. 160 (1948).

[38] 48 U.S. (7 How.) 283, 509–10 (1849) (Daniel, J., dissenting).

[39] *See* California v. United States, 104 F.3d 1086, 1090 & n.3 (9th Cir. 1997). The court found the issue to be a nonjusticiable political question. *See id.* at 1089.

[40] *See* Arizona v. United States, 104 F.3d 1095, 1096 (9th Cir. 1997), *cert. denied*, 522 U.S. 806 (1997); New Jersey v. United States, 91 F.3d 463, 468–69 (3d Cir. 1996); Padavan v. United States, 82 F.3d 23, 28 (2d Cir. 1996); Chiles v. United States, 874 F. Supp. 1334, 1335–36 (S.D. Fla. 1994), *aff'd*, 69 F.3d 1094 (11th Cir. 1995), *cert. denied*, 517 U.S. 1188 (1996); *see also* Texas v. United States, 106 F.3d 661 (5th Cir. 1997) (seeking federal monies based on alleged constitutional and statutory violations resulting from failure of U.S. government to adequately enforce immigration laws).

One might argue that the federal government must be permitted to regulate immigration in order to fulfill its obligations to the states under the Invasion Clause. This, of course, implicitly treats all migrants as unwanted "invaders" and plays into the concept that immigrants are a social problem. *See* Chapter 1 and 2. Despite the rhetoric employed by some restrictionists, the flow of undocumented immigrants are difficult to categorize as an "invasion" for constitutional purposes.

Ultimately, it is a stretch to claim that the War and Invasion Clauses of the Constitution allow for Congress to regulate immigration by Congress. Some immigration decisions may impact U.S. relations with nations with which it is at war. However, U.S. involvement in war is fortunately the exception rather than the rule. It therefore proves difficult to hinge the federal power to regulate immigration on the congressional power to declare war.

e.   Summary

Nothing in the U.S. Constitution clearly enumerates the federal power to regulate immigration. Nonetheless, federal regulation of immigration continues. There appears to be no going back. Efforts at state and local action in the field have provoked great controversy.

However, the naturalization, commerce, and war and related powers afforded to Congress under Article I, in combination offer support for federal laws regulating immigration. Together with the foreign affairs and other sovereign powers inherent in the U.S. Constitution, which are discussed below, it seems sensible in the U.S. constitutional scheme for Congress to regulate immigration.

2.   Implied Powers

a.   Foreign Affairs Power

Commentators often refer to the implied power of the Executive Branch over foreign affairs to authorize federal regulation of immigration.[41] In *Chae Chan Ping v. U.S.* (The Chinese Exclusion Case),[42] the Supreme Court in 1889 emphasized the federal government's power over foreign affairs as the foundation for its power to regulate immigration and upheld a federal immigration law that, among other things, excluded most immigrants from China from the U.S. shores. See Chapters 2 and 6 for further analysis of this important case.

In the *Chinese Exclusion Case*, Justice Field linked the power to regulate immigration with the power of the federal government to conduct foreign affairs: "[T]he United States, in their *relation to foreign countries* and their subjects or citizens, are one nation, invested with powers which belong to independent

---

[41] *See, e.g.*, Raquel Aldana, *The September 11 Immigration Detentions and Unconstitutional Executive Legislation*, 29 S. ILL. U. L.J. 5, 14–21 (2005); Anne Y. Lee, *The Unfettered Executive: Is There an Inherent Presidential Power to Exclude Aliens?*, 39 COLUM. J.L. & SOC. PROBS. 223, 245–48 (2005); Nancy E. Powell, *The Supreme Court as Interpreter of Executive Foreign Affairs Power*, 3 CONN. J. INT'L L. 161, 184–87 (1987).

[42] 130 U.S. 581, 609 (1889).

nations . . . . [F]or national purposes, embracing our *relations with foreign nations*, we are but one people, one nation, one power."[43] The Court explained that "[t]he power of exclusion of foreigners [is] *an incident of sovereignty belonging to the government of the United States, as a part of those sovereign powers delegated by the Constitution* . . . ."[44] The Court further emphasized

> [t]hat the government of the United States . . . can exclude aliens from its territory is a proposition which we do not think open to controversy. *Jurisdiction over its own territory to that extent is an incident of every independent nation. It is a part of its independence. If it could not exclude aliens, it would be to that extent subject to the control of another power.*[45]

However, similar to its treatment of the immigration power, the Constitution fails to expressly mention the foreign affairs power.[46] In *United States v. Curtiss-Wright Export Corp.*,[47] the Supreme Court clearly distinguished between powers delegated to the federal government in the Constitution and inherent sovereign powers, which it found includes the federal government's foreign affairs power. Although commentators have questioned *Curtiss-Wright*,[48] almost all assume that some foreign affairs power exists in the federal government.

The federal government's exclusive power to conduct foreign affairs has led courts to invalidate *state* statutes that attempt to regulate immigration. The classic statement of this position occurs in the 1875 decision of *Chy Lung v. Freeman*:

> The passage of laws which concern the admission of citizens and subjects of foreign nations to our shores belongs to Congress, and not to the States. It has the power to regulate commerce with foreign nations; the responsibility for the character of those regulations, and for the manner of their execution, belongs solely to the national government. If it be otherwise, a single State can, at her pleasure, embroil us in disastrous quarrels with other nations.[49]

---

[43] 130 U.S. at 604, 606 (emphasis added).

[44] *Id.* at 609 (emphasis added).

[45] *Id.* at 603–04 (emphasis added).

[46] *See* LOUIS HENKIN, FOREIGN AFFAIRS AND THE CONSTITUTION 16–18 (1972); *see also* Curtis A. Bradley, *Executive Power Essentialism and Foreign Affairs*, 102 MICH. L. REV. 545, 660–64 (2004) (reviewing debate at Constitutional Convention over the foreign affairs powers of the President); Michael D. Ramsey, *The Power of the State in Foreign Affairs: The Original Understanding of Foreign Policy Federalism*, 75 NOTRE DAME L. REV. 341, 396–99 (1999) (describing how foreign relation powers were not allocated nor mentioned in Constitution); Michael D. Ramsey, *The Myth of Extraconstitutional Foreign Affairs Power*, 42 WM. & MARY L. REV. 379, 403–06 (2000) (asserting that extraconstitutional foreign affairs power is unnecessary); Michael P. Van Alstine, *Executive Aggrandizement in Foreign Affairs Lawmaking*, 54 UCLA L. REV. 309, 316–20 (2006) (examining President's foreign affairs power with the Constitution's limited guidance).

[47] 299 U.S. 304, 315–18 (1936). Cleveland analyzes the evolution of the concept of inherent federal power over foreign affairs. *See* Cleveland, *supra* note 3.

[48] *See* HENKIN, *supra* note 46, at 23–26; Charles A. Lofgren, United States v. Curtiss-Wright Export Corporation: *An Historical Reassessment*, 83 YALE L.J. 1 (1973); Note, *Constitutional Limits on the Power to Exclude Aliens*, 82 COLUM. L. REV. 995 (1982).

[49] 92 U.S. 275, 280 (1875); *see* Hines v. Davidowitz, 312 U.S. 52 (1941) (invalidating Pennsylvania's

Similarly, in *Nishimura Ekiu v. United States*,[50] the Supreme Court upheld the Immigration Act of 1891 and stated that

> [*i*]*t is an accepted maxim of international law, that every sovereign nation has the power, as inherent in sovereignty, and essential to preservation, to forbid the entrance of foreigners within its dominations, or to admit them only in such cases and upon such conditions as it may see fit to prescribe. In the United States, this power is vested in the national government, to which the Constitution has committed the entire control of international relations, in peace as well as in war.*[51]

The Court decided these cases at the time when Congress had enacted a comprehensive immigration law and fully occupied the field. The Court saw immigration as affecting the nation's foreign relations but also relied on justifications for the federal government's exercise of the power.

The Supreme Court continues to invoke the foreign relations power as a justification for deferring to the federal exercise of authority over immigration.[52] In *Sale v. Haitian Centers Council, Inc.*,[53] for example, the Court cited *United States v. Curtiss-Wright Export Corp.* and upheld the U.S. government's interdiction of Haitians on the high seas, despite strong arguments that it violated international and domestic law, and emphasized that "we are construing treaty and statutory provisions that may involve *foreign and military affairs* for which the President has unique responsibility."

b.   Necessity and Structural Justifications

One leading immigration law casebook suggests that, because federal power over immigration is *necessary* to the successful operation of the U.S. Constitution, the power may be implied into the Constitution:

> The primary purpose of the constitution is to establish a system of government for a nation, a nation encompassing territory and members ("citizen"). A system of government is the process by which citizens establish rules of conduct for persons within the territory. From these premises, two sorts of structural arguments may follow. First, to be a

---

Alien Registration Act and emphasizing "[t]hat the supremacy of the national power in the general field of foreign affairs, including power over immigration, naturalization and deportation, is made clear by the Constitution, was pointed out by the authors of the Federalist in 1787, and has since been given continuous recognition by this Court") (footnotes omitted).

[50] 142 U.S. 651 (1892).

[51] *Id.* at 658 (emphasis added).

[52] *See, e.g.*, INS v. Aguirre-Aguirre, 526 U.S. 415, 425 (1999) ("We have recognized that judicial deference to the Executive Branch is especially appropriate in the context where officials 'exercise especially sensitive political functions that implicate questions of foreign relations.'") (quoting INS v. Abudu, 485 U.S. 94, 110 (1999)); Mathews v. Diaz, 426 U.S. 67, 81 (1976) (to the same effect); Harisiades v. Shaughnessy, 342 U.S. 580, 588–89 (1952) (noting that immigration policy is "virtually and intricately interwoven" with foreign relations, war power, and maintenance of a republican form of government); *see also* Hampton v. Mow Sun Wong, 426 U.S. 88, 101–02 n.21 (1976) ("The power over aliens is of a political character and therefore subject only to narrow judicial review.").

[53] 509 U.S. 155, 188 (1993) (emphasis added).

sovereign nation, a people must have control over their territory. A nation of open borders runs the risk of not being able to govern itself because its sovereignty, to some extent, is in the hands of the other nations of the world. It seems reasonable to believe that the persons who wrote and ratified the Constitution thought (or hoped) they were creating a nation that would be able to take its place among other nations as an equal; one that would possess the powers of sovereignty generally possessed by all other nations . . . .

A second structural argument may be based on the notion of citizenship and the relationship of the citizen to the nation. Citizens, through the process of government, argue about, protect and further values. This discussion of values is essentially a process of national self-definition. The regulation of immigration may be crucial to the process of self-definition. Not only do immigration decisions give citizens the ability to regulate who the participants in the discussion will be, such decisions themselves are an act of self-definition. By deciding whom we permit to enter the country, we say much about who we are as a nation.[54]

There arguably is no real alternative but for the federal government to regulate immigration — especially in the modern world with relatively easy travel and heavy migration pressures. Although it is true that federal immigration regulation did not exist in its current form for the first century of the nation's existence,[55] that was a different time. We have a nation that no longer promotes settlement of the great frontier and in which movement of people, generally speaking, is no longer as difficult and dangerous as in the past. Modern times is a time of easy migration and movement around the world. One might query what choice is there today but for Congress to regulate immigration?

The nation's sovereign powers over immigration echo similar justifications for the federal power over foreign relations that the Court relied upon in *The Chinese Exclusion Case*. The need for sovereign control over borders to ensure a nation as well as the power to define a national identity, are legitimate goals for a government. Nonetheless, whatever their common sense appeal, the powers to pursue these goals are not expressly spelled out in the U.S. Constitution.

B.   THE SCOPE OF THE FEDERAL POWER TO REGULATE IMMIGRATION

In the last decades of the nineteenth century, Congress passed laws that comprehensively regulated immigration. By the end of the century, the federal government firmly was in charge of immigration regulation. The question then is the scope of the federal power over immigration. As it turns out, despite the lack of clear constitutional authority to regulate immigration, the Supreme Court has declared the scope of the federal power to regulate immigration to be broad and

---

[54] T. Alexander Aleinikoff, David A. Martin, Hiroshi Motomura & Maryellen Fullerton, Immigration and Citizenship: Process and Policy 208–09 (6th ed. 2008).

[55] *See* Neuman, *supra* note 11.

expansive, with the role of the Judiciary in reviewing the immigration laws passed by Congress, and the implementation by the Executive, exceedingly narrow.

1.　The "Plenary Power" Doctrine

The judicially created "plenary power" doctrine, emerging originally to shield from review the laws barring Chinese immigration in the late nineteenth century, protects from judicial scrutiny the substantive decisions of Congress on immigration admissions criteria. In *The Chinese Exclusion Case*,[56] the Supreme Court rejected a constitutional challenge to racial discrimination in the Chinese Exclusion Act and emphasized that courts lack power to review congressional exercise of its "plenary power" over immigration. Note the incongruity: as we have seen, it is difficult to find a constitutional justification for the federal power to regulate immigration, but the Court implies that power and, at the same time, concludes that the power is "plenary," not subject to ordinary constitutional limitations.

Born with the emergence of the federalization of immigration, the Supreme Court aggressively later invoked the plenary power doctrine in cases decided in the midst of the Cold War.[57] Scholars have consistently criticized the doctrine, see Chapter 6, which allows noncitizens to be treated in ways that would be patently unconstitutional if they were citizens.[58]

To date there have been no successful challenges to laws passed by Congress that refuses admission to classes of noncitizens or authorizes the removal of noncitizens from the country. Under the plenary power doctrine, discussed in Chapter 6, the courts generally defer to the political branches of government. The Supreme Court has stated unequivocally that: " '[O]ver no conceivable subject is the legislative power of Congress more complete than it is over' the admission of aliens."[59] The Supreme Court, for example, has upheld exclusions and deportations

---

[56] *See generally* Gabriel J. Chin, Chae Chan Ping *and* Fong Yue Tin: *The Origins of Plenary Power in* IMMIGRATION STORIES 7 (David A. Martin & Peter H. Schuck ed., 2005). Chae Chin Ping v. United States (*The Chinese Exclusion Case*), 130 U.S. 581, 609 (1889). The Chinese exclusion laws capped the federalization of the immigration laws. For an explanation of their genesis that differs from the conventional wisdom, see Kerry Abrams, *Polygamy, Prostitution and the Federalization of Immigration Law*, 105 COLUM. L. REV. 641, 642 (2005) ("The regulation of marriage and morality played a pivotal role in the federalization of immigration law."); *see also* Matthew Lindsay, *Preserving the Exceptional Republic: Political Economy, Race, and the Federalization of American Immigration Law*, 17 YALE J.L. & HUMANITIES 181 (2005) (analyzing the federalization of immigration law).

[57] *See, e.g.*, United States *ex rel*. Knauff v. Shaughnessy, 338 U.S. 537 (1950) (refusing to admit wife to U.S. citizen based on secret evidence); Shaughnessy v. United States *ex rel*. Mezei, 345 U.S. 206 (1953) (allowing long-term lawful permanent resident to be subject to indefinite detention upon seeking reentry into the United States).

[58] For critical analysis of the doctrine, *see* Stephen H. Legomsky, *Immigration Law and the Principal of Plenary Congressional Power*, 1984 S. CT. REV. 255; Gabriel J. Chin, *Segregation's Last Stronghold: Race, Discrimination and the Constitutional Law of Immigration*, 46 UCLA L. REV. 1 (1998). The U.S. government, however, invoked the doctrine with vigor after the events of September 11, 2001. *See infra* text accompanying notes 126–34.

[59] Fiallo v. Bell, 430 U.S. 787, 792 (1977) (citation omitted).

of certain races and nationalities, and noncitizens with particular political views and upheld indefinite detention of immigrants.[60]

Recent years had seen cracks in the plenary power doctrine. Three immigration cases decided by the Court in 2001 suggested the decline of unfettered plenary power over immigration. In *Zadvydas v. Davis*,[61] for example, the Court refused to invoke the doctrine to shield from review the Executive Branch's indefinite detention of noncitizens awaiting deportation from the United States. Stating that Congress's power over immigration is "subject to important constitutional limitations,"[62] the Court decided the case on statutory grounds and held that a reasonable time limitation on post-removal detention must be inferred because "a statute permitting indefinite detention would raise a serious constitutional problem."[63] The Court thus suggested that the Constitution applies to the terms of detention of immigrants. Similarly, in that same term, the Court emphasized that Congress must clearly state the elimination of judicial review of removal orders; because Congress had not (and because to do so would raise "serious constitutional questions"), the Court found that reform legislation had not eliminated habeas corpus review of a removal order.[64] Finally, in *Nguyen v. INS*,[65] the Court upheld a distinction in the Immigration and Nationality Act between illegitimate children of U.S. citizen fathers and mothers but applied the same scrutiny it applies to gender classifications under ordinary constitutional law. The Court did not invoke the plenary power doctrine, emphasizing it need not address the "wide deference accorded to Congress in the exercise of its immigration and naturalization power."[66]

In light of these cases, some immigration scholars declared that the plenary power doctrine was in decline.[67] This optimism turned out to be premature. The tragic events of September 11, 2001 marked the plenary power doctrine's comeback. After September 11, the Bush administration expressly relied on the plenary power doctrine in targeting Arab and Muslim noncitizens for special rules

---

[60] *See, e.g.*, Chae Chin Ping v. United States (*The Chinese Exclusion Case*), 130 U.S. 581, 609 (1889) (refusing to disturb Chinese exclusion law); Harisiades v. Shaughnessy, 342 U.S. 580 (1952) (upholding deportation of former Communist party members); Shaughnessy v. United States *ex rel.* Mezei, 345 U.S. 206 (1953) (allowing long term lawful permanent resident to be subject to indefinite detention upon reentry into the United States).

[61] 533 U.S. 678, 695–96 (2001).

[62] *Id.* at 695.

[63] *Id.* at 690.

[64] *See* INS v. St. Cyr, 533 U.S. 289, 310–14 (2001).

[65] 533 U.S. 53 (2001).

[66] *Id.* at 72–73.

[67] *See, e.g.*, Cornelia T.L. Pillard & T. Alexander Aleinikoff, *Skeptical Scrutiny of Plenary Power: Judicial and Executive Branch Decision Making in Miller v. Albright*, 1998 Sup. Ct. Rev. 1 (1999); Peter J. Spiro, *Explaining the End of Plenary Power*, 16 Geo. Immigr. L.J. 339 (2002); Gabriel J. Chin, *Is There a Plenary Power Doctrine? A Tentative Apology and Prediction for Our Strange but Unexceptional Constitutional Immigration Law*, 14 Geo. Immigr. L.J. 257 (2000). Some disagreed. *See* Kevin R. Johnson, *Race and Immigration Law and Enforcement: A Response to "Is There a Plenary Power Doctrine?"*, 14 Geo. Immigr. L.J. 289 (2000).

and procedures in put in place in connection with the "war on terror."[68] In so doing, it emphasized that "[t]he political branches of the government have plenary authority in the immigration area."[69] In *Demore v. Kim*,[70] the Supreme Court in 2003 upheld the mandatory detention of certain noncitizens pending their deportation and firmly emphasized that "this Court has firmly and repeatedly endorsed the proposition that Congress may make rules as to aliens that would be unacceptable if applied to citizens."

The Supreme Court also has invoked the plenary power doctrine to immunize from meaningful judicial review federal laws that discriminate against immigrants who live in the United States. For example, in finding that Congress could limit the eligibility of lawful immigrants for a federal medical benefits, the court emphasized that

> [*i*]*n the exercise of its broad power over naturalization and immigration, Congress regularly makes rules that would be unacceptable if applied to citizens.* The exclusion of aliens and the reservation of the power to deport have no permissible counterpart in the Federal Government's power to regulate the conduct of its own citizenry. The fact that an Act of Congress treats aliens differently from citizens does not itself imply that such disparate treatment is "invidious."[71]

In short, there is a long history continuing through to this day of judicial deference to decisions by Congress and the Executive Branch on issues of immigration and the treatment of immigrants. As we shall see later in this Chapter, judicial intervention in the U.S. immigration laws has ordinarily been limited to ensuring that proper procedural protections are in place in removal and other hearings. In the end, Congress and the Executive Branch generally have the final say on U.S. immigration law and policy. The courts ordinarily decline to interfere with the substantive decisions of the political branches of government.

At the same time, there is some room for judicial review of immigration decisions. In *McNary v. Haitian Refugee Center*,[72] for example, the Supreme Court held that challenges to the constitutionality of the practices, procedures, and

---

[68] *See, e.g.*, Registration and Monitoring of Certain Nonimmigrants, 67 Fed. Reg. 52,584 (Aug. 12, 2002) (requiring "special registration" of certain noncitizens from nations populated predominantly by Arabs and Muslims).

[69] *Id.* at 52,585 (citing Fiallo v. Bell, 430 U.S. 787, 792 (1977); Mathews v. Diaz, 426 U.S. 67, 80–82 (1976)).

[70] 538 U.S. 510, 522 (2003) (citations omitted); *see* M. Isabel Medina, Demore v. Kim — *A Dance of Power and Human Rights*, 18 Geo. Immigr. L.J. 697 (2004) (criticizing Court's decision in *Demore v. Kim*); Margaret H. Taylor, Demore v. Kim: *Judicial Deference to Congressional Folly, in* Immigration Stories, *supra* note 56, at 343 (contending that Court's decision in *Demore v. Kim* was a product of the times, namely the Court was influenced by the "war on terror" after September 11, 2001 and was reluctant to interfere with the U.S. government's detention of noncitizens that it viewed to be a threat to public safety).

[71] Mathews v. Diaz, 426 U.S. 67, 79–80 (1976) (emphasis added) (footnotes omitted); *see, e.g.*, Demore v. Kim, 538 U.S. 510, 521–22 (2003) (quoting *Mathews v. Diaz*). Reno v. Flores, 507 U.S. 292, 305–06 (1993) (invoking plenary power doctrine in upholding regulation limiting release from detention of juvenile noncitizens); Fiallo v. Bell, 430 U.S. 787, 792 (1977) (quoting *Mathews v. Diaz*).

[72] 498 U.S. 479 (1991).

policies of the Immigration and Naturalization Service were proper subjects for judicial review. Courts continue to review the practices, procedures, and policies of immigration authorities even though Congress has attempted to restrict judicial review. *See* Chapter 6. In 2001, the Court warned that a "strong presumption in favor of judicial review of administrative action" exists and the Immigration & Naturalization Service must overcome "the longstanding rule requiring a clear statement of congressional intent to repeal habeas jurisdiction."[73]

2.   Federal Preemption of State and Local Regulation of Immigration

Since 1875, the federal government has comprehensively regulated immigration. The states had regulated migration into their jurisdictions in certain respects, with a particular focus on discouraging the poor and criminals from entering their respective jurisdictions.[74]

In *DeCanas v. Bica*,[75] the Supreme Court held that federal law did not preempt state law barring the employment of undocumented immigrants. This was before 1986 when Congress enacted the Immigration Reform and Control Act,[76] which provided for the imposition of sanctions on employers of undocumented immigrants. *See* Chapter 13. However, the Court further acknowledged that "[p]ower to regulate immigration is *unquestionably a federal power.*"[77]

Increasingly, state and local governments have challenged federal primacy over immigration matters. This trend began in earnest in 1994, when California voters passed Proposition 187, a measure that effectively was designed to regulate immigration by denying public benefits to undocumented immigrants.[78] A federal court struck down most of the measure as preempted by federal law.[79] The power of state and local governments to regulate immigration remains a contentious issue, especially as those governments increased their activity in this area with the failure of comprehensive immigration reform in 2007. *See* Chapter 4. This is a

---

[73]   INS v. St. Cyr, 533 U.S. 289, 298 (2001) (citations omitted).

[74]   *See* Neuman, *supra* note 11.

[75]   424 U.S. 351 (1976).

[76]   Pub. L. No. 99-603, 100 Stat. 3359 (1986).

[77]   *DeCanas v. Bica*, 424 U.S. at 354 (citing *Passenger Cases*, 48 U.S.(7 How.) 283 (1849); Henderson v. Mayor of New York, 92 U.S. 259 (1976); Chy Lung v. Freeman, 92 U.S. 275 (1876); Fong Yue Ting v. United States, 149 U.S. 698 (1893)) (emphasis added). The Court held at the same time that state regulation consistent with federal immigration legislation was not preempted.

[78]   *See, e.g.*, Linda S. Bosniak, *Opposing Proposition 187: Undocumented Immigrants and the National Imagination*, 28 CONN. L. REV. 555 (1996); Kevin R. Johnson, *An Essay on Immigration Politics, Popular Democracy, and California's Proposition 187: The Political Relevance and Legal Irrelevance of Race*, 70 WASH. L. REV. 629, 646 (1995); Kevin R. Johnson, *Public Benefits and Immigration: The Intersection of Immigration Status, Ethnicity, Gender, and Class*, 42 UCLA L. REV. 1509 (1995); Gerald L. Neuman, *Aliens as Outlaws: Government Services Proposition 187 and the Structure of Equal Protection*, 42 UCLA L. Rev. 1925 (1995); Ruben J. Garcia, Comment, *Critical Race Theory and Proposition 187: The Racial Politics of Immigration Law*, 17 CHICANO-LATINO L. REV. 138 (1995).

[79]   *See* League of United Latin American Citizens v. Wilson, 997 F. Supp. 1244 (C.D. Cal. 1997).

much publicized issue, with courts in recent years reaching different conclusions.[80] One way of rationalizing the role of the two coordinate bodies of government is to allow the federal government to regulate admission and enforce the immigration laws while permitting state and local governments to assist in the integration of immigrants into U.S. society.[81]

3.   Constitutional Limitations on the Federal Power to Regulate Immigration and Immigrants

Noncitizens at the border have limited rights. The Supreme Court has restated the essence of the plenary power doctrine that "an alien seeking initial admission has *no* constitutional rights regarding his application, for the power to admit or exclude aliens is a sovereign prerogative."[82] Noncitizens within the territory of the United States have more rights but not as many as citizens. Commentators have called for greater protection of the rights of immigrants residing in the United States.[83]

---

[80] *Compare* Lozano v. Hazleton, 496 F. Supp. 2d 477 (M.D. Pa. 2007) (invalidating city immigration ordinance on federal preemption grounds), *with* Gray v. City of Valley Park, 2008 U.S. Dist. LEXIS 7238 (E.D. Mo. Jan. 31, 2008) (holding that similar city ordinance was not preempted by federal law). For critical analysis of local attempts to regulate immigration, see Michael A. Olivas, *Immigration-Related State and Local Ordinances: Preemption, Prejudice, and the Proper Role for Enforcement*, 2007 U. CHI. LEGAL F. 27; *see also* Orde F. Kittrie, *Federalism, Deportation, and Crime Victims Afraid to Call the Police*, 91 IOWA L. REV. 1449 (2006) (analyzing federalism issues raised in immigration enforcement); Michael A. Olivas, *Preempting Preemption: Foreign Affairs, State Rights, and Alienage Classifications*, 35 VA. J. INT'L L. 217 (1994) (arguing for adherence to rule that state regulation of immigration is preempted by federal law); Huyen Pham, *The Inherent Flaws in the Inherent Authority Position: Why Inviting Local Enforcement of Immigration Laws Violates the Constitution*, 31 FLA. ST. U.L. REV. 965 (2004) (contending that local governments cannot constitutionally enforce immigration laws); Michael J. Wishnie, *Laboratories of Bigotry? Devolution of the Immigration Power, Equal Protection, and Federalism*, 76 N.Y.U. L. REV 49 (2001) (discussing states as possibly increasing discrimination against immigrants); *see also* Rose Cuison Villazor, *What Is a "Sanctuary"?*, 61 SMU L. REV. 133 (2008) (analyzing the "sanctuary" cities that exist in the United States).

Recent years have seen increased calls by scholars for greater state and local involvement in immigration regulation. *See, e.g.*, Huntington, *supra* note 1; Kris W. Kobach, *The Quintessential Force Multiplier: The Inherent Authority of Local Police to Make Immigration Arrests*, 69 ALB. L. REV. 179 (2005) (contending that local police can enforce immigration laws); Peter H. Schuck, *Taking Immigration Federalism Seriously*, 2007 U. CHI. LEGAL F. 57 (seeing increased role for state and local governments in immigration regulation); Peter J. Spiro, *The States and Immigration in an Era of Demi-Sovereignties*, 35 VA. J. INT'L L. 121 (1994) (calling for a greater role of states in immigration regulation); *see also* Matthew Parlow, *A Localist's Case for Decentralizing Immigration Policy*, 84 DENV. U. L. REV. 1061 (2007) (contending that local governments should be permitted to regulate immigration in a manner consistent with federal immigration law and policy).

[81] *See* Cristina Rodriguez, *The Significance of the Local in Immigration Regulation*, 106 MICH. L. REV. 567 (2008).

[82] Landon v. Plasencia, 459 U.S. 21, 32 (1982) (citing, *inter alia*, United States *ex rel* Knauff v. Shaughnessy, 338 U.S. 537, 542 (1950); Fiallo v. Bell, 430 U.S. 787, 799 (1977); Kleindienst v. Mandel, 408 U.S. 753 (1972) (emphasis added).

[83] *See, e.g.*, Aldana, *supra* note 41; Victor C. Romero, *The Congruence Principle Applied: Rethinking Equal Protection Review of Federal Alienage Classifications After* Adarand Constructors, Inc. v. Pena, 76 OR. L. REV. 425 (1997); *Developments in the Law — Immigration Policy and the Rights of Aliens*, 96 HARV. L. REV. 1286, 1408 nn.57–58 (1983).

a.   Individual Rights

i.   Procedural Due Process

Aliens in removal (often referred to as deportation) proceedings long have been entitled to the protections of the Due Process Clause.[84] The Court initially defined due process rights narrowly — e.g., finding that the lack of knowledge of English in a hearing conducted in English did not violate due process[85] — but the due process rights of noncitizens has expanded over time consistent with the general expansion of due process rights. This resulted in part from the growing sensitivity to the weighty individual interests at stake in removal proceedings.[86] In addition, certain returning aliens in seeking entry into the United States are entitled to due process.

The Supreme Court has extended Due Process rights to certain categories of noncitizens.[87] In 1982, the Supreme Court in *Landon v. Plasencia* held that the question whether a lawful permanent resident who had briefly left the country could be denied entry and have her right to return decided in a hearing that comported with due process. The Court adhered to its holding in *Rosenberg v. Fleuti*[88] that an "innocent, casual and brief excursion" outside the United States by a lawful permanent resident would not, upon her return, mean that she was engaged in a new "entry" into the country. The question of the nature and meaning of the "excursion," however, need not be resolved in a deportation hearing, which generally affords the noncitizen greater procedural protections; the immigration statute in place "clearly reflect[s] a congressional intent that, whether or not the alien is a permanent resident, admissibility shall be determined in an exclusion hearing."[89] The issue of Plasencia's alleged "entry" could therefore be resolved in an exclusion hearing, which at the time provided fewer rights to the alien than deportation hearings, so long as it comported with due process.

The Court restated the essence of the plenary power doctrine that "an alien seeking initial admission has *no* constitutional rights regarding his application, for the power to admit or exclude aliens is a sovereign prerogative."[90] However, the Court went on to observe that "once an alien gains admission to our country and begins to develop the ties that go with permanent residence, his constitutional

---

[84] *See The Japanese Immigrant Case*, 189 U.S. 86, 100–01 (1903).

[85] *Id.* at 101–02.

[86] *See* Fong Haw Tan v. Phelan, 333 U.S. 6, 10 (1948) ("Deportation is a drastic measure and at times the equivalent of banishment or exile."); Bridges v. Wixon, 326 U.S. 135, 147 (1945) (emphasizing that "deportation may result in the loss 'of all that makes life worth living' ") (citation omitted).

[87] *See* Landon v. Plasencia, 459 U.S. 21 (1982) (holding that lawful permanent resident was entitled to due process in hearing).

[88] 374 U.S. 449, 462 (1963).

[89] *Landon v. Plasencia*, 459 U.S. at 28. Parts of this discussion are adapted from Kevin R. Johnson, *Maria and Joseph Plasencia's Lost Weekend: The Case of Landon v. Plasencia, in* IMMIGRATION STORIES, *supra* note 56, at 221.

[90] *Landon v. Plasencia*, 459 U.S. at 32 (citing, *inter alia*, United States *ex rel.* Knauff v. Shaughnessy, 338 U.S. 537, 542 (1950); Fiallo v. Bell, 480 U.S. 787, 799 (1977); Kleindienst v. Mandel, 408 U.S. 753, 765–66 (1972)) (emphasis added).

status changes accordingly. Our cases have frequently suggested that a continuously present resident alien is entitled to a fair hearing when threatened with deportation . . . ."[91] It emphasized that "[w]e need not now decide the scope of [the plenary power doctrine precedent]; it does not govern this case, for Plasencia was absent from the country only a few days, and *the United States has conceded that she has a right to due process.*"[92]

The Court preceded to state that the flexible *Mathews v. Eldridge* balancing test — the general test previously articulated by the Court for evaluating whether governmental procedures comply with due process — applied to determining the specific procedures that Due Process required in Plasencia's case:

> the courts must consider the interest at stake for the individual, the risk of an erroneous deprivation of the interest through the procedures used as well as the probable value of additional or different procedural safeguards, and the interest of the government in using the current procedures rather than additional or different procedures.[93]

Although declining to itself strike the balance in Plasencia's case, the Court noted that she had a "weighty" interest as stake because she "stands to lose the right 'to stay and live and work in this land of freedom' " and "may lose the right to rejoin her immediate family, a right that ranks high among the interests of the individual."[94] It further observed that "[t]he government's interest in efficient administration of the immigration laws at the border also is weighty."[95] The Court reminded the lower court that, on remand, it could only decide "whether the procedures meet the essential standard of fairness under the Due Process clause and [could not impose] procedures that merely displace congressional choices of policy."[96]

The Supreme Court's landmark decision in *Landon v. Plasencia* has had a mixed legacy in the lower courts. The courts dutifully abided by the Court's holding that, when seeking re-entry into the country, a lawful permanent resident's claim of

---

[91] *Landon v. Plasencia*, 459 U.S. at 32. (citations omitted). One of the authorities relied on by the Court for this proposition was *Johnson v. Eisentrager*, 339 U.S. 763, 770 (1950), a case that later was much-debated in connection with the indefinite detention after September 11, 2001 of two U.S. citizens, Jose Padilla and Yaser Hamdi, who the Bush administration classified as "enemy combatants." *See* Hamdi v. Rumsfeld, 542 U.S. 507 (2004) (ruling that U.S. citizen held as "enemy combatant" had the right to a hearing to challenge that classification); Rumsfeld v. Padilla, 542 U.S. 426 (2004) (finding that the court in which action was filed lacked jurisdiction over Padilla and could not entertain a challenge to his detention as an "enemy combatant"); *see also* Hamdan v. Rumsfeld, 548 U.S. 557 (2006) (holding that military tribunals created by Bush administration were unlawful). In *Eisentrager*, the Court highlighted that the rights of a noncitizen who had resided in the United States ordinarily increased with the length of residence, which stood in stark contrast to the rights of "enemy aliens" in times of war.

[92] *Landon v. Plasencia*, 459 U.S. at 34 (citing transcript to Oral Argument 6, 9, 14 and Brief for Petitioner 9–10, 20–21) (emphasis added).

[93] *Landon v. Plasencia*, 459 U.S. at 34 (citing Mathews v. Eldridge, 424 U.S. 319, 334–35 (1976)).

[94] *Landon v. Plasencia*, 459 U.S. at 34 (citations omitted).

[95] *Id.*

[96] *Id.* at 34–35.

admissibility must be determined in proceedings that comply with Due Process.[97] Some courts, however, also viewed *Landon v. Plasencia* as standing for the proposition that the rights of lawful permanent residents increased as the length of their time in the country grew and thus were greater than those of first-time entrants.[98] In contrast, some courts have taken language from the decision to support Congress's plenary power with respect to the procedures afforded certain noncitizens seeking initial entry into the country.[99]

Importantly, courts understood *Landon v. Plasencia* to require that the *Mathews v. Eldridge* balancing test applied to evaluate whether hearing procedures were consistent with due process.[100] In 1988, the Board of Immigration Appeals ruled that a returning lawful permanent resident like Plasencia in exclusion proceedings must be given reasonable notice of the charges, as well as a procedurally fair hearing with the government bearing the burden of proof; the lawful permanent resident could be excluded only upon a showing of clear, unequivocal, and convincing evidence,[101] procedures that differed dramatically from those afforded to Maria Plasencia.

Some immigration law scholars read *Landon v. Plasencia* as opening the door for expanded constitutional rights for noncitizens seeking entry into the United States.[102] They see the decision as a "crack" in the plenary power doctrine. Other commentators, however, are more circumspect, emphasizing that *Landon v. Plasencia* included strong plenary power doctrine language but failed to define the constitutional rights of lawful permanent residents with any specificity.[103]

Prompted by *Landon v. Plasencia*, Congress in 1996 amended the immigration statute to provide that returning lawful permanent residents seeking to enter the country are generally not subject to the same procedures and inadmissibility grounds as first-time entrants. The new law provides that a lawful permanent

---

[97] *See, e.g.*, INS v. Phinpathya, 464 U.S. 183, 193 (1984); Ali v. Reno, 22 F.3d 442, 448 (2d Cir. 1994).

[98] *See, e.g.*, Rhoden v. United States, 55 F.3d 428, 432 (9th Cir. 1995); Campos v. INS, 961 F.2d 309, 316 (1st Cir. 1992).

[99] *See, e.g.*, Cuban Am. Bar Ass'n v. Christopher, 43 F.3d 1412, 1428 (11th Cir.), *cert. denied*, 516 U.S. 913 (1995); Haitian Ctrs. Council v. McNary, 969 F.2d 1326, 1340 (2d Cir. 1992), *vacated sub nom. as moot*, 509 U.S. 918 (1993).

[100] *See, e.g.*, Zadvydas v. Davis, 533 U.S. 678, 694 (2002); Flores v. Meese, 934 F.2d 991, 1013 (9th Cir. 1990), *rev'd on other grounds*, 507 U.S. 291 (1993).

[101] *See* Matter of Huang, 19 I. & N. Dec. 749, 753–54 (BIA 1988); *see, e.g.*, Khodagholian v. Ashcroft, 335 F.3d 1003, 1006 (9th Cir. 2003); Rosendo-Ramirez v. INS, 32 F.3d 1085, 1090 (7th Cir. 1994).

[102] *See, e.g.*, David A. Martin, *Due Process and Membership in the National Community: Political Asylum and Beyond*, 44 U. PITT. L. REV. 165, 214–15 (1983); Hiroshi Motomura, *The Curious Evolution of Immigration Law: Procedural Surrogates, for Substantive Constitutional Rights*, 92 COLUM. L. REV. 1625, 1652–56 (1992) [hereinafter Motomura, *The Curious Evolution of Immigration Law*]; Hiroshi Motomura, *Immigration Law After a Century of Plenary Power: Phantom Constitutional Norms and Statutory Interpretation*, 100 YALE L.J. 545, 578–780 (1990); Michael Scaperlanda, *Partial Membership: Aliens and the Constitutional Community*, 81 IOWA L. REV. 707, 744–45 (1996).

[103] *See* T. Alexander Aleinikoff, *Immigrants in American Law: Aliens, Due Process and "Community Ties": A Response to Martin*, 44 U. PITT. L. REV. 237, 260 n.65 (1983); Legomsky, *supra* note 58, at 260 nn.25–26; Peter H. Schuck, *The Transformation of Immigration Law*, 84 COLUM. L. REV. 1, 62–63 & n.342 (1984).

resident stopped at the border generally is *not* treated as seeking admission into the country;[104] this shifts the legal focus to whether the alien has been admitted into the country previously[105] and entitles most lawful permanent residents at the border to a removal proceeding with broader procedural protections than they would have enjoyed in the the past. Consequently, a beneficial dialogue between the Supreme Court in *Landon v. Plasencia* and Congress ultimately secured greater rights for lawful permanent residents and arguably made immigration procedures more consistent with mainstream constitutional norms.

ii. Substantive Due Process

Noncitizens in the United States — like citizens in certain respects — have limited substantive due process rights.[106] In *Flores v. Reno*,[107] the Supreme Court rejected the substantive due process claim of unaccompanied minors to be released to persons not their parents, close relatives, or legal guardians. *Flores* involved a substantive due process claim forbidding infringement of fundamental liberty interests and claimed that a regulation required noncitizen minors to be released from custody to parents, close relatives, or a legal guardian. The Court found no substantive due process violation, emphasizing that only the rights of *aliens* were at stake.[108]

In subsequent detention cases, the Court has vacillated in the substantive due process rights afforded noncitizens in detention. In *Zadvydas v. Davis*,[109] the Court refused to invoke the plenary power doctrine to shield from review the indefinite detention of noncitizens awaiting deportation and held that regular review for possible release was required. In *Demore v. Kim*,[110] however, the Court upheld mandatory detention of certain noncitizens pending their deportation. One explanation for the different results in the two cases is that the tragic events of September 11, 2001 raised to the fore, national security concerns that did not previously have such urgency.[111]

---

[104] Immigration & Nationality Act § 101(a)(13)(C), 8 U.S.C. § 1101(a)(13)(C) (amended Illegal Immigration Reform and Immigrant Responsibility Act of 1996 by § 301(a), Pub. L. No. 104-208, 110 Stat. 3009-546, 3009-575 (1996)), provides that a lawful permanent resident ordinarily "shall not be regarded as seeking admission into the United States for purposes of the immigration laws unless the alien . . . ."

[105] *See* David A. Martin, *Graduated Application of Constitutional Protections for Aliens: The Real Meaning of* Zadvydas v. Davis, 2001 SUP. CT. REV. 47, 64–66.

[106] For analysis of the state of substantive due process doctrine, see Daniel O. Conkle, *Three Theories of Substantive Due Process*, 85 N.C. L. REV. 63 (2006); Michael A. Scaperlanda, *Illusions of Liberty and Equality: An "Alien's" View of Tiered Scrutiny, Ad Hoc Balancing, Governmental Power, and Judicial Imperialism*, 55 CATH. U.L. REV. 5 (2005).

[107] 507 U.S. 292 (1993).

[108] *See id.* at 301–06 (citing, *inter alia*, Mathews v. Diaz, 426 U.S. 67, 81 (1976) and related plenary power doctrine cases).

[109] 533 U.S. 678, 695–96 (2001). In *Clark v. Martinez*, 543 U.S. 371 (2005), the Court extended *Zadvydas* to aliens deemed inadmissible.

[110] 538 U.S. 510, 522 (2003).

[111] *See* Taylor, *supra* note 70.

iii.   Equal Protection

The Equal Protection rights of noncitizens living in the United States under the Fifth and Fourteenth Amendments are diluted when it comes to noncitizens. The Supreme Court also has invoked the plenary power doctrine to immunize from meaningful judicial review federal laws that discriminate against immigrants who live in the United States. For example, in finding that Congress could limit the eligibility of lawful immigrants for a federal medical insurance program, the Supreme Court emphasized that "[i]*n the exercise of its broad power over naturalization and immigration, Congress regularly makes rules that would be unacceptable if applied to citizens* . . . . The fact that an Act of Congress treats aliens differently from citizens does not itself imply that such disparate treatment is 'invidious.' "[112] Still, the Court applied rational basis review to the federal alienage classification,[113] demonstrating that noncitizens in the United States possess *some* Equal Protection rights.

In a variety of cases, Supreme Court has struck down limitations on the rights of aliens on Equal Protection grounds.[114] The Court at various times has employed strict scrutiny to review *state* laws that discriminated against lawful permanent residents.[115] However, the Court has permitted state governments to impose citizenship requirements on state jobs that perform a "political function."[116] By executive order, the federal government has barred noncitizens from federal civil service jobs.[117] After September 11, the Aviation and Transportation Security Act[118] made U.S. citizenship a qualification for airport security.

---

[112]   Mathews v. Diaz, 426 U.S. 67, 79–80 (1976) (emphasis added) (footnotes omitted).

[113]   *Id.* at 81–82.

[114]   *See, e.g.*, Yick Wo v. Hopkins, 118 U.S. 356 (1886) (holding that discriminatory enforcement of local ordinances against persons of Chinese ancestry violated Equal Protection Clause); Takahashi v. Fish & Game Comm'n, 334 U.S. 410, 420 (1948) (striking down state law restricting fishing by noncitizens); Truax v. Raich, 239 U.S. 33 (1915) (invalidating Arizona law requiring certain number of employees in workplace to be citizens).

[115]   *See, e.g.*, Bernal v. Fainter, 467 U.S. 216, 220 (1984) (applying strict scrutiny holding that state citizenship requirement for notary publics was unconstitutional); Sugarman v. Dougall, 413 U.S. 634, 641–46 (1973) (finding aliens to be a discrete and insular minority, applying strict scrutiny, and invalidating citizenship requirement for state civil service position); Graham v. Richardson, 403 U.S. 365, 370–76 (1971) (applying strict scrutiny to an alienage classification and striking down a bar of state welfare benefits to lawful residents).

[116]   *See, e.g.*, Cabell v. Chavez-Salido, 454 U.S. 432 (1982) (upholding a state law requiring "peace officers" to be U.S. citizens); Ambach v. Norwick, 441 U.S. 68 (1970 (public school teacher); Foley v. Connolie, 435 U.S. 291 (1978) (police officers).

[117]   *See* Mow Sow Wong v. Campbell, 626 F.2d 739 (9th Cir. 1980), *cert. denied sub nom.*, Lum v. Campbell, 450 U.S. 959 (1981) (rejecting constitutional challenge); Jalil v. Campbell, 590 F.2d 1120 (D.C. Cir. 1978) (per curiam); (same); Vergara v. Hampton, 581 F.2d 1281 (7th Cir. 1978), *cert. denied sub nom.* Vergara v. Chairman, Merit System Protection Board, 441 U.S. 905 (1979). For an explanation of the history culminating in the Executive Order, see Motomura, *The Curious Evolution of Immigration Law, supra* note 102, at 690 n.335.

[118]   Pub. L. 107-71, § 111(a)(2), 115 Stat. 597, 617 (2001). Congress later amended the Act to expand eligibility for federal airport screening positions to U.S. nationals. *See* Pub. L. No. 107-296, § 1603, 116 Stat. 2135, 2313 (2002).

The highwater mark of noncitizen rights under the Equal Protection Clause probably is *Plyler v. Doe*,[119] which held that undocumented children could not constitutionally be denied access to elementary and secondary public schools. The Court emphasized that "[a]liens, even aliens whose presence in the country is unlawful, have long been recognized as 'persons' guaranteed due process of law by the Fifth and Fourteenth Amendments . . . . Indeed, we have clearly held that the Fifth Amendment protects aliens whose presence in this country is unlawful from invidious discrimination by the Federal Government."[120] The Court further stated that "[i]t would be incongruous to hold that the United States . . . is barred from invidious discrimination with respect to unlawful aliens, while exempting the States from a similar limitation."[121] Although not finding undocumented immigrants to be a suspect class,[122] or that education is a fundamental right,[123] the Court found that the Texas law that would have effectively barred many undocumented children from the public elementary and secondary schools could not be justified and violated the Equal Protection Clause.

Discrimination based on alienage can have disparate impacts on particular national origin groups. This is especially the case in light of the fact that the vast majority of today's immigrants are from Latin America and Asia. In *Cabell v. Chavez-Salido*,[124] the Supreme Court rejected an equal protection challenge to a California law requiring probation officers to be citizens. For that reason, Los Angeles County declined to hire a lawful permanent resident for more than twenty-five years who had been born in Mexico. In dissent, Justice Blackmun lamented: "I can only conclude that California's exclusion of these appellees from the position of deputy probation officer stems solely from state parochialism and hostility toward foreigners who have come to this country lawfully."[125]

The dangers of discrimination can be seen vividly in the various measures implemented by the federal government after September 11, in the so-called "war on terror." There was legal precedent for the measures. In *Narenji v. Civiletti*,[126] while a group of Americans were held hostage in Iran, a court of appeals in 1979 upheld special procedures requiring all nonimmigrant Iranians attending post-secondary school to report to the local Immigration and Naturalization Service office. The court emphasized that "classifications among aliens based upon nationality are consistent with due process and equal protection if supported by a rational basis."[127] The court found that the regulation satisfied that test and stated that "it is not the business of courts to pass judgment on the decisions of the

---

[119] 457 U.S. 202 (1982); *see* Michael A. Olivas, Plyler v. Doe, *The Education of Undocumented Children, and the Polity, in* IMMIGRATION STORIES, *supra* note 56, at 197 (analyzing background of case).

[120] *Plyler v. Doe*, 457 U.S. at 210 (citing, *inter alia*, Yick Wo v. Hopkins, 118 U.S. 356, 369 (1886) and Mathews v. Diaz, 426 U.S. 67, 77 (1973)).

[121] *Plyler v. Doe*, 457 U.S. at 210 (citation omitted).

[122] *See id.* at 219.

[123] *See id.* at 221.

[124] 454 U.S. 432 (1982).

[125] *Id.* at 463 (Blackmun, J., dissenting).

[126] 617 F.2d 745, 746–47 (D.C. Cir. 1979).

[127] *Id.* at 748; *see* Ghaelian v. INS, 717 F.2d 950, 953 (6th Cir. 1983); Nademi v. INS, 679 F.2d 811

President in the field of foreign policy."[128] Later, the President responded to the Iraqi invasion of Kuwait by requiring fingerprinting and photographing of virtually all nonimmigrants with Iraqi and Kuwaiti travel documents.[129]

After the tragic events of September 11, 2001, the President instituted a "special registration" program[130] — known as the National Security Entry-Exit Registration System — applicable to certain noncitizens from nations populated predominantly by Arabs and Muslims and emphasizing that "[t]he political branches of the government have plenary authority in the immigration area." The courts refused to disturb the special registration program.[131]

For example, in *Kandamar v. Gonzales*,[132] the court of appeals rejected a constitutional challenge and emphasized that

> [p]ossibly, the events of September 11, 2001, and terrorist activities around the world, inform the degree of scrutiny to be applied, but we in any event give deference to the Attorney General's requirement that young males from certain countries be subject to special registration. We hold that a special registration system serves legitimate government objectives of monitoring nationals from certain countries to prevent terrorism and is rationally related to achieving these monitoring objectives. [citing *Narenji v. Civiletti*].

The invocation of the plenary power doctrine by the Bush administration in support of special registration is consistent with other claims by the administration that ordinary principles of law do not govern the Executive Branch in the "war on terror."[133] But even if the plenary power doctrine did not preclude judicial review,

---

(10th Cir. 1982); Dastmalchi v. INS, 660 F.2d 880, 892 (3d Cir. 1981); Malek-Marzban v. INS, 653 F.2d 113 (4th Cir. 1981).

[128]   *Narenji v. Civiletti*, 617 F.2d at 748.

[129]   56 Fed. Reg. 1566 (1991) (codified at 8 C.F.R. pt. 264).

[130]   Registration and Monitoring of Certain Nonimmigrants, 67 Fed. Reg. 52,584, 52,585 (Aug. 12, 2002) (citing Fiallo v. Bell, 430 U.S. 787, 792 (1977); Mathews v. Diaz, 427 U.S. 67, 80–82 (1976)).

[131]   *See, e.g.*, Kandamar v. Gonzales, 464 F.3d 65, 73–74 (1st Cir. 2006) (rejecting Equal Protection challenge to registration program); Ahmed v. Gonzales, 447 F.3d 433, 439–40 (5th Cir. 2006) (same); Ali v. Gonzales, 440 F.3d 678, 681–82 (5th Cir. 2006) (finding, in removal case, that special registration did not violate Equal Protection guarantee); Roudnahal v. Ridge, 310 F. Supp. 2d 884, 892 (E.D. Ohio 2003) (refusing to disturb program and finding no Equal Protection violation even though program was directed primarily at Arab and Muslim noncitizens). For specific criticism of "special registration," see Ty S. Wahab Twibell, *The Road to Internment: Special Registration and Other Human Rights Violations of Arabs and Muslims in the United States*, 29 Vt. L. Rev. 407, 527–35 (2005) (identifying problems generated by racial profiling in immigration enforcement, including in special registration); Kathryn Lohmeyer, Note and Comment, *The Pitfalls of Plenary Power: A Call fror Meaningful Review of NSEERS "Special Registration,"* 25 Whittier L. Rev. 139 (2003); Heidee Stoller et al., Developments in Law and Policy, *The Costs of Post-9/11 National Security Strategy*, 22 Yale L. & Pol. Rev. 197, 220–22 (2004) (analyzing the history of the special registration program and its reliance on racial profiling); *see also* Hiroshi Motomura, *Immigration and We the People After September 11*, 66 Alb. L. Rev. 413, 420–21 (2003) (calling for a coherent understanding of immigration and citizenship decisions to prevent the campaign against terrorism from dividing the nation).

[132]   464 F.2d 65, 73–74 (1st Cir. 2006).

[133]   *See* Diane Marie Amann, *Abu Ghraib*, 153 U. Pa. L. Rev. 2085 (2005); Diane Marie Amann, *Guantanamo*, 42 Colum. J. Transnat'l L. 263 (2004); Erwin Chemerinsky, *The Assault on the*

it has been debated whether the U.S. Constitution in fact applies in evaluating the lawfulness of the various measures taken by the U.S. government in the war on terror.[134]

b.   Separation of Powers

i.   Limits on Judicial Review

The courts have seen a variety of limits on judicial review imposed over the years. Both the plenary power doctrine and *Chevron* deference, discussed in Chapter 6, limit the scope of judicial review of the immigration laws and their administration. In addition, Congress frequently has enacted "court stripping" provisions limiting — at times radically curtailing — judicial review of various immigration decisions. These provisions are discussed in Chapter 6.

ii.   INS v. Chadha

In *INS v. Chadha*,[135] the Supreme Court found that a provision of the Immigration & Nationality Act authorizing Congress to reverse a decision of the agency in a deportation case violated separation of powers principles. Chadha entered the United States lawfully on a nonimmigrant student visa in 1966, but the government initiated deportation proceedings after his visa expired. The immigration court suspended Chadha's deportation due to extreme hardship, a decision vetoed by Congress as permitted by the Immigration & Nationality Act. The Supreme Court found that this veto power violated separation of powers:

> Disagreement with the Attorney General's decision on Chadha's depor-
> tation — that is, Congress' decision to deport Chadha — no less than
> Congress' original choice to delegate to the Attorney General the authority
> to make that decision, involves determinations of policy that Congress can
> implement in only one way; bicameral passage followed by presentment to
> the President. Congress must abide by its delegation of authority until that
> delegation is legislatively altered or revoked.[136]

The Supreme Court's decision in *Chadha* establishes important limits on Congress's role in intervening in the administration of the immigration laws. Since the case was decided, Congress has avoided direct intervention in the decisions of the immigration bureaucracy.

Constitution: Executive Power and the War on Terrorism, 40 U.C. DAVIS L. REV. 1 (2006).

[134] *See* Bruce Ackerman, *The Emergency Constitution*, 113 YALE L.J. 1029 (2004); Eric A. Posner & Adrian Vermeule, *Accommodating Emergencies*, 46 STAN. L. REV. 605 (2003); *see also* Richard Posner, NOT A SUICIDE PACT: THE CONSTITUTION IN A TIME OF NATIONAL EMERGENCY (2006) (contending that the U.S. Constitution permits most of Bush administration's counterterrorism measures).

[135] 462 U.S. 919 (1983).

[136] 462 U.S. 919, 954–55 (1983).

C. THE RELAXATION OF FEDERAL PREEMPTION: THE DEVOLUTION DOCTRINE

Recent years have seen the federal government's attempt to devolve to the states increasing immigration functions. Local police traditionally have not been involved in immigration enforcement; many localities for law enforcement reasons, had rules that officers should not inquire into the immigration status of witness, victims, suspects or perpetrators. The U.S. government in recent years has solicited the assistance of state and local official and police in immigration enforcement. *See* Chapter 4.

Proposition 187, an initiative passed by California voters in 1994 sought to restrict public benefits available to undocumented immigrants.[137] Not long after, Congress passed welfare reform in 1996 that restricted benefits to lawful as well as unlawful immigrants.[138] The reform afforded authority to the states to determine immigrant eligibility for certain benefit programs, with states taking varying approaches.[139] Misconceptions about immigrant benefit recipients contributed to the reform's passage.[140]

Employers have been called on increasingly to lend a hand in enforcing the immigration laws. The Immigration Reform and Control Act used the threat of employer sanctions to halt the employment of undocumented immigrants. In recent years, local governments have sought to prohibit the employment of undocumented immigrants and for landlords not to rent to undocumented immigrants.[141]

---

[137] *See supra* text accompanying notes 78–79 (citing authorities).

[138] *See* Personal Responsibility and Work Opportunity Reconciliation Act of 1996, Pub. L. No. 104-193, 110 Stat. 2105.

[139] *See* Peter H. Schuck, *Taking Immigration Federalism Seriously*, 2007 U. Chi. Leg. F. 57, 60–61; *Developments in the Law Jobs and Borders*, 118 Harv. L. Rev. 2171, 2248–51 (2005); *see also* Emilie Cooper, Note, *Embedded Immigrant Exceptionalism: An Examination of California's Proposition 187, the 1996 Welfare Reforms and the Anti-Immigrant Sentiment Expressed Therein*, 18 Geo. Immigr. L.J. 345, 351–57 (2004) (summarizing impact of welfare reform on immigrants). *See generally* Sheryll D. Cashin, *Federalism, Welfare Reform, and the Minority Poor: Accounting for the Tyranny of State Majorities*, 99 Colum. L. Rev. 552 (1999) (analyzing impacts of devolution of federal benefit programs to the states).

[140] *See* Bill Ong Hing, *Don't Give Me Your Tired, Your Poor: Conflicted Immigrant Stories and Welfare Reform*, 33 Harv. C.R.-C.L. L. Rev. 159 (1998).

[141] *See* Huyen Pham, *The Private Enforcement of Immigration Laws*, 96 Geo. L.J. 777 (2008); Rigel C. Oliveri, *Between a Rock and a Hard Place: Landlords, Latinos, Anti-Illegal Immigrant Ordinances, and Housing Discrimination*, 62 Vand. L. Rev. 55 (2009) (analyzing critically local ordinances prohibiting private landlords from renting to undocumented immigrants).

Chapter 4

STATE AND LOCAL INVOLVEMENT IN IMMIGRATION AND POLICY: FEDERALISM AND ALIENAGE LAW

SYNOPSIS

A. The Alien Land Laws
B. Firearm Alienage Restrictions
C. Alienage Suffrage
D. The Special Public Interest Doctrine
E. The Political-Function Exception
F. Private Employment
G. Public Benefits
H. Public Education
  1. K-12 Education
  2. Higher Education
I. Worker Rights
  1. State Employment and Labor Laws
  2. Day Laborers
J. Driver's Licenses
K. Landlord/Tenant Immigration Ordinances
L. The Official English/English-Only Laws
M. Local Immigration Enforcement
N. Family Law
O. Conclusion

Until 1875[1], with the exception of the short-lived Alien and Sedition Acts of 1798,[2] Congress left the U.S. international borders open, and states, not the federal government, attempted to restrict immigration flows. States imposed restrictions on transborder movement on the basis of crime, health, public morals, poverty, disability, and ideology or race.[3] Then, in a series of nineteenth century decisions,

---

[1] In 1875, Congress restricted immigration for the first time by including a convict and prostitution immigration restriction a federal statute. Act of Mar. 3, 1875 (Page Law), ch. 141, 18 Stat. 477 (repealed 1974).

[2] The package of legislation included three statutes directed specifically at aliens: the Naturalization Act of 1798, Act of June 18, 1798, ch. 54, 1 Stat. 566; the Alien Enemies Act, Act of July 6, 1798, ch. 66, 1 Stat. 577; and the Alien (or Alien Friends) Act, Act of June 25, 1798, ch. 58, 1 Stat. 570.

[3] *See* Kerry Abrams, *Polygamy, Prostitution, and the Federalization of Immigration Law,* 105

the Court invalidated certain state immigration restrictions,[4] ultimately declaring in 1889 in the *Chinese Exclusion Case* that immigration control is an exclusive federal power.[5]

The *Chinese Exclusion Case* originated the doctrine of federal plenary immigration power, but the doctrine did not end state regulation of immigrants. Unable to directly control transborder movement, states turned to restricting the living conditions of immigrants, who were perceived as a threat to the well-being of white native residents. In the late nineteenth and early twentieth centuries, these state efforts included employment and property ownership restrictions against mostly Japanese and Chinese immigrants,[6] as well as language restrictions that targeted German and other Eastern and Southern European immigrants.[7] These and other state alienage restrictions have continued throughout much of the twentieth century until today, usually heightening in times of economic depression or war. Most recently, the September 11th attacks led several states and local governments to pass thousands of such alienage measures, most of which aim to rid localities of undocumented immigrants through tough restrictions or regulations of certain public goods and services, jobs, and housing, or through increased local immigration law enforcement.[8]

From the beginning, constitutional challenges to anti-immigrant measures have raised equality concerns as well as questions of preemption. Initially, the preemption arguments focused on state infringement upon the federal government's commerce- or treaty-making powers. With few exceptions, courts upheld these early local ordinances, holding that they did not conflict with treaty obligations[9] or interfered with commerce,[10] and further, that states could legitimately discriminate and reserve for their citizens the distribution of public moneys and wealth, among which were the access to natural resources and public

---

COLUM. L. REV. 641 (2005); Marvin H. Morse and Lucy M. Moran, *Troubling the Waters: Human Cargos*, 33 J. MAR. L. & COM. 1 (2002); and Gerald L. Neuman, *The Lost Century of American Immigration Law (1776–1875)*, 93 COLUM. L. REV. 1833 (1993).

[4] *See, e.g.*, the Passenger Cases, 48 U.S. (7 How.) 283 (1849) (striking down state taxes on certain categories of arriving immigrants); Henderson v. Mayor of New York, 92 U.S. (Otto) 259 (striking down state taxes on certain categories of arriving immigrants).

[5] Chae Chan Ping v. U.S., 130 U.S. 581 (1889).

[6] Keith Aoki, *No Right to Own?: The Early Twentieth-Century "Alien Land Laws" as a Prelude to Internment*, 40 B.C. L. REV. 37 (1998); SUCHENG CHAN, THIS BITTER-SWEET SOIL: THE CHINESE IN CALIFORNIA AGRICULTURE, 1860–1910 (1986); ROGER DANIELS, THE POLITICS OF PREJUDICE: THE ANTI-JAPANESE MOVEMENT IN CALIFORNIA AND THE STRUGGLE FOR JAPANESE EXCLUSION (2d. ed. 1977).

[7] Lupe S. Salinas, *Immigration and Language Rights: The Evolution of Private Racists Attitudes into American Public Law and Policy*, 7 NEV. L.J. 895, 917 (2007).

[8] *See, e.g.*, Raquel Aldana & Steve Bender, SALT Statement on Post 9/11 Anti-Immigrant Measures, *available at* http://www.saltlaw.org/~salt2007/files/uploads/2007_SALT_immigrationordinances_0.pdf; Michael J. Wishnie, *State and Local Police Enforcement of Immigration Laws*, 6 U. PA. J. CONST. L. 1084 (2004).

[9] *See, e.g.*, Hauenstein v. Lynham, 100 U.S. 483 (1880); Blythe v. Hinckley, 180 U.S. 333(1901); Patsone v. Pennsylvania, 232 U.S. 138 (1914); Crane v. New York, 239 U.S. 195 (1915); Heim v. McCall, 239 U.S. 175 (1915); and Terrace v. Thompson, 263 U.S. 197 (1923).

[10] McCready v. Virginia, 94 U.S. 391 (1877).

service jobs.[11]

As federal immigration power solidified and expanded, preemption challenges focused instead on state infringement upon federal immigration power. Generally, the success of federal immigration power preemption claims has been greater when Congress has legislated in the area and when state regulation conflicts with federal law or policies.[12] Preemption successes also occur when states deny rights or benefits to documented immigrants, especially lawful permanent residents, in the absence of authorizing federal legislation.[13] In contrast, state laws are likely to be upheld when they target the undocumented, are consistent with federal immigration laws or policies, and/or are considered to involve an overriding, and thus domestic, state interest.[14] At times, the federal immigration power preemption doctrine has yielded contradictory judicial results.[15] Such results have prompted scholars to critique the doctrine as unworkable because the line between noncitizen regulation affecting domestic affairs and affecting foreign affairs is impossible to draw.[16]

As equal rights doctrine also evolved, equality challenges to state alienage restrictions enjoyed greater success, with courts recognizing that alienage-based distinctions are suspect and deserving of strict scrutiny protection.[17] Protection, however, has generally extended only to lawful U.S. residents and, with the exception of undocumented children for purposes of K-12 education, has excluded the undocumented.[18] Thus, states have had a wide margin to discriminate against the undocumented, at least when the distinction denies what courts deem a privilege or benefit.[19] Further, Congress has, at least with regard to public benefits, devolved to states its authority to discriminate even against lawful residents[20] As a result, some states have seized on this statutory authority to discriminate against lawful residents in the area of public benefits.[21] Finally, states are able to discriminate freely against all noncitizens as to voting and in certain

---

[11] *See, e.g.*, Lynham, 100 U.S. at 495–86; Patsone, 232 U.S. at 143–44; McCall, 239 U.S. at 188–193; Thompson, 263 U.S. at 214–224.

[12] *See generally* subsections B. Firearm Alienage Restrictions, G. Public Benefits, and H.2. Higher Education.

[13] *See generally* subsections D. The Special Public Interest Doctrice and G. Public Benefits.

[14] *See generally* B. Firearm Alienage Restrictions, C. Alienage Suffrage, E. The Political-Function Exception, F. Private Employment, G. Public Benefits, H. Public Education, I. Worker Rights, J. Driver's Licenses, and K. Landlord/Tenant Immigration Ordinances.

[15] *See generally* subsections B. Firearm Alienage Restrictions, F. Private Employment, H.2. Higher Education, I. Worker Rights, and K. Landlord/Tenant Immigration Ordinances.

[16] *See, e.g.*, Christina M. Rodríguez, *The Significance of the Local in Immigration Regulations*, 106 MICH. L. REV. 567, 616–640 (2008); Pratheepan Gulasekaram, *Aliens with Guns: Equal Protection, Federal Power, and the Second Amendment*, 92 IOWA L. REV. 891, 929–40 (2007).

[17] Graham v. Richardson, 403 U.S. 365, 371–72 (1971).

[18] Plyler v. Doe, 457 U.S. 202, at 221–26 (1982).

[19] *See generally* F. Private Employment and G. Public Benefits.

[20] *See generally* G. Public Benefits.

[21] *Id.*

public jobs based on principles of federalism, as these areas are viewed as exclusive local political functions.[22]

A. THE ALIEN LAND LAWS

Since early times, land ownership became one significant area of local alienage regulation. The early American colonies adopted from the English common law the alien land laws, which excluded noncitizens from land ownership.[23] Then, from U.S. independence until the late nineteenth century, a tendency to abolish alien land restrictions emerged.[24] This trend was followed, however, by the enactment of several waves of anti-alien land laws at both the federal and state levels in response to perceived threats of foreign land ownership to national and local interests. Based on fears that large foreign-owned ranches would jeopardize statehood for the territories, Congress passed the Territorial Land Act of 1787[25] which forbade extensive alien landholding in the organized territories, except by immigrant farmers who had applied for citizenship. Eleven states passed similar laws as a necessary response to a depressed agricultural condition and to guard against absentee ownership of land.[26]

At the turn of the twentieth century, the Japanese represented an economic threat to native whites in Western states, particularly in agriculture.[27] As a result, in 1913, California adopted the California Alien Land Law. California extended the law in 1920, and several states followed suit, from Washington and Oregon to Kansas, then further east.[28] These laws, *inter alia*, barred "aliens ineligible for citizenship," which affected almost exclusively the Japanese, not solely from owning, but also from leasing and transferring in trust, agricultural land.[29] In a series of four cases decided in 1923, the Court upheld the constitutionality of these laws, finding that they neither violated U.S. treaty obligations with Japan nor equal protection.[30] In their reasoning, the Court completely ignored the *Yick Wo v. Hopkins*[31] precedent, which struck down California's ordinance barring the Chinese from operating laundry mats, and distinguished *Truax v. Raich*,[32] which struck down an Arizona ordinance restricting the employment of noncitizens.[33] The

---

[22] *See generally* C. Alienage Suffrage and E. The Political-Function Exception.

[23] Polly J. Price, *Alien Land Restrictions in the American Common Law: Exploring the Relative Autonomy Paradigm*, 43 Am. J. Legal Hist. 152, 155–66 (1999). *See also* Mark Shapiro, Note, *The Dormant Commerce Clause: A Limit on Alien Land Laws*, 20 Brook. J. Int'l L. 217, 220 (1993).

[24] Shapiro, *supra* note 23, at 220.

[25] 48 U.S.C. §§ 1501–08 (1988).

[26] Shapiro, *supra* note 23, at 221.

[27] Aoki, *supra* note 6, at 38–55. *See also* Shapiro *supra* note 23, at 222.

[28] Aoki, *supra* note 6, at 53.

[29] *Id.* at 38–9.

[30] *See* Terrace v. Thompson, 263 U.S. 197 (1923); Porterfield v. Webb, 263 U.S. 225 (1923); Webb v. O'Brien, 263 U.S. 313 (1923); Frick v. Webb, 263 U.S. 326 (1923).

[31] Yick Wo v. Hopkins, 118 U.S. 356 (1886).

[32] 239 U.S. 33 (1915).

[33] *See infra* notes 101–108 and accompanying text (discussing the *Yick Wo* and *Truax v. Raich* cases).

Court distinguished *Truax* by contrasting the 14th Amendment right to earn a living from the privilege of owning or controlling agricultural land within the state.[34] Moreover, the Court held that controlling the quality and allegiance of those who own and occupy farm lands are matters of the highest importance to states.[35] Then, not surprisingly, anti-Japanese sentiment intensified during World War II, prompting some states to enact restrictive alien law statutes aimed specifically at preventing Japanese from moving into states following their release from internment.[36]

After World War II, the Court took initial steps to repeal alien land laws based on equal protection grounds. In *Oyama v. California*, the Court indicated in *dicta* that equal protection did not allow California to prohibit land ownership by foreign nationals who were ineligible for citizenship.[37] Several state supreme courts followed suit and declared their alien land laws unconstitutional in violation of the Fourteenth Amendment,[38] while other state legislatures repealed their laws. More importantly, by 1952, no foreign national was ineligible for citizenship on the basis of race or national origin.[39] As a result, most laws restricting land ownership based on citizenship ineligibility would not facially discriminate based on national origin.

Another wave of alien land laws was enacted during the Cold War to limit the rights of foreigners to receive land by inheritance. The purpose of such laws was to prevent the diversion of U.S. wealth to communist governments.[40] In 1968, however, the Supreme Court severely limited this practice when it struck down an Oregon statue that conditioned a foreign national's rights of inheritance on a showing of reciprocal rights granted to U.S. citizens in that national's country of origin.[41] This time, the basis for the challenge was the law's unconstitutional intrusion into the field of foreign affairs.[42]

The most recent wave of alien land laws occurred in the 1970s, when a number of states reacted to a surge in farmland foreign investment by restricting the *situs* and the amount of land that could be purchased.[43] To date, no court has struck down the validity of these statutes. Moreover, state cases during this era distinguished *Oyama* based on the absence of facial national origin discrimination in the alien land law restrictions.[44]

---

[34] *Thompson*, 263 U.S. at 222.

[35] *Id.*

[36] *See, e.g.*, Gabriel J. Chin, *Citizenship and Exclusion: Wyoming's Anti-Japanese Alien Land Law in Context*, 1 Wyo. L. Rev. 497, 498–503 (2001).

[37] 332 U.S. 633 (1948).

[38] *See, e.g.*, Sei Fujii v. State, 242 P.2d. 617, 625 (Cal. 1952); State v. Oakland, 287 P.2d 39, 42 (Mont. 1955); Kenji Namba v. McCourt, 204 P.2d 569, 614 (Or. 1949).

[39] McCarran-Walter Act of 1952, Pub. L. No. 82-414, 66 Stat. 163.

[40] Shapiro, *supra* note 23, at 222.

[41] Zschernig v. Miller, 389 U.S. 429 (1968).

[42] *Id.* at 432.

[43] Shapiro, *supra* note 23, at 222 (citing to laws enacted in Iowa and Nebraska).

[44] *See* Lehndorff Geneva, Inc. v. Warren, 246 N.W. 2d 815, 824 (Wis. 1976).

Many states, even today, continue to have laws that restrict to some degree the rights of noncitizens to own property.[45] The greatest restrictions pertain to the acquisition of agricultural land by nonresident foreign nationals or foreign corporations, while other states limit the number of acres that can be owned or simply impose reporting requirements.[46] Non-agricultural restrictions on real property similarly impose limits on the number of acres that can be owned, limit the number of years the property may be held, or impose reporting requirements.[47] Finally, a few states still have laws restricting the right of foreign nationals to receive inheritances.[48]

Despite the number of constitutional challenges available, none are likely to strike down most remaining alien land laws for several reasons. First, the vast majority of current alien land laws restrict from owning land only nonresident foreign nationals or foreign corporations, and whether these laws are equally susceptible to constitutional challenges based on equal protection grounds remains unclear.[49] Moreover, very few statutes impose reciprocity provisions on other nations or any other provision that would trample on the federal government's foreign affairs powers, including statutes that would deny foreign nationals specific rights granted to them by treaty.[50] Another potential challenge could be based on preemption based on the powers of the federal government to regulate commerce and foreign affairs, and perhaps also in its taxing powers.[51] To date, however, no federal statute that could pertain to alien property restrictions[52] has been employed to challenge state alien land laws, perhaps because the rights of foreign nationals

---

[45] *See, e.g,* Price, *supra* note 23, at 152 (reporting that approximately half the states have laws that restrict noncitizen access to real property). A 1990 American Bar Association Study reported that about thirty states imposed some type of alien land restriction ranging from requiring registration upon purchase to limiting prospecting on public lands to inherence limitations. AMERICAN BAR ASSOCIATION, COMMITTEE ON FOREIGN INVESTMENT IN U.S. REAL ESTATE, FOREIGN INVESTMENT IN U.S. REAL ESTATE: A COMPREHENSIVE GUIDE (Timothy E. Powers, ed. 1990). Since the ABA study, a few states have repealed or changed their statues. These include Kansas, Kan. Stat. Ann. § 59–511 (2002) (repealing law that allowed transmission and inheritance of property only when provided for by treaty); Montana, Mon. Code. Ann. § 77-2-306 (2003) (deleting portion of its statute which had required noncitizens to declare intention to become citizens before acquiring public land); New Mexico (repealing N.M. Const. Art. II, § 22, which had prohibited acquisition of land by noncitizens ineligible for U.S. citizenship); and Wyoming (repealing Wyo. Sta. § 34-15-101 (Supp. 1989), which barred non-resident noncitizens from acquired land unless there was reciprocity but still prohibiting them from taking land through inheritance or testamentary disposition).

[46] Price, *supra* note 23, at 223.

[47] *Id.*

[48] *Id.*

[49] Shapiro, *supra* note 23, at 226.

[50] *Id.* at 228–229.

[51] *Id.* at 230–31.

[52] The statutes include the Alien Property Custodian Regulations, 26 C.F.R. § 303.1; 28 C.F.R. § 167; 31 C.F.R. §§ 520.101, 520.102 (1992); the Foreign Asset Control Regulation, 50 U.S.C. §§ 1-44 (1988); the AFIDA, 7 U.S.C. §§ 3501–08 (1988); the International Investment and Trade in Services Survey Act of 1976, 22 U.S.C. §§ 3101–08 (amended 1990); the Foreign Investment in Real Property Tax Act of 1980, 22 U.S.C. § 3104 (c). *Id.* at 231–6; and the Agricultural Foreign Investment Disclosure Act, 7 U.S.C.A. § 3501 (1978).

with respect to real property have been primarily a matter of state regulation.[53] Moreover, Congress has not expressly manifested its intent to preempt state alien land regulation, even when it has legislated to regulate foreign ownership of U.S. real property.[54]

B.   FIREARM ALIENAGE RESTRICTIONS

Laws that restrict noncitizen's possession, use, and/or transport of firearms occupy another important area of alienage state regulation. Historically, state legislatures enacted these gun laws within the first decades of the twentieth century based on fear and prejudices against immigrants. Newly arrived Italian immigrants and so-called foreign anarchists during the red-scare era were objects of such fear.[55] Although many of these laws have been amended or repealed, today over twenty states still impose some form of restriction on noncitizens' possession, use, and/or transport of firearms.[56] In addition, the federal Gun Control Act (GCA), adopted originally in 1968 and amended in 1993,[57] currently forbids ownership, possession, or transport of firearms by nonimmigrants (temporary legal migrants), undocumented immigrants, and former citizens who have renounced their citizenship.[58] Congress enacted the GCA in order to prevent firearms from getting into the hands of perceived dangerous individuals, and noncitizens were included along with persons with prior felony convictions.[59]

Constitutional challenges to firearm alienage restriction laws in a handful of states have focused mostly on equal protection or preemption grounds, with few others raising a right to bear arms under state constitutions. The results have been varied. Courts invalidating state firearm alienage restrictions have relied mostly on equal protection grounds[60] or on the fundamental right to bear arms.[61] Cases upholding state firearm alienage restrictions have either viewed the state police power as creating an exemption to equal protection restrictions,[62] or have rejected

---

[53] AMERICAN JURISPRUDENCE, SECOND EDITION, Aliens and Citizens, § 2075, Real Property Rights.

[54] Shapiro, *supra* note 23, at 231–36.

[55] Gulasekaram, *supra* note 16, at 908–09.

[56] *Id.* at 895. The first gun control act that mentions noncitizens is the Omnibus Crime Control and Safe Streets Act of 1968, Pub. L. No. 90-351, tit. IV, 82 Stat. 197, 234 (1968) (codified at 18 U.S.C. §§ 921–30 (2000)). Karen A. Michalson, *Constitutional Law — Is 18 U.S.C. § 922 (0)(1) Constitutional? Mere Possession of Self-Created Objects and the Reach of the Commerce Clause*, 28 W. NEW ENG. L. REV. 133, 144 (2005).

[57] Brady Handgun Violence Prevention Act, Pub. L. No. 103-159, 107 Stat. 1536 (1993).

[58] 18 U.S.C. § 922 (g)(5)(A) (2000).

[59] *See* William J. Vizzard, *The Gun Control Act of 1968*, 18 ST. LOUIS U. PUB. L. REV. 79, 87–90 (1999); Franklin E. Zimring, *Firearms and Federal Law: The Gun Control Act of 1968*, 4 J. LEGAL STUD. 133, 140–43 (1975).

[60] *See* Chan v. Troy, 559 N.W.2d 374, 376 (Mich. 1997); State v. Chumphol, 634 P.2d 451 (Nev. 1981); Sandiford v. Com., 217 Va. 117 (Va. 1974); and People v. Rappard, 28 Cal. App. 3d 302 (Cal. App. 1972).

[61] *See* People v. Zerillo, 189 N.W. 927 (Mich. 1922).

[62] *See* Ex Parte Rameriz, 226 P. 914 (Cal. 1994); People v. Cannizaro, 31 P.2d 1066 (Cal. App. 2d Dist. 1974); Utah v. Vlach, 645 P.2d 677 (Utah 1982); Utah v. Beorchia, 530 P.2d 813 (Utah 1974) and State v. Rheaume, 116 A. 758 (N.H. 1922).

preemption challenges based on the interplay between state and federal firearm alienage restrictions.[63] Congress specifically contemplated concurrent state firearm regulation when it enacted the Gun Control Act.[64] In effect, Section 927 of the Act declares that viable preemption challenges are limited to conflict preemption; that is, state laws that are in direct conflict with federal legislation; and not field preemption; that is, state laws that are otherwise consistent with or expand on federal alienage gun restrictions.[65] Thus, a preemption problem would likely arise only if states decreased federal alienage gun restrictions, which currently apply to the undocumented, nonimmigrants, and persons who have denounced their citizenship. In contrast, preemption would not apply if states sought to expand the restriction also to certain lawful permanent residents.[66]

Challenges to federal alienage gun restrictions based on the right to bear arms or on equal protection have also been rejected, namely because a right to bear arms has not been considered an individual right.[67] Interestingly, the recent Supreme Court case, *District of Columbia v. Heller*,[68] which recognized the right of an individual to bear arms in the Second Amendment, could alter this analysis. On the other hand, the reference to the word "people" in the text of the Second Amendment[69] could very well lead to an interpretation of the right as belonging solely to citizens or to a narrow group of legal immigrants. The *Heller* Court certainly hints at this possibility by citing to *U.S. v. Verdugo-Urquidez*,[70] a case involving the meaning of the word "people" in the Fourth Amendment.[71] There, in *dicta*, the Court defined the term as referring to "a class of persons who are part of a national community or who have otherwise developed sufficient connection with this country to be considered part of that community."[72] To some scholars, a citizenship-based reading of the right to bear arms would be inconsistent with the important role that noncitizens today have in arms-bearing public functions, including their substantial military service and the requirement that they must register for selective service.[73]

---

[63] *See* State v. Hermandez-Mercado, 879 P.2d 283 (Wash. 1994).

[64] 18 U.S.C. § 927 (2000).

[65] Gulasekaram, *supra* note 16, at 927.

[66] *Id.*

[67] *See* Lewis v. U.S., 445 U.S. 55, 65 (1980) (reviewing firearm restrictions under rational basis and noting that legislative restrictions on the use of firearms do not trench upon any constitutionally protected liberty); U.S. v. Toner, 728 F.2d 115, 128 (2d Cir. 1984) (holding that the right to possess a gun is a not a fundamental right and that the statute making it a felony for an "illegal alien" to possess or transport "in commerce or affecting commerce . . . any firearm" did not violate the Fifth Amendment right to equal protection).

[68] 128 S. Ct. 2783, 2791 (2008).

[69] The Second Amendment reads: "A well regulated Militia, being necessary to the security of a free State, the right of the people to keep and bear Arms, shall not be infringed." U.S. Const., amend. II. Along with the U.S. Constitution, seventeen state constitutions also reference "the people," with the rest explicitly referencing citizens or persons. Gulasekaram, *supra* note 16, at 906.

[70] 494 U.S. 259 (1990).

[71] *Heller*, 128 S. Ct. at 2791.

[72] *Id.* at 265.

[73] Gulasekaram, *supra* note 16, at 907.

C. ALIENAGE SUFFRAGE

Historically, states determined who was eligible to vote in both state and federal elections[74] with few exceptions, such as when Congress promoted alien suffrage to encourage immigration in certain U.S. territories.[75] States did not restrict voting to citizens from the founding throughout much of the nineteenth century.[76] Early support for alienage suffrage was motivated by both democratic and instrumental principles. Not only did states send the message that newcomers would not be excluded from political participation, as it was a natural right (instead exclusion rested on race, gender, property, and wealth), but states hoped that enfranchising noncitizens would encourage their rapid state settlement.[77]

Wars and the changing faces and needs of immigration into the United States, however, led to a rise in nativism, as well as more restrictive views about who should participate in the community's process of political self-definition.[78] By 1928, no state afforded noncitizen suffrage in statewide or federal elections,[79] a situation that persists until today, save in the ability of noncitizens to vote in a few U.S. municipalities, towns, or in school district elections.[80]

Throughout the history of alienage suffrage, the battle to enfranchise noncitizens has been political rather than legal, and the preference has been for state discretion over judicial intervention. Historically, neither the Supreme Court nor lower courts have declared the practice of inclusion unconstitutional.[81] Rather, numerous state courts endorsed alienage suffrage,[82] and even the U.S. Supreme Court indirectly signaled acceptance of the practice based on federalism principles.[83] This treatment of alienage suffrage as a political question appears consistent with constitutional

---

[74] Gerald L. Neuman, *"We are the People": Alien Suffrage in German and American Perspective*, 13 MICH. J. INT'L L. 259, 294 (1992).

[75] Jasmin B. Raskin, *Legal Aliens, Local Citizens: The Historical, Constitutional and Theoretical Meanings of Alien Suffrage*, 141 U. PA. L. REV. 1391, 1402, 1407 (1993) (discussing the Northwest Ordinance of 1787 and the organic acts for the Oregon and Minnesota territories which granted noncitizens the rights to vote in order to produce immigration in those respective territories). Similarly, though Congress did not extend voting rights to noncitizens in lands taken from Mexico during the Mexican war, it did include provisions for alienage suffrage for persons willing to declare their intent to naturalize. *Id.* at 1407–08.

[76] Leon E. Aylsworth, *The Passing of Alien Suffrage*, 25 AM. POL. SCI. REV. 114, 114–16 (1931) (documenting that during the nineteenth century the constitutions of at least twenty-two states and territories granted noncitizens the right to vote).

[77] Raskin, *supra* note 75, at 1395.

[78] *See* Neuman, *supra* note 74, at 296–99; Raskin, *supra* note 75, at 1403–15; Virginia Harper-Ho, *Noncitizen Voting Rights: The History, the Law and Current Prospects for Change*, 18 LAW & INEQ. 271, 276 (2000) (discussing the effect of the War of 1812, the Civil War and WWI on alienage suffrage in the United States).

[79] Aylsworth, *supra* note 76, at 114.

[80] Elise Brozovich, *Prospects for Democratic Change: Non-citizen Suffrage in America*, 23 HAMLINE J. PUB. L. & POL'Y 403, 440–44 (2002).

[81] Raskin, *supra* note 75, at 1417.

[82] *Id.*

[83] *Id.* at 1717–20 (discussing Dred Scott v. Sanford, 60 U.S. (19 How.) 393, 405 (1856); Minor v. Happersett, 88 U.S. (21 Wall.) 162 (1874); Pope v. Williams, 193 U.S. 621 (1904)).

text. Under the U.S. Constitution, alien suffrage is neither constitutionally compelled nor constitutionally forbidden.[84] One oblique reference appears in Article I, which reads that members of the House of Representatives shall be "chosen every second Year by the People of several states,"[85] with "People" possibly being read as narrower than person and imposing a citizenship restriction.[86] The various suffrage amendments (the Fifteenth, Nineteenth, Twenty-fourth, and Twenty-sixth) make explicit reference to citizens.[87] Their language, however, proscribes the exclusion of citizens from voting without prohibiting the inclusion of others. Indeed, just four years after the adoption of the Fifteenth Amendment, the Court in *Minor v. Happersett* did not interpret the word "citizen" to invalidate the common and visible practice of alienage suffrage in several states.[88]

Contemporary arguments over alienage suffrage continue to emphasize the State's discretion to define the political community, even as restrictive voting qualifications as applied to citizens (e.g., literacy or residency requirements) face strict scrutiny equal protection challenges.[89] Local arguments for inclusion have generally focused on the legitimate interest of resident noncitizens in having a say in the rules that govern their conduct and affect their interests in light of their status as subjects of U.S. laws, and their degree of contributions and stakes in the community.[90] In contrast, those who oppose alienage suffrage insist on citizenship as an essential precondition for voting and cast doubt on the loyalty of those who decline to declare their allegiance and full commitment to the United States.[91]

The contemporary practice of exclusion is likely to be upheld as courts continue to view alienage suffrage as involving political decisions rather than legal mandates.[92] Some scholars have even projected that were Congress to prohibit alienage suffrage, such law would be upheld under modern constitutional law and federal immigration power.[93] Moreover, despite early arguments to the contrary,[94] equal

---

[84] Neuman, *"We are the People"*, *supra* note 74, at 292.

[85] U.S. Const. art. I, § 2, cl. 1.

[86] Neuman, *"We are the People"*, *supra* note 74, at 292. *See also* notes 70–73 and accompanying text (discussing the U.S. Supreme Court holding in *Verdugo-Urquidez*).

[87] Other constitutional provisions cited in the alienage suffrage debate includes Article IV, § 4, the Republican Guaranty Clause ["The United States shall guarantee to every State in this Union a Republican Form of Government . . . "] and the Fourteenth Amendment, Cl. 1, the Privileges and Immunities Clause ["Not state shall make or enforce any law which shall abridge the privileges and immunities of citizens of the United States."]. Alienage suffrage, however, does not contravene the text of either provision. Harper-Ho, *supra* note 78, at 289–290.

[88] 88 U.S. at 177. *See also* Raskin, *supra* note 75, at 1424–30 (arguing that the suffrage amendments to not require states to confine voting to U.S. citizens).

[89] Neuman, *"We are the People"*, *supra* note 74, at 313–22.

[90] Raskin, *supra* note 75, at 1441–45. *See also* Harper-Ho, *supra* note 78, at 294–98.

[91] Neuman, *"We are the People"*, *supra* note 74, at 325–30.

[92] Indeed, more recent equal protection challenges to laws prohibiting alien suffrage in local elections have been unsuccessful. *See, e.g.*, Park v. State, 528 P.2d 785 (Alaska 1974) (upholding law that restricted voting in state elections to citizens); Padilla v. Allison, 38 Cal. App. 3d 784 (Cal. App. 1974) (upholding California's Constitutional provision making citizenship a prerequisite to voting).

[93] Neuman, *"We are the People"*, *supra* note 74, at 324. *But cf.* Haper-Ho, *supra* note 78, at 288–89; Raskin, *supra* note 75, at 1430–31.

protection challenges to state alienage suffrage restrictions would likely fall under the political-function exception doctrine,[95] under which alienage discrimination has been upheld in areas of government and politics.[96]

D. THE SPECIAL PUBLIC INTEREST DOCTRINE

For most of U.S. history, states have been free to reserve resources for their own citizens or to share them with noncitizens. Throughout the seventeenth century, for example, some states restricted access to natural resources and commercial licenses solely to citizens.[97] What would become known as the special public interest doctrine was subsequently extended into areas of private and public employment, as well as in the area of public benefits.[98] While the original special public interest doctrine did not survive equal protection and preemption scrutiny,[99] even today some states continue to bar all noncitizens (including lawful permanent residents) or certain immigrants (i.e., temporary or undocumented) from private and public jobs, from state institutions of higher learning, and from public benefits.[100]

The first time the Court struck down a special public interest ordinance was in 1886 in *Yick Wo v. Hopkins*.[101] A San Francisco local ordinance, while neutral on its face, was used to deny commercial licenses almost exclusively to Chinese laundry mat owners, some of whom had operated their businesses for more than twenty years.[102] The Court acknowledged the racial animus behind the ordinance and applied the Fourteenth Amendment to strike it down.[103] *Yick Wo*, however, did not rid states of the special public interest exception. Many statutes barring noncitizens from jobs or natural resources continued to be upheld by the courts.[104] As well, courts justified certain types of alienage commercial restrictions based on the states' police powers, which they could employ to protect the health, safety, welfare, and morals of the community.[105]

---

[94] Gerald Rosberg, *Aliens and Equal Protection: Why Not the Right to Vote?*, 75 MICH. L. REV. 1092, (1977) (arguing that equal protection should be read to guarantee the right of resident noncitizens to vote at all levels of government).

[95] Brozovich, *supra* note 80, at 421–26.

[96] *See generally infra* subsection E. The Political-Function Exception.

[97] *See, e.g.*, McCready v. Virginia, 94 U.S. 391 (1877) (local ordinance barring noncitizens from catching and planning oysters in local river).

[98] *See generally infra* subsections E. The Political-Function Exception, F. Private Employment, and G. Public Benefits.

[99] *See infra* subsections E. The Political-Function Exception, F. Private Employment, G. Public Benefits, and H.2. Higher Education.

[100] *See generally infra* notes 275–313 and accompanying text.

[101] Yick Wo v. Hopkins, 118 U.S. 356 (1886).

[102] *Id.* at 358.

[103] *Id.* at 368.

[104] *See, e.g.*, Crane v. New York, 239 U.S. 195 (1915) (government contracts); Heim v. McCall, 239 U.S. 175 (1915) (subway contracts); McCready v. Virginia, 94 U.S. 391 (1876) (Oysters at a local river); Patsone v. Commw. of Pennsylvania, 232 U.S. 138 (1914) (hunting wild game).

[105] *See, e.g.*, Trageser v. Gray, 20 A. 905 (Md. 1890) (upholding restriction on selling liquor given the inherent danger of the business). *But see* Templer v. Michigan State Bd. of Examiners of Barbers, 90

In 1915, the Court limited somewhat the public interest doctrine in *Truax v. Raich* when it struck down an Arizona statute forbidding private businesses of more than five persons from filling their work force with more than twenty percent noncitizens.[106] The Court held that states could not bar noncitizens from the "common occupations of the community,"[107] though it left open the permissibility of alienage restrictions in areas outside employment.[108] States thus continued to carve out exceptions to *Truax*, excluding noncitizens from operating certain businesses or engaging in certain occupations by arguing that such alienage restrictions constituted reasonable police regulation to protect the public interest. These exceptions elicited mixed holdings from the courts. In 1927, for example, the Court upheld an Ohio law that barred noncitizens from operating pool halls, considering such places to be potential locations of depravity,[109] while state courts upheld certain alienage restrictions in areas of public employment,[110] transportation services,[111] fishing,[112] and labor union positions.[113] In other states, similar restrictions on commercial licenses or occupations, however, did not survive courts' skepticism that the nature of the business threatened the public welfare, and such laws were struck down as violating equal protection or treaty obligations.[114]

Not until thirty years after *Truax* did the Court again reject a public interest rationale for discriminating against noncitizens. In 1948, in *Takahashi v. Fish & Game Commission*, the Court struck down a California law that denied fishing licenses to foreign nationals ineligible for citizenship.[115] The Court required California to establish a rational relation test to the restriction and articulate the state special public interest of regulating the supply of fish.[116] In striking down the law, however, the Court refused to consider the racist legislative purpose of the statute, which targeted the Japanese.[117] The Court did, however, hold that the

---

N.W. 1058 (Mich. 1902) (striking down restriction on noncitizens from becoming barbers as unnecessary to protect health).

[106] Truax v. Raich, 239 U.S. 33 (1915).

[107] *Id.* at 41.

[108] *Id.* at 41–43.

[109] State of Ohio ex rel. Clarke v. Deckeback, 274 U.S. 392, 396 (1927). Prior state cases have also upheld similar restrictions. *See* Anton v. Winkle, 197 F. 340 (D.C. Or. 1924); State ex rel. Balli v. Carrel, 124 N.E. 129 (Ohio 1919).

[110] People v. Crane, 108 N.E. 427 (N.Y. 1915); Lee v. City of Lynn, 111 N.E. 700 (Mass. 1916); Cronelius v. City of Seattle, 213 P. 17 (Wash. 1923), overruled by Harriott v. City of Seattle, 500 P.2d 101 (Wash. 1972).

[111] Morin v. Numan, 103 A. 378 (N.J. Sup. 1918) (denying licenses to transport passengers for hire).

[112] Alsos v. Kendall, 227 P. 286 (Or. 1924).

[113] American Fed'n of Labor v. Mann, 188 S.W. 2d 276 (Tex. Civ. App. 1945).

[114] Abe v. Fish and Game Comm'n of Cal., 49 P.2d 608 (Cal. App. 4 Dist. 1935) (commercial fishing license); Magnai v. Harnett, 14 N.Y. 2d 107 (N.Y. A.D. 3 Dept. 1939) (chauffeur licenses); Wormen v. Moss, 29 N.Y. 2d 798 (1941) (massage parlor operators); State ex rel. Quisor v. Ellis, 184 P.2d 860 (Or. 1947) (barber shop).

[115] 334 U.S. 410 (1948).

[116] *Id.* at 418–20.

[117] *Id.* at 418 (it is "unnecessary to resolve this controversy concerning the [racial] motives that prompted enactment of the legislation").

fishing restriction was preempted by the federal government's plenary power to regulate noncitizens, stressing that "the power of the state to apply its laws exclusively to its alien inhabitants as a class is confined within narrow limits."[118] In the meantime, some states continued to rely on the public interest doctrine, at times unsuccessfully, to discriminate against noncitizens, including by barring them from certain jobs.[119]

Takahashi cast doubt on the special public interest doctrine, but more than two decades passed before the Court rejected the doctrine and granted noncitizens, at least lawful permanent residents, a suspect class status. In 1971, in *Graham v. Richardson*, the Court struck down two state welfare statutes that denied benefits to noncitizens, including legal permanent residents (LPRs), by applying a strict scrutiny analysis and declaring that "classifications based on alienage . . . are inherently suspect and subject to close judicial scrutiny."[120] The Court also relied on preemption as another reason for invalidating the statutes, stating that laws that restrict welfare eligibility of noncitizens "conflict with . . . . overriding national policies in an area constitutionally entrusted to the Federal Government."[121]

Some scholars have dated the death of the special public interest doctrine as early as 1948 or at least 1971, with the Court's holdings in *Takahashi* and *Graham*, respectively.[122] Different doctrines, however, have emerged, such as the political-function exception or the expansion of the federal plenary power doctrine over immigration and its devolution to the states, which has permitted states to restrict their resources for citizens, at least as to certain public jobs or certain public benefits in nearly the same scope as was permitted under the special public interest doctrine.[123] Moreover, since *Graham*, recent constitutional holdings have more clearly narrowed the application of equal protection to a narrower group of noncitizens, primarily lawful permanent residents, allowing states wide discretion, with the exception of K-12 public education, to exclude undocumented immigrants from the enjoyment of state resources.[124] Further, limitations on the preemption doctrine have expanded the ability of states to discriminate against undocumented or temporary foreign residents, particularly in the area of private employment.[125]

---

[118] *Id.* at 420.

[119] *See, e.g.*, Perotta v. Gregory, 158 N.Y. S.2d 221 (1957) (upholding alienage restriction for garbage collector job); Purdy and Fitzpatric v. State, 456 P.2d 645 (Cal. 1969) (striking down statute that prohibited noncitizen employment on public works based on preemption); Dep't of Labor and Industry v. Cruz, 212 A.2d 545 (N.J. 1965) (striking down based on equal protection a statute banning noncitizen employment in public works employment); Hsieh v. Civil Serv. Comm'n of City of Seattle, 488 P.2d 555 (Wash. 1971) (striking down citizenship requirement to be a civil engineer); Herriott v. City of Seattle, 500 P.2d 101 (Wash. 1972) (striking down citizenship requirement to become city transit operator.).

[120] 403 U.S. 365, 371–72 (1971).

[121] *Id.* at 378.

[122] *See* Michael Scaperlanda, *Partial Membership: Aliens and the Constitutional Community*, 81 Iowa L. Rev. 707, 735 (1996).

[123] *See generally infra* subsections E. The Political-Function Exception, F. Private Employment, and G. Public Benefits.

[124] *See generally infra* subsections G. Public Benefits, H.2. Higher Education, I. Worker Rights, J. Driver's Licenses, and K. Landlord/Tenant Immigration Ordinances.

[125] *See generally infra* subsection F. Private Employment.

E. THE POLITICAL-FUNCTION EXCEPTION

For public service jobs, the U.S. Supreme Court carved out a political-function exception, which has permitted states to restrict certain public jobs for their citizens. The first Supreme Court case to allude to the political-function doctrine was *Sugarman v. Dougall*, which struck down a New York State law that limited state competitive civil service positions to U.S. citizens.[126] The Court rejected the broad application of the special public interest doctrine that had earlier restricted noncitizen access to certain public rights and resources,[127] requiring instead a substantial state interest and a narrowly tailored law to achieve that interest.[128] *Sugarman*, however, left open the possibility that a citizenship requirement for some public jobs in which the state had a legitimate interest — i.e., "where citizenship bears some rational relationship to the special demands of a particular position" — could pass constitutional muster.[129] This prerogative, the Court explained, resides in a State's power and responsibility "to preserve the basic conception of a political community,"[130] and pertains "not only to the qualification of voter, but also to persons holding state elective or important nonelective executive, legislative, and judicial positions."[131] Such public officers, the Court considered, "perform functions that go to the heart of representative government[s]."[132]

After *Sugarman*, the Court began to carve out areas where states could require citizenship in public employment. In essence, the political-function exception permitted states to show only a rational relationship between the alienage restriction and the interest sought to be protected.[133] In *Foley v. Connelie*, decided just a year after *Sugarman*, police officers became the first exception, which the Court justified on the basis that police, while they do not formulate policy, use a high degree of judgment and discretion that affect the lives of citizens, and that, moreover, citizens are presumed to be more familiar and sympathetic to American traditions.[134] Both Justice Blackmun's concurrence and Justice Marshall's dissent in *Foley* expressed concern over the watering down of the requirement that important positions must involve policy making, not merely policy execution.[135] Similarly, a year after *Foley*, in *Amback v. Norwick*, the Court extended the political-function exception to teachers employed in public schools, reasoning that teaching fulfills "a most fundamental objective of government to its constituency" and is "so bound up with the operation of the state."[136] The Court came to this

---

[126] 413 U.S. 634 (1973).

[127] John E. Richards, *Public Employment Rights of Aliens*, 31 BAYLOR L. REV. 371, 372–74 (1982).

[128] *Sugarman*, 413 U.S. at 641–46..

[129] *Id.* at 647 (quoting from Judge Lumbaards' lower court's separate concurrence opinion).

[130] *Id.* (quoting from Dunn v. Blumstein, 405 U.S. 330, 344 (1972)).

[131] *Id.*

[132] *Id.*

[133] Foley v. Connelie, 435 U.S. 291, 297 (1978).

[134] *Id.* at 297–300.

[135] *Id.* at 301 (Blackmun, J. concurring); *Id.* at 303–13 (Marshall, J., dissenting).

[136] Amback v. Norwick, 441 U.S. 68, 69–72 (1979).

conclusion because teachers as role models have a unique opportunity "to influence the attitudes of students toward government, the political process and citizens' social responsibility."[137] *Amback* provoked a strong four-member dissent returning again to the requirement that important public employees must participate directly in policy setting, a role that teachers did not fulfill.[138]

The Court's most recent decision, *Cabell v. Chavez-Salido*, not only extended the exception to probation officers,[139] but created an even more flexible rule permitting states to apply the political-function exception to broadly worded statutes.[140] The statute actually precluded noncitizens from jobs as peace officers, which, in addition to probation officers, included seventy different types of jobs such as toll takers, cemetery sextons, fish and game wardens, furniture and bedding inspectors, and Board of Dental Examiners.[141] Thus, the Court announced a two-pronged test to decide the issue: first, to examine whether the classification was inclusive (i.e., narrowly tailored); and second, whether the classification involved a nonelective government position of someone who participated directly in the formulation, operation or review of broad public policy.[142] As to the first prong, the Court rejected a standard based solely on the general reach of the statute, inquiring instead into "whether the restriction reaches so far and is so broad and haphazard as to belie the state's claim that it is only attempting to ensure that an important function of the government be in the hands of [citizens]."[143] In essence, as the dissent pointed out, this approach changed the standard of review of alienage classifications challenge as overbroad from one of strict scrutiny to only a requirement of "substantial fit."[144] Thus, while the Court acknowledged that some of the categories had, at best, a "tenuous" connection to usual police activities, it emphasized that the general arrest authority theoretically accorded all peace officers to find the statute "sufficiently tailored" to the aims sought.[145] As to the second prong, the Court reasoned that probation officers' tremendous discretionary and coercive authority over those who have been found to have violated the norms of social order met the requirement of the job's political function.[146] Here too, the four-member dissent reiterated similar concerns to the ones expressed in *Amback* because probation officers also do not directly engage in policy making, nor were their coercive powers over lawbreaking citizens unique.[147] With *Cabell*, the dissenting Justices feared, almost every judicial and bureaucratic position would qualify for the political-function exception.[148]

---

[137] *Id.* at 79.

[138] *Id.* at 83.

[139] Cabell v. Chavez-Salido, 454 U.S. 432, (1982).

[140] *Id.*

[141] *Id.* at 450.

[142] *Id.* at 441.

[143] *Id.* at 442.

[144] *Id.* at 453.

[145] *Id.* at 444.

[146] *Id.* at 446.

[147] *Id.* at 453.

[148] *Id.* at 461–62. Some lower courts, however, will still strike down broadly worded statutes that ban

The Court has, however, rejected the political-function exception in a few cases, primarily involving noncitizen access to professional licenses. In *In re Griffiths*, decided the same day as *Sugarman*, the Court struck down a citizenship requirement of admission to the Connecticut bar and rejected the argument that lawyers, as officers of the court, were formulators of governmental policy.[149] Until then, an overwhelming majority of states prevented even lawful permanent residents from gaining admission to the bar.[150] Similarly, in *Bernal v. Fainter*, the Court rejected the political-function exception as applied to public notaries.[151]

The political-function exception has been justified as means to preserve the significance of citizenship within a community, which requires drawing lines between community and outsiders.[152] Disagreement arises still as to where exactly that line should be drawn, as every public employee could suddenly be transformed into a policymaker to exclude noncitizens.[153] Many caution, moreover, that courts have employed the rhetoric of preserving the political community to discriminate against noncitizens who are stereotyped as disloyal and unwilling to adopt U.S. values.[154]

F. PRIVATE EMPLOYMENT

For jobs falling outside the scope of the political-function exception, *Graham v. Richardson* immediately led to the defeat of many state laws imposing alienage employment restrictions based on equal protection and/or preemption grounds.[155] In 1976, for example, the Court struck down a Puerto Rico statute that restricted the practice of private civil engineering to U.S. citizens.[156] That same year, however, the Court decided *Decanas v. Bica*, which upheld a California statute that prohibited employers from knowingly employing noncitizens not entitled to lawful residence in the United States if such employment would adversely affect lawful

---

noncitizens from all public employment, even if as applied they pertain to professions that the Court has found to have a "political function." *See, e.g.*, Chang v. Glynn County School Dist., 457 F. Supp. 2d 1378 (2006) (striking down Georgia's statute that barred noncitizens from all public employment when applied to fire noncitizen public school teacher plaintiffs).

[149] In re Griffiths, 413 U.S. 717, 729 (1973).

[150] Kiyoko Kamio Knapp, *Disdain of Alien Lawyers: History of Exclusion*, 7 SETON HALL CONST. L.J. 103, 121–40 (1996).

[151] 467 U.S. 216 (1984). For a critique of *In re Griffith, see* Sanford Levinson, *National Loyalty, Communalism, and the Professional Identity of Lawyers*, 7 YALE J.L. & HUMAN. 49 (1995).

[152] *See* Kiyoko Kamio Knapp, *The Rhetoric of Exclusion: The Art of Drawing a Line Between Aliens and Citizens*, 10 GEO. IMMIGR. L.J. 401, 412 (1996); Scaperlanda, *supra* note 122, at 736–37.

[153] Knapp, *supra* note 152, at 412.

[154] *Id.* at 418–23. *See also* KENNETH L. KARST, BELONGING TO AMERICA: EQUAL CITIZENSHIP AND THE CONSTITUTION 87 (1989).

[155] *See* Herriot v. City of Seattle, 500 P.2d 101 (1972) (on transit operators); Sundram v. City of Niagara Falls, 357 N.Y. S.2d 943 (1973) (taxi cab drivers); Mohamed v. Parks, 352 F. Supp. 518 (D. Ma. 1973) (counselors); Wong v. Hohnstrom, 405 F. Supp. 727 (D. Minn. 1975) (pharmacists); C.D.R. Enterprises, LTD., et al., v. Bd. of Educ. of the City of New York, 412 F. Supp. 1164 (1976) (painting contractors with public contract).

[156] Exam'g Bd. of Eng'rs, Architects and Surveyors v. Otero, 426 U.S. 572 (1976).

resident workers.[157]

The *Decanas* challenge focused on preemption because the California statue was said to encroach upon and interfere with Congress' exercise of its exclusive power over immigration.[158] *DeCanas* established a three-prong test to assess preemption. First, courts must determine whether the state regulation is invalid as a "regulation of immigration."[159] Second, even if the legislation does not regulate immigration, it is still preempted if Congress has shown a "clear and manifest purpose" to completely enact an "ouster of state power — including state power to promulgate laws not in conflict with federal laws."[160] Third, the state law is preempted if it "stands as an obstacle to the accomplishment and execution of the full purposes and objectives of Congress."[161]

In applying the test, the *DeCanas* Court generously interpreted the preemption test in favor of the states. On the first prong, the *DeCanas* Court reasoned that the "[p]ower to regulate immigration is unquestionably exclusively a federal power,"[162] but it cautioned that "not every state enactment which in any way deals with aliens is a regulation of immigration" and is *per se* preempted by federal law.[163] The Court further narrowed the regulation of immigration to include "essentially a determination of who should or should not be admitted into the country, and the conditions under which a legal entrant would remain."[164] The Court, moreover, characterized the California statute as implicating the state's broad policing powers to regulate the employment relationship to protect workers within the state.[165] Given this rationale, the Court held that it could not conclude that preemption is required because "the nature of the . . . subject matter (regulation of employment of illegal aliens) permits no other conclusion . . . ."[166] While *DeCanas* did not extend to bar Congress from regulating the employment of noncitizens, another decade would pass before Congress would make it illegal to hire undocumented workers.[167] Thus, as to the second prong, the Court also could not find preemption given that "Congress ha[d] [not] unmistakably so ordained that result."[168] Finally, as to the third prong, *DeCanas* chose to remand the case due to the lack of a complete record on the issue.[169]

---

[157] 424 U.S. 351 (1976).

[158] *Id.* at 353–54.

[159] *Id.* at 354.

[160] *Id.* at 357.

[161] *Id.* at 363.

[162] *Id.* at 354.

[163] *Id.* at 355.

[164] *Id.*

[165] *Id.* at 356.

[166] *Id.*

[167] *See infra* notes 171–73 and accompanying text (discussing the Immigration Reform and Control Act of 1986).

[168] *DeCanas*, 424 U.S. at 356.

[169] *Id.* at 363.

Post-*DeCanas*, and in the absence of federal legislation regulating the employment of noncitizens, state laws imposing sanctions on private employers for hiring noncitizens survived preemption or equal protection challenges but only when these laws pertained to undocumented workers, not to permanent or temporary residents authorized to work in the United States.[170] Then, in 1986, Congress passed the Immigration Reform and Control Act of 1986 (IRCA) imposing for the first time federal civil and criminal sanctions on employers for "knowingly" hiring undocumented workers.[171] The rationale for the law was that jobs in the United States attracted undocumented immigrants, which in turn depressed wages and worsened working conditions for eligible U.S workers.[172] Intended to control unauthorized immigration by deterring unauthorized workers, IRCA expressly preempted state or local laws "imposing civil or criminal sanctions (other than through licensing and similar law) upon those who employ, or recruit or refer for a fee for employment, unauthorized aliens."[173]

Despite IRCA's express preemption clause, particularly post-9/11, when hostility against immigrants increased, a few states, frustrated over federal under enforcement of IRCA, enacted their own laws imposing sanctions on employers for hiring unauthorized workers. For example, in 2006, the City of Hazleton, Pennsylvania enacted Ordinance 2006–10, which sought to deny or suspend business licenses to employers who employed unauthorized workers.[174] Similarly, in 2007, Arizona enacted the Legal Arizona Workers Act, which similarly would suspend or revoke an employer's business license for knowingly or intentionally hiring the undocumented.[175] Other states followed suit and passed similar laws alone or as part of broader anti-immigrant measures, including South Carolina,[176] Oklahoma,[177] Missouri,[178] and Tennessee.[179] These laws, as well as the laws of several other states, require employers to use the federal E-verify database to check the immigration status of their employees and/or new hires.[180] In contrast, at least one state, Illinois,

---

[170] *See, e.g.*, C.D.R. Enterprises, LTD. v. Bd. of Educ. of City of New York, 412 F. Supp. 1164 (D.C. N.Y 1976) (striking down as in violation of equal protection a New York labor law providing that employment in the construction of public works must be given to citizens); Rogers v. Larson, 563 F.2d 617 (C.A. V.I. 1977) (striking down as preempted a Virgin Islands statute requiring the termination of nonimmigrant workers authorized to work with resident workers).

[171] Pub. L. No. 99-603, 100 Stat. 339 (1986).

[172] Michael J. Wishnie, *Prohibiting the Employment of Unauthorized Immigrants: The Experiment Fails*, 2007 U. CHI. LEGAL F. 193, 195–6 (2007).

[173] 8 U.S.C. § 1324a(h)(2) (2000).

[174] Lozano v. City of Hazleton, 496 F. Supp. 2d 477 (M.D. Pa. 2007).

[175] A.R.S. § 23–211 to 23–214 (Supp. 2007).

[176] SOUTH CAROLINA ILLEGAL IMMIGRATION REFORM ACT, S. 392, 117th Sess. (2007–2008), *available at* http://www.scstatehouse.net/sess117_2007-2008/bills/392.htm.

[177] THE OKLAHOMA TAXPAYER AND CITIZEN PROTECTION ACT OF 2007, H.B. 1804, 51st Leg., 1st Sess. (2007).

[178] MISSOURI OMNIBUS IMMIGRATION ACT, S.B. 348 (Aug. 28, 2007), *available at* http://www.senate.mo.gov/07info/BTS_Web/Bill.aspx?SessionType=r&BillID=6818.

[179] TENNESSEE HOUSE BILL 729 (Jan. 1, 2008), *available at* http://www.legislature.state.tn.us/bills/currentga/BILL/HB0729.pdf.

[180] These other states include Georgia, Colorado, Missouri, Mississippi, Rhode Island, Utah, and Minnesota. *See* Paul Hastings, I *mmigration News: Recent E-Verify Developments*, May 20, 2008,

has passed legislation to restrict the use of E-verify subject to database improvements.[181]

Preemption challenges to state laws imposing employer sanctions for the hiring of the undocumented have yielded mixed results. For example, while two federal district courts upheld Arizona's and Missouri's laws as within the permissible licensing restriction exemption of IRCA's preemption provision,[182] another federal district court rejected this very argument by the City of Hazleton, restricting the availability of a local licensing restriction as a response to an IRCA, not a local law violation.[183] An Oklahoma federal district court also enjoined the enforcement of that state's employer sanction laws against a challenge that IRCA's preemption provisions violated the state's lawmaking autonomy without proper constitutional authority.[184] It is likely that the Third, Ninth, and Tenth Circuits will weigh in on the issue soon.[185]

Preemption challenges to state mandates to use E-verify for employee's work eligibility have come up in the context of state employer-sanction laws.[186] In upholding Arizona's employer-sanctions laws, the federal district courts also rejected the argument that making E-verify mandatory under state law conflicts with the purposes and objectives of Congress, given that E-verify is voluntary under federal law.[187] A Missouri's district court also rejected conflict preemption challenges, which were based on claims of Missouri's' higher verification requirements and different procedural requirements for employee verification.[188] At times, the district court agreed with the noted differences but held overall that "every slight difference in emphasis between the federal requirement and the local requirements" did not create a conflict where the clear intent of Congress is that all

---

available at http://www.paulhastings.com/publicationDetail.aspx?publicationId=906.

[181] Illinois Public Act 095-0138, H.B. 1744, 820 Ill. Comp. Stat. 55/1, et at seq., § 12(a) (an act amending the Right to Privacy in the Workplace Act), *available at* www.ilga.gov/legislation/publicacts/fulltext.asp?Name=095-0138 ("Employers are prohibited from enrolling in any Employment Eligibility Verification System . . . until the Social Security Administration (SSA) and Department of Homeland Security (DHS) databases are able to make determination of 99% of the tentative nonconfirmation notices issued to employers within 3 days, unless otherwise required by law.").

[182] Arizona Contractor's Ass'n, Inc. v. Candelaria, 534 F. Supp. 2d 1036, 1045–55 (D. Ariz. 2008); Gray v. City of Valley Park, 2008 WL 294294, *10–12 (E.D. Mo. 2008).

[183] Lozano v. City of Hazleton, 496 F. Supp. 2d 477, 519 (M.D. Pa. 2007).

[184] Chamber of Commerce of the U.S. of America, et al., v. Henry, et al., 208 U.S. Dist. LEXIS 44168, *12 (W.D. OK. June 4, 2008).

[185] As of this writing, the Third Circuit had agreed to hear the Hazleton case by a three-judge panel. John J. Moser, *Hazleton's Anti-Illegal Immigrant Law Back in Court*, The Morning Call, Sept. 9, 2008, *available at* www.mcall.com/news/local/all-a1_immigrant.6580053sep09,0,5874170.story. Oklahoma is also asking the Tenth Circuit to reverse the district court's injunction. Ron Jenkins, *AG Defends Immigration Law*, Assoc. Press, Aug. 29, 2008, *available at* www.kansas.com/news/state/story/510977.html. As well, plaintiffs in the Arizona case have filed appeal with the Ninth Circuit. ACLU Press Release, Challenge to Arizona Employer Sanctions Law Continues in Appellate Court, Feb. 7, 2008, *available at* http://www.aclu.org/immigrants/discrim/34021prs20080207.html.

[186] Neither the Oklahoma nor the Pennsylvania district courts reached the issue of E-verify directly, having considered the entire employer-sanctions laws preempted.

[187] *Candelaria*, 534 F. Supp. 2d at 1055–57.

[188] *City of Valley Park*, 2008 WL 294294, at 13–19.

employees be subject to employment verification requirements.[189] Furthermore, DHS has challenged Illinois' restriction on employer's voluntary use of E-verify on the basis that it conflicts with federal law by imposing additional conditions not imposed by Congress on Illinois employers who wish to verify employee's work eligibility[190] and creates an obstacle to the federal government's ability to evaluate the effectiveness of E-verify.[191] At least while that litigation is pending, Illinois suspended enforcement of its law before it even came into effect.[192]

Aside from preemption, another piece of the puzzle on the issue of mandatory E-verification is whether and how states may use E-verify results against employers to punish them for "knowingly" hiring undocumented workers. At least the Ninth Circuit cast doubt on this issue when it recently upheld an arbitration determination that no-match letters on social security numbers sent to employers from the Social Security Administration (SSA) did not constitute "convincing information" of knowingly hiring undocumented workers.[193] E-verify, of course, relies in great part on SSA records, which the Ninth Circuit noted, were not intended to be used to verify work eligibility, and, furthermore, contain inaccurate or incomplete employer records.[194]

Plaintiffs also have unsuccessfully raised due process and/or equality challenges in the employer-sanctions laws. The equality challenge has been based on the adverse effect of ordinances on Latino hiring based on employers' fear that person might be undocumented and/or on the alleged intent of the law to discriminate against Latinos.[195] Courts, however, have found neither discriminatory intent, nor a discriminatory purpose, even if the ordinances have a disparate impact.[196] Due process challenges have focused on the potential deprivation of employer's businesses without providing adequate standards or guidance for compliances or sufficient procedures to challenge adverse findings.[197] Here, too, courts have found the law to provide adequate standards for liability and procedural due process to employers.[198]

---

[189] *Id.* at *15.

[190] Complaint, U.S. v. Illinois, D.C. of Ill., Springfield, at ¶¶ 34–40, a *available at* http://www.dhs.gov/xlibrary/assets/US_v_Illinois_Complaint_092407_to_File.pdf.

[191] *Id.* at ¶ 43.

[192] DHS Notice for Illinois Employers about E-Verify, *available at* www.dhs.gov/ximgtn/programs/gc_1199120920203.shtm.

[193] Aramark Facilities Serv's v. Serv. Employee Int'l Union, Local 1877, AFL-CIO, 530 F.3d 817, 828 (9th Cir. 2008).

[194] *Id.* at 826.

[195] Lozano v. City of Hazleton, 496 F. Supp. 2d 477, 540 (M.D. Pa. 2007); *City of Valley Park*, 2008 WL 294294 *26.

[196] *City of Hazleton*, 496 F. Supp. 2d at 541–42; *City of Valley Park*, 2008 WL 294294 *26.

[197] *City of Valley Park*, 2008 WL 294294 *27; *Candelaria*, 534 F. Supp. 2d at 1057.

[198] *City of Valley Park*, 2008 WL 294294 *27–29; *Candelaria*, 534 F. Supp. 2d at 1057–60.

G.   PUBLIC BENEFITS

Congress, and before that states, regulated immigrants' consumption of public benefits principally by barring the migration of "paupers" or persons likely to become a public charge[199] but not by denying them access to public benefits. In fact, most states conferred public benefits to most of indigent residents irrespective of their immigration status based on policy considerations[200] and on state or constitutional or statutory provisions that recognize a duty to aid indigents or the needy who reside in their territory.[201] Similarly, prior to 1996,[202] legal noncitizens were automatically eligible for almost all federally-funded public benefits,[203] although fewer programs remained accessible to the undocumented.[204]

Some states, as well as the federal government, however, have restricted public benefits eligibility even for lawful permanent residents. In *Graham*, for example, the equal protection and preemption challenges were to an Arizona statute that imposed a fifteen year residency requirement on lawful permanent residents for the receipt of federal assistance programs and to a Pennsylvania statute that restricted to citizens the receipt of a general assistance program funded solely with state funds.[205] Congress began to enact alienage restrictions on access to public benefits principally in the 1970s.[206] Unlike states, however, the federal government has enjoyed broader discretion to impose alienage restrictions on access to federal public benefits. In 1976, five years after *Graham*, in *Matthews v. Diaz*, the Court upheld as a legitimate exercise of federal immigration power Congress' imposition of a five year residency federal requirement on lawful permanent residents seeking Medicare Supplemental Medical Insurance.[207] *Graham*, in fact, foreshadowed the result in *Diaz*. *Graham*, which also considered a preemption challenge, held that states may not "add to nor take from the conditions lawfully imposed by Congress

---

[199] Neuman, *The Lost Century of American Immigration Law*, *supra* note 3, at 1848 (discussing state pauper immigration restrictions); Richard A. Boswell, *Restrictions on Non-citizens' Access to Public Benefits: Flawed Premise, Unnecessary Response*, 42 U.C.L.A. L. Rev. 1475, 1481–87 (1995) (discussing federal economic based immigration restrictions).

[200] *See* Peter L. Reich, *Public Benefits for Undocumented Aliens: State Law into the Breach Once More*, 21 N.M. L. Rev. 219, 242–48 (1991) (discussing policy reasons for granting public benefits to all immigrants, including health risks to the public when vulnerable groups lack access to basic medical services; the greater contributions as compared to costs of immigrants to U.S. society; and humanitarian values).

[201] *See id.* at 228–41.

[202] In 1996, Congress revamped the entire welfare system and also restricted federal welfare program eligibility for lawful permanent residents. *See infra* notes 227–37 and accompanying text.

[203] Reich, *supra* note 200, at 221, 232–34 (discussing pre-1996 access restrictions to immigrants except permanent residents or persons "permanently residing in the United States color of law"). *See also* Evangeline G. Abriel, *Rethinking Preemption for Purposes of Aliens and Public Benefits*, 42 U.C.L.A. L. Rev. 1597, 1660–62 (1995); Boswell, *supra* note 199, at 1487–92.

[204] Reich, *supra* note 200, at 237; Boswell, *supra* note 199, at 1498–1500.

[205] Graham v. Richardson, 403 U.S. 365, 366–380 (1971). Before *Graham*, citizenship was a classification for old age assistance in Texas. Vernon's Ann. Texas Const. Art. 3, § 51-a. After *Graham*, the legislature amended its statute. *Id.* However, even after *Graham*, Mississippi has not overturned its law requiring one year state residency in order to receive old age assistance. Miss. Code Ann. § 43-9-7.

[206] Boswell, *supra* note 199, at 1492–97.

[207] Matthews v. Diaz, 426 U.S. 67 (1976).

upon admission, naturalization and residence of aliens in the United States . . . "[208] Similarly, the *Diaz* Court affirmed that the "relationship between the United States and our alien visitors has been committed to the political branches of the Federal Government."[209] Thus, the Court applied the same lenient rational basis test to federal alienage public benefits restriction that had traditionally applied in the immigration context.[210]

The *Diaz* Court's rationale falls within a broader conception of immigration control. Measures that exclude immigrants from access to rights and benefits of U.S. society are viewed as both indirect means of controlling immigration, but also as a proper preservation of the benefits of membership for those deemed to belong within the moral boundaries of the national community.[211] Critics of *Diaz* question, however, the deterrence immigration control claims, in that immigrants do not ordinarily come to the United States to obtain benefits, but rather, to work.[212] Moreover, when immigrants live and work in the political community, they should be treated as members of the community, at least when the sovereign consented to their admission in the first place.[213] The mirror image critique is directed at *Graham*, in that states should be allowed to discriminate in favor of citizens who are the sole full members of the community.[214] Those who defend *Graham* do so for the same reasons that *Diaz* is criticized and emphasize, at least with respect to lawful residents, that noncitizens too have strong claims to membership.[215]

Post-*Diaz*, Congress continued to impose further public benefits restrictions on noncitizens. For example, the 1986 IRCA reforms also granted lawful status to undocumented persons residing in the United States since before 1982, but it disqualified them from any federal or joint federal-state assistance program for five years from the date of legalization.[216] Similarly, the Immigration Act of 1990 created a new "temporary protected status" for persons fleeing armed conflict or natural disasters in their home, but prohibited the beneficiaries from participating in most federal benefit programs.[217]

Some states also attempted to duplicate and impose even greater restrictions on noncitizen public benefit eligibility than under federal law, but restricted these

---

[208] *Graham*, 403 U.S. at 378.

[209] *Diaz*, 426 U.S. at 81.

[210] *Id.* at 79–80.

[211] Linda Bosniak, *Membership, Equality, and the Difference that Alienage Makes*, 69 N.Y.U. L. Rev. 1047, 1053 (1994).

[212] Kevin R. Johnson, *Public Benefits and Immigration: The Intersection of Immigration Status, Ethnicity, Gender and Class*, 42 U.C.L.A. L. Rev. 1510, 1513, n.18 (1995) (citing to several social science studies linking migration patterns to jobs and family unification, not public benefits). *See also* Reich, *supra* note 200, at 226 (same).

[213] Michael Walzer, *The Distribution of Membership, in* Boundaries: National Autonomy and Its Limits 1, 23–32 (Peter J. Brown & Henery Sur, eds., 1981).

[214] Gerald L. Neuman, *Aliens as Outlaws: Government Services, Proposition 187, and the Structure of Equal Protection Doctrine*, 42 U.C.L.A. L. Rev. 1425, 1427 (1995).

[215] *Id.*

[216] 8 U.S.C.A. § 1255(h)(1)(A) (Supp. 1991).

[217] Pub. L. No. 101-649, 104 Stat. 4978 (1990).

measures to undocumented immigrants in light of *Graham*. Proposition 187, which California voters overwhelmingly approved in 1994,[218] *inter alia*, barred the undocumented from a host of social services and health care provisions and imposed mandatory reporting provisions to immigration and other state agencies when ineligible persons sought these benefits.[219] Proposition 187 took on highly inflated rhetoric blaming "illegal aliens for the ills of the state;" proponents of the measure in the official Ballot pamphlet warned of an "illegal alien invasion" that would reduce California to "economic bankruptcy."[220] Ironically, the projected enforcement costs of Proposition 187 would have dwarfed any projected savings.[221]

The first challenge to Proposition 187 (*Lulac I*) sought to declare Proposition 187 unconstitutional mostly based on preemption as applied to the undocumented and on equal protection grounds as applied to undocumented children.[222] *Lulac I, inter alia*, struck down as preempted Proposition 187's public benefits verification and reporting requirements as these created "an entirely independent set of criteria by which to classify individuals based on immigration status"[223] and which criteria were aimed solely at reporting violations to effectuate removal.[224] In addition, *Lulac I* held that federal legislation preempted the provision in Proposition 187 that denied state administration of federally funded public social services to the undocumented.[225] In contrast, *Lulac I* upheld Proposition 187's denial of public benefits when based on federal determinations of immigration status.[226]

The partial defeat of Proposition 187 was short-lived because shortly thereafter Congress adopted the Personal Responsibility and Work Opportunity Reconciliation Act of 1996 (PRWORA).[227] Some, in fact, consider Proposition 187 as the impetus for the 1996 anti-immigrant reform.[228] In general, the PRWORA did four things. First, it restricted the eligibility of "qualified aliens,"[229] including lawful

---

[218] Proposition 187 was approved by a 59-41% margin. California Secretary of State, Statement of Vote, Nov. 8, 1994, at 115.

[219] These services included child welfare and foster care benefits, county general assistance, battered women's counseling and publicly-funded health services. Johnson, *Public Benefits and Immigration, supra* note 212, at 1562–63.

[220] Arguments in Favor of Proposition 187, in Proposition 187: Illegal Aliens — Ineligibility for Public Services — Verification and Reporting, § 10, 1994 Cal. Adv. Leg. Serv. B-43 (Deering). *See also* Johnson, *supra* note 212, at 1558–61 (discussing the anti-immigrant animus of Proposition 187).

[221] Johnson, *Public Benefits and Immigration, supra* note 212, at 1568–71.

[222] League of United Latin Am. Citizens v. Wilson (Lulac I), 908 F. Supp. 755, 764 (C.D. Cal. 1995).

[223] *Id.* at 770 (striking down as preempted Sections 4 through 9 in the preamble).

[224] *Id.* at 771.

[225] *Id.* at 786.

[226] *Id.* at 776.

[227] Pub. L. No. 104-193, 110 Stat. 2105 (1996).

[228] Peter J. Spiro, *Learning to Live with Immigration Federalism*, 29 Conn. L. Rev. 1627, 1641–46 (1997) (discussing the "steam-valve" effect of preemption, under which state preferences, frustrated at the local level, are revisited by Congress).

[229] PRWORA classified all foreign nationals into two categories of eligibility for federal, state, or local public benefits: "qualified aliens" and "not-qualified aliens." "Qualified aliens" included, among others, LPRs, those granted refugee or asylum status, and certain battered spouses or children. "Not-qualified aliens" include the undocumented, as well as persons with temporary visas or nonimmigrant status,

permanent residents, to receive several federally funded public benefits.[230] Second, it authorized, but did not require states to deny locally funded benefits to "qualified aliens,"[231] despite *Graham's* precedent.[232] Third, the legislation tightened restrictions on the few public benefits once available to certain persons now considered "not qualified," including undocumented persons.[233] In fact, the PRWORA proscribed states from conferring benefits to the undocumented persons except through affirmative legislative enactment.[234] Finally, the PRWORA delegated to states the administration of public benefits programs, including the requirement to verify applicant's immigration status and mandatory reporting requirements to immigration authorities for three federal programs (social security income, public housing, and Temporary Assistance for Needy Families) when the agency knows that the applicant is not lawfully present in the United States.[235] In light of the PRWORA, then California Governor Pete Wilson appealed *Lulac I* and moved for reconsideration.[236] However, *Lulac II* found that the PROWA itself preempted most provisions of the state law. The foundation that had supported the initiative also appealed, but the Ninth Circuit affirmed.[237]

With some exceptions, state responses to PRWORA have been to restore certain benefits to legal immigrants. Over half of the states are spending their own money to cover at least some of the immigrants who are ineligible for federally funded

---

those granted temporary protected status, and other persons who have applied for but not yet received legal immigration status. PRWORA § 431[b].

[230] For example, the PRWORA barred "qualified aliens" from receiving supplemental security income (SSI) and food stamps, at least until those eligible attain citizenship or meet additional requirements. PRWORA §§ 401 and 402[a][1]). Certain classes of "qualified aliens" were exempted from SSI and food stamps restrictions: (1) refugees, asylees, and individuals granted withholding of deportation, but only for the first five years after being granted that status; (2) active duty service members, veterans, and their direct family members; and (3) LPRs who could prove they had worked at least forty qualifying quarters, or ten years, for social security purposes. PRWORA § 402[a][2]. PRWORA also restricted lawful permanent residents access to other federal means-tested programs, such as Medicaid and Temporary Assistance for Needy Families (TANF) for the first five years after entry or admission PRWORA § 401[a].

[231] 8 U.S.C. § 1612(b)(1) (2000) (authorizing states to "determine the eligibility" of qualified aliens for Medicaid, TANF, and Title XX block grants); and *id.* § 1622 (a) (authorizing states to "determine the eligibility for any State Public Benefits" or certain qualified and certain nonqualified aliens).

[232] Legislative history, in fact, suggests that *Graham* was an explicit target of several provisions of the PRWORA. Michael J. Wishnie, *Laboratories of Bigotry? Devolution of the Immigration Power, Equal Protection, and Federalism*, 76 N.Y.U. L. REV. 493, 512–14 (2001).

[233] Under law prior to PRWORA, foreign nationals were eligible to receive Medicaid, SSI, and Aid to Families with Dependent Children (now TANF) if they were "permanently residing in the United States under color of law." PRWORA disallowed such aid. "Not-qualified aliens" are still eligible for some public benefits, however. These include: emergency Medicaid; immunizations; diagnosis and treatment of communicable diseases; short-term, in-kind, noncash emergency or disaster relief services; school lunch, breakfast, and other child nutrition programs. STEVEN W. BENDER, ET AL., EVERYDAY LAW FOR LATINOS/AS, 205–206 (2008).

[234] PRWORA § 1621[c] and [d]).

[235] *Id.*, at § 404, amended by Balanced Budget Act of 1997, §§ 564, 5581(a).

[236] United Latin Am. Citizens v. Wilson, 997 F. Supp. 1244, 1252 (C.D. Cal. 1997).

[237] League of United Latin Am. Citizens v. Wilson, 131 F.3d 1297, 1309 (9th Cir. 1997).

programs, although these programs offer fewer benefits.[238] In addition, some states have also passed legislation to provide a few public benefits even to the undocumented, such as prenatal care and medical insurance for the elderly, for the disabled, and for children.[239] In contrast, some states have heeded the federal government's invitation to strip lawful permanent residents of even greater public benefits than under the PRWORA,[240] while others are imposing stricter verification and mandatory reporting requirements. For example, on November 2, 2004, Arizona voters approved Proposition 200, also known as the Arizona Taxpayer and Citizen Protection Act.[241] Proposition 200 included provisions to deny to undocumented benefits, for which they were already ineligible under the PRWORA and to require all Arizona agencies responsible for administering public benefits, subject to civil and criminal sanctions, to verify the immigration status of any applicant and report to the immigration authorities any applicant unable to provide it.[242] Proposition 200 proponents claimed that undocumented immigrants cost the state tens of millions of dollars based on unsubstantiated allegations of pernicious fraud for seeking benefits, for which they did not qualify.[243] Here too any questionable savings would have been dwarfed by the millions of tax dollars necessary to implement the verification requirements.[244] After Arizona's initiative, more than twenty states considered or introduced similar measures to the ones of Proposition 200.[245]

The *Diaz* precedent has foreclosed challenges to Congress' authority to enact the PRWORA and deny public benefits to noncitizens.[246] Some scholars argue, nevertheless, that Congress could not legislate to undermine *Graham* simply by devolving its powers to discriminate against noncitizens to states through the PRWORA.[247] After the PRWORA, however, courts have resisted equal and preemption protection challenges to restrictive state public benefits measures, as long as the states have followed PRWORA guidelines.[248] A federal district court, for example, lifted its restraining order against Proposition's 200 public benefit provisions after Arizona's Attorney General clarified that the public benefits

---

[238] THE NATIONAL IMMIGRATION LAW CENTER (NILC), GUIDE TO IMMIGRANT ELIGIBILITY FOR FEDERAL PROGRAMS 3, 102–103, 108, 122–27, 134–35 (4th ed. 2002).

[239] *Id.* at 124–27.

[240] California barred unqualified immigrants from 200 programs. Wendy Zimmerman & Karen C. Tumlin, *Patchwork Policies: State Assistance for Immigrants Under Welfare Reform*, 1999 URB. INST. 39–41 (1999), available at http://www.urban.org/UploadedPDF/occ24.pdf. Maine cut off immigrant access to health insurance. *Id.* at 41. Minnesota and Maine barred undocumented immigrants from general assistance. *Id.*

[241] Proposition 200, *available at* http://www.azsos.gov/elections/2004/info/PubPamphlet/Sun-Sounds/english/prop200htm (last visited Jan. 25, 2007) (current version at Ariz. Rev. Stat. Ann. § 46-140.01).

[242] *Id.* at § 6.A.

[243] Raquel Aldana, *Federal Citizenship and the "Alien,"* 46 WASHBURN L.J. 263, 276–277 (2007).

[244] *Id.* at 275.

[245] *See* Protect America Now website to promote initiatives in other states, *available at* http://www.pan2004.com/whatshot_stateinitiatives.html.

[246] *See* Michael J. Wishnie, *Laboratories of Bigotry?, supra* note 232, at 518.

[247] *Id.* at 528–58.

[248] Aldana, *supra* note 243, at 286–88.

restrictions applied only to those public benefits programs already governed by federal law and did not include the state's medical insurance or many other state programs.[249] Subsequently, the Ninth Circuit vacated the district court's order and held that the Arizona employee plaintiffs lacked standing to enjoin enforcement of Arizona Proposition 200 for failing to show a "genuine threat of imminent prosecution."[250] As of this writing, Proposition 200's public benefits provisions remain in force in Arizona. A few challenges to post-PRWORA restrictions on state public benefits have been successful, but the challenges have been based on state constitutional challenges. The state of New York, for example, has interpreted its State Constitution as creating a right to welfare, which trumps federal legislation mandating or permitting state discrimination against noncitizens.[251]

Moreover, pro-immigrant public benefits state measures seeking to restore PRWORA-stripped benefits to immigrants through state funds have been struck down based on preemption.[252] These courts view the PRWORA as such a comprehensive regulatory scheme in the area of public benefits to noncitizens that states have no power to legislate in the area unless through express Congressional authority.[253]

The debate of whether states should be able to freely deny public benefits to undocumented immigrants is made more difficult by undocumented immigrants' unauthorized entry, as well as the inability or unwillingness of the federal government to control the border. To some, these factors justify state discrimination when states disproportionately bear the "costs" of the presence of unauthorized migrants who have no right to claim membership in the community.[254] Those who favor equal protection for the undocumented highlight the disparate impact of public benefits restrictions on the most vulnerable subgroup of immigrants, namely poor people of color and women, few of whom are eligible to immigrate legally to the United States despite strong pull factors from U.S. employers for these workers.[255] Moreover, their unrepresented, unlawful status and foreignness makes the undocumented the most vulnerable to nativist outbursts of anti-immigrant sentiments and hostile discrimination that requires judicial protection.[256]

---

[249] Friendly House v. Napolitano, No. CV 04-649 TUC DCB (D. Ariz. Dec. 22, 2004) (order).

[250] Friendly House v. Napolitano, 419 F.3d 930, 932 (2008).

[251] *Id.* at 301–302.

[252] Aldana, *supra* note 243, at 286–87.

[253] *Id.*

[254] *See* Johnson, *Public Benefits and Immigration*, *supra* note 212, at 1538–40.

[255] *Id.* at 1542–58.

[256] Neuman, *Aliens as Outlaws*, *supra* note 214, at 1440–50.

H. PUBLIC EDUCATION

1.   K-12 Education

Access to public education from kindergarten through twelfth grade (K-12) is another area that some states have attempted to restrict, at least to undocumented students and at times also to nonimmigrants. In 1975, for example, Texas passed legislation to bar undocumented children from K-12 public schools or charge them tuition.[257] A group of undocumented children challenged the law on preemption and equal protection grounds[258] in *Plyler v. Doe*, a case the U.S. Supreme Court would ultimately decide in their favor in 1982 in a 5-4 margin.[259] The Court declared that unlike public benefits, access to K–12 education is a quasi-fundamental right, and that the Texas law violated equal protection under the Fourteenth Amendment of the U.S. Constitution.[260] The *Plyler* Court recognized that undocumented immigrants are "persons" under the Fourteenth Amendment; however, it explicitly denied that they constitute a "suspect" class.[261] Nevertheless, the Court accorded undocumented children special status (quasi-suspect) in that children should not be punished for their parents' choice to break the immigration laws.[262] Then, applying intermediate scrutiny,[263] the Court dismissed the State's argument that the law was necessary to preserve the State's "limited resources for the education of its lawful residents,"[264] particularly when the State failed to show significant savings for the state during trial.[265] The Court also rejected the state's justification of the law as a deterrent against unlawful immigration, finding it a "ludicrously ineffectual attempt to stem the tide of illegal immigration"[266] and also an infringement into Congress' exclusive power over immigration.[267] Finally, while the *Plyler* Court was divided on the constitutional question, it was unanimous about the inadvisability to the Texas law, namely its potential of creating a permanent cast of undocumented residents with no hope of advancement in U.S. society.[268]

At a minimum, *Plyler* requires K–12 schools not to adopt policies or take actions that would deny access to or dissuade the enrollment of undocumented children in

---

[257] Tex. Educ. Code Ann. Tit. 2, § 21.031 (Vernon 1976). For a more detailed explanation of Texas' law, *see* Michael A. Olivas, *Plyler v. Doe, the Education of Undocumented Children, and the Policy, in* Immigration Stories 198–199 (David A. Martin and Peter H. Schuck, eds. 2005).

[258] For an explanation of the *Plyler* litigation and principal players, *see id.* at 199–208.

[259] 457 U.S. 202 (1982).

[260] *Id.* at 221–28.

[261] *Id.* at 218–219.

[262] *Id.* at 220.

[263] The Court employs a rational basis argument but actually applies a test that is best characterized as intermediate scrutiny in that the State had to meet a "substantial goal." *Id.* at 223–24.

[264] *Id.* at 227.

[265] *Id.* at 229.

[266] *Id.* at 228.

[267] *Id.* at 225–36.

[268] *Id.* at 218–19.

public schools. *Plyler* also entitles undocumented students to varied benefits provided by a number of special programs.[269] These rights of undocumented students' access to K–12 public education are settled in the legal domain, despite post-*Plyler* attempts by some states to sidestep the decision. In clear violation of *Plyler*, for example, California's Proposition 187 included provisions barring undocumented children from public schools,[270] which were struck down as unconstitutional early in the litigation.[271] Moreover, in 1996, Congress considered federal legislation to reverse *Plyler*, known as the Gallegly Amendment,[272] although ultimately the PRWORA preserved *Plyler* by prohibiting states from denying children access to elementary public schools.[273] Still, some states have chosen to deny access to K-12 schools to nonimmigrant children given that *Plyler* did not directly address the issue,[274] while others have focused on calculating the cost of educating undocumented children in the hope of overturning *Plyler* on the facts — i.e., showing a substantial financial interest to educate lawful residents.[275]

2.   Higher Education

States' involvement in noncitizen access to higher education has implicated issues of admission, in-state tuition, and other financial benefits eligibility, such as financial aid and scholarships. It is well-settled law that states that deny any of these benefits to lawful permanent residents run afoul of equal protection. In 1977, in *Nyquist v. Mauclet*, the Court applied strict scrutiny equal protection analysis to strike down a New York state financial assistance program that was limited solely to citizens or certain noncitizens who were either refugees or had applied or intended to apply for citizenship.[276] Challenges to denial of these same benefits to nonimmigrants and the undocumented, however, have been tested solely for preemption validity, not equality or substantive due process principles. In 1982, in *Toll v. Moreno*, the Court struck down on preemption grounds a 1973 Maryland statute that granted in-state tuition benefits solely to U.S. citizens and lawful permanent residents.[277] The plaintiffs in that case, who held "G-4" nonimmigrant visa status, challenged the legislation on the basis that it conflicted with federal

---

[269] These programs include: (1) the Emergency Immigrant Education Program (No Child Left Behind Act of 2001, 115 Stat. 1425 at §§ 3241–3248); (2) programs that receive funds under Section 204 of the Immigrant Reform and Control Act (SILG Funds); (3) bilingual or English-language learning programs; (4) Chapter 1 funds, which are used to supplement the educational services provided to low-achieving students in low-income neighborhoods; (5) Head Start programs; (6) special education; and (7) free and reduced meal programs.

[270] Section 7 of Proposition 187, California ballot Pamphlet: General Election Nov. 8, 1994, at 92 (1994) (adding Cal. Educ. Code § 48125).

[271] *League of United Latin American Citizens v. Wilson*, 908 F. Supp. 755 (C.D. Cal. 1995).

[272] H.R. 4134, 104th Cong. § 1 (1996).

[273] 8 U.S.C. §§ 1643(a)(2) (2000).

[274] BENDER, ET AL., *supra* note 233, at 89.

[275] *Id.* at 89–90.

[276] 432 U.S. 1 (1977). *See also* Jagnandan v. Giles, 379 F. Supp. 1178 (1974) (declaring a Mississippi statute classifying all noncitizens, including permanent resident plaintiffs, as nonresidents for purposes of charging them higher tuition and fees, unconstitutional under equal protection and due process).

[277] 458 U.S. 1, 3–4 (1982).

immigration policy under which, in contrast to other nonimmigrant holders, they were permitted to establish domicile in the U.S.[278] The Court agreed that barring domiciled nonimmigrants from acquiring in-state status for purposes of college tuition violated the Supremacy Clause.[279] The case, however, did not address the law's legality as applied to non-domiciled nonimmigrants under federal immigration law or undocumented students. Subsequent state cases addressing states' ability to employ federal immigration criteria to postsecondary in-state tuition determinations, moreover, yielded mixed results.[280] This area of the law, which has become increasingly pertinent as states legislate to either grant or deny these benefits to undocumented students, remains unsettled. Since 2001, at least ten states have legislated to grant undocumented students in-state tuition,[281] while three have legislated against it,[282] with several others formally considering the issue.[283] In addition, states' Attorney Generals, Board of Regents, or Departments of Education have weighed in on the issue with mixed results.[284]

To date, the debate over the legality of in-state tuition for undocumented students has centered on whether states who charge in-state tuition to undocumented students are preempted by the Illegal Immigration Reform and Immigrant Responsibility Act of 1996 (IIRIRA).[285] Chapter 14 of IIRIRA, which deals with restricting welfare and public benefits, contains two provisions relevant to noncitizens in postsecondary education. Section 1621 included in the definition of restricted "[s]tate or local public benefit[s]" "any . . . postsecondary education . . . benefit for which payments or assistance are provided to an individual, household, or family eligibility unit by an agency of a State or local government or by appropriated funds of a State or local government."[286] Section 1621 further prescribes that only states which have specifically enacted legislation after August 22, 1996 to affirmative grant eligibility could make such state or local public benefits available to noncitizens excluded from benefits under the

---

[278] *Id.* at 7–8.

[279] *Id.* at 17.

[280] Challenges based on preemption to California's decision in the 1980s to allow undocumented students establish residency for tuition purposes, for example, produced inconsistent rulings in California courts. For a thorough examination of this litigation, *see* Michael A. Olivas, *Storytelling Out of School: Undocumented College Residency, Race, and Reaction,* 22 HASTINGS CONST. L.Q. 1019, 1051–1060 (1995).

[281] *See* University of Houston, Institute for Higher Education Law and Governance, http://www.law.uh.edu/ihelg/state.html. The first two states were Texas and California in 2001, followed suit by Utah and New York in 2002, Washington, Oklahoma and Illinois in 2003, Kansas in 2004, New Mexico in 2005, and Nebraska in 2006. *Id.*

[282] These states are Arizona, Georgia, and Mississippi. *Id.*

[283] *Id.*

[284] *Compare* Ark. Op. Atty. Gen. No. 2008-109, 2008 WL 4198411 (Ark. A.G.) (concluding that colleges and university may enroll undocumented students and are not obliged to verify citizenship in the absence of a rule or regulation to the contrary) with Co. Atty. Gen., Formal Opinion No. 06-01, 2006 WL 1370998 (Colo. A.G.) (concluding that community colleges lack statutory authority to establish a policy or regulating granting in-state tuition status to undocumented students).

[285] Illegal Immigration Reform and Immigrant Responsibility Act (IIRIRA) of 1996, Pub. L. No. 104-208, div. C, 110 Stat. 3009-546-3009-724.

[286] *Id.* at § 1621.

legislation.[287] More on point, Section 1623 of IIRIRA provides that "an alien who is not lawfully present in the United States shall not be eligible on the basis of residency within a State (or a political subdivision) for any postsecondary education benefit unless a citizen or national of the Unites States is eligible for such a benefit (in no less an amount, duration, and scope) without regard to whether the citizen or national is such a resident."[288]

Professor Kris W. Kobach has relied on IIRIRA § 1623 to publish articles and to participate in litigation to challenge state laws that offer in-state college tuition to undocumented students.[289] Kobach argues, *inter alia*, that the plain text of § 1623 displaces state laws that offer in-state tuition to undocumented students without offering the same to out-of-state residents through express preemption.[290] Most states offering in-state tuition to undocumented students, however, do so not on the basis of residency but rather contingent upon attending high school in the state for three years.[291] Kobach views this approach as states' attempt to evade § 1623.[292] He argues that Congress intended the phrase "eligible on the basis of residence within the State . . . for any postsecondary education benefit" to expressly bar undocumented students from resident tuition rates, discounts, and scholarships available to state residents.[293] Any other reading of the statute, Kobach characterizes as implausible because it allows states to create a semantic loophole to obliterate the proscription so long as the word "residence" is avoided, which in turn violates the "whole act" rule of statutory construction by ignoring the rest of the IIRIRA and the manifest intent of Congress.[294] As a matter of public policy, Kobach espouses the view that persons who have violated federal immigration laws should not be rewarded with taxpayer-subsidized tuition in light of limited resources and the increasing financial burden born by U.S. taxpayers and U.S. citizen parents to educate their children.[295]

Professor Michael A. Olivas adopts different constitutional, statutory, and policy approaches to the issue of in-state resident tuition policies for noncitizens. Olivas views states' apportionment of tuition benefits and state residency determinations

---

[287] *Id.* ("A State may provide that an alien who is not lawfully present in the United States is eligible for any State or local public benefit which such alien would otherwise be ineligible under subsection (a) of this section only through the enactment of State law after August 22, 1996, which affirmatively provides for such eligibility.").

[288] *Id.* at § 1623.

[289] Kris W. Kobach, *Immigration Nullification: In-State Tuition and Lawmakers who Disregard the Law*, 10 N.Y.U. J. Legis. & Pub. Pol'y 473, 503–17 (2006–2007). Kobach represents the U.S. citizens plaintiffs challenging the laws granting in-state tuition to undocumented students in Kansan and California. *Id.* at FNa1.

[290] *Id.* at 507–08. Kobach also makes an argument for implied preemption through other provisions of the INA in that such laws conflict with the objectives of Congress to curtail undocumented migration, represent a general obstacle to enforcement, and require state officers to make independent judgments about students' immigration status. *Id.* at 513–17.

[291] *Id.* at 506.

[292] *Id.*

[293] *Id.* at 510.

[294] *Id.* at 511.

[295] *Id.* at 498–503.

as appropriately a state role when such laws incorporate but do not determine immigrant status.[296] Indeed, for more than a century, states have exercised sole authority to set admission and resident tuition policies at public universities.[297] Moreover, in-state residency is solely a state-determined benefit or status as no federal funds attach to the classification.[298] Thus, Olivas rejects the argument that in-state tuition laws for undocumented students are impinging on federal immigration powers.[299] Olivas also does not read IIRIRA as precluding states from granting in-state tuition to undocumented students. Olivas reads Sections1621 and 1623 of IIRIRA together (the latter which Kobach mostly ignores) to conclude that IIRIRA allows states to confer (or not to confer) residency status upon the undocumented in their public postsecondary institutions.[300] Section 1623 merely modifies the authority of states to confer state postsecondary benefits such that undocumented students are not favored over out-of-state residents.[301] All ten state statutes currently conferring in-state tuition to undocumented students require of them state high school attendance and three years residency, which are not required of citizen non-residents.[302] As such, undocumented students are not favored over other nonresident applicants. Further, Olivas reads the term "benefit" as used in both provisions as proscribing monetary postsecondary benefits, not status-based residency classifications.[303] As a matter of public policy, Olivas challenges the overstated claims of U.S. citizen student displacement by undocumented students and critiques the short-sightedness of opposing the integration of long-term undocumented students as productive contributors of society.[304]

Plaintiffs on either side of the debate are relying on the Supremacy Clause to challenge the validity of laws that grant or deny in-state tuition or other postsecondary benefits to undocumented students. For example, students and unincorporated organizations challenged Virginia's post-secondary institutions' policy of denying admissions to undocumented students based, *inter alia*, on preemption,[305] while nonresident citizen students asserted preemption to challenge a Kansas statute allowing undocumented students to attend Kansas universities

---

[296] Michael A. Olivas, *Lawmakers Gone Wild? College Residency and the Response to Professor Kobach*, 61 S.M.U. L. Rev. 99, 106 (2008).

[297] *See* Michael A. Olivas, *Storytelling Out of School: Undocumented College Residency, Race, and Reaction*, 22 Hastings Const. L. Q. 1019, 1027 (1995) (tracing court cases dating back to 1882 that held that only states can set residency and tuition policies for institutions of higher learning).

[298] Olivas, *Lawmakers Gone Wild, supra* note 296, at 122.

[299] *Id.*

[300] *Id.*

[301] *Id.* at 123.

[302] *Id.*

[303] To make this argument, Olivas examines the textual modifications of "benefit" employed in the provisions — such as "for which payments or assistance are provided to an individual, household, or family eligibility . . . under 1621(c) (1)(B) and "amount, duration, and scope" in section 1623. *Id.* at 124.

[304] Olivas, *Storytelling Out of School, supra* note 297, at 1085–86.

[305] Equal Access Education v. Merten, 305 F. Supp. 2d 585 (2004).

and pay in-state tuition.[306] The Kansas litigation never reached the merits because the Tenth Circuit affirmed the district court's case dismissal for lack of standing.[307] Virginia's federal district court holding applies the *DeCanas* three-prong preemption test[308] to uphold the validity of admission denials to postsecondary schools to undocumented students. Like Olivas, the court affirmed that federal immigration laws and those more specifically pertaining to noncitizen postsecondary benefits do not preclude state regulation of noncitizen access to higher education benefits.[309] In dicta, however, on the specific interpretation of IIRIRA Section 1623, the court inferred that "aliens cannot receive in-state tuition unless out-of-state United States citizens receive this benefit,"[310] a reading that is more consistent with Kobach's interpretation of the same. Interestingly, a recent ICE letter to North Carolina's Attorney General's office on the issue of federal laws' regulation of higher education benefits to the undocumented concluded that "*admissions* to public post-secondary educational institutions is not one of the benefits regulated by the [IIRIRA] and is not a public benefit under the [PWORA]."[311] The letter did not address the issue of in-state tuition benefits. The latest ruling on point is from a California district court, which declared California's grant of in-state tuition benefits to certain undocumented students preempted by Section 1623, in so far as in-state tuition constituted a benefit on the basis of residence which was not made available to all nonresident students.[312] Having considered in-state tuition an included benefit under the IIRIRA, the court also found California's law preempted by the formal requirements of Section 1621 to

---

[306] Day v. Bond, 511 F.3d 1030 (10th Cir. 2007).

[307] *Id.* at 1139. Another case in Oklahoma against a statute that included fourteen distinct anti-immigration sections, including Section Eleven denying resident tuition, financial aid, and scholarship to undocumented students was also dismissed for lack of standing. That case, however, did not include student plaintiffs challenging that specific provision of the law. Nevertheless, it is worth noting that while certain other undocumented persons denied driver's licenses or who faced eviction from their homes based on their status could prove injury, they were denied standing nonetheless on a theory of "unclean hands." The decision reads in relevant part:

> An Illegal alien, in willful violation of federal immigration law, is without standing to challenge the constitutionality of a state law, when compliance with federal law would absolve the illegal alien's constitutional dilemma . . . ."

National Coalition of Latino Clergy, Inc., et al. v. Henry, 2007 WL 43906650 (N.D. Okla. 2007). This same logic could apply to deny standing to undocumented students challenging laws that deny them in-state tuition.

[308] 424 U.S. 351 (1976). *See infra* notes 159–161 and accompanying text for a description of the *DeCanas* test.

[309] For example, the court rejects the argument that state determinations of students' immigration status is preempted by federal immigration law because Virginia adopts federal immigration classifications. *Merten*, 305 F. Supp. at 603. As well, the court rejects that Virginia is attempting to regulate in a field that is completely occupied by the federal government. *Id* at 605.

[310] *Id.* at 606–07.

[311] Letter from Sheriff (Ret.) Jim Pendergraph, Executive Director, Office of State and Local Coordination, U.S. Dept. of Homeland Security to Thomas J. Ziko, Special Deputy Attorney General, N.C. Department of Justice (July 9, 2008) (cited in Ark. Op. Atty. Gen. No. 2008-109, 2008 WL 4198411, at *3 (Ark. A.G.)).

[312] Martinez v. Regents of the Univ. of California, 2008 WL 4194303 (Cal. App. 3 Dist.), at *14–25.

affirmatively legislate conferring a benefit to unqualified noncitizens.[313] None of these decisions and/or opinions definitively resolves the issue of whether federal law or state law governs issues of admission and/or in-state tuition benefits for undocumented students.

Congress could ultimately legislate to definitively "occupy" the field of postsecondary education benefits for noncitizens. Since 2001, Congress has attempted, but failed to pass the legislation most commonly known as the Development Relief and Education for Alien Minors (DREAM) Act, to permit states to offer in-state tuition rates to undocumented students and to offer legalization to noncitzens who possess good moral character, can establish five year residency in the U.S., are under 21 years of age, earn a high school degree, and complete at least two years of college or military service.[314] Were this law to pass, it would preempt inconsistent state legislation, although states might still be able to regulate to grant or deny benefits to undocumented students ineligible for benefits under the DREAM Act.

I. WORKER RIGHTS

1. State Employment and Labor Laws

Prior to IRCA's passage, worker rights and benefits, with the exception of unemployment benefits,[315] have generally been available to all workers, regardless of immigration status.[316] Since IRCA's passage, however, a number of employers challenged workers' compensation claims by unauthorized workers, although generally state courts found no conflict between IRCA's employer sanctions for the hiring of undocumented persons and state laws protecting workers.[317] In passing IRCA, in fact, legislative history leaves clear that the law's intention was not to limit workplace protections afforded to undocumented workers.[318]

Despite IRCA's legislative history, in 2002 the U.S. Supreme Court decided *Hoffman Plastic Compounds, Inc. v. National Labor Relations Board*[319] and held that an undocumented worker fired in retaliation for his support of union organizing was ineligible for backpay (i.e., lost wages resulting from unlawful termination) because such an award would conflict with IRCA's bar on the hiring of undocumented workers. *Hoffman Plastic* was a departure from the Court's

---

[313] *Id.* at * 27.

[314] *See* Regini Shah, *Sharing the Dream: Toward Formalizing the Status of Long-Term Undocumented Children in the United States*, 39 Colum. Hm. Rts. L. Rev. 637 (2008).

[315] *See, e.g.*, Alonso v. State of California, 50 Cal. Rptr. 536 (Cal. App. 1975); Pinilla v. Bd. of Review in Dep't of Labor, 382 A.2d 921 (N.J. Super. A.D. 1978); Flores v. Dep't of Jobs and Training, 411 N.W. 2d 499 (Minn. 1987); and Ruiz v. Unemployment Compensation Bd. of Review, 911 A.2d 600 (Pa. Cmmw. 2006) (barring unauthorized workers from unemployment benefits).

[316] *See* Anne Marie O'Donovon, *Immigrant Workers and Workers' Compensation After Hoffman Plastics Compounds, Ind. v. N.L.R.B.*, 30 N.Y.U. Rev. L. & Soc. Change 299, 303–04 (2006).

[317] *Id.*

[318] H.R. Rep. No. 99-682, pt. 1, at 49; H.R. Rep. No. 99-682, pt. 2, at 8–9.

[319] 535 U.S. 137 (2002).

decision nearly two decades earlier in 1984 in *Sure-Tan, Inc. v. NLRB*,[320] in which the Court found no difficulty harmonizing NLRA coverage with a worker's violation of the immigration laws.[321] *Sure-Tan* held that undocumented workers are "employees" under the NLRA, and thus, found that NLRA statutory remedies applied equally to undocumented workers.[322] But even in *Sure-Tan*, decided pre-IRCA, the issue of backpay was more controversial, ultimately leading to a 5-4 majority disapproving an award of six months backpay for workers who had accepted voluntary departure in lieu of deportation based on concerns over undermining the deterrence of unauthorized migration embodied in the immigration laws.[323] *Hoffman Plastic*, however, did not rely on *Sure-Tan* to deny backpay remedies, choosing instead to conclude that IRCA has significantly altered the "legal landscape,"[324] for it has "'forcefully' made combating the employment of illegal aliens central to '[t]he policy of immigration law.'"[325]

Post-*Hoffman Plastics*, some states have relied on the opinion's IRCA interpretation to deny state worker rights to undocumented workers, while other states have rejected the expansion of *Hoffman Plastics* to state workplace laws.[326] For example, while almost all state workers' compensation statutes cover undocumented workers,[327] some courts have relied on *Hoffman Plastics* to deny some or all workers' compensation remedies to undocumented workers, focusing on the worker's wrongdoing of working without authorization and IRCA's goal of deterring unauthorized migration.[328] In addition, a few state legislatures have contemplated proposals to exclude the undocumented from worker compensation

---

[320] 467 U.S. 883 (1984).

[321] *Id.* at 893–94.

[322] *Id.*

[323] *Id.* at 903.

[324] *Hoffman Plastic*, 535 U.S. at 147 (quoting INS v. Nat'l Ctr. For Immigrants' Rights, Inc., 502 U.S. 183, 194 & n.8 (1991)).

[325] *Id.* at 148.

[326] *See generally* María Pabón López, *The Place of the Undocumented Workers in the United States Legal System After Hoffman Plastics Compounds: An Assessment and Comparison with Argentina's Legal System*, 15 IND. INT'L & COMP. L. REV. 301 (2005).

[327] Jeffrey Klamut, *The Invisible Fence: De Facto Exclusion of Undocumented Workers from State Workers' Compensation Systems*, 16 KANS. J. L. & PUB. POL'Y 174, 182 (2006–7) (explaining that many statutes include undocumented workers explicitly in their statutory definition of employee, while others do so only implicitly through broad language that includes all workers employed under a contract of hire). Still, most undocumented workers are de facto excluded from coverage because most work in industries where statutory exemptions and employer evasion schemes limit access to worker compensation benefits. *Id.* at 188–204.

[328] *See, e.g.*, Sanchez v. Eagle Alloy, Inc. 658 N.W. 2d 510, 515 (Mich. Ct. App. 2003) (limiting undocumented worker's compensation benefits to the date when his undocumented status was discovered because of the worker's criminal act of obtaining employment fraudulently); Reinforced Earth Co. v. Workers' Com. Appeal Bd. (Astudillo, 810 A.2d 99, 108–09 & n.12 (Pa. 2002) (holding that while *Hoffman Plastics* did not bar medical benefits for injuries sustained by undocumented workers, it did suspend their eligibility for wage replacement benefits); Tarango v. State Indus. Ins. Sys., 25 P.3d 175 (Nev. 2001) (holding while undocumented workers are eligible for medical compensation for injuries, not so for vocational rehabilitation because of their unauthorized entry).

benefits.[329] Several states, however, have refused to extend *Hoffman Plastics* to state worker compensation statutes reasoning that it is the role of states to regulate workplace safety and finding strong policy grounds to protect workers within the state.[330] Similarly, tort actions filed by undocumented workers against employers for work injuries have yielded mixed results, at least as to lost wages resulting from the injury.[331] Those courts denying lost wages view this remedy as similar to backpay, given that it awards damages for "would have" rather than already earned wages in contravention of IRCA.[332] Courts that have granted lost wages emphasize instead the prevalence of the states' interest in protecting workers, absent an explicit mandate from Congress.[333] In addition, some state courts have denied worker remedies for wrongful termination under state anti-discrimination statutes based also on IRCA's deterrence rationale.[334] In the same way that the undocumented worker in *Hoffman Plastics* was eligible for compensation for work already performed, less affected have been worker protections for work already performed, such as state prevailing wage requirements or laws imposing penalties for unpaid wages.[335]

---

[329] Klamut, *supra* note 327, at 204–207 (discussing proposals in South Carolina and Maryland).

[330] *See, e.g.*, Madeira v. Affordable Hous. Found., Inc., 469 F.3d 219, 228 (2d Cir. 2006) (concluding that states enjoy broad authority under their police powers to enact laws affecting occupational health and safety and holding that undocumented worker was eligible for lost earnings damages); Farmers Bros. Coffee v. Workers' Comp. Appeals Bd., 133 Cal. App. 4th 533 (Cal. App. 2 Dist. 2005) (reasoning that the purpose of California's Workers' Compensation Act is to furnish, expeditiously and inexpensively, treatment and compensation for persons suffering workplace injury, irrespective of the fault of any party, and to secure workplace safety). *See also* Balbuena v. IDR Realty LLC, 6 N.Y. 3d 338 (N.Y. 2006) (awarding lost earnings); Design Kitchen & Baths v. Lagos, 882 A.2d 817 (Md. 2005) (awarding medical benefits); Correa v. Waymouth Farms, Inc., 664 N.W. 2d 324 (Minn. 2003) (awarding temporary total disability benefits to undocumented worker); Cherokee Indus., Inc. v. Alvarez, 84 P.3d 798 (Okla. Civ. App. Div. 3 2003) (awarding total disability benefits).

[331] *Compare* Veliz v. Rental Serv. Corp. USA, 313 F. Supp. 2d 1317, 1337 (M.D. Fla. 2003) *and* Hernandez-Cortez v. Hernandez, 2003 U.S. Dist. LEXIS 19780 (D. Kan. 2003) (relying on *Hoffman Plastics* to deny lost wages as a remedy for the work-related death of a worker) *with* Majlinger v. Casino Contracting Corp., 25 A.D.3d 14 (N.Y.A.D. 2 Dept. 2005) *and* Tyson Foods, Inc. v. Guzman, 116 S.W.3d 233 (Tex. App. 2003) (awarding lost wages to undocumented worker).

[332] *Veliz*, 313 F. Supp. 2d at 1337.

[333] *Majlinger*, 25 A.D. 3d at 14.

[334] Crespo v. Evergo Corp., 841 A.2d 471 (N.J. Super. Ct. App. Div. 2004) (denying remedies to undocumented worker fired for being pregnant); Morenjon v. Hinge, No. BC255537, 2003 WL 22482036 at *1 (Ca. Ct. App. Nov. 21, 2003) (unpublished) (denying remedies to undocumented worker who was fired after requesting leave to undergo surgery to treat ovarian cancer).

[335] *See, e.g.*, Coma Corp. v. Kansas Dept. of Labor, 154 P.3d 1080 (Kan. 2007) (holding that IRCA did not preempt Kansas Wage Payment Act on the issue of earned but unpaid wages and that employer was subject to statutory penalty for willfully failing to pay undocumented worker his earned wages); Reyes v. Van Elk, Ltd., 56 Cal. Rptr. 3d 68 (Cal. App. 2 Dist. 2007) (holding that IRCA did not preempt the states wage and hour legislation in undocumented workers' claim for unpaid prevailing wages); Pineda v. Kel-Tech Const., Inc. 832 N.Y.S.2d 386 (N.Y. Sup. 2007) (upholding the right of undocumented worker to prevailing wages for work performed).

2. Day Laborers

Local governments have also acted to regulate the growing presence of day laborers in their communities. Day laborers who generally congregate at informal hiring places such as a street corner, parking lot, sidewalk, or park to wait for temporary or permanent employment are overwhelmingly Latino and undocumented.[336] Their visibility has created tensions in communities, especially with some anti-immigrant groups who portray them as violent criminals and sexual harassers[337] or simply as public nuisances or traffic safety hazards.[338] As well, localities have been concerned over day laborer's all too common experiences of labor exploitation and other types of victimization, including hate crimes.[339]

Localities have either moved to harass or displace day laborers or they have attempted to improve their lot by imposing license restrictions on those who hire them or promoting and regulating work centers that provide improved facilities, education, and legal representation to exploited workers.[340] Either response has faced court challenges with mixed results.

One common type of regulation, for example, has been laws or ordinances that impose a traffic violation on day laborers or persons who hire them for congregating at informal hiring places to seek jobs or for picking up the workers at these places.[341] Such laws have been successfully struck down under First Amendment challenges as impermissible content–based regulation (of protected commercial speech),[342] or, even if deemed content-neutral, for lacking a substantial state interest,[343] or for not being narrowly tailored to meet that interest.[344] In contrast, First Amendment challenges to registration requirements based on a theory of impermissible prior restraints on the commercial speech of those who employ day laborers have not been successful, as long as the law establishes clear guidelines and accords sufficient due process to registrants, including judicial review.[345]

---

[336] Abel Valenzuela Jr., et al., *On the Corner: Day Labor in the United States* (2006), *available at* http://www.sscnet.ucla.edu/issr/csup/uploaded_files/Natl_DayLabor-On_the_Corner1.pdf.

[337] *See, e.g.*, http://www.daylaborers.org/index.htm (website portraying daylaborers as violent criminals and sexual deviants).

[338] Mauricio A. España, *Day Laborers, Friend or Foe: A Survey of Community Responses*, 30 Fordham Urb. L.J. 1979, 1993–2000 (2003).

[339] *Id.* at 1991–1993, 2001–2002.

[340] *See, e.g.*, Victor Narro, *Impacting Next Wave Organizing: Creative Campaign Strategies of the Los Angeles Worker Center*, 50 N.Y.L. Sch. L. Rev. 465, 486–95 (2005–2006) (describing the work of worker centers with day laborers). *See also* Rodriguez, *supra* note 16, at 597–99 (same).

[341] *See, e.g.*, § 72.17(C) of the Town of Cave Creek, Arizona Code (Oct. 24, 2007) (making it unlawful for "[any] person []to stand on or adjacent to a street or highway and solicit, or attempt to solicit, employment, business or contributions from the occupant of any vehicle").

[342] Lopez v. Town of Cave Creek, AZ, 559 F. Supp. 2d 1030 (D. Ariz. 2008).

[343] Coalition for Humane Immigrant Rights of Los Angeles v. Burke, 2000 WL 1481467 (C.D. Cal. 2000) (unpublished opinion).

[344] Comite Jornaleros de Redondo Beach v. City of Redondo Beach, 475 F. Supp. 2d 952 (C.D. Cal. 2006).

[345] *See, e.g.*, Calderon v. City of Vista, 2006 WL 2265112 (S.D. Cal. 2006) (unpublished opinion).

Equal protection challenges have also been raised against selective law enforcement practices by local police or against ordinances designed to curb day labor practices. For example, a successful equal protection challenge was brought against the mayor and police of the Village of Mamaroneck in New York after they waged an intense law enforcement campaign to reduce the number of workers that included increasing police presence in the area, intimidating workers, and aggressively issuing traffic tickets to contractors who entered the area to pick up day laborers.[346] In contrast, another court upheld a housing overcrowding ordinance adopted by the Town of Jupiter, Florida, which was then enforced against properties primarily occupied by Hispanic residents in an effort to drive out day laborers congregating in the neighborhood.[347] The different outcomes in the cases turned on whether plaintiffs factually proved to the court that selective enforcement was intentionally racist against Latinos as opposed to discriminatory based on non-suspect characteristics.[348]

The public sponsorship of work centers for day laborers has also been challenged. In the town of Herndon, for example, taxpayers sponsored by Judicial Watch, a conservative political group, raised a preemption challenge arguing that the work centers facilitate the hiring of undocumented workers in violation of IRCA.[349] This litigation ultimately became moot when the town of Herndon closed the center's doors in 2007 after facing significant public pressure against it.[350]

J. DRIVER'S LICENSES

Post 9/11, the issue of driver's license restrictions for noncitizens took center stage.[351] With few exceptions, prior to that time, most noncitizens could obtain driver's licenses notwithstanding their immigration status.[352] Suddenly, however, driver's licenses became an issue of national security, rather than a local road safety regulation.[353] In fact, in 2004, Congress signed into law the Intelligence Reform and

---

[346] *See, e.g.,* Doe v. Vill. of Mamaroneck, 462 F. Supp. 2d 520, 527 (S.D. N.Y. 2006).

[347] Young Apartments, Inc. v. Town of Jupiter, Florida, 2007 WL 1021133 (S.D. Fla. 2007).

[348] *Compare Vill. of Mamanoreck,* 462 F. Supp. 2d at 547–553 *with Young Apartments, Inc.,* 2007 WL 1021133, at *5.

[349] *See, e.g.,* Karunakarum v. Town of Herndon, 2006 WL 408389 (Va. Cir. Ct. 2006) (unpublished opinion) (granting standing to taxpayers). For the background to the litigation *see* Margaret Hobbins, Note, *The Day Laborer Debate: Small Towns, U.S.A. Takes on Federal Immigration Law Regarding Undocumented Workers,* 6 Conn. Pub. Int. L.J. 111, 113–117 (2006).

[350] Rodríguez, *supra* note 16, at 599.

[351] Aldana, *supra* note 243, at 281–82. *See also* María Pabón López, *More than a License to Drive: State Restrictions on the Use of Driver's Licenses by Noncitizens,* 29 S. Ill. U. L.J. 9, 95–109 (2005).

[352] Some exceptions included Illinois and California which, since the 1970s and 1990s respectively, required applicants for driver's licenses to have social security numbers. *See* Doe v. Edgar, 1989 WL 91805 (1989) (unpublished) (discussing Ill. Rev. Stat. Ch. 95 ½, para 6_1.06); Lauderbach v. Zolin, 41 Cal. Rprtr. 2d 434 (1995) (discussing California's 1992 Trial Court Realignment and Efficiency Act). *See also* Kevin R. Johnson, *Driver's Licenses and Undocumented Immigrants: The Future of Civil rights Law?,* 5 Nev. L.J. 213, 232 (2004) (discussing the anti-immigrant animus behind California's law).

[353] Aldana, *supra* note 243, at 282.

Terrorism Prevention Act (IRTPA)[354] and the REAL ID Act in 2005,[355] which "federalized" driver's licenses by imposing national standards for their issuance.[356] The REAL ID Act specifically affected noncitizens by imposing Social Security Numbers (SSN) and legal residency requirements on state-issued driver's licenses for these to be used as a form of identification before federal agencies for official purposes.[357] As well, the REAL ID act contemplated only temporary driver's licenses and identification cards for noncitizens with temporary visas or those whose petitions were pending with an expiration date matching that of the visa or after one year if there was no definite end period.[358]

By the time Congress acted, at least twenty-four states had already legislated to require lawful presence for the issuance of driver's licenses, with only eleven states that expressly did not.[359] The federalization of driver's licenses, however, also prompted many more states to legislate in the area,[360] despite significant concerns over costs and other burdens on states.[361] States restrict noncitizen access to driver's licenses either by requiring an SSN, with or without exceptions for the issuance of a license, or by imposing a lawful presence requirement through legislation and/or agency practice. By May of 2008, for example, all fifty states require a SSN, although only South Dakota does so without exception.[362] In addition, thirty states have a lawful presence requirement by legislation, while fourteen more create this requirement by agency policy or by the combination of documents required of driver's license applicants.[363] Thirty-two states also require that driver's licenses expire at the same time as the applicant's length of authorized immigration status.[364] Thus, hardly any state makes driver's licenses available to noncitizens. As of May 2008, only Hawaii, Maryland, New Mexico, and Washington do not have a lawful presence requirement and permit exceptions to the SSN requirement when the applicant is ineligible for a SSN.[365] In addition, at least two states, Tennessee and Utah, opted to issue driving certificates or driving privilege

---

[354] Pub. L. No. 108-458, § 7212(b)(2)(A)-(F), 118 Stat. 3638 (Dec. 17, 2004).

[355] Pub. L. No. 109-13, 119 Stat. 231 (May 10, 2005).

[356] Aldana, *supra* note 243, at 282.

[357] Real ID Act, supra note 355, at § 202(c).

[358] *Id.*

[359] Aldana, *supra* note 243, at 282.

[360] Within four months of the REAL ID Act's passage, twenty-four states introduced legislation to conform state law to the federal requirements *Id.* at 283.

[361] *See* National Governors Association, National Conference of State Legislatures, American Association of Motor Vehicle Administration, The Real ID Act: National Impact Analysis 2 (Sept. 2006), *available at* http://www.ncsl.org/print/statefed/Real_ID_Impact_Report_FINAL_Sept19.pdf (concluding that Real ID would cost more than $11 billion over five years and have a major impact on services to the public and impose unrealistic burden on state compliance).

[362] Nat'l Immig. L. Center, *Overview of States' Driver's License Requirements, available at* http://www.nilc.org/immspbs/DLs/state_dl_rqrmts_ovrvw_2008-05-18.pdf (last visited June 17, 2008).

[363] *Id.*

[364] *Id.*

[365] *Id.*

cards to undocumented drivers.[366] These documents are good to operate a vehicle on the road, but are not valid for identification.

Proponents of granting driver's licenses to all noncitizens challenge the claim that their exclusion would improve national security; as well they raise civil liberties and state rights concerns.[367] The conferral of driver's license to noncitizens would create a fuller record of the identity of undocumented persons in the U.S., furthering the government's law enforcement goals.[368] In contrast, the denial of identification to undocumented persons affects their ability to conduct the most "ordinary living" tasks, such as driving, opening up a bank account, or renting an apartment.[369] Moreover, racial and anti-immigrant animus has motivated many of the local driver's license restriction legislation, which is viewed as a type of immigration control.[370] Undocumented persons, however, do not go away and find alternatives to live and drive without U.S. driving authorization and identification. The consequences of this fact not only deteriorate road safety but expose immigrants to harm, such as increased exploitation, profiling, and criminalization.[371]

A number of states have also openly opposed the federalization of driver's licenses, citing in addition to cost, state sovereignty, road safety, and privacy concerns.[372] In January of 2008, Maine became the first state to pass a resolution in opposition of REAL ID compliance, joined subsequently by Arkansas, Idaho, Montana, and Washington.[373] In addition, at least twenty-four other states have considered opting out of REAL ID or placing conditions on their participation.[374]

Court challenges to state noncitizen driver's license restrictions have generally been unsuccessful because those affected are not treated as a protected group and the restriction is not considered a fundamental right. The Sixth Circuit, for example, upheld Tennessee's driver certificate program against an equal protection challenge filed by temporary residents.[375] To do so, the court declined to extend suspect class status to nonimmigrants or to recognize driver's license denials as

---

[366] Spencer Garlick, Note, *License to Drive: Pioneering a Compromise to Allow Undocumented Immigrant Access to the Roads*, 31 SETON HALL LEGIS. J. 191, 205–06 (2006).

[367] *See, e.g.*, Raquel Aldana & Sylvia R. Lazos Vargas, *"Aliens" in Our Midst Post 9-11: Legislating Outsiderness Within the Border*, 38 U.S.C. DAVIS L. REV. 1683, 1711–19 (2005).

[368] Donal Kervin & Margaret D. Stock, *The Role of Immigration in a Coordinated National Security Policy*, 21 GEO. IMMIGR. L.J. 383, 411–13 (2007).

[369] Johnson, *Driver's Licenses and Undocumented Immigrants*, *supra* note 352, at 223–232.

[370] *Id.* at 223–24.

[371] *Id.* (documenting, *inter alia*, the imposition of criminal sanctions for driving without a license).

[372] *See* Manoj Govindaich, *Driver Licensing Under the Real ID Act: Can Current Technology Balance Security and Policy*, 2006 U. ILL. L.J. L. TECH. & POL'Y 201 (2006) (discussing Real ID's privacy concerns).

[373] Tyler Moran, Nat'l Immig. L. Ctr., *Anti-Real ID Measures Enacted in Five States So Far* (April 2007), *available at* http://www.nilc.org/immspbs/DLs/DL036.htm.

[374] Nat'l Immig. L. Ctr., 2007 State REAL ID Legislation (April 2007), *available at* http://www.nilc.org/immspbs/DLs/state_real_id_proposals_2007-04-23.pdf.

[375] LULAC v. Bredesen, 500 F.3d 523 (6th Cir. 2007).

violating the fundamental right to travel.[376] Similar results have occurred in Iowa, Georgia, and North Dakota where bars to driver's licenses to undocumented persons have been upheld against equal protection challenges, despite the absence of a driving certificate.[377] Substantive due process challenges also have not succeeded, because the denial of driver's license is viewed as a privilege to drive, not as a fundamental liberty interest.[378] Separate right to travel challenges have also been dismissed, at least for undocumented persons, whose presence in the U.S. in violation of federal law makes their "right to travel" claims untenable to some courts.[379] Several challenges have been addressed to motor vehicle departments alleging misapplication of statutes or administrative overreach when their practices have imposed requirements that immigrant applicants have been unable to meet to obtain driver's licenses.[380] These challenges are unlikely to continue, however, as legislatures enact laws to comply with the REAL ID Act's specific requirements.

K. LANDLORD/TENANT IMMIGRATION ORDINANCES

Immigrant communities have already been disproportionately affected by facially neutral housing code ordinances, such as those that purport to limit nontraditional family units or occupancy rates.[381] Beginning in 2006, however, localities began to adopt ordinances that explicitly sought to bar undocumented immigrants from rental properties based on their immigration status.[382] Hazleton, Pennsylvania became the first municipality to adopt an anti-immigrant tenancy ordinance, and it became the model to hundreds of other localities in about 29 states considering similar provisions.[383] By mid-2008, localities had passed at least 42 ordinances containing immigrant tenancy restrictions,[384] relying on states' police

---

[376] *Id.* The right to travel challenge in this case was made more difficult by Tennessee's issuance of driving certificates, which the court viewed as hardly an attempt of the state to deter or penalize travel. *Id.*

[377] Sanchez v. Iowa, 692 N.W.2d 812 (Iowa 2005); John Doe 1 v. Georgia Dep't of Pub. Safety, 147 F. Supp. 2d 1369 (N.D. Ga. 2001); Doe v. Edgar, 1989 WL 91805 (N.D. Ill. 1989) (unpublished opinion). *But see* People v. Quiroga-Puma, 848 N.Y. S.2d 853 (N.Y. Just. Ct. 2007) (applying equal protection strict scrutiny to a New York statute that resulted in the denial of driver's licenses to undocumented persons).

[378] *Sanchez*, 692 N.W. 2d at 819–20.

[379] *Doe v. Georgia Dep't of Pub. Safety*, 147 F. Supp. 2d at 1373–75. *See also* LULAC v. Bredesen, 500 F.3d 523 (6th Cir. 2007) (dismissing right to travel claim when driving certificates had been issued).

[380] Cubas v. Martinez, 870 N.E.2d 133 (2007) (upholding New York's DMV's statutory authority for proof-of identity requirements); Fahy v. Comm'n, New Hampshire Department of Safety, 2006 WL 176346 (2006) (unpublished opinion) (striking down practice of imposing a shorter expiration date on driver's licenses for, *inter alia*, lawful permanent residents when practice not statutorily mandated nor authorized); Villegas v. Silverman, 832 N.E.2d 598 (2005) (enjoining Indiana's Bureau of Motor Vehicles identification requirements based on overreach of statutory authority and violation of administrative rule-making procedures); Lauderbach v. Zolin, 41 Cal. Rptr. 2d 434 (1995) (upholding San Francisco's DMV's statutory authority to require social security numbers for the issuance of driver's licenses).

[381] Guadalupe T. Luna, *Immigrants, Cops and Slumlords in the Midwest*, 29 S. Ill. U. L.J. 61, 73–77 (2005).

[382] Rigel C. Oliveri, *Between a Rock and a Hard Place: Landlords, Latinos, Anti-Illegal Immigrant Ordinances, and Housing Discrimination*, 62 Vand. L. Rev. 55, 59–72 (2009).

[383] *Id.* at 60.

[384] *Id.*

power to protect the health, safety, and welfare of their citizens.[385]

Generally, these tenancy ordinances include renting to certain noncitizens as part of the definition of "harboring"[386] and impose on the tenants proof of legal citizenship and/or residency requirements.[387] Under some ordinances, such as the City of Farmers Branch, landlords directly would be responsible for immigration verification and recordkeeping.[388] Other ordinances, such as Hazleton's, require that all tenants obtain an occupancy permit from the City, which they could obtain only after providing proof of immigration eligibility.[389] Or, as in the case of the City of Escondido, some ordinances sough to rely on federal cooperation or resources for immigration verification.[390] Generally, enforcement relies on any individual filing a complaint with the municipality that a resident of a dwelling unit is an unauthorized immigrant.[391] In addition, in some cases, landlords may exercise a "safe harbor" provision and seek to verify a tenant's immigration eligibility even without a complaint.[392] In all cases, tenants unable to comply with immigration eligibility to rent are subject to eviction within days,[393] while landlords who fail to evict must face suspension of their licenses to rent,[394] civil penalties,[395] or, in some cases, criminal sanctions.[396]

---

[385] *See, e.g.*, Villas at Parkside Partners v. The City of Farmers Branch, 577 F. Supp. 2d 858 (N.D. Tex. 2008) (citing to the preamble of Ordinance 2892, which read in part that "the city of Farmers has determined that it is a necessity to adopt . . . immigration certification . . . for apartment complexes to safeguard the public . . . ").

[386] *See, e.g.*, City of Hazleton Ordinance 2006–18, The Illegal Immigration Relief Act Ordinance (IIRA), Sept. 21, 2006, at § 5 and 7.B, *available at* http://clearinghouse.wustl.edu/detail.php?id=5472; Okla. Stat. tit. 21, § 446 (2007); and City of Escondido Ordinance No. 2006-38R, "Establishing Penalties for Harboring of Illegal Aliens in the City of Escondido," § 3, 16E-1, *available at* http://www.ci.escondido.ca.us/immigration/Ord-2006-38R.pdf.

[387] *See, e.g.*, City of Farmers Branch, Ordinance No. 2892, "An Ordinance Amending Chapter 26, Businesses, Article IV Apartment Complex Rental, Mandating a Citizenship Certification Pursuant to 24 CFR 5 et seq . . . ;" § 2, *available at* www.ci.farmers-branch.tx.us/Communication/Ordinance%20No%202892.html; City of Hazleton Ordinance 2006–13, Establishing a Registration Program for Residential Rental Properties . . . " "Tenant Registration Ordinance," Aug. 15, 2006, at 7.b.1.g.

[388] City of Farmer's Branch Ordinance No. 2892, *supra* note 387, at § 2, (2)-(4).

[389] Hazleton Ordinance 2006–13, *supra* note 387, at 7.b.1.g. Another example is Valley Park. *See* Oliveri, *supra* note 382, at 63–64.

[390] City of Escondido Ordinance No. 2006-38R, *supra* note 386, at § 3, 16E-2(c).

[391] Oliveri, *supra* note 382, at 62–63 (describing complaint procedures under ordinances enacted by Hazleton, Cherokee County, Escondido, Riverside, and Valley Park).

[392] *Id.* at 62 (discussing Hazleton's "safe harbor" provision).

[393] *Id.* at 62–63 (describing procedures leading up to eviction in Hazleton, Cherokee County, Riverside, and Valley Park).

[394] *See, e.g.*, Escondido Ordinance No. 2006-38R, *supra* note 386, at § 3, 16E-2(d); Hazleton Ordinance, 2006–18, *supra* note 386, at § 5.B(4).

[395] *See, e.g.*, Hazleton Ordinance, 2006–13, *supra* note 387, at § 10.b ($1,000.00 fine for each occupant without a permit and $100 per day per occupant not evicted). *See also* Oliveri, *supra* note 382, at 63 n.22 (discussing fines imposed by Valley Park, Farmer's Brahcn, Escondido, and Riverside).

[396] *See, e.g.*, Farmers Branch Ordinance No. 2892, *supra* note 387 at § 4 (misdemeanor punishable with a $500 per day per violation).

As of this writing, about seven tenancy ordinances have been challenged in court,[397] with some being dismissed after localities voluntarily amended or withdrew the ordinances.[398] Legal challenges have raised constitutional claims of preemption, due process and equal protection violations, as well claims based on federal civil rights statutes and state laws. To date, with the exception of an Oklahoma federal district court, which denied standing to sue based on their undocumented immigration status,[399] courts have either enjoined localities from enforcing the tenancy ordinances or declared the ordinances unconstitutional. One of the first rulings came from a California federal district court, which enjoined the implementation of the City of Escondido's tenancy ordinance based on preemption and due process concerns.[400] Then, on July 26, 2007 a Pennsylvania district court struck down the Hazleton ordinance and this ruling is awaiting appeal in the Third Circuit.[401] Most recently, in August of 2008, a Texas federal district court made final and permanent[402] an earlier issued injunction against the enforcement of the City for Farmers Branch ordinance based on legitimate concerns over preemption and due process.[403]

On the due process claims, the ordinances have raised significant due process concerns by failing to provide adequate notice and hearings,[404] or for failing to adequately define the offense.[405] On the preemption claims, courts found the ordinances preempted for different reasons in response to the different provisions in the ordinances. Courts disagreed, for example, on whether the respective tenancy ordinances constituted a "regulation of immigration," in violation of *DeCanas'* first prong. The California federal district court said no, because the Escondido ordinance still relied on federal agencies to determine whether individuals could remain in the country.[406] In contrast, the Farmers Branch ordinance adopted Department of Housing and Urban Development immigration classification standards and burdened landlords and city officials with immigration verification functions, prompting the court to declare it a "regulation of immigration."[407] Yet, the Texas court found the Farmers Branch field and conflict preempted, the former because federal legislation already provides for fines and criminal penalties for the harboring of unauthorized immigrants, and the latter, because the ordinance

---

[397] Oliveri, *supra* note 382, at 65–72 (discussing litigation in Hazleton, Pennsylvania, Valley Park, Missouri, Farmers Branch, Texas, Cherokee County, Georgia, Escondido, Texas, Riverside, New Jersey). In addition, tenant plaintiffs filed a complaint in Oklahoma. Nat'l Coal. of Latino Clergy, Inc., et al., v. Henry, 2007 WL 4390650 (N.D. Okla. 2007).

[398] *Id.* at 65, note 38 (discussing the results in Valley Parks, Cherokee Country, Escondido, Riverside, and Farmer's Branch).

[399] *Na'l Coal. of Latino Clergy*, 2007 WL 4390650 at *9.

[400] Garrett v. City of Escondido, 465 F. Supp. 2d 1043 (S.D. Cal. 2006).

[401] Lozano v. City of Hazleton, 496 F. Supp. 2d 477 (M.D. Pa. 2007).

[402] Villas at Parkside Partners v. City of Farmers Branch, 577 F. Supp. 2d 581, 582 (2008).

[403] Villas at Parkside Partners v. City of Farmers Branch, 577 F. Supp. 2d 858, 866–77 (2008)

[404] *City of Escondido*, 465 F. Supp. 2d at 1059; *Lozano*, 496 F. Supp. 2d at 537–38.

[405] *City of Farmers*, 577 F. Supp. 2d at 876–77.

[406] *City of Escondido*, 465 F. Supp. 2d at 1055–56.

[407] Oliveri, *supra* note 382, at 56–68.

sought to rely on federal agencies and/or databases (i.e., the Systematic Alien Verification for Entitlements Program, SAVE), without a clear federal authority to do so.[408] The Hazleton ordinance also included a "harboring" provision, but the court did not address the field preemption issue. Instead, the court declared the Hazleton ordinance "harboring" provisions and tenant registration requirements conflict preempted, because all unauthorized immigrants seeking tenancy are presumed removable and are denied the right to reside in the city without the benefit of a formal immigration hearing during which they may be permitted to remain in the United States.[409] Further, reliance on city employees for immigration verification conflicted with federal immigration procedures, under which immigration judges are the sole and exclusive procedure for determining a person's admissibility and/or removability.[410] Interestingly, the federal harboring provision[411] had not been employed against landlords for renting to the undocumented until recently. In May of 2008, in the first criminal case, federal prosecutors in Kentucky charged four landlords with twenty-four counts of harboring undocumented immigrants and twenty-four counts of encouraging undocumented immigration for renting to unauthorized immigrants.[412] After a Kentucky federal district court ordered that the crimes charged required intent to violate immigration laws,[413] however, a jury found all defendants not guilty of the crimes charged.[414]

In addition to due process and preemption, the Hazleton litigation also considered equal protection and other statutory challenges to the ordinance. The court rejected the equal protection challenge, however, because plaintiffs failed to demonstrate the ordinance's discriminatory intent,[415] and any disparate impact directed at undocumented persons, an unprotected class, was rationally related to the "aim of limiting the social and public safety problems caused by the presence of people without authorization."[416] On the statutory challenges, the court found that

---

[408] *City of Escondido*, 465 F. Supp. 2d at 1056–57. The California federal district court declined to consider the second and third *DeCanas* prongs in light of the court's ruling with respect to the first prong. *City of Farmers*, 577 F. Supp. 2d at 871–74.

[409] *Lozano*, 496 F. Supp. 2d at 531–32.

[410] *Id.* at 533.

[411] 8 U.S.C. § 1324 (a)(1)(A)(iii) (2000) (providing that any person who "knowing or in reckless disregard of the fact that an alien has come to, entered, or remains in the United States in violation of the law, conceals, harbors, or shield from detection, or attempts to conceal, harbor, or shield from detection, such alien in any place, including any building or any means of transportation . . . " shall be punished).

[412] U.S. v. William Jerry Hadden, et al., Criminal Action No. 08-50-KSF, Order of June 17, 2008, on file with author. As of this writing, a separate federal non-criminal complaint against landlords for allegedly renting to undocumented tenants is pending in New Jersey after plaintiffs represented by the Immigration Reform Law Institute filed suit in June of 2008 under federal and state RICO and housing laws. Maribel Delrio-Mocci, et al., v. Connolly Properties, Inc., et al., Civ. Action 2:08-cv-02753-WJM-MF, Complaint, at 2, on file with author.

[413] Hadden, et. al., June 17 Order, *supra* note 412, at 4.

[414] U.S. v. Willam Jerry Hadden, et al., Criminal Action No. 08-5-S-KSf, Verdict, June 27, 2008, on file with author.

[415] *Lozano*, 496 F. Supp. 2d at 540.

[416] *Id.* at 542. For similar reasons, the court also did not find an equal protection violation under the Fair Housing Act. *Id.* at 545–46.

the ordinance violated the right to contract under 42 U.S.C. § 1981 by prohibiting undocumented persons from entering into leases,[417] but failed to find a violation under the state's Landlord and Tenant Act.[418]

At least one locality, the City of Farmers Branch, passed a new housing resolution in response to the adverse litigation in an effort to rid the ordinances of its constitutional problems.[419] The City of Farmers Branch describes Ordinance 2952[420] as different from the old ordinance because it defines who can rent an apartment in reference to federal law and removes from landlords the responsibility to verify the tenant's immigration status.[421] Opponents disagree with this factual characterization or that the changes remedy the law's constitutional flaws, and hope to resolve the issue in recent litigation filed in federal district court.[422]

L.　THE OFFICIAL ENGLISH/ENGLISH-ONLY LAWS

State Official English/English-only laws date back to 1811, when Louisiana became the first state to adopt English as the state's official language.[423] During the early 1900s a few states followed suit, motivated by a growing hostility toward immigrants from southern and eastern Europe.[424] A new wave of similar laws surfaced in the 1980s, spearheaded by organizations such as U.S. English,[425] this time directed toward Latino/a and Asian immigrants.[426] Those efforts lost momentum by the end of the decade, when, in fact, some legislatures even adopted multilingual resolutions.[427] The success of the California's Proposition 187 campaign, however, led many other states to adopt Official English or English-Only laws.[428] More recently, the post-9/11 anti-immigrant climate has also resulted, as of the time of this writing, in at least six more states joining the twenty-four others that already had such laws (for a total of thirty),[429] in addition to twelve more states

---

[417]　*Id.* at 547–48.

[418]　*Id.* at 552–54.

[419]　*City of Farmers*, 577 F. Supp. 2d at 859–60. *See also* Anabelle Garay, *Judge Rules Against Immigration-Related Rental Ban*, The Assoc. Press, Aug. 20, 3008, *available at* www.chron.com/disp/story.mpl/ap/tx/5974403.htm.

[420]　City of Farmers Ordinance 2952, *available at* http://www.ci.farmers-branch.tx.us/Communication/Ordinance%20No%202952.doc.

[421]　Frank Trejo, *Farmers Branch Sued Over Latest Attempt to Ban Illegal Immigrants from Rentals*, The Dallas Morning News, Sept. 4, 2008, *available at* www.dallasnews.com/sharedcontent/dws/news/localnews/stories/DN-fbordinance_04met.ARTO.Central.Edition1.4d7ad65.html.

[422]　*Id.*

[423]　Louisiana Enabling Act, 2 U.S. Stat. 641 § 3 (1811).

[424]　Steven W. Bender, *Consumer Protection for Latinos: Overcoming Language Fraud and English-Only in the Marketplace*, 45 Am. U. L. Rev. 1027, 1046–47 (1996).

[425]　Kenya Hart, *Defending Against a "Death by English": English-Only, Spanish-Only, and A Gringa's suggestions for Community Support of Language Rights*, 14 Berkeley La Raza L.J. 177, 178–79 (2003).

[426]　Bender, *supra* note 424, at 1047.

[427]　*Id.* at 1047–48 (discussing multilingual measures in New Mexico, Oregon and Washington).

[428]　Bender, *supra* note 424, at 1048–49.

[429]　The thirty states and date of adoption of the latest law in that state are as follows: Louisiana

that are considering such legislation.[430]

Official English/English-only laws have been adopted by states as constitutional amendment, as a statute, or through referendum. A more recent trend has only involved the enactment of English-only laws through ordinances by cities and other localities.[431] The language of these laws differs substantially from state to state, which may determine the reach of its implementation as well as its legality, neither of which is settled.[432] There are, for example, several states whose laws simply declare English the "official" state language,[433] with others adding enforcement provisions,[434] while the majority of states specifically bar or limit the use of any language other than English to conduct state business.[435] Certainly, the latter tend to be the most restrictive, but even those laws solely declaring English the official language are not always purely symbolic and have prompted some legislatures or agencies to adopt English-only policies as a direct result of the law's adoption.[436] As well, some state agencies have adopted English-only policies, even in the absence of Official English/English only laws in the state, such as, for example, no Spanish rules in schools.[437] In addition, some states, have adopted special laws barring

---

(1811); Nebraska (1920); Illinois (1969); Massachusetts (1975); Hawaii (1978, note with native Hawaiian); Virgina (1981 & 1996); Kentucky (1984); Indiana (1984); Tennessee (1984); California (1986); Georgia (1986 & 1996); Arkansas (1987); Mississippi (1987); North Carolina (1987); North Dakota (1987); South Carolina (1987); Colorado (1988); Florida (1988); Alabama (1990); Montana (1995); New Hampshire (1995); South Dakota (1995); Wyoming (1996); Alaska (1998); Missouri (1998); Utah (2000); Iowa (2002); Arizona (2006); Idaho (2007); and Kansas (2007). States with Official English Laws, U.S. English, *available at* http://www.us-english.org/view/13 (last visited 7/14/2008).

[430] These states are: Delaware, Maryland, Michigan, Minnesota, New Jersey, Ohio, Oklahoma, Pennsylvania, Rhode Island, Wisconsin, and West Virginia. U.S. English maintains a per state database of existing Official English/English-Only laws or pending bills at http://www.us-english.org/view/364 (last visited July, 14, 2008).

[431] *See* Lupe S. Salinas, *Immigration and Language Rights: The Evolution of Private Racist Attitudes into American Public Law and Policy*, 7 NEV. L.J. 895, 926–927 (stating that at least fifty local governments have adopted or are planning to adopt similar Official English/English-Only ordinances).

[432] Bender, *supra* note 424, at 1049.

[433] These include: Hawaii, Illinois, Indiana, Kentucky, Massachusetts, North Dakota, and Mississippi.

[434] These include: Alabama, Arkansas, California, Colorado, Florida, Missouri, and North Carolina.

[435] These include: Alaska, Kansas, Louisiana, Georgia, Idaho, Iowa, Montana, Nebraska, New Hampshire, Tennessee, South Carolina, South Dakota, Utah, Virginia, and Wyoming.

[436] Such was the case, for example, where the Alabama Department of Public Safety decided to administer the driver's license examination only in English after the state adopted a constitutional amendment declaring English the official language of the state. Alexander v. Sandoval, 532 U.S. 275, 278–79 (2001). *See also* Bender, *supra* note 424, 1054 ("Once enacted, a 'symbolic' Official English law may remain unchallenged on constitutional grounds due to its apparent lack of impact, yet still cause pernicious injury to language minorities.").

[437] This was the case in Kansas, for example, where a school district barred students from speaking Spanish prior to that state's adoption of its English-only law. Rubio v. Turner Unified Sch. Dist. No. 202, 453 F. Supp. 2d 1295 (D. Kan. 2006). Kansas adopted its English-only statute in 2007. KAN. STAT. ANN. § 73–28 (2801–2807). Historically, schools have been used as the language battleground against non-native English speakers with the adoption of strict English-only policies. *See, e.g.,* Juan F. Perea, *Bucando America: Why Integration and Equal Protection Fail to Protect Latinos*, 117 HARV. L. REV. 1420, 1429 (2004) (discussing the no Spanish policies in Puerto Rican schools). *See also* Salinas, *supra* note 431, at 917 (discussing the history of No Spanish Rule in Texas public schools).

bilingualism or multilingualism in specific government functions, such as, for example, a prohibition against bilingual instruction in schools.[438]

Challenges to English-Only laws, policies, or practices have been brought under free speech and equal protection, the latter generally under federal civil rights statutes. In 1923, the U.S. Supreme Court struck down a Nebraska statute that forbade any teacher "to teach any subject to any person in any language other than the English language" for infringing on the free speech right of the teacher to teach and the equivalent right of the students to receive foreign language instruction.[439] Since then, however, the Supreme Court definitive resolution on the merits in these cases has been frustrated by procedural impediments. Such was the case, for example, in Arizona, where the U.S. Supreme Court ultimately vacated a successful First Amendment challenge to Arizona's English-only statute in the Ninth Circuit on the basis that the case became moot when the plaintiff ceased to be a state employee.[440] As well, the U.S. Supreme Court vacated a successful discrimination Title VI of the Civil Rights Act of 1964 challenge against Alabama's English-only driving test policy in the Eleventh Circuit when it held that there is no private right of action under the statute to enforce disparate impact regulations.[441] Despite the Supreme Court actions, these circuit holdings have been instructive to subsequent litigation on the merits or have prompted states to alter their policies. Such was the case, for example, in Alabama, where the Department of Public Safety stopped its English-only administration of driving exams following the Eleventh Circuit ruling.[442] As well, an Arizona Superior Court[443], the Oklahoma[444] and the Alaska Supreme Courts[445] relied on the Ninth Circuit First Amendment holding to find similar free speech, as well as equal protection, violations in Arizona's English-only constitutional amendment.

Free speech challenges have been successful when English-only laws broadly have required use of English by all government officials and employees in all levels of government.[446] Such laws have been found to infringe upon the rights of non-English speaking persons to petition their own government;[447] the speech rights of legislators and other elected official to communicate with their non-English speaking constituents;[448] and the right of employees to comment on

---

[438] Consider, for example, California's Proposition 227, adopted in 1998, which amended the California Education Code to replace bilingual education with immersion programs. California Teachers Ass'n v. Davis, 64 F. Supp. 2d 945, 948 (C.D. Cal. 1999).

[439] Meyer v. Nebraska, 262 U.S. 390 (1923).

[440] Arizonans for Official English v. Arizona, et al, 520 U.S. 43 (1997).

[441] Alexander v. Sandoval, 523 U.S. 275 (2001).

[442] Cole et al., v. Riley, 989 So. 2d 1001 (Ala. 2007).

[443] Ruiz v. Hull, 957 P.2d 984, 988 (Ariz. 1998).

[444] In re Initiative Petition No. 366, 46 P.3d 123, 126 (Okla. 2002).

[445] Alaskans for a Common Language, Inc. v. Kritz, 170 P.3d 183, 200 (Alaska 2007).

[446] *Id.* at 197–99.

[447] *Id.* at 200; *Ruiz v. Hull*, 957 P.2d at 997.

[448] *Kritz*, 170 P.3d at 202–03; *Ruiz v. Hull*, 957 P.2d at 997–98.

matters of public concern.[449] In contrast, public employees' speech on matters of only personal interest is generally not thought to enjoy free speech protection, such that bilingual public employees do not have a *per se* right to communicate to one another in Spanish, unless the employer intended to quash expression on a matter of public concern.[450] Further, these laws have been categorized as implicating more than merely form of speech regulations, since by their nature, they also regulate content, and, as such, these laws have been subjected to strict scrutiny.[451] Still, courts have found that the stated purpose of English-only laws — namely of promoting unity through a common language — is compelling.[452] As such, the problem with the laws has really been their overly-broad scope.[453] More narrowly tailored laws, however, that impose an English-Only requirement in highly specific situation could survive free speech scrutiny under the state-as-speaker doctrine, under which governments have been permitted to control the content, form, and manner of speech under certain circumstances.[454] As well, legislation that relieves states of the responsibility to provide services in languages other than English could also be upheld.[455] What these special circumstances may be is still largely undefined and likely to vary from jurisdiction to jurisdiction.[456]

Equal protection challenges to Official English/English-Only laws have been fewer, in great part, given the difficult task of proving discriminatory intent in the adoption of language restrictions.[457] Moreover, most courts miss or reject the connection between language discrimination and race, and, instead, characterize language discrimination not as racist, but rather as discrimination based on national origin, culture, or worse, as "race-neutral."[458] For example, in *Hernandez v. New York*, a more recent Supreme Court case, to apply equal protection to language discrimination, the Court upheld a prosecutor's use of peremptory strikes against bilingual jurors, reasoning that the uncertainty of the juror's ability to accept the official translation of Spanish-language testimony provided a valid race-neutral reason for the practice.[459] Similarly, the Ninth Circuit rejected that California's

---

[449] *Kritz*, 170 P.3d at 203–04; *Ruiz v. Hull*, 957 P.2d at 997–98.

[450] Maldonado v. City of Altus, 433 F.3d 1294, (10th Cir. 2006), abrogated on other grounds by Metzler v. Fed. Home Bank of Topeka, 464 F.3d 1164 (10th Cir. 2006) (rejecting a free speech challenge to English only policy applying to "all work related and business communications during the work day . . . with the exception of those circumstances where it is necessary and prudent to communicate with [the public]."). *See also Kritz*, 170 P.3d at 203.

[451] *Kritz*, 170 P.3d at 206; *Ruiz v. Hull*, 957 P.2d at 999.

[452] *Kritz*, 170 P.3d at 206–07.

[453] *Id.* at 207–08.

[454] *Id.* at 199.

[455] *Id.* at 208.

[456] In dicta, for example, the Alaska Supreme court included the publication of official government documents and the administration of driving licensing examinations solely in English as permissible under the government-as-speaker doctrine. *Id.* at 199.

[457] *See* Margaret Robertson, Comment, *Abridging the Freedom of Non-English Speech: English-Movement Legislation and the Free Speech Rights of Government Employees*, 2001 B.Y.U. L. REV. 1641, 1645 (2001).

[458] Perea, *supra* note 437, at 1434–35.

[459] 500 U.S. 352 (1991).

prohibition against bilingual education was racially-motivated, even if it dispropor-tionately affected Latinos, finding instead that it represented an effort to remedy a "pedagogically flawed educational system."[460] Some courts, however, have applied strict scrutiny to equal protection challenges to English-Only laws when these laws have also been found to impinge on free speech.[461] Such cases, however, do not address the potential race-based motivation of the legislation or practice.

M. LOCAL IMMIGRATION ENFORCEMENT

Every month, the United States Immigration and Customs Enforcement (ICE) Law Enforcement Support Center (LESC) responds to over 60,000 queries from local law enforcement about foreign nationals they encounter in the course of their daily duties.[462] This trend coincides with the "force multiplier" that has resulted from the involvement of local law enforcement in enforcing federal immigration laws, particularly post-9/11.[463] Local police, state troopers, correctional facilities staff, and other law enforcement assist ICE to detect, arrest, detain, and turn-over foreign nationals who are present in the United States in violation of civil or criminal immigration laws. Local police are not only asking persons detained and/or arrested during their routine police work for their immigration status,[464] but they are, alone or in collaboration with ICE, executing immigration raids,[465] or conducting raids,[466] road blocks,[467] street sweeps, or other investigations that target noncitizens for violations of the federal immigration laws.[468]

---

[460] Valeria v. Davis, 307 F.3d 1036, 1041 (9th Cir. 2002), *rehearing en banc denied by* Valeria v. Davis, 320 F.3d 1014 (9th Cir. 2003).

[461] *See, e.g.*, *Ruiz v. Hull*, 957 P.2d. at 1000–1001.

[462] *287(g) Program: Ensuring the Integrity of America's Border Security System Through Federal-State Partnerships: Before the House Committee on Homeland Security Committee on Management, Integration, and Oversight*, July 27, 2005, at 5 (statement of Paul M. Kilcoyne, Deputy Assistant Director of Investigative Serv. Div., USCIS), http://www.ice.gov/doclib/pi/news/testimonies/050727kilcoyne.pdf.

[463] *See* Kris W. Kobach, *The Quintessential Force Multiplier: The Inherent Authority of Local Police to Make Immigration Arrests*, 69 ALB. L. REV. 179 (2005–2006).

[464] *See, e.g.*, Muelher v. Mena, 544 U.S. 93 (2005) (involving the questioning of detainee about her immigration status during the execution of a gang-related warrant in a home); Farm Labor Org. Comm. v. Ohio State Highway Patrol, 991 F. Supp. 85 (N.D. Ohio 1997) (involving asking occupants in a car during a traffic stop about their immigration status); U.S. v. Esparza-Mendoza, 386 F.3d 953 (10th Cir. 2004) (involving the discovery of an outstanding immigration warrant during a community care-function encounter).

[465] *See, e.g.*, Flores v. Wallas Walla Police, No. CV-06-166-MWL., 2006 WL 2850010 (E.D. Wash. Oct. 2, 2006) (involving local police arrest based on a federal immigration warrant).

[466] *See, e.g.*, U.S. v. Vite-Espinoza, 342 F.3d 462, 464 (6th Cir. 2003) (involving the execution of a home raid with a federal immigration search warrant during a joint federal, state, and local police task force investigating the counterfeiting of immigration and identification documents).

[467] *See, e.g.*, State v. Bolton, 301 P.2d 98 (N.M. App. 1990) (involving participation of ICE agents in state road block).

[468] U.S. v. Perez-Sosa, 164 F.3d 1082 (8th Cir. 1998) (involving state trooper's consensual encounter that lead to probable cause based on report that person was transporting undocumented persons).

To enforce federal immigration laws, local law enforcement agencies rely on either express statutory authority or claim inherent powers. Congress cannot compel local enforcement of immigration laws, but it can, and has, conferred express authority to permit federal local law enforcement officers to voluntarily enforce certain provisions of the Immigration and National Act (INA). To date, Congress has chosen to confer this power only with respect to a limited number of criminal provisions in the INA. These sections are: (1) INA § 274 (Arrest authority to enforce prohibitions against transporting and harboring certain aliens);[469] INA § 276 (Authority to arrest and detain re-entry offenders; that is, previously deported immigrants with a felony conviction who are found present in the United States;[470] and INA § 103(a)(8) (Emergency Powers authorizing "any State or local law enforcement officer" to enforce federal immigration laws in the event the Secretary certifies that "an actual or imminent mass influx of aliens arriving off the coast of the United States, or near a land border" exists.).[471]

In addition, the Illegal Immigration Reform and Immigrant Responsibility Act of 1996 ("IIRAIRA") added Section 287(g) to the INA. This provision authorizes the Secretary of the Department of Homeland Security ("DHS") to enter into agreements, known as Memorandum of Agreement ("MOA"), with state and local law enforcement agencies and to permit trained officers to perform immigration enforcement functions under the supervision of ICE officers, at the expense of the state or political subdivision, and to the extent consistent with state and local law.[472] As of June 2008, 55 local law enforcement agencies, 765 officers in all, in 18 states have entered into such agreements, with approximately 80 more with pending requests.[473] ICE credits the program with identifying more than 60,000 persons since January of 2006, mostly in jails, who are suspected of being in the country without authorization.[474] These MOAs have delegated to local law enforcement nearly all of ICE's enforcement powers, including the authority (1) to interrogate any person believed to be an alien as to his right to be or remain in the United States (INA § 287(a)(1) and 8 C.F.R. § 287.5(a)(1)); (2) to make warrantless arrest for unlawful entry at the border or within the U.S. for reasonable belief that a person has violated the immigration laws (INA § 287(a)(2) and 8 C.F.R. 287.5(c)(1)); (3) to make warrantless arrest for immigration felonies (INA § 287(a)(4) and 8 C.F.R. § 287.5(c)(2)); (4) to serve arrest warrants for immigration violations pursuant to 8 C.F.R. § 287.5(e)(3); (5) to administer oaths or take and consider evidence; book a noncitizen for immigration violations and interview and prepare affidavits and sworn statements from noncitizens (INA § 287(b) and 8 C.F.R. § 287(a)(2)); (6) to prepare charging documents (INA Section 239, 8 C.F.R. § 239.1; INA Section 238; 8 C.F.R. § 238.1; INA Section 241(a)(5), 8 C.F.R. § 241. INA

---

[469] 8 U.S.C § 1324 (2000).

[470] 8 U.S.C. 1256(c) (2000), *amended by* Illegal Immigration Reform and Immigrant Responsibility Act of 1996 (IIRIRA), Pub. L. No. 104-208, § 372(3), 110 Stat. 3009.

[471] 8 U.S.C. § 1103(a)(8) (2000), *amended by* Illegal Immigration Reform and Immigrant Responsibility Act of 1996 (IIRIRA), Pub. L. No. 104-208, § 372(3), 110 Stat. 3009.

[472] 8 U.S.C § 1357(g) (2000).

[473] ICE, Partners, *Delegation of Immigration Authority Section 287(g) Immigration and Nationality Act*, April 18, 2008, www.ice.gov/partners/287g/Section287_g.htm.

[474] *Id.*

Section 235 (b)(1), 8 C.F.R. § 235.3); (7) to issue immigration detainers (8 C.F.R. § 287.7) and I-213 Record of Deportable/Inadmissible Alien, for processing aliens in categories established by ICE supervisors; and (8) to detain and transport arrested aliens to ICE-approved detention facilities (8 C.F.R. § 287.5(c)(6)).[475]

The MOAs greatly differ in terms of their nature and scope. The broadest of them take on all of the eight powers/functions to allow trained local law enforcement officers to enforce both civil and criminal immigration laws.[476] Others also pertain to all types of immigration violations, but may exclude certain of the delegated powers, usually the power to serve immigration warrants or the power to conduct warrantless arrests.[477] Most MOAs, however, restrict the cooperation agreement to assist ICE with criminal investigations in general or to certain types of criminal investigations, such as human trafficking, gangs, drugs, identity theft; to capture "criminal aliens;" or to address counter-terrorism and domestic security needs.[478] There are also quite a few agreements with detention facilities.[479] Thus, the MOA itself defines the scope and limitations of the authority to be designated to the local law enforcement agency, as well as the number of local officers trained and authorized to enforce federal immigration laws. Some MOAs are quite broad and grant all available powers to the local officers, while others are restricted to specific types of enforcement and adopt only some or a few of the enforcement powers. No one is monitoring how these agreements are actually being implemented, however, which raises concern over potential enforcement of immigration laws beyond those expressly spelled out in the agreement.[480]

The newness of these cooperation agreements and the limited resources for their implementation are the reasons why most local law enforcement agencies still rely on claims of inherent authority to make arrests for violations to most federal immigration laws. The question on inherent authority is whether states have the power to make arrests for violations to either criminal or civil federal immigration law or both without express congressional authorization. In practice, local police need not rely on any claimed inherent power to conduct law enforcement encounters with noncitizens. First, courts will frequently treat inquiries, including by local law enforcement agents, into the detainees' immigration status as consensual encounters.[481] Therefore, such inquiries do not constitute a separate immigration-

---

[475] *See, e.g.*, Memorandum of Agreement between the ICE and the Arizona Department of Public Safety, at 2–3, *available at* http://islandia.law.yale.edu/wirc/287g_foia.html.

[476] *See, e.g.*, Memorandum of Agreement between ICE and Washington County, Arkansas, Sheriff's Office, at 2–3, *available at* http://islandia.law.yale.edu/wirc/287g_foia.html.

[477] *See, e.g.*, Memorandum of Agreement between ICE and the State of Alabama at 2(no serving warrants, but power arrest without a warrant), *available at* http://islandia.law.yale.edu/wirc/287g_foia.html.

[478] *See, e.g.*, Memorandum of Agreement between ICE and State of Florida, at 2, (counter-terrorism and domestic security), *available at* http://islandia.law.yale.edu/wirc/287g_foia.html.

[479] *See, e.g.*, Memorandum of Agreement between ICE and the Jail Board of the Prince William — Manassas Regional Adult Detention Center, *available at* http://islandia.law.yale.edu/wirc/287g_foia.html.

[480] American Immigration Lawyers Association, Fact Sheet — "287(g)" Agreements, *available at* http://www.aila.org/search/default.aspx?searchterm=fact%20sheet%20287(g).

[481] *See, e.g.*, Muelher v. Mena, 544 U.S. 93 (2005) (involving the police questioning of a handcuffed

related seizure, at least not under the Fourth Amendment.[482] Second, much of local immigration enforcement occurs in the course of ordinary local policing work; e.g., during traffic stops or in the course of community policing functions or other criminal investigations. Thus, local law enforcement officers generally possess an independent state ground, even if pretextual,[483] for detaining or even arresting the immigrant. Such independent state ground increasingly involves state crimes that adversely affect undocumented noncitizens as applied, including driving without a license[484] or trespassing.[485]

When local police rely on a federal immigration ground to seize or search an immigrant without congressional authorization, there is fierce disagreement on whether they possess an inherent authority to do so. While some defend states' inherent right to make both civil and criminal immigration arrests,[486] others conclude that no such state inherent power exists because the enforcement of immigration law is an exclusive federal power that must be enforced uniformly by one sovereign in light of immigration laws' implications on foreign policy.[487] At a minimum, these scholars maintain that states can enforce federal immigration laws only to the degree that express congressional delegation authorizes.[488] Congress' delegation of some immigration enforcement powers to states, without more, does not put to rest whether states are able to act beyond those delegated powers. The Supreme Court[489] and several federal appellate courts, including the Second,[490] the Fifth,[491] and the Seventh Circuits,[492] have long recognized that state law controls

---

detainee not named in the warrant about her immigration status during the execution of a gang-related warrant in a home).

[482] *Id.* at 102.

[483] Whren v. United States, 517 U.S. 806, 811 (1996) (holding that pretextual motives need not invalidate police conduct that is otherwise justified by reasonable belief that a violation of law has occurred).

[484] Johnson, *Driver's License and Undocumented Immigration, supra* note 352, at 224–228.

[485] *See, e.g.*, Michael R. Boland, Jr., Comment, *No Trespassing: The States, the Supremacy Clause, and the Use of Criminal Trespass Law to Fight Illegal Immigration*, 111 PENN. ST. L. REV. 481 (2006).

[486] *See, e.g.*, Kobach, *The Quintessential Force Multiplier, supra* note 463.

[487] *See, e.g.*, Huyen Pham, *The Inherent Flaws in the Inherent Authority Position: Why Inviting Local Enforcement of Immigration Laws Violates the Constitution*, 31 FLA. ST. U. L. REV. 965, 978–1000 (2004). *See also* Michael J. Wishnie, *State and Local Police Enforcement of Immigration law*, 6 U. PA. J. CONST. L. 1084, 1092–95 (2004). *See, e.g.*, U.S. Senator Jeff Session & Cynthia Hayden, *The Growing Role for State & Local Law Enforcement in the Real of Immigration Law*, 16 STAN. L. & POL'Y REV. 323 (2005).

[488] Wishnie, *State and Local Police Enforcement of Immigration Law, supra* note 487, at 1092–95.

[489] U.S. v. Di Re, 332 U.S. 581, 591 (1948) ("No act of Congress lays down a general federal rule for arrest without a warrant for federal offenses. None purports to supersede state law. And none applies to this arrest which, while for a federal offense, was made by a state officer accompanied by federal officers who had the power to arrest. Therefore the New York statute provides the standard by which this arrest must stand or fall."). *See also* Miller v. U.S., 357 U.S. 301, 305 (1958) (in the circumstance of an arrest for violation of federal law by state peace officers, " . . . the lawfulness of the arrest without warrant is to be determined by reference to state law").

[490] U.S. v. Haskins, 228 F.3d 151, 152 (2d Cir. 2000), *cert denied*, 531 U.S. 1175 (2001).

[491] U.S. v. Bowdach, 561 F.2d 1160, 1168 (5th Cir. 1977).

[492] U.S. v. Janik, 723 F.2d 537, 548 (7th Cir. 1983).

the validity of state law warrantless arrests for federal crimes, even when Congress has not directly authorized it. In the immigration context, however, only three federal circuit courts, the Ninth, the Tenth, and the Fifth, have weighed on the specific question of whether local law enforcement possesses inherent authority to make arrests for immigration offenses which have not been preempted by federal law.[493] A circuit split exists between the Ninth Circuit recognizing an inherent, non-preempted local law enforcement power to make such arrests, but restricting it to violations of federal criminal immigration laws[494] and the Fifth[495] and Tenth Circuits[496] subsequently concluding similarly on the preemption issue, but without drawing the same distinction between civil and criminal offenses. In addition, the Third Circuit recently upheld the legality of a warrantless arrest executed by local law enforcement for an immigration criminal violation without expressly addressing local law enforcement's authority to engage in that type of law enforcement in the first place.[497]

The uncertainty of states' authority to make arrests for immigration violations has been made worse by conflicting opinions on the issue issued by the Office of Legal Counsel (OLC). In 1996, after the Ninth and Fifth, but before the Tenth Circuit opinions, the OLC accepted the Ninth Circuit limits and concluded that state and local police may constitutionally detain or arrest persons who have violated criminal provisions of the INA, subject to state law, but may not do so solely for civil violations.[498] After the September 11 attacks on the World Trade Center and the Pentagon, however, the OLC issued a new 2002 opinion retracting its earlier position and concluding that state and local police possess inherent authority to make arrests for both criminal and civil violations which would render that person removable.[499] The 2002 OLC opinion remained unpublished until July 2005, when it was released after the Second Circuit granted a FOIA request,[500] although allowing some redactions to the opinion.[501]

The distinction between civil and criminal immigration enforcement continues to be relevant not only to the question of inherent local authority to enforce federal immigration laws, but also to the permissible and/or actual scope of MOAs under INA § 287(g). However, in many instances this dichotomy under federal immigra-

---

[493] Sessions and Hayden, *supra* note 487, at 332–336.

[494] Gonzalez v. City of Peoria, 722 F.2d 468, 475–77 (9th Cir. 1983). The Ninth Circuit held, for example, that the enforcement authority must distinguish illegal entry, which is a criminal immigration violation, from illegal presence, such as overstaying a visa, which is only a civil violation. *Id.* at 477.

[495] Lynch v. Cannatella, 810 F.2d 1363, 1366, 1371 (5th Cir. 1987).

[496] *See* U.S. v. Vasquez-Alvarez, 176 F.2d 1294, 1295–1300 (10th Cir. 1999); U.S. v. Santana-Garcia, 264 F.3d 1188, 1190–1194 (10th Cir. 2001).

[497] U.S. v. Laville, 480 F.3d 187 (2007).

[498] Theresa Wynn Roseborough, Deputy Assistant Att'y Gen., Office of Legal Counsel, U.S. Dep't of Justice, *Assistance by State and Local Police in Apprehending Illegal Aliens* (memorandum opinion for U.S. Attorney, S.D. Cal.) (Feb. 5, 1996), http://www.usdoj.gov/olc/immstopo1a.htm.

[499] Sessions & Hayden, *supra* note 487, at 337.

[500] Nat'l Council of La Raza v. Dep't of Justice, 411 F.3d 350 (2nd Cir. 2005).

[501] Dep't of Justice, Office of Legal Counsel, *Non-preemption of the Authority of State and Local Law Enforcement Officials to Arrest for Immigration Violations* (Apr. 3, 2002), *available at* www.aclu.org/FilesPDFs/ACF27DA.pdf.

tion law is unworkable as increasingly what were once treated as purely civil immigration violations now also result in criminal penalties, subject to the discretion of ICE. In fact, there are at least forty-seven criminal provisions in the sections of federal immigration law.[502] In addition, increasingly, ICE is relying on federal identity theft or fraud statutes to charge noncitizens for the possession or use of false, or a third party's, immigration documents or social security numbers.[503] Thus, while ICE is likely to simply institute removal proceedings against most persons apprehended through collaboration with local law enforcement, the potential applicability of a federal crime to any, or most actions, by the noncitizen is likely to conflate civil and criminal immigration enforcement to such degree as to make the distinction untenable.

Another layer of complexity is the relationship between a state's arrest warrant requirement and the inherent authority of local law enforcement to enforce immigration laws. The issue is that since some state statutes authorize warrantless arrests for misdemeanors solely when the crime is committed in the presence of the arresting officer, then warrantless arrests of noncitizens for federal immigration violations, whether for civil or minor crimes, violate this law.[504] Warrantless arrests that do not comply with state law requirements have been challenged in motions to suppress in federal criminal cases when defendants have been arrested by local law enforcement based solely on immigration violations. At least the Third Circuit, however, has denied remedy, even after it recognized that a violation to the state law has occurred. That case involved a member of the Marine Unit of the Virgin Islands Police Department (VIPD), who arrested the defendants and turned them over to ICE to be tried for alien smuggling offenses.[505] The Third Circuit affirmed the district court's finding that the arrest was illegal under state law because it was for a misdemeanor, which required the crime to be committed in the presence of the officer to justify a warrantless arrest.[506] Nevertheless, the Third Circuit reversed the initial grant of a motion to suppress on the basis that "an arrest that is unlawful under state or local law is [not] unreasonable *per se* under the Fourth Amendment."[507] As part of its rationale, the Third Circuit noted that a different holding would lead to the anomaly that the same arrest would be legal so long as local police conduct it jointly with ICE, given that ICE must not comply with the same presence requirement under federal law.[508]

---

[502] Kobach, *The Quintessential Force Multiplier, supra* note 463, at 220, Table 1.

[503] Press Release, U.S. Immigration and Customs Enforcement, Fact Sheet: Frequently Asked Questions About Worksite Enforcement (Oct. 15, 2007), http://www.ice.gov/pi/news/factsheets/worksite.htm.

[504] *See, e.g.,* Cecilia Renn, *State and Local Enforcement of the Criminal Immigration Statutes and The Preemption Doctrine,* 41 U. Miami L. Rev. 999, 1005 (1987).

[505] U.S. v. Laville, 480 F.3d 187 (3rd Cir. 2007).

[506] *Id.* at 191.

[507] *Id.* Other courts grappling with the same issue have simply given the "presence" requirement an extremely broad interpretation, such that an officer who acts quickly in response to an alert to arrest a noncitizen for a misdemeanor immigration violation still meets the "presence" requirement. *See, e.g.,* U.S. v. Daigle, No. CRIM. 05-29-B-W, 2005 WL 1692648 (D. Me. Jul. 19, 2005).

[508] *Laville,* 480 F.3d at 193.

Not all localities have heeded the call to enforce immigration laws. At the same time that localities and/or local law enforcement agencies are engaging in the enforcement of immigration laws, other local entities, including state and city governments, have adopted "sanctuary policies" restricting local law enforcement collaboration with ICE on the detection and detention of unauthorized immigrants. Most of the largest cities in the United States today have some variation of such sanctuary policies.[509] In all, about forty-nine cities and towns and about three states have some type of sanctuary law.[510] Such sanctuary policies are generally of three types: (1) they limit inquiries into a person's immigration status (don't ask); (2) they limit arrests or detention for violation of immigration law (don't enforce); and (3) they limit provision to federal authorities of immigration status information (don't tell).[511] Localities promulgate these policies through various means, including by adopting city council resolutions, municipal ordinances, mayoral executive orders, and police chief memoranda.[512] The issues that arise with sanctuary policies are whether they are preempted by federal immigration law, as well as whether they are invalidated or made moot by conflicting local policies that seek greater local enforcement of immigration laws, including through adoption of INA § 287(g) agreements.

Several potential conflicts exist between sanctuary policies and federal law. Some suggest, for example, that sanctuary policies violate the federal anti-harboring provision.[513] The resolution is likely to depend on the federal court that decides the issue given that circuit courts interpret the harboring provision quite differently.[514] The issue might turn on whether courts view "sanctuary policies" as active concealment, which has been required by the Sixth Circuit, as opposed to most other circuits (the Second, the Fifth, the Eighth, and the Ninth) that include in the definition of harboring the provision of services and the mere omission to report that person to immigration authorities.[515] From a political perspective, however, such challenge is unlikely.[516]

---

[509] These include: Baltimore, Chicago, Denver, Detroit, Houston, Los Angeles, Minneapolis, New York City, Philadelphia, San Francisco, Seattle, and Washington, D.C. Orde F. Kittrie, *Federalism, Deportation, and Crime: Victims Afraid to Call the Police*, 91 Iowa L. Rev. 1449, 1466–74 (2006).

[510] Nat'l Immigration Law Ctr., Annotated Chart of Laws, Resolutions, and Policies, Instituted Across the U.S. Protecting Residents from Local Enforcement of Immigration Laws (2004).

[511] Kittrie, *supra* note 509, at 1455. *See also* Huyen Pham, *The Constitutional Right Not to Cooperate? Local Sovereignty and the Federal Immigration Power*, 74 U. Cin. L. Rev. 1373, 1388–91 (2006) (describing the characteristics of sanctuary policies as follows: no discrimination; no enforcement civil immigration laws; no inquiry into citizenship status; and no notifying federal immigration authorities).

[512] *Id.* at 1474.

[513] This provision imposes criminal penalties on "[a]ny person who . . . knowing or in reckless disregard of the fact that an alien has come to, entered, or remains in the United States in violation of law, conceals, harbors, or shields from detection, or attempts to conceal, harbor, or shield from detection, such alien in nay place, including any building or any means of transportation." 8 U.S.C. § 1324(a)(1)(A)(iii) (2000).

[514] Kittrie, *supra* note 509, at 1493–95.

[515] *See id.*

[516] *Id.* at 1495.

Congress, however, passed two laws in 1996 explicitly to counter local sanctuary policies.[517] The first, Section 1373, mandates that "a Federal, State, or local government entity or official may not prohibit, or in any way restrict, any government entity or official from sending to, or receiving from, [ICE] information regarding the citizenship or immigration status, lawful or unlawful, of any individual."[518] Section 1644 includes much of the same language as section 1373, and states that "no State or local government entity may be prohibited, or in any way restricted, from sending to or receiving from the Immigration and Naturalization Service information regarding the immigration status, lawful or unlawful, of an alien in the United States."[519] Essentially, the broader provision, Section 1373, prohibits a government entity or official from restricting disclosure of immigration status to ICE. Section 1644 only prohibits the proscription as applied to government entities. In 1999, the Second Circuit decided the only case to date, *City of New York v. United States*[520] that assesses the application of these provisions to sanctuary policies. In that case, the Giuliani administration sought to enjoin the 1996 laws arguing that these laws violated the Tenth Amendment by forcing New York City to collaborate with federal immigration enforcement and the Guarantee Clause of the Constitution by interfering with the City's chosen form of government.[521] The Second Circuit disagreed and found that the federal provisions preempted the City's sanctuary policy which proscribed voluntary cooperation with ICE by local police in immigration enforcement. Essentially, "don't tell" sanctuary policies are vulnerable to preemption challenges in light of the Second Circuit opinion.[522] In contrast, "don't ask" and "don't enforce" sanctuary policies are not vulnerable to preemption.[523] Federal prohibition of such sanctuary policies, moreover, would run afoul of the anti-commandeering doctrine, under which the federal government could not require that state and local officials engage in immigration law enforcement.[524]

Local protection against immigration enforcement by local police responds to the strong policy objective of building trust and cooperation between immigrant communities and police.[525] The effectiveness of these so-called sanctuary policies, however, is weak for several reasons, including that violations to these policies by local police are not enforced, and individual immigrants can not prevent their removal once they have been turned over to ICE.[526]

---

[517] Pham, *The Constitutional Right Not to Cooperate?*, *supra* note 511, at 1384–85.

[518] 8 U.S.C. § 1373 (2000).

[519] 8 U.S.C. § 1644 (2000).

[520] 179 F.3d 29 (2nd Cir. 1999).

[521] *Id.* at 33.

[522] Kittrie, *supra* note 509, at 1498. *See also* Pham, *The Constitutional Right Not to Cooperate?*, *supra* note 511, at 1391–95.

[523] Kittrie, *supra* note 509, at 1499.

[524] *Id.* at 1487–93, 1499–1500.

[525] *Id.* at 1475–80.

[526] *Id.* at 1480–84.

N.   FAMILY LAW

Some states are denying couples marriage licenses or are considering legislation to do so on the basis of the immigration status of one or both persons.[527] Sometimes, the inability of at least one of the marriage license petitioners to produce certain types of identification only available to citizens, such as social security numbers or driver's licenses, becomes the basis for the denial.[528] In some states, however, existing practice or pending legislation does or would require proof of legal immigration status for the issuance of driver's licenses.[529] At least one federal district court in Pennsylvania enjoined the practice of requiring proof of legal immigration status to apply for a marriage license as unconstitutional based on a substantive due process and equal protection grounds.[530] In doing so, the court applied strict scrutiny analysis also to the equal protection challenge irrespective of whether the classification created a suspect class.[531]

Immigration status is also influencing the way that courts resolve traditional family matters, including determinations of divorce and child custody.[532] Professor David B. Thronson has documented that courts openly, or at times underhandedly, discriminate against undocumented immigrants to deny them family-based funda-mental rights, including custody; or manipulate family proceeding outcomes purportedly to achieve certain immigration results, such as in divorce proceedings that could affect the legal status of the immigrant spouse; or simply tailor the decision to accommodate the immigration circumstances that follow from the family law decision, such as awarding alimony payments to a non-working spouse who is

---

[527] Christopher D. Nelson, Comment, *Protecting the Immigrant Family: The Misguided Policies, Practices and Proposed Legislation Regarding Marriage License Issuance*, 4 U. St. Thomas L.J. 643, 644–656 (documenting marriage licenses denials and similar proposed legislation in Pennsylvania, Minnesota, Virginia, Tennessee, and Connecticut). Family law is not the only substantive area where immigration status has influenced local laws or local judicial decision-making. For instance, legislatures are increasingly considering immigration status to restrict discretionary leniency in criminal proceed-ings, such as probation or alternative punishment schemes or bail generally available to criminal defendants. *See, e.g.*, Ruvulcaba v. State, 143 P.3d 468, 470 (Nev. 2006) (considering undocumented status of defendant to deny him probation); Arizona 2006 Proposition 100 (amending the state Constitution to prohibit bail for illegal aliens who are charged with a serious felony (defined in statute as those of classes one, two, three and four, as well as aggravated DUI), *available at* http://www.azsos.gov/election/2006/ Info/pubpamphlet/english/Prop100.htm. As well, some localities have relied on immigration status to seek to deny or restrict certain tort remedies that are still available to citizens. Arizona 2006 Proposition 102 (amending the state Constitution to prohibit a person who is in Arizona in violation of federal immigration law from being awarded punitive damages in any civil lawsuit filed in the state. Eligibility of illegal immigrants to file for compensatory damages is not affected. Referred by Legislature (SCR 1001, 2006 Reg. Sess.), *available at* http://www.azsos.gov/election/2006/Info/pubpamphlet/english/ Prop102.htm.

[528] Nelson, *supra* note 527, at 645–651.

[529] *Id.* at 656.

[530] Buck v. Stankovic, 485 F. Supp. 2d 576, 582 (M.D. Pa. 2007) (citing Zablocki v. Redhail, 434 U.S. 374, 386 (1978) to affirm the fundamental character of the right to marry).

[531] *Id.* at 583.

[532] *See, e.g.*, David B. Thronson, *Custody and Contradictions: Exploring Immigration law as Federal Family Law in the Context of Child Custody*, 59 Hastings L.J. 453 (2008); David B. Thronson, *Of Borders and Best Interests: Examining the Experiences of Undocumented Immigrants in U.S. Family Courts*, 11 Tex. Hisp. J. L. & Pol'y 45 (2005).

ineligible to work under immigration law.[533] Thronson cautions against this approach based on either its implications on equality or other family-based fundamental rights or on the erroneous assumption that judges make based on their poor understanding of complex immigration laws to make decisions.[534] Rather, Thronson advocates for a transformation of immigration law in ways that more fully recognize the "mixed status" immigration composition of U.S. families and the detrimental implications of immigration enforcement on the parent-child relationship.[535]

O. CONCLUSION

States have always engaged in the regulation of immigrants. The exponential increase in local laws pertaining to immigrants and immigration,[536] a trend likely to continue in the face of failed immigration reform policies and continued migration, questions the premise, at least as a descriptive matter, that immigration control is the sole responsibility of the federal government. Normatively, however, immigration scholars cannot agree on whether this is a good or a bad trend. Further, immigration scholars (and judges) have been criticized for selectively choosing either federalism or national uniformity values based on their personal outcome preference, rather than a true commitment to a robust debate over the novel questions raised by immigration federalism.[537] Unfortunately, those immigration scholars, who have engaged in a more "functional account" (as opposed to outcome-determinative critique) of this new immigration federalism are still principally relying on selective anecdotal examples to support their functional value-claims, where the empirical evidence is either absent or mixed.[538] Thus, much more empirical research is needed to resolve the tensions created by localized immigration control.

One claimed benefit of decentralization of immigration powers is that it encourages experimentation and innovation.[539] Here, the claim is that such experimentation and innovation, by accommodating and reflecting a greater variety of view on citizens, could actually mitigate pressure on the federal government to enact legislation that reflects extreme positions at either end of the political spectrum.[540] Another cited benefit is that local experimentation can lead to quick

---

[533] Thronson, *Of Borders and Bests Interests, supra* note 532, at 54–71.

[534] *Id.*

[535] *See generally,* David B. Thronson, *Choiceless Choices: Deportation and the Parent-Child Relationship,* 6 NEV. L.J. 1165 (2006).

[536] Consider, for example, that as March 31, 2008, at least 1,106 immigration-related bills had been in 44 states. Overview of State Legislation Related to Immigrants and Immigration, January-March 2003, National Congress of State Legislatures, Immigrant Policy Project, April 24, 2008, *available at* http://www.ncsl.org/programs/immig/immigreportapril2008.htm.

[537] Clare Huntington, *The Constitutional Dimension of Immigration Federalism,* 61 VAND. L. REV. 787, 830 (2008).

[538] *See, e.g.,* Huntington, *supra* note 537; Rodriguez, *supra* note 16.

[539] Huntington, *supra* note 537, at 827.

[540] *Id.* at 831. The other side of the coin, that quenching decentralization through preemption, could lead to more restrictive immigration policies has been advanced by Peter Spiro with his "steam-valve"

lessons for states — i.e., a mass exit of workers from states — which could lead towns to repeal their anti-immigrant laws.[541] In short, there is no basis to favor uniformity over experimentation, at least not if the reason is that one level of government will better protect the rights of citizens over another.[542] In contrast, those who favor preemption view a strong national government as serving an interest in uniformity, as well as fairness and equality, values that matter greatly in matters implicating foreign affairs.[543] The difficulty here is that the argument for uniformity has the most salience in areas of traditional immigration law — that is, the regulation of who comes in, must leave, or can become a full member of the U.S. society. This argument loses its value, however, the more immigration law touches on areas of traditional state concern, such as access to education or the distribution of state public resources.[544]

A second claimed federalism benefit is that competition among localities enhances efficiency and effectiveness; when local governments respond to local preferences the possibility of exit encourages efficiency.[545] As an example of economic efficiency, scholars cite the possibility that decentralized experimentation could fine-tune the connection between immigration and labor, such that localities could tailor their immigration supply to respond to the local demand for labor.[546] In contrast, those who favor preemption also claim that economic interests are better served by a strong national government, including by safeguarding against race-to-the-bottom phenomena.[547] Going back to the example of labor, the free movement of workers could be essential to a robust, globalized economy, and states could thwart immigration policy if immigrants allowed into the country are not welcomed by individual states.[548]

A third claimed benefit of decentralization of immigration laws is that it furthers political accountability and participation when the interests of smaller groups are satisfied and more individuals are able to participate.[549] In contrast, those who favor more centralized decision-making express worry over parochialism, as well as increasing negative externalities in the decision-making process.[550] Here, however, more empirical data is necessary to examine whether the national or local governments are better placed to offer greater political accountability to immigrants. This argument is further complicated by the fact that noncitizens generally cannot vote in either federal or local elections. Rather than electoral participation, therefore, data that must be examined includes non-electoral noncitizen participa-

---

metaphor. *See* Spiro, *supra* note 228 and accompanying text.

[541] Huntington, *supra* note 537, at 832. *See also* Matthew Parlow, *A Localist's Case for Decentralizing Immigration Policy*, 84 Denv. U. L. Rev. 1061, 1069–73 (2007).

[542] Huntinton, *supra* note 537, at 831.

[543] *Id.* at 828–29.

[544] *Id.*

[545] *Id.* at 828.

[546] *Id.* at 833.

[547] *Id.* at 829.

[548] *Id.* at 834.

[549] *Id.* at 828.

[550] *Id.* at 835.

tion, as well as the effectiveness of immigrant civil rights groups vs. anti-immigrant groups to influence local vs. national politics.

Decentralization is finally credited with better promoting both states' rights and individual rights insofar as states act as a check against national power.[551] In direct conflict with this claim, some place greater faith that the national government is better placed to protect the fundamental rights of immigrants against vociferous, nativist local groups.[552] Here too, proponents on either side of the argument suffer from selectively pointing out to pro- or anti-immigrant local legislation to prove their claims.[553] What is true, however, is that the different legal regimes governing the application of equal protection or due process doctrines as between the federal (i.e., rational review irrespective of classification and/or existence of a fundamental right) and state governments (strict scrutiny at least for suspect or quasi-suspect classifications and for fundamental rights) could mean greater judicial accountability at the local levels.[554] Whether judicial accountability could be sufficient to turn the anti-immigrant tide, or whether doctrines would eventually shift to resemble those at the federal level remains to be seen.

---

[551] *Id.* at 828.

[552] *Id.* at 829.

[553] *See, e.g.,* Rodríguez, *supra* note 16, at 569–70.

[554] Aldana, *supra* note 243, at 306.

Chapter 5

IMMIGRATION ACTORS: FEDERAL AGENCIES AND COURTS

A. THE POLITICAL BRANCHES OF THE FEDERAL GOVERNMENT IN REGULATING IMMIGRATION

1. Congress

It has long been recognized that Congress has plenary power over immigration matters. This power is derived from various provisions of the Constitution.[1] The plenary power of Congress also is based on the sovereign power of the federal government; and it is shared by both the legislative and executive branches. The plenary power of Congress includes the authority to decide the requirements for

---

[1] Art. I, § 8, Cl. 4 grants Congress the power to establish a uniform rule of naturalization; Art. I, § 8, cl. 3 grants Congress the power "to regulate Commerce with foreign Nations;" Art. 1, § 9, cl. 1 the Migration and Importation clause; and Art. § 8, cl. 11 the War Power clause.

entry into, the conditions for remaining in and the grounds for removal from the United States. This power is quite broad and under this doctrine the actions of the federal government in immigration matters largely are immune from constitutional scrutiny. The plenary power doctrine is discussed in detail in Chapter 3.

2.   The President and Executive Branch

The Executive Branch and the President, as the head of the branch, share immigration power with Congress. The President's power is derived from statutory authority, the delegated power of Congress, and the plenary power doctrine. The President of the United States directs several aspects of immigration law. The President directs the operation of the entire executive branch using the appointments power, with the advice and consent of the Senate, of Article II of the U.S. Constitution.[2] This includes all of the federal departments and agencies involved in immigration matters: the Department of State, the Department of Homeland Security, the Department of Justice, the Department of Labor and the Department of Health and Human Services.

The President establishes the number of refugees who can be admitted into the United States in each fiscal year under INA § 207(b). The President also may issue a proclamation to suspend the entry of all noncitizens or any group of noncitizens if their entry is deemed to be "detrimental to the interests of the United States" under INA § 212(f). This proclamation authority has been used by Presidents to further foreign policy goals of the U.S. In 1996 President Clinton banned the entry of noncitizens and their immediate family members from Burma who participated in political repression in that country.[3] Similar proclamations were issued by both President George W. Bush in 2001 and President Clinton in 1999 relating to the Western Balkans, including Bosnia-Herzegovena and Kosovo.[4]

The most criticized use of the presidential proclamation authority involves the interdiction of vessels containing migrants from Haiti and, later from Cuba.[5] Presidential proclamations to interdict vessels in international waters and return the noncitizen passengers were issued by President Reagan in 1981 and by President Bush in 1991 and 1992.[6] Those seeking asylum were forced to raise their claims in offshore refugee camps.[7] Chapter 11 covers refugees and asylum in the United States.

---

[2] Art. II, Sec. 2, Cl. 2.

[3] 61 Fed. Reg. 52,233 (1996) (The notice stated that "[t]he regime has failed to enter into serious dialogue with the democratic opposition and representatives of the country's ethnic minorities, has failed to move toward achieving national reconciliation, and has failed to meet internationally recognized standards of human rights.").

[4] 2001 Pres. Proc. No. 7452, 66 Fed. Reg 34,775 (June 29, 2001); 1999 Pres. Proc. No. 7249, 64 Fed. Reg. 62561 (1999).

[5] *See* Harold Koh, *Americas Offshore Refugee Camps*, 29 U. RICH. L. REV. 139 (1995).

[6] 1981 Pres. Proc. No. 4865, 46 Fed. Reg. 48,107 (1981); Executive Order No. 12801, 57 Fed Reg. 2313. The Attorney General also has authority, in urgent circumstances, to direct state and local officials to respond to "an actual or imminent mass influx of aliens arriving off the coast" under INA § 103(a)(10).

[7] This policy was upheld in *Jean v. Nelson*, 472 U.S. 846 (1985).

B. THE ADMINISTRATIVE STRUCTURE OF IMMIGRATION LAW

1.   A Brief History of the Rise and Fall of the INS

Immigration functions are managed by a number of executive branch departments. Today, the Department of Homeland Security directs the majority of immigration functions. The Department of Labor, the Department of State and Department of Justice also play an important role in the immigration system. Before 2003, most of the immigration functions were within the Department of Justice under the aegis of the Immigration and Naturalization Service (INS).

Federal regulation of immigration matters began during the late 1800s. The first one hundred years of U.S. history, (1776–1875), was a period of open immigration. Immigrants were welcomed and admitted to the U.S. with minimal restrictions. States managed the admission processing during this time period. In 1891, the Superintendent of Immigration within the Department of Treasury began managing federal immigration matters, and took over this role from the states. The immigration function was transferred to the Department of Commerce and Labor in 1903. When a new Department of Labor was created in 1913, it housed two separate operations: a Bureau of Immigration; and a Bureau of Naturalization. In 1933, these two bureaus were consolidated into the Immigration and Naturalization Service.

In 1940, the Attorney General of the Justice Department was assigned the role of supervising immigration matters including the INS which was transferred from the Department of Labor. The Attorney General directed both the INS and the Executive Office of Immigration Review. Other immigration functions were housed in the Department of Labor as well as the State Department. The INS managed both the enforcement of immigration law, and the processing of immigration benefits. The INS enforcement function included inspection of arriving passengers, prosecution at administrative hearings, border patrol, and detention of noncitizens. The INS immigration benefits function included the adjudication of petitions for naturalization, as well as other services relating to noncitizens in the U.S. on a temporary basis or as lawful permanent residents.

The INS headquarters office in Washington D.C. directed a vast system of local district offices, regional adjudication centers and Border Patrol operations. This headquarters office managed operations, budget, policy-setting, the drafting of regulations, and liaising with Congress and other agencies. Local district offices operated throughout the United States, and regional offices primarily adjudicated immigration benefits applications. The district offices were divided into units relating to both enforcement functions, such as investigations, as well as adjudication functions such as the review of initial petitions for naturalization. Enforcement in the interior of the country also was managed through the district offices to apprehend undocumented noncitizens in the United States, investigate employers who employed unauthorized workers, and detain noncitizens pending hearings before Immigration Judges. Asylum adjudicators were located in separate offices. Asylum adjudication was moved from the district offices in 1990 to ensure trained asylum officers adjudicated applications.

The Border Patrol also operated within the INS structure. The Border Patrol managed enforcement along the land borders of the United States with Mexico and Canada. The Border Patrol was separate from the district offices and its principal focus was to prevent unauthorized entry into the United States, including the apprehension of undocumented noncitizens near the border. The district offices oversaw more than 350 ports of entry into the United States at airport terminals and land border crossings. Immigration officers admitted noncitizens into the United States after an inspection; generally, a brief series of questions about the noncitizen's plans in the U.S.

The INS also shared the management of immigration matters with other agencies within the Executive Branch, and DHS continues to work with these agencies today. The State Department was and continues to be involved in the issuance of visas in its embassies and consulate offices located worldwide. The Department of Labor was and continues to be involved in assessing labor needs for some lawful permanent residents and some temporary workers.

Criticism of the large bureaucracy for immigration decisionmaking has been ongoing since the 1940s when the INS was consolidated within the Justice Department. The 1997 Report of the Commission on Immigration Reform suggested a reorganization of the immigration system.[8] The primary issues had been the dual mission of the INS (service and enforcement), the overlap of authority with other agencies within the federal government, and management.[9] In the 1990s, the INS had failing information management systems leading to significant backlogs in processing applications for immigration benefits. Regulatory and legislative attempts to reorganize the immigration benefits functions often created more inefficiencies. The enforcement function of the INS also was burdened as Congress increased funding in the late 1990s to enhance border protection. Many proposals were debated including whether to split apart the enforcement and immigration benefits functions entirely or whether a Cabinet level agency should be established.[10]

The impetus for change increased dramatically after September 11, 2001. Congress adopted a comprehensive reorganization of all national security functions, including immigration, as part of the Homeland Security Act of 2002 which was signed into law on November 25, 2002.[11]

---

[8] U.S. Commission on Immigration Reform, Becoming An American: Immigration and Immigrant Policy 148–169 (Report to Congress 1997).

[9] Papademetriou, Aleinikoff, & Meyers, *Reorganizing the U.S. Immigration Function: Toward a New Framework for Accountability*, Carnegie Endowment for International Peace (1998); *See also* Papademetriou, Aleinikoff, & Meyers, *Reorganizing the Immigration Function: Toward a New Framework For Accountability*, 75 INTER. REL. 501 (Apr. 13, 1998); Gene McNary, *No Authority, No Accountability: Don't Abolish the INS, Make It An Independent Agency*, 74 INTER. REL. 1281 (Aug. 25, 1997); David A. Martin, *Immigration Policy and The Homeland Security Act Reorganization: An Early Agenda for Practice Improvements*, 17 INTER. REL. 601 (April 28, 2003).

[10] *Id.*

[11] Homeland Security Act of 2002 (HSA), Pub. L. No. 107-296, 116 Stat. 2135 (2002).

2.   Department of Homeland Security

The Homeland Security Act of 2002 (HSA) consolidated twenty-two federal agencies dealing with immigration and national security into one Executive Branch cabinet level department. HSA abolished the INS, and the immigration function formerly within U.S. Department of Justice was moved almost entirely to the new Department of Homeland Security (DHS). Congress restructured all of the immigration functions and mandated a complete separation of immigration benefits services from the enforcement operations. One immigration function has remained with the Justice Department: the Executive Office of Immigration Review.

As of March 1, 2003, the service and benefit functions of the INS transitioned into the Department of Homeland Security as the Bureau of Citizenship and Immigration Services (USCIS).[12] The two immigration enforcement units within DHS that began operations on March 1, 2003 are the Bureau of Immigration and Customs Enforcement (ICE) and the Bureau of Customs and Border Protection (CBP). ICE primarily deals with interior immigration enforcement operations, and CBP deals with border enforcement. This massive overhaul of all homeland security functions has required extensive, on-going oversight. For example, the Government Accounting Office has issued numerous reports since 2003.[13]

The authority of the Secretary of Homeland Security relating to immigration matters is identified in INA § 103. HSA consolidated the authority to issue regulations, and administer and enforce the INA, under the Department of Homeland Security. HSA also transfers authority from the State Department to DHS for final decisions regarding the issuance of visas, as discussed below.

a.   Citizenship and Immigration Services — USCIS

USCIS began conducting the service and benefit functions of the INS on March 1, 2003.[14] It is responsible for the administration of immigration and naturalization adjudication functions, and establishing the policies and priorities for immigration services.[15] USCIS has oversight of approximately 250 offices and fifteen thousand employees. USCIS is responsible for all of the adjudications formerly within the INS including decisions by immigration examiners, asylum officers, regional service centers and application support centers.

There is an appellate review body for some benefits decisions located within USCIS: the Administrative Appeals (AAO). The AAO formerly existed within the INS to provide appellate review of decisions by regional offices regarding petitions for nonimmigrant status and permanent residence primarily under the

---

[12] HSA § 451; 69 Fed. Reg. 60,937 (Oct. 13, 2004) (changing the name).

[13] *See, e.g. Department of Homeland Security: Progress Report on Implementation of Mission and Management Functions* (GAO-07-454, August 2007); *Department of Homeland Security: Progress Report on Implementation of Mission and Management Functions* (GAO-07-454, August 2007) (noting over 400 GAO reports on DHS major departmental programs in 2003–2007).

[14] The Director of USCIS reports directly to the Deputy Secretary of DHS.

[15] U.S. Citizenship and Immigration Services, www.uscis.gov/portal/site/uscis/aboutuscis. USCIS adjudications include immigrant visa petitions, naturalization petitions, asylum and refugee applications, service center adjudications, and all other adjudications performed by the former INS.

employment-based immigrant categories.[16] Many other decisions are appealed to the AAO.[17] Other decisions are reviewed by Immigration Judges within the Executive Office of Immigration Review (EOIR). Generally, appeals of removal orders are heard by the Board of Immigration Appeals (BIA). The regulations determine which decisions must be appealed to the BIA or to the AAO.[18] The EOIR is discussed in greater detail below.

The Office of the Secretary of DHS includes the Citizenship and Immigration Services Ombudsman. This position is designed to resolve individual and employer problems with USCIS, as well as increase efficiencies in administering citizenship and immigration services.

b.   Immigration and Customs Enforcement — ICE

ICE's immigration enforcement activities include: apprehending, detaining, and removing criminal and undocumented noncitizens; disrupting and dismantling organized smuggling of humans and contraband as well as human trafficking; investigating and prosecuting those who engage in benefit and document fraud; blocking and removing employers' access to undocumented workers; and enforcing compliance with programs to monitor visitors.[19] ICE takes custody of noncitizens detained during removal proceedings, and serves as one of the largest jailors in the nation.[20] ICE is the largest investigative branch of DHS. It is composed of special agents of the former INS and Customs Office, INS detention and deportation officers, the INS immigration litigation section, including trial attorneys representing the government in immigration court, and Federal Protective Service employees.

ICE includes the Office of Detention and Removal Operations (DRO). It transports noncitizens, manages their custody while waiting for cases to be processed, and removes unauthorized noncitizens from the U.S. The DRO also is responsible for conducting reviews and annual inspections to ensure compliance with National Detention Standards adopted by the former INS.[21] Most ICE detainees are held in state and local jails with general population inmates.[22] As of 2007, detainees also were held in eight ICE-owned service processing centers, six contract detention facilities operated by private contractors specifically for ICE detainees, nineteen contract detention facilities for juveniles, and three contract

---

[16] Some family sponsored petitions can be appealed to the AAO including battered spouse and children self-petitions. *See* 8 C.F.R. § 103.1(f).

[17] 8 C.F.R. §§ 103.1, 103.3, 103.4 (certification of a case is possible to higher officials).

[18] 8 C.F.R. §§ 1003.3(b), 103.3.

[19] *See* 34 INTER. REL. 2137 (Sept. 17, 2007) (discussing GAO report entitled *Department of Homeland Security: Progress Report on Implementation of Mission and Management Functions* (GAO-07-454, August 2007)).

[20] *See* ALIENIKOFF, MARTIN, MOTOMURA & FULLERTON, IMMIGRATION AND CITIZENSHIP, PROCESS AND POLICY 272 (6th ed. 2008).

[21] The Natural Detention Standards were adopted by INS in 2000 and are based on standards from the American Correctional Association.

[22] ICE detainees are held in approximately 300 state and local jails according to the GAO. *See infra* note 19.

family detention facilities. The detention of noncitizens has increased dramatically in recent years. The total number of noncitizens in removal proceedings who spend some time in detention per year increased from 95,214 in 2001 to 283,115 in 2006.[23]

c.   Customs and Border Protection — CBP

CBP is responsible for border enforcement including the inspection of goods, all cargo and agricultural products, and the screening of noncitizens requesting admission. CBP officers review passports and visas at all ports of entry into the U.S. (both at airports and land borders), and at a select number of prescreening posts in Canada and the Caribbean. CBP officers inspect and admit as many as 400–500 million persons each year, including both noncitizens and U.S. citizens.[24] CPB is responsible for the 5,525 mile border with Canada and a 1,989 mile border with Mexico. CPB's border security activities also include: detecting and preventing terrorists and terrorist weapons from entering the U.S.; interdicting illegal drugs and other contraband; and apprehending individuals who attempt to enter the U.S. without inspection within a reasonable distance from the border.[25] A Director of Shared Services was established to coordinate resources of the immigration benefits and enforcement functions within USCIS, CBP and ICE.

CPB oversees a large-scale effort to increase border security using enhanced technology, the construction of fencing along the Mexican border and other measures. A 2007 GAO Report found that CPB had achieved modest progress on border security as a result of delays in the implementation of many new programs.[26] These efforts have faced strong opposition from local property owners along the border, immigrant rights advocates, and non-governmental organizations. According to the GAO and Army Corps of Engineers, as of August 2008, ninety-seven landowners along the border refused to sell their land, and the cost of the fencing was $7.5 million per mile.[27] This is covered in Chapter 13.

---

[23] *Alien Detention Standards: Telephone Access Problems Were Pervasive at Detention Facilities; Other Deficiencies Did Not Show a Pattern of Noncompliance*, GAO-07-875 (July 6, 2007) (In FY 2007, ICE received $953 million in funding for detention services).

[24] *See* ALIENIKOFF, MARTIN, MOTOMURA AND FULLERTON, *supra* note 20. In fiscal year 2005, approximately 400,000 noncitizens were denied admission into the U.S. and either withdrew their applications for admission upon receiving CBP permission or were placed in removal proceedings to determine eligibility for admission. *See* TRAC, Immigration Inspections When Arriving in the U.S. (2006), *available at* http://trac.syr.edu/immigration/reports/142.

[25] *See* 34 INTER. REL. 2137 (Sept. 17, 2007) (discussing GAO report entitled *Department of Homeland Security: Progress Report on Implementation of Mission and Management Functions* (GAO-07-454, August 2007)).

[26] *Department of Homeland Security: Progress Report on Implementation of Mission and Management Functions* (GAO-07-454, August 17, 2007).

[27] *Noteworthy* 85 INTER. REL. 2800 (Oct. 20, 2008).

3.   Department of State

The Department of State Bureau of Consular Affairs historically has managed the overseas process for noncitizens prior to entry into the United States. This process involves millions of visas issued annually.[28] State Department consular officers in over 200 offices located worldwide perform this initial screening function.[29] DHS monitors the issuance of visas by consular officers and now has veto authority due to perceived weaknesses in the visa issuance system before September 11, 2001.[30] The authority of the Secretary of the State Department relating to immigration matters is in INA § 104.

Consular officers review applications for visas to enter the U.S. and issue visas allowing a noncitizen to present herself for entry into the U.S. under INA §§ 221 and 222. Consular officers have extraordinarily broad discretion in the issuance of visas.[31] Their visa decisions are subject to random review procedures by supervising officers at the consular post overseas. In any case where the denial of a visa raises a question of law, a consular officer's decision can be reviewed by a visa review board in Washington D.C.[32] There are noncitizens who are exempt from the visa requirement, however most noncitizens must apply for a visa prior to entry.

The visa does not guarantee admission into the United States. It is merely the first step in the process, and provides the required documentation for airline travel to the U.S.[33] Generally, a noncitizen must present her visa in order to request admission into the U.S. at a border port of entry. The various procedures for admission into the U.S. are covered in Chapter 10. The regulations for the State Department are set forth in 22 C.F.R. Parts 40–53 and instructions relating to the code are published in the Foreign Affairs Manual (FAM).

The Visa Office of the State Department also tracks the annual number of immigrant visas issued under INA § 201 through the publication of a monthly visa bulletin.[34] The National Visa Center (NVC) of the State Department manages the immigrant visa application process prior to the final immigrant visa interview at a

---

[28] Since 2001, over 5 million visas have been issued annually. Dep't of State Reports of Visa Office, *available at* http://travel.state.gov.

[29] INA § 101(a)(9) defines consular officer to include any consular, diplomatic or other officer or employee designated under the regulations for the purpose of issuing immigrant or nonimmigrant visas, or adjudicating nationality of individuals outside of the U.S.

[30] DHS may not require a consular officer to issue a visa if the consular officer has refused.

[31] The doctrine of consular non-reviewability is covered in Chapter 10.

[32] INA § 104(a)(1). This lack of review by the Secretary of State, the chief officer of the department, is designed to insulate consular officers from political pressure in visa issuance decisions. The random review of decisions began in 2006 to ensure professionalism and uniformity of decisions. *See* 22 C.F.R. §§ 41.113(i), 41.121(c), 71 Fed. Reg. 37494 (2006).

[33] *See* INA § 273 (it is unlawful for any person, including any transportation company, to bring to the U.S. any alien who does not have a valid passport and unexpired visa, if a visa is required).

[34] The monthly visa bulletin charts immigrant visa availability by immigrant visa category under INA § 203, and, in some cases by country based on the per-country limit calculations under INA § 202. *See* U.S. Dept. of State, Visas, *available at* http://travel.state.gov/visa/frvi/bulletin/bulletin.

consular post overseas. These issues relating to immigrant visas are covered in Chapter 5.

The State Department has other units dealing with immigration matters. The Bureau of Population, Refugee and Migration (PRM) manages key parts of the refugee admissions process including assistance to refugees in overseas camps, and the admission of refugees into the U.S. through refugee resettlement programs. The Bureau of Educational and Cultural Affairs (ECA) manages programs to enhance the mutual understanding among nations. It supervises exchange programs that send U.S. citizens overseas, as well as the numerous programs that sponsor noncitizen exchange visitors to the U.S. as nonimmigrant visitors. Noncitizens who participate in these programs are known as J-1 Exchange Visitors and they are admitted as nonimmigrants under INA § 101(a)(15)(J). Nonimmigrant visas and related matters are covered in Chapter 8.

4. Department of Justice

The Justice Department retained the EOIR after the HSA reorganization of immigration functions. The EOIR contains three units: the Office of the Chief Immigration Judge; the BIA; and the Office of the Chief Administrative Hearing Office (OCAHO). A Director of the EOIR is appointed by the Attorney General and manages all three units.[35] The Attorney General has direct authority over the EOIR.

All of the EOIR units hold hearings to make decisions on individual immigration matters. The Office of the Chief Immigration Judge supervises the immigration judges located throughout the U.S. Appeals of the decisions by immigration judges are heard by the BIA. Trial attorneys, now within ICE, represent the government in these hearings. Both the BIA and Immigration Judges are discussed in more detail below.

The OCAHO consists of administrative law judges who hold hearings under the employer sanctions regime established by the Immigration Reform and Control Act of 1986 (IRCA).[36] IRCA prohibits the knowing hire of unauthorized noncitizens and imposes employer sanctions. A major concern when IRCA was enacted was the possibility of employer discrimination based on national origin or citizenship status when verifying employment eligibility of workers. A second office created by IRCA, the Office of Special Council for Immigration Related Unfair Employment Practices, ensures compliance with IRCA's antidiscrimination provisions. This office is part of the Civil Rights Division of the Justice Department.

a. Immigration Courts

Many decisions about the removal of noncitizens from the United States are made immigration judges who are defined in INA § 101(b)(4). Immigration Judges must be attorneys and they are appointed by the Attorney General.[37] The INA

---

[35] 8 C.F.R. § 1003.0.

[36] Immigration Reform and Control Act (IRCA), Pub. L. 99-603, 100 Stat. 3359 (1986).

[37] 8 C.F.R. § 1003.10 (immigration judges are attorneys appointed by the Attorney General as

states that immigration judges shall conduct proceedings for deciding the inadmissibility or deportability of a noncitizen under INA § 240(a)(1).

Before 1956, decisions about immigration matters initially were made by inspections officials not lawyers. Many were concerned about this dual authority of inspections officials to make initial decisions at the point of entry into the U.S., as well conduct hearings after this initial decision. However, neither the Administrative Procedures Act nor the Constitution require the separation of enforcement and adjudication functions.[38] The Department of Justice gradually imposed a separation of these functions. The HSA is the first statute to recognize the EOIR as a separate entity within the Justice Department. The HSA effectively has created a statutory separation of functions by housing the EOIR in the Justice Department and moving the rest of the INS functions to DHS.

Before HSA, the Justice Department used its regulatory authority to organize immigration court functions. As of 1956, some officers were assigned to present evidence on behalf of the government and other officers were assigned to render decisions. The INS required special inquiry officers to have law degrees in 1956. In 1962, the Justice Department established a staff of trial attorneys to represent the government. The special inquiry officers were designated as immigration judges in 1973 by regulation. In 1983, the Department of Justice established the Executive Office of Immigration Review to separate immigration judges from the INS entirely. This change was designed to ensure neutral and independent decision-making by immigration judges.[39]

The corp of immigration judges has increased significantly in the last twenty years from 85 judges in 1992 to over 200 judges in 2006 who are located in 54 immigration courts throughout the U.S. The judges' have very large caseloads of removal proceedings, bond and detention determinations, and motions decisions. One on-going problem is the lack of secretarial and other administrative support; judges frequently issue long oral opinions from the bench because of this problem. Federal courts have highlighted the problems faced by immigration judges in terms of caseload and support, and some have criticized the of job performance of immigration judges.[40] Numerous media reports about abusive immigration judges were published in 2005 and 2006.[41] In response, Attorney General Gonzalez

---

administrative judges who conduct specified classes of proceedings including removal proceedings under INA § 240).

[38] *See* Wong Yang Sung v. McGrath, 339 U.S. 33 (1950) (holding that the separation of enforcement and adjudication functions was required by the Administrative Procedures Act (APA)). In response to *Wong Yang Sung v. McGrath*, Congress amended the APA to specifically exempt immigration proceedings from this APA requirement.

[39] Uniform rules of practice were adopted by the EOIR in 1987.

[40] Judge Richard Posner has been a strong critic of the bureaucratic decision-making process within the EOIR. *See, e.g.*, Benslimane v. Gonzales, 430 F.3d 828, 829–30 (7th Cir. 2005); Iao v. Gonzales, 400 F.3d 530, 534–535 (7th Cir. 2005); Mekhael v. Mukasey, 509 F.3d 326, 328 (7th Cir. 2007); Kadia v. Gonzales, 501 F.3d 817, 821 (7th Cir. 2007).

[41] *See, e.g.*, Adam Liptak, *Courts Criticize Judges Handling of Asylum Cases*, N.Y. TIMES, Dec. 26, 2005, at A1; Pamela A. MacLean, *Immigration Judges Come Under Fire*, NAT'L L.J., Jan. 30, 2006, at 1; Errol Lewis, *It's Time for U.S. to Bridle Unfair Judges*, NEW YORK DAILY NEWS, Aug. 15, 2006, *available at* http://www.nydailynews.com/archives/opinions/2006/08/15/2006-08-

ordered a comprehensive review of immigration judge and BIA operations in January 2006. The Justice Department introduced a 22-point reform plan in August 2006 including better training of Immigration Judges and EOIR staff, a formal code of conduct, and regular performance evaluations of immigrations judges.[42] The reform plan also addressed BIA operations and this aspect of the plan is discussed below.

A 2008 report of the effectiveness of these 2006 reforms discovered that many reform measures were not implemented. The report stated that the EOIR failed to conduct performance evaluations of immigration judges, or review the summary appeals procedures of the BIA and had not implemented a code of judicial conduct.[43] Widespread criticism of EOIR operations continues. In 2008, the Justice Department also was criticized for using political affiliation and other improper factors to appoint immigration judges.[44]

The Attorney General, under the Homeland Security Act of 2002 amendments, retains authority with respect to all questions of law in immigration matters.[45] However, the authority to issue regulations, administer and enforce the INA is assigned to DHS. The Attorney General also exercises final review authority over BIA decisions upon a request by the BIA or the Secretary of DHS, and when the A.G. chooses to exercise this authority in a particular case.[46]

b.   Board of Immigration Appeals

The BIA rules on appeals from decisions of immigration judges. A right of appeal to the BIA exists for noncitizens found removable by immigration judges under 8 C.F.R. 1003.1(b). The BIA has appellate jurisdiction to hear final decisions of immigration judges in most removal cases and cancellation of removal applications, decisions involving fines and penalties, waivers of inadmissibility for nonimmigrants, decisions relating to bond and detention in removal, and asylum decisions.

Some decisions by USCIS immigration examiners can be appealed to the BIA. The appeal of some DHS decisions are heard by the AAO of the DHS (discussed

---

15_it_s_time_for_u_s__to_bridle.html (last visited Jan. 22, 2009) (describing immigration judges as "incompetents, bigots and bullies").

[42] *See Attorney General Outlines Reforms for Immigration Courts*, 83 INTER. REL. 1725 (Aug. 14, 2006).

[43] The report was produced by the Transactional Records Access Clearinghouse (TRAC) supported by Syracuse University and the Carnegie Foundation and found that six of the twenty-two initiatives were not completed including performance evaluations for judges and BIA members, the completion of a code of judicial conduct, and a final rule limiting BIA affirmances without opinion. *See* Spencer S. Hsu and Carrie Johnson, *Effort on Immigration Courts Faulted*, Washington Post A06 (Mon. Sept. 8, 2008). Pamela A. Maclean, *DOJ Falls Short on Promised Immigration Judge Reform, Report Says*, *available at* http://www.law.com (Sept. 17, 2008).

[44] A DOJ Inspector General Report found that internet searches to determine political campaign contributions, voting patterns and affiliations were part of the screening process for immigration judges. *See* Spencer S. Hsu and Carrie Johnson, *Effort on Immigration Courts Faulted*, WASHINGTON POST, Sept. 8, 2008, at A8.

[45] Homeland Security Act of 2002 Amendments, P.L. 108-7, 117 Stat. 11 (Feb. 20, 2003).

[46] 8 C.F.R. § 1003.1(h).

above) and are not reviewed in immigration court. Immigration Judges may consider matters when a removal hearing begins if an application is renewed before the Immigration Judge. In that case, the application is considered *de novo*; for example, an asylum application or an adjustment of status application.[47]

An appeals process for immigration decisions regarding admission and removal has existed since 1921 when the Department of Labor managed immigration matters. The transfer of immigration functions to the Justice Department in 1940 included the transfer of the appeals board. It was named, at that time, the Board of Immigration Appeals and it operated independently from the INS. Decisions by the BIA were made by panels of three judges. As the caseload of appeals increased over the years so did the composition of the BIA from its original five members. In 1987, BIA membership increased to fifteen members and later to twenty-one members. The backlog of cases continued to grow and the BIA was the subject of a great deal of criticism. In 1999, the Board adopted a streamlining mechanism to lessen the backlog of appeals.[48] A key feature of this streamlined procedure allowed one BIA member to review an appeal.

In 2002 further efforts to decrease the appeals backlog were adopted under Attorney General Ashcroft. Currently, the regulations permit review by a single member of the BIA in a majority of cases.[49] A single member of the BIA may summarily dismiss an appeal, affirm an immigration judge's decision without an opinion, or issue an abbreviated opinion. These summary procedures have been upheld.[50] The Attorney General exercises final review authority over BIA decisions, although this authority is rarely exercised. A case may be referred to the Attorney General for a final decision when the Chairman of the BIA or a majority of the BIA members decide a case should be referred, when the Attorney General decides to take a case on referral, or when the Secretary of DHS requests a referral.[51]

The substantial criticisms about immigration adjudications in 2005 and 2006 included the BIA streamlined procedures.[52] Proposed BIA reforms included increasing the size to 15 permanent judges and using temporary members assigned to the BIA for periods of up to one year. The 2006 Justice Department 22-point reform plan dealing with immigration judges and other EOIR reforms also included reform of the affirmance without opinion procedure to reduce the number

---

[47] 8 C.F.R. § 208.14(c)(1) (asylum applications); 8 C.F.R. § 245.2(a)(5)(ii) (adjustment of status applications to LPR).

[48] Single member review was permissible upon a finding "that the result reached in the decision under review was correct; that any errors in the decision under review were harmless or nonmaterial." 64 Fed. Reg. 56,135, 56,136 (Oct. 18, 1999).

[49] 67 Fed. Reg. 54,878 (Aug. 26, 2002).

[50] *See, e.g.*, Zhang v. U.S. Dept of Justice, 362 F.3d 155, 157 (2d Cir. 2004) (finding summary affirmance by one BIA member does not deprive an asylum applicant of due process and citing cases from the 10th, 8th, 9th, 7th, 11th, 5th and 1st circuits also upholding the streamlining provisions).

[51] 8 C.F.R. § 1003.1(h).

[52] *See e.g.*, *Overwhelmed Circuit Courts Lashing Out at the BIA and Selected Immigration Judges: Is Streamlining to Blame*, 48 INTER. REL. 2005 (2005) (in the period ending March 2003 petitions for review for immigration cases filed in federal courts had increased 379%).

of cases subject to this form of review. The 2008 TRAC report found that a final rule had not been implemented.[53]

5.   Department of Labor

The Department of Labor (DOL) is involved in immigration functions in three different areas. A substantial part of DOL's immigration function occurs in the labor certification process for many employment-based immigrants.[54] Labor certification from the DOL is required before the USCIS will process these immigrant visa petitions. Employers seeking to hire a noncitizen in these employment-based categories must first obtain DOL certification that there are no workers who are able, willing, qualified or available for a position and that the employment of the noncitizen will not adversely affect the wages and working conditions of U.S. workers similarly employed. Denials of certification are reviewed within DOL by the Board of Alien Labor Certification Appeals (BALCA). Three-judge panels of administrative law judges review these cases. The labor certification process is covered in Chapter 7.

A second area where DOL has a significant immigration function is the employment of certain temporary workers. DOL oversees the initial process for nonimmigrants who enter as specialty occupational temporary workers or as other lower-skilled temporary workers.[55] Employers of these temporary workers, who remain in the U.S. for an extended period of time, must first process an application the DOL before filing a nonimmigrant visa petition with USCIS. Nonimmigrants are covered in Chapter 8.

The third area of DOL immigration activity relates to the employment authorization of both citizens and noncitizens. The Wage and Hour Division monitors and investigates employer compliance with immigration control recordkeeping requirements, and minimum wage and maximum hour laws.

6.   Department of Health and Human Services — Office of Refugee Resettlement

The Homeland Security Act moved the jurisdiction over unaccompanied minors to the Office of Refugee Resettlement within the Department of Health and Human Services. The Office of Refugee Resettlement (ORR) provides assistance to refugees who are resettled in the U.S. under INA § 412. ORR administers domestic refugee resettlement programs that provide assistance to new refugees including employment training, English language training, and financial assistance. ORR has the responsibility for the care and custody of unaccompanied minors in immigration proceedings.

---

[53] *See* Spencer S. Hsu and Carrie Johnson, *Effort on Immigration Courts Faulted*, WASHINGTON POST, Sept. 8, 2008, at A6.

[54] INA §§ 212(a)(5)(A), 203(b)(2) (advanced degree professionals or persons of exceptional ability), 203(b)(3) (skilled workers, professionals and other workers).

[55] INA §§ 101(a)(15)(H)(i)(b) (requires a labor condition application to be filed with the DOL for H-1B specialty occupational workers); 101(a)(15)(H)(ii), 20 C.F.R. §§ 651.10, 655 (requiring temporary labor certification for H-2A agricultural workers and H-2B seasonal workers).

C. THE JUDICIAL ROLE IN IMMIGRATION LAW

The judicial review of immigration decisions is not widely available due primarily to 1996 and 2005 amendments to the INA.[56] Despite this, federal courts have an important role in the review of removal orders and other immigration decisions. Federal courts do have jurisdiction using a writ of habeas corpus for persons "in custody in violation of the Constitution or laws . . . of the United States."[57] The availability of a writ of habeas corpus is guaranteed by the U.S. Constitution in the Suspension Clause of Article I.[58] Noncitizens seeking habeas review must be in physical custody and petitions for writs of habeas corpus traditionally were a primary source of jurisdiction for the review of agency decisions.[59] The 1952 initial codification of immigration laws did not have a judicial review provision for removal orders. After the passage of the INA, however, declaratory and injunctive relief to challenge an exclusion or deportation became available under the Administrative Procedures Act.[60]

For nearly 35 years, until 1996 amendments to the INA, the path for judicial review was defined by former INA § 106. In 1961, Congress enacted § 106 establishing a grant of judicial review in U.S. Courts of Appeal for final deportation orders and establishing an explicit habeas corpus review provision. Under the 1996 IIRIRA amendment to the INA, Congress adopted a new scheme for judicial review found in INA § 242, and eliminated § 106.

The 1996 IIRIRA legislation retains judicial review in U.S. Courts of Appeal by petition for review. Judicial review of many immigration decisions is barred through jurisdiction-stripping provisions.[61] Entire categories of cases are barred from judicial review under these amendments including those dealing with certain criminal offenses.[62] In addition, many of the numerous discretionary decisions by DHS and immigration judges are not subject to judicial review, including inadmissibility waivers, relief from removal, and the adjustment of status to permanent resident. Congress adopted extremely deferential standards in the new judicial

---

[56] REAL ID Act of 2005, Title B of the Emergency Supplemental Appropriations Act for Defense, The Global War on Terror, and Tsunami Relief, 2005, 109 Pub. L. No. 12, 110 Stat. 231 (2005); Illegal Immigration Reform and Immigrant Responsibility Act, Pub. L. No. 104-208, 110 Stat. 3009 (1996) (IIRIRA); Antiterrorism and Effective Death Penalty Act, Pub. L. No. 104-132, 100 Stat. 1214 (1996) (AEDPA).

[57] 28 U.S.C.A. § 2241(c)(3)(2008).

[58] U.S. CONST., art. I, Sec. 9, Cl.2 states "The privilege of the writ of habeas corpus shall not be suspended, unless when in Cases of Rebellion or Invasion the public Safety may require it."

[59] See Heikkila v. Barber, 345 U.S. 229 (1953) (habeas corpus was the only way of challenging deportation under the INA at that time).

[60] See Brownell v. Shung, 352 U.S. 180 (1956) (exclusion); Schnaughnessy v. Pedreiro, 349 U.S. 48 (1955) (deportation). The Administrative Procedures Act, 5 U.S.C.A. § 701 et. seq. generally permitting judicial review of final administrative decisions unless specifically precluded from review or some other mechanism for review is provided by statute. Review under the APA eliminated the requirement of physical custody of the noncitizen required in habeas corpus review.

[61] INA § 242(a)(2).

[62] Antiterrorism and Effective Death Penalty Act, Pub. L. No. 104-132, 100 Stat. 1214 (1996) (AEDPA).

review scheme as well.[63] This is discussed in greater detail in Chapter 6.

Federal courts of appeal have jurisdiction to review constitutional claims and questions of law such as applying the wrong standard.[64] As noted above, after 1996, district courts continued to have jurisdiction to decide habeas petitions, including those brought by criminal noncitizens.[65] The 2005 REAL ID Act revised the jurisdiction of federal courts and requires U.S. Courts of Appeal to function as the sole means for judicial review, thus eliminating district court habeas corpus jurisdiction in nearly all cases.[66] Now, petitions of review of removal orders must be filed with federal courts of appeal and jurisdiction extends only to questions of law or constitutional claims. Further, the federal courts of appeal must decide cases based on the administrative record alone without any factual development.[67] This is covered in Chapter 6.

---

[63] *See, e.g.,* INA § 242(b)(4)(D) (asylum decisions by the Attorney General [through Immigration Judges and the BIA] are "conclusive unless manifestly contrary to the law and an abuse of discretion).

[64] *See* Liu v. INS, 508 F.3d 716, 720–22 (2d Cir. 2007); Jean-Pierre v. U.S. Att'y Gen., 500 F.3d 1315, 1320–22 (11th Cir. 2007).

[65] INS v. St. Cyr, 533 U.S. 289 (2001) (bar on judicial review in courts of appeal in INA § 242 does not preclude habeas corpus petitions in district courts).

[66] INA § 242(a)(2)(D) (added by the REAL ID Act) (eliminating habeas corpus jurisdiction, mandamus jurisdiction, and jurisdiction under the All Writs Act, 28 U.S.C. § 1651, but permitting district court jurisdiction over nationality claims).

[67] INA § 241(a)(1).

Chapter 6

JUDICIAL REVIEW

SYNOPSIS

A.   A BRIEF INTRODUCTION TO THE CURRENT CONTROVERSY OVER JUDICIAL REVIEW

Generally speaking, the judiciary has taken a hands-off approach to the decisions of Congress and the President on immigration matters. The extreme deference of the courts has a long history, beginning in earnest with the Supreme Court deferring to congressional enactment of a series laws excluding Chinese immigrants from U.S. shores in the late 1800s, which were discussed in Chapters 2 and 3.[1] Most recently, the unwillingness of the judiciary to intervene in immigration matters could be seen in the courts' deferential responses to the various measures directed at Arab and Muslim noncitizens in the "war on terror" that followed the tragic events of September 11, 2001.[2]

Two major doctrines discussed in this Chapter require judicial deference to the Executive and Legislative Branches of the federal government on immigration matters and have indelibly shaped modern immigration law. The twin doctrines of deference weave themselves throughout the immigration case law, often serving as background influences on judicial decisions even if not expressly mentioned by the courts:

1.   **The "Plenary Power" Doctrine**: This doctrine requires the courts to defer to the substantive — and, at times, procedural — immigration decisions of Congress and the Executive Branch, which the Supreme Court has declared to possess "plenary power" over immigration. The doctrine has shielded Congress's determinations about which noncitizens to admit to, and exclude and deport from, the United States.

2.   ***Chevron* Deference**: The courts ordinarily defer to the work of administrative agencies, which the Supreme Court's evolving administrative law

---

[1] *See, e.g.*, Chae Chin Ping v. United States (*The Chinese Exclusion Case*), 130 U.S. 581, 609 (1889) (rejecting a constitutional challenge to racial discrimination in the Chinese Exclusion Act and emphasizing that courts lack power to review exercise of congressional "plenary power" over immigration).

[2] *See, e.g.*, Roudnahal v. Ridge, 310 F. Supp. 2d 884, 892 (E.D. Ohio 2003) (rejecting constitutional challenge to special registration program directed primarily at Arab and Muslim noncitizens); Kandamar v. Gonzales, 464 F.3d 65 (1st Cir. 2006) (rejecting argument that evidence obtained through registration should be suppressed based on constitutional violations); Ali v. Gonzales, 440 F.3d 678, 681–82 (5th Cir. 2006) (finding, in removal case, that special registration did not violate Equal Protection guarantee). At times, the Supreme Court has been willing to intervene to halt the excesses of the Bush administration's various security measures. *See, e.g.*, Boumediene v. Bush, 128 S. Ct. 2229 (2008) (holding that detainees had right to seek writ of habeas corpus to challenge their detention at Guantánamo Bay, Cuba); Hamdan v. Rumsfeld, 548 U.S. 557 (2006) (holding that military tribunals created by Bush administration violated the law); Hamdi v. Rumsfeld, 542 U.S. 507 (2004) (ruling that U.S. citizen held as "enemy combatant" had right to judicial determination of the propriety of that classification); *see also* Rumsfeld v. Padilla, 542 U.S. 426 (2004) (finding that court in which action was filed lacked jurisdiction over U.S. citizen defendant to entertain challenge to indefinite detention of U.S. citizen classified as "enemy combatant").

Some precedent arguably supported the targeted nature of the latest security measures. In the Iranian hostage crisis during President Carter's administration, the courts upheld special immigration regulations applicable only to Iranian students. *See* Ghaelian v. INS, 717 F.2d 950, 953 (6th Cir. 1983); Nademi v. INS, 679 F.2d 811 (10th Cir. 1982); Dastmalchi v. INS, 660 F.2d 880, 892 (3d Cir. 1981); Malek-Marzban v. INS, 653 F.2d 113 (4th Cir. 1981); Narenji v. Civiletti, 617 F.2d 745 (D.C. Cir. 1979), *cert. denied*, 446 U.S. 957 (1980).

jurisprudence — especially what is known as *Chevron* deference[3] — increased in both breadth and depth in the decades closing the twentieth century.[4]

As discussed later in this Chapter, Congress itself has imposed significant limits on judicial review of immigration decisions, especially in immigration reform laws passed in 1996 and 2005.[5] These limits — often derided as "court stripping" provisions — have provoked considerable controversy and much commentary.[6] Congress intended the reforms, generally speaking, to eliminate perceived excessive delays and "frivolous" appeals. As amended by Congress, the Immigration and Nationality Act now limits judicial review of immigration decisions in a variety of significant ways. New immigration reform proposals almost invariably include provisions that would further restrict judicial review.

A combination of recent developments has made judicial review even more controversial. In 2002, then-Attorney General John Ashcroft reduced the number of members sitting on the Board of Immigration Appeals (BIA), the sole appellate body in the immigration adjudicatory bureaucracy from 23 to 11, expedited the review of cases, and increased the numbers of summary dispositions by the Board.[7] In reducing the size of the Board, "[t]he axe fell entirely on the most 'liberal' members of the BIA, as measured by percentages of their rulings in favor of noncitizens."[8]

---

[3] *See* Chevron USA, Inc. v. Natural Resources Defense Council, Inc., 467 U.S. 837 (1984).

[4] Parts of this chapter are adapted from Kevin R. Johnson, *Protecting National Security Through More Liberal Admission of Immigrants*, 2007 U. CHI. LEGAL. F. 157.

[5] For critical appraisal of the restrictions on judicial review, *see* Professor Lenni Benson's scholarship, *You Can't Get There From Here: Managing Judicial Review of Immigration Cases*, 2007 U. CHI. LEGAL F. 405 [hereinafter Benson, *You Can't Get There From Here*]; *Making Paper Dolls: How Restrictions on Judicial Review and the Administrative Process Increase Immigration Cases in the Federal Courts*, 51 N.Y. L. SCH. L. REV. 37 (2006/07) [hereinafter Benson, *Making Paper Dolls*]; *The New World of Judicial Review of Removal Orders*, 12 GEO. IMMIGR. L. REV. 233 (1998) [hereinafter Benson, *The New World*]; *Back to the Future: Congress Attacks the Right to Judicial Review of Immigration Proceedings*, 29 CONN. L. REV. 1411 (1996) [hereinafter Benson, *Back to the Future*]. For a basic summary of current law on judicial review, *see* Gerald Seipp, *Federal Court Jurisdiction to Review Immigration Decisions: A Tug of War Between Three Branches*, IMMIGRATION BRIEFINGS (Apr. 2007).

[6] *See, e.g.*, Symposium, *Immigration Appeals and Judicial Review*, 55 CATH. U.L. REV. 905 (2006).

[7] *See* Stephen H. Legomsky, *Deportation and the War on Independence*, 91 CORNELL L. REV. 369, 375 (2006). *See generally* Susan Burkhardt, *The Contours of Conformity: Behavioral Decision Theory and the Pitfalls of the 2002 Reforms of Immigration Procedures*, 19 GEO. IMMIGR. L.J. 35, 80–83 (2004) (analyzing critically BIA reforms, including shortening deadlines for deciding appeals, reducing size of BIA, eliminating oral arguments, and summary dispositions of appeals); Michael M. Hethmon, *Tsunami Watch on the Coast of Bohemia: The BIA Streamlining Reforms and Judicial Review of Expulsion Orders*, 35 CATH. U. L. REV. 999 (2006) (reviewing impact of BIA streamlining immigration cases in court of appeals); Shruti Rana, *"Streamlining" the Rule of Law: How the Department of Justice is Undermining Judicial Review of Agency Action*, 2009 U. ILL. L. REV. (forthcoming) (to the same effect). For analysis of court decisions analyzing various streamlining measures, *see* Drew Marksity, Comment and Casenote, *Judicial Review of Agency Action: Federal Appellate Review of Board of Immigration Appeals Streamlining Decisions*, 76 U. CIN. L. REV. 645 (2008).

[8] Legomsky, *supra* note 7, at 376 (footnote omitted).

The result of the so-called "streamlining" has been nothing less than a surge of appeals brought by noncitizens ordered removed from the country in the federal courts, which responded by instituting special rules for reviewing immigration cases.[9] At the same time, as will be discussed later in this Chapter, the federal courts have repeatedly criticized the poor quality of the BIA and immigration court decisions.

1. Criticism of Immigration Adjudication by the Immigration Bureaucracy

Until the spring of 2003, the Immigration & Naturalization Service (INS), which was part of the U.S. Department of Justice, was the primary federal agency in charge of administering and enforcing the Immigration and Nationality Act (INA). For decades, immigrant rights advocates contended that the INS over-emphasized enforcement and failed to fairly and efficiently provide the service to immigrants that was mandated by the law (including, but not limited to, fair and timely processing of visa applications and naturalization petitions). Reviewing courts frequently rejected INS policies and decisions, which suggested structural problems within the agency. One empirical study of judicial review of immigration decisions concluded that successful impact lawsuits — class actions designed to remedy perceived patterns and practices of law-breaking, "coupled with Congress' failure to overturn their results, provide a clear signal that some important aspects of the INS' administrative performance are deeply and systematically flawed."[10]

Since the spring of 2003, the Department of Homeland Security (DHS) has been primarily charged with enforcing the immigration laws.[11] The jury remains out about whether the DHS is any better than the INS at serving the needs of noncitizens and ensuring border enforcement and homeland security. Some commentators contend that the situation now is worse with the DHS mission of ensuring "homeland security" and fighting terrorism, with immigration enforcement dominating any other immigration objectives.[12] Immigration enforcement actions of agencies in DHS are frequent subjects of criticism.[13]

---

[9] *See, e.g.*, Lenni Benson, *Introduction to Seeking Review: Immigration Law and Federal Court Jurisdiction Symposium*, 51 N.Y.L. SCH. L. REV. 3, 5 (2006/07) (discussing surge of immigration appeals and special rules adopted in Second Circuit designed to improve efficiency of deciding appeals).

[10] Peter H. Schuck & Theodore H. Wang, *Continuity and Change: Patterns of Immigration Litigation in the Courts, 1979–1990*, 45 STAN. L. REV. 115, 177 (1992).

[11] *See* Homeland Security Act, Pub. L. No. 107-296, 116 Stat. 2135 (2002).

[12] For criticism of the Department of Homeland Security handling of immigration matters, *see* M. Isabel Medina, *Immigrants and the Government's War on Terrorism*, 6 CENTENNIAL 225, 230–32 (2006); Victor Romero, *Race, Immigration, and the Department of Homeland Security*, 19 ST. JOHN'S J. LEGAL. COMMENT. 51 (2004). *See generally* Thomas W. Donovan, *The American Immigration System: A Structural Change With a Different Emphasis*, 17 INT'L. J. REFUGEE L. 574 (2005) (recognizing added complaints of inefficiency arising from shift of immigration authority from Immigration & Naturalization Service to Department of Homeland Security); Noel L. Griswold, Note, *Forgetting the Melting Pot: An Analysis of the Department of Homeland Security Takeover of the INS*, 39 SUFFOLK U. L. REV. 207 (2005) (arguing that shift from INS to Department of Homeland Security turned immigration matters into national security issues); Jeffrey Mans, *Reorganization as a Substitute for Reform: The Abolition of INS*, 112 YALE L.J. 145 (2002) (asserting that reallocation of power from INS to DHS will refocus

Existing separately from the DHS, an administrative adjudicatory system decides the claims of noncitizens seeking, among other things, to resist removal from the United States. It is housed in the Executive Office for Immigration Review within the U.S. Department of Justice headed by the U.S. Attorney General. Immigration courts hear evidence and decide removal and other immigration matters; the Board of Immigration Appeals (BIA) hears administrative appeals of immigration court decisions.[14] See Chapter 5 for further details.

Similar to the INS, the immigration courts and Board of Immigration Appeals (BIA) have been the subject of sustained, often harsh, criticism.[15] The Board, part of the U.S. Department of Justice, long has been challenged for, among other things, a lack of independence and neutrality. Other criticisms run the gamut from poor quality rulings (most charitably attributed to overwork), to bias against noncitizens, to simple incompetence, ineptitude, and sloppiness. Such criticism, not coincidentally, increased after the BIA, during the Bush administration, changed its procedures to expedite its rulings and attempted to reduce a large backlog of cases, which in turn led to a flood of appeals in the federal courts.[16]

A most articulate spokesperson for the critics has been none other than respected court of appeals judge Richard Posner, who Republican President Ronald Reagan appointed to the federal bench.[17] As Judge Posner succinctly stated in one immigration appeal, "[a]t the risk of sounding like a broken record, we reiterate our oft-expressed concern with adjudication of asylum claims by the Immigration Court and the Board of Immigration Appeals and with the defense of

---

immigration priorities to national security concerns); *see also* Jennifer M. Chacón*Unsecured Borders: Immigration Restrictions, Crime Control and National Security*, 39 CONN. L. REV. 1827, 1184–87 (2007) (contending that current immigration policies are counterproductive to making nation safer); Kevin R. Johnson & Bernard Trujillo, *Immigration Reform, National Security After September 11, and the Future of North American Integration*, 91 MINN. L. REV. 1369, 1396–1403 (2007) (arguing that the "war on terror" unfortunately came to dominate the much-needed national discussion of immigration reform).

[13] *See, e.g.*, Stephanie Francis Ward, *Illegal Aliens on I.C.E.: Tougher Immigration Enforcement Tactics Spur Challenges*, A.B.A. J., June 2008, at 44 (questioning aggressive immigration enforcement measures); *The Shame of Postville*, N.Y. TIMES, July 13, 2008, at WK11 (criticizing raid of meatpacking plant in Postville, Iowa).

[14] *See* 8 C.F.R. §§ 1002–1003.11 (2006).

[15] *See, e.g.*, Pamela A. MacLean, *Immigration Judges Come Under Fire*, NAT'L L.J., Jan. 30, 2006, at 1; Christina B. LaBrie, *Third Circuit Describes "Disturbing Pattern of IJ Misconduct" in Asylum Cases*, IMMIGRATION DAILY, Oct. 22, 2005, at *see, e.g.*, Sukwanputra v. Gonzales, 434 F.3d 627, 637–38 (3d Cir. 2006); Wang v. Attorney General, 423 F.3d 260 (3d Cir. 2005); Nuru v. Gonzales, 404 F.3d 1207, 1229 (9th Cir. 2005).

[16] For an in-depth empirical study of the increase in appeals of Board of Immigration Appeals decisions, *see* John R.B. Palmer, Stephen W. Yale-Loehr, & Elizabeth Cronin, *Why Are So Many People Challenging Board of Immigration Appeals Decisions in Federal Court? An Empirical Analysis of the Recent Surge in Petitions for Review*, 20 GEO. IMMIGR. L.J. 1 (2005); ABA COMM'N ON IMMIGRATION POLICY, PRACTICE & PRO BONO, SEEKING MEANINGFUL REVIEW: FINDINGS AND RECOMMENDATIONS IN RESPONSE TO DORSEY & WHITNEY STUDY OF BOARD OF IMMIGRATION APPEALS PROCEDURAL REFORMS (2003), *available at* http://www.abanet.org/immigration/bia.pdf.

[17] *See, e.g.*, Benslimane v. Gonzales, 430 F.3d 828, 829–30 (7th Cir. 2005); Iao v. Gonzales, 400 F.3d 530, 534–35 (7th Cir. 2005). For analysis of Judge Posner's immigration jurisprudence, *see* Adam B. Cox, *Deference, Delegation, and Immigration Law*, 74 U. CHI. L. REV. 1671 (2007).

the BIA's asylum decisions in this court. . . . "[18] In another appeal, he stated "[w]e understand the Board's staggering workload. But the Department of Justice cannot be permitted to defeat judicial review by refusing to staff the Immigration Courts and the Board of Immigration Appeals with enough judicial officers to provide reasoned decisions."[19] In still another immigration appeal, Judge Posner emphasized that "[d]eference is earned; it is not a birthright. Repeated egregious failures of the Immigration Court and the Board to exercise care commensurate with the stakes in an asylum case can be understood, but not excused, as consequences of a crushing workload that the executive and legislative branches of the federal government have refused to alleviate."[20]

Along these lines, a recent empirical study of the asylum adjudication system has shown widely disparate results between immigration judges.[21] Along with the reversals in the courts, the evidence suggests a chronic problem in the quality of the immigration court and BIA decisions. The quality problems create a lack of confidence in the decisions and place its very legitimacy in question.

In late 2005, the criticism of the agency adjudication of immigration matters reached a crescendo pitch when the *New York Times* ran a front page story about how immigration judges at times in mean-spirited and disrespectful ways, disposed of the cases of noncitizens.[22] The voracity and consistency of the critics of the immigration courts, along with the surrounding national publicity, ultimately provoked Attorney General Alberto Gonzales to instruct the immigration judges to clean up their acts.[23]

2.   Congressional Restrictions on Judicial Review

Over roughly the same general time period that criticism of immigration adjudication was on the rise, Congress anomalously has engaged in a concerted effort to limit judicial review of agency immigration decisions. As discussed later in this Chapter, in immigration reform legislation in 1996 and 2005, Congress dramatically restricted the authority of the courts to review the removal decisions of the immigration bureaucracy — in some instances, purporting to eliminate all

---

[18] Pasha v. Gonzales, 433 F.3d 530, 531 (7th Cir. 2005) (Posner, J.) (citation omitted); *see* Lynne Marek, *Posner Blasts Immigration Courts as "Inadequate" and Ill-Trained*, NAT'L L.J., Apr. 22, 2008 (reporting on Judge Posner's criticism of asylum adjudication system in speech to Chicago Bar Association).

[19] Mekhael v. Mukasey, 509 F.3d 326, 328 (7th Cir. 2007).

[20] Kadia v. Gonzales, 501 F.3d 817, 821 (7th Cir. 2007).

[21] *See* Jaya Ramji-Nogales, Andrew I. Schoenholtz, & Philip G. Schrag, *Refugee Roulette: Dispari-ties in Asylum Adjudication*, 60 STAN. L. REV. 295 (2007). For commentary on the study, *see* Stephen H. Legomsky, *Learning to Live with Unequal Justice: Asylum and the Limits of Consistency*, 60 STAN. L. REV. 413 (2007); Margaret H. Taylor, *Refugee Roulette in An Administrative Law Context: The Deja Vu of Decisional Disparities in Agency Adjudication*, 60 STAN. L. REV. 475 (2007).

[22] *See* Adam Liptak, *Courts Criticize Judges' Handling of Asylum Cases*, N.Y. TIMES, Dec. 26, 2005, at A1.

[23] *See* Memorandum from U.S. Attorney General Alberto Gonzales to Immigration Judges (Jan. 9, 2006), *available at* http:///www.immigration.com/newsletter1/attgenimmjudge.pdf. For discussion of the memorandum, *see* Cham v. Attorney General, 445 F.3d 683, 686–89 (3d Cir. 2006).

judicial review over certain removal decisions.[24] After the 1996 reforms, litigation continued for years about what, if any, judicial review was permitted in certain removal cases in which Congress seemed to eliminate all judicial review; the U.S. government consistently and aggressively argued for limited, or no, judicial review in the cases of noncitizens convicted of certain crimes.[25]

Today, as we shall see later in this Chapter, the immigration agencies make numerous final immigration decisions on a variety of matters. An influential immigration law scholar describes what has transpired in limiting agency and judicial review through a variety of mechanisms as nothing less than a "war on [the] independence" of adjudication of immigration cases.[26] Serious questions exist over the fairness and impartiality of agency immigration adjudication.

It might strike the uninitiated reader as peculiar that Congress has consistently moved toward *less* — not *more* — judicial review at the same time that the administrative immigration decision-making bodies have suffered consistent — even increasing — criticism. Indeed, one could most forcefully argue that careful judicial review is *most* necessary when the agency's competence, independence, and impartiality have been seriously questioned. Especially when critically important decisions affecting a discrete and insular (and disenfranchised) minority are at stake, basic fairness concerns militate in favor of meaningful judicial review.[27] In such circumstances, limits on the power of courts to review administrative decisions adverse to noncitizens can only make matters worse for noncitizens, as well as for the perceived legitimacy of the agency's actions.[28]

All this said, let us look at some of the history of judicial review of immigration decisions and the modern statutory framework.

---

[24] *See* REAL ID Act of 2005, Title B of the Emergency Supplemental Appropriations Act for Defense, the Global War on Terror, and Tsunami Relief, 2005, 109 Pub. L. No. 12, 110 Stat. 231 (2005); Illegal Immigration Reform and Immigrant Responsibility Act, Pub. L. No. 104-208, 110 Stat. 3009 (1996); Antiterrorism and Effective Death Penalty Act, Pub. L. No. 104-132, 100 Stat. 1214 (1996).

[25] *See* Nancy Morawetz, *Back to Back to the Future? Lessons Learned from Litigation over the 1996 Restrictions on Judicial Review*, 51 N.Y.L. Sch. L. Rev. 113 (2006) (analyzing litigation over judicial review); *see also* Lenni Benson, *Back to the Future*, *supra* note 5, at 1438 (discussing Congress' concern about noncitizens convicted of crimes and adoption of 1996 legislation).

[26] Legomsky, *supra* note 7 (arguing that 1996 Congressional restrictions on judicial review and Attorney General's changes to BIA served to diminish judicial decisional independence).

[27] *See* Kevin R. Johnson, *Hurricane Katrina: Lessons About Immigrants in the Administrative States*, 45 Hous. L. Rev. 11, 40–43 (2008). Many commentators have advocated careful judicial review of law affecting noncitizens, a "discrete and insular minority," who cannot participate directly in the political process. *See, e.g.*, John Hart Ely, Democracy and Distrust 135–79 (1980); David Cole, *Enemy Aliens*, 54 Stan. L. Rev. 953, 981 (2007); Neal Katyal, *Equality in the War on Terror*, 59 Stan. L. Rev. 1365, 1383–84 (2002).

[28] For thoughtful analysis of the need for reform of the current system of judicial review, *see* Benson, *You Can't Get There From Here*, *supra* note 5.

B.   CONSTITUTIONAL SCOPE AND LIMITS ON JUDICIAL REVIEW OF IMMIGRATION DECISIONS

This section will first review the constitutional requirements for judicial review of immigration decisions. It then proceeds to look at the statutory provisions for judicial review in the Immigration and Nationality Act, with a particular emphasis on the restrictions on judicial review imposed by Congress in recent years.

1.   Constitutional Mandates on Judicial Review

The Supreme Court has interpreted the Constitution as affording different degrees of judicial review of different types of immigration decisions. At one time, there were two types of proceedings.[29] As traditionally known, exclusion hearings involved noncitizens seeking admissions into the United States.[30] Deportation hearings involved efforts to remove noncitizens from the United States.[31] Congress and the Supreme Court allocate different rights and protections to noncitizens in these hearings. Now both are referred to as removal hearings.[32] Both possess different bundles of constitutional rights.

Despite the lack of constitutional guarantees, immigrants excluded from the United States generally are afforded hearings to establish whether they are admissible. Immigrants in removal proceedings, as well as some in exclusion proceedings, have a right to Due Process and a hearing that comports with Due Process.[33] There are exceptions to this general rule, however. For example, an "expedited removal" procedure added in 1996, discussed later in this Chapter, limits judicial review of the decision to deny entry to particular noncitizens.[34]

a.   Review of the Right to Enter

There are not many constitutional requirements on judicial review of the decisions of the U.S. government denying noncitizens entry into the country. Returning lawful permanent residents, however, have been afforded a right to a hearing complying with Due Process.

---

[29] *See* Landon v. Plasencia, 459 U.S. 21, 25 (1982) (noting two types of removal proceedings: deportation hearings and exclusion hearings) (citing Leng May Ma v. Barber, 357 U.S. 185, 187 (1958)).

[30] *See* Leng May Ma v. Barber, 357 U.S. 185, 187 (1958) (describing exclusion hearings as determining whether a noncitizen is allowed to enter United States).

[31] *See id.* at 187 (defining deportation proceedings as expulsion hearings).

[32] *See* INA § 240, 8 U.S.C. § 1229a.

[33] *See* Landon v. Plasencia, 459 U.S. 21 (1982) (holding that lawful permanent resident was entitled to due process in exclusion hearing). Parts of this discussion have been adapted from Kevin R. Johnson, *Maria and Joseph Plasencia's Lost Weekend: The Case of* Landon v. Plasencia, *in* IMMIGRATION STORIES (David A. Martin & Peter H. Schuck eds., 2005).

[34] *See* INA § 235(b), 8 U.S.C. § 1225(b); *see* Lisa J. Laplante, *Expedited Removal at U.S. Borders: A World Without a Constitution*, 25 N.Y.U. REV. L. & SOC. CHANGE 213, 213–16 (1999) (describing limits on judicial review of expedited removals).

Two Cold War decisions reflect a very narrow conception of the constitutional rights of noncitizens. In *United States* ex rel. *Knauff v. Shaughnessy*,[35] the Supreme Court refused to intervene in a case involving the denial of admission of a noncitizen spouse of a U.S. citizen based on secret evidence and emphasized that "[w]hatever the procedure authorized by Congress, it is due process as far as an alien denied entry is concerned." In *Shaughnessy v. United States* ex rel. *Mezei*,[36] the Court reiterated this holding in an even more extreme case, that is, where the noncitizen denied entry into the United States based on secret evidence faced the prospect of indefinite detention (because his native country refused to allow his return).[37]

The Supreme Court's 1982 decision in *Landon v. Plasencia*[38] is the most significant subsequent development in the due process rights of lawful permanent residents. The Court held that the question whether a lawful permanent resident who had briefly left the country could be denied entry must have her right to return decided in a hearing that comported with due process. The Court went on to make an important acknowledgment that "once an alien gains admission to our country and begins to develop the ties that go with permanent residence, his constitutional status changes accordingly. Our cases have frequently suggested that a continuously present resident alien is entitled to a fair hearing when threatened with deportation. . . . "[39] It further emphasized that "[w]e need not now decide the scope of [the plenary power doctrine precedent]; it does not govern this case, for Plasencia was absent from the country only a few days, and *the United States has conceded that she has a right to due process*."[40] At the same time, the Court restated the essence of the plenary power doctrine that "an alien seeking initial admission has *no* constitutional rights regarding his application, for

---

[35] 338 U.S. 537, 544 (1950).

[36] 345 U.S. 206 (1953); *see* Charles D. Weisselberg, *The Exclusion and Detention of Aliens: Lessons from the Lives of Ellen Knauff and Ignatz Mezei*, 143 U. PA. L. REV. 933 (1995). For criticism of *Knauff* and *Mezei*, see Henry Hart, *The Power of Congress to Limit the Jurisdiction of the Federal Courts: An Exercise in Dialectic*, 66 HARV. L. REV. 1362, 1391–96 (1953). *See also* STEPHEN H. LEGOMSKY, IMMIGRATION AND THE JUDICIARY: LAW AND POLITICS IN BRITAIN AND AMERICA 199–201 (1987); T. Alexander Aleinikoff, *Aliens Due Process, and "Community Ties": A Response to Martin*, 44 U. PITT. L. REV. 237, 237–39, 258–60 (1983); David A. Martin, *Due Process and Membership in the National Community: Political Asylum and Beyond*, 44 U. PITT. L. REV. 165, 173–80 (1983).

[37] *See Mezei*, 345 U.S. at 212 (quoting *Knauff*, 338 U.S. at 544).

[38] 459 U.S. 21 (1982).

[39] *Id.* at 32 (citations omitted). One of the authorities relied on by the Court for this proposition was *Johnson v. Eisentrager*, 339 U.S. 763, 770 (1950), a case that later was much-debated in connection with the indefinite detention after September 11, 2001 of two U.S. citizens, Jose Padilla and Yaser Hamdi, who the Bush administration classified as "enemy combatants." *See* Hamdi v. Rumsfeld, 542 U.S. 507 (2004) (ruling that U.S. citizen held as "enemy combatant" had the right to a hearing to challenge that classification); Rumsfeld v. Padilla, 542 U.S. 426 (2004) (finding that the court in which action was filed lacked jurisdiction over Padilla and could not entertain a challenge to his detention as an "enemy combatant"); *see also* Hamdan v. Rumsfeld, 548 U.S. 557 (2006) (holding that military tribunals created by Bush administration were unlawful). In *Eisentrager*, the Court highlighted that the rights of a noncitizen who had resided in the United States ordinarily increased with the length of residence, which stood in stark contrast to the rights of "enemy aliens" in times of war.

[40] *Landon v. Plasencia*, 459 U.S. at 34 (citing transcript to Oral Argument 6, 9, 14 and Brief for Petitioner 9–10, 20–21) (emphasis added).

the power to admit or exclude aliens is a sovereign prerogative."[41]

The Court proceeded to state that the flexible *Mathews v. Eldridge* balancing test — the general test previously articulated by the Court for evaluating whether governmental procedures complied with due process — applied to determining the specific procedures that due process required in Plasencia's immigration case:

> [T]he courts must consider the interest at stake for the individual, the risk of an erroneous deprivation of the interest through the procedures used as well as the probable value of additional or different procedural safeguards, and the interest of the government in using the current procedures rather than additional or different procedures.[42]

Although declining to itself strike the balance in Plasencia's case, the Court noted that she had a "weighty" interest at stake because she "stands to lose the right 'to stay and live and work in this land of freedom' " and "may lose the right to rejoin her immediate family, a right that ranks high among the interests of the individual."[43] It further observed that "[t]he government's interest in efficient administration of the immigration laws at the border also is weighty."[44] At the same time, the Court cautioned the lower court that, on remand, it could only decide "whether the procedures meet the essential standard of fairness under the Due Process Clause and [could not impose] procedures that merely displace congressional choices of policy."[45]

The courts have dutifully abided by the Court's holding in *Landon v. Plasencia* that, when seeking re-entry into the country, a lawful permanent resident's claim of admissibility must be determined in exclusion proceedings.[46] Some courts have viewed *Landon v. Plasencia* as standing for the proposition that the rights of lawful permanent residents increased as the length of their time in the country grows and thus were greater than those of first-time entrants.[47] In contrast, some courts have taken language from the decision to support Congress's plenary power with respect to the procedures accorded certain noncitizens seeking initial entry into the country.[48]

---

[41] *Landon v. Plasencia*, 459 U.S. at 32 (emphasis added).

[42] *Landon v. Plasencia*, 459 U.S. at 34 (citing Mathews v. Eldridge, 424 U.S. 319, 334–35 (1976)); *see also* Nimrod Pitsker, Comment, *Due Process for All: Applying* Eldridge *to Require Appointed Counsel for Asylum Seekers*, 95 CAL. L. REV. 169 (2007) (contending that *Mathews v. Eldridge* due process blancing test required appointed counsel for noncitizens seeking asylum in the United States).

[43] *Landon v. Plasencia*, 459 U.S. at 34 (citations omitted).

[44] *Id.*

[45] *Id.* at 34–35.

[46] *See, e.g.*, INS v. Phinpathya, 464 U.S. 183, 193 (1984); Ali v. Reno, 22 F.3d 442, 448 (2d Cir. 1994). In *Rafeedie v. INS*, 880 F.2d 506, 519–24 (D.C. Cir. 1989), the court of appeals held that only when the trip was *lengthy* could a returning lawful permanent resident be deprived of due process.

[47] *See, e.g.*, Rhoden v. United States, 55 F.3d 428, 432 (9th Cir. 1995); Campos v. INS, 961 F.2d 309, 316 (1st Cir. 1992).

[48] *See, e.g.*, Cuban Am. Bar Ass'n v. Christopher, 43 F.3d 1412, 1428 (11th Cir.), *cert. denied*, 516 U.S. 913 (1995); Haitian Ctrs. Council v. McNary, 969 F.2d 1326, 1340 (2d Cir. 1992), *vacated sub nom. as moot*, 509 U.S. 918 (1993).

Importantly, courts understood *Landon v. Plasencia* to require that the *Mathews v. Eldridge* balancing test applied to evaluate whether hearing procedures were consistent with due process.[49] In 1988, the BIA ruled that a returning lawful permanent resident like Plasencia must be given reasonable notice of the charges, as well as a procedurally fair hearing with the government bearing the burden of proof; the lawful permanent resident could be excluded only upon a showing by clear, unequivocal, and convincing evidence of excludability.[50]

Some immigration law scholars read *Landon v. Plasencia* as opening the door for expanded constitutional rights for noncitizens seeking entry into the United States[51] and thus as a "crack" in the plenary power doctrine. Other commentators, however, are more circumspect, emphasizing that the Supreme Court included strong plenary power doctrine language and failed to define the constitutional rights of lawful permanent residents with any degree of specificity.[52]

Prompted by *Landon v. Plasencia*, Congress in 1996 amended the Immigration & Nationality Act to provide that returning lawful permanent residents seeking to enter the country are generally not subject to the same procedures and inadmissibility grounds as first-time entrants.[53] This entitles most lawful permanent residents at the border to a removal proceeding, with broader procedural protections than previously enjoyed. Consequently, a beneficial dialogue between the Supreme Court in *Landon v. Plasencia* and Congress ultimately secured greater rights for lawful permanent residents and arguably made immigration procedures more consistent with mainstream constitutional norms.

b. Removal

Aliens physically present in the United States are entitled to a hearing that complies with Due Process before they can be deported. Given the weighty interests at stake, removal hearings, which are sometimes referred to as

---

[49] *See, e.g.*, Zadvydas v. Davis, 533 U.S. 678, 694 (2002); Flores v. Meese, 934 F.2d 991, 1013 (9th Cir. 1990), *rev'd on other grounds*, 507 U.S. 291 (1993).

[50] *See* Matter of Huang, 19 I. & N. Dec. 749, 753–54 (BIA 1988); *see, e.g.*, Khodagholian v. Ashcroft, 335 F.3d 1003, 1006 (9th Cir. 2003); Rosendo-Ramirez v. INS, 32 F.3d 1085, 1090 (7th Cir. 1994).

[51] *See, e.g.*, David A. Martin, *Due Process and Membership in the National Community: Political Asylum and Beyond*, 44 U. Pitt. L. Rev. 165, 214–15 (1983); Hiroshi Motomura, *The Curious Evolution of Immigration Law: Procedural Surrogates for Substantive Constitutional Rights*, 92 Colum. L. Rev. 1625, 1652–56 (1992) [hereinafter Motomura, *The Curious Evolution of Immigration Law*]; Hiroshi Motomura, *Immigration Law After a Century of Plenary Power: Phantom Constitutional Norms and Statutory Interpretation*, 100 Yale L.J. 545, 578–780 (1990) [hereinafter Motomura, *Immigration Law After a Century of Plenary Power*]; Michael Scaperlanda, *Partial Membership: Aliens and the Constitutional Community*, 81 Iowa L. Rev. 707, 744–45 (1996).

[52] *See* T. Alexander Aleinikoff, *Immigrants in American Law: Aliens, Due Process and "Community Ties": A Response to Martin*, 44 U. Pitt. L. Rev. 237, 260 n.65 (1983); Stephen H. Legomsky, *Immigration Law and the Principal of Plenary Congressional Power*, 1984 S. Ct. Rev. 255, 260 nn.25–26; Peter H. Schuck, *The Transformation of Immigration Law*, 84 Colum. L. Rev. 1, 62–63 & n.342 (1984).

[53] *See* Immigration & Nationality Act § 101(a)(13)(C), 8 U.S.C. § 1101(a)(13)(C) (amended by the Illegal Immigration Reform and Immigrant Responsibility Act of 1996, Pub. L. No. 104-208 § 301(a), 110 Stat. 3009-546–3009-575 (1996)).

deportation hearings, must comply with due process.[54] As discussed later in the Chapter, the Supreme Court has emphasized that the general rule is that the Constitution requires *some* judicial review of a removal order.

C. LIMITS ON JUDICIAL REVIEW

There are two important judicially created limits on the judicial review of immigration decisions — the "plenary power" doctrine and the ordinary deference to administrative agencies known as *Chevron* deference. In addition, congressional restrictions on immigration decisions, which will be discussed in the next part of this Chapter, narrow the review — as well as the scope of the review — of immigration decisions by the courts.

1. The "Plenary Power" Doctrine

The judicially created "plenary power" doctrine, emerging originally to shield from review the laws barring Chinese immigration in the late nineteenth century, has protected from judicial scrutiny the decisions of Congress on immigration admissions criteria as well as, in certain instances, the procedures afforded noncitizens seeking entry into the United States.[55]

> If . . . the government of the United States, through its legislative department, considers the presence of foreigners of a different race in this country, who will not assimilate with us, to be dangerous to its peace and security,. . . . [i]ts determination is conclusive on the judiciary.[56]

Scholars have consistently criticized the doctrine,[57] which allows noncitizens to be treated in ways that would be patently unconstitutional if they were citizens. As discussed later in the Chapter, although some "cracks" have emerged in the plenary power doctrine, it remains the law of the land.

The Bush administration expressly relied on the plenary power doctrine in targeting Arab and Muslim noncitizens for special rules and procedures in the "war on terror" put into place in response to the tragic events of September 11, 2001.[58]

---

[54] *See* Yamataya v. Fisher (*The Japanese Immigrant Case*), 189 U.S. 86 (1903); *see also* Fong Haw Tan v. Phelan, 333 U.S. 6, 10 (1998) ("Deportation is a drastic measure and at times the equivalent of banishment or exile."); Bridges v. Wixon, 326 U.S. 135, 147 (1945) (emphasizing that "deportation may result in the loss ' of all that makes life worth living' ") (citation omitted).

[55] *See, e.g.*, Chae Chin Ping v. United States (*The Chinese Exclusion Case*), 130 U.S. 581, 609 (1889) (rejecting a constitutional challenge to racial discrimination in the Chinese Exclusion Act and emphasizing that courts lack power to review congressional exercise of its plenary power over immigration). *See generally* Gabriel J. Chin, Chae Chan Ping and Fong Yue Ying: *The Origins of Plenary Power, in* IMMIGRATION STORIES, *supra* note 33, at 7.

[56] *The Chinese Exclusion Case*, 130 U.S. at 606.

[57] *See, e.g.*, T. ALEXANDER ALEINIKOFF, SEMBLANCES OF SOVEREIGNTY: THE CONSTITUTION, THE STATE, AND AMERICAN CITIZENSHIP (2002); GERALD L. NEUMAN, STRANGERS TO THE CONSTITUTION — IMMIGRANTS, BORDERS, AND FUNDAMENTAL LAW (1996); Michael Scaperlanda, *Polishing the Tarnished Golden Door*, 1993 WIS. L. REV. 965; Kif Augustine-Adams, *The Plenary Power Doctrine After September 11*, 38 U.C. DAVIS L. REV. 701 (2005).

[58] *See, e.g.*, Registration and Monitoring of Certain Nonimmigrants, 67 Fed. Reg. 52584, 52585 (Aug.

In the 2003 decision of *Demore v. Kim*,[59] the Supreme Court upheld the mandatory detention of certain noncitizens pending their deportation and reiterated that the "this Court has firmly and repeatedly endorsed the proposition that Congress may make rules as to aliens that would be unacceptable if applied to citizens."

Consider some prominent examples of the plenary power doctrine at work. In *United States* ex rel. *Knauff v. Shaughnessy*,[60] the Supreme Court in a case involving the noncitizen spouse of a U.S. citizen emphasized that "[w]hatever the procedure authorized by Congress, it is due process as far as an alien denied entry is concerned." In *Shaughnessy v. United States* ex rel. *Mezei*,[61] the Court reiterated this holding in an even more extreme case — and refused to intervene in a case in which the noncitizen denied entry into the United States would not be accepted by native country and thus faced the prospect of indefinite detention.

Besides invoking the doctrine in evaluating the *procedures* for admission in immigration cases, the Supreme Court, as it did in the *Chinese Exclusion Cases*, also has applied the plenary power doctrine in upholding the grounds for deportation established by Congress. For example, in *Harisiades v. Shaughnessy*,[62] the Court upheld the deportation of lawful permanent residents who had been affiliated with the Communist Party (before the law provided that the affiliation could result in deportation) and emphasized that

> any policy toward aliens is vitally and intricately interwoven with contemporaneous policies in regard to the conduct of foreign relations, the war power, and the maintenance of a republican form of government. Such matters are so exclusively entrusted to the political branches of government as to be largely immune from judicial inquiry or interference.

More recently, in *Fiallo v. Bell*,[63] the Court in 1977 upheld gender discrimination in the immigration laws and emphasized that

---

12, 2002) (rationalizing special registration of noncitizens from nations populated predominantly by Arabs and Muslims by emphasizing that "[t]he political branches of the government have plenary authority in the immigration area") (citing Fiallo v. Bell, 430 U.S. 787, 792 (1977); Mathews v. Diaz, 426 U.S. 67, 80–82 (1976)).

[59] 538 U.S. 510, 522 (2003) (citations omitted).

[60] 338 U.S. 537, 544 (1950).

[61] 345 U.S. 206, 212 (1953); *see* Charles D. Weisselberg, *The Exclusion and Detention of Aliens: Lessons from the Lives of Ellen Knauff and Ignatz Mezei*, 143 U. PA. L. REV. 933 (1995). For criticism of *Knauff* and *Mezei*, *see* Hart, *supra* note 36, at 1391–96. *See, e.g.*, LEGOMSKY, *supra* note 36, at 199–201; Aleinikoff, *supra* note 52, at 237–39, 258–60; Martin, *supra* note 51, at 173–80.

[62] 342 U.S. 580, 566–89 (1952) (footnote omitted). In a chilling concurrence, Justice Frankfurter emphasized that "[w]hether immigration laws have been crude and cruel, whether they may have reflected xenophobia in general or anti-Semitism or anti-Catholicism, the responsibility belongs to Congress." *Harisiades*, 342 U.S. at 597 (Frankfurter, J., concurring); *see also* Galvan v. Press, 347 U.S. 522, 531 (1954) (deporting lawful permanent resident who had been affiliated with an organization deemed to be communist). *See generally* Kevin R. Johnson, *The Anti-Terrorism Act, the Immigration Reform Act, and Ideological Regulation in the Immigration Laws: Important Lessons for Citizens and Noncitizens*, 28 ST. MARY'S L.J. 833 (1997) (analyzing ideological regulation under U.S. immigration laws).

[63] 430 U.S. 787, 792 (1977) (refusing to invalidate a provision of immigration laws discriminating against fathers of illegitimate children over mothers). In 2001, the Court upheld a distinction in the INA between illegitimate children of U.S. citizen fathers and mothers but applied the same scrutiny it applies

it is important to underscore the limited scope of judicial inquiry into immigration legislation. This Court has repeatedly emphasized that "over no conceivable subject is the legislative power of Congress more complete than it is over" the admission of aliens. . . . Our cases "have long recognized the power to expel or exclude alien as a fundamental sovereign attribute exercised by the Government's political departments largely immune from judicial control." . . . Our recent decisions have not departed from that rule.

The Supreme Court, however, has not always been entirely consistent in its invocation of the plenary power doctrine. In *Zadvydas v. Davis*,[64] for example, the Court refused to invoke the doctrine to shield from review the indefinite detention of noncitizens awaiting deportation from the United States.

Courts, at times, have employed limited rationality review in interpreting the immigration laws. In *Francis v. INS*,[65] for example, the court of appeals exercised rational basis review under the Equal Protection Clause of the Fourteenth Amendment to ensure relief was available to a noncitizen under the immigration laws.

The inconsistent treatment of the legal rights of immigrants, and frequent resort to the plenary power doctrine, by the Court suggests an ambivalence about their status in the United States, which permeates all of U.S. immigration law.[66]

Generally speaking, the courts have deferred to the major immigration decisions of Congress and the Executive Branch. As discussed previously, the Supreme Court, for example, upheld one of the Chinese exclusion laws — one of Congress's early forays in the federalization of immigration regulation, *see* Chapter 2, emphasizing that if Congress "considers the presence of foreigners of a different race in this country, who will not assimilate with us, to be dangerous to its peace and security . . . , [Congress's] determination is conclusive upon the judiciary."[67] More recently, in *Sale v. Haitian Centers Council, Inc.*,[68] the Court upheld the U.S. government's much-criticized interdiction of Haitians on the high seas, in the face of strong arguments that it violated international and domestic law, and emphasized that "we are construing treaty and statutory provisions that may involve foreign

---

to gender classifications under ordinary constitutional law. *See* Nguyen v. INS, 533 U.S. 53 (2001).

[64] 533 U.S. 678, 695–96 (2001); *see also* Clark v. Martinez, 543 U.S. 371 (2005) (extending *Zadvydas v. Davis* to other classifications of noncitizens). *But see* Demore v. Kim, 538 U.S. 510, 522 (2003) (invoking plenary power doctrine to uphold mandatory detention of noncitizens pending removal).

[65] 532 F.2d 268 (2d Cir. 1976); *see, e.g.,* Cato v. INS 84 F.3d 597 (2d Cir. 1996); Varlamparambill v. INS, 831 F.2d 1362, 1364 (7th Cir. 1987); Augustin v. Sava, 735 F.2d 32 (2d Cir. 1984); Tapia-Acuna v. INS, 640 F.2d 223, 225 (9th Cir. 1981).

[66] *See generally* LINDA S. BOSNIAK, THE CITIZEN AND THE ALIEN: DILEMMAS OF CONTEMPORARY MEMBERSHIP (2006) (analyzing this ambivalence).

[67] Chae Chan Ping v. United States (*The Chinese Exclusion Case*), 130 U.S. 581, 606 (1889).

[68] 509 U.S. 155, 188 (1993) (citing United States v. Curtiss-Wright Export Corp., 299 U.S. 304 (1936)). For commentary on the case, *see* Harold H. Koh, *The "Haiti Paradigm" in United States Human Rights Policy*, 103 YALE L.J. 2391, 2391 (1994); Harold H. Koh, *Reflections on Refoulment and Haitian Centers Council*, 35 HARV. INT'L L.J. 1 (1994).

and military affairs for which the President has unique responsibility." *See* Chapter 3.

a.   The Plenary Power Doctrine and Resident Aliens

As seen in the cases involving the deportation of alleged communists, the Supreme Court has held that, in certain instances, the plenary power doctrine also serves to immunize from meaningful judicial review *federal* laws that discriminate against noncitizens who are physically present in the United States. In finding that Congress could limit the eligibility of lawful immigrants for a federal medical insurance program, the Supreme Court emphasized that

> [i]n the exercise of its broad power over naturalization and immigration, Congress regularly makes rules that would be unacceptable if applied to citizens. The exclusion of aliens and the reservation of the power to deport have no permissible counterpart in the Federal Government's power to regulate the conduct of its own citizenry. The fact that an Act of Congress treats aliens differently from citizens does not itself imply that such disparate treatment is "invidious."[69]

But, again we see some ambivalence in the Court's constitutional jurisprudence surrounding aliens, at least when it comes to *state* laws that discriminate against noncitizens. In *Plyler v. Doe*,[70] for example, the Supreme Court found that a Texas law effectively barring undocumented children from the public elementary and secondary schools, violated the Fourteenth Amendment. Similarly, in *Graham v. Richardson*,[71] the Court applied strict scrutiny to a law discriminating against noncitizens and struck down under the Equal Protection Clause state laws barring certain legal immigrants from receiving public benefits. For a further discussion generally of the constitutional rights of immigrants living in the United States, *see* Chapter 3.

In sum, there is a long tradition of judicial deference to decisions by Congress and the Executive Branch on issues of immigration and the treatment of immigrants (at least by the federal government). Judicial intervention in the immigration laws has ordinarily been limited to ensuring that proper procedural protections are in place in removal and other hearings, rather than guaranteeing meaningful review of substantive immigration decisions in the laws passed by Congress.[72]

---

[69] Mathews v. Diaz, 426 U.S. 67, 79–80 (1976) (footnotes omitted); *see* Reno v. Flores, 507 U.S. 292, 305–06 (1993) (invoking plenary power doctrine in upholding regulation limiting release from detention of juvenile noncitizens).

[70] 457 U.S. 202 (1982).

[71] 403 U.S. 365 (1971).

[72] *Compare* Landon v. Plasencia, 459 U.S. 21 (1982) (holding that lawful permanent resident was entitled to due process in exclusion hearing), *with* Demore v. Kim, 538 U.S. 510, 517–33 (2003) (finding that Congress could lawfully conclude that noncitizens subject to removal on certain criminal grounds could be detained pending deportation), *and* Kleindienst v. Mandel, 408 U.S. 753 (1972) (refusing to intervene in case in which U.S. government denied temporary entry to Belgian journalist allegedly because of his advocacy of communism and emphasizing that Congress has "'plenary power to make rules for the admission of aliens and to exclude those who possess those characteristics which Congress has forbidden.'") (citation omitted).

b.   The Impacts of the Plenary Power Doctrine

One of the results of the hands-off approach of the courts in reviewing the Executive and Legislative Branches' immigration decisions is a body of immigration law that discriminates against groups of noncitizens that would be unconstitutional if applied to citizens. As discussed in Chapter 2, the poor, unhealthy, political dissidents, disabled, gays and lesbians, and many other categories of noncitizens have been — and some continuing to be — disadvantaged by the U.S. immigration laws.[73] Moreover, unlike other areas of constitutional law, there has been precious little dialogue between the courts and Congress on substantive immigration matters. The lack of dialogue has in certain respects distorted some aspects of immigration law and, in certain circumstances, led to more extreme immigration laws.[74] Judicial review in a plenary power regime has not served as a significant moderating influence on Congress and the Executive Branch in formulating immigration law and policy or immigration enforcement.

The bottom line is that, in the end, Congress and the Executive Branch generally have the final say on immigration law and policy. And the courts ordinarily decline to interfere with the substantive decisions of the political branches of government.

2.   Chevron *Deference*

For the most part, administrative agencies within the Executive Branch enforce U.S. immigration law. In immigration cases, federal courts tend to defer to agencies both in the interpretation and in the application of the law. Along these lines, general administrative law principles, as they emerged in the later part of the twentieth century, have called for significant deference to the factual and legal determinations of administrative agencies.

Judicial deference to the fact-finding of administrative agencies is well-established.[75] In *INS v. Elias Zacarias*,[76] for example, the Court articulated a

---

[73] *See generally* KEVIN R. JOHNSON, THE "HUDDLED MASSES" MYTH: IMMIGRATION AND CIVIL RIGHTS (2004).

[74] For exploration of the results of the lack of a dialogue between the courts, Congress, and the Executive Branch, *see* Motomura, *Immigration Law After a Century of Plenary Power, supra* note 51, and Motomura, *The Curious Evolution of Immigration Law, supra* note 51.

[75] *See, e.g.*, Chevron v. Natural Resources Defense Council, Inc., 467 U.S. 837 (1984); United States v. Mead, 533 U.S. 218 (2001). For analysis of *Chevron* deference in immigration law, *see* Brian G. Slocum, *The Immigration Rule of Lenity and* Chevron *Deference*, 17 GEO. IMMIGR. L.J. 515 (2003) (discussing the conflict between immigration rule of lenity and *Chevron* deference); Estella F. Chen, Note, *Judicial Deference After* United States v. Mead: *How Streamlining Measures at the Board of Immigration Appeals May Transform Traditional Notions of Deference in Immigration Law*, 20 GEO. IMMIGR. L.J. 657 (2006) (discussing administrative law deference standards to immigration decisions).

[76] 502 U.S. 478, 481 (1992) (citing NLRB v. Columbian Enameling & Stamping Co., 306 U.S. 292 (1939)) (footnote omitted). For analysis of *Zacarias, see* Deborah Anker et al., *The Supreme Court's Decision in* INS v. Elias-Zacarias: *Is There Any "There" There?*, 69 INTERPRETER RELEASES 289 (1992); Kevin R. Johnson, *Responding to the "Litigation Explosion": The Plain Meaning of Executive Branch Primacy Over Immigration*, 71 N.C. L. REV. 413, 461–72 (1993); Stephen M. Knight, *Shielded From Review: The Questionable Birth and Development of the Asylum Standard of Review Under* Elias-Zacarias, 20 GEO. IMMIGR. L.J. 133, 133 (2005); Karen Musalo, *Irreconcilable Differences? Divorcing Refugee Protections from Human Rights Norms*, 15 MICH J. INT' L L. 1179 (1994).

strong form of deference to the fact-finding of the Board of Immigration Appeals and held that, to reverse a Board fact determination, the asylum applicant must show that the evidence "was such that a reasonable fact-finder would have to conclude that the requisite fear of persecution existed." Congress codified the Court's deferential holding in 1996.[77]

The Supreme Court extended deference to certain *legal* interpretations of administrative agencies in the landmark decision of *Chevron USA v. Natural Resources Defense Council, Inc.*[78] In *Chevron*, the Court pronounced that the courts must defer to the agency's interpretation of a statute that Congress has delegated the power to interpret.[79] *Chevron* "dramatically expanded the circumstances in which courts must defer to agency interpretations of statutes."[80] This new form of deference is in tension with the declaration in *Marbury v. Madison* that it is the Judiciary's obligation "to say what the law is."[81]

The courts often apply *Chevron*, as well as related forms of agency deference, to BIA immigration decisions.[82] (This is true even though, as discussed earlier in this Chapter, the BIA's decisions have been much-criticized.). In *INS v. Aguirre-*

---

[77] *See* INA § 242(b)(4)(B), 8 U.S.C. § 1252(b)(4)(B) ("[T]he administrative findings of fact are conclusive unless any reasonable adjudicator would be compelled to conclude to the contrary.") (enacted as part of the Illegal Immigration Reform and Immigrant Responsibility Act of 1996 (IIRIRA), Pub.L. No. 104-208, 110 Stat. 3009-546); *see, e.g.*, Korytnyuk v. Ashcroft, 396 F.3d 272, 286 (3d Cir. 2005); Dia v. Ashcroft, 353 F.3d 228, 248 (3rd Cir. 2003); Stephen M. Knight, *Shielded From Review: The Questionable Birth and Development of the Asylum Standard of Review Under* Elias-Zacarias, 20 Geo. Immigr. L.J. 133, 133 (2005).

[78] 467 U.S. 837, 865–66 (1984).

[79] In the Court's words,

> Judges are not experts in the field, and are not part of either political branch of the Government. . . . [A]n agency to which Congress has delegated policymaking responsibilities may, within the limits of that delegation, properly rely upon the incumbent administration's views of wise policy to inform its judgments. *While agencies are not directly accountable to the people, the Chief Executive is, and it is entirely appropriate for this political branch of the Government to make such policy choices* — resolving the competing interests which Congress itself either inadvertently did not resolve, or intentionally left to be resolved by the agency charged with the administration of the statute in light of everyday realities.

Id. (emphasis added).

Chevron is "[t]he best known judicial decision in administrative law" and that, since decided, "it [as of 2006] has been cited in more than 8000 judicial opinions." Allison Marston Danner & Adam Marcus Samaha, *Judicial Oversight in Two Dimensions: Charting Area and Intensity in the Decisions of Justice Stevens*, 74 Fordham L. Rev. 2051, 2067–68 (2006).

The Supreme Court in *United States v. Mead*, 533 U.S. 218 (2001), held that *Chevron* deference was not warranted to an agency decision because Congress in the governing statute did not intend to delegate interpretative authority to the U.S. Customs Service on a tariff classification ruling. *See, e.g.*, Gonzales v. Oregon, 546 U.S. 243, 255–56 (2006); Alaska Dep't of Environmental Conservation v. EPA, 540 U.S. 461, 487–88 (2004).

[80] Thomas W. Merrill & Kristin E. Hickman, Chevron's *Domain*, 89 Geo. L.J. 833, 833 (2001).

[81] 5 U.S.(1 Cranch) 137, 177 (1803).

[82] *See, e.g.*, INS v. Aguirre-Aguirre, 526 U.S. 415, 424–25 (1999) (holding that court of appeals erred in failing to afford Chevron deference to agency's interpretation of the Immigration & Nationality Act); INS v. Elias-Zacarias, 502 U.S. 478, 481 (1992) (ruling that agency fact-finding that asylum applicant was not eligible for relief could be reversed only if the reviewing court found that "a reasonable factfinder would have to conclude that the requisite fear of persecution existed") (citation and footnote omitted).

Aguirre,[83] for example, the Supreme Court reversed a court of appeals decision that the Board had improperly denied relief to an applicant for asylum and withholding of deportation because he had committed "serious nonpolitical crimes" that, under the applicable statutory language, rendered the applicant ineligible for relief. The Court held that

> the Court of Appeals failed to accord the required level of deference to the interpretation of the serious nonpolitical crime exception adopted by the Attorney General and the BIA. Because the Court of Appeals confronted questions implicating "an agency's construction of the statute which it administers," the court should have applied the principles of deference described in *Chevron U.S.A. Inc. v. Natural Resources Defense Council, Inc.* . . . [84]

The Court further emphasized that "we have recognized that judicial deference to the Executive Branch is especially appropriate in the immigration context where officials 'exercise especially sensitive political functions that implicate questions of foreign relations.' "[85] This, of course, sounds of the plenary power doctrine, which was discussed earlier in this Chapter and in Chapter 3.

A reviewing court, however, will not defer to an agency interpretation of the law that is contrary to Congressional intent.[86] In *INS v. Cardoza-Fonseca*,[87] the Supreme Court rejected the Board of Immigration Appeal's interpretation of the INA's provisions governing the burden on an asylum-seeker in establishing the requisite fear of persecution. *See* Chapter 11. The Court found that Congress intended the "well-founded fear of persecution" standard for asylum to be "more generous" than the clear probability of persecution standard necessary to establish entitlement to withholding of deportation.[88] Because the Court found that the agency's interpretation was contrary to the intent of Congress as determined through reliance on "traditional tools of statutory construction," it refused to apply *Chevron* deference to the BIA's interpretation.[89]

---

[83]   526 U.S. 415, 424 (1999).

[84]   *Id.* (citation omitted).

[85]   *Id.* at 425 (quoting INS v. Abudu, 485 U.S. 94, 110 (1988)). *See* Chapter 3 for discussion of the foreign relations power under the Constitution as a possible rationale for the federal power to regulate immigration.

[86]   *See* INS v. Cardoza-Fonseca, 480 U.S. 421, 444–50 (1987) (rejecting Board of Immigration Appeal's interpretation of asylum provisions of immigration laws as contrary to the intent of Congress); *see, e.g.*, Gen. Dynamics Land Sys., Inc. v. Cline, 540 U.S. 581, 600 (2004); Singh v. Gonzales, 451 F.3d 400, 403–04 (6th Cir. 2006); Ucelo-Gomez v. Gonzales, 448 F.3d 180, 185–88 (2d Cir. 2006); Zheng v. Gonzales, 422 F.3d 98, 112–20 (3d Cir. 2005); Soliman v. Gonzales, 419 F.3d 276, 281–86 (4th Cir. 2005); Gao v. Ashcroft, 299 F.3d 266, 271–72 (3d Cir. 2002); Chowdhury v. INS, 249 F.3d 970, 972–73 (9th Cir. 2001).

[87]   480 U.S. 421 (1987); *see, e.g.*, Sale v. Haitian Centers Council, Inc., 509 U.S. 155, 162 (1993); INS v. Aguirre-Aguirre, 526 U.S. 415, 427–28 (1999); Osorio v. INS, 18 F.3d 1017, 1021–23 (2d Cir. 1994).

[88]   *See Cardoza-Fonseca*, 480 U.S. at 430.

[89]   *See id.* at 446. In interpreting the INA, the Court relied on the language of the statute, legislative history, and international law. *See id.* at 427–43. The Court has had an ongoing debate over the propriety of considering legislative history and international law in interpreting statutes. *See, e.g.*, William N. Eskridge, Jr., *The New Textualism*, 37 UCLA L. Rev. 621 (1990); William N. Eskridge, Jr., *Public Values in Statutory Interpretation*, 137 U. Pa. L. Rev. 1007 (1989); Cass R. Sunstein, *Interpreting*

Similarly, in *INS v. St. Cyr*,[90] the Supreme Court refused to extend *Chevron* deference to the BIA's interpretation of a provision of the 1996 immigration reforms restricting judicial review because it found that "there was no ambiguity in the statute for an agency to resolve," a prerequisite for such deference. The Court also found that "substantial constitutional questions" would arise if the agency position — no judicial review of a removal decision — were followed.[91]

D.   THE IMMIGRATION & NATIONALITY ACT PROVISIONS ON JUDICIAL REVIEW

1.   A Brief History of Statutory Judicial Review Provisions

The Immigration and Nationality Act provides for judicial review of removal orders as well as a variety of other immigration decisions. The general rule is that a noncitizen has a right to *some* form of judicial review of an order of removal by the Executive Branch.[92] This is no small part because of the weighty individual interests at stake.[93] The precise nature of that review has changed over time, however.

The original Immigration & Nationality Act of 1952 (INA) lacked any provision for judicial review of removal orders. The district courts reviewed deportation orders through writs of habeas corpus filed in a district court.[94] The U.S. Constitution guarantees the writ of habeas corpus.[95] Article I, § 9, clause 2

Statutes in the Regulatory State, 103 HARV. L. REV. 405 (1989); Michael P. Van Alstine, *Dynamic Treaty Interpretation*, 146 U. PA. L. REV. 687 (1998).

[90]   533 U.S. 289, 320 n.45 (2001).

[91]   *See id.* at 300.

[92]   *See generally* Benson, *Back to the Future, supra* note 5 (discussing importance of judicial review in immigration proceedings and how recent legislation such as AEDPA have eliminated such review); Legomsky, *supra* note 7 (analyzing the challenge to decisional independence of immigration decision-making); M. Isabel Medina, *Judicial Review — A Nice Thing? Article III, Separation of Powers and the Illegal Immigration Reform and Immigrant Responsibility Act of 1996*, 29 CONN. L. REV. 1525 (1997) (discussing constitutional problems created by statutes that limit judicial review for noncitizens).

[93]   *See* Fong Haw Tan v. Phelan, 333 U.S. 6, 10 (1998) ("Deportation is a drastic measure and at times the equivalent of banishment or exile."); Bridges v. Wixon, 326 U.S. 135, 147 (1945) (emphasizing that "deportation may result in the loss 'of all that makes life worth living' ") (citation omitted).

[94]   *See* Heikkila v. Barber, 345 U.S. 229, 235 (1953) (stating that habeas corpus is sole way of challenging deportation order under then-existing statute); *see, e.g.,* United States *ex rel.* Fells v. Garfinkel, 158 F. Supp. 524 (W.D. Pa. 1957), *aff'd*, 251 F.2d 846 (3d Cir. 1958); United States *ex rel.* Athanasopoulous v. Reid, 110 F. Supp. 200 (D.C. 1953). In a response to recent congressional efforts to limit judicial review of certain removal decisions, commentary on the use of habeas corpus review flourishes. *See, e.g.,* Benson, *The New World, supra* note 5; Benson, *Back to the Future, supra* note 5; David Cole, *Jurisdiction and Liberty: Habeas Corpus and Due Process as Limits on Congress's Control of Federal Jurisdiction*, 86 GEO. L.J. 2481 (1998); Richard H. Fallon, *Applying the Suspension Clause to Immigration Cases*, 98 COLUM. L. REV. 1068 (1998); M. Isabel Medina, *Judicial Review–A Nice Thing? Article III, Separation of Power and the Illegal Immigration Reform and Immigrant Responsibility Act of 1996*, 29 CONN. L. REV. 1525 (1997); Gerald L. Neuman, *Habeas Corpus, Executive Detention, and the Removal of Aliens*, 98 COLUM. L. REV. 961 (1998). *See generally* LARRY W. YACKLE, FEDERAL COURTS–HABEAS CORPUS (2003).

[95]   One of the classic discussions of habeas corpus review is Hart, *supra* note 36, at 1386–96. In 2001,

provides: "The Privilege of the Writ of Habeas Corpus shall not be suspended, unless when in Cases of Rebellion or Invasion the public Safety may require it."

In 1961, Congress created a specific statutory provision for judicial review, former INA § 106(a).[96] Under that procedure, which is similar in important respects to the procedure employed in the review of other agency decisions, the noncitizen filed a "petition for review" in the court of appeals, without any review in the district court. In 1996, the Illegal Immigration Reform and Immigrant Responsibility Act (IIRIRA) replaced INA § 106 with INA § 242, 8 U.S.C. § 1252. Under Section 242, the petition for review in the court of appeals generally remains the exclusive mode of judicial review of an administratively final removal order. However, as discussed later in this Chapter, IIRIRA purported to bar judicial review of whole categories of removal orders and erected several other barriers to judicial review of administrative immigration decisions. The REAL ID Act further narrowed judicial review and responded to a Supreme Court decision ensuring habeas corpus review of certain removal decisions.[97]

2.   Statutory Limits: "Court Stripping" Provisions in the 1996 Immigration Reforms and the REAL ID Act

In 1996, Congress passed back-to-back pieces of immigration reform legislation[98] that significantly narrowed judicial review of immigration decisions and resulted in years of litigation over the availability of judicial review over certain kinds of immigration decisions.

In Section 440(a) of the Antiterrorism and Effective Death Penalty Act (AEDPA), Congress barred review of final deportation orders for noncitizens convicted of certain crimes: "Any final order of deportation against an alien who is deportable by reason of having committed [certain crimes, including "aggravated felonies," see INA § 101(a)(43), 8 U.S.C. § 1101(a)(43)] shall not be subject to review by any court." Later that year, Congress passed the Illegal Immigration Reform and Immigrant Responsibility Act (IIRIRA), which incorporated and expanded AEDPA's limitations on judicial review of immigration decisions.[99]

In *INS v. St. Cyr*,[100] the Supreme Court in 2001 — culminating years of litigation — found that the bars on judicial review for noncitizens convicted of

---

the Supreme Court interpreted one of the bars on judicial review in the 1996 immigration reforms as not foreclosing habeas corpus review. *See* INS v. St. Cyr, 533 U.S. 289 (2001).

[96] Congress added this provision in no small part in response to the perceived abuse of judicial review for purposes of delay by, among others, reputed mobster Carlos Marcello. *See* Daniel Kanstroom, *The Long, Complex, and Futile Deportation Saga of Carlos Marcello, in* IMMIGRATION STORIES, *supra* note 33, at 113; *see also* Marcello v. Bonds, 349 U.S. 302 (1955) (affirming deportation order); United States *ex rel.* Marcello v. District Dir., 634 F.2d 964, 974 (5th Cir. 1981) (reviewing Marcello's request for suspension of deportation); Kevin R. Johnson, *Los Olvidados: Images of the Immigrant, Political Power of Noncitizens, and Immigration Law and Enforcement*, 1993 B.Y.U. L. REV. 1139, 1229–30 (1993).

[97] *See* INS v. St Cyr, 533 U.S. 289 (2001).

[98] *See* Illegal Immigration Reform and Immigrant Responsibility Act, Pub. L. No. 104-208, 110 Stat. 3009 (1996); Antiterrorism and Effective Death Penalty Act, Pub. L. No. 104-132, 110 Stat. 1214 (1996).

[99] *See* INA § 242(a)(2)(B-C), 8 U.S.C. § 1252(a)(2)(B-C).

[100] 533 U.S. 289 (2001).

certain crimes did not preclude them from challenging their removal through *habeas corpus* proceedings in the district courts, with the rulings subject to appeal to the court of appeals, and found that Congress had failed to make a "clear statement" eliminating habeas review; the court, by allowing habeas review, avoided "substantial constitutional questions."[101] In response to the Court's decisions, Congress eliminated habeas corpus review of removal decisions in the district courts in the REAL ID Act of 2005, Title B of the Emergency Supplemental Appropriations Act for Defense, the Global War on Terror, and Tsunami Relief.[102] The Act directed review of removal orders to proceed in the court of appeals, not the district courts.[103] Since passage of the REAL ID Act, courts have dismissed habeas corpus reviews of removal orders.[104]

Section 242(a)(5) of the Immigration and Nationality Act, 8 U.S.C. § 1252(a)(5), which is entitled "exclusive means of review," provides that:

> Notwithstanding any other provision of law (statutory or nonstatutory), including section 2241 of title 28, or any other habeas corpus provision, and sections 1361 and 1651 of such title, a petition for review filed with an appropriate court of appeals in accordance with this section *shall be the sole and exclusive means for judicial review*. . . . (emphasis added).

INA § 242(a)(2)(D), 8 U.S.C. § 1252(a)(2)(D) further provides that:

> Nothing in [the provisions that limit or eliminate judicial review] shall be construed as precluding review of *constitutional claims or questions of law* raised upon a petition for review filed with an appropriate court of appeals in accordance with this section. (emphasis added).

Thus, the INA currently provides for review of "constitutional claims" as well as "questions of law." Omitted from this is any review of agency fact-findings.

Judicial review of a removal order under Section 242, as amended by the REAL ID Act, thus rests in large part on whether a court classifies a claim as "factual" or "legal." As in many areas of law, the lines between questions of "law" and "fact" are often difficult to discern — and are downright murky — in immigration law.[105]

---

[101]　*Id.* at 300.

[102]　109 Pub. L. No. 12, 119 Stat. 231 (2005).

[103]　*See* Gerald L. Neuman, *On the Adequacy of Direct Review After the REAL ID Act of 2005*, 51 N.Y. SCH. L. REV. 133 (2006/07).

[104]　*See, e.g.*, Iasu v. Smith, 511 F.3d 881, 891 (9th Cir. 2007); Nunes v. Ashcroft, 375 F.3d 810, 811 (9th Cir. 2004); Zalawadia v. Ashcroft, 371 F.3d 292, 294 (5th Cir. 2004). For discussion, *see* Hiroshi Motomura, *Immigration Law and Federal Court Jurisdiction Through the Lens of Habeas Corpus*, 91 CORNELL L. REV. 459 (2006); Neuman, supra note 103.

[105]　*See*, Aaron G. Leiderman, Note, *Preserving the Constitution's Most Important Human Right: Judicial Review of Mixed Questions Under the Real ID Act*, 106 COLUM. L. REV. 1367, 1369–77 (2006) (discussing the legislative intent behind questions of law and questions of fact under the Real ID Act); Sarah A. Moore, Note, *Tearing Down the Fence Around Immigration Law: Examining the Lack of Judicial Review and the Impact of the Real ID Act While Calling for a Broader Reading of Questions of Law to Encompass "Extreme Cruelty"*, 82 NOTRE DAME L. REV. 2037, 2047–51 (2007) (exploring definition of "questions of law" under the REAL ID Act).

a. Questions of "Law" or "Fact"?

As the REAL ID amended INA § 242, pure fact questions are not subject to judicial review.[106] In contrast, "constitutional claims" and "questions of law" are clearly subject to review. Courts have exercised jurisdiction over constitutional challenges to the immigration laws.[107] Pure legal questions can be straight-forward. However, legal questions can be intertwined with factual determinations. For example, the U.S. Court of Appeals for the Seventh Circuit held that it had jurisdiction over a claim that the Board of Immigration Appeals applied the incorrect legal standard reviewing the immigration judge's fact-finding.[108]

A circuit split is now emerging as to what is a "mixed" question of law and fact that is subject to judicial review.[109] The Ninth Circuit in *Ramadan v. Gonzales*[110] held that it had jurisdiction to challenge a determination that a noncitizen had failed to show changed circumstances to excuse the untimely filing of an asylum application. The court held that it had jurisdiction to review "questions of law" including "questions involving the application of statutes or regulations to undisputed facts, sometimes referred to as *mixed questions of fact and law*."[111] The court concluded that, under REAL ID, it had jurisdiction to review these mixed questions.[112]

In contrast, the Second Circuit held that it lacked jurisdiction over an asylum claim that the immigration judge found was not filed in a timely manner.[113] It treated the issue as more fact, than legal, and thus not subject to review.

b. The Standards of Review

Once judicial review has been established, the question then is the scrutiny of the review or, in other words, how closely to review BIA decisions. The appropriate scrutiny is determined by the standard of review applied by the reviewing court.

---

[106] *See, e.g.*, Rodrigues-Nascimento v. Gonazles, 485 F.3d 60, 62 (1st Cir. 2007) (holding that determination of "hardship" was finding of fact, and thus the court lacked appellate jurisdiction); Chen v. U.S. Dep't of Justice, 471 F.3d 315 (2d Cir. 2006) (holding that the REAL ID Act barred judicial review of agency fact-finding).

[107] *See* Patel v. Gonzales, 470 F.3d 216, 219–20 (6th Cir. 2006) (finding that constitutional claim gave rise to jurisdiction); Flores-Ledezma v. Gonzales, 415 F.3d 375, 380 (5th Cir. 2005) (holding that constitutional challenge to statute is subject to review).

[108] *See* Guevara v. Gonzales, 472 F.3d 972, 974–75 (7th Cir. 2007).

[109] For analysis of this issue, *see* Leiderman, *supra* note 105.

[110] 479 F.3d 646 (9th Cir.2007); *see, e.g.*, Mirzoyan v. Gonzales, 457 F.3d 217, 220 (2d Cir. 2006) (per curiam) (reviewing de novo mixed questions of law and fact of whether mistreatment suffered by asylum applicant constituted persecution); Chen v. Ashcroft, 381 F.3d 221 (3d Cir. 2004) (holding that court had jurisdiction to review BIA's determination that statutory asylum protection did not extend to women undergoing forced abortions to an unmarried partner).

[111] *Ramadan*, 479 F.3d at 650 (emphasis added).

[112] *See id.* at 651–54; *see also* Moirzoyan v. Gonzales, 457 F.3d 217, 220 (2d Cir. 2006) (per curiam) (reviewing "mixed" questions of law and fact de novo); Secaida-Rosales v. INS, 331 F.3d 297, 307 (2d Cir. 2003) (same).

[113] *See* Liu v. INS, 508 F.3d 716 (2d Cir. 2007).

INA § 242(b)(4), 8 U.S.C. § 1252(b)(4), sets forth deferential judicial review standards for factual determinations. "[A]dministrative findings of fact are conclusive unless any reasonable adjudicator would be compelled to conclude the contrary." INA § 242(b)(4)(B), 8 U.S.C. § 1252(b)(4)(B). As discussed earlier, this codifies the Supreme Court's decisions in *INS v. Elias-Zacarias*. "[A] decision that an alien is not eligible for admission to the United States is conclusive unless manifestly contrary to law."[114] For *asylum* decisions, the standard is that the Attorney General's judgment whether to grant asylum "shall be conclusive unless manifestly contrary to the law and an abuse of discretion." INA § 242(b)(4)(D), 8 U.S.C. § 1252(b)(4)(D).

Courts exercise "de novo," or independent, review over questions of law.[115] However, as discussed previously in this Chapter, courts must afford *Chevron* deference to an agency interpretation of the Immigration & Nationality Act.[116] As also discussed earlier in this Chapter, the courts generally defer to the legal interpretations of the BIA.

c. Commencing Proceedings or Stays of Removal

INA § 242(g), as added by IIRIRA, bars judicial review of decisions as whether to commence removal proceedings, which might be characterized as the exercise of prosecutorial discretion, and whether to execute a removal order.[117] In *Reno v. American-Arab Anti-Discrimination Committee*,[118] the Supreme Court ruled that INA § 242(g), 8 U.S.C. § 1252(g) barred judicial review of a claim of selective

---

[114] INA § 242(b)(4)(C), 8 U.S.C. § 1252(b)(4)(C).

[115] *See, e.g.*, Arca-Pineda v. Attorney General, 527 F.3d 101, 103–04 (3d Cir. 2008); Mendez-Mendez v. Mukasey, 525 F.3d 828, 832 (9th Cir. 2008); Ochieng v. Mukasey, 520 F.3d 1110, 1113 (10th Cir. 2008); Puentes Fernandez v. Keisler, 502 F.3d 337, 344–45 (4th Cir. 2007); Gao v. United States Att'y Gen., 500 F.3d 93, 98 (2d Cir. 2007); Manzur v. U.S. Dep't of Homeland Security, 494 F.3d 281, 288–89 (2d Cir. 2007); Uwais v. United States Att'y Gen., 478 F.3d 513, 517 (2d Cir. 2007); Sanusi v. Gonzales, 474 F.3d 341, 345 (6th Cir. 2007); Blanco de Belbruno v. Ashcroft, 362 F.3d 272, 278 (4th Cir. 2004); Kankamalage v. INS, 335 F.3d 858, 861 (9th Cir. 2003).

[116] *See, e.g.*, Estrada-Rodriguez v. Mukasey, 512 F.3d 517, 519–20 (9th Cir. 2007) (citing Kanka-malage v. INS, 335 F.3d 858, 862 (9th Cir. 2003)); Segran v. Mukasey, 511 F.3d 1, 5 (1st Cir. 2007); Ortega-Cervantes v. Gonzales, 501 F.3d 1111, 1113 (9th Cir. 2007); Abebe v. Gonzales, 493 F.3d 1092, 1100–01 (9th Cir. 2007); Vo v. Gonzales, 482 F.3d 363, 366 (5th Cir. 2007).

[117] *See* Reno v. American-Arab Anti-Discrimination Committee, 525 U.S. 471 (1999); *see, e.g.*, Barahona-Gomez v. Reno, 236 F.3d 1115, 1118 (9th Cir. 2001); Schaeuble v. Reno, 87 F. Supp. 2d 383, 392 (D.N.J. 2000); Maldonado v. Fasano, 67 F. Supp. 2d 1170, 1175 (S.D. Cal. 1999), *aff'd*, 225 F.3d 1100 (9th Cir. 2000); Barapind v. Reno, 72 F. Supp. 2d 1132, 1156 (E.D. Cal. 1999); Botezatu v. INS, 195 F.3d 311, 313 (7th Cir. 1999). For thoughtful analysis of § 242(g), *see* Nancy Morawetz, *Predicting the Meaning of INA* § 242(b)(9), 14 Geo. Immigr. L.J. 453 (2000); Hiroshi Motomura, *Judicial Review in Immigration Cases after AADC: Lessons from Civil Procedure*, 14 Geo. Immigr. L.J. 385 (2000); Leti Volpp, *Court-Stripping and Class-Wide Relief: A Response to Judicial Review in Immigration Cases After AADC*, 14 Geo. Immigr. L.J. 463 (2000).

[118] 525 U.S. 471 (1999). For analysis of the discussion, *see* Benson, *The New World*, *supra* note 5; Berta E. Hernández-Truyol, *Nativism, Terrorism, and Human Rights-The Global Wrongs of Reno v. American-Arab Anti-Discrimination Committee*, 31 Colum. Hum. Rts. L. Rev. 521 (2000); John A. Scanlan, *American-Arab — Getting the Balance Wrong — Again*, 52 Admin. L. Rev. 347 (2000) Adrien K. Wing, Reno v. American-Arab Anti-Discrimination Committee, 31 Colum. Hum. Rts. L. Rev. 561 (2000).

prosecution of the immigration laws based on the speech of the noncitizens.[119]

d.   Class Actions

Impact class actions brought on behalf of a group of noncitizens long have been brought in immigration cases in attempts to change institutional practices. In *McNary v. Haitian Refugee Center, Inc.*,[120] the Supreme Court addressed a class action in which the plaintiffs alleged a pattern or practice of procedural due process violations in Immigration & Naturalization Service administration of the special agricultural worker (SAW) legalization program in the Immigration Reform and Control Act of 1986. The statutory provision at issue in that case, INA § 210(e), 8 U.S.C. § 1160(e), provides that

> There shall be no administrative or judicial review of a determination respecting an application for [legalization] under this section except in accordance with this subsection. . . . *There shall be judicial review of such a denial only in the judicial review of an order of exclusion or deportation.* . . . (emphasis added).

The Court read this language not to preclude class action challenges to agency practices and policies used in processing applications. It therefore held that the district court had jurisdiction to hear the class action. The Court recognized that postponing adjudication until individual deportation orders were entered and reviewed "would foster the very delay and procedural redundancy that Congress sought to eliminate in passing" the provision limiting judicial review.[121]

Since *McNary v. Haitian Refugee Center*, however, Congress has limited the courts' ability to order class-wide injunctive relief in immigration cases. The Immigration Reform and Immigrant Responsibility Act of 1996 added INA § 242(f)(1), 8 U.S.C. § 1252(f)(1), which provides that

> no court (other than the Supreme Court) shall have jurisdiction to enjoin or restrain the operation of [certain provisions of the immigration laws, as amended in 1996] other than with respect to the application of such provisions to an individual alien against whom proceedings . . . have been initiated.

There has been much literature on the impact of this provision.[122]

---

[119] Section 242(g), 8 U.S.C. § 1252(g) provides that

> No courts shall have jurisdiction to hear any cause or claim on behalf of any alien arising from the decision or action by the Attorney General to commence proceedings, adjudicate cases, or execute removal orders against any alien under the Act.

For applications of § 242(g), *see*, for example, Chapinski v. Ziglar, 278 F.3d 718, 720–21 (7th Cir. 2002) (ruling that court lacked jurisdiction to hear a class action to compel government to commence removal proceedings); Tefel v. Reno, 180 F.3d 1286, 1298 (11th Cir. 1999), *cert. denied*, 530 U.S. 1228 (2000) (finding that § 242(g) did not bar class action challenging rules for seeking relief from deportation); Sadhvani v. Chertoff, 460 F. Supp. 2d 114, 121–25 (D.D.C. 2006) (holding that court lacked jurisdiction to hear challenge to Immigration & Custom Enforcement decision to execute removal order).

[120] 498 U.S. 479 (1991).

[121] *Id.* at 490 (quoting court of appeals).

[122] *See* Jill E. Family, *Another Limit on Federal Court Jurisdiction? Immigrant Access to*

The key question is the extent to which *McNary* survives the new Section 242. Impact class actions still are brought on immigration matters.[123] Immigrant workers have brought class actions under other statutes.[124]

Another section of the INA might be read as restricting multiparty actions. Section 242(b)(9), 8 U.S.C. § 1251(b)(9) provides that:

> Judicial review of all questions of law and fact, including interpretation of constitutional and statutory provisions, arising from any action taken or proceeding brought to remove an alien from the United States . . . shall be available only in judicial review of a final order under this section.

Commentators are split on whether Section 242(b)(9) deprives a court of jurisdiction to hear multi-party litigation against the government until after final removal orders are entered.[125]

To this point, the Supreme Court after *McNary* has not addressed directly whether plaintiffs may bring class actions for injunctive or declaratory relief in challenges to the immigration laws. Nothing in the REAL ID Act appears to amend the law on "pattern and practice" litigation. Immigration class actions continue to be brought.[126]

Class-Wide Injunctive Relief, 53 CLEV. ST. L. REV. 11 (2005–06); Gerald L. Neuman, *Immigration: Federal Courts Issues in Immigration Law*, 78 TEX. L. REV. 1661, 1679–87 (2000); Volpp, *supra* note 117, at 467–75; *see also* Benson, *Back to the Future*, *supra* note 5, at 1454 ("Congress probably intended [8 U.S.C. § 1252(f)(1)] to prevent class-wide injunctions such as those which have prevented the [federal government] from removing large numbers of people or from implementing changes in the past.").

[123] *See, e.g.*, Barahona-Gomez v. Reno, 236 F.3d 1115, 1118–21, 1233–34 (9th Cir. 1999) (holding that court had jurisdiction to hear class actions for violation of due process rights); Tefel v. Reno, 180 F.3d 1286, 1298 (11th Cir. 1999) (holding that INA § 242(g) "does not alter the jurisdiction . . . over class-wide allegations"), *cert denied*, 530 U.S. 1228 (2000). For analysis of the § 242 and class actions, *see* Motomura, *supra* note 117; Family, *supra* note 122; Volpp, *supra* note 117. For analysis suggesting that Section 242 (f)(1) also bars a declaratory judgment against the government with regard to a particular policy or practice, *see* Gerald L. Neuman, *Federal Courts Issues in Immigration Law*, 78 TEX. L. REV. 1661, 1684–87 (2001).

[124] *See, e.g.*, Enkhbayar Choimbol v. Fairfield Resorts, Inc., 475 F. Supp. 2d 557 (E.D. Va. 2006) (certifying class of immigrant workers); Farm Labor Organizing Committee v. Ohio State Highway Patrol, 308 F.3d 523 (16th Cir. 2001) (reviewing class action suit seeking to enjoin alleged racial profiling by state highway patrol officers); *see* Janet Herold, *Fighting the Good Fight: Prosecuting and Defending Class Wage Claims for Immigrant Workers*, 10 EMP. RTS. & EMP. POL'Y J. 487 (2006).

[125] *Compare* Motomura, *supra* note 117, at 434–38 (reading § 242(b)(9) narrowly), *with* David A. Martin *Behind the Scenes on a Different Set: What Congress Needs to Do in the Aftermath of* St. Cyr *and* Nguyen, 16 GEO. IMMIGR. L.J. 313, 321–24 (2000) (commenting that § 242(b)(9) has broader preclusive impact). *See, e.g.*, Detroit Free Press v. Ashcroft, 195 F. Supp. 2d 948, 954–55 (E.D. Mich. 2002), *aff'd*, 303 F.3d 681 (6th Cir. 2002) (holding that court has jurisdiction to hear multi-party litigation before removal orders are entered); Hillcrest Baptist Church v. U.S., 2007 U.S. Dist. LEXIS 12782, at ** 25–26, (W.D. Wash. Feb. 23, 2007) (holding that § 242(b)(9) does not preclude court's judicial review of decisions made outside of removal proceedings).

[126] *See, e.g.*, Aparicio v. Blakeway, 302 F.3d 437 (5th Cir. 2002) (class action involving applications for special agricultural worker status); Walters v. Reno, 145 F.3d 1032 (9th Cir. 1998) (class of immigrant plaintiffs alleging denial of due process due to inadequate notice of removal procedures), *cert. denied*, 526 U.S. 1003 (1999).

e.   Habeas Corpus Review

As discussed earlier, the Supreme Court in recent years has ensured, at a minimum, habeas corpus review of removal decisions.[127] In *INS v. St. Cyr*,[128] the Court held that the district courts retained habeas corpus jurisdiction in the face of government arguments that the 1996 amendments barred jurisdiction over appeals of deportation orders of aggravated felons. As discussed earlier in this Chapter, the REAL ID Act, as it amended Section 242(a), re-established petitions for review in the courts of appeals as the exclusive vehicle for court review of final removal orders.[129] The Act expressly eliminated habeas corpus jurisdiction, mandamus jurisdiction, and jurisdiction under the All Writs Act, 28 U.S.C. § 1651, over removal orders.[130] There is one important exception, however. Courts that have interpreted INA § 242(a)(2) appear to allow habeas jurisdiction to review the *detention* of noncitizens.[131]

One benefit of habeas corpus is that it allows for the development of a factual record. Congress however, expressly precluded any fact-finding other than by the agency. According to INA § 242(a)(1), a reviewing "court may not order the taking of additional evidence. . . . " INA § 242(b)(4)(A) further provides that "the court of appeals shall decide the petition only on the administrative record on which the order of removal is based."[132] Thus, there is no room for factual development in the court of appeals in petitions to review removal orders.

3.   The Nuts-and-Bolts of Judicial Review

a.   Petitions for Review

INA § 242(a)(1) provides that "[j]udicial review of a final order of removal is governed only by chapter 158 of title 28 of the United States Code," known as the Hobbs Act, which permits a "petition for review" in the court of appeals. The petition for review, which is filed in the circuit that has jurisdiction over the geographical area in which the removal hearing was held,[133] must be filed no later than 30 days after the final removal order.[134] This time limit has been treated as a

---

[127] For a review of habeas corpus jurisdiction in judging measures taken in the war on terror, *see* Richard H. Fallon & Daniel J. Meltsner, *Habeas Corpus Jurisdiction, Substantive Rights, and the War on Terror*, 120 HARV. L. REV. 2029 (2007).

[128] 533 U.S. 289 (2001).

[129] For discussion of the various provisions of the REAL ID Act, *see* generally Hiroshi Motomura, *Immigration Law and Federal Court Jurisdiction Through the Lens of Habeas Corpus*, 91 CORNELL L. REV. 459 (2006).

[130] *See* INA § 242(a)(5); 8 U.S.C. § 1252(a)(5).

[131] *See, e.g.*, Hernandez v. Gonzales, 424 F.3d 42, 42–43 (1st Cir. 2005) (quoting H.R. Conf. Rep. No. 109-72, at 175 (2005)); Del Toro-Chacon v. Chertoff, 2008 U.S. Dist. LEXIS 18807 (W.D. Wash. March 10, 2008); Jeanty v. Bulger, 204 F. Supp. 2d 1366, 1373–74 (S.D. Fla. 2002), *aff'd sub nom.*, 321 F.2d 1336 (11th Cir.), *cert denied*, 540 U.S. 1016 (2003).

[132] There is an exception under INA § 242(b)(5)(B) for nationality claims, which may be transferred to a district court.

[133] *See* INA § 242(b)(2).

[134] *See* INA § 242(b)(1).

jurisdictional bar, i.e., the court lacks jurisdiction to review the petition if it was not filed in a timely manner.[135]

As amended, the filing of a petition for review does not automatically stay the noncitizen's removal pending disposition of the appeal; the noncitizen must file a motion for a stay. *See* INA § 242(b)(3)(B).[136] This has great practical significance and requires a stay motion to be filed in every case in which a petition for review is filed.[137]

Section 242(a)(1) makes the petition for review in the court of appeals the "sole and exclusive" procedure for reviewing removal orders. INA § 242(b)(9), which the Supreme Court has referred to as an "unmistakable 'zipper' clause,"[138] consolidates for review all questions of law or fact "arising from any action taken or proceeding brought to remove an alien from the United States. . . . " In *Madu v. Attorney General*,[139] however, the court of appeals found that Section 242(b)(9) did not apply to a challenge to Madu's detention and impending removal on the ground that there was no removal order in place. The court reasoned that Section 242(b)(9) applies only to review of an order of removal.[140]

---

[135] *See, e.g.*, Stone v. INS, 514 U.S. 386, 394–95 (1995) (holding that filing a timely motion with the BIA does not toll the time to petition for review); Dakane v. United States Attorney General, 399 F.3d 1269, 1272 n.3 (11th Cir. 2005) (per curiam).

[136] *See* Teshome-Gebreegziabher v. Mukasey, 528 F.3d 330, 331–32 (4th Cir. 2008) (recognizing that § 242(b)(3)(B) eliminates automatic stays of orders of removal when petition for review is filed); Rivera v. Mukasey, 508 F.3d 1271, 1277–78 (9th Cir. 2007) (acknowledging that filing of a petition for review does not automatically stay the removal of an alien pending the court's decision).

[137] *See* Teshome-Gebreegziabher v. Mukasey, 528 F.3d 330, 332 n.1 (4th Cir. 2008) ("The majority of circuits which have considered this issue have held that the traditional preliminary injunction balancing test" focusing on the likelihood of success on the merits and the relative harms to the parties, applies to requests for stays of removal.) (citing Tesfamichael v. Gonzales, 411 F.3d 169 (5th Cir. 2005); Hor v. Gonzales, 400 F.3d 482 (7th Cir. 2005); Douglas v. Ashcroft, 374 F.3d 230 (3d Cir. 2004); Lim v. Ashcroft, 375 F.3d 1011 (10th Cir. 2004); Arevalo v. Ashcroft, 344 F.3d 1 (1st Cir. 2003); Mohammed v. Reno, 309 F.3d 95 (2d Cir. 2002); Bejjani v. INS, 271 F.3d 670 (6th Cir. 2001); Andreiu v. Ashcroft, 253 F.3d 477 (9th Cir. 2001) (en banc)); Tesfamichael v. Gonzales, 411 F.3d 169, 171–78 (5th Cir. 2005) (stating that "one who is seeking review of a deportation order must ask the reviewing court for a stay of removal" and reviewing law on the standard for securing a stay of removal), *cert. denied sub nom.*, 128 S. Ct. 353 (2007). *But see* Bin Weng v. United States Att'y Gen., 287 F.3d 1335 (11th Cir. 2002) (requiring that noncitizen demonstrate by "clear and convincing evidence" that removal order violates the law). Sitting as a Circuit Justice, Justice Kennedy has acknowledged the split in the circuits on the appropriate standard for a stay of removal but concluded that the case before him was an inappropriate vehicle for resolving the split because the petitioner would have failed to satisfy either stay standard. *See* Kenyeres v. Ashcroft, 538 U.S. 1301, 1305–07 (2003) (Kennedy, J.).

[138] Reno v. American-Arab Anti-Discrimination Committee, 525 U.S. 471, 483 (1999). As Gerald Neuman explained, "[t]he term 'zipper clause' comes from labor law, where it refers to a provision in a collective bargaining agreement that prohibits further collective bargaining during the term of the agreement or, more generally, that limits the agreement of the parties to the four corners of the contract." Gerald L. Neuman, *Jurisdiction and the Rule of Law After the 1996 Immigration Act*, 113 Harv. L. Rev. 1963, 1984–85 (2000).

[139] 470 F.3d 1362, 1367 (11th Cir. 2006).

[140] *See also* Khorrani v. Rolince, 493 F. Supp. 2d 1061, 1067 (N.D. Ill. 2007) (similar reasoning). *See generally* Motomura, *supra* note 117, at 409–30 (urging a narrow reading of § 242(b)(9) that allows review of significant independent matters).

b.   Exhaustion of Administrative Remedies

Consistent with ordinary administrative law principles, INA § 242(d)(1), 8 U.S.C. § 1252(d)(1), provides that "[a] court may review a final order of removal only if . . . *the alien has exhausted all administrative remedies* available to the alien as of right."[141] (emphasis added). This is an easy requirement to satisfy in most cases in which a removal order has been entered. Courts have recognized various exceptions to the exhaustion requirement.[142]

c.   Limits on Judicial Review

i.   Consular Absolutism

Although removal decisions ordinarily are subject to judicial review, other immigration decisions are not. Importantly, visa denials by U.S. State Department consular officers are immune from judicial review.[143] The rule that a consular officer's decision to deny a visa is not reviewable by *any* court and that any review is limited to appeals within the agency, is known as "consular absolutism."[144] This rule can have far-reaching consequences for would-be immigrants who, for example, claim to be eligible to rejoin family, or to pursue employment, in the United States and claim to be eligible for an immigrant visa.

"[C]ourts have identified a limited exception to the doctrine [of consular absolutism] where the denial of a visa implicates the constitutional rights of American citizens."[145] The exception is founded in *Kleindienst v. Mandel*,[146] which

---

[141] The exhaustion requirement "is based on the need to allow agencies to develop the facts, to apply the law in which they are particularly expert, and to correct their own errors. The rule ensures that whatever judicial review is available will be informed and narrowed by the agencies' own decisions. It also avoids duplicative proceedings, and often the agency's ultimate decision will obviate the need for judicial intervention." Schlesinger v. Councilman, 420 U.S. 738, 756–57 (1975); *see, e.g.*, Soberanes v. Comfort, 388 F.3d 1305, 1309–10 (10th Cir. 2004*)*; Jordan v. Ashcroft, 296 F. Supp. 2d 249, 251–53 (D. Conn. 2003); Beresford v. INS, 299 F. Supp. 2d 106, 109 (E.D.N.Y. 2004).

[142] *See, e.g.*, Zhong v. U.S. Dep't of Justice, 480 F.3d 104, 116–25 (2d Cir. 2007) (stating that cases can be considered in "extraordinary situations" even when remedies have not been exhausted); Beharry v. Ashcroft, 329 F.3d 51, 56 (2d Cir. 2003) (recognizing that "the judicial common law exhaustion doctrine is discretionary and includes a number of exceptions"); Iddir v. INS, 301 F.3d 492, 498–99 (7th Cir. 2002) (listing various exceptions to exhaustion rule); Castro-Cortez v. INS, 239 F.3d 1037, 1044–45 (9th Cir. 2001) (finding that exhaustion requirement had been satisfied even though one avenue for protesting decision had not been pursued).

[143] *See, e.g.*, Saavedra Bruno v. Albright, 197 F.3d 1153, 1156 (D.C. Cir. 1999); Li Hing of Hong Kong, Inc. v. Levin, 800 F.2d 970, 971 (9th Cir. 1986); United States *ex rel.* Ulrich v. Kellog, 30 F.2d 984, 986 (D.C. Cir. 1929); Ruston v. Dep't of State, 29 F. Supp. 2d 518, 522 (E.D. Ark. 1998); *see also* Stephen H. Legomsky, *Fear and Loathing in Congress and the Courts: Immigration and Judicial Review*, 78 Tex. L. Rev. 1615, 1619–23 (2000) (mentioning well-settled precedent that courts lack jurisdiction to review visa denials by consular officers). For a study with recommendations for change, *see* James A.R. Nafziger, *Review of Visa Denials by Consular Officers*, 66 Wash. L. Rev. 1 (1991).

[144] For criticism of the rule of consular absolutism based on an abuse of power in an individual case, *see* David Ngaruri Kenney & Philip G. Schrag, Asylum Denied: A Refugee's Struggle for Safety in America 319–22 (2008).

[145] Bustamante v. Mukasey, 531 F.3d 1059, 1061 (9th Cir. 2008) (citing Adams v. Baker, 909 F.2d 643, 647–48 (1st Cir. 1990); Burrafato v. United States Dept. of State, 523 F.2d 554, 556–57 (2d Cir. 1975);

allowed U.S. citizens who claimed that their First Amendment rights were infringed because of the government's denial of a visa to Belgium journalist and Marxian theoretician and held that the Executive Branch could base a decision on admissibility on the basis of a facially legitimate and "bona fide reason."

ii.   Criminal Grounds

One important limit on judicial review involves removal of noncitizens convicted of certain crimes. Reflecting the fact that there are few defenders of "criminal aliens" in the political process,[147] Congress has consistently imposed restrictions on the judicial review of removal orders of this category of immigrants.[148] Under INA § 242(a)(2)(C), "no court shall have jurisdiction to review" a removal order if the person "is removable" on almost any of the crime-related grounds, such as the ever-expanding "aggravated felony" category. *See* INA § 101(a)(43), 8 U.S.C. § 1101(a)(43); Chapter 11. Importantly, INA § 242(a)(2)(D), 8 U.S.C. § 1252(a)(2)(D) specifies that the various limitations on judicial review do not preclude "review of constitutional claims or questions of law raised upon a petition for review. . . . "

Courts have consistently interpreted Section 242(a)(2)(C) as *not* barring review of whether the person is, in fact, subject to removal.[149] Thus, for example, if the removal ground is conviction of an "aggravated felony," the determination of whether the crime in question in fact constitutes an aggravated felony under the INA remains reviewable.[150] The same holds true for crimes of moral turpitude

---

Saavedra Bruno v. Albright, 197 F.3d 1153, 1163 (D.C. Cir. 1999)).

[146] Kleindienst v. Mandel 408 U.S. 753, 770 (1972).

[147] *See* JOHNSON, *supra* note 73, at 111–18: Kevin R. Johnson, *Los Olvidados: Images of the Immigrant, Political Power of Noncitizens, and Immigration Law and Enforcement*, 1993 BYU L. REV. 1139, 1169 (1993).

[148] *See, e.g.*, Gonzales v. Duenas-Alvarez, 549 U.S. 183 (2007); Lopez v. Gonzales, 549 U.S. 47 (2006); Leocal v. Ashcroft, 543 U.S. 1 (2004). *See generally* Andrew David Kennedy, Note, *Expedited Injustice: The Problems Regarding the Current Law of Expedited Removal of Aggravated Felons*, 60 VAND. L. REV. 1947 (2007).

[149] *See, e.g.*, Mahadeo v. Reno, 226 F.3d 3, 9 (5th Cir. 2000) (recognizing that § 242(a)(2)(C) would not prevent court from reviewing whether defendant is "an alien, removable, and removable because of a conviction for a qualifying crime") (citations omitted); Fierro v. Reno, 217 F.3d 1, 3 (1st Cir. 2000) (stating that "this court's authority to review removal orders based on an alien's commission of an aggravated felony has recently been restricted, . . . but this does not bar Fierro's claim on review that he is a citizen rather than an alien") (citation omitted); Anic v. Reno, 114 F. Supp. 2d 871, 877 (E.D. Mo. 2000) (stating that § 242(a)(2)(C) "permits substantial judicial review of the legality of an alien's removability").

[150] *See, e.g.*, Ortiz-Magana v. Mukasey, 523 F.3d 1042, 1046 (9th Cir. 2008); Penuliar v. Ashcroft, 395 F.3d 1037, 1040 (9th Cir. 2005); Gomez-Diaz v. Ashcroft, 324 F.3d 913, 916 (7th Cir. 2003); Valansi v. Ashcroft, 278 F.3d 203, 207–08 (3d Cir. 2002); Dalton v. Ashcroft, 257 F.3d 200, 203 (2d Cir. 2001); Nehme v. INS, 252 F.3d 415–42 (5th Cir. 2001); Guerrero-Perez v. INS, 242 F.3d 727, 729–30 (7th Cir. 2001); Drakes v. Zimski, 240 F.3d 246, 247–51 (3d Cir. 2001); Lewis v. INS, 194 F.3d 539, 541–46 (4th Cir. 1999). *But see* Berehe v. INS, 114 F.3d 159, 161 (10th Cir. 1997).

The government conceded the point in *Calcano-Martinez v. INS*, 533 U.S. 348, 350 n.2 (2001), and the Supreme Court reviewed the criminal grounds for removal in Leocal v. Ashcroft, 543 U.S. 1 (2004).

under INA § 237(a)(2).[151]

iii. Expedited Removal

Decisions of expedited removal at ports of entry, added in 1996 reform legislation,[152] are not subject to judicial review. INA § 235(b)(1) authorizes "expedited removal" of arriving noncitizens whom immigration inspectors believe to be inadmissible on documentary or fraud grounds. The Attorney General has the discretion to extend the expedited removal procedure to those who are present in the United States and unable to prove two years continuous physical presence, INA § 235(b)(1)(A)(iii), and has exercised that authority on several occasions.[153] INA § 242(a)(2)(A) provides that courts lack jurisdiction to review expedited removal orders. However, INA § 242(e)(2) provides that a court may exercise habeas corpus to review a claim that the person is a U.S. citizen (and thus not subject to expedited removal), that the person was not in fact the subject of an expedited removal order, or that the expedited removal procedure should not have been used because the person was a returning lawful permanent resident. *See* INA § 242(e)(2) and the previous discussion of *Landon v. Plasencia.*

Congress also imposed limits on class actions challenging expedited removal. INA § 235(e)(3) prohibits actions to challenge the legality of INA Section 235(b), or of any regulations or other written policies issued to implement Section 235(b), more than 60 days after the challenged section was implemented. During the 60-day period in which such challenges could be brought, only the District Court for the District of Columbia had jurisdiction, and no such challenge may be brought by class action. *See* INA § 242(e)(1)(B). A challenge to expedited removal was brought and dismissed on standing grounds.[154]

iv. Discretionary Relief

One of the most important limits on judicial review concerns the exercise of discretion by the agents. INA § 242(a)(2)(B), 8 U.S.C. § 1252(a)(2)(B) denies judicial review of any form of relief "specified . . . to be in the discretion of the Attorney General or the Secretary of Homeland Security other than the granting of relief under section 208(a) [which governs asylum, *see* Chapter 11]." INA § 242(d), 8 U.S.C. § 1252(d) provides, however, that nothing "shall be construed as precluding review of constitutional claims or questions of law raised upon a petition for review filed with the appropriate court of appeals. . . . "

---

[151] *See, e.g.,* Notash v. Gonzales, 427 F.3d 693, 695–96 (9th Cir. 2005); Sosa-Martinez, 420 F.3d 1338, 1340–41 (11th Cir. 2005); Patel v. Ashcroft, 401 F.3d 400, 405–07 (6th Cir. 2005); Carty v. Ashcroft, 395 F.3d 1081, 1082–83 (9th Cir. 2005).

[152] *See* Laplante, *supra* note 34, at 213–16; Ebba Gebisa, Comment, *Constitutional Concerns with the Enforcement and Expansion of Expedited Removal,* 2007 U. Chi. Legal F. 565.

[153] See Gebisa, *supra* note 152, at 571–74 (summarizing expansion of use of expedited removal); Thomas J. White Center on Law & Government, *The Expedited Removal Study: Report on the First Three Years of Implementation of Expedited Removal,* 15 Notre Dame. J.L. Ethics & Pub. Pol'y 1, 17–18 (2001) (same).

[154] *See* American Immigration Lawyers Ass'n v. Reno, 199 F.3d 1352 (D.C. Cir. 2000) (dismissing challenge to expedited removal provision on standing grounds).

Section 242(a)(2)(B)(i) bars judicial review of any judgment of relief under the waiver provisions in § 212(h) and § 212(i), cancellation of removal, voluntary departure, and adjustment of status. See Chapter 11. INA § 242(a)(2)(B)(ii) bars judicial review of any other decisions or actions, not including nationality and naturalization decisions, to be in the discretion of the Attorney General or Secretary of Homeland Security.[155] Section 242(a)(2)(B), however, does not preclude judicial review of "constitutional claims or questions of law." INA § 242(a)(2)(D). In addition, an exception leaves judicial review available for asylum decisions, but the statute specifies a highly deferential standard of review. See INA § 242(b)(4)(D) ("[T]he Attorney General's discretionary judgment whether to grant relief under section 208(a) [asylum] shall be conclusive unless manifestly contrary to the law and an abuse of discretion.").[156]

In *Montero-Martinez v. Ashcroft*,[157] the Ninth Circuit held that under § 242(a)(2)(B)(i) it could review whether the immigrant was ineligible for cancellation of removal. However, the court held that whether "exceptional and extremely unusual hardship" exists is a discretionary judgment not subject to judicial review.[158]

As *Montero-Martinez* suggests, it is settled that the bar on review is limited to the discretionary components of the named remedies. As for review of agency factfinding, several courts construed the pre-REAL ID Act version of section 242(a)(2)(B)(i) as not barring judicial review of administrative findings of fact concerning eligibility for affirmative relief.[159] Nothing in the REAL ID Act changes those results.

It is not clear whether Section 242(b)(2)(B)(ii) reaches those Attorney General decisions that are authorized by regulation rather than by statute. Several courts have expressly held that denials of motions to reopen removal procedings, which are authorized by regulation,[160] are reviewable for abuse of discretion.[161] The

---

[155] *See, e.g.*, Singh v. Gonzales, 451 F.3d 400, 410 (6th Cir. 2006); Tang v. Chertoff, 493 F. Supp. 2d 148, 153 (D. Mass. 2007); Grinberg v. Swancina, 478 F. Supp. 2d 1350, 1353–54 (S.D. Fla. 2007); Zheng v. Pogash, 416 F. Supp. 2d 550, 554–56 (S.D. Tex. 2006). For a thorough discussion of the definition of "discretionary" immigration decisions, *see* DANIEL KANSTROOM, DEPORTATION NATION: OUTSIDERS IN AMERICAN HISTORY 228–40 (2007).

[156] *See generally* Daniel Kanstroom, *Surrounding the Hole in the Doughnut: Discretion and Deference in U.S. Immigration Law*, 71 TUL. L. REV. 703 (1997) (analyzing exercise of agency discretion in immigration cases).

[157] 277 F.3d 1137, 1141–44 (9th Cir. 2002); *see, e.g.*, Fernandez v. Gonzales, 439 F.3d 592, 603 (9th Cir. 2006); Sepulveda v. Gonzales, 407 F.3d 59, 62–63 (2d Cir. 2005); Morales-Morales v. Ashcroft, 384 F.3d 418, 423 (7th Cir. 2004).

[158] *See also* Fernandez v. Gonzales, 439 F.3d 592, 603 (9th Cir. 2006); Martinez-Rosas v. Gonzales, 424 F.3d 926, 929–30 (9th Cir. 2005); Romero-Torres v. Ashcroft, 327 F.3d 887, 889–92 (9th Cir. 2003).

[159] *See, e.g.*, Reyes-Vasquez v. Ashcroft, 395 F.3d 903, 907–09 (8th Cir. 2005) (holding that BIA finding of no "continuous physical presence" for cancellation of removal purposes was not discretionary and therefore subject to judicial review); Morales-Morales v. Ashcroft, 384 F.3d 418, 421–23 (7th Cir. 2004) (same); Sabido Valdivia v. Gonzales, 423 F.3d 1144, 1149 (10th Cir. 2005) (same); Mireles-Valdez v. Ashcroft, 349 F.3d 213 (5th Cir. 2003) (same); Sepulveda v. Gonzales, 407 F.3d 59, 63 (2d Cir. 2005) (holding that "INA did not bar judicial review of nondiscretionary, or purely legal, decisions regarding an alien's eligibility for adjustment of status").

[160] *See* 8 C.F.R. § 103.3 (2008).

courts are split with respect to the reviewability of the decisions of immigration judges denying continuances by *regulation*, which are in the discretion of the immigration court.[162]

v. Detention Decisions

While removal proceedings are pending, administrative officials have the discretion whether to detain the noncitizen, release him or her on bond, or grant parole without requiring bond. See INA § 236(a), 8 U.S.C. § 1226(a). However, detention is mandatory for noncitizens who are deportable under most of the criminal provisions. See INA § 236(c), which the Supreme Court upheld in the face of a constitutional challenge in *Demore v. Kim*.[163]

Under INA § 236(e), "[n]o court may set aside any action or decision of the Attorney General under this section regarding the detention or release of any alien or the grant, revocation, or denial of bond or parole."[164] The REAL ID Act did not amend INA § 236(e), and the conference committee report stated that the Act "would not preclude habeas review over challenges to detention that are independent of challenges to removal orders."[165]

---

[161] *See* Singh v. Gonzales, 404 F.3d 1024, 1026–27 (7th Cir. 2005); Zhao v. Gonzales, 404 F.3d 295, 302–04 (5th Cir. 2005); Medina-Morales v. Ashcroft, 362 F.3d 1263, 1268–71 (9th Cir. 2004); *see also* Barker v. Ashcroft, 382 F.3d 313, 315 (3d Cir. 2003) (holding denials of motion to reopen reviewable but not addressing the distinction between discretionary authority conferred by statute and that conferred by regulations).

[162] *Compare* Zafar v. U.S. Att'y Gen., 461 F.3d 1357, 1360–62 (11th Cir. 2006) (holding that court had jurisdiction to review decision to deny continuance of removal proceedings); Zhao v. Gonzalez, 404 F.3d 295, 302–04 (5th Cir. 2005) (holding that § 1252(a)(2)(B)(ii) does not bar judicial review of decision to deny motion to reopen removal proceedings); Subhan v. Ashcroft, 383 F.3d 591, 594–96 (7th Cir. 2004) (holding that court of appeals can review decision to deny continuance as part of review of final removal order); Medina-Morales v. Ashcroft, 371 F.3d 520, 528–29 (9th Cir. 2004) (holding that § 1252(a)(2)(B)(ii) does not deprive court of appeals of jurisdiction to review denial of motion to reopen), *with* Yerkovich v. Ashcroft, 381 F.3d 990, 993–95 (10th Cir. 2004) (holding that § 1252(a)(2)(B)(ii) precludes judicial review of decision to deny continuance of removal proceedings); Onyinkwa v. Ashcroft, 376 F.3d 797, 799–800 (8th Cir. 2004) (concluding that court of appeals lacks jurisdiction to review denial of requests to continue removal proceedings). *See generally* Tarik Naber, *Judicial Review Under 8 U.S.C. § 1252(a)(2)(B)(ii): How a Minority of Federal Circuit Courts Are Keeping Non-Citizens Out of Court*, 40 U.C. Davis L. Rev. 1515 (2007).

[163] 538 U.S. 510 (2003).

[164] The Court in *Demore v. Kim*, 538 U.S. 510, 516–17 (2003), read the provision as permitting the use of habeas corpus to challenge the constitutionality of Section 236.

[165] House Rep. No. 109-72, at 175, 109th Cong., 1st Sess. (2005).

Chapter 7

IMMIGRANT VISAS

A. THE FUNDAMENTALS

The INA establishes an elaborate system to manage the total worldwide level of immigration for those seeking permanent residence in the United States. The following discussion relates only to permanent residence — the system for immigrant visas.

There are worldwide quotas, per-country limits and visa category restrictions. The worldwide allocation of visas is divided among the preference categories for family-sponsored and employment-based immigrants, and the diversity immigrant category. Immediate relatives of U.S. citizens are in distinct class of immigrants outside of the worldwide allocation. Several categories of "special immigrants" also are treated differently in the allocation of immigrant visas. Refugees and asylees become lawful permanent residents under a separate numerical system. This Chapter covers immigrant visa categories and the visa allocation system.

1. Worldwide Quotas and Preference Categories

Worldwide numerical restrictions on immigrant admissions have existed since 1921 under the discriminatory national origins quota system. The national origins quota system from 1921 to 1965 favored certain countries by allocating more visas to Western European nations, and by excluding most Asian countries almost entirely. Chapter 2 covers the history and evolution of immigration law and policy.

Today, the immigrant visa system relies on an annual nondiscriminatory worldwide distribution as well as per-country quotas in each of the family-sponsored and employment-based preference categories. Diversity visas are within the worldwide allocation but have different per-country limits. The current system was established by the 1990 amendments to the INA. The 1990 Act reorganized the family-sponsored preference categories, added new employment-based preference categories, and established the diversity visa category. It also increased the total number of annual immigrant visas.

The worldwide annual visa allocation system is set forth in INA § 201 and establishes a baseline for total annual immigrant visas of 675,000 for family-sponsored, employment-based, and diversity visas.[1] The per-country limits in INA § 202 ensure equal access to immigrant visas by all nations.

To understand the worldwide annual visa allocation system it is useful to think of immigrants as divided into two categories: (1) immigrants subject to numerical restrictions; and (2) immigrants who obtain immigrant visas without numerical limitation. Those admitted without numerical restriction include immediate relatives of United States citizens,[2] returning permanent residents[3] and special immigrants along with a limited group of other permanent residents.[4] Immediate relatives are a special class within the visa allocation system, and they represent the majority of immigrants entering without numerical restriction. The immediate relative category includes the children, spouses, and parents of U.S. citizens who are at least 21 years of age.[5]

---

[1] INA §§ 201(c)(1)(A)(i) (480,000 baseline for family-sponsored visas); 201(d)(1)(A) (140,000 baseline for employment-based visas); 201(e) (55,000 baseline for diversity visas).

[2] INA § 201(b)(2)(A).

[3] INA § 101(a)(27)(A).

[4] INA § 201(b). Noncitizens not subject to the worldwide levels or numerical limits include: special immigrants who are returning from temporary visits abroad (INA § 101(a)(27)(A)) and former U.S. citizens who will apply to reacquire citizenship (INA § 101(a)(27)(B)); refugees under INA § 207 or asylees who have adjusted status under INA § 209; LPRs who were beneficiaries under IRCA under INA §§ 210 or 245A; LPRs who are beneficiaries of cancellation of removal under INA § 240A; and special registry LPRs who entered before 1972 under INA § 249.

[5] INA § 101(b)(1) (definition of a child); § 201(b)(2)(A) defines immediate relatives to include some widows and widowers; a lawful permanent resident's child born outside of the U.S. while on a temporary trip abroad; and a child who enters separately from a parent who was granted permanent residence, when the child is following to join that parent.

The total worldwide number of immigrant visas issued in each fiscal year varies, and regularly is above the 675,000 baseline.[6] For example, in 2006, the total number of immigrant admissions was 1,266,264 and in 2007 the total number of immigrant admissions was 1,052,415.[7] The worldwide levels fluctuate due to a number of reasons. A major factor accounting for the range of total immigrant admissions is the number of immediate relatives and the statutory requirement of a minimum number of 226,000 visas for the family preference categories. This statutory minimum is discussed below. The system also is designed to capture unused visas in the employment-based and family-sponsored preferences, and reallocate those in the following fiscal year.[8] Another major reason is bureaucratic processing delays.

Immigrant visas are issued on a fiscal year basis beginning on October 1st each year.[9] An immigrant visa is assigned to an individual when a noncitizen is admitted at a port of entry after consular processing or when an adjustment of status application is approved.[10] Immigrant visas are assigned to the principal beneficiary of a visa petition and that person's spouse and children who are admitted at the same time as derivative beneficiaries.[11] Visa numbers are used quickly in each preference category as visas are assigned to principal immigrants and their derivative beneficiaries.

a.   Family-Sponsored Visas

The number of immediate relative admissions, although not subject to numerical restrictions, are tallied under the worldwide system. Immediate relatives represent the majority of immigrants entering without numerical restriction.[12] The immediate relative category includes the children, spouses, and parents of U.S. citizens who are at least 21 years of age.[13]

---

[6] INA § 201(c)(1)(A)(i) (480,000 baseline for family-sponsored visas); § 201(d)(1)(A) (140,000 baseline for employment-based visas); § 201(e) (55,000 baseline for diversity visas).

[7] Dept. of Homeland Sec., *Yearbook of Immigration Statistics*, *available at* http://www.dhs.gov/ximgtn/statistics/publications/yearbook.shtm (last visited Oct. 16, 2008). To compare: in 2000, total immigrant admissions were 849,807; in 2001 total immigrant admissions were 1,064,318. Dept. of Homeland Sec., *Archives*, *available at* http://www.dhs.gov/ximgtn/statistics/publications/archive.shtm#1 (last visited Oct. 16, 2008).

[8] INA § 201(c).

[9] The fiscal year is October 1 through September 31st.

[10] *See* Chapter 10.

[11] INA § 203(d). Noncitizen spouses and children may also "follow to join" the principal beneficiary of a petition who entered earlier as long as they are still eligible under the definition of "spouse" or "child" in INA § 101(b).

[12] Immediate Relative Admissions were 436,802 in 2005; were 581,106 in 2006; and were 494,920 in 2007. Dept. of Homeland Sec., *Yearbook of Immigration Statistics*, *available at* http://www.dhs.gov/ximgtn/statistics/publications/yearbook.shtm (last visited Oct. 16, 2008).

[13] INA §§ 101(b)(1); 201(b)(2)(A)(i).

The annual worldwide allocation of immigrant visas to the family categories is set at a baseline of 480,000.[14] These 480,000 visas are allocated to immediate relative admissions, which are not limited, and the family-sponsored preference category admissions which are numerically limited. There is a ceiling on the number of immediate relative admissions that can be allocated from the total 480,000 annual family-sponsored visas. The annual visas for the other family-sponsored preference categories may not be lower than 226,000.[15] This ensures that immediate relative admissions do not use up all of the family-sponsored preference visas in any fiscal year.[16]

This floor of 226,000 family-sponsored visas plus the unlimited immediate relative visas creates the annual variability in total immigrant visas. As a result, the total actual number of family visas issued in a fiscal year regularly is above the 480,000 family-sponsored baseline. Once immediate relative admissions rise above the floor of 226,000, then the total number of family visas issued will rise above 480,000, as needed, to accommodate all of the immediate relatives who seek admission in a given year. If immediate relative visas are below the floor, then more visas are available to the family-sponsored preferences categories.

The minimum number of 226,000 visas for the four family-sponsored preference categories are allocated under INA 203(a).[17] The four family-sponsored preference categories include:

- **First Preference** for unmarried sons and daughters over the age of 21 of U.S citizens (23,400 visas per year);
- **Second Preference** for two categories: the spouses and children (2-A) and unmarried sons and daughters (2-B) of permanent residents (114,200 visas per year);
- **Third Preference** for married sons and daughters of U.S. citizens and their spouses and children (23,400 visas per year); and
- **Fourth Preference** for brothers and sisters of U.S. citizens at least 21 years of age, and their spouses and children (65,000 visas per year).

Only one family-sponsored category is available to LPRs. The second preference category allows LPRs to bring in close family members. In the second preference category, the allocation of the family-sponsored visas favors LPR spouses and children under the age of 21. Seventy-five percent (75%) of the second preference visas must be allocated to the 2-A category for spouses and children.[18]

---

[14] INA § 201(c). The annual allocation includes any unused employment-based visas from the prior fiscal year.

[15] INA § 201(c)(2) establishes a "floor" of 226,000 visas for the family-sponsored preference categories.

[16] INA § 201(c)(1)(B)(ii). Family-sponsored admissions also are reduced by the number of noncitizens who were paroled into the US. under INA § 212(d)(5) and who have not departed within 365 days and who did not acquire permanent residence in the preceding two fiscal years.

[17] Note more than 226,000 visas might be available in a fiscal year if immediate relative admissions are below the floor.

[18] INA § 202(a)(2) establishes a floor for the second preference 2-A category for spouses and children of permanent residents to accommodate the demand for visas from the large number of petitions filed

b.   Employment-Based Visas

The worldwide level of employment-based immigrant visas allocated each fiscal year is 140,000.[19] The 1990 amendments to the INA increased the number of employment-based visas from 54,000 to the current level of 140,000. There are "spill-down" provisions to reallocate unused visas among the employment-based preference categories annually.[20]

The five employment based preference categories for immigrant visas are:

- **Priority Workers (EB-1)** including three types of workers: (1) persons of extraordinary ability in the sciences, arts, education, business or athletics; (2) outstanding researchers; (3) multinational executives and managers (28.6% of the total number or approximately 40,000);[21]
- **Members of the Professions with Advanced Degrees and Noncitizens with Exceptional Ability (EB-2)** including physicians working in shortage areas (28.6% of the total number plus any unused visas from the EB-1 category or approximately 40,000);[22]
- **Skilled Workers, Professionals and Other Workers (EB-3)** (28.6% of total number plus any unused visas in the EB-1 and EB-2 categories or approximately 40,000);[23]
- **Certain Special Immigrants** (7.1% of the total number; unused special immigrant visas are allocated to the EB-1 category or approximately 10,000); and
- **Employment Creation Visas** (7.1% of the total number or approximately 10,000).

2.   Per-Country Ceilings and the Visa Bulletin

The per-country numerical visa limitations on individual countries are set forth in INA § 202. The per-country limit system is extraordinarily complex. Generally, each country will receive 7% of the total annual visas allocated to the preference catgories. In 2007, this was 26,120 immigrant visas. This does not mean that each of the 180+ countries of the world have 26,000 visas annually. The per-country limits exist to ensure that high demand in one country does not use up all of the available worldwide visas.[24] The per-country limits apply only to family-sponsored

---

by permanent residents for their spouses and children, and the hardship caused by long delays in the availability of visas for close family members.

[19] INA § 201(d). The annual allocation includes any unused family-sponsored visas from the prior fiscal year. If not all of the employment-based numbers are used in a fiscal year, then the surplus visas are added to the total family-sponsored visas to be allocated in the following fiscal year.

[20] INA § 203(b).

[21] Each category of priority workers has equal access to the annual 40,000 visa allotment under INA § 203(b)(1).

[22] *Id.*

[23] The term "profession" is defined at INA § 101(a)(32).

[24] Under INA § 202(e) there is a separate complex formula to ensure that visas for countries with high demand are spread out among the family-sponsored and employment-based categories.

and employment-based categories. Immediate relatives are not included in the per country limit, nor are diversity immigrants.

The Visa Office of the U.S. Department of State publishes a monthly visa bulletin that charts immigrant visa availability by preference category, and, in some cases by country, based on a per-country limit calculation.[25] [See Appendix 7-1.] Some countries regularly reach the per-country limit for the allocation of visas in some of the preference categories. These backlogs are created because there are more approved immigrant visa petitions relative to the availability of visas under the per-country limits and worldwide allocation limits. The countries that typically have backlogs in the availability of visas include Mexico, India, China, and the Philippines.

An immigrant visa is available to each noncitizen according to the priority date (the waiting list) in the Visa Bulletin. A priority date is assigned when the noncitizen's family member files a visa petition or when the employer files a petition or labor certification application to begin the processing. The Visa Bulletin is issued monthly during the fiscal year to chart the movement of priority dates in the waiting list.

For example, the August 2008 Visa Bulletin has a date of September 8, 1997 for the fourth preference family-sponsored visa category (brothers and sisters of U.S. citizens). Immigrant visas are available to a noncitizen whose brother or sister filed an immigrant visa petition on or before September 8, 1997. Noncitizens from the Philippines, for example, who are eligible under the fourth preference family-sponsored visa category have an even longer backlog in the availability of visas. The priority date for Filipino fourth preference petition beneficiaries is March 6, 1986, representing a much greater backlog.

B.   FAMILY IMMIGRATION

Family members of U.S. citizens and permanent residents are eligible for immigrant visas either as immediate relatives or within one of the family-sponsored preference categories set forth in INA § 203(a).

There are a few key issues that affect all of the family-sponsored preference categories. First, only U.S. citizens may petition for extended family members in the first, third and fourth preference categories. Permanent residents may only petition for their spouses, children under the age of 21, and adult, unmarried sons and daughters. Second, in most of the preference categories there are significant backlogs in the availability of immigrant visas, as long as a decade. This situation has led to the suggestion that the third and fourth preference categories should be eliminated and those visas could be reallocated to close family members.[26] It is anticipated that this reallocation would eliminate the constant backlogs in the second preference category.

---

[25] Dept. of State, *Visa Bulletin*, *available at* http://travel.state.gov/visa/frvi/bulletin/bulletin_1360.html (last visited Oct. 16, 2008).

[26] U.S. Commission on Immigration Reform, *Becoming an American: Immigration and Immigrant Policy* (Report to Congress 1997).

The four family-sponsored preference categories include:

- **First Preference** for unmarried sons and daughters over the age of 21 of U.S citizens (23,400 visas per year);
- **Second Preference** for the spouses, children and unmarried sons and daughters of permanent residents (114,200 visas per year);
- **Third Preference** for married sons and daughters of U.S. citizens and their spouses and children (23,400 visas per year); and
- **Fourth Preference** for brothers and sisters of U.S. citizens at least 21 years of age, and their spouses and children (65,000 visas per year).

1.   Marriage-Based Immigration

Marriage is a key family relationship for immigration benefits under the INA, however the term "marriage" is not defined. Marriages are a major source of the annual immigrant admissions either as immediate relatives or within a preference category. Spouses and children also immigrate as derivative beneficiaries on employment-based petitions.[27]

There are two eligibility issues that arise in marriage-based immigrant cases. First, the marriage must be valid in the place where it took place. A common-law marriage is recognized as long as it is valid in the location where it existed.[28] Similarly, marriages that take place in foreign countries are recognized if the marriage is valid under the laws of the foreign country.[29]

Second, the marriage must qualify under the INA, even if the marriage is valid where it took place. Same-sex marriages, although these may be valid in the locale where the ceremony occurs, have not been recognized for immigration benefits. This denial of immigration benefits is inconsistent with the immigration policies of many other nations.[30] For example, the United Kingdom has recognized same-sex relationships of more than four years since 1997.

In *Adams v. Howerton*, 673 F.2d 1036 (9th Cir. 1982), *cert denied*, 458 U.S. 1111 (1982), a gay couple was married after receiving a marriage license from the county clerk in Boulder, Colorado and a ceremony was performed by a minister. Adams filed an immediate relative petition for his same-sex partner, Sullivan. The INS denied the petition and the BIA affirmed. The Ninth Circuit affirmed the BIA decision by interpreting the INA and Congressional intent in using the term marriage. The court concluded that the ordinary construction of the term marriage included only a man and a woman.[31]

---

[27] INA 203(b).

[28] *Matter of Darwish*, 14 I. & N. Dec. 307 (BIA. 1973).

[29] *Matter of L__*, 7 I. & N. Dec. 587 (BIA 1957).

[30] *See* Thomas Alexander Alienikoff, David A. Martin, Hiroshi Motomura & Maryellen Fullerton, *Immigration and Citizenship, Process and Policy* 331 (6th ed. 2008). As of 2006, same-sex immigration benefits were available in Australia, Belgium, Brazil, Canada, Denmark, Finland, France, Germany, Iceland, Israel, the Netherlands, New Zealand, Norway, Portugal, South Africa, Spain, Sweden, Switzerland, and the United Kingdom.

[31] The 1996 Defense of Marriage Act permits federal recognition only of marriages between a man

The problem of sham marriages entered for immigration benefits has long been a concern of Congress. Before the 1986 amendments to the Act, the INS adopted two approaches to identify fraudulent marriages. A marriage was deemed fraudulent if the parties did not intend to establish a life together when they entered the marriage. Marriages also were deemed invalid if "factually dead" due to separation or other change in circumstances despite the intent of the husband and wife when they married. Before 1986, the INS conducted lengthy investigations of marriage relationships to determine whether a couple intended to establish a life together or to identify whether a marriage was factually dead.[32]

For example, in *Bark v. INS*, 511 F.2d 1200 (9th Cir. 1975), the Ninth Circuit reviewed an Immigration Judge's decision that a sham marriage existed. Bark and his wife were "sweethearts" in Korea before she immigrated. After Bark came to the U.S. in 1968 (as a business visitor and as a student), he and his wife renewed their relationship. The couple was married in 1969 (less than one year after his business visit). Both Bark and his wife testified at the hearing that they married for love and not to obtain immigration benefits.

In *Bark*, the Immigration Judge decided a sham marriage existed because the couple had separated at one point and there was evidence that "the wife could and did leave as she pleased when they were together." The BIA affirmed and the Ninth Circuit reversed and remanded the case. The court noted that a sham marriage exists if the couple did not intend to establish a life together, and the mere fact that the couple separated is not an indication of whether they intended to establish a life together *when they are married.*[33] Further, a bona fide marriage does not require any particular kind of relationship between a couple.

Congress addressed the problem of fraudulent marriages and intrusive investigations in the 1986 Immigration Marriage Fraud Act [IMFA], and established an entirely new process.[34] Now, conditional permanent residence is granted to noncitizens if the marriage was entered into less than two years before the immigrant visa is issued under INA § 216.[35] Marriages over two years at the time an immigrant visa is issued are not subject to the conditional residency requirement. Conditional residence is accorded to marriages in the family-sponsored second preference category and the immediate relative category.

IMFA establishes a procedure for removal of the condition. The conditional resident and petitioning spouse must file a joint petition to remove the condition during the ninety-day period prior to the second anniversary of obtaining permanent resident status.[36] The joint petition must establish that the couple has

---

and a woman. Pub. L. No. 104-199, 110 Stat. 2419 (Sept. 21, 1996).

[32] *See* Dabaghian v. Civilietti, 607 F.2d 868 (9th Cir. 1979) (rejecting the INS denial of immigration benefits based on a finding that a marriage was "factually dead but legally alive" because, in part, of the likely invasion of privacy by INS investigators).

[33] The case was remanded to the Immigration Judge to assess whether Bark and his wife intended to establish a life together at the time of their marriage. *Bark*, 511 F.2d at 1202.

[34] Pub. L. No. 99-639, 100 Stat. 3537 (Nov. 10, 1986).

[35] INA § 216(g).

[36] INA § 216(c)(1)(a).

a qualifying marriage that: (1) is valid under the laws where it took place; (2) has not been judicially annulled or terminated other than through death of a spouse; and (3) was not entered for immigration benefits.[37] The couple may be required to appear for a personal interview before approval of the joint petition.[38]

Failure to file the petition before the two-year anniversary is permissible only if the noncitizen establishes good cause and extenuating circumstances.[39] Failure to file a joint petition or failure to appear for an interview, other than for good cause, results in termination of permanent residence as of the two-year anniversary.[40] If the joint petition is denied, permanent residence is terminated on the date of the second anniversary.[41] If the residence is terminated, then the noncitizen is removable under INA § 237(a)(1)(D).[42]

The noncitizen can request a waiver of the joint petition requirement.[43] A hardship waiver to remove the condition is available when one of the requirements of a qualifying marriage can not be established. The noncitizen's waiver application must establish either: (1) extreme hardship would result if the noncitizen is removed; (2) the marriage was entered in good faith but has been terminated and the noncitizen was not at fault in failing to meet the requirements for removal of the condition; or (3) the marriage was entered in good faith by the noncitizen and during the marriage the noncitizen was subject to extreme cruelty or battery, and the noncitizen was not a fault in failing to meet the requirements for removal of the condition.[44]

Another mechanism to prevent sham marriages was added in the 1986 IMFA amendments relating to subsequent marriages and immigration benefits.[45] An LPR who obtained residence based on a marriage is prohibited from filing a marriage petition for a new spouse until five years have elapsed, unless special circumstances exist.[46]

2.   Domestic Violence

One major concern about the conditional residence procedure was the possibility that victims of domestic abuse might feel forced to stay with an abusive spouse in order to remove the condition on their permanent residence status. The 1990 Act

---

[37] INA § 216(d)(1)(A).

[38] INA § 216(d)(3). The personal interview requirement can be waived when deemed appropriate. 8 C.F.R. § 216.4(b)(1) (2008).

[39] INA § 216(d)(2)(B).

[40] INA § 216(c)(2).

[41] INA § 216(c)(3)(C).

[42] *See* Chapter 11.

[43] INA § 216(c).

[44] INA § 216(c)(4).

[45] INA § 204(a)(2)(A).

[46] An LPR can avoid this bar if clear and convincing evidence exists that the prior marriage was not entered for purposes of obtaining immigration benefits or evading any provision of immigration laws. This spousal second preference petition limitation does not apply if the prior marriage was terminated by death of the U.S. citizen or LPR spouse. INA § 204(a)(2)(B).

added the third extreme hardship waiver ground to the joint petition requirement for battered spouses.[47] Subsequent amendments to the INA in 2000, 2005 and 2006 have expanded the protection of victims of domestic abuse.[48] Spouses, parents and children who are subject to extreme cruelty or are battered may file their own petitions for permanent residence.

Another domestic abuse situation was addressed by 1994 amendments to the INA. The 1994 Violence Against Women Act (VAWA) permits a battered spouse, either documented or undocumented, who is eligible for a marriage-based immigrant visa petition to file a petition on her own behalf.[49] A battered spouse or child is eligible to self-petition if she is a person of "good moral character;" she entered the marriage in good faith, and resided in the United States with the U.S. citizen or permanent resident spouse; and the spouse or child was subject to a battering or extreme mental cruelty during the marriage.[50] Victims of abuse are eligible based on physical and emotional abuse as well as the threat of abuse.[51] A self-petition also may be filed by: (1) battered children up to the age of 25 of a U.S. citizen or permanent resident, and (2) elderly abuse victims of a U.S. citizen or permanent resident.[52]

This self-petition process avoids the involvement of an abusive spouse, who may have refused to file a petition or threatened to withdraw a petition for an immigrant visa. The Battered Immigrant Women Protection Act of 2000 (VAWA 2000) amendments to the INA made it easier for battered spouses and children to self-petition in the event of a divorce before the self-petition is filed.[53] VAWA 2000 also eliminated the requirement that the self-petitioning spouse or child establish deportation would result in extreme hardship.[54] Divorced victims of abuse also are eligible to self-petition.

VAWA and other related amendments to the INA provide other forms of relief to battered spouses and children.[55] Certain grounds of inadmissibility and

---

[47] INA § 216(c)(4)(C).

[48] Victims of Trafficking and Violence Protection Act (VTVPA) (Battered Immigrant Women Protection Act, Pub. L. No. 106-386, 114 Stat. 1464 (Oct. 28, 2000); Violence Against Women and DOJ Reauthorization Act of 2005, Pub. L. No. 109-162, 119 Stat. 2960 (Jan. 5, 2006); Violence Against Women Reauthorization Act-Technical corrections, Pub. L. No. 109-271, 120 Stat. 750 (Aug. 12, 2006).

[49] Violence Against Women Act (VAWA), Pub. L. No. 103-322, 108 Stat. 1902–1955 (Sept. 13, 1994).

[50] INA § 204(a)(1)(A)-(B).

[51] 8 C.F.R. § 216.5(e)(3)(i) defines extreme cruelty and a battered person to include, but not be limited to, forcible detention, psychological or sexual abuse, or exploitation which results in physical or mental injury or the threat of injury.

[52] INA §§ 204(a)(1)(D)(v); 204(a)(1)(A)(vii).

[53] INA § 204(a)(1)(B)(v). The marriage must be terminated within two years immediately preceding the filing of the self-petition.

[54] Battered Immigrant Women Protection Act of 2000 (VAWA 2000), Pub. L. No. 106-386, 114 Stat. 1464 (Oct. 28, 2000). The Act also allows a self petition in the case of invalid marriages entered in good faith but found to be bigamous. See INA § 204(a)(1)(A)(iii).

[55] The International Marriage Brokers Regulation Act of 2005 requires certain international marriage brokers to conduct background checks on U.S. patrons and provide information to noncitizen spouses. 8 U.S.C. § 1375a (2006).

deportation may not apply if connected to the spousal battery or cruelty.[56] Special relief from removal provisions apply to battered spouses and children.[57] VAWA 2000 added two nonimmigrant visa categories for victims of trafficking and victims of other criminal activity.[58] These are discussed in Chapter 8.

3.   Other Family Members

Some family members of both lawful permanent residents and U.S. citizens are eligible for immigrant visas; namely spouses and children.[59] The extended family members of U.S. citizens may immigrate, including parents, married or unmarried sons and daughters, and siblings. The second preference category for lawful permanent resident family members only includes children and unmarried sons and daughters. There are significant visa backlogs in many of these categories.[60]

Immigrant children are particularly affected by the backlog in visa availability. Children under the age of 21 are eligible for classification as immediate relatives, and second preference immigrants.[61] A frequent problem occurs when a child "ages-out" and turns 21 rendering her ineligible for an immigrant visa as a child.[62] The immigrant visa petition can be transferred to an adult son or daughter category but these categories often have even longer backlogs.[63] Longstanding bureaucratic processing delays have exacerbated the problem of children aging-out. The 2002 Child Status Protection Act, addressed this problem by changing the timeframe for determining whether a noncitizen is a child for derivative beneficiaries and the children of lawful permanent residents.[64]

Another major issue is the definitions of the key terms in the family-sponsored categories. The definition of terms such as child, parent, spouse are extremely complex. For example, the definition of a "child" includes children who are

---

[56] *See* INA §§ 212(a)(6)(A)(ii); 212(a)(9)(B)(iii)(IV), 212(a)(9)(C)(ii), and 237(a)(7).

[57] INA § 240A(b)(2).

[58] INA § 101(a)(15)(T)-(U).

[59] *See* INA § 101(b)(1).

[60] For example, in August 2008, visas were available for married sons and daughters of U.S. citizens who had filed petitions before June 8, 2000; visas were available for siblings of U.S. citizens who had filed petitions before September 8, 1997. Dept. of State, *Visa Bulletin, available at* http://travel.state.gov/visa/frvi/bulletin/bulletin_1360.html (last visited Oct. 16, 2008).

[61] INA §§ 201(b)(2)(A)(i), 203(a)(2)(A).

[62] INA § 203(h).

[63] The child of a U.S. citizen who ages out will convert to the first preference unmarried son or daughter or the third preference married son or daughter family-sponsored category (INA § 203(a)(1)), and the child of an LPR who ages out will convert to the second preference adult unmarried son or daughter category (INA § 203(a)(2)(B)).

[64] Pub. L. No. 107-208, 116 Stat. 927 (Aug. 6, 2002). *See* INA § 203(h). The child's age for immediate relative petitions is deemed to be the age of the child when the parent filed the petition. The child's age for second preference petitions filed by permanent residents and derivative beneficiary admissions is the age of the child on the date on which an immigrant visa number become available, subject to some limitations. For a detailed explanation of these provisions, *see* 79 Interpreter Releases 1433, 1503, 1520 (2002) and 80 Interpreter Releases 243 (2003).

adopted, born out of wedlock, and stepchildren.[65] There is a large body of caselaw interpreting these terms and other aspects of family relationships.[66]

Generally, Congress has broad, plenary power to draw distinctions among family members in creating preference categories. For example, in *Fiallo v. Bell*, 430 U.S. 787 (1977), unwed fathers challenged the constitutionality of the definition of those parents and children eligible for immigration benefits. In 1977, INA § 101(b)(1) defined the term child to only recognize nonmarital children and their natural mothers for immigration benefits.[67] The Supreme Court upheld the definition using only minimal scrutiny despite the apparent gender and illegitimacy classification.[68] The Court relied upon the plenary power doctrine and noted that only a facially legitimate and bona fide reason is required to support the asserted discrimination against nonmarital natural fathers and their children.[69]

4. Special Juvenile Status

There is a special immigrant category, created in 1990, for children who have been declared dependents on a juvenile court or placed in the custody of a state. This includes juveniles who have been placed in foster care for whom family reunification is no longer a viable option. This category principally applies to children who have been abandoned, neglected or abused.[70] Juveniles in DHS or ORR custody, either actual or constructive, must receive DHS consent before a state juvenile court may assert jurisdiction. DHS will consent only if it determines that the jurisdiction of the juvenile court is not for the purpose of obtaining permanent residence.

Immigrant visas are available to a juvenile if there has been a determination, in an administrative or judicial proceeding, that it would not be in the juvenile's best interest to be returned to her or her parent's previous country of nationality or country of last habitual residence. State juvenile courts make this determination whether family reunification is no longer viable. A juvenile is eligible if she is under 21.

---

[65] INA §§ 101(b), 101(c).

[66] *See, e.g.*, Young v. Reno, 114 F.3d 879 (9th Cir. 1997) (adopted child may not apply for immigration benefits on behalf of a natural sibling).

[67] Before 1986, INA § 101(b)(1) defined "child" as "an unmarried person under the age of twenty-one who is a legitimate or legitimated child, a stepchild, an adopted child or an illegitimate child seeking preference by virtue of his relationship with his natural mother." A 1986 amendment to INA § 101(b)(1)(D) provided immigration benefits to natural fathers with bona fide relationships with their nonmarital children. *See* Matter of Vizcaino, 19 I. & N. Dec. 644 (BIA 1988).

[68] A dissenting opinion by Justice Marshall, joined by Justice Brennan, criticized the deference to Congress in the case of "invidious and irrational" discrimination among citizens. *Fiallo*, 430 U.S. at 800.

[69] *Cf.* Nguyen v. INS, 533 U.S. 53 (2001) upholding a gender classification regarding citizenship eligibility, but applying intermediate scrutiny, when nonmarital fathers and mothers were treated differently in regard to proof of parentage.

[70] INA § 101(a)(27)(J).

C. EMPLOYMENT-BASED PREFERENCE CATEGORIES

The 1990 amendments to the INA restructured the immigrant visa system and made major changes to the employment-based preference categories. The annual number of employment-based visas more than doubled to a total of 140,000. The 1990 Act also created new categories for immigrant investors who create employment in the U.S. and for advanced degree professionals. The employment-based preference categories include:

- **First Preference:** Priority Workers (EB-1) including three types of workers: (1) persons of extraordinary ability in the sciences, arts, education, business or athletics; (2) outstanding researchers; (3) multinational executives and managers;
- **Second Preference:** Members of the Professions with Advanced Degrees and Noncitizens with Exceptional Ability (EB-2) including physicians working in shortage areas;
- **Third Preference:** Skilled Workers, Professionals and Other Workers (EB-3);
- **Fourth Preference:** Certain Special Immigrants (discussed in Section D below); and
- **Fifth Preference:** Employment Creation Visas.

A key feature of the employment-based immigration system is the labor certification process to test the labor market and ensure that the permanent employment of a noncitizen will not have an adverse affect on U.S. workers.[71] The employment-based system can be divided into those categories subject to labor certification and those categories exempt from labor certification. Typically those categories exempt from labor certification have a streamlined procedure and short visa backlogs, if any.

Labor certification is designed to protect the wages and working conditions of U.S. workers by determining, on an individual basis, whether there are available, able, willing or qualified U.S. workers to fill positions offered to noncitizens. Labor certification also is designed to determine whether the employment of the individual noncitizen will adversely affect the wages and working conditions of U.S. workers.[72]

Another feature of the employment-based preference system is the similarity of the permanent resident categories to many nonimmigrant visa categories.[73] Often, a noncitizen will enter the U.S. initially as a nonimmigrant and then decide to pursue permanent residence. The nonimmigrant categories and immigrant categories interrelate and allow a seamless transition for some noncitizens from temporary to permanent residence, including some EB-1 priority workers, some EB-2 exceptional and advanced degree professional workers, and some EB-3 professionals. For example, the O-1 outstanding person nonimmigrant visa category requires

---

[71] INA § 101(a)(31) defines "permanent" to mean "a relationship of continuing or lasting nature" even though the relationship may be dissolved eventually.

[72] INA § 212(a)(5)(i). A U.S. worker is defined as a U.S. citizen, U.S. national, or a noncitizen legally permitted to work permanently in the U.S., including refugees and asylees. 20 C.F.R. § 656.3 (2008).

[73] Compare priority worker multinational executives and managers under INA § 203(b)(1) with L intracompany transferees under INA § 101(a)(15)(L).

very similar evidence to the EB-1 employment-based person of extraordinary ability category.[74] There is a similar symmetry between the professionals in both the second and third employment-based preferences and the H-1B Specialty Occupational Worker nonimmigrant category.[75] This creates the possibility of a transition from nonimmigrant temporary worker to permanent resident worker for higher skilled workers which is unavailable to lower skilled workers.

1. Priority Workers (EB-1)

Priority workers under the employment-based first preference (EB-1) immigrant visa category includes three types of workers, all of whom are exempt from the labor certification requirement. These are: (1) persons of extraordinary ability in the sciences, arts, education, business or athletics; (2) outstanding professors and researchers; and (3) multinational executives and managers. Regulations list the evidence required for each of these priority worker categories.[76] Persons of extraordinary ability may establish eligibility with evidence of a one-time internationally recognized award (e.g., an Oscar or Pulitzer Prize) or combined evidence of lesser international recognition.[77] Noncitizens in the extraordinary ability category do not require a job offer from a U.S. entity and can self-petition to establish eligibility.[78] Outstanding professors and researchers who are internationally recognized and who have at least three years of experience are eligible if there is an offer of employment from a prospective U.S. employer.[79] Multinational executives and managers, who are intracompany transferees, are eligible if they function at a senior level in an organization as defined by the INA.[80]

2. Members of the Professions with Advanced Degrees and Noncitizens with Exceptional Ability (EB-2)

The second employment-based preference category (EB-2) includes noncitizens of exceptional ability in the sciences, arts or business, and advanced degree professionals.[81] The labor certification requirement applies to this preference category.[82] Advanced degree professionals must hold a degree beyond a

---

[74] INA §§ 101(a)(15)(O), 203(b)(1)(A).

[75] INA § 101(a)(15)(H)(1).

[76] 8 C.F.R. § 204.5 (2008).

[77] 8 C.F.R. § 204.5(h)(3) allows evidence in at least three of the following categories: nationally or internationally recognized awards or prizes for excellence; membership in associations; published material about the noncitizen; participation by the noncitizen judging the work of other in his or her field; original contributions of major significance.

[78] 8 C.F.R. § 204(h)(5) (2008). A noncitizen demonstrating extraordinary ability must also demonstrate she will continue to work in her area of expertise.

[79] 8 C.F.R. § 204.5(i) (2008).

[80] INA § 101(a)(44) defines managerial capacity and executive capacity for both employment-based priority workers and the L-1 intracompany transferee nonimmigrant visa category in INA § 101(a)(13)(L).

[81] INA § 203(b)(2) permits noncitizens with the equivalent of an advanced degree to petition under this category.

[82] INA § 212(a)(5)(A).

baccalaureate degree or its equivalent.[83] Persons of exceptional ability must establish that their work in the U.S. will substantially benefit the national economy, cultural, or educational interests, or welfare of the U.S.

National interest waivers are one way in which a noncitizen in the EB-2 category can avoid the lengthy labor certification process. These waivers are only available to second employment-based preference beneficiaries and the noncitizen may file a waiver application on his or her own behalf. The employment offer requirement is waived if the prospective work of the noncitizen is in the national interest.[84] If a waiver is granted, then the labor certification requirement also is waived.[85] These waivers are difficult to obtain because the noncitizen's prospective work must have a substantial and national impact.[86]

3.   Skilled Workers, Professionals and Other [Unskilled] Workers (EB-3)

The third employment-based preference category (EB-3) includes skilled workers, professionals without advanced degrees and other workers (unskilled workers). The labor certification requirement applies to this category. A profession is defined in the INA to "include but not be limited to architects, engineers, lawyers, physicians, surgeons, and teachers in elementary or secondary schools, colleges, academies and seminaries."[87] The terms "profession" and "professional" are terms of art defined through a large body of caselaw and administrative decisions. Generally, a profession has been interpreted to include occupations for which at least a baccalaureate degree in the field is required for entry.

The skilled worker category is available to individuals who possess and are filling an employment position requiring at least two years of training or experience.[88] The "other workers" category is set aside for those performing unskilled labor which is not of a temporary or seasonal nature. There are only 10,000 visas allotted to the other worker category annually, which has resulted in longstanding, severe backlogs in the availability of visas for these workers.[89]

---

[83] 8 C.F.R. § 204.5(k)(2) (2008).

[84] National interest waivers are also available to physicians working in shortage areas or veterans facilities under INA § 203(b)(2)(B)(ii).

[85] INA § 203(b)(2)(B). The regulations specify that a national interest waiver of the job offer requirement also waives the labor certification requirement. 8 C.F.R. § 204.5(k)(4)(ii) (2008). Although the noncitizen who obtains a national interest waiver does not require a job offer, often, an employer is involved.

[86] In *Matter of New York State Dept. of Transportation (NYSDOT)*, 22 I. & N. Dec. 215 (BIA 1998), the Administrative Appeals Office found that an employer seeking a national interest waiver of the job offer requirement and labor certification requirement, must establish that: the noncitizen will be employed in an area of substantial intrinsic merit; the proposed benefit of that employee will be national in scope; and the national interest would be adversely affected if labor certification were required for the noncitizen. The last prong of the test makes it virtually impossible for all but very few noncitizens to obtain national interest waivers.

[87] INA § 101(a)(32).

[88] INA § 203(b)(3)(A)(i); 8 C.F.R. § 204.5(l)(2) (2008).

[89] Only 5,000 visas are available in this category. Nicaraguan Adjustment and Central American

4.   Employment Creation [Investor] Visas (EB-5)

The fifth employment-based preference category (EB-5) includes immigrant investors who create employment in the United States. This category requires investment of one million dollars and the creation of at least ten full-time employment positions for U.S. citizens, permanent residents or other authorized noncitizen workers. The required investment is reduced in targeted rural or other high unemployment areas. More than the one million dollar investment can be required by the Attorney General in high employment areas. Investors are granted conditional permanent residence, similar to family-sponsored marriage cases, and there are criminal provisions of the INA prohibiting immigration-related entrepreneurship fraud.[90]

5.   Labor Certification

Labor certification is a prerequisite for many of the employment-based categories. The INA lists the lack of certification as an inadmissibility grand.[91] Labor certification applies to all of the employment-based third preference. Labor certification is required for the employment-based second preference category, except in the case of a national interest waiver or Schedule A precertification (discussed below). The labor certification process is a mechanism to evaluate the impact on the U.S. labor market of employment offers to noncitizens.[92] The U.S. Department of Labor [DOL] determines whether the employment of a particular noncitizen will produce an adverse impact on the wages and working conditions of U.S. workers. It is presumed that there is no adverse affect if there are no available, able, willing or qualified U.S. workers to fill the permanent position to be offered to the noncitizen.[93]

The labor certification requirement may be waived under Schedule A precertification. Schedule A is a list of occupations the DOL already has determined are shortage occupations, therefore the employment of a noncitizen would not adversely affect the wages and working conditions of U.S. workers.[94] Under Schedule A, Group I, licensed physical therapists and professional nurses are precertified occupations.[95] A noncitizen may be eligible as a person of exceptional ability in the sciences or arts under Schedule A, Group II. Only the labor certification requirement is waived; an offer of employment is still required. The Schedule A requirements for exceptional ability differ slightly from second preference employment-based exceptional ability.

Relief Act (NACARA) Pub. L. No. 105-100, 111 Stat. 2160 (Nov. 19, 1997).

[90] INA § 275(d).

[91] INA § 212(a)(5)(i).

[92] INA § 101(a)(31) defines "permanent" to mean "a relationship of continuing or lasting nature" even though it may be dissolved eventually.

[93] INA § 212(a)(5)(i).

[94] 20 C.F.R. §§ 656.5(b)(1), 656.15 (2008).

[95] 20 C.F.R. § 656.15(c) (2008).

The traditional labor certification process, from 1965 to March 2005, was a time-consuming procedure involving review by state workforce agencies and a regional office of the DOL. The local state workforce agency (SWA) began the labor certification process by examining each individual job offer to determine whether it was a bona fide job opportunity. The SWA would supervise recruitment to ensure a good faith process. The DOL also would review the entire process, and determine whether additional information was needed, and ultimately whether to grant or deny certification. Significant processing backlogs developed during 1990s, creating problems for both employers and their noncitizen employees.[96]

As of March 28, 2005, the DOL has implemented a new system to address the enormous backlogs: PERM, the Program Electronic Review Management system.[97] The PERM system relies on the same substantive requirements as traditional labor certification, however, PERM significantly changes the procedure. SWAs only provide wage determinations to ensure an offered position reflects the prevailing wage in the local geographic area. The employer's recruitment process occurs before filing the labor certification application and, as a result, with no oversight by the SWA. Employers must attest to following the rules and they are required to maintain documentation of the recruitment effort.[98] The DOL will conduct audits on a random or selective basis to review this documentation.

The labor certification application includes information about the job offer and information about the noncitizen beneficiary on whose behalf certification is sought, including prior employment experience and education. The DOL will use the information about the noncitizen to review whether the employer has a valid job offer or one that is tailored to the noncitizen's background.

Employers are required to offer the prevailing wage for a position in the local geographic area.[99] The SWA determines the prevailing wage and an employer can challenge the SWA's determination.[100] Generally, a lower wage will not be accepted unless unusual circumstances exist. For example, in *Matter of Tuskegee University*, the DOL denied certification for an associate professor position

---

[96] Many noncitizens are employed in nonimmigrant status with a specific time limit, such as H-1B workers. The labor certification application is just the first step in the process of immigrant visa classification under the second and third employment-based categories. After certification, an immigrant visa petition (Form I-140) had to be filed, and in the 1990s backlogs in adjudicating these petitions also existed.

[97] Other attempts to streamline the labor certification process such as "Reduction-in-Recruitment," [RIR] were developed. RIR eliminated the state agency supervision of recruitment in straightforward cases. RIR was phased out when PERM was introduced, although some cases still remain in the adjudication pipeline.

[98] *See* 20 C.F.R. § 656.17 (2008). Regulations require advertising and posting requirements for the offered permanent employment position. The employer evaluates job applicants and prepares a detailed recruitment report specifying the recruitment steps taken, the job applicants, the number of hires, and the number of workers who were rejected based on lawful, job-related reasons.

[99] 20 C.F.R. § 656.40 (2008).

[100] The employer can challenge the SWA's prevailing wage determination. For example, the SWA conducts surveys and maintains databases of wages within its local area and this information is used to determine the appropriate prevailing wage. Employers may challenge the SWA's prevailing wage determination by providing their own surveys and other information.

because the university did not offer a wage comparable to other colleges in the local geographic area.[101] Tuskegee University argued that its offered wage was well-above the prevailing wage among the 43 schools in the United Negro College Fund and this group should be the comparison group for the prevailing wage determination. The Board of Alien Labor Certification Appeals [BALCA] agreed with Tuskegee University and granted certification.[102]

Employers may not tailor a job offer to the background of the noncitizen beneficiary of the labor certification application. The minimum requirements for offered positions may not be unduly restrictive in terms of the years and types of education or prior work experience required. The DOL makes its determinations about unduly restrictive requirements using the O*NET (Occupational Information Network), an online database of occupations with information about the normally required education and experience.[103] An employer can establish that its minimum requirements are justified by business necessity to counter a DOL finding of unduly restrictive requirements.[104]

O*NET contains job descriptions and the normal education and experience requirements for employment positions. The position descriptions include a number that corresponds to the years of education and experience required: the SVP (specific vocational preparation) number. If a job requires more experience and education than the SVP number in O*NET, or the job includes a combination of occupations or degree requirements, the employer may need to provide a business necessity justification.[105] Foreign language requirements are presumptively restrictive and, under PERM, a specific business necessity justification is required.[106]

In The Matter of Information Industries, Inc. is the leading case on the issue of whether the job requirements in a labor certification application are unduly restrictive and tailored to the background of a noncitizen.[107] The employer sought certification for a systems engineer position requiring two specific educational degrees; both a B.S. in Engineer and an M.S. in Computer Science. The DOL

---

[101] 5 Imm. L. & Proc. Rep. B3-172 (BALCA, Feb. 23, 1988).

[102] BALCA did not follow *Matter of Tuskegee University* in later cases. In *Matter of Hathaway Children's Services*, 91-INA-388, 1994 WL 29778 (BALCA, Feb. 4, 1994), BALCA reviewed the wage for a "maintenance repairer" job in a nonprofit treatment center for disabled children. The Board stated it did not see any justification for paying a different wage for positions with the same job duties. The center argued that the comparison group for the prevailing wage determination should be other United Way non-profit organizations.

[103] *See* http://www.onetcener.org or www.flcdatacenter.com. O*NET incorporates information from the Dictionary of Occupational Titles which had been used for decades by DOL.

[104] Business necessity exists if the job requirements bear a reasonable relationship to the occupation in the context of the employer's business, and are essential to perform the job duties in a reasonable manner.

[105] 20 C.F.R. § 656.17 (2008).

[106] 20 C.F.R. § 656.17 states that business necessity for a foreign language may be based on the nature of the occupation, e.g., a translator, or the need to communicate with a large majority of the employer's customers, contractors, or employees who cannot communicate effectively in English.

[107] *In the Matter of Information Industries, Inc.*, 88-INA-82 (BALCA 1989).

denied certification finding the dual degree requirement to be unduly restrictive and not justified by a business necessity.[108]

BALCA found that business necessity exists if an employer to demonstrate that the job requirements bear a reasonable relationship to the occupation in the context of the employer's business, and are essential to perform, in a reasonable manner, the job duties as described by the employer.[109] In *Information Industries*, BALCA found that the two degree requirement did not conflict with the Dictionary of Occupational Titles [now O*NET].[110] The Board remanded back to the DOL Regional Certifying Officer to determine whether the job requirements were justified by business necessity. On remand, certification was denied again because the two degree requirement were unduly restrictive.[111]

Unduly restrictive requirements will cause a denial of certification.[112] After review of the application, the DOL Certifying Officer will approve the application, request additional information, select the application for audit, or deny the application. Denials are appealed to the Board of Alien Labor Certification Appeals [BALCA]. Employers are subject to sanctions for abuse of the process, such as misrepresentations or violation of the regulations pertaining to recordkeeping. Review in federal court is available after exhaustion of all administrative procedures under the Administrative Procedure Act.

Upon approval of a labor certification application, an employer files an I-140 Immigrant Visa Petition on behalf of the noncitizen beneficiary. The employer files the immigrant visa petition with a USCIS Regional Service Center. The labor certification approval is valid for a period of 180 days.[113] The USCIS will examine whether the noncitizen meets the minimum job requirements for the offered position in the labor certification application. USCIS also will review whether the employer has the ability to pay the prevailing wage. The USCIS does not have authority to reevaluate the test of the labor market conducted by the DOL.

---

[108] The DOL regulation at issue, 20 C.F.R. 656.21(b)(2), has a nearly identical provision under the PERM regulations, 20 C.F.R. 656.17(h). Under 20 C.F.R. 656.21(b)(2), the job opportunity can not be unduly restrictive, unless justified by business necessity, and the requirements: "shall be those normally required for the job in the United States; shall be those defined for the job in the DOL Dictionary of Occupational Titles [incorporated today in O*NET] and shall not include requirements for foreign languages."

[109] BALCA adopted an interpretation of the business necessity standard after considering the use of the term in other statutory contexts. For example, under Title VII of the 1964 Civil Rights Act, business necessity is established only when the essence of a business operation is undermined.

[110] *See* http://www.onetcenter.org or www.flcdatacenter.com.

[111] The noncitizen subsequently moved to another DOL region and obtained certification. T. Alienikoff, *supra* note 30 at 375.

[112] Denials also occur if the DOL determines that the noncitizen received on-the-job training for the offered position, and therefore was at an advantage compared to U.S. workers applying for the job.

[113] An approved labor certification on or after July 16, 2007 expires if it is not filed in support of an I-140 Immigrant Visa Petition within 180 days. 20 C.F.R. 656.30(b)(1) (2008).

D.   CERTAIN SPECIAL IMMIGRANTS (EB-4)

The fourth employment-based preference category (EB-4) includes certain special immigrants identified in INA § 101(a)(27)(C) through (M). This hodgepodge group includes: ministers and other religious workers: certain foreign medical graduates; certain overseas employees and retirees of the U.S. government, American Institute of Taiwan, Panama Canal Company or Canal Zone Authority, and specified international organizations including NATO; certain juvenile court dependents; some members of the military; and certain broadcasters. Congress added translators with U.S. Armed Forces as a category of special immigrants in 2006.[114] Only Iraqi or Afghani translators are eligible and they must have worked for a period of at least 12 months. In 2008, Congress added another special immigrant category for Iraqis employed by or on behalf of the U.S. in Iraq after March 20, 2003.[115] The eligibility requirements for each of these categories of special immigrant are set forth in INA § 101(a)(27). Special immigrants file their own visa petitions (form I-360) with USCIS.

Noncitizens eligible for special juvenile immigrant status are discussed in Section 4 of this Chapter.

E.   DIVERSITY VISAS AS SET FORTH IN INA § 203(C)

Under the Diversity Visa Lottery Program, 55,000 visas are allocated using a random selection system.[116] This immigrant category was added to the system in 1990, in part, to address low immigration from Western European countries.[117] The diversity visas are allocated by dividing countries and regions of the world into high admission or low admission areas. Countries with fewer than 50,000 immigrants to the United States over the preceding five-year period may be designated low admission countries. High admission countries can not participate at all in the diversity immigrant visa system. Diversity visas are distributed differently to low admission countries in low admission regions and low admission countries in high admission regions. The high admission and low admission countries are identified annually.[118]

Noncitizens are eligible for diversity visas if they have at least a high school education or its equivalent, or at least two years of work experience in an occupation requiring two years of training or experience. There is a separate diversity visa

---

[114]   Natural Defense Authorization Act for Fiscal Year 2006, Pub. L. No. 109-163, 119 Stat. 3136 (Jan. 6, 2006).

[115]   Iraqis Providing Faithful and Valuable Service to U.S., Pub. L. No. 110-181, 122 Stat. 3 (Jan. 28, 2008).

[116]   INA § 201(b)(2)(A). The number of diversity visas issued is reduced by up to 5,000 visas in order to allocate visas under NACARA. *See supra* note 90.

[117]   Early lottery programs in 1988 and 1989 were ad-hoc measures available only to a narrow group of noncitizens. The history of the diversity immigrant category is discussed in Chapter 2.

[118]   In FY 2008, the high admission countries included Brazil, Canada, China (mainland); Colombia; Dominican Republic; El Salvador; Haiti; India; Jamaica; Mexico; Pakistan; Philippines; Peru; Poland, Russia; South Korea; United Kingdom (except Northern Ireland); and Vietnam.

lottery each year. Only one application may be filed per year by a noncitizen.[119] The DOS website provides instructions and timetables for applications. If an applicant is selected, she is notified by the DOS. Spouses and children are eligible as derivative beneficiaries.[120] The immigrant visa must be issued within the fiscal year and more applicants are selected than the number of visas available. Delays in processing or an excessive number of applicants can use up all of the visas before the fiscal year ends. As a result, some selected applicants may not receive a diversity visa.

F. ASYLEES AND REFUGEES

Noncitizens who have a "well founded fear of persecution based on race, religion, nationality, membership in a social group or political opinion" may become permanent residents.[121] Noncitizens who have been granted asylum in the United States or who have entered the U.S. as refugees are eligible to adjust status to permanent resident after one year under INA § 209. There is a separate system for the allocation of immigrant visas to refugees who have established a well founded fear through an overseas refugee program. The President of the United States makes an annual recommendation of the number of refugee admissions.[122] Noncitizens who have applied for asylum in the United States based one of the five grounds above and have established a well-founded fear in the U.S. are asylees. Asylees are eligible to adjust status to LPR without any numerical limit. Prior to the 2005 REAL ID Act, there were annual limits on the number of asylee adjustments.[123]

---

[119] The DOS usually specifies a one or two-month period for the online submission of applications. For example, the 2009 Lottery registration period was October 3 through December 2, 2007. Lottery winners were notified by mail between May and July 2008. DOS, *Diversity Visa (DV) Lottery Instructions, available at* http://travel.state.gov/visa/immigrants/types/types_1318.html. (last visited Oct. 16, 2008).

[120] INA § 203(d).

[121] INA § 1010(a)(42)(A).

[122] INA § 207.

[123] REAL ID Act of 2005, Pub. L. No. 109-13, 119 Stat. 231 (May 11, 2005).

Chapter 8

NONIMMIGRANT VISAS

SYNOPSIS

Immigration law recognizes several categories of nonimmigrants who enter the United States, for specific purposes and for limited time periods, without an intent to remain in the country permanently. Nonimmigrant visas far outnumber immigrant visas. Criteria for admission to the United States with nonimmigrant visas are less restrictive than admission with immigrant visas because it is the nature of the activity and the permitted length of stay that restrict the nonimmigrant visa. Nonimmigrant visa applicants may seek waivers for most grounds of inadmissibility.[1]

INA § 101(a)(15) lists the categories of nonimmigrants allowed into the United States. These categories include family; business, employment and commercial; educational; and victims of violence. The name of the visa typically corresponds to

---

[1] INA § 212(d)(3).

the subsection of INA § 101(a)(15) in which each visa is described. For the most part, noncitizens seeking admission are presumed to be immigrants unless they can show they fit within one of the nonimmigrants categories listed in INA § 101(a)(15).[2] Nonimmigrant visa applicants must show that their intended stay is temporary and that their activities in the United States are consistent with those allowed for the claimed nonimmigrant status. A nonimmigrant's long-term desire to remain in the United States permanently, however, has been recognized in the dual intent doctrine. The doctrine holds that a nonimmigrant may have both a long-term intent to remain in the United States permanently as well as a short-term intent to leave in compliance with the visa requirement.[3]

With certain exceptions, nonimmigrants can change status from one nonimmigrant category to another. Nonimmigrants who overstay their visas or are otherwise unlawfully present in the United States for six months or more are ineligible to change status. The following categories of immigrants are not allowed to change status to another nonimmigrant classification: C (transit), D (crewmen), K (fiancée), J (exchange visitor/student, if subject to the two-year foreign residency requirement), S (informant), visa waiver program entrant or those who entered in transit without a visa. Moreover, M-1 (vocational student) visa holders cannot change status to F-1 (student) or to H-1, if H-1 is based on the training received as M-1. None of the restrictions on changing status apply to those who seek a change in status to T (trafficking) or U (crime victim) status.

A. FAMILY

1.   The V Visa

Congress created the V visa to allow for the reunification of families during the long wait time for an immigrant visa. The V visa allows spouses and children of permanent residents to live and work in the United States while awaiting either approval of an immigrant visa petition, processing of an immigrant visa, or adjustment of status. The V visa is a transitional visa that allows legal status in the United States until the visa holder can obtain immigrant status. Because the V visa was envisioned as a temporary measure, its provisions were made available only to those whose sponsors petitioned for them on or before December 21, 2000. The LIFE Act, which created the V visa, allowed beneficiaries of second preference petitions filed on or before December 21, 2000 to apply for nonimmigrant status as long as three years had passed since the petitions were filed. This means that the visas would be available only until December 21, 2003. The visas were made available to those whose I-130 petitions were pending, those whose I-130 petitions were approved but whose visa numbers were not yet available, and those whose I-130 petitions were approved and whose adjustment of status was pending.

---

[2] INA § 214(b).

[3] Matter of H-R-, 7 I. & N. Dec. 651, 654 (R.C. 1958); Matter of Hosseinpour, 15 I. & N. Dec. 191, 192 (BIA 1975) (the "mere desire . . . to obtain permanent residence in the future does not, by itself, automatically disqualify an alien from admission as a nonimmigrant").

There are three categories of V visas: the V-1 is reserved for spouses of permanent residents; the V-2 is reserved for children of the permanent resident petitioner; the V-3 is reserved for derivative children of either a V-1 or V-2 visa holder. A person in V status can apply for work authorization.[4] A person can lose V status if the underlying I-130 petition or adjustment of status application is denied, withdrawn, or revoked.

2. The Fiancé Visa: K Visa

The K visa is sometimes known as a hybrid because the K visa holder is allowed to enter as a nonimmigrant and apply for permanent residence under certain conditions. K visas are available for fiancés of U.S. citizens and their children under 21 years of age, or for spouses of U.S. citizens and their children under 21.

There are three categories of K visa holders. The K-1 visa is reserved for fiancés of U.S. citizens. It allows a fiancé to enter the United States for a 90-day period to marry the petitioner and apply for permanent residence. A K visa can be issued only after a petition for sponsorship has been approved by DHS. The petitioner must show that the parties met previously, in person, within two years of the date of the filing of the petition (unless a waiver is granted).[5] This fraud prevention measure was implemented with the passage of the Immigration Marriage Fraud Amendments of 1986.[6] The requirement is waivable on a showing of extreme hardship to the petitioner, or a showing of long-held social, religious, or cultural custom.[7] The parties must also show that they have a bona fide intention to marry and are legally able and willing to marry within 90 days after the fiancé's arrival in the U.S.

If the marriage does not occur within the 90 day period, the K nonimmigrant must leave the United States. The 90 day period is a strict time limit, although at least one court has held that the period can be tolled when circumstances beyond the control of the visa holder make it impossible to meet the deadline.[8] Once the marriage takes place, the K-1 nonimmigrant must apply for adjustment of status. A child accompanying or following to join may be admitted as a K-2 nonimmigrant.

The K-3/K-4 visas were created by the LIFE Act of 2000 to speed the process of entry for spouses and children of U.S. citizens awaiting entry into the United States. The K-3/K-4 visas allow spouses and children of U.S. citizens who are the beneficiaries of approved I-130 petitions to be admitted to the U.S. initially as nonimmigrants while they wait to adjust status. Previously, these applicants had to wait outside the United States until their immigrant visas were processed. Applicants can enter the United States once an I-130 has been filed and await the

---

[4] INA § 214(o)(1)(A).

[5] INA § 214(d).

[6] Publ. L. 99-639, 100 Stat. 3537.

[7] 8 C.F.R. 214.2(k)(2).

[8] Moss v. I.N.S., 651 F.2d 1091, 1093 (5th Cir. 1981) (court noted that purpose of K visa was to show intent to marry rather than to enforce an "absolute and mandatory period of time within which [to marry]").

approval of the I-130 and the processing of the immigrant visa or adjustment of status in the United States. K-3/K-4 nonimmigrants are admitted for a period of two years, and can seek extensions.

B. BUSINESS, EMPLOYMENT, AND COMMERCIAL

1. Temporary Business or Pleasure Visitors

Visas for temporary visitors, known as B-1/B-2 visitors, are reserved for those visiting the United States temporarily for business or pleasure. INA § 101(a)(15)(B) makes clear that this type of visa is not available for those planning to study in the United States, those performing skilled or unskilled labor, or those representing foreign media. A B-1/B-2 applicant must show that s/he has a residence in a foreign country which s/he has no intention of abandoning. The applicant must also show that s/he has an intention to depart at the expiration of his/her stay, and that s/he has adequate financial resources to carry out the purpose of the visit. A B-1/B-2 visitor is admitted for up to one year with extensions of six months available.[9]

A B-1 visitor for business is admissible if entering the United States to engage in commercial transactions not involving gainful employment. Such activities as negotiating contracts, consulting with clients or business associates, attending conferences, and participating in board of directors meetings are considered activities of a commercial or business nature. If a business activity involves full-time management of a U.S. business, however, a B-1 visa is not appropriate.[10] The regulations governing nonimmigrant visas define business as a legitimate commercial or professional activity, not local employment or labor for hire.[11] The regulations require that the applicant show a clear intent to continue foreign residence, intent to enter the United States for a specified limited duration of time, and that the principal place of business and actual profit accrual occurs in a foreign country.[12] The B-1 applicant must show documentation that s/he meets each of these requirements.

A person entering as a B-1/B-2 visitor cannot attend school as an F-1 student without first obtaining a change in status within the United States, or an F-1/M-1 visa abroad.[13]

2. Visas for Business Personnel

There are several categories of visas available for those who enter the United States to work. This section discusses H, L, E, I, O, P, Q, and R visas. Each of these visas permits employment in the United States, and permits stays longer

---

[9] 8 C.F.R. § 214.2(b)(2).

[10] Matter of Lawrence, 15 I. & N. Dec. 418, 420 (BIA 1975).

[11] 22 C.F.R. § 41.31(b).

[12] 22 C.F.R. § 41.31(b).

[13] Memo, Williams, Ex. Assoc. Comm. Field Ops., HQISD 70/6.2.2 P (April 12, 2002), reprinted in 79 No. 17 Interpreter Releases 595, 605–07 (Apr. 22, 2002).

than the B visa allows. Some provide a path to permanent residency. The categories define the type of work, profession, or business that the applicant seeks to perform in the United States.

a.   The Professional Visas: H-1, L, O, and P

H visa applicants are those coming temporarily to work in the United States in specialty occupations (H-1B); as professional nurses in health profession shortage areas (H-1C); as temporary agricultural workers (H-2A); as skilled/unskilled workers in occupations where U.S. citizens or residents are unavailable (H-2B); as trainees (H-3); or accompanying family members with H visas (H-4). Each visa category maintains a yearly cap. Although the visa requires intent to return to one's home country, it does not preclude seeking legal permanent residence for H-1B holders. Often, an H-1B visa holder also qualifies for an employment immigrant visa but, because the wait times for obtaining legal permanent resident status are so long, Congress made explicit in the Immigration Act of 1990 that a person whose skills are needed today can seek both permanent resident status and an H-1B visa. This dual intent is not considered, "evidence of an intention to abandon foreign residence for purposes of obtaining" an H-1B visa.[14]

The H-1B visa category includes persons in specialty occupations, fashion models of distinguished merit and ability, or persons participating in Department of Defense cooperative projects. A specialty occupation is defined as one that requires the application of highly specialized knowledge and a bachelor's degree or higher in that particular specialty.[15] The position must meet one of the following criteria: a bachelor's degree is the employer's minimum requirement for the entry into the position; a bachelor's degree is usually required of this position in the industry; the employer normally requires a degree or its equivalent, or the duties are so specialized and complex that the knowledge required for the position is associated with a degree.[16]

This category of visas requires that the applicant submit a labor condition application (LCA), also known as an "attestation" to the U.S. Department of Labor (DOL).[17] The application must state that the employer will offer the greater of the actual wage paid to similar employees or the prevailing wage for the occupation in the area to the applicant seeking a visa; that the working conditions of similarly situated workers will not be affected; that there is not a strike or lockout at the place of employment; that the employer has provided notice of the filing of the visa application to the appropriate bargaining representative, or by public posting to affected employees. The employer must attest that it is not displacing and will not displace a U.S. worker within the period beginning 90 days before the filing and ending 90 days after the filing of the application.[18] The employer must show that it has taken good faith steps to recruit U.S. workers at the same or greater salary as

---

[14] INA § 214(h).

[15] INA § 214(i)(1); 8 C.F.R. § 214.2(h)(4)(ii).

[16] 8 C.F.R. § 214.2(h)(4)(iii)(A).

[17] INA § 212(n).

[18] INA § 212(n)(1)(E).

is being offered to the noncitizen, and has offered the job to any U.S. worker who applies and is equally or better qualified.[19] An employer must show that it filed the attestation; DOL approval is not required. The Department of Labor typically provides the applicant with a certification unless the application is incomplete or inaccurate.[20]

Until 1990 there was no cap on nonimmigrant categories, including the H-1B category. When Congress passed the Immigration Act of 1990, it set caps for H-1B recipients at 65,000. This limitation caused much frustration for employers, especially those experiencing the industry boom and labor shortages in the information technology fields. Congress temporarily raised the H-1B caps for 1999, 2000, and 2001.[21] The caps were increased to up to 115,000 in 1999 and 2000, and 107,500 in 2001. Congress again raised the caps in 2000 to 195,000 for the fiscal years 2001 through 2003, and created a cap exemption for higher education institutions and government or nonprofit research institutions.[22] After an economic slowdown, Congress allowed the caps to revert to 65,000 in fiscal year 2004. For the past several years, the H-1B visa caps have been reached on the first day of the fiscal year or close to it. Every year, there are calls for a reform of the immigration system to address problems in labor flow caused by the caps. Congress has also responded to calls to address employer dependence on H-1B workers by imposing up to a $1,000 fee on H-1B petitions. The fees are used for workforce training programs for U.S. workers. Congress has also made H-1B visas portable, allowing visa holders to change jobs after their arrival to avoid perceived employer exploitation of visa holders.

The L visa serves functions similar to those of the H-1B visa but is reserved for intracompany transferees who are entering the United States to further the business needs of foreign or multinational corporations. The purpose of the L visa is to facilitate transfers of executives or employees with specialized knowledge between foreign-based offices to U.S. branches or subsidiaries. The L visa requires that a person "render his services . . . in a capacity that is managerial, executive, or involves specialized knowledge."[23] Specialized knowledge is defined by the statute as "special knowledge of the company product or its application in international markets or . . . an advanced level of knowledge of processes and procedures of the company."[24] L visa applicants must show that they have been employed continuously for one of the previous three years by the company who seeks their services.[25] L visa holders are granted up to three years stay, and can

---

[19] INA § 212(n)(1)G).

[20] 8 C.F.R. § 214.2(h)(4)(i)(B)(1).

[21] American Competitiveness and Workforce Improvement Act of 1998, Pub. L. 105-277, 112 Stat. 2681 (Oct. 21, 1998).

[22] American Competitiveness in the Twenty-First Century Act of 2000, Pub. L. 106-313, 114 Stat. 1251 (Oct. 17, 2000).

[23] INA § 101(a)(15)(L).

[24] INA § 214(c)(2)B).

[25] INA 101(a)(15)(L).

extend their stay for up to seven years for managers or five years for those with specialized knowledge.[26]

Concern over whether the L visa category was being used to circumvent the labor attestation requirements and caps of the H-1B category prompted Congress to limit eligibility for L visas based on specialized knowledge.[27] Congress limits the placement of employees with specialized knowledge to worksites principally controlled by the employer.[28]

Closely related to the H-1B visa category are the O and P categories. The O category covers athletes, entertainers, and performers or others in the arts, sciences, business, or education, who have exhibited "extraordinary ability" demonstrated by "sustained national or international acclaim."[29] The O category also covers immediate relatives and support staff of the principal O visa recipient. An O visa is available initially for a three year period with the possibility of one year extensions.[30]

The P category contains several subcategories of recognized athletes and entertainers. The P-1 category is reserved for internationally recognized athletes or entertainment groups performing in specific events. The P-2 category is reserved for artists and entertainers seeking to enter the United States under reciprocal exchange programs. The P-3 category is used by artists or entertainers providing "culturally unique" programs.

P-1 visa holders are admitted for up to five years, with the possibility of up to a five year extension.[31] The rest of the P categories are admitted initially for one year and can seek one year extensions.

b.   Lesser Skilled Workers: H-2 Visas

The H-2 visa category is reserved for less skilled workers who enter the United States seasonally or for temporary work to fill a demonstrated temporary labor need. The H-2 category requires that an employer show that the nonimmigrant is needed on a seasonal or temporary basis "to perform agricultural labor or services"[32] or "to perform temporary service or labor if unemployed person capable of performing such service or labor cannot be found in this country."[33]

The H-2A category is reserved for agricultural workers. This visa category carries the legacy of guest worker programs such as the "Bracero program," infamous for its lack of labor protections for its foreign workers.[34] Until 1986,

---

[26] INA § 214(c)(2)(D); 8 C.F.R. § 214.2(l)(7); 8 C.F.R. § 214.2(l)(15)(ii).

[27] INA § 214(c)(2)(F).

[28] *Id.*

[29] INA § 101(a)(15)(O).

[30] 8 C.F.R. 214.2(o)(6)(iii); 8 C.F.R. 214.2(0)(12)(ii).

[31] 8C.F.R. § 214.2(p)(8)(iii)(A); 8 C.F.R. § 214.2(p)(14)(ii)(A).

[32] INA § 101(a)(15)(H)(2)(A).

[33] INA § 1019A)(15)(H)(2)(B).

[34] For history and analysis of the Bracero program and similar guest worker initiatives, *see* Mae

employers could seek agricultural workers only through the general low-skill worker visa. Agricultural employers found the process for obtaining general visas too cumbersome, and, as a result, rarely sought visas for their workers. Much of the agricultural industry operated with undocumented workers. Congress attempted to remedy the problem by creating the H-2A program through the Immigration Reform and Control Act of 1986.[35] Congress made the process more accessible and streamlined. An employer must file a labor certification application with the DOL showing that "(A) there are not sufficient workers who are able, willing and qualified, and who will be available at the time and place needed, to perform the labor or services involved in the petition and (B) the employment of the alien in such labor or services will not adversely affect the wages and working conditions of workers in the United States similarly employed."[36] Once a labor certification is granted, the USCIS must approve the petition before individual workers can obtain visas. The DOL establishes a yearly adverse effect wage rate which sets the minimum hourly wage for H-2A workers for each state. In 2008, the hourly wage ranged from $8.41 in Arkansas and Louisiana to $10.86 in Hawaii.[37] Also, H-2A workers must be provided with housing, meals or cooking facilities, return transportation, and workers' compensation insurance or its equivalent.[38]

The H-2B program covers lesser-skilled workers outside of the agricultural industry. An H-2B visa is available for temporary employment for a job that is temporary in nature.[39] The need must be a "one-time occurrence, a seasonal need, or an intermittent need."[40]

H-2B visas are capped at 66,000, not including workers' families.[41] No more than 33,000 of the visas are available in each half of the fiscal year.[42] H-2B visa holders are admitted for up to one year, and can get extensions up to a total three year stay.[43] An H-2B visa is available only if an "unemployed person capable of performing such service or labor cannot be found in this country."[44] Employers seeking H-2B workers must seek either a certification from the DOL that "qualified workers in the United States are not available and that the alien's

---

Ngai, IMPOSSIBLE SUBJECTS 138–166 (2005); Michael A. Olivas, *The Chronicles, My Grandfather's Stories, and Immigration Law: The Slave Traders Chronicle as Racial History*, 34 ST. LOUIS U. L.J. 425, 435–39 (1989-1990); Gilbert Paul Carrasco, *Latinos in the United States — Invitation and Exile, in* IMMIGRANTS OUT! THE NEW NATIVISM AND THE ANTI-IMMIGRANT IMPULSE IN THE UNITED STATES 190–204 (Juan Perea, ed., 1997).

[35] *See* INA § 101(a)(15)(H)(ii)(a).

[36] INA § 218(a)(1).

[37] 73 Fed. Reg. 10289 (Feb. 26, 2008).

[38] INA § 218(c)(4); 20 C.F.R. §§ 655.102(b)(9), 655.107; 655.102(b)(4), 655.102(b)(5)(ii); INA § 218(b)(3).

[39] 8 C.F.R. § 214.2(h)(6)(ii); Matter of Artee Corp, 18 I. & N. Dec. 366 (BIA 1982); Sussex Engineering v. Montgomery, 825 F.2d 1084 (6th Cir. 1987). "Temporary" is defined as a year or less. 8 C.F.R. § 214.2(h)(6)(ii)(B).

[40] 8 C.F.R. § 214.2(h)(6)(ii)(B).

[41] INA § 214(g)(2).

[42] INA § 214(g)(1)(B); INA § 214(g)(10).

[43] 8 C.F.R. § 214.2(h)(9)(iii)(B).

[44] 8 C.F.R. § 214.2(h)(1)(ii)(D).

employment will not adversely affect wages and working conditions of similarly employed United States workers," or a notice "detailing the reasons why such certification cannot be made. Such notice shall address the availability of U.S. workers in the occupation and the prevailing wages and working conditions of U.S. workers in the occupation."[45] In fiscal year 2006, the vast majority of H-2B visa holders worked in the landscaping industry.[46] Other high volume H-2B industries include housekeeping, construction work, and forestry. To deal with backlogs, the DOL implemented the Program Electronic Review Management ("PERM") system in 2005, in order to speed up the processing of labor certifications for both immigrant and H-2 visas.[47]

c.   Treaty Traders and Investors, and Free Trade Agreement Professionals: The E and TN Visas

The E and TN visas accommodate those who enter the United States pursuant to international trade and commerce and free trade agreements. E visas are available for those who seek to participate in international trade and investment opportunities in the United States. The E-1 category is for treaty traders; the E-2 category is reserved for treaty investors. The principal requirement for an E visa is that the visa holder be a citizen or national of a country that maintains a treaty of commerce or navigation which provides for the applicant's trade or investment. A treaty trader must carry out substantial international trade, principally between the United States and the treaty country. A treaty investor must invest, or be in the process of investing, significant capital in an enterprise s/he will direct and which will not be a marginal enterprise entered into solely to make a living.

Several treaties meet the definition of commerce and navigation, but the Immigration and Nationality Act itself also confers E visa benefits on citizens of Australia and Sweden. Trade is defined as transactions involving goods and services, as well as technology-related services.[48]

An E visa holder is admitted for up to two years initially, and may remain indefinitely on two year extensions as long as s/he continues to operate the activities for which entry was initially granted. This distinctive character of the E visa makes it preferable in some instances to an L or H-1B visa. As with H-1B and L visa holders, an E visa holder does not have to maintain a foreign residence that s/he does not intend to abandon.[49] An E visa holder's spouse may work.[50]

TN visas were created by Congress upon the passage of the North American Free Trade Agreement ("NAFTA"). There are four categories of businesspeople covered under NAFTA. They parallel the business visitor, the treaty trader or

---

[45] 8 C.F.R. § 214.2(h)(6)(iv).

[46] Office of Foreign Labor Certification, Department of Labor, Foreign Labor Certification: International Talent Helping Meet Employer Demand 18 (2007).

[47] Office of Foreign Labor Certification, Department of Labor, Foreign Labor Certification: International Talent Helping Meet Employer Demand 18 (2007).

[48] INA § 101(a)(15)(E)(i).

[49] 8 C.F.R. § 214.2(e)(5).

[50] 8 C.F.R. § 214.2(e)(6).

investor, the intra-company transferee, and the professional categories found in the general immigration statute. NAFTA incorporated free trade-related businesspeople into the general B-1, E-1, E-2, and L visa categories. NAFTA created a TN visa for professionals, which parallels the H-1B visa, except that employers seeking Canadian citizens need not file labor attestations or preliminary applications with DHS. Employers seeking Mexicans must go through a more involved process to obtain TN visas for their employees.[51]

Similar visa procedures have been set up pursuant to trade agreements with Chile and Singapore. Pursuant to these agreements Congress established a new H1-B1 "fast track" visa category that eliminates some of the procedural requirements of the H-1B.[52]

d. Other Workers: I, Q, and R Visas

Workers who seek to come to the United States to exchange culture, history, or traditions of a country, as well as for employment and to provide practical training, are eligible for Q visas. These are popularly known as Disney visas, named after the company that lobbied for their creation in the Immigration Act of 1990. The visas allowed for sponsorship of an employee whose work inherently calls for the exchange of cultural information, regardless of skill level. The requirements for the visa include: (1) the employer must be actively engaged in the business of cultural exchange, and not merely an agent or broker; (2) the employer must attest that it will provide Q visa holders with the wages and working conditions comparable to those afforded domestic workers;(3) the visa holder must be at least 18 years of age and have the skills and language ability to communicate the cultural attributes of the country; and (4) the visa holder must have resided and been physically present outside the U.S. if previously admitted on a Q visa. The program must be a structured program in a school, museum, or business; must contain a cultural component that is essential to the visa holder's employment or training; and cannot include training independent of a cultural component. The visa is available for up to 15 months initially, with extensions granted only up to a total of 15 months.

Q-2 visas are visas available under a program approved by the Secretary of State and the Attorney General for those residing in Northern Ireland who are 35 years old or younger and who seek to come to the U.S. to participate in a cultural and training program for the purpose of providing training, employment, and the experience of coexistence and conflict resolution in a diverse society.

R visas are available to religious workers. Those who are eligible include ministers, persons in a professional religious capacity, persons working for religious organizations, and those who were, for two years before applying, a member of a bona fide religious organization. Entry is limited to five years and a

---

[51] Ranko Shiraki Oliver, *In the Twelve Years of NAFTA, the Treaty Gave to Me . . . What Exactly?: An Assessment of Economic, Social and Political Developments in Mexico Since 1994 and Their Impact on Mexican Immigration into the United States*, 10 HARV. LATINO L. REV. 53, 126–127 (2007) (describing the differences in procedures for obtaining TN visas between Canadians and Mexicans).

[52] INA § 101(a)(15)(H)(i)(b); § 214(g)(8).

visa is available for spouses and children accompanying or following to join the principal applicant.

I visas are available to bona fide representatives of the foreign press, radio, or information media entering solely to engage in their profession. The visa is available for those applicants whose countries have reciprocal agreements with the United States. A visa holder is admitted for up to one year, with indefinite one year extensions. There are no restrictions on adjustment. Spouses and children can accompany or follow to join, but they must apply independently for employment authorization if they wish to work in the United States.

C. TOURISTS

B-2 visitors for pleasure can enter the United States temporarily and for specified periods of time. Pleasure is defined in the regulations as "legitimate activities of a recreational character, including tourism, amusement, visits with friends or relatives, rest, medical treatment and activities of a fraternal, social, or service nature."[53]

Examples of visitors for pleasure include tourists, a social visitor in the U.S. to see friends or relatives, someone seeking entry for health purposes, convention participants, amateur sports or similar event participants, dependents of U.S. military personnel, those accompanying B-1 or D nonimmigrants, and those entering the United States to marry U.S. citizens who will depart, or to marry nonimmigrants, who will then receive derivative status.

D. EDUCATIONAL: STUDENTS AND SCHOLARS

This section discusses academic and nonacademic student status in the United States. Academic student status is conferred through an F-1 visa. The F-1 visa is granted to an individual,

> having a residence in a foreign country which he has no intention of abandoning, who is a bona fide student qualified to pursue a full course of study and who seeks to enter the United States temporarily and solely for the purpose of pursuing such a course of study at an established college, university, seminary, conservatory, academic high school, elementary school, or other academic institution or in a language training program in the United States . . . .[54]

An applicant must show that s/he has no intention to immigrate into the United States. The applicant must be studying at a designated educational institution approved by U.S. Immigration and Customs Enforcement and in compliance with the Student and Exchange Visitor Information System ("SEVIS"). The SEVIS is a reporting and monitoring system that tracks student's status, reporting violations, school transfers, and course of study. The system reflects the government's views that student visa systems need more potent security dimensions, especially after

---

[53] 22 C.F.R. § 41.31(b)(2).

[54] INA § 101(a)(15)(F).

9/11. The system was implemented in order to more closely monitor the entry, exist and movement of international students in the United States.

In order to apply for F-1 status, a student must submit a SEVIS Form I-20 issued by a school approved by USCIS.[55] The applicant must show that s/he has sufficient financial resources available to cover expenses while in the United States.[56] The applicant must show that s/he has the credentials to attend the chosen institution and that the applicant is proficient in English or will receive training to become proficient.[57] The applicant must show that s/he will carry a full course of study.[58]

F-2 status is available to spouses and children of F-1 visa holders. As this is a derivative status, F-2 visa holders lose their status if the principal F-1 visa holder violates his/her status. An F-2 visa holder cannot attend post-secondary educational institutions on an F-2 visa. A dependent child can attend elementary and high school, but cannot attend a post-secondary school without changing his/her status to F-1.

F-3 status is available to students from Canada and Mexico who are not residing in the United States.[59] These border commuting students are subject to SEVIS.[60] They cannot sponsor spouses or children for F-2 status.

Several activities may place an F-1 student out of status. A student who is employed without authorization, transfers schools without permission, or fails to complete a course of study in time and has run out of extensions is out of status and subject to removal.[61] A student who drops below a full course of study without prior permission of the designated school official is out of status.[62]

A nonimmigrant visa is available for vocational students. The M visa is available for students who seek to study in a community college, a post-secondary vocational/ business school which confers a degree, a vocational school such as a flight school, or a cooking school. An M applicant must present a SEVIS Form I-20 and is admitted for the time necessary to meet the course of study or one year, whichever is less.[63] The applicant may get extensions up to 3 years from the original start date to complete the program.[64]

Just as with the F visas, an M-1 visa holder may sponsor a spouse and children who are accompanying or following to join the applicant to the United States. These

---

[55] 8 C.F.R. § 214.2(f)(1)(i)(A).

[56] 22 C.F.R. § 41.61(b)(1)(ii).

[57] 9 FAM 41.61 N. 7.

[58] A student can reduce his/her course load only once and with permission from the designated school official to no less than six semester/quarter hours, or a half-time load. 8 C.F.R. § 214.2(f)(6)(iii).

[59] INA § 101(a)(15(F)(iii).

[60] 68 Fed. Reg. 28129, 28130 (May 23, 2003).

[61] 8 C.F.R. § 214.2; Matter of Yazdani, 17 I. & N. Dec. 626 (BIA 1981).

[62] 8 C.F.R. § 214.2(f)(6)(iii).

[63] 8 C.F.R. § 214.2)(m)(5).

[64] 8 C.F.R. § 214.2(m)(10).

applicants hold M-2 visas. They cannot obtain employment or engage in full-time study without a change of status to M-1. A child with M-2 status can still attend elementary and high school.

M-1 status is more restrictive than F-1 status. An M-1 visa holder can only be authorized a reduced course load for medical reasons and only for a maximum aggregate period of five months. S/he can only attend school with extensions for a maximum of 3 years and can transfer schools only within the first 6 months unless circumstances beyond the student's control are involved.[65] Unlike F-1 visas holders, M-1 visa holders cannot accept employment, outside of practical training, after completing a course of study.[66] An M-1 visa holder cannot change status to H if the basis of the H was training received as an M-1 student.[67] Nor can an M-1 change status to F.[68]

The J visa is an education-related visa reserved for those who seek to enter the United States on a scholarly exchange. A J visa holder is one who has no intention of abandoning a foreign residence and is a bona fide student, scholar, trainee, teacher, professor, research assistant, specialist, or leader in a field of specialized knowledge. The J visa holder is coming temporarily to the United States on a program designated by the U.S. Information Agency for the purpose of teaching, training, studying or conducting research.[69] The J applicant must show that s/he has sufficient funds and English fluency to complete the intended program.[70] The J program is administered by the U.S. Department of State's Bureau of Educational and Cultural Affairs ("ECA") and its Office of Exchange Coordination and Designation ("ECD"). The ECD is responsible for designating qualifying governmental and private programs and maintaining an adequate participation process. The categories of potential participants range from secondary school students to scholars, and include trainees, au pairs, and camp counselors.

A J-1 visa holder may seek employment authorization with advance written approval if during her/his stay an urgent and unforeseen financial need has arisen and the employment does not interfere with full-time progress toward the educational objective of the visit.[71]

J-2 visas are available for spouses and children following to join the principal visa holder. J-2 visa holders are eligible for employment authorization for the duration of the visa stay.[72]

Certain J visa holders are required to return to their home country for two years upon completion of their training in the United States before they can seek to adjust

---

[65] 8 C.F.R. § 214.2(m)(11).

[66] 8 C.F.R. § 214.2(m)(13).

[67] 8 C.F.R. § 248.1(d). This prohibition does not apply to M-2 visa holders.

[68] 8 C.F.R. § 248.1(c). This prohibition does not apply to M-2 visa holders.

[69] INA § 101(a)(15(J).

[70] 22 C.F.R. §§ 41.62(a)(2), (3).

[71] 22 C.F.R. § 62.23(g).

[72] 8 C.F.R. § 214.2(j)(1)(v)(B).

status, change status to H or L status, or apply for an immigrant visa.[73] These include visa holders whose participation was financed in whole or part by a U.S., or the participant's home country government, agency, or whose occupation was listed on the Department of State's skills list at the time of admission. Those who came to the U.S. or acquired J status after January 10, 1977 to receive graduate medical education are also required to meet the two year foreign residency requirement.[74]

The H-3 visa is available to workers who are invited to the United States by an individual or organization to receive instruction or training, other than graduate medical training. The training received in the United States must not be "designed primarily to provide productive employment."[75] An applicant seeking H-3 status must show that s/he has a foreign residence to which s/he will return. S/he must also show that the proposed training is not available in the home country, that the applicant will not be placed in a position that regularly employs U.S. citizens and residents, and that the training will benefit the applicant in pursuing a career outside the U.S.[76] An H-3 visa recipient will receive a visa for the length of time of the training, but no longer than two years.[77] An H-3 visa holder is limited in the type of extension or change of status s/he can seek. Importantly, the visa holder must remain and reside outside the country for at least six months before applying for an extension or change of status.[78]

E. HUMAN TRAFFICKING AND OTHER VICTIMS OF VIOLENCE

In 2000, Congress passed the Victims of Trafficking and Violence Protection Act of 2000 ("VTVPA"),[79] which created two categories of nonimmigrant visas available to victims of human trafficking and serious crimes in the United States. The purpose behind the visas was largely humanitarian, but also law-enforcement related: to encourage undocumented noncitizens to step forward and cooperate in law enforcement investigations and/or prosecutions of criminal activity in the United States.[80] The T visa was meant to identify and capture perpetrators of forced sex and forced labor trafficking. The U visa was meant to identify and protect victims of an enumerated set of serious crimes.

---

[73] The person may be able to obtain a waiver of the requirement. INA § 212(e); 8 U.S.C. § 1182(e); Freidberger v. Schultz, 616 F. Supp. 1315 (D.C. Pa. 1985).

[74] INA § 212(e).

[75] INA § 101(a)(15)(H)(iii).

[76] 8 C.F.R. § 214.2(h)(7)(ii)(A).

[77] 8 C.F.R. § 214.2(h)(9)(iii)(C)(1).

[78] 8 C.F.R. § 214.2(h)13)(iv).

[79] Pub. L. 106-386, 114 Stat. 1464.

[80] See Victims of Trafficking and Violence Protection Act of 2000, section 102 (the purpose of this Act is to "combat trafficking in persons, . . . to ensure just and effective punishment of traffickers, and to protect their victims").

1.   T Visas

Congress made 5,000 nonimmigrant visas available pursuant to the VTVPA for victims of sex trafficking or of severe forms of trafficking. To be eligible, a T visa applicant must show that s/he is or has been a victim of a severe form of trafficking in persons, is physically present in the U.S. because of such trafficking, and is under the age of 18 or has complied with any reasonable request for assistance in the investigation or prosecution of trafficking. The applicant must also show that s/he would suffer extreme hardship involving unusual or severe harm upon removal.[81]

A severe form of trafficking is defined under the Act as

(A) sex trafficking in which a commercial sex act is induced by force, fraud, or coercion, or in which the person induced to perform such act has not attained 18 years of age; or

(B) the recruitment, harboring, transportation, provision, or obtaining of a person for labor or services, through the use of force, fraud, or coercion for the purpose of subjection to involuntary servitude, peonage, debt bondage, or slavery.[82]

The Act defines sex trafficking as "the recruitment, harboring, transportation, provision, or obtaining of a person for the purpose of a commercial sex act."[83]

The T visa is available for four years, and allows for extensions as long as the person is still needed in the investigation or prosecution of a crime. Congress has provided T visa holders the opportunity to seek adjustment to permanent resident status after three years.[84] The T visa has been granted in few instances. Since its inception, the number of visas granted is in the hundreds, even though up to 5,000 are available every year.[85]

2.   U Visas

The U visa is available to someone who "suffers substantial physical and mental abuse as a result of having been a victim of criminal activity."[86] To be eligible the victim must possess information concerning the criminal activity, and a law enforcement official must certify that the victim "has been helpful, is being helpful, or is likely to be helpful" in the investigation or prosecution of a crime. Any law enforcement agency may so certify, including police departments, prosecutors, judges, or other federal, state, and local authorities.[87] The regulations specifically

---

[81] INA § 101(a)(15(T)(i).

[82] 22 U.S.C. § 7102(8) (2000).

[83] 22 U.S.C. § 7108(9) (2000).

[84] INA § 245(l).

[85] INA § 214(o)(2).

[86] INA § 101(a)(15(U).

[87] INA § 101(a)(15)(U).

name the EEOC, the DOL, and child protective services as agencies that can issue this certification.

The enumerated crimes range from sex-related crimes to labor-related crimes.[88] They include rape, torture, trafficking, incest, domestic violence, sexual assault, abusive sexual contact, prostitution, sexual exploitation, female genital mutilation, being held hostage, peonage, involuntary servitude, slave trade, kidnapping, abduction, unlawful criminal restraint, false imprisonment, blackmail, extortion, manslaughter, murder, felonious assault, witness tampering, obstruction of justice, perjury, or any similar activity considered criminal under local, state or federal law.[89]

A U visa recipient is eligible for the visa for four years. The visa holder is eligible to adjust to permanent resident status after three years.[90]

The U visa regulations were finally implemented in September 2007, seven years after the passage of the VTVPA. Before the regulations were in place, U visa-eligible persons were granted interim relief in the form of deferred action for one year increments along with employment authorization documents.

Several critics of the U visa process point to the difficulty in balancing between the law enforcement purpose and the victim protection purpose of the Act in determining how U visas are disseminated.[91] Some of this balancing difficulty is evident in the regulations, which, for example, require each law enforcement agency to designate a person responsible for signing law enforcement certifications. Presumably this requirement limits the number of applicants who will receive law enforcement certification, which is the first step in seeking a U visa.

F. OTHER NONIMMIGRANT VISAS

There exist several visas that are very narrow in scope. The C visa covers those nonimmigrants in transit between two non-U.S. destinations. This category in-cludes diplomats in transit and certain visitors to and from the United Nations headquarters in New York. D visas allow nonimmigrant crew members on airplanes and vessels to enter the United States temporarily in connection with their work or to take shore leave. The S visa is available to informants and witnesses in criminal and counter-terrorist investigations and prosecutions.

---

[88] *See* Leticia M. Saucedo, *A New U: Organizing Victims and Protecting Immigrant Workers*, 42 University of Richmond Law Review 891 (2008).

[89] INA § 101(a)(15)(U)(iii).

[90] INA § 214(p).

[91] *See e.g.*, Grace Chang and Kathleen Kim, *Reconceptualizing Approaches to Human Trafficking: New Directions and Perspectives from the Field(s)*, 3 Stan. J.C.R.-C.L. 317 (2007); Dina Haynes, *(Not) Found Chained to a Bed in a Brothel: Conceptual, Legal and Procedural Failures to Fulfill the Promises of the Trafficking Victims Protection Act*, 21 Geo. Immig. L.J. 337 (2007); Jennifer Chacon, *Misery and Myopia; Understanding the Failures of U.S. Efforts to Stop Human Trafficking*, 74 Fordham L. Rev. 2977, 3019 (2006).

Chapter 9

INADMISSIBILITY GROUNDS AND WAIVERS

Even though an applicant for admission may meet the requirements to qualify for a particular immigration category, for example as the spouse of a U.S. citizen or professional of extraordinary ability, the person may still be precluded from the issuance of an immigrant visa if he or she falls within one of the grounds of inadmissibility. The grounds of inadmissibility are found in INA § 212.

A. IMMIGRATION CONTROL

A substantial number of inadmissibility grounds pertain to disqualifying factors related to immigration controls such as visa fraud, alien smuggling, and unlawful presence in the United States. In other words, violation of an immigration law itself can be a ground of inadmissibility.

1. Smugglers of Aliens

Under INA § 212(a)(6)(E), an alien who at any time "knowingly has encouraged, induced, assisted, abetted or aided" any other noncitizen to enter or try to enter the United States is inadmissible. Amendments in 1990 eliminated a requirement of smuggling "for gain" from the concept of alien smuggling. Thus, although the prior law was clearly aimed at punishing professional smugglers, the language of the current provision conceivably covers anyone who helps or encourages another alien to try to cross the border without inspection, even when payment is not contemplated. So individuals who have helped their own family members across the border surreptitiously are inadmissible under this provision.

A waiver of this ground of admissibility is available only to a lawful permanent resident who assisted a spouse, parent, son, or daughter to enter illegally, or to an alien seeking admission or adjustment of status as an immediate relative or family preference immigrant (except for the sibling category).

There is a particular problem if the individual is actually criminally convicted of alien smuggling, harboring, or transporting under INA § 274(a)(1)(A) or (2). Such a conviction is considered an aggravated felony, even if the defendant was not paid and was simply helping a friend or relative, and even if no sentence was imposed. The only exception is for first offense smuggling of a spouse, child, or parent.[1]

2. Visa Fraud

Under INA § 212(a)(6)(C), an alien who "by fraud or willfully misrepresenting a material fact, seeks to procure (or has sought to procure or has procured) a visa, other documentation, or admission into the United States" is inadmissible. Documentation includes not only the specified visa, but the supporting documents such as birth, marriage, and divorce certificates, work experience letters, and school records.

---

[1] Matter of Ruiz-Romero, Int. Dec. No. 3376 (BIA 1999).

A charge based on procurement of a visa or other documentation is not sustainable unless the fraud was practiced on an authorized United States government official.[2] A willful misrepresentation must be made with knowledge of its falsity and with actual intent to deceive so that an advantage under the immigration laws might be gained to which the alien would not have otherwise been entitled.[3]

Even though the misrepresentation is willful, the alien is not inadmissible unless the misrepresentation is material. In determining whether a misrepresentation is material, the attorney general has suggested the following three-part inquiry:

- Does the record establish that the alien is excludable on the true facts? If it does, then the misrepresentation was material; the inquiry ends. If it does not, then the second and third questions must be considered.
- Did the misrepresentation tend to shut off a line of inquiry which is relevant to the alien's eligibility? A misrepresentation as to identity or place of past residence, for example, would almost necessarily shut off an opportunity to investigate part or all of the alien's past history, and thus have shut off a relevant investigation. However, a remote, tenuous, or fanciful connection between a misrepresentation and a line of inquiry which is relevant to the alien's eligibility is insufficient to satisfy this aspect of the test of materiality.
- If a relevant line of inquiry has been cut off, might that inquiry have resulted in a proper determination that the alien be excluded? On this aspect of the question the alien bears the burden of persuasion and proof. Having made a willful misrepresentation which tends to cut off a relevant line of investigation, he cannot now try out his eligibility as if nothing had happened. One who, by an intentional and wrongful act, has prevented or restricted an inquiry into relevant facts bears the burden of establishing the true facts and the risk that any uncertainties from the person's own obstruction of the inquiry may be resolved unfavorably.[4]

A waiver of the visa fraud ground of inadmissibility is available to applicants if they are a spouse, son, or daughter of a U.S. citizen or lawful permanent resident and refusal of admission would result in extreme hardship to that relative.

3.　　Document Fraud

Under INA §§ 212(a)(6)(F), a person who is subject to a final order and penalties related to document fraud proceedings is inadmissible. Under INA § 274C, it is unlawful for a person to knowingly forge or alter any document or to "use, attempt to use, possess, obtain, accept, or receive or provide" any false document for the purpose of obtaining any benefit under the immigration laws. This includes using a false document or borrowing someone else's document, such as a visa to gain entry or a social security card to complete an I-9 form to obtain a

---

[2] *Cf.* Matter of Shirdel, Int. Dec. No. 2958 (BIA 1984).

[3] Matter of G-G-, 7 I.&N. Dec. 161 (BIA 1956).

[4] Matter of S-&B-C-, 9 I.&N. Dec. 436, 448–49 (A.G. 1961).

job. Document fraud also occurs when a noncitizen uses a false document to board an airplane or other transport and then destroys the document en route to the United States.

Document fraud also covers those who assists others "to prepare, file, or assist another in preparing or filing, any application for benefits under this Act, or any document required under this Act, or any document submitted in connection with such application or document, with knowledge or in reckless disregard of the fact that such application or document was falsely made or, in whole or in part, does not relate to the person on whose behalf it was or is being submitted."[5]

INA § 274C defines document fraud and sets forth rules for a civil hearing before an administrative hearing officer. The officer will issue a final order against a person if the person either (a) waives the right to the civil hearing, or (b) is found to have committed document fraud. This is a civil penalty. For an applicant to be inadmissible for document fraud, the person must have been notified to attend the document fraud hearing and be subject to a final order from that hearing.[6]

4.   False Claim to U.S. Citizenship

Any applicant who falsely claims to be a U.S. citizen is inadmissible under INA § 212(a)(6)(C)(ii). A noncitizen must not falsely claim to be a U.S. citizen for any purpose or benefit under the Immigration and Nationality Act, including the act's employment authorization attestation requirements or under any other federal or state law. This ground of inadmissibility requires a showing that the false representation was made for a specific purpose — to satisfy a legal requirement or obtain a benefit that otherwise would not be available to the noncitizen.

The inadmissibility ground related to false claims to U.S. citizenship does not apply in the following circumstances: (a) when each of the applicant's natural or adopted parents is or was a U.S. citizen; (b) if the applicant began to reside permanently in the United States prior to the age of sixteen; and (c) if the applicant reasonably believed at the time of such statement, violation, or claim that he or she was a U.S. citizen.

5.   Stowaways

Under INA § 212(a)(6)(D), a person who obtains transportation without consent and through concealment is inadmissible. A passenger with a valid ticket is not a stowaway. No waiver is available for this ground of inadmissibility. Stowaways do not have a right to an inadmissibility hearing, unless they apply for asylum.[7]

---

[5] INA § 274C(5).

[6] *See* Walter v. INS, 159 F.3d 1349 (2d Cir. 1998).

[7] INA § 273(d).

6.   Unlawful Presence in the United States

Under INA § 212(a)(9), any alien, other than an alien lawfully admitted for permanent residence, who has been unlawfully present in the United States for a period of more than 180 days but less than a year, and who voluntarily departed prior to any removal proceedings, is barred from admission for three years. Any alien who has been unlawfully present in the United States for a year or more and who is seeking readmission will be barred for ten years. Any person removed is subject to the ten year bar if they were unlawfully present for more than 180 days. Thus, in order to be subject to the three or ten-year bars, the person must have departed from the United States and is seeking readmission to the United States. Unlawful presence includes those who have overstayed their visas as well as those who entered without proper inspection. A person who has been unlawfully present does not fall within this inadmissibility category if he or she has not departed and is eligible for adjustment of status in the United States.

The 180 days or year must be continuous. A person who is in unlawful status for four months, then leaves and comes back to new unlawful status for five months, has not spent six months in continuous unlawful presence and does not come within the three or ten year bar.

Unlawful presence does not include any period of time that the person was under age eighteen, any time during which the alien had a bona fide asylum application pending, any time during which the alien had a nonfrivolous application pending for a change or extension of status and did not work without authorization, or any time during which the alien was a beneficiary of family unity protection. This ground of inadmissibility also does not apply to an alien who was a victim of spousal or parental abuse when the unlawful presence is related to the abuse.

Time spent in proceedings before an immigration judge or higher appellate authority is not necessarily a period of authorized stay. When a person enters without inspection, unlawful presence begins to accrue at entry and continues to accrue while such a person is in proceedings. When a nonimmigrant bearing a date-certain Form I-94 (entry-departure form) remains in the United States beyond the date noted on that form, unlawful presence begins to accrue as of the date the Form I-94 expired. A nonimmigrant bearing a date-certain Form I-94 who is placed in removal proceedings will not begin to accrue time unlawfully present until the date noted on the Form I-94 has been reached or the immigration judge orders the alien removed, whichever is earlier. When an alien successfully contests the charges of inadmissibility or removability brought by ICE in a proceeding, the alien will be deemed not to have accrued any periods of unlawful presence in the United States during the pendency of the proceedings.

The unlawful presence ground of inadmissibility can be waived as a matter of discretion if the prospective immigrant is the spouse, son, or daughter of a U.S. citizen or lawful permanent resident and the refusal to admit would result in extreme hardship to the spouse or parent. The waiver is not available to a parent of a citizen or lawful permanent resident. The waiver decision is entirely within the discretion of immigration authorities and is not subject to judicial review.[8]

A more severe, permanent bar to admission applies to those who have been unlawfully present in the United States for an aggregate period of more than one year, depart, and then enter or attempt to reenter the United States without permission.[9] These individuals cannot even apply for a discretionary waiver of this provision until ten years has elapsed since their last departure from the United States.

7.   Prior Removal or Deportation

In general, any alien who has been ordered removed from the United States when attempting to seek admission is inadmissible for five years from the date of such removal. An alien who has been removed from the United States after having gained admission is inadmissible for ten years from the date of such removal. However, if the person has already been removed at least once in the past, or if the alien was removed due to a conviction for an aggravated felony, the person is inadmissible for twenty years.[10] Aliens who were previously removed, deported, or excluded from the United States and who reenter without permission are guilty of a felony under INA § 276.

Under INA § 212(a)(6)(B), an alien who fails or refuses to attend a removal proceedings is inadmissible for five years.

B. POLITICAL AND NATIONAL SECURITY

Under INA § 212(a)(3), activities considered threatening to U.S. security trigger inadmissibility. Those activities include espionage, sabotage, terrorist activity, and genocide. The preclusion also applies to those who were Nazis or members in Communist or totalitarian parties. The law also excludes those whose entrance would have "serious adverse foreign policy consequences."

Terrorist activity includes any activity that is unlawful under the laws of the place where committed involving highjacking or sabotage of any conveyance; seizing or detaining, and threatening to kill, injure, or continue to detain, another individual in order to compel a third person (including a governmental organization) to do or abstain from doing any act as an explicit or implicit condition for the release of the individual seized or detained; assassination; the use of any biological agent, chemical agent, or nuclear weapon or device, or explosive or firearm with the intent to endanger the safety of one or more individuals or to cause substantial damage to property.

The USA PATRIOT Act, enacted in response to 9/11, added new grounds of inadmissibility for representatives (and their spouses and children) of foreign terrorist organizations or any group that publicly endorses acts of terrorist activity.

---

[8] INA § 212(a)(9)(B)(v).

[9] INA § 212(a)(9)(C).

[10] INA § 212(a)(9).

Noncitizens are denied admission if they "endorse or espouse terrorist activity," or "persuade others to support terrorist activity or a terrorist organization," in ways that the State Department determines impede U.S. efforts to combat terrorism.The Act defines "terrorist activity" expansively to include support of otherwise lawful and nonviolent activities of almost any group that used violence. Noncitizens are deportable for wholly innocent associational activity, excludable for pure speech, and subject to incarceration without a finding that they pose a danger or flight risk. Foreign nationals can be detained for up to seven days while the government decides whether or not to file criminal or immigration charges. The Attorney General has broad preventive detention authority to incarcerate noncitizens by certifying there are "reasonable grounds to believe" that a person is "described in" the antiterrorism provisions of the immigration law, and the individual is then subject to potentially indefinite detention. The Attorney General also can detain noncitizens indefinitely even after prevailing in a removal proceeding "until the Attorney General determines that the noncitizen is no longer a noncitizen who may be certified [as a suspected terrorist.]"

INA § 219 allows the State Department to designate an organization as a terrorist organization if the group (1) is a foreign organization; (2) engages in terrorist activity; and (3) threatens the security of U.S. nationals or the national security of the United States. The State Department must notify Congress of the intent to designate a particular organization as terrorist and publish the designation in the Federal Register. The designation of an organization as a terrorist organization will last for two years, at which time the State Department may redesignate the organization for another two years. Congress, however, may block or revoke a designation at any time. An organization that is designated as a terrorist organization may, within 30 days of the date of designation, seek judicial review of the designation in the U.S. Court of Appeals for the District of Columbia Circuit.

Under INA § 212(a)(3)(E), any alien who has engaged in conduct defined as genocide for purposes of the International Convention on the Prevention and Punishment of Genocide is inadmissible. The convention defines the term "genocide" as any of the following acts committed with the intent to destroy, in whole or in part, a national, ethnic, racial, or religious group by killing members of the group; causing serious bodily or mental harm to members of the group, deliberately inflicting on the group conditions of life calculated to bring about its physical destruction in whole or in part, importing measures intended to prevent births within the group, and forcibly transferring children of the group to another group. Directing, inciting, or conspiring to commit genocide also fall within this section.

Applicants who are permanently ineligible for U.S. citizenship also are inadmissible under INA 212(a)(8). Draft dodgers and deserters fall within this provision. However, the provision does not include those who merely failed to register with the Selective Service. Also, those draft dodgers or deserters during the Vietnam War era who were granted amnesty by President Carter are not inadmissible.

Unlawful voting contrary to federal, state, or local laws renders an applicant inadmissible under INA § 212(a)(10). Generally, these laws require that the person knew that he or she was not eligible to vote. This inadmissibility ground does not apply to a person (1) whose parents were U.S. citizens, (2) who began residing permanently in the United States prior to age sixteen, or (3) who reasonably believed that he or she was a U.S. citizen.

C. CRIMINAL

1. Moral Turpitude Crime

Under INA § 212(a)(2)(A)(i)(I), an alien who has been convicted of, or who has admitted the commission of, a crime involving moral turpitude is inadmissible. The statute does not distinguish between misdemeanors and felonies. The term "moral turpitude" is difficult to define with precision. Various courts have suggested that the term includes crimes that evince depravity and baseness, that are malum in se, morally and inherently wrong, or that would be viewed as involving moral turpitude in the common conscience of the community.[11] Whether a crime involves moral turpitude depends on what must be proven to establish guilt. A crime involves moral turpitude if, from the statutory definition and the material allegations of the information or indictment, the crime necessarily or inherently involves moral turpitude. For example, if the statute is divisible in that not every violation of it would necessarily involve moral turpitude, then it is proper to examine the record of conviction (including the indictment or information, plea, verdict or judgment, and sentence). Such an examination would not be proper, however, when a person is charged with a crime involving moral turpitude but plea bargains to a lesser or different charge that does not necessarily involve moral turpitude.

Crimes that have been determined to involve moral turpitude include murder, voluntary manslaughter, aggravated assault, rape, kidnapping, theft, lewd conduct, bigamy, fraud, and other crimes having as an element the intent to defraud. An aggravated assault against a peace officer that resulted in bodily harm to the victim and involved knowledge by the offender that his force was directed at an officer performing an official duty, has been held to involve moral turpitude.[12] Under certain circumstances, involuntary manslaughter could involve moral turpitude.[13] Being an accessory to murder can be a moral turpitude crime when the defendant admitted that he knew the principal had intentionally committed murder and that he intentionally assisted the principal in avoiding detention.[14] Making false statements on a driver's license application was a crime involving moral turpitude when the elements of materiality and knowledge were shown.[15] Furthermore, it makes no difference whether the moral turpitude offense was motivated by economic hardship or the need to feed a family during time of war.[16]

---

[11] *See* Jordan v. DeGeorge, 341 U.S. 223 (1951).

[12] Matter of Danesh, Int. Dec. No. 3068 (BIA 1988).

[13] Franklin v. INS, 72 F.3d 571 (8th Cir. 1995).

[14] Cabral v. INS, 15 F. 3d 193 (1st Cir. 1994).

[15] Zaitona v. INS, 9 F. 3d 432 (6th Cir. 1993).

[16] Chiaramonte v. INS, 626 F.2d 1093 (2d Cir. 1980); Matter of De La Nues, 18 I.&N. Dec. 140 (BIA 1981).

On the other hand, crimes such as voluntary manslaughter, joyriding, and simple assault have been held not to involve moral turpitude. Structuring financial transactions to avoid currency reports was determined not a crime involving moral turpitude because the statute involved did not make intent to defraud the government an essential element of the offense; the defendant could have been convicted even if he was not aware that his conduct was illegal.[17]

Under the statute, the alien's admission of all the essential elements of a crime involving moral turpitude is sufficient to trigger inadmissibility, notwithstanding the absence of a conviction. The alien must understand the full nature and elements of the crime to which he or she is admitting. However, even if the alien was charged and acquitted, the subsequent admission may fall within the ground of inadmissibility.

Several statutory exceptions to the moral turpitude ground of inadmissibility are contained in the statute.

a.   Political offense. Those crimes that are purely political offenses are exempted under INA § 212(a)(2)(A)(i)(I). The State Department Foreign Affairs Manual provides examples where the aliens concerned were considered to have been convicted of "purely political offenses:

- An alien convicted by a South African court of robbery and assault because he helped to overpower his guards and forcefully took possession of a government car in attempting to escape from a civilian internment camp.
- An alien convicted by a Netherlands court of having executed false ration coupons in order to benefit the underground during World War II.
- An alien who was a member of the German SS and sentenced by a Soviet court to nine years for theft of paper bags.
- An alien convicted in Italy of participating in a riot protesting lack of flour distribution when the court held that the acts were not one for personal reasons or for individual gain.

b.   Juvenile offense. Juvenile offenders are exempted from the moral turpitude exclusion if they have committed only one crime involving moral turpitude while under the age of eighteen. However, at least five years must have elapsed since the date of commission of the offense since the date of release from confinement, whichever is later. Conduct underlying a foreign conviction for an offense that constitutes an act of juvenile delinquency under U.S. standards, however treated by the foreign court, is not a crime for purposes of exclusion.

c.   Petty offense. An alien is exempted from the moral turpitude exclusion if convicted of only one crime and the maximum penalty for the crime did not exceed imprisonment for one year and if the alien was not sentenced to a term of imprisonment in excess of six months.

Under INA § 212(h), an alien inadmissible because of the commission of a crime involving moral turpitude may be admitted as a matter of discretion if one of two

---

[17] Goldeshtein v. INS, 8 F.3d 645 (9th Cir. 1993).

conditions is met: (1) the crime for which the person is inadmissible occurred more than 15 years ago, the admission would not be contrary to national safety and security, and the person has been rehabilitated; or (2) the person is the spouse, parent, son, or daughter of a U.S. citizen or a lawful permanent resident, and the inadmission would result in extreme hardship to the relative. The waiver is not available to someone who has been convicted of, or who admits committing, a murder or criminal acts involving torture.

2.   Narcotics and Marijuana

Persons who have committed offenses relating to narcotics and marijuana are extremely disfavored under U.S. immigration laws. For example, under INA § 212(a)(2)(A)(i)(II), aliens convicted of violating any law or regulation relating to a controlled substance is inadmissible. This includes solicitation to commit a crime relating to a controlled substance.[18] Furthermore, the statute also renders inadmissible aliens whom the consular or DHS official "knows or has reason to believe" are or have been traffickers. For example, an arrest for a controlled substance offense that does not result in a conviction may form the basis for a reasonable belief that the alien was a trafficker.[19]

As discussed below, aliens who are drug addicts or drug abusers also are inadmissible.

Waivers of inadmissibility for narcotics are quite limited. An INA § 212(h) waiver is available only to marijuana offenders who have committed a single offense involving simple possession of not more than 30 grams. The waiver is a matter of discretion and one of two sets of conditions must be met: (1) the crime for which the person is inadmissible occurred more than 15 years ago, the admission would not be contrary to national safety and security, and the person has been rehabilitated; or (2) the person is the spouse, parent, son, or daughter of a U.S. citizen or a lawful permanent resident, and the inadmission would result in extreme hardship to the relative.

3.   Multiple Criminal Convictions

Aliens who have been convicted of two or more offenses, regardless of whether moral turpitude or drugs were involved, are inadmissible under INA § 212(a)(2)(B) if the aggregate sentence to confinement actually imposed was five years or more. This inadmissibility ground includes misdemeanors and felonies. It makes no difference if the convictions resulted from a single trial or involved offenses from a single scheme of misconduct.

The waivers available for the moral turpitude inadmissibility are also available for this ground of inadmissibility.

---

[18] Matter of Beltran, Int. Dec. No. 3179 (BIA 1992).

[19] Nunez-Payan v. INS, 815 F.2d 384 (5th Cir. 1987).

4.   Prostitution and Commercialized Vice

Under INA § 212(a)(2)(D), aliens who are prostitutes or procurers, or entering to engage in other unlawful commercialized vice, and who have engaged in prostitution or procuring within ten years of the application for admission are inadmissible. The provision also covers aliens coming to the United States to engage in commercialized vice such as loan sharking or gambling. There need not have been a conviction, and the alien is not exempt from the exclusion if prostitution was legal at the place engaged in or in the place to which the alien is coming to the United States.

Persons falling within the prostitution inadmissibility may apply for the discretionary family waiver of INA § 212(h). One of two conditions must be met: (1) the crime for which the person is inadmissible occurred more than 15 years ago, the admission would not be contrary to national safety and security, and the person has been rehabilitated; or (2) the person is the spouse, parent, son, or daughter of a U.S. citizen or a lawful permanent resident, and the inadmission would result in extreme hardship to the relative.

D.   ECONOMIC

One of the most commonly raised grounds of inadmissibility is under INA § 212(a)(4), which raises the issue of whether an applicant is likely to become a public charge. Consular and USCIS officials have tremendous discretion in determining whether an applicant is likely to become a public charge. Yet that discretion is not absolute and there must be some support for the decision.[20] Some of the factors generally considered are age, ability and willingness to work, promise of a job, close relatives in the United States, and mental and physical health. A healthy person in the prime of life ordinarily should not be considered likely to become a public charge.[21]

In making their likelihood of public charge determinations, consular and USCIS officials generally refer to income poverty guidelines published by the Department of Health and Human Services and updated annually. The applicant must establish a level of income or assets, essentially with income of at least 125 percent of the federal poverty guidelines.

Past receipt of public assistance can be relevant to whether the applicant is likely to become a public charge. DHS follows a set of interim rules that have been in place for a number of years:

- DHS may not consider use of non-cash benefits (such as Medicaid or Food Stamps) by an applicant as a basis for public charge. However, if a person has received or is likely to receive long-term publicly funded institutionalization (such as placement in a nursing home or mental hospital), then DHS can consider that as one factor in a public charge decision.

---

[20] Matter of Perez, 15 I.&N. Dec. 136 (BIA 1974); Matter of Harutunian, 14 I.&N. Dec. 583 (Reg. Comm'r 1974).

[21] Matter of Martinez-Lopez, 10 I.&N. Dec. 409 (A.G. 1964).

- DHS may consider the receipt of cash benefits in the public charge determination if they are received for the purpose of income maintenance. This includes programs such as Temporary Assistance for Needy Families (TANF), General Assistance (GA), or Supplemental Security Income (SSI).
- If the cash benefits for maintenance were received by an applicant's family members, these cannot be considered in the applicant's public charge determination unless the applicant was relying on the cash benefits as his or her sole means of support.
- One-time cash grants and cash designated for other purposes such as child car or job training should not be considered in public charge decisions. Similarly, benefits that are earned, e.g., Social Security retirement or veterans benefits, are not to be considered.

Since 1996, any applicant immigrating through a family visa petition must have an affidavit of support (Form I-864) submitted as part of the file from a U.S. family member. The affidavit of support is legally enforceable and is used to help the applicant establish sufficient assets and income. Under INA § 213A(f)(1), the sponsor who signs the affidavit of support must be a citizen or national of the United States or a lawful permanent resident, of at least 18 years of age. The sponsor must live in the United States or in a U.S. territory or possession. The U.S. citizen or lawful permanent resident who is filing the petition in a family immigration situation must file an affidavit of support, even if the petitioner's income is low.

The sponsor must establish that he or she has "the means to maintain an annual income equal to at least 125% of the federal poverty line" for his or her own household plus the intending immigrant and family members immigrating with the applicant. Sponsors who are active in the U.S. Armed Forces only need to demonstrate support at 100 percent of the poverty line. To establish income, the sponsor must provide a social security number and copies of three years of tax returns.[22]

If the petitioner sponsor does not earn enough income alone to meet the 125 percent of the poverty income guidelines requirement, three other mechanisms are possible: (1) adding household members' income; (2) finding a joint sponsor; and/or (3) using significant assets.

The income of the petitioning sponsor's household members may be added to the sponsor's income in order satisfy the applicant's public charge challenge. The income of these contributing household members can be added: any person (including the intending immigrant) who has lived in the sponsor's household for at least the previous six months and is related to the sponsor by birth, marriage or adoption, and dependents listed on the sponsor's tax return. These household members must also sign the I-864A affidavit of support, thereby become jointly and severally liable to help support the applicant.

Joint sponsors must meet the same requirements as the original petitioning sponsor. Under INA § 213A(f), the joint sponsor must be a lawful permanent resident or a U.S. citizen at least eighteen years old who lives in the United States or a U.S. territory or possession. The joint sponsor must sign a separate affidavit

---

[22] INA § 213A(6)(A)(i), (B).

of support and become legally obligated to support the applicant. The joint sponsor must make 125 percent of the income needed to support both his or her household and the intending immigrant.

When income is not sufficient, the availability of significant assets can still satisfy the public charge ground of inadmissibility. The intending immigrant's assets also can be counted. Savings accounts, stocks and bonds, certificates of deposit, life insurance policies, real estate, and personal property are examples of acceptable significant assets. There are two requirements: (1) the assets must be convertible to cash within one year, and (2) the net worth of the assets must be five times the difference between the sponsor's actual income and the income the sponsor is required to have. A sponsor, joint sponsor, or household member can use significant assets to meet or help meet the 125 percent requirement.

The Form I-864 affidavit of support is legally enforceable against the sponsor, as well as any joint sponsor or contributing household member.[23] Any federal, state or local government can sue the sponsor to recover the costs of federal or state means-tested public benefits that were received by the immigrant during the period of enforcement of the affidavit of support. Reimbursement for benefits received by the immigrant more than ten years earlier cannot be sought.[24] Federal mean-tested public benefits have been defined to include Medicaid, the State Children's Health Insurance Program (SCHIP), Temporary Assistance for Needy Families, SSI, and Food Stamps. The sponsored immigrant also can sue the sponsor to seek support at a level equivalent to 125 percent of the poverty guidelines.[25]

The sponsor's obligation under the affidavit of support ends when:

1. The sponsored immigrant becomes a U.S. citizen,
2. The sponsored immigrant is credited for forty "qualifying quarters" of employment as reflected by social security payments (i.e., a minimum of ten years),
3. The sponsored immigrant ceases to be a lawful permanent resident and has left the United States, or the sponsored immigrant dies, or
4. The sponsor files for bankruptcy.[26]

The sponsor's obligation does not end due to divorce, because the immigrant disappears and does not communicate with the sponsor, or for other personal reasons. Although the obligation ends if the sponsor dies, the sponsor's estate may have to pay obligations that arose before the sponsor died. Similarly, even after the sponsor's obligation ends, the sponsor remains liable for debts that arose before the support obligation ended.

While the general rule is that all family immigration applicants must have a qualified affidavit of support submitted on their behalf by the petitioner and, if needed, a join sponsor, a few exceptions are provided.

---

[23] INA § 213A(a)(1)(B).

[24] INA § 213A(b)(2)(C).

[25] INA § 213A(a)(1)(B), (e)(1).

[26] INA § 213A(a)(3).

1. Self-petitioning battered spouses and children. A noncitizen who has been battered or abused by a U.S. citizen or permanent resident spouse or child can "self-petition" under the Violence Against Women Act (VAWA) provisions. These self-petitioners do not need to have an I-864 affidavit of support filed on their behalf. Unlike other family immigrants, the need only meet the general public charge test.[27]

2. When the petitioner has died. If a petitioner dies after the petition is approved but before the family member immigrates, in some cases the government will reinstate or maintain the petition for humanitarian reasons. In that case, other family members can become substitute sponsors for purposes of submitting an affidavit of support.[28]

3. Child automatically derives U.S. citizenship upon becoming lawful resident. Some noncitizen children automatically become U.S. citizens at the moment they become lawful permanent residents through the citizenship of the parent (derivative citizenship under INA § 340). Because they become citizens upon admission, an affidavit of support is not required.

4. Immigrant has earned or inherits forty quarters of qualifying income. An affidavit of support is not required for applicants who already have or can be credited with forty qualifying quarters of qualifying income.[29] Of course, many immigrants have worked in the United States with authorization. However, even those who worked without authorization can get credit for the quarters worked if they paid into the social security system. And in some circumstances, some individuals can claim quarters of work done by relatives. For example, children can credit the quarters that their parents (including stepparents) earned from the date of the parent's birth until the date the child turns eighteen. A spouse can credit the quarters earned by the other spouse from the date of their marriage.

E. PUBLIC HEALTH AND MORALS

Inadmissibility grounds related to health can be divided into four categories: communicable diseases, failure to obtain vaccinations, mental or physical disorder, and drug addiction or abuse.

1. Communicable Diseases

Under INA § 212(a)(1)(A)(i), an applicant with a communicable disease is inadmissible. For example, tuberculosis and sexually transmitted disease such as gonorrhea and syphilis are bases for inadmissibility. A person testing positive for these illnesses can have the disease treated and cured and then qualify to immigrate. In the alternative, if an illness such as tuberculosis cannot be quickly cured, under certain circumstances, the applicant may qualify for a waiver and gain admission.

---

[27] INA § 212(a)(4)(C)(i).

[28] INA § 213A(2)(f)(5)(B).

[29] 78 Interpreter Releases 994 (June 11, 2001); 79 Interpreter Releases 385 (Mar. 11, 2002).

An applicant with acquired immune deficiency syndrome (AIDS) is also inadmissible. Individuals who are HIV-positive are inadmissible, but under certain conditions, they also may qualify for a waiver.

2.   Failure to Prove Vaccinations

Under INA § 212(a)(1)(A)(ii), an applicant is inadmissible for failing to present evidence of vaccination against preventable diseases: mumps, measles, rubella, polio, tetanus and diphtheria toxoids, pertussis, influenza type B, and hepatitis B. This provision may be waived if the applicant obtains a vaccination, or if a civil surgeon or similar official certifies that the vaccination would not be medically appropriate, or if the vaccination would be contrary to the person's religious or moral beliefs.[30]

3.   Mental or Physical Disorder

Under INA § 212(a)(1)(A)(iii), applicants are inadmissible if they have a mental or physical disorder and related behavior that may threaten the property, welfare, and safety of themselves or others, or who have had such a disorder in the past that is likely to recur. For example, this ground of inadmissibility may apply to an applicant who has been committed to a mental institution for violent behavior, or to someone who has been diagnosed as a sexual predator, or even to someone who is suicidal.

Alcoholism can be a basis for inadmissibility under this provision, and a drunk driving conviction can serve as evidence of alcoholism. Some U.S. consulate offices have denied visa applications under this provision on the basis of one or two arrest for driving under the influence of alcohol. Pursuant to standards established by the Center for Disease Control, an applicant must have been free of alcoholic behavior for two years in order to avoid this ground of inadmissibility.

Under INA § 212(a)(10)(B), an applicant who is accompanying a separate applicant who has been deemed inadmissible due to physical or mental disability also is inadmissible if the applicant is needed for the protection or guardianship of the helpless person.

4.   Drug Addicts and Drug Abusers

Under § 212(a)(1)(A)(iv), drug addicts and drug abusers are inadmissible. This inadmissibility ground applies to current, not past, abuse or addiction. The statute charges the Department of Health and Human Services with the responsibility of defining drug abuse or addiction. The Center for Disease Control, and HHS agency, has adopted a very controversial test for determining drug abuse. In its view, any drug use that goes beyond mere "experimentation" with drugs is drug abuse. Since CDC views experimentation as "taking an illegal drug one time," its definition has led to the inadmissibility of applicants who have tried a drug more than one time.

---

[30] INA § 212(g)(2).

In order to determine if an applicant for a visa is inadmissible under any of the health-related ground, DHS requires the applicant to take a medical examination given by a doctor approved by DHS or, in consular processing, a doctor approved by the U.S. consulate. If the examining physician suspects the applicant of drug abuse, the applicant must be referred to a drug abuse expert for more evaluation. Only drug incidents that have occurred within the last three years are to be considered.

F. SPECIAL RULES

1. Asylum and Refugee Status

As we will see in Chapter 11, applicants with a well founded fear of persecution may qualify to remain in or enter the United States as asylees or refugees. However, even though a well founded fear of persecution is established, an applicant can still be barred from obtaining asylum or refugee status if the applicant has persecuted others, been convicted of a particularly serious crime, committed a serious non-political crime prior to entering the United States, or is a danger to U.S. security. Applicants may also be denied status if they have firmly resettled in a third country or have an offer of safe haven from a third country.

a. Persecution of Others

Under INA § 208(b)(2)(A)(i), an applicant is ineligible for refugee status or asylum if the person has "ordered, incited, assisted, or otherwise participated in the persecution of any person on account of race, religion, nationality, membership in a particular social group, or political opinion." An applicant has not "persecuted others" if he or she simply participated as a regular soldier and fought against other combatants in a war. Also, in *Matter of Rodriguez-Majano*,[31] the BIA held that a truck driver who was forced to deliver supplies for the guerrillas, and who was later forced to join the guerrillas until he could desert after two months, was not ineligible for asylum.

b. Conviction of a Particularly Serious Crime

Under INA § 208(b)(2)(A)(ii), no one who has been convicted of a particularly serious crime in the United States and therefore constitutes a danger to the community will be granted refugee or asylee status. In *Matter of Frentescu*,[32] involving an applicant who had been convicted of the crime of burglary in Illinois, the BIA ruled that the following factors should be considered in determining whether a particularly serious crime was involved: the nature of the conviction, the circumstances and underlying facts of the conviction, the type of sentence imposed, and whether the type and circumstances of the crime indicate that the alien will be a danger to the community. The BIA further stated that, although there may be instances when crimes against property will be considered "particularly serious,"

---

[31] Int. Dec. No. 3088 (BIA 1988).

[32] 18 I.&N. Dec. 244 (BIA 1982).

crimes against persons are more likely to be categorized as such. Also, the sentence imposed would be relevant to the issue of the seriousness of the alien's danger to the community.

Using these factors, the BIA concluded in *Frentescu* that the applicant had not been convicted of a particularly serious crime. The crime was an offense against property, the dwelling was not occupied, the applicant was not armed, and there were not aggravating circumstances. Furthermore, the applicant received a suspended sentence after serving only three months.

On the other hand, in *Matter of Garcia-Garrocho*,[33] the BIA held that a New York conviction for residential burglary in the first degree was per se a particularly serious crime because the statute involved one or more aggravating circumstances, including physical injury or potentially life-threatening acts. To the BIA, the determination of whether a crime is particularly serious essentially turns on whether the crime is one that, by its nature, represents a danger to the community.

Conviction of an aggravated felony is an absolute bar to asylum. As reviewed in Chapter 11, aggravated felonies include such things as drug trafficking, document fraud with a sentence of at least one year imposed, alien smuggling, crimes of violence or theft or burglary with a sentence of at least one year imposed, child molestation, money laundering (over $10,000), and murder.

Although unlawful trafficking in controlled substances presumptively constitutes a particularly serious crime, the Attorney General has stated that an exception can be made when there are extenuating circumstances that are both extraordinary and compelling.[34]

c.   Commission of a Serious Non-Political Crime

Under INA § 241(b)(3)(B)(iii), an applicant is ineligible for asylum if there are "serious reasons" to believe that the applicant has committed a serious non-political crime prior to entering the United States. The disqualification applies even without evidence of a conviction, and the crime can be less serious than a "particularly serious crime."

In *INS v. Aguirre-Aguirre*,[35] the Supreme Court reinstated a BIA decision holding that a serious non-political crime had occurred in an incident that involved throwing store merchandise on the floor and burning ten buses, along with moving hesitant passengers off the buses before the vehicles were destroyed. The court rejected the use of a balancing test in such cases, maintaining that whether the applicant faced persecution in his home country had no bearing on whether a serious non-political crime had occurred.

---

[33] Int. Dec. No. 3022 (BIA 1987).

[34] Matter of Y-L-, A-G-,R-S-L-, 23 I.&N. Dec. 270 (A.G. 2002).

[35] 526 U.S. 415 (1999).

d.   Danger to U.S. Security

Under INA § 208(b)(2)(A)(iv), an applicant is barred from asylum if "there are reasonable grounds for regarding the alien as a danger to the security of the United States." No person who has been involved in terrorist activity will be granted refugee or asylee status. After 9/11, the definition of who is a "terrorist" is quite broad. For example, the term could be interpreted to cover people who have provided food or other "material support" to guerillas or others trying to overthrow the government, or people who have given money to organizations whose aims the U.S. government believes are, at least in part, terrorist in nature.

The USA PATRIOT Act provisions are relevant here as well. Noncitizens are denied admission if they "endorse or espouse terrorist activity," or "persuade others to support terrorist activity or a terrorist organization," in ways that the State Department determines impede U.S. efforts to combat terrorism. The Act defines "terrorist activity" expansively to include support of otherwise lawful and nonviolent activities of almost any group that used violence. Noncitizens are deportable for wholly innocent associational activity, excludable for pure speech, and subject to incarceration without a finding that they pose a danger or flight risk. Foreign nationals can be detained for up to seven days while the government decides whether or not to file criminal or immigration charges. The Attorney General has broad preventive detention authority to incarcerate noncitizens by certifying there are "reasonable grounds to believe" that a person is "described in" the antiterrorism provisions of the immigration law, and the individual is then subject to potentially indefinite detention. The Attorney General also can detain noncitizens indefinitely even after prevailing in a removal proceeding "until the Attorney General determines that the noncitizen is no longer a noncitizen who may be certified [as a suspected terrorist.]."

e.   Firm Resettlement or Offer of Safe Haven

Even though an asylum applicants may meet the definitional requirements for "refugee," under INA § 208(b)(2)(A)(vi), an applicant will be barred if he or she has "firmly resettled in another country prior to arriving in the United States."[36] The regulations provide the following guidance in determining whether the applicant has firmly resettled:

> An alien is considered to be firmly resettled if, prior to arrival in the United States, he entered into another nation with, or while in that nation received, an offer of permanent resident status, citizenship, or some other type of permanent resettlement unless he establishes: (a) that his entry into that nation was a necessary consequence of his flight from persecution, that he remained in that nation only as long as was necessary to arrange onward travel, and that he did not establish significant ties in that nation; or (b) that the conditions of his residence in that nation were so substantially and consciously restricted by the authority in the country of refugee that he was not in fact resettled. In making his determination, the Asylum Officer or Immigration Judge shall consider the conditions under which

---

[36] *See also* Matter of Lam, 18 I&N. Dec. 15 (BIA 1981).

other residents of the country live, the type of housing made available to the refugee, whether permanent or temporary, the types and extent of employment available to the refugee, and the extent to which the refugee received permission to hold property and to enjoy other rights and privileges, such as travel documentation including a right of entry and/or reentry, education, public relief, or naturalization, ordinarily available to others resident in the country.[37]

In addition to these regulatory guidelines, a significant amount of existing case law interprets the firmly resettled concept,[38] which was upheld by the Supreme Court under prior law as a central theme of refugee legislation.[39] Arguably, the government bears the initial burden of establishing firm resettlement.[40]

In *Cheo v. INS*,[41] two brothers from Cambodia were denied their asylum claims because they had resided peacefully in Malaysia for three years prior to coming to the United States, suggesting that Malaysia had allowed them to stay indefinitely. Similarly, in *Matter of Portales*,[42] the applicants were Cubans requesting asylum. However, prior to their seeking asylum in the United States, they resided for sixteen months in Peru, where they were granted refugee status. With that status, they were entitled to work, attend school, practice their religion, and were required to pay taxes. They were issued refugee documents by Peru that were valid for two years and could return to Peru. On those facts, the BIA concluded that the applicants were firmly resettled in Peru, especially because there was no indication that the Peruvian government intended to terminate their refugee status.

Related to, but quite distinct from, the firmly resettled preclusion is a discretionary basis for denial of asylum when there is an outstanding offer of resettlement by a third nation in which the applicant will not be subject to persecution. The policy has no basis in statute, and a regulatory reference to the policy was removed in 1990. The Ninth Circuit also disfavors such a policy, as evidenced by its decision in *Damaize-Job v. INS*.[43] In that case a Nicaraguan Miskito Indian's claim was not undermined, even though he had stopped in other countries before entering the United States.

However an applicant is barred from asylum if the Attorney General determines that the applicant may be removed, pursuant to a bilateral or multilateral agreement, to a country in which the person has access to a fair procedure for applying for asylum or equivalent protection. Of course, the person's life or freedom cannot be threatened in the third country.[44]

---

[37] 8 C.F.R. § 208.15.

[38] *See, e.g.*, Matter of Guiragossian, 17 I.&N. 161 (BIA 1979).

[39] Rosenberg v. Chien Woo, 402 U.S. 49 (1971).

[40] Salazar v. Ashcroft, 359 F.3d 45, 50 n.3 (1st Cir. 2004).

[41] 162 F.3d 1227 (9th Cir. 1998).

[42] 18 I.&N. Dec. 239 (BIA 1982).

[43] 787 F.2d 1332 (9th Cir. 1986).

[44] INA § 208(a)(2)(A).

2.   Domestic Violence

Abused spouses and children of U.S. citizens and lawful permanent resident aliens who self-petition under VAWA are not inadmissible under the unlawful presence ground of inadmissibility (e.g., three and ten-year bars). They must, however, demonstrate a connection between the abuse and the unlawful status.[45]

Other grounds of inadmissibility under INA § 212(a) deserve special consideration. Under INA § 212(h), a special VAWA can be found those who are inadmissible because of a criminal past. The special waiver for VAWA self-petition set forth. In INA § 204(a)(1)(A), (B) relieves the applicant of a showing of extreme hardship to a qualifying relative. The waiver is discretionary, of course, and when the applicant's crime is violent or dangerous, favorable discretion is not likely unless there are extraordinary circumstances.[46]

When it comes to the public charge ground of inadmissibility, VAWA self-petitioners are exempted from the requirement of submitting an affidavit of support. Also, USCIS cannot consider for public charge purposes any benefits a self-petitioner received because of her status as an abused immigrant.[47]

A VAWA-specific waiver for the fraud or misrepresentation ground of inadmissibility is also provided if the person can demonstrate extreme hardship to themselves or to a lawful parent or child.[48]

3.   Special Juvenile Status

Children who are under the jurisdiction of a juvenile court and who are eligible for long term foster care may apply for adjustment of status as special immigrants. This means that they can become lawful permanent residents without having a U.S. citizen or permanent resident parent petition and without having to wait for a priority date. The court does have to rule that returning the child to the country of origin would not be in the child's best interest.[49]

Certain grounds of inadmissibility are waived (public charge, labor certification, documentation).[50] A waiver of most of the other noncriminal and nonsecurity grounds is available.

4.   Nonimmigrant Visas

Nonimmigrants must also satisfy the grounds of inadmissibility in INS § 212(a). However, special mention must be made of INA § 214(b) which provides that "every alien . . . shall be presumed to be an immigrant until he establishes to the satisfaction of the consular officer . . . that he is entitled to a nonimmigrant

---

[45] INA § 212(a)(6)(ii).

[46] 8 C.F.R. 212.7(d).

[47] INA 212(p).

[48] INA § 212(i).

[49] INA §§ 101(a)(27)(J), 203(b)(4).

[50] INA § 245(h)(1); 8 C.F.R. § 245.1(e).

status." Thus, it is the nonimmigrant's burden to establish that he or she qualifies. This provision has become synonymous with the concept of immigrant intent because the majority of nonimmigrant visa refusals are for visitor or student visas that carry with them the nonimmigrant intent requirement such as the need to maintain a residence abroad.

However, some nonimmigrant categories contain no such nonimmigrant intent provisions, including, for instance, the O-1 category (person with extraordinary science, business or athletic ability). Yet, a consular officer could deny an O-1 visa application on § 214(b) grounds.

Another ground of denial falls under INA § 221(g) that provides that a consular officer should not issue a visa if (1) from the visa application or supporting documentation, it appears that the applicant is ineligible to receive it, (2) the application fails to comply with the statute or regulations, or (3) the consular officer knows or has reason to believe that the applicant is ineligible under INA § 212 or any other provision of law. Normally, consular officers rely on INA § 212(g) when an applicant fails to provide sufficient documentation to obtain a visa but there are insufficient grounds to deny it under INA § 214(b) and/or it appears that additional evidence could demonstrate the applicant's eligibility. Denials under INA § 221(g) also occur at border posts when the consular officer feels unable to adjudicate the application and wants the applicant to apply at his or her home post.[51]

---

[51] Susan K. Wehrer, M Mercedes Badia-Tavas, & Judy J. Lee, *Studies in Chaos Theory: Guiding Clients through Appropriate uses of the Temporary Visitor Visa Categories, in* IMMIGRATION & NATIONALITY LAW HANDBOOK, 2007–08 ED., at 314–15 (Richard Link, et. al, eds.).

Chapter 10

ADMISSION PROCEDURES

A. OVERVIEW

Admissions procedures vary for the different categories of nonimmigrants and immigrants, and other noncitizens who request admission into the United States. Generally the noncitizen must establish eligibility for admission in one of the qualifying immigrant, nonimmigrant or other categories, and she must establish she is not inadmissible under INA § 212(a).

Most noncitizens are admitted into the United States using a two-stage procedure: applying for a visa at a U.S. Embassy or Consular Office overseas; and applying for admission into the United States at an approved port of entry. This two-stage procedure involves scrutiny by a DOS consular officer overseas and scrutiny by a DHS immigration officer upon request for admission at the border. In the case of admission into the U.S. by adjustment of status, from nonimmigrant to immigrant status, only the DHS is involved in the process. Other noncitizens requesting admission into the U.S., including those fleeing persecution and unauthorized migrants, are addressed in Chapters 11 and 13. Lawful presence in the U.S. under a discretionary procedure such as parole or deferred action is discussed in this Chapter.

Noncitizens must possess appropriate travel documents to board an airplane bound for the U.S. and apply for admission a port of entry. The required documentation varies. Generally, all noncitizens must possess a visa (either a nonimmigrant visa in their passport or the "green card" Form I-551 for LPRs). Most nonimmigrants must submit a visa application to a U.S. Embassy or Consular Office to obtain a visa in their passport before arriving at an approved port of entry into the United States. Nonimmigrants in certain categories may apply for admission directly at the border without a visa. Applicants for admission, as a result, bear the burden of establishing eligibility for admission in one of the immigrant or nonimmigrant categories.

Some nonimmigrant categories and nearly all immigrant visa categories require an approved visa petition before submitting a visa application at a Consular Office overseas, and/or applying for admission into the United States. Visa petitions for nonimmigrants and immigrants are discussed separately below.

After the noncitizen receives the visa, or if a visa is not required, she may travel to a U.S. port of entry and apply for admission. A DHS immigration officer conducts an inspection of each noncitizen requesting admission under INA § 235. The officer will determine if an inadmissibility ground under INA § 212(a) is applicable, and verify whether any computer system maintained by DHS has information about the individual.[1]

The term admission is defined in INA § 101(a)(13) to mean a lawful entry of a noncitizen into the U.S. after inspection and authorization by an immigration officer. All noncitizens who have not been admitted after inspection are deemed to be applicants for admission. This includes noncitizens who arrive a port of entry to apply for admission and those apprehended inside the United States.[2] The admission process at the border is discussed below.

B. NONIMMIGRANTS

Most nonimmigrants who seek admission into the United States must follow the two-step procedure of applying for a visa at a U.S. Embassy or Consular Office overseas and applying for admission at an approved port of entry. Some nonimmigrants are exempt from the visa requirement, and, therefore, they may seek

---

[1] The DHS databases include the Arrival and Departure Information System (ADIS), the Interagency Border Inspection System (IBIS), and the National Automated Immigration Lookout System (NAILS), among others. The State Department maintains a database, the Consular Lookout and Support System (CLASS).

[2] INA §§ 101(a)(15), 235.

admission directly at a port of entry. This includes nationals of countries in the Visa Waiver Program, discussed below. Most nationals of Canada and Mexico also are exempt from the visa requirement.

1.   Nonimmigrant Visa Applications and Admissions

Most nonimmigrants must obtain a visa in their passports by submitting a visa application to a U.S. Embassy or Consular Office abroad.[3] The visa application process identifies whether the noncitizen is eligible for the category under INA § 101(a)(15). Consular officers also must determine whether the nonimmigrant has the proper intent. Under INA § 214(b), all applicants for admission are presumed to be immigrants (lawful permanent residents).[4] The burden is on the noncitizen to establish the intent to visit the U.S. temporarily in a specific nonimmigrant visa category under INA § 101(a)(15). For example, a B Tourist Visitor under INA § 101(a)(15)(B)(2) must intend to visit temporarily and to engage only in tourist activities.

The visa application process further requires the noncitizen to establish she is not inadmissible under any of the categories in INA § 212(a). The questions on a visa application mirror the INA § 212(a) inadmissibility provisions. Many nonimmigrant categories require the noncitizen to establish her intent to return to her home country. In some nonimmigrant categories, the DOS and DHS recognize a noncitizen may have a dual intent to remain in the U.S. temporarily and intend to remain permanently if, at some future time, the process for an immigrant visa is completed.[5]

Some nonimmigrant categories require an approved nonimmigrant visa petition prior to submitting a visa application to a U.S. Embassy or Consular Office abroad, and prior to applying for admission into the United States.[6] Other nonimmigrant categories may require additional documentation prior to applying for a visa.[7] For example, students in the F category, under INA § 101(a)(15)(F), must obtain a document from the school they will attend in the United States.[8]

Visa applications are submitted in person at the U.S. Embassy or Consular Office overseas. Congress requires everyone between the ages of 15 and 79 to

---

[3] INA § 222 covers the requirements for a visa application.

[4] INA § 214(b) presumes that a nonimmigrant applicant for a visa or admission into the U.S. is an immigrant (lawful permanent resident). Generally, this means the nonimmigrant must establish her intent to return to her home country. The INA § 214(b) presumption does not apply to nonimmigrant applicants under INA §§ 101(a)(15)(H), (L), and (V).

[5] The dual intent doctrine permits a nonimmigrant to begin the permanent residence process while maintaining valid nonimmigrant status. This doctrine only applies to nonimmigrants under INA §§ 101(a)(15)(E), (H)(i)(b), (L), (O), (P), and (V). *See also* Matter of Hosseinpour, 15 I. & N. Dec. 191 (B.I.A. 1975).

[6] Nonimmigrants under INA §§ 101(a)(15)(H), (L), (K), (O), (P), (Q) must file a nonimmigrant visa petition, Form I-129.

[7] Nonimmigrants under INA §§ 101(a)(15)(F), (M), (J).

[8] An F-1 student must obtain a Form I-20 issued by the school in which she will enroll and this form must be presented to the DOS to obtain an F visa, and to the DHS at the port of entry to be admitted.

appear for an in-person interview when requesting a nonimmigrant visa.[9] As of October 2005, visa applicants must provide photos and fingerprints under the Biometric Visa Program [BIOVISA]. The State Department uses BIOVISA to create an electronic version of visa applications and this database is used by DHS immigration officers at ports of entry.[10]

Consular officers have broad discretion in visa issuance and their scrutiny is the first screening of whether a noncitizen is inadmissible.[11] This is discussed further below in Section D.1. However, the visa application process, after September 11, 2001, includes greater oversight of visa issuance by the DHS.[12] DHS immigration officers are located in U.S. Embassies and Consular Offices abroad, and DHS officers can veto the issuance of a visa. The denial of visas by consular officers is covered in Section C.2, Review of Visa Denials, of this Chapter.

Upon approval of the visa application by the consular officer, a visa sticker is placed in the noncitizen's passport. Nonimmigrant visas have a specific validity period, generally determined by the statutory requirements for each nonimmigrant category. Often, visas allow multiple entries. For example, one might have an F-1 multiple-entry student visa valid for the duration of status as a student, or a three-year H-1B specialty worker visa based on the period of validity of the underlying H-1B nonimmigrant visa petition.[13] A multiple entry visa will allow an individual to travel to the U.S. on numerous visits.

The visa is a required travel document for most noncitizens. The visa allows a person to travel to the United States and apply for admission at a port of entry. Airlines often perform the initial review of travel documents before an individual may board a flight to the U.S. The noncitizen will present the visa to a DHS Immigration officer to apply for admission at the port of entry. The visa does not guarantee admission into the United States.

a.   Visa Waiver Program Admissions

Under the Visa Waiver Program, business or tourist visitors from specified countries may apply for admission without a visa. The Visa Waiver Program [VWP] is set forth in INA § 217. Countries in the program are those Congress has determined have a low incidence of visa overstays or other immigration system abuses. Nationals of VWP countries may seek admission for up to 90 days. There are 27 countries in the VWP program.[14]

---

[9] INA § 222(h) was added by the Intelligence Reform and Terrorism Prevention Act of 2004, Pub. L. No. 108-458, 118 Stat. 3638 (Dec. 17, 2004). Before this Act, the personal appearance requirement could be waived.

[10] INA § 221(a)(2), 8 U.S.C. § 1201(a)(2) (2006).

[11] INA § 101(a)(9) defines "consular officer" to mean any consular, diplomatic or other officer or employee of the U.S. designated for the purpose of issuing immigrant or nonimmigrant visas, and in some cases for the purpose of adjudicating nationality.

[12] DHS has authority over visa policy and regulations governing visas.

[13] INA §§ 101(a)(15)(F), (H)(1).

[14] As of August 2008, the countries participating in the VWP include Andorra, Australia, Austria, Belgium, Brunei, Denmark, Finland, France, Germany, Iceland, Ireland, Italy, Japan, Liechtenstein,

VWP tourist or business visitors waive their right to extend their stay, to change their nonimmigrant visa status under INA § 248, or to adjust status under INA § 245(a) (except for immediate relatives). VWP visitors also waive their right to a removal hearing under INA § 217(b).

The Visa Waiver program was initially established as a pilot program in 1986. Congress made the program permanent in 2000. After September 11, 2001, amendments to the VWP enhanced the documentary requirements. Noncitizens entering under the VWP must have passports with integrated circuit chips containing biographic data and a biometric identifiers such as a digitized photograph.[15]

b.   Western Hemisphere Admissions

Most Canadian noncitizens under the North American Free Trade Agreement [NAFTA] do not require a visa to apply for admission, however, most require a passport.[16] There are other longstanding systems designed to accelerate the admissions process for some noncitizens, for example travel for citizens of the U.S., Canada, and Bermuda. Generally, Canadians and Mexicans also may visit the U.S. for business or as tourists with a Border Crossing Card [BCC] containing biometric data. Mexicans entering the U.S. for a period up to 30 days may travel with a BCC within 25 miles of the border region, except those entering Arizona who may travel within 75 miles of the border region.

The ease of travel within the Western Hemisphere has changed due to increased documentary requirements. As of January 2007, the Western Hemisphere Travel Initiative (WHTI) established by the DHS now requires everyone (U.S. citizens and noncitizens) travelling by air from Canada, Mexico, the Caribbean and Bermuda to present a passport or other approved identification to enter the U.S.[17] The WHTI passport requirement will be extended to all persons entering the U.S. by land or by sea on June 1, 2009.

2.   Nonimmigrant Visa Petitions

Generally, noncitizens who will work in the U.S. temporarily must have an approved visa petition. Those nonimmigrant categories requiring an approved visa petition prior to visa application and application for admission into the United States under INA § 101(a)(15) include:

Luxembourg, Monaco, Netherlands, New Zealand, Norway, Portugal, San Marino, Singapore, Slovenia, Spain, Sweden, Switzerland, and the United Kingdom.

[15] This applies to passports issued after October 26, 2006. Passports issued prior to October 26, 2006 must be machine-readable. Any noncitizen who does not possess a machine-readable passport, or, if applicable, a passport with the integrated circuit chip, must obtain a visa to enter the U.S. *See* Enhanced Border Security and Visa Entry Reform Act, Pub. L. No. 107-173, 116 Stat. 543 (May 14, 2002) (requiring machine-readable, tamper-resistant passports with biometric data).

[16] NAFTA categories for the admission of Mexicans and Canadians include tourist visitors, some intracompany transferees, and some professionals. 8 C.F.R. § 214.2(b)(4) (2006).

[17] 71 Fed. Reg. 68,412 (Nov. 24, 2006). WHTI is a joint Department of State (DOS) and Department of Homeland Security (DHS) plan to implement a 9/11 Commission recommendation for visa exempt noncitizens.

- H Specialty Occupation Workers, Temporary Workers and Trainees;
- K Fiance, Fiancees, and Spouses of United States citizens;
- L Intracompany Transferees;
- O Outstanding Individuals in the sciences, arts, education, businesss, or athletics;
- P Artists and Entertainers; and
- Q International Cultural Exchange performers.

USCIS Regional Service Centers in the United States review nonimmigrant visa petitions to determine whether the petitioner (usually the employer) and beneficiary of the petition meet the statutory requirements for that particular category. For example, H-1B specialty worker nonimmigrant visa petitions are filed by prospective employers who must establish the position to be filled is a "specialty occupation" and the noncitizen meets the statutory and regulatory requirements to fill the position.[18] Premium processing of employment-related nonimmigrant petitions is available under INA § 286(u).[19]

Upon approval of the visa petition by the USCIS Regional Service Center, a noncitizen may submit a visa application overseas to a Consular Office, or a change of status application in the United States.[20] For example, an F-1 student in the United States might change her status to H-1B specialty worker without leaving the country. The change of status application can be submitted at the same time as the H-1B visa petition, and the decision to approve the petition will occur simultaneously with the decision to change the noncitizen's status. The noncitizen in this example would have to apply for an H-1B visa at a U.S. Consular Office on her next trip outside of the U.S. in order to return and be admitted in H-1B status.

C. IMMIGRANTS

1.   Immigrant Visa Petitions

Generally, the first step in all immigrant visa cases is the submission of an immigrant visa petition to a USCIS Regional Service Center having jurisdiction over the petitioner under INA § 204(a).[21] The petitioner must establish the required relationship exists between the petitioner and beneficiary under the particular immigrant visa category under INA § 203. Some noncitizens may self-petition under the employment-based and family-sponsored categories.[22] Some employment-based categories require labor certification from the Department of

---

[18] INA § 101(a)(15)(H)(1)(B).

[19] Applicants for premium processing pay a fee of $1000 in addition to the regular processing fee.

[20] INA § 248 allows change of status for nonimmigrants in lawful status who are admissible, except in certain categories (nonimmigrants under § 101(a)(15)(C), (D), (K), (S), (J) who are subject to a two-year foreign residence requirement; nonimmigrants in the VWP and tourist or business visitors to Guam are ineligible to change status).

[21] An I-130 Petition is submitted for the family-sponsored immigrant visa categories, and an I-140 Petition is submitted for the employment-based categories.

[22] See, e.g., INA §§ 204(a)(1)(A)(ii) (noncitizens who have been battered or subject to extreme cruelty), 204(e) (priority workers under INA § 203(b)(1)(A), 204(g) (certain special immigrants);

Labor before the immigrant visa petition is filed.[23] After a labor certification application is approved, an immigrant visa petition is filed with USCIS.

The burden of proof is on the petitioner to establish eligibility in the immigrant visa petition. The decision to approve or deny the petition is based only on the statutory criteria for the immigrant visa category (family-sponsored or employment-based) not the inadmissibility grounds of INA § 212(a). A petition is automatically revoked if the petitioner withdraws the petition or, generally, if the petitioner dies.[24]

Approval of the immigrant visa petition completes the first stage of the permanent resident process. Upon approval of the immigrant visa petition by a USCIS Regional Service Center, the beneficiary will opt for either consular visa processing at a U.S. Embassy or Consular Office abroad or adjustment of status in the United States. Lawful permanent residence status is granted upon admission into the U.S. at the conclusion of consular processing or upon approval of an adjustment of status application. Both consular processing and adjustment of status are discussed below.

a. Processing Delays

Lengthy delays in immigrant visa petition and adjustment of status application processing led Congress to adopt many ameliorative measures during the past fifteen years. The long delays became a significant problem in the 1990s when resources were redirected to speed up the naturalization processing times. These delays created significant hardships for petitioners and noncitizen beneficiaries.

In 2000, a new K-3 nonimmigrant category was created for spouses of U.S. citizens in the Legal Immigration Family Equity Act [LIFE].[25] The K-1 visa category existed for fiancés and fiancées of U.S. citizens, but there was no category for the spouses of U.S. citizens.[26] Although immigrant visas are immediately available to immediate relatives, a backlog in processing petitions can cause a long separation for newly married couples. The K-3 nonimmigrant visa category is available to these spouses. The U.S. citizen must have filed an immigrant visa petition on behalf of his spouse and the spouse is admitted pending the approval of the petition. The LIFE Act also established the V nonimmigrant visa to address long processing delays. The V nonimmigrant category under § 101(a)(15)(V) is

---

201(b)(2)(A) (the spouses, parent or child of a member of the armed forces killed in combat). An I-360 Petition is filed by many self-petitioners.

[23] The labor certification process in INA § 212(a)(5)(A)(i) is required for employment-based immigrant visas under §§ 203(b)(2) (advanced degree professionals), and 203(b)(3) (skilled workers, professionals, and other workers).

[24] There is a humanitarian exception to the revocation of a petition when the petitioner dies. 8 C.F.R. § 205.1(a).

[25] Pub. L. No. 106-553, 114 Stat. 2762 (Dec. 21, 2000).

[26] Before the LIFE amendment, spouses of U.S. citizens were forced to enter the U.S. using another nonimmigrant visa, usually a B-1 business or B-2 tourist visa. The spouses always faced the potential problem of violating their nonimmigrant visas because of their intent to become lawful permanent residents. The only other option was for the noncitizen spouse to endure a long separation from the U.S. citizen spouse pending the processing of the immigrant visa petition.

available to the spouses and children of lawful permanent residents when there is a delay of three years or more.[27]

The problem of children aging-out of an immigrant visa petition (turning 21 years of age) was also addressed by Congress.[28] The Child Status Protection Act of 2002 provides that a beneficiary of an immediate relative petition filed by a U.S. citizen will continue to be eligible for an immigrant visa even if she reaches the age of 21.[29] The children of lawful permanent residents who are beneficiaries of immigrant visa petitions also are aided by a relaxed determination of when a child ages out as a beneficiary.[30] This is discussed in greater detail in Chapter 8.

Congress also adopted measures to assist H-1B nonimmigrant specialty occupation workers who have employment-based immigrant visa petitions filed by employers. Employers can pay a substantial fee for premium processing of the immigrant visa petition under INA § 286(u), although there is no mechanism to accelerate the visa issuance process (by adjustment of status or consular processing).[31]

2.   Immigrant Visa Consular Processing

The final stage of the permanent resident process for most noncitizens is the first admission into the U.S. as a permanent resident. There are two possible avenues for this first admission either consular visa processing or adjustment of status. Consular processing refers to a noncitizen's application for her immigrant visa abroad initially at the U.S. Embassy or Consular Office and then her application for admission at an approved port of entry into the United States. The alternative procedure, an application to adjust of status, usually from nonimmigrant to immigrant, occurs while remaining in the United States. Adjustment of status is a discretionary procedure and not all noncitizens are eligible as discussed below.

The consular processing begins after a visa petition is approved and the approved petition is forwarded to the National Visa Center [NVC] for management

---

[27] Under § 101(a)(15)(V), a V nonimmigrant visa is available if an I-130 petition was filed prior to December 21, 2000 and the petition is pending for three years or more, or the petition was approved but three or more years have elapsed, and where an immigrant visa is not available or a jointly-filed visa petition and adjustment of status application is still pending.

[28] INA § 101(b)(1) defines a child to mean "an unmarried person under twenty-one years of age."

[29] Pub. L. No. 107-208, 116 Stat. 927 (Aug. 6, 2002).

[30] *Id.* If the LPR petitioner naturalizes while the immigrant visa petition is pending, the date of naturalization is used to determine whether or not the child continues to be eligible for an immigrant visa. Other provisions were designed to protect children under the family-sponsored categories, as well as children who were derivative beneficiaries under the employment-based categories.

[31] Other measures have eased the transition for H-1B workers to lawful permanent residents. *See,* 21st Century Department of Justice Appropriations Act, Pub. L. No. 107-273, 116 Stat. 1758 (Nov. 2, 2002). In 2000, Congress had extended the six-year limit for beneficiaries of employment-based petitions filed under the first, second, or third preferences (INA § 203(b)(1)-(3)) if a backlog in immigrant visas existed due to per-country limits. American Competitiveness in the 21st Century Act, Pub. L. No. 106-313, 114 Stat. 1251 (Oct. 17, 2000); Pub. L. No. 106-311, 114 Stat. 1247 (Oct. 17, 2000).

of the final stage of the process.[32] When an immigrant visa is available, based on the priority date established by the visa petition or labor certification application, the NVC will forward a notice to the noncitizen with detailed instructions about the submission of additional documents.[33] See Chapter 7. An affidavit of support is required for family-based immigrants to establish that the noncitizen is not likely to become a public charge, which would render her inadmissible.[34] All of the required documents are submitted to the NVC, and then the final immigrant visa interview is scheduled.[35] A medical exam must be performed overseas just prior to the final visa interview.

The second phase of consular processing is the visa interview at the consular post. Usually the interview is scheduled at the consular office in the last place of residence abroad.[36] At this interview, the consular officer will verify that the documents presented establish eligibility for the immigrant visa category.[37] The approval of the immigrant visa petition by USCIS establishes eligibility and the visa interview represents a verification of eligibility.[38] At this visa interview, the Consular Officer will evaluate whether the immigrant visa applicant is inadmissible under any of the categories in INA § 212(a).[39] The DHS is involved in the immigrant visa interview. DHS, under the Homeland Security Act of 2002, has authority to review any visa application, conduct investigations and require a denial of a visa.[40]

The final phase in consular processing of an immigrant visa is the initial application for admission into the United States as a permanent resident. Upon approval of the immigrant visa application at the Consular Office, the noncitizen is given a sealed packet to present to the DHS immigration officer at an approved port of entry into the U.S.[41] At the border, the noncitizen again bears the burden of establishing she is admissible under INA § 212(a).

If the noncitizen is admissible, the DHS immigration officer will place an I-551 stamp on the I-94 biographical data card that is completed by all noncitizens who enter the U.S. The I-94 card is stapled to the passport. The I-551 stamp on the card is the temporary "green card" verifying the individual is a lawful permanent

---

[32] The visa petition is approved by a USCIS Regional Service Center and then forwarded to the USCIS National Visa Center.

[33] Certified copies of documents, police records from the jurisdictions in which the noncitizen has lived, evidence of the payment of U.S. taxes, if applicable, etc.

[34] INA § 212(a)(4).

[35] INA § 212(a)(4).

[36] 9 FAM 42.61.

[37] INA §§ 221, 222.

[38] Approval of the petition by USCIS establishes prima facie eligibility for a particular immigrant visa, and consular officers are instructed to defer to this decision unless reasonable suspicion exists about its validity.

[39] The questions on the immigrant visa application mirror the inadmissibility provisions of INA § 212(a).

[40] INA § 221(a)(2).

[41] The noncitizen must apply for entry within six months of the issuance of this immigrant visa packet under INA § 221(c).

resident. The actual card, now pink rather than green, is mailed to the noncitizen usually within three to four months of the initial admission.

a. Review of Visa Denials

Consular officers will deny a visa application if it appears from statements in the application or other documents that the noncitizen is ineligible for either a nonimmigrant or immigrant visa.[42] A consular officer may also deny an immigrant or nonimmigrant visa if the officer has reason to believe the noncitizen is ineligible.[43] The noncitizen must be given a written explanation of the grounds for denial.[44] Denials of immigrant and nonimmigrant visa applications at the U.S. Embassy or Consular Office historically have not been subject to judicial review.[45] The State Department regulations require notice of the reasons for denial of the visa.[46] Visa denials are reviewed by more senior consular officers. If the denial is based on a question of law, an advisory opinion may be requested from the DOS Visa Office. The Secretary of State does not have authority to review individual visa decisions under INA § 104. The only review of visa decisions by consular officers is the review by a supervisor, discretionary review by the Visa Office, or random reviews conducted by supervisors in a given consular office.[47]

In a few limited instances, judicial review of a visa denial has occurred. In *Kleindeinst v. Mandel*, 408 U.S. 753 (1972), the Supreme Court found it had jurisdiction to hear a claim in which U.S. citizens asserted a First Amendment right to hear a noncitizen professor who was denied a nonimmigrant visa. The Supreme Court recognized the U.S. citizens had standing to bring a claim into federal court, however the Court upheld the Department of State's denial of the nonimmigrant visa by finding a facially legitimate, bona fide reason existed for the denial.[48]

This lack of appellate review has been criticized by many.[49] Under this system, an individual applying for an immigrant visa who has established eligibility through the immigrant visa petition approval process is in no better position than a tourist visitor applying for a nonimmigrant visa. The 1997 Report of U.S. Commission on Immigration Reform recommended formal administrative review

---

[42] INA § 221(g).

[43] *Id.*

[44] *See* INA § 212(b), 22 C.F.R. § 42.81(b) (2006).

[45] *See* Pena v. Kissenger, 409 F. Supp 1182 (S.D.N.Y. 1976); Saavedra Bruno v. Albright, 197 F.3d 1153, 1158–64 (D.C. Cir. 1999); Li Hing of Hong Kong, Inc. v. Levin, 800 F.2d 970 (9th Cir. 1986).

[46] 22 C.F.R. § 42.81(b) (2006).

[47] 22 C.F.R. § 42.121(d)(2006).

[48] *See also* Academy of Religion v. Chertoff, 463 F. Supp. 2d 400, 416–19 (S.D.N.Y. 2006) (First Amendment challenge by academic organizations to denial of visa based on security concerns regarding an Islamic scholar); Abourezk v. Reagan, 785 F.2d 1043 (D.C. Cir. 1986), *aff'd per curiam by an equally divided court*, 484 U.S. 1 (1987) (District Court for the D.C. Circuit found it had jurisdiction to review a visa denial; INA provision at issue in this case has since been repealed); Martinez v. Bell, 468 F. Supp. 719 (S.D.N.Y. 1979).

[49] *See* Stephen H. Legomsky, *Fear and Loathing in Congress and the Courts*, 78 TEX. L. REV. 1615 (2001).

of all immigrant visa denials and some nonimmigrant visa denials.[50]

3.   Adjustment of Status

Adjustment of status under INA § 245 is an alternative procedure to consular processing for the final stage of becoming a lawful permanent resident.[51] A noncitizen who applies to adjust status from nonimmigrant to immigrant is not required to attend a visa interview abroad. The noncitizen's application for initial admission as a lawful permanent occurs entirely inside of the United States.

Adjustment of status is a discretionary procedure developed to accommodate nonimmigrants in the United States and avoid costly overseas visits to apply for an immigrant visa. These applications are a routine part of the permanent residence process, despite the DHS discretion whether to grant or deny adjustment. The vast majority of adjustments occur following the criteria set forth in INA § 245(a). Some noncitizens are eligible to adjust under the grandfathered provisions of INA § 245(i), discussed below. Adjustment also is available to noncitizens in special adjustment categories.[52] Adjustment of status is available to refugees and asylees.[53] Adjustment before an immigration judge through cancellation of removal is possible under INA § 240A.

An applicant for adjustment must establish she meets the separate requirements for adjustment, as well as all of the admissibility grounds under INA § 212(a). The adjustment of status applicant also must verify eligibility for the particular immigrant visa category under INA § 203, e.g., eligibility as an immediate relative, brother of a U.S. citizen, or in an employment-based category. Noncitizens barred from adjustment of status must follow the consular processing procedure to become a permanent resident.

A nonimmigrant in the U.S. may apply for adjustment of status when his or her priority date is current and an immigrant visa, therefore, is immediately available.[54] The application, Form I-485, may only be filed after approval of the immigrant visa petition by USCIS or, if the priority date is current, an adjustment of status application can be filed concurrently with the immigrant visa petition.

The adjustment of status application contains many identical questions to the immigrant visa application filed at the Consular Office overseas. The questions are designed to determine if a noncitizen is inadmissible under § 212(a). The adjustment applicant, similar to the consular processing immigrant visa applicant,

---

[50] U.S. Commission on Immigration Reform, Becoming An American: Immigration and Immigrant Policy 181–82 (Report to Congress 1997) (recommending review for nonimmigrant categories "where there is a petitioner in the United States who is seeking the admission of the visa applicant," such as employer petitioners for H-1B specialty occupations and L-1 intracompany transferees, or universities for J-1 exchange visitors).

[51] INA § 245.

[52] Special adjustment categories include employment-based immigrants who have engaged in unauthorized employment or otherwise failed to maintain continuous lawful status (INA § 245(k)); victims of trafficking (INA § 245(l)), or victims of crimes against women (INA § 245(m)).

[53] INA § 209.

[54] 8 C.F.R. § 245.1(g) (2006).

must provide certified copies of documents, police reports, an affidavit of support under INA § 212(d)(4), if required, and complete a medical exam. In addition, the adjustment applicant must pass security clearances.

Eligibility for adjustment of status is determined by the noncitizen's current status in the U.S. when the application is filed, apart from immigrant visa eligibility and admissibility. Under INA § 245(a), the noncitizen must have maintained valid nonimmigrant status during all periods of stay in the United States. The adjustment applicant must have been inspected by a DHS immigration officer, and admitted or paroled into the U.S. Those who enter without inspection or at a location other than an approved port of entry are not eligible to adjust under § 245(c).

Other noncitizens are barred from applying for adjustment of status under § 245(c).[55] Noncitizens, other than immediate relatives, who have engaged in unauthorized employment before filing or who are in "unlawful immigration status" are ineligible to adjust.[56] This means noncitizens are barred from adjusting status if they have violated the terms of their nonimmigrant visa, usually working without authorization for any period of time.[57] The INA provides a safe harbor for applicants who failed to maintain lawful status through no fault of their own or for technical reasons.[58] Immediate relatives are exempt from this bar to adjustment of status under INA § 245(c)(2).[59] Other noncitizens are ineligible to adjust. For example, the INA bars business and tourist visitors who enter under the Visa Waiver Program from adjustment.[60]

There are some major benefits to the adjustment of status procedure. The applicant can be accompanied by an attorney to the adjustment of status interview in the United States. From a practical standpoint, the most important benefit is the opportunity to renew the adjustment of status application in a removal proceeding.[61] Therefore, greater procedural protection exists for the adjustment applicant vis-à-vis the consular processing applicant. A noncitizen may apply to adjust status in the first instance before an Immigration Judge as a form of relief from removal. This is discussed in Chapter 9.

---

[55] INA § 245(c) lists all of the noncitizens who are barred from adjusting their status.

[56] Under INA § 245(c)(7) noncitizens who are beneficiary of an employment-based petition are barred from adjustment if they are "not in a lawful nonimmigrant status" thereby excluding those who entered without inspection or are otherwise present in the U.S.

[57] Under INA § 245(k) a noncitizen beneficiary of an employment-based petition may adjust if the failure to maintain lawful status, unauthorized employment or other violation is 180 days or less.

[58] Technical violations of nonimmigrant status are permitted such as a USCIS delay in processing of a nonimmigrant extension of stay or change of status application. See 8 C.F.R. § 245.1(d)(2).

[59] Generally, immediate relatives, battered spouses and children, and special immigrants under INA § 101(a)(27)(H) are exempt from the requirement to maintain valid status in INA §§ 245(c)(2), (7), and (8).

[60] Immediate relatives who enter under the VWP are eligible to adjust under INA § 245(c)(4). INA § 245(c) also bars terrorists deportable under § 237(a)(4)(B), noncitizens transit without a visa under § 101(a)(15)(C), and criminal investigation informants under INA § 101(a)(15)(S).

[61] 8 C.F.R. §§ 103.5, 245.2(a)(5)(ii).

There is no judicial review of the denial of an adjustment application. Adjustment of status is a discretionary decision by USCIS. Under INA 242(a)(1)(B)(ii), there is no judicial review of discretionary decisions. Adjustment of status can be rescinded within five years if the noncitizen was not eligible to adjust. After five years, lawful permanent resident status may be terminated, effectively rescinding the adjustment application, if an order of removal is entered.[62]

a.   Adjustment Under 245(i)

INA § 245(i) expanded the group of noncitizens eligible to adjust status. Under § 245(i), those individuals, who would have obtained lawful permanent residence through the consular processing procedure, could adjust status if they paid a substantially increased fee and were not otherwise ineligible.[63] This option was very popular among prospective immigrants because they could avoid the expense and inconvenience of traveling abroad. Congress added this option in 1994 and included a three-year sunset provision. The 1994 expansion by Congress was part of a wide-ranging effort to increase funding for the INS. The INS was faced with major problems with its computer database and information systems. One solution was to increase its fee structure for many petitions and other benefits.

The INA § 245(i) adjustment option became a critical vehicle to obtain permanent residence after the 1996 IRRIRA amendments to the INA. The 1996 amendments added unlawful presence as a new ground of inadmissibility under § 212(a)(9)(B) with the possibility of being barred from admission for three or ten years.[64] Prior to the 1996 IIRIRA amendments, noncitizens who violated their nonimmigrant status or entered the U.S. without inspection could become permanent residents using the consular processing method. These noncitizens, although ineligible to adjust, could satisfy the qualifying criteria for an immigrant visa as family-sponsored or employment-based immigrants and were admissible under INA § 212(a) before 1996. These noncitizens could be admitted into the United States as permanent resident using consular processing because mere unlawful presence was not an inadmissibility ground before the 1996 IIRIRA amendments.

The 1996 IIRIRA amendment drastically altered the position of noncitizens who were beneficiaries of immigrant petitions but who had not maintained lawful status. If a noncitizen, who was never in lawful status or had fallen out of lawful status, was required to leave the United States to follow the consular processing procedure, then upon return he or she would be inadmissible under § 212(a)(9)(B), unless they obtained a waiver. For this group, the § 245(i) adjustment benefit is the only mechanism to become a lawful permanent resident unless they are eligible for a waiver under INA § 212(a)(9)(B)(v).[65]

---

[62] INA § 246(a).

[63] Under INA § 245(i), a noncitizens must comply with the requirements of INA § 245(d)-(f).

[64] INA § 212(a)(9)(B)(i)(I)-(II) (unlawful presence of more than 180 days but less than one year means noncitizen may not seek readmission within three years of departure; unlawful presence of one year or more means noncitizen may not seek readmission within ten years of departure).

[65] INA § 212(a)(9)(B)(v) (waiver of unlawful presence inadmissibility ground requires extreme hardship to a citizen or LPR spouse or parent).

In September 1997, just before the sunset provision of September 30, 1997, Congress adopted a grandfather clause to extend this benefit. The grandfather clause allowed any noncitizen to adjust under § 245(i) if a visa petition or labor certification application was filed on or before January 14, 1998. Congress chose not to extend 245(i) permanently although there was significant support for such action. Those opposed to a permanent extension argued that § 245(i) was similar to an amnesty provision.

Adjustment of status under § 245(i) was extended again by Congress in the Legal Immigrant Family Equity Act of 2000 (LIFE Act).[66] Under this extension, INA § 245(i) grandfathers noncitizens who were in the United States on December 21, 2000 and had a visa petition or labor certification application filed by April 30, 2001.[67] The extension of this benefit resulted in a tremendous surge in the filing of labor certification applications and family-sponsored petitions before the deadline.

D. ACTUAL ADMISSION

1. Admissions at the Border

Generally, a noncitizen must either possess a visa or fit within one of the visa-exempt categories in order to board an airplane to travel to the U.S. The admission process at the border requires a noncitizen to present her passport with a biometric visa stamp at approved port of entry to apply for admission. An individual is defined as an applicant for admission if: she is present in the U.S. but has not been admitted, if she is at the border seeking admission; she is interdicted and brought to the U.S. even if she is not seeking admission; or she is a returning lawful permanent resident deemed an applicant for admission under INA § 101(a)(13)(C).[68] All applicants for admission who are noncitizens must be inspected by an immigration officer.[69]

Nonimmigrants entering the U.S. fill out a I-94 Form (Arrival-Departure Record) containing basic biographical information. This I-94 Form is stamped by the DHS immigration officer and it contains a notation about the visa category in which the noncitizen has entered and the permissible term of stay. For example, a B Tourist Visitor under INA § 101(a)(15)(B) may request admission for a six month period, however the notation on the I-94 card will determine the end of the valid term of stay in the U.S. Immigrants generally do not fill out I-94 Forms, except in connection with their first application for admission as a permanent resident. Immigrants present their immigrant visa card, Form I-551 (the "green card").[70]

---

[66] Pub. L. No. 106-553, 114 Stat. 2762 (Dec. 21, 2000).

[67] The LIFE Act also created a new nonimmigrant V category to accommodate family members of § 245(i) adjustment applicants; it is available to spouses and children of lawful permanent residents who have filed a family-sponsored immigrant visa petitions prior to December 21, 2000. INA § 101(a)(15)(V).

[68] INA § 235(a)(1).

[69] INA § 235(a)(3).

[70] INA §§ 211(g), 101(a)(13) (defining "admission" for LPRs).

The inspections process for noncitizen is set forth in INA § 235. At the border, all noncitizens have the burden of proving they are eligible for admission. Possession of an immigrant or nonimmigrant visa does not guarantee admission into the U.S. The inadmissibility provisions of INA § 212(a) apply to all noncitizens seeking admission, regardless of whether the noncitizen seeks admission as a lawful permanent resident, a nonimmigrant, a parolee, or a refugee. Some returning LPRs are not applicants for admission as defined in INA § 101(a)(13).

All nonimmigrants requesting admission at the border also have the burden of establishing they are not intending immigrants. Under INA § 214(b) there is a presumption that all persons requesting admission or applying for a visa intend to become lawful permanent residents. As a result, the noncitizen bears the burden of establishing she has sufficient ties to her home country which she has no intention of abandoning in order to establish true a bona fide temporary intent. This presumption of intending immigrant status applies to all nonimmigrants.[71]

Lawful permanent residents who arrive at a port of entry are not applicants for admission for purposes of immigration law except in certain circumstances set forth in INA § 101(a)(13).[72] If a returning lawful permanent resident is deemed an applicant for admission under INA § 101(a)(13), then she is subject to the inadmissibility provisions of INA § 212(a). This significantly alters the position of those residents who are defined as seeking admission upon return to the U.S. This group of permanent residents who must apply for admission under INA § 101(a)(13) includes noncitizens: who have abandoned or relinquished their status; who are absent for a continuous period of more than 180 days; who have engaged in illegal activity after departing the U.S.; who depart from the U.S. during removal proceedings; who previously violated INA § 212(a) and have not received a waiver or received relief from removal; those who attempted to enter at a place other than a port of entry.

Noncitizens arriving at a port of entry and seeking admission into the United States must establish "clearly and beyond doubt" they are entitled to be admitted under INA § 235(b)(2)(A), except returning lawful permanent residents. If a noncitizen can not satisfy this burden of proof, then she will be placed in ordinary removal proceedings under INA § 240.[73] The removal hearing process is covered in Chapter 12.

At the border, an Immigration Officer may admit a noncitizen, remove her under the expedited removal procedure of INA § 235, parole her into the U.S. for humanitarian reasons under INA § 212(d)(5), require deferred inspection to obtain further information to make a decision about admission, or place her in ordinary removal proceedings under INA § 240. At that time, if the noncitizen is not admitted she may be placed in detention as discussed below. A noncitizen also may

---

[71] *See supra* note 4.

[72] INA § 101(a)(13) codifies, in part, the Supreme Court's decision in *Rosenberg v. Fleuti*, 374 U.S. 499 (1963) (brief, innocent, and casual trips abroad do not interrupt the lawful permanent residence presence in the U.S.).

[73] INA § 235(a)(2) provides exceptions to the mandatory detention of arriving noncitizens who are crew members or stowaways when such noncitizens seek asylum or demonstrate a credible fear of persecution.

decide to withdraw her application for admission. Each of these options is discussed below.

A noncitizen applying for admission may decide to withdraw her application for admission under INA § 235(a)(4). The option to withdraw an application for admission is available at the initial inspection, at the deferred inspection and at a removal hearing to determine admission into the U.S.[74] The Immigration Officer has the authority to grant or deny the request to withdraw an application for admission. If a noncitizen withdraws the application for admission her visa can be cancelled and physically crossed out of her passport.[75]

Deferred or secondary inspection is another option available at the border. A secondary inspection occurs when further information is required from a noncitizen and the individual is taken aside at the port of entry for further questioning. A deferred inspection often will occur within a few days of the application for admission.[76] DHS immigration officer's decision to allow deferred inspection permits the noncitizen to present additional evidence of admissibility.

If a noncitizen is not admitted into the United States by an immigration officer, there are several different procedures that may apply under the INA. These are discussed in Section 3, Denial of Admission, below.

a.   National Security & Admissions

The inspections and admissions process at the border changed significantly after September 11, 2001. Many measures were introduced to address enhanced security concerns. Today, numerous databases are maintained by the DHS and are available to DHS immigration officers at border ports of entry.

The USA PATRIOT Act contained a number of provisions designed to ensure data sharing among U.S. agencies and departments.[77] DHS and DOS receive information from the FBI National Crime Information Center database to check the criminal background of an applicant for admission or a visa applicant. The Enhanced Border Security and Visa Entry Reform Act of 2002 increased the required data available at border ports of entry.[78] The Department of State provides an electronic version of each visa application to DHS inspectors at ports of entry.[79]

---

[74] 8 C.F.R. § 235.4 (2006).

[75] 22 C.F.R. § 41.122(h) (2006).

[76] 8 C.F.R. § 235.2 (2006).

[77] Pub. L. No. 107-56, 115 Stat. 343–45 (Oct. 26, 2001).

[78] Enhanced Border Security and Visa Entry Reform Act, Pub. L. No. 107-173, 116 Stat. 543 (May 14, 2002).

[79] Other systems exist. An interagency database system, the Interagency Border Inspection System (IBIS), is available at the border. The DOS Consular Lookout and Support System (CLASS) is similar. The Arrival and Departure Information System (ADIS) is a centralized database containing information about each person's arrival and departure from the U.S. There are specialized databases for visa waiver admissions, refugees, and terrorists and others.

The USA PATRIOT Act requires the INS and the State Department to implement a comprehensive entry and exit data system. The DHS initially created the National Security Entry-Exist Registration System [NSEERS] to track noncitizens in the U.S. from admission until departure in 2002.[80] NSEERS required special registration noncitizens from designated countries.[81] Noncitizens subject to this special registration had to register every time they entered or departed the U.S., and within 10 days of each change of address.

US-VISIT, the U.S. Visitor and Immigrant Status Indicator Technology Program system, is the principal tracking system for the entry and exit of noncitizens. The US-VISIT program is designed to collect, maintain, and share data. The data collected includes biometric identifiers such as digital fingerprints. As of November 2007, the DHS requires international visitors who enter through the US-VISIT designated airports to submit a ten-fingerprint scan. The noncitizen's biometric identifiers, fingerprints and photographs will also be compared to other databases managed by CBP. This system was mandated by the 1996 IIRIRA amendments but was not implemented due to data systems problems.[82]

As of January 2004, nonimmigrants, must comply with the US-VISIT requirements if they apply for admission at designated air and seaports or at the 50 busiest land border ports of entry to the United States.[83] The system tracks the arrival every noncitizen visitor at designated ports of entry. The system was initially implemented at air and seaports, and has been extended to all ports of entry as of December 31, 2005. As of August 2008, the US-VISIT system does not track the exits of noncitizens.

One problem that arises with all of these systems is inaccurate information. There are mechanisms for challenging the records. DHS has a US-VISIT Program Privacy Officer who will review requests to change records.[84] Two 2007 GAO Reports about the program have identified concerns about the effectiveness and implementation of this system.[85]

---

[80] INA § 263. The INA requires all noncitizens in the U.S. for more than 30 days to be registered and fingerprinted, although before September 11, 2001 this requirement typically was waived. INA §§ 261–266.

[81] Nationals or citizens of designated countries are required to register with NSEERS. Designated countries include Afghanistan, Algeria, Bahrain, Eritrea, Iran, Iraq, Lebanon, Libya, Morocco, North Korea, Oman, Qatar, Somalia, Sudan, Syria, Tunisia, United Arab Emirates, and Yemen. Noncitizens from other countries may be requested to register in NSEERS by immigration or consular officers. 8 C.F.R. § 264.1 (2006).

[82] 69 Fed. Reg. 468 (Jan. 5, 2004). See also DHS Office of Inspector General, Implementation of the United States Visitor and Immigrant Indicator Technology Program at Land Border Ports of Entry, available at http://www.dhs.gov (February 2005).

[83] 69 Fed. Reg. 53,318 (Aug. 31, 2004).

[84] 69 Fed. Reg. 2608 (Jan. 16, 2004). There are procedures to challenge the records in other database systems.

[85] See Homeland Security: US-VISIT Program Faces Operational, Technological, and Management Challenges, G.A.O. Rpt. 07-632T0 (Mar. 2007); Homeland Security: Prospects for Biometric US-VISIT Exit Capability Remain Unclear, G.A.O. Rpt. 07-1044T (Jun. 2007).

Other systems have been adopted to facilitate admissions. One goal is to separate arriving noncitizens into those who possess documents and those who do not possess documents. The Port Passenger Acceleration Service System [PortPASS] includes a number of programs designed for this purpose. Some of the programs included in PortPASS are the INS Passenger Accelerated Service System [INSPASS] and the Secure Electronic Network for Travelers Rapid Inspection [SENTRI]. The PortPASS system is used for both U.S. citizens and noncitizens. It is a separate system for admission available at certain ports of entry and requires an application for admission into the program.

The INSPASS system has been used since 1993 to facilitate the entry of low-risk, frequent travelers into the U.S. INSPASS is a voluntary program and it allows passengers to go directly to inspection at a kiosk that reads the individual's hand geometry biometric image in the database. An individual must apply for entry into the program. Participation is available to citizens of the U.S., Canada, Bermuda and Visa Waiver Program countries. INSPASS operations (kiosks) are located in some large ports of entry.[86]

b. Denial of Admission

The INA provides several procedures for noncitizens who apply for admission and are found inadmissible. A noncitizen is inadmissible unless she can establish she is "clearly and beyond doubt" entitled to be admitted under INA § 235(b)(2)(A), unless the oncitizen is a returning LPR.[87] If the noncitizen can not satisfy this burden of proof, then she will be detained pending an ordinary removal hearing under INA § 240.[88] Noncitizens who seek entry from Canada and Mexico may may be returned to Canada or Mexico pending the removal hearing.[89] LPRs who apply for admission and are found inadmissible are in a distinct position vis-à-vis the government. DHS has the burden of proof to establish an LPR is inadmissible and LPRs have full due process rights at their removal hearing.[90]

A noncitizen may be permitted to withdraw her application for admission and return to her home country on the next flight at her expense.[91] If the noncitizen is found inadmissible because she lacks proper entry documentation or has committed fraud or misrepresentation then she will be subject to separate expedited removal procedure under INA § 235(b)(1). This is discussed below.

Most other noncitizens denied admission at the border may request a removal hearing under INA § 240 except suspected terrorists and those requesting

---

[86] Los Angeles, California; Newark, N.J.; New York, New York; San Francisco, California; and Washington, D.C. It is also available at U.S. pre-inspection sites at airports in Vancouver and Toronto, Canada.

[87] DHS has the burden of proof to establish the inadmissibility ground applies to a returning LPR.

[88] INA § 235(a)(2) provides exceptions to the mandatory detention of arriving noncitizens who are crew members or stowaways when such noncitizens seek asylum or demonstrate a credible fear of persecution.

[89] INA § 235(b)(2)(C).

[90] Landon v. Plasencia, 459 U.S. 21 (1982).

[91] INA § 235(a)(4).

admission under the Visa Waiver Program. Noncitizens who are suspected terrorists may be subject to removal without a hearing as a criminal or suspected terrorist, or subject to removal by a special Terrorist Removal Court. Removal using expedited removal (INA § 235(b)(1)) or ordinary removal (INA § 240(b)) bars the noncitizen from seeking admission within five years of the date of the removal under INA § 212(a)(9)(A). The procedures for expedited removal are discussed below. Removal hearings are discussed in Chapter 12.

2.   Expedited Removal

Before the 1996 IRRIRA amendments to the INA, all noncitizens arriving at a port of entry and applying for admission could challenge their exclusion before an immigration judge. At the exclusion hearing, the noncitizen could be represented by counsel and some procedural protection was required by INS regulations.

The 1996 IRRIRA amendments redesigned the entire admissions process. Separate exclusion hearings no longer take place. All hearings before an immigration judge, whether to decide the admission of a noncitizen or to remove a noncitizen who is already admitted into the U.S., are now called removal hearings.

More significantly, the 1996 IIRIRA amendments reclassified some applicants for admission and these groups no longer have an opportunity to challenge the initial admission decision before an immigration judge. These applicants for admission are subject to a separate expedited removal procedure. Under INA § 235(b)(1), if an noncitizen applicant for admission lacks proper documents, possesses fraudulent or invalid documents, or committed fraud or misrepresentation at any time, she is this subject to the expedited removal procedure. In this case, the DHS immigration officer makes an inadmissibility determination at the border that INA § 212(a)(6)(C) or (7) applies to a noncitizen. Very limited exceptions to the expedited removal process exist for noncitizens who are inadmissible under INA §§ 212(a)(6)(C) or (7).[92] Some Cubans and unaccompanied minors are exempt from expedited removal.[93]

There are alternatives to the expedited removal procedure for noncitizens who are inadmissible under INA § 212(a)(6)(C) or (7). The noncitizen may be permitted to withdraw her application for admission.[94] It is possible to obtain a waiver of the inadmissibility ground requiring proper documentation if unforeseen emergency circumstances exist. This waiver can be granted at the border by the immigration officer in lieu of entering an expedited removal order.[95] If a noncitizen expresses a fear of persecution if she were returned to her home country, then an expanded

---

[92] Nearly all noncitizens who are inadmissible under INA § 212(a)(6)(C) or (7) are subject to expedited removal. Under INA § 235(b)(1)(F), some Cubans and unaccompanied minors who may be inadmissible under § 212(a)(6)(C) or (7) are not subject to expedited removal. VWP applicants are also not subject to expedited removal. See 8 C.F.R. § 235.3 (2006).

[93] INA § 235(b)(1)(F).

[94] INA § 235(a)(4).

[95] INA § 212(d)(4)(A). Emergency documentary waivers may be granted when there is a medical emergency or the noncitizen's documents have been lost or stolen within 48 hours of departure to the U.S.

inspection process involving a credible fear interview is required. The credible fear interview is discussed below.

Under the expedited removal procedure, the DHS immigration officer immediately conducts the hearing at the port of entry by advising the noncitizen of the inadmissibility charges against her and giving the noncitizen an opportunity to respond. If a removal order is issued by the inspecting immigration officer, the order is reviewed by a supervisory officer before it is considered final. The INA precludes review of the inspector's decision and states "the officer shall order the alien removed from the United States without further hearing or review . . . " unless the noncitizen expresses intent to apply for asylum or a fear of persecution.[96]

Noncitizens present in the U.S., who have not been admitted or paroled as defined in INA 101(a)(13), are subject to expedited removal.[97] The Secretary of DHS has "sole and unreviewable discretion" to decide whether to apply expedited removal noncitizens in the interior of the U.S.[98] The INA states that expedited removal can apply to a noncitizen who has not been admitted or paroled and who can not establish to the satisfaction of an immigration officer that she has been present in the U.S. continuously for the prior two years. Under this provision, DHS must decide whether to apply expedited removal to those with less than two years of continuous physical presence. The regulations require the Secretary of DHS to publish a notice in the Federal Register if he or she intends to apply expedited removal procedures to noncitizens apprehended within the United States who have not been admitted.[99]

DHS has applied expedited removal at locations other than an approved port of entry in two circumstances. In August 2004, the DHS published a notice explaining that the expedited removal procedure would be applied to noncitizens who are present in the U.S. within 100 miles of the U.S. border with Canada or Mexico, and who can not establish that they have been physically present in the U.S. continuously for a 14 day period before the encounter.[100] DHS also has applied this expedited removal procedure in all coastal areas, specifically to exclude Haitian asylum seekers.[101]

---

[96] INA § 235(b)(1)(A)(i).

[97] INA § 235(b)(1)(A)(iii). Expedited removal also applies to other arriving noncitizens in addition to those applying for admission at a port of entry. These additional categories of arriving noncitizens include those seeking transit through the U.S., those interdicted in international or U.S. waters, and those brought to the U.S. by any means.

[98] INA § 235(b)(1)(A)(iii).

[99] 8 C.F.R. § 235.3(b)(1)(ii).

[100] 69 Fed. Reg. 488877 (Aug. 11, 2004). In January 2006 DHS announced that expedited removal was expanded to include the northern border of the U.S. *Department of Homeland Security Streamlines Removal Process Along Entire U.S. Border*, available at http://www.dhs.gov/xnews/releases/ press_release_0845.shtm (last visited Jan. 30, 2006).

[101] *Secure Border Initiative*, available at http://www.cbp.gov/xp/cgov/border_security/sbi/ sbi_information/ (last visited Jan. 1, 2007).

Review of an expedited removal order is limited. Generally, there is no administrative appeal of immigration officer's decision.[102] Judicial review is available only if a noncitizen claims she is a lawful permanent resident, refugee, asylee or a U.S. citizen.[103] In this case, a habeas corpus proceeding under INA § 242(e) is available but the scope of review is very limited.[104] The only other form of review of the expedited removal order is the limited review available to noncitizens who receive a negative credible fear determination as described below.

An expedited removal order issued by a DHS immigration officer has the same weight as a removal order issued by an Immigration Judge. A noncitizen who was removed after an expedited removal order is inadmissible for five years under INA § 212(a)(9)(A)(i), unless a waiver is granted.

Suspected terrorists and noncitizens who threaten foreign policy or national security are subject to a distinct form of expedited removal under INA § 235(c). If an immigration officer or an Immigration Judge suspects that an arriving noncitizen is inadmissible under terrorist or national security grounds, then a removal order will be issued and the immigration officer or IJ may "not conduct any further inquiry or hearing until ordered by the Attorney General."[105] The Attorney General is required to review these removal orders and is authorized to remove the noncitizen without further inquiry or hearing. The Attorney General may rely on confidential information and consultation with "appropriate security agencies of the United States Government" to determine whether a terrorist or national security ground of inadmissibility applies. If the Attorney General does not order removal, then the A.G. must specify the type of further inquiry or hearing to be conducted.

a.   Credible Fear Determinations

A modified expedited removal process exists for a noncitizen, inadmissible under INA § 212(a)(6)(C) or (7), who asserts a fear of persecution upon return to her home country or an intent to file an asylum application. Under INA § 235(b)(1)(B), the noncitizen must have an opportunity to demonstrate she possesses a credible fear of persecution. This occurs in an interview with a DHS asylum officer, usually in the airport or in a detention facility. An applicant demonstrates a credible fear if there is "a significant possibility, taking into account the credibility of the statements made by the alien in support of the alien's claim and such other facts as are known to the officer, that the alien could establish eligibility for asylum under section 208."[106]

---

[102] INA § 235(c). Administrative review is required for LPRs, asylees, and refugees.

[103] INA § 242(e) (judicial review by habeas corpus proceeding). 8 C.F.R. § 235.3(b)(5)(i) (2006).

[104] Under INA § 242(e)(2), the court may determine only: (1) whether the person is a noncitizen; (2) whether the noncitizen was ordered removed under the expedited review procedures; and (3) whether the noncitizen has shown by a preponderance of the evidence that she is a lawful permanent resident, is a refugee under INA § 207, or has been granted asylum under INA § 208 (and asylum status has not been terminated).

[105] INA § 235(c); expedited removal applies to noncitizens inadmissible under INA §§ 212(a)(3)(A) (other than clause (ii)), (B) or (C).

[106] INA § 235(b)(1)(B)(v).

If the DHS asylum officer finds no credible fear exists, then the applicant can request review by an immigration judge of the credible fear determination.[107] The review by an Immigration Judge must occur within seven days. No other administrative review is available of the initial credible fear determination. If the Immigration Judge agrees that no credible fear exists, there is no further administrative review on the merits of the fear of persecution. If the noncitizen establishes a credible fear of persecution, she will be referred for an ordinary removal hearing under INA § 240. The INA requires that a noncitizen "shall be detained pending a final determination of credible fear of persecution."[108] Once an applicant is referred for an ordinary removal hearing, she may be released from detention under discretionary parole. This is discussed below. Removal Hearings and Procedures are covered in Chapters 9 and 10.

There are on-going concerns about expedited removal, particularly the credible fear process.[109] A 2005 report of the U.S. Commission on International Religious Freedom [CIRF] expressed concern about potential asylum applicants feeling intimidated by the DHS initial questioning, or lack comprehension about the significance of the interview as the only opportunity to convey a fear of persecution.[110] It recommended videotaping DHS initial interviews, and guidance for consistent assessments of whether a credible fear exists. A 2007 CIRF report confirmed that DHS had done little to implement the recommendations.

3.   Before an Immigration Judge

Noncitizens who are found inadmissible generally may challenge the DHS immigration officer's decision in an ordinary removal hearing under INA § 240. The 1996 IIRIRA amendments created one unified hearing, a removal hearing, for all inadmissibility or deportability determinations.[111] As a result of this unified hearing, there are some additional procedural protections for those who challenge the inadmissibility determination of a DHS immigration officer.

Once removal proceedings have begun, the noncitizen may be able to prove that she is in fact admissible because the inadmissibility ground is inapplicable, or because she has been granted a waiver of inadmissibility. The Immigration Judge will decide whether an inadmissibility ground is inapplicable. Some waiver applications can be decided by an IJ in a removal hearing and others must be decided by DHS. An applicant for admission who is placed in removal proceedings before an Immigration Judge may seek to adjust status. As noted above, she may

---

[107] INA § 235(b)(1)(B)(iii)(III).

[108] *Id.*

[109] *See* Orantes-Hernandez v. Gonzales, 504 F. Supp. 2d 825 (C.D.Cal. 2007); *See also* Michele R. Pistone, *Justice Delayed Is Justice Denied: A Proposal for Ending the Unnecessary Detention of Asylum Seekers*, 12 HARV. HUM. RS. J. 197 (1999) (criticizing the detention of asylum seekers in the expedited removal process under INA § 235(a)).

[110] U.S. Commission on International Religious Freedom was created by the International Religious Freedom Act, Pub. L. 105-292, 112 Stat. 2787 (1998). It is a bipartisan independent agency.

[111] IIRIRA went into effect on April 1, 1997.

renew her adjustment application if it was denied by DHS, or she may file an application initially before the Immigration Judge.[112]

If a noncitizen is ordered removed by an IJ, because she is found inadmissible, then she is barred from readmission to the U.S. for five years under INA § 212(a)(9)(A)(i). The noncitizen may be admitted sooner if the Secretary of DHS consents to her readmission.

4. Detention and Parole

Detention is required for many noncitizens seeking admission into the United States if they are denied admission.[113] An individual is an applicant for admission if she is present in the U.S. but has not been admitted and if she is at the border seeking admission under INA § 101(a)(13)(C).[114] All applicants for admission must be inspected by immigration officers.[115]

There are a variety of removal procedures for applicants seeking admission.[116] Detention pending removal is determined by the reason for removal in a particular case. Most often, a noncitizen who is found inadmissible by an immigration officer will be placed either in ordinary removal proceedings under INA § 240 or expedited removal proceedings under INA § 235(b)(1). Other removal proceedings exist for criminals and suspected terrorists. All removal procedures are discussed in Chapter 12.

The DHS decision whether to detain or release a noncitizen on parole may depend on the availability of detention facilities, and the concern about the likelihood of a noncitizen appearing at future hearing dates. This can result in different parole policies of various DHS districts across the country. Priority is given to noncitizens subject to mandatory detention under the INA including noncitizens who are criminals or suspected terrorists.[117] Those in expedited removal proceedings, including lawful permanent residents, are subject to mandatory detention.[118] Mandatory detention is discussed in Chapter 12.

Noncitizens placed in ordinary removal proceedings under INA § 240, may request parole for release from detention under INA 212(d)(5).[119] Historically, parole was granted regularly to arriving noncitizens pending a hearing before an Immigration Judge. A noncitizen applying for admission at the border may be

---

[112] 8 C.F.R. § 245.2(a)(1).

[113] INA § 235(b)(2).

[114] INA § 235(a)(1). Applicants for admission also includes noncitizens interdicted and brought to the U.S., and returning lawful permanent residents deemed applicants for admission under INA § 101(a)(13).

[115] INA § 235(a)(3).

[116] See supra Section D(iii) discussing Denial of Admission.

[117] INA § 236(c).

[118] 8 C.F.R. 235.3(b)(5)(i) (release from mandatory detention through parole is available but only to meet a medical emergency or for a legitimate law enforcement objectives).

[119] INA § 212(d)(5). Parole is available to those inspected by an immigration officer under INA § 235(b) and those apprehended inside the U.S. who are deemed to by "arriving" under INA § 235(a).

paroled into the U.S. for "urgent humanitarian reasons" or if a significant public health benefit exists under INA § 212(d)(5)(A).[120] Parole permits an noncitizen to enter the territory of the United States, however it is not admission into the U.S. as defined in INA § 101(a)(13). It is often granted during the pendency of a removal hearing or other DHS determination, or for emergency medical reasons. A noncitizen may reside for many years in the U.S. as a parolee under the "legal fiction" of an applicant for admission. Immigration Judges do not have jurisdiction to review parole decisions regarding noncitizens arriving at a port of entry and seeking admissions, including those who claim to be lawful permanent residents.[121]

Noncitizens subject to expedited removal must be detained pending the decision whether an expedited removal order and pending the execution of the removal order. This mandatory detention requirement is applied to all noncitizens subject to expedited removal including lawful permanent residents.[122] Detention also is required for noncitizens asserting a credible fear until a final decision is made whether a credible fear exists, and if a negative decision is made, until the order is executed.[123] Release from mandatory detention through parole is available but only for a medical emergency or for a legitimate law enforcement objective, or if the noncitizen is referred for an ordinary removal hearing under INA § 240.[124]

---

[120] Prior to the 1996 IIRIRA amendments, the criteria for parole were either the existence of "emergent reasons" or "reasons deemed strictly in the public interest."

[121] INA § 236(c); 8 C.F.R. § 236.1(c)(11) (2006).

[122] *See* Matter of Collado-Munoz, 21 I&N Dec. 1061 (BIA 1997) (an LRP arriving at a border post of entry and seeking admission is not entitled to a bond hearing before an Immigration Judge).

[123] INA § 235(b)(1)(B)(iii)(IV).

[124] 8 C.F.R. 253.3(b)(5)(i) (2006).

Chapter 11

REMOVAL

    a.   **Deferred Action**

    b.   **Voluntary Departure**

    c.   **Stays of Removal**

A. GENERAL CONSIDERATIONS

Removal proceedings are the principal method by which the United States removes or expels people from its borders. Before 1996, such proceedings were categorized as either deportation or exclusion proceedings, depending on the presence of the noncitizen within the United States. Noncitizens who were seeking admission into the United States and were not physically present within the borders of the country were subject to exclusion proceedings. Those who had entered and were present, with or without authorization, were subject to deportation proceedings. In 1996, Congress passed the Illegal Immigration Reform and Immigrant Responsibility Act ("IIRAIRA"), which, among other things, replaced deportation and exclusion proceedings with removal proceedings. The biggest practical consequence of the shift has been that those who have entered without inspection and are caught inside U.S. borders are now subject to the grounds of inadmissibility rather than the grounds of deportability.[1]

1. History and Theory of Deportation

Originally, deportation was the method used to correct errors in admission or to expel alien enemies.[2] Until the mid-nineteenth century, immigration control was considered a police power of the individual States rather than of the federal government.[3] States continued to control immigration exclusively or in conjunction with the federal government until the passage of the first comprehensive federal immigration law, the Immigration Act of 1882.[4] The law mandated the exclusion of several undesirable categories of noncitizens, including convicts, "lunatics," and people unable to care for themselves.[5]

The power of the federal government to control immigration and exclusion policies was expanded by the Supreme Court in *Chae Chan Ping v. United States*,[6] known as the Chinese Exclusion Case. In deciding whether the federal government had the power to exclude someone who was lawfully admitted, the Supreme Court held that the power to exclude foreigners is an "incident of sovereignty belonging to the government of the United States."[7] The 1891 Immigration Act further consolidated immigration power in the federal government, and extended deportation policy to cover those who were later discovered to have been subject to exclusion at entry. That law was followed in 1892 by a law requiring all Chinese to

---

[1] INA § 212(a)(6) (a).

[2] Alien and Sedition Acts of 1798.

[3] DAN KANSTROOM, DEPORTATION NATION: OUTSIDERS IN AMERICAN HISTORY 92 (2007).

[4] KANSTROOM, *supra* note 3, at 94.

[5] Immigraton Act of Aug. 3, 1882, 22 Stat. 214; KANSTROOM, *supra* note 3, at 94.

[6] 130 U.S. 581 (1889).

[7] *Id.* at 609.

register and to prove their legality. To prove their legality, Chinese had to produce the testimony of at least one credible white witness. The Supreme Court found the law constitutional in *Fong Yue Ting v. United States.*[8] The *Fong Yue Ting* Court reaffirmed and expanded the holding of *Chae Chan Ping*, finding "[t]he right to exclude or to expel all aliens, or any class of aliens . . . [is] an inherent and inalienable right of every sovereign and independent nation."[9] The Court established that the federal government has as much of a right to expel and deport foreigners as it has to prevent them from entering in the first place.

Ever since the passage of the Alien and Sedition Acts of 1798, Congress has continued to enhance the government's power to expel aliens for violating entry laws and to expel temporary aliens.[10] This power has incrementally increased over the years to include the deportation of those who had entered with proper documentation, but who behaved improperly once within the United States. Thus, despite the Supreme Court's proclamation in *Fong Yue Ting* that an "order of deportation is not a punishment for crime,"[11] deportation's punitive character has assumed greater and greater significance over time as Congress adds to the list of grounds for which a noncitizen may be expelled once in the United States with proper documentation.

Before Congress changed the landscape with its passage of IIRAIRA in 1996, the law classified a noncitizen according to whether s/he had "entered" the United States. If the noncitizen had not entered, s/he was considered someone seeking admission and was subject to the inadmissibility grounds under INA § 212. If the noncitizen had physically entered, whether lawfully or not, s/he was not seeking admission, but rather was subject to the deportation grounds of INA § 237.

Deportation policy has historically taken on a civil character, even as Congress has moved toward increasing the crime-related grounds for deportability. IIRAIRA and its companion, the Antiterrorism and Effective Death Penalty Act ("AEDPA"), have substantially altered immigration policy, moving it radically toward a policy that punishes those who are present for criminal behavior through deportation. Nonetheless, deportation policy and deportation procedures have never carried the constitutional protections reserved for criminal proceedings because the Supreme Court has held that both exclusion and deportation proceedings are civil in character.[12] Several commentators, both before and after passage of the 1996 law, have reasoned that to the extent that deportation procedures are increasingly used to punish, they should be accompanied by the constitutional protections of criminal proceedings.[13]

---

[8] Fong Yue Ting v. United States, 149 U.S. 698 (1893).

[9] *Id.* at 711.

[10] CHARLES GORDON, STANLEY MAILMAN, AND STEPHEN YALE-LOEHR, IMMIGRATION LAW AND PROCEDURE, § 71.01[2].

[11] *Fong Yue Ting*, 149 U.S. at 730.

[12] Chae Chan Ping v. United States, 130 U.S. 581 (1889) (exclusion proceedings are civil in nature); Fong Yue Ting v. United States, 149 U.S. 698 (1893) (expulsion proceedings are civil in nature).

[13] *See, e.g.,* Daniel Kanstroom, *Deportation, Social Control, and Punishment: Some Thoughts About Why Hard Laws Make Bad Cases*, 113 HARV. L. REV. 1889, 1998 (2000); Peter L. Markowitz, *Straddling the Civil-Criminal Divide: A Bifurcated Approach to Understanding the Nature of Immigration*

2.   The 1996 Law

When Congress passed IIRAIRA in 1996, it created several obstacles to admission and to lawful presence in the United States, all relevant to the deportation and exclusion categories. The following are some of the highlights of IIRAIRA relevant to removal:

a.   Bars to Admissibility

Congress added a provision to the inadmissibility grounds of the INA prohibiting the re-entry of certain noncitizens who had entered the country unlawfully and who subsequently left the country. The provision is known as the "three- and ten- year bar" because of the sanctions it imposes. The law states that any alien who was unlawfully present for a period of more than 180 days but less than one year, and who voluntarily departed the United States before commencement of removal proceedings, is barred from seeking admission into the United States for three years from the date of his or her departure.[14] Any alien who was unlawfully present for one year or more is barred from seeking admission for ten years.[15] For purposes of this provision, unlawful presence means presence after the expiration of an authorized stay, or presence without admission or parole.[16] The unlawful presence period started to count six months after enactment of IIRAIRA, on April 1, 1997.[17] There are some limited exceptions to the unlawful presence definition, in which certain periods do not count as unlawful presence. These include the time period before a noncitizen turns 18, the time period that an asylum applicant's application is pending, and the time period that a beneficiary of family unity protection holds such status.[18] The unlawful presence definition does not apply to trafficking victims or to victims of domestic violence who violated the terms of their nonimmigrant visas because of the domestic violence.[19] This inadmissibility ground can be waived by the Attorney General if the noncitizen can show that refusal of admission will result in extreme hardship to the citizen or lawful permanent resident spouse or parent of the noncitizen.

b.   Expedited Removal

IIRAIRA created a new expedited removal process which allows government authorities to summarily remove anyone attempting to enter the country with no documents[20] or with false documents.[21] If an immigration officer finds that an arriving noncitizen has attempted to enter the country with false or no documents,

---

Removal Proceedings, 43 HARV. C.R.C.L. L. REV. 289, 290–295 (2008); Stephen H. Legomsky, *The Alien Criminal Defendant*, 14 SAN DIEGO L. REV. 105, 121–127 (1977).

[14] INA § 212(a)(9)(B)(i)(I).

[15] INA § 212(a)(9)(B)(i)(II).

[16] INA § 212(a)(9)(B)(ii).

[17] IIRAIRA § 309.

[18] INA § 212(a)(9)(B)(iii).

[19] INA § 212(a)(9)(B)(iii).

[20] INA § 212(a)(7).

[21] INA § 212(a)(6)(C).

the officer may order the noncitizen removed without further hearing or review unless the noncitizen seeks asylum or makes a credible claim of fear of persecution.[22]

An immigration officer can also apply expedited removal to persons who have not been admitted or paroled, and who cannot show to the officer's satisfaction that they have been physically present in the United States continuously for two or more years.[23] There are several exceptions to the expedited removal process in addition to asylum seekers, including Cuban citizens, lawful permanent residents or persons lawfully admitted, and minors who are not aggravated felons or who have not been formerly removed.

c.   Removal Proceedings

IIRAIRA replaced the pre-1996 procedures of "deportation" and "exclusion" with the "removal" proceeding, which now covers both those cases in which a noncitizen has not been admitted and those in which an admitted noncitizen is being expelled.[24] Where someone is not covered by expedited removal procedures, s/he is entitled to removal proceedings pursuant to INA § 240. While the statute no longer makes distinctions between those seeking admission and those subject to deportation, it does continue to differentiate between the burden of proof for someone who is seeking admission and someone subject to deportation. In addition, the grounds of removal still depend on one's status with respect to admission.

d.   Cancellation of Removal

The 1996 law replaced the pre-1996 relief from expulsion known as "suspension of deportation" with the procedure now known as "cancellation of removal."[25] Cancellation of removal covers those cases in which the government seeks to remove lawful permanent residents and those in which the government seeks to remove various categories of noncitizens. Significantly, the cancellation of removal procedure is more stringent than its predecessor. The suspension of deportation rules allowed a noncitizen who had been present in the United States for at least seven years to show that the noncitizen or his/her citizen or LPR spouse, parent, or child would suffer extreme hardship upon deportation. An immigration judge would then have the discretion to suspend the deportation. Under the cancellation of removal procedure, a nonpermanent resident must show that s/he has been in the United States for at least ten years, and that removal will cause an "exceptional and extremely unusual" hardship to a citizen or LPR spouse, parent, or child. Unusual hardship to the noncitizen is not sufficient for cancellation of removal under the new standard.

---

[22] INA § 235(b)(1).

[23] INA § 235(b)(1)(A)(iii)(II).

[24] INA § 240.

[25] INA § 240A.

e. Meaning of "Entry" and "Admission"

IIRAIRA repealed the definition of "entry" and replaced it with a definition of "admission."[26] Before 1996, a noncitizen seeking "entry" into the United States was subject to exclusion proceedings, while a noncitizen who had already entered was subject to deportation proceedings. Many important deportation grounds used the term entry, e.g., "entry without inspection" and "inadmissible at entry." When IIRAIRA replaced entry with admission, most of the importance surrounding entry was lost. Entry still exists in certain immigration provisions, but its importance is greatly reduced.

Admission is now the more important concept for immigration law. Admission is defined in INA § 101(a)(13) as "the lawful entry of the alien into the United States after inspection and authorization by an immigration officer." Both admitted and non-admitted noncitizens are now subject to removal proceedings. However, admission is important in determining whether the noncitizen will be subject to the grounds of inadmissibility or the grounds of deportability, which are different and can prove very important. Thus, physical presence within the United States has become less important than legal presence, i.e., one's status as admitted or not admitted.

B. REMOVAL GROUNDS AND WAIVERS

This section explores the three broad categories of removal grounds that could subject noncitizens to removal proceedings. Grounds of removal, whether for inadmissibility or for deportability, fall into three conceptual categories: immigration control, criminal grounds, and other grounds. This section covers the removal grounds that are based on deportability. The separate section on inadmissibility in this book covers parallel removal grounds of inadmissibility.

1. Immigration Control Grounds

Immigration control rationales for exclusion and expulsion can be found in the inadmissibility[27] as well as in the deportability grounds for removal.[28] These sets of rules are meant to maintain the integrity of the immigration control system established in the statute. The immigration control grounds of deportation, found at INA § 237, are in place in order to enforce the rest of the grounds of removal found in the statute. As with inadmissibility, these grounds of deportability focus on border control issues. Some of the provisions deal with errors upon entry, while others deal with post-entry immigration control issues.

---

[26] INA § 101(a)(13).

[27] *See, e.g.,* INA § 212(a)(6); INA § 212(a)(7).

[28] *See, e.g.,* INA § 237(a)(1); INA § 237(a)(3).

a.   Correcting Errors in Admission upon Entry

Before the 1996 law, entry without inspection was a deportable act.[29] Congress repealed the entry without inspection deportability ground, replacing it with the unlawful presence provision in the grounds of inadmissibility.[30] Reflecting the error correction function of deportation policy, INA§ 237(a)(1) renders deportable a noncitizen who "at the time of entry or adjustment of status was within one or more of the classes of aliens inadmissible by the law existing at such time."

This deportability ground covers inadmissibility due to immigration control issues. Recall that noncitizens who arrive at unauthorized points of entry are inadmissible.[31] Likewise, immigrants and nonimmigrants seeking to enter the United States without valid documentation of their status are inadmissible.[32] A noncitizen is inadmissible for making false representations about his or her immigration status. Any noncitizen who commits fraud or willfully misrepresents a material fact in order to obtain a visa, admission, documentation, or any other benefit provided by immigration law is inadmissible.[33] The Attorney General may waive the application of this provision for a VAWA petitioner or any other noncitizen who (1) is the spouse, parent, son, or daughter of a U.S. Citizen or LPR and (2) was in possession of an immigrant visa or equivalent document and was otherwise admissible to the United States at time of admission.[34]

In addition to incorporating the inadmissibility grounds, the deportability grounds for removal deem a noncitizen removable for various other violations of immigration law. A noncitizen who is unlawfully present in the United States, or whose nonimmigrant visa has been revoked, is deportable.[35]

The statute includes a deportability ground for marriage fraud. This provision operates in one of two ways. First, if a noncitizen obtains an immigrant visa based on a marriage that is less than two years old when the noncitizen enters the country and the marriage is terminated or annulled within two years after the noncitizen is admitted, the noncitizen will be considered to have obtained the visa by fraud.[36] The noncitizen has the burden of proof to show that the marriage was not entered into for the purpose of perpetrating immigration fraud. Second, if the Attorney General finds that the noncitizen has failed to fulfill the marriage obligations because the marriage was entered into for immigration purposes, the noncitizen will be found deportable.[37]

---

[29] *See* INA § 241(a)(1)(B) (pre-1996).

[30] INA § 212(a)(6).

[31] INA § 212(a)(6).

[32] INA 212(a)(7). A waiver of this provision is available upon evidence that the noncitizen did not know of his or her inadmissibility. INA § 212(k).

[33] INA § 212(a)(6)(C).

[34] INA § 237(a)(1)(H).

[35] INA § 237(a)(1)(B).

[36] INA § 237(a)(1)(G)(i).

[37] INA § 237(a)(1)(G)(ii).

b.   Post-Entry Immigration Control

In keeping with the immigration control function, the INA deems any non-citizen who smuggles, or encourages, induces, or aids and abets smuggling, deportable.[38] This deportability ground has a humanitarian waiver provision for LPRs who smuggled immediate family members – spouse, parent, son, or daughter.[39] It also makes exceptions for immigrants who were present in the United States and who smuggled immediate family members eligible for family reunification immigration benefits.[40]

The grounds of deportability apply to actions taken after entry, such as noncompliance with the conditions of entry. A conditional resident whose conditional status is terminated after entry, for example, is deportable.[41] Likewise, a noncitizen who was inadmissible at the time s/he received adjustment of status is also deportable.[42]

There are several provisions in the statute that require those who have lawfully entered to maintain their status by registering with the government, reporting address changes, and similar activities aimed at facilitating the monitoring of immigrants.[43] Violations of these provisions render a noncitizen deportable.[44] Willful violations of these provisions are also criminal offenses subject to fines or imprisonment.[45]

2.   Criminal Grounds

The criminal grounds of removal have continued to grow through the years, as Congress increasingly relies on deportation to punish those who acquire criminal records after admission. The immigration-crime intersection is complex, requiring analysis at several different points. Most of the deportability grounds require a conviction, and there are several inquiries into whether there has been a conviction in many cases. The deportability grounds include conviction for a crime involving moral turpitude. Volumes have been written analyzing whether particular offenses qualify as such. The aggravated felony grounds of deportability are surrounded by their own set of complex inquiries.

---

[38] INA § 237(a)(1)(E).

[39] INA § 237(a)((1)(E)(iii).

[40] INA § 237(a)(1)(E)(ii).

[41] INA § 237(a)(1)(D). This provision applies to noncitizens who have received conditional residence as spouses or sons and daughters under INA§ 216, or to conditional residents who received conditional residence as entrepreneurs, spouses and children pursuant to INA § 216A.

[42] INA § 237(a)(1)(A).

[43] INA §§ 261–266.

[44] INA § 237(a)(3)(A); INA § 237(a)(3)(B).

[45] INA § 266.

a.   Crimes Involving Moral Turpitude and Aggravated Felonies

A noncitizen convicted of a crime involving moral turpitude that was committed within five years after the date of admission is deportable if the crime is one for which a sentence of one year or longer may be imposed.[46] A similar provision makes a noncitizen inadmissible, although the deportability ground is more stringent; it focuses on the *possible* sentence rather than the *actual* sentence in determining a noncitizen's deportability. Even if a noncitizen is actually sentenced to less than one year, s/he is still deportable under this provision for a crime involving moral turpitude if the offense carried a possible term of one year or more.

The crime involving moral turpitude provision states that the crime must have been committed within five years after the date of admission. Understanding the term "admission" in this context can be complicated. An adjustment of status is considered an admission for purposes of this provision.[47] If a person entered the United States without authorization, committed a qualifying crime, and then adjusted status to LPR, however, the conviction did not occur after admission because admission was not effectuated until the adjustment of status.[48]

The term "moral turpitude" has never been legislatively defined, since its introduction into the immigration statute in 1891. The Supreme Court held that the term was not unconstitutionally vague in a case involving the deportation of a noncitizen for criminal convictions involving fraud. In *Jordan v. DeGeorge*, the Court was asked to decide whether the term "moral turpitude" was unconstitutionally vague in a case involving the crime of conspiracy to defraud the United States of taxes on distilled spirits, the elements of which involve fraud.[49] That particular crime, the Court held, was squarely within the definition of a crime involving moral turpitude, "[w]hatever else the phrase 'crime involving moral turpitude' may mean in peripheral cases."[50]

Since then, courts have consistently defined moral turpitude as "involving conduct that is base, vile, or depraved, and contrary to the private and social duties man owes to his fellow men or to society in general."[51]

In determining whether a crime charged can be considered a crime involving moral turpitude or an aggravated felony, courts have used categorical analysis.[52]

---

[46] INA § 237(a)(2)(A)(i). The statute states that for those who obtained permanent residence through S visas, a CIMT conviction will trigger deportation if committed ten years after admission.

[47] Matter of Rosas-Ramirez, 221 I &N Dec. 616 (BIA 1999).

[48] Matter of Rosas-Ramirez, 22 I. & N. Dec. 616, 623 (BIA 1999) ("[T]he reference in section 237(a)(2)(A)(iii) of the Act to 'after admission' includes both those aliens who are 'admitted' at the time of entry . . . as well as those who are 'lawfully admitted for permanent residence' . . . ").

[49] Jordan v. DeGeorge, 341 U.S. 223 (1951).

[50] *Id.* at 232.

[51] Navarro-Lopez v. Gonzales, 503 F.3d 1063, 1068 (9th Cir. 2007).

[52] This approach was first introduced in *Taylor v. United States*, 495 U.S. 575, 601–02 (1990). The Supreme Court instructed other courts to look "only to the fact of conviction and the statutory definition

Under this approach, an immigration court does not conduct a thorough review of the facts giving rise to the criminal conviction, but rather relies exclusively on the elements of the statutory offense to determine whether they constitute a crime involving moral turpitude. If a noncitizen is convicted of a crime under a divisible statute — one that includes multiple crimes phrased in the disjunctive or included as distinct subsections — the court may look into a limited record of conviction to whether the criminal conviction is a crime involving moral turpitude. The documents that constitute the record of conviction include "the statutory definition, charging document, written plea agreement, transcript of plea colloquy, and any explicit factual finding by the trial judge to which the defendant assented."[53] Mere accusations contained in these documents are not considered part of the facts of the case, especially if they go beyond the elements needed for a conviction of the crime.[54]

A noncitizen who, any time after admission, commits two or more crimes involving moral turpitude is deportable. There is an exception for purely political offenses and for multiple offenses arising out of a single scheme of criminal misconduct. The Second, Third, and Ninth Circuits require the government to carry the burden of proving that the crimes did not arise out of a single scheme of conduct. The BIA has interpreted the single scheme provision to cover separate and distinct crimes performed in furtherance of a single criminal episode, lesser included offenses, and instances where two crimes flow from and are the natural consequence of a single act of criminal misconduct.[55]

Another category of general crimes for which admitted noncitizens can be deported is the aggravated felony category. While this category was initially a narrow one, it has expanded to include behaviors and actions that are not considered particularly egregious or aggravated in the criminal law context. Aggravated felony is defined at INA § 101(a)(43). The definition includes what are traditionally considered egregious crimes, such as murder, rape, sexual abuse of a minor, illicit trafficking in a controlled substance, crimes of violence, and theft offenses. It also includes activities such as forging a passport, counterfeiting, obstruction of justice or perjury, and failure to appear in court to answer for a felony charge. As with crimes of moral turpitude, whether a crime is an aggravated felony depends on a categorical analysis of the convicted offense.

b.   Controlled Substances, Firearms, and Domestic Violence

Convictions of controlled substance, firearms, or domestic violence offenses make a noncitizen deportable. These deportability provisions are all examples of post-entry social control. A noncitizen convicted of any state, federal, or foreign country law related to controlled substances, other than possession for personal

---

of the prior offense" in order to avoid the "practical difficulties and potential unfairness" of a lengthy and detailed factual review of the offense.

[53] Shepard v. United States, 544 U.S. 13, 16 (2005).

[54] Matter of Perez-Contreras, 20 I. & N. Dec. 615 (BIA 1992).

[55] Matter of Adetiba, 20 I. & N. Dec. 506, 509 (BIA 1992).

use of 30 grams or less of marijuana, is deportable.[56] The statute also makes a noncitizen who anytime after admission becomes a drug abuser or addict deportable.[57]

Just as broad in its application is the provision which makes conviction of a firearms offense after admission a deportable offense. The law states that "[a]ny alien who at any time after admission is convicted under any law of purchasing, selling, offering for sale, exchanging, using, owning, possessing, or carrying . . . any weapon, part, or accessory which is a firearm . . . in violation of any law is deportable."[58] Probably the most far-reaching criminal deportability ground is the domestic violence ground. A noncitizen convicted of any domestic violence offense at any time after admission is deportable.[59] Domestic violence offenses include domestic violence, stalking, and child abuse, neglect or abandonment. Moreover, the statute makes anyone who violates a protection order involving threats of violence, whether civil or criminal, deportable.[60]

c.   Other Enumerated Crimes

The statute enumerates several other crimes for which conviction makes a noncitizen deportable, including failure to register as a sex offender; high speed flight from an immigration checkpoint; crimes related to espionage, treason and sedition; and certain violations of the Trading with the Enemy Act or the Military Selective Service Act.

The deportability ground is triggered by a conviction of any one of these crimes. IIRAIRA added a definition of conviction to the statute in 1996. A conviction is defined under 8 U.S.C. § 1101(a)(48) as a formal judgment of guilt by a court, or if adjudication has been withheld, where (1) a judge or jury has found the alien guilty or the alien has entered a plea of guilty or *nolo contendere* or has admitted sufficient facts to warrant a finding of guilt, and (2) the judge has ordered some form of punishment, penalty, or restraint on the alien's liberty.

Under this definition, dismissals, juvenile court dispositions, and convictions that are on direct appeal are not considered "convictions." Completion of a pre-trial diversion program, upon which charges are dismissed, is not a conviction, as long as no plea of guilty or *nolo contendere* has been entered at any time.

A conviction that is vacated on the basis of procedural or substantive infirmities is not a conviction for immigration purposes.[61] A conviction vacated for

---

[56] INA § 237(a)(2)(B)(i).

[57] INA § 237(a)(2)(B)(ii).

[58] INA § 237(a)(2)(C).

[59] INA § 237(a)(2)(E)(i).

[60] INA § 237(a)(2)(E)(ii).

[61] In re Adamiak, 23 I. & N. Dec. 878, 880–81 (BIA 2006) (The BIA held that a conviction vacated by the trial court because of a defect in the underlying criminal proceedings, i.e., the failure of the court to advise the defendant of possible immigration consequences of a guilty plea, was no longer a conviction for immigration purposes. In so holding, the BIA recognized that it did not "share the view" of the 5th Circuit Court of Appeals on the effectiveness of vacating a conviction for immigration purposes.). *But see* Renteria Gonzalez v. I.N.S., 322 F.3d 804, 813–14 (5th Cir. 2002) ("a vacated conviction, federal or state,

rehabilitative or immigration reasons, however, will still be considered a conviction for immigration purposes.[62]

3. Other Removal Grounds

The statute includes several miscellaneous removal grounds that do not fit into the immigration control or criminal categories. These grounds include health-related, economic, and moral grounds for removing admitted noncitizens. For example, the deportability grounds target nonimmigrant status violators or those who entered lawfully but have since failed to comply with the requirements imposed by a health-related waiver upon entry.[63] A noncitizen is also deportable for abusing drugs or being a drug addict.[64] A noncitizen can be removed under certain circumstances if he or she becomes a public charge within five years after entry.[65] Each of these provisions has the effect of maintaining scrutiny over an immigrant even after admission.

C. RELIEF FROM REMOVAL

Noncitizens in removal proceedings may be eligible for several forms of relief from removal that allow them to stay in the United States. The concept of relief from removal is analogous to an affirmative defense in a judicial setting. The noncitizen can demonstrate that other factors, such as length of stay in the United States, should outweigh the grounds of removability s/he faces. This section discusses the eligibility requirements as well as the possible obstacles to relief from removal. Some obstacles are common to several forms of relief. For example, aggravated felons cannot seek forms of relief such as cancellation of removal, voluntary departure, or registry.[66] Likewise, anyone who (1) receives a Notice to Appear (NTA) at a removal hearing and fails to appear, (2) accepts voluntary departure but fails to depart, or (3) re-enters the United States without authorization after being removed, is rendered ineligible for these remedies for ten years.[67]

---

remains valid for purposes of the immigration laws").

[62] Pickering v. Gonzales, 465 F.3d 263, 266 (6th Cir. 2006) (holding that the BIA "correctly interpreted the law by holding that, when a court vacates an alien's conviction for reasons solely related to rehabilitation or to avoid adverse immigration hardships . . . the conviction is not eliminated for immigration purposes").

[63] INA § 237(a)(1)(C).

[64] INA § 237(a)(2)(B)(ii).

[65] INA § 237(a)(5).

[66] *See* INA § 240A(a)(3); § 240A(b)(1)(c) (cancellation of removal); § 240B(a)(1) (voluntary departure); § 249 (registry). Section 212(c) relief continues to be available for persons in proceedings prior to April 1, 1997, the date of IIRAIRA's enactment. It is also available to those who pled guilty to a crime prior to April 1, 1997. INS v. St. Cyr, 533 U.S. 289 (2001).

[67] INA § 240(b)(7), § 240B(d), § 241(a)(5).

1.   Lasting Relief

a.   Cancellation of Removal

IIRAIRA added section 240A to the INA in 1996, creating a type of relief known as cancellation of removal. At the same time, Congress eliminated suspension of deportation and section 212(c) relief, both of which existed under previous versions of the statute.[68] These forms of relief were folded into the now-existing cancellation provisions of the statute. Congress capped the number of cancellations available each year at 4,000.[69]

Section 240A of the INA contains two types of cancellation of removal. The first, found in section 240A(a), allows certain lawful permanent residents to remain in the United States after an order of removal. This remedy is typically invoked when a lawful permanent resident (LPR) has committed a crime rendering him or her deportable. The second, found in section 240A(b), is available to "certain nonpermanent residents," and is available either to out-of-status noncitizens, or to lawful permanent residents who do not fit into the requirements of section 240A(a).

Cancellation of removal is more restrictive than either suspension of deportation or relief under section 212(c). In particular, unlike previous similar relief provisions, the new provision requires that any nonpermanent resident seeking relief must show exceptional and extremely unusual hardship to a citizen spouse, parent, or child.[70] On the other hand, the provision resolves many questions that had historically arisen under the interpretation of section 212(c) regarding its differential applicability in deportation and exclusion cases. Years of legal debate surrounding when and how section 212(c) could be used to protect deportable or inadmissible noncitizens was resolved when Congress implemented the cancellation of removal provision, which applies both to noncitizens subject to deportation and those subject to exclusion.

i.   Lawful Permanent Residents (Cancellation of Removal Part A)

Cancellation of removal is available for certain lawful permanent residents who can show that they (1) have been admitted for permanent residency at least five years; (2) have resided continuously in the United States for seven years after having been admitted in any status; and (3) have not been convicted of an aggravated felony. A person who was admitted temporarily or as a nonimmigrant will be considered to have been "admitted in any status" for purposes of the seven

---

[68] For a description of the remedies available before cancellation of removal, see Elwin Griffith, *The Road Between the Section 212(c) Waiver and Cancellation of Removal under Section 240A of the Immigration and Nationality Act — The Impact of the 1996 Reform Legislation*, 12 GEO. IMMIGR. L.J. 65 (1997); Lory D. Rosenberg and Denise Sabagh, *A Practitioners' Guide to INA § 212(c)*, IMMIGRATION BRIEFINGS (April 1993).

[69] INA § 240A(e). The cap does not include grants of cancellation for certain nationals of Guatemala, El Salvador, the Soviet Union and its successor republics, and most Eastern European countries. INA § 240(e)(3)(A).

[70] INA § 240A(b)(1)(D).

year requirement. A person who is served with an NTA before the seven years of continuous residence will not be eligible for cancellation, however.[71] Nor will a person who committed an offense rendering him/her inadmissible under INA § 212(a)(2) or removable under INA § 237(a)(2) or § 237(a)(4) prior to the seven year period.[72] In other words, the time period stops accruing at the time of the commission of the crime.

In determining whether a noncitizen should be granted cancellation of removal, the discretionary criteria previously used in section 212(c) relief cases continues to be used in cancellation of removal cases to determine eligibility. The positive criteria include family ties in the United States, residency of long duration in the country, evidence of hardship to the respondent's family if deportation occurs, military service, history of employment, existence of value and service to the community, proof of genuine rehabilitation if a criminal record exists, and evidence of good character. Negative factors include the nature and underlying circumstances of exclusion grounds, additional significant violations of the INA, existence of a criminal record, and other evidence of bad character. Once cancellation of removal is granted, the noncitizen returns to his/her previous LPR status.

ii.   Nonpermanent Residents (Cancellation of Removal Part B)

Cancellation of removal is available for nonpermanent residents, although the eligibility requirements render it a more limited remedy for this class of noncitizens. The relief is available for those who are deportable or inadmissible. Those whose removal is cancelled under this provision can also seek adjustment of status as part of their relief.[73] Cancellation of removal is available for nonpermanent residents who can show they (1) have been physically present in the United States continuously for ten years immediately prior to the cancellation application; (2) have exhibited good moral character for the ten year period; (3) have not been convicted of a crime listed in the criminal provisions of the inadmissibility and deportability grounds in the INA; and (4) can show that removal would result in exceptional and extremely unusual hardship to a citizen or LPR spouse, parent, or child.[74] The statute requires that the 10-year continuous presence period end when an NTA is served on the noncitizen.[75] The statute also defines continuous physical presence for purposes of this provision. It states that a single departure of more than 90 days destroys continuous physical presence, as do cumulative absences totaling more than 180 days.[76] Courts have held that voluntary departure in lieu of removal will also destroy continuous physical

---

[71] INA § 240A(d)(1); Matter of Nolasco, 22 I. & N. Dec. 632 (BIA 1999).

[72] INA § 240A(d)(1)(B).

[73] INA§ 240A(b)(1).

[74] INA § 240A(b)(1).

[75] INA § 240A(d)(1).

[76] INA § 240A(d)(2).

presence.[77]

The hardship requirement in this provision of cancellation is more restrictive than the requirement for suspension of deportation, its predecessor relief mechanism. Under previous versions of suspension of deportation, eligibility for relief required a showing of *economic detriment* to the citizen/LPR spouse, parent, or child of the respondent. It was later transformed to a showing of *extreme hardship* to the applicant. With the passage of IIRAIRA, Congress now requires the applicant to show *exceptional and extremely unusual hardship* to the applicant's immediate relatives. Not only is this standard more restrictive than the previous standards, but a judge's decision on whether the standard has been met is not reviewable.[78] This limitation makes the current standard much more difficult for respondents to meet.

This form of relief is not available to certain categories of noncitizens, including crew members, J visa exchange visitors, and those who are inadmissible or deportable on political or national security grounds.

iii.   Victims of Domestic Violence

Certain victims of domestic violence are eligible for cancellation of removal under special rules that apply because of their victim status. This form of relief is available for a noncitizen who can show s/he has been battered or subjected to extreme cruelty by a citizen or LPR spouse or parent.[79] The noncitizen must also show continuous physical presence for the three years immediately preceding the application. The issuance of an NTA does not toll the three year continuous residence period as it does for those seeking cancellation of removal under INA § 240A(b).[80] The noncitizen must show good moral character during the three-year period as well. S/he is ineligible for relief if s/he has committed an aggravated felony, a crime defined in INA § 212(a)(2) or 212(a)(3), marriage fraud, or a crime defined under INA § 237(a)(2)-(4). The noncitizen must also show "extreme hardship" (as opposed to "exceptional and extremely unusual hardship") to him/herself, or to the noncitizen's child or parent.[81]

The continuous physical presence requirement in the domestic violence provision allows an exception for those who cannot meet the requirement for reasons related to the violence or abuse. Any absence shown to be linked to the violence or abuse will not be counted in determining whether the noncitizen meets the continuous physical presence requirement. With respect to good moral character, the Attorney General can waive any conviction for a crime that was connected to the noncitizen having been abused or battered if it may otherwise be

---

[77] Matter of Romale-Alcaide, 23 I. & N. Dec. 423 (BIA 2002); Reyes-Vasquez v. Ashcroft, 395 F.3d 903, 907 (8th Cir. 2005).

[78] INA § 242(a)(2)(B)(i); Romero-Torres v. Ashcroft, 327 F.3d 887 (9th Cir. 2003); Gonzalez-Oropeza v. U.S. Attorney General, 321 F.3d 1331, 1332–33 (11th Cir. 2003).

[79] INA § 240A(2). This relief is also available to battered spouses whose marriage is not legitimate because of bigamy. INA § 240A(2)((A)(i)(III).

[80] INA § 240A(b)(2)(A)(ii).

[81] INA § 240A(b)(2)(a)(v).

a bar to a finding of good moral character. In addition, the children of battered spouses who obtain cancellation of removal will be paroled and considered beneficiaries of an application for adjustment of status once the cancellation applicant has been granted adjustment.[82]

iv. NACARA

In 1997, Congress passed the Nicaraguan Adjustment and Central American Relief Act (NACARA), providing relief to thousands of Central Americans and others fleeing civil unrest in their home countries.[83] NACARA provides for a form of cancellation of removal, known as special rule cancellation. It is available to nationals of Guatemala, El Salvador, the Soviet Union and its successor republics, and most Eastern European nations, who entered before a specified date in 1990. The requirements for special rule cancellation are less restrictive than the general cancellation of removal requirements. They are the same as the requirements for the pre-IIRAIRA suspension of deportation. Special rule cancellation requires seven years of continuous physical presence, compared to ten under regular cancellation for nonpermanent residents. It also requires "extreme hardship" to oneself or immediate relatives, rather than the strict "exceptional and extremely unusual" standard in regular cancellation. The rule that continuous physical presence ends with the filing of an NTA or with the commission of a crime does not apply to special rule cancellation. The applicant must also show good moral character for the seven years immediately preceding the filing of the application.[84]

A separate provision of NACARA created an amnesty program for Nicaraguan and Cuban nationals who were continuously present in the United States since December 1995. Applications had to be filed by April 1, 2000. The person had to be admissible, although certain inadmissibility grounds, such as public charge, lack of labor certification, and present without admission, were waived.

b. Adjustment of Status

As seen in the cancellation of removal context, adjustment of status for nonpermanent residents is available as affirmative relief from removal. A noncitizen in removal proceedings is eligible for adjustment of status if s/he is otherwise admissible. Waivers are available for certain grounds of inadmissibility. As with affirmative applications for adjustment of status, those who are out of status are not eligible for adjustment, unless they are immediate relatives of citizen sponsors, or are employment-based preference immigrants who have not been out of status more than 180 days.

An eligible noncitizen already in removal proceedings can apply for adjustment of status with the immigration judge directly.[85] The judge has the discretion to

---

[82] INA § 240A(b)(4).

[83] Pub. L. 105-100; 111 Stat. 2160, 2193.

[84] Cuadra v. Gonzales, 417 F.3d 947, 950–52 (8th Cir. 2005).

[85] 8 C.F.R. § 245.2(a)(1).

deny removal and grant adjustment of status; that decision is reviewable by the Board of Immigration Appeals.[86]

c.   Asylum and Withholding of Removal

Asylum and withholding of removal may be sought in removal proceedings by persons fleeing persecution in their home countries. This section describes each form of relief and the law that has developed around concepts within each form of relief. Asylum-related relief draws from international as well as domestic sources of law for its existence. The United States is a signatory to the 1967 United Nations Protocol Relating to the Status of Refugees, which governs the treatment of asylees and refugees. Although the Protocol and similar international agreements are not self-executing,[87] they do provide persuasive authority for issues that arise in asylum-related cases.

Asylum is a form of relief available to those noncitizens in removal proceedings who face persecution or have a well-founded fear of persecution upon removal because of race, religion, nationality, membership in a particular social group, or political opinion.[88] Asylum is not available, however, to "any person who ordered, incited, assisted, or otherwise participated in the persecution of any person on account of race, religion, nationality, membership in a particular social group, or political opinion."[89] The statute lists several additional reasons for which a court can deny asylum, including conviction of a serious crime which creates a danger to the community, conviction of a serious crime outside the United States, security grounds, or that the asylum applicant was firmly resettled in a third country before arriving in the United States.[90]

The respondent in a removal case has the burden to show that s/he has a well-founded fear of persecution on account of one of the enumerated categories.[91] The feared persecution must arise at the hands of the government or by persons or organizations the government is unwilling or unable to control.[92] The "on account of," or "nexus," requirement requires evidence that the persecution or threatened persecution is because of, or premised on, race, religion, nationality, political opinion, or membership in a particular social group.

---

[86] 8 C.F.R. § 1003.1(b)(3).

[87] They do not go into full effect without action by Congress to enact them through accompanying legislation. *See* Haitian Refugee Center v. Baker, 949 F.2d 1109 (11th Cir. 1991).

[88] INA §§ 208, 235. *See* INA § 101(a)(42) for the definition of refugee. An asylum applicant has the burden to show s/he meets the refugee definition. INA § 208(b)(1)(B).

[89] INA § 101(a)(42)(B).

[90] INA § 208(b)(2).

[91] I.N.S. v. Elias-Zacarias, 502 U.S. 478 (1992); Sangha v. I.N.S., 103 F.3d 1482, 1486–87 (9th Cir. 1997).

[92] *See, e.g.,* Favlova v. I.N.S., 441 F.3d 82, 91–92 (2d Cir. 2006) (reversing BIA denial of asylum where applicant showed that Russian government was unwilling to control religiously motivated persecution of Baptists); Fiadjoe v. Attorney General, 411 F.3d 135, 160–63 (reversing BIA asylum denial where country report noted it would be futile to report slave practices of religious sect to police who were not willing to stop such persecutory practices); Singh v. I.N.S., 94 F.3d 1353, 1360 (9th Cir. 1996).

Well-founded fear of persecution has been defined by the courts as a reasonable possibility of persecution.[93] In *I.N.S. v. Cardoza-Fonseca*, the Supreme Court, in determining the definition of well-founded fear in INA § 101(a)(42), noted that this subjective standard is lower than the objective "more likely than not" standard which the INS advocated.[94] The BIA and lower courts have since interpreted a fear as well-founded if "a reasonable person in [the applicant's] circumstances would fear persecution."[95] A person seeking asylum must have suffered past persecution or fear future persecution because of his/her status in one or more of the protected categories in the statute. Persecution has been defined as a threat to the life or freedom of, or the infliction of suffering or harm upon, those who differ in a way regarded as offensive.[96]

The persecution or fear of persecution claimed by the respondent has both objective and subjective components. The asylum applicant must show that s/he considers government action or inaction persecutory. It is the persecution viewed from the point of view of the asylum applicant that is relevant. The intent of the persecutor, moreover, is not relevant, as long as the act is objectively considered persecution, and the applicant him/herself considers it persecution or threatened persecution.[97] The objective component can be met by showing as little as a 10% chance of persecution. The immigration regulations establish a rebuttable presumption that evidence of past persecution creates a well-founded fear of future persecution.[98] The government can rebut the presumption by showing either a "fundamental change in circumstances" (e.g., a change in country conditions), or that the applicant could "avoid future persecution by relocating to another part of the applicant's country . . . and it would be reasonable to expect the applicant to do so."[99]

The statute requires that an asylum applicant file an application for asylum within one year of arriving in the United States. Procedurally, an applicant must show by "clear and convincing evidence" that an application for asylum was filed within one year of arrival[100], that there are "changed circumstances which materially affect the applicant's eligibility for asylum,"[101] or that the delay in filing an application was because of "extraordinary circumstances."[102]

---

[93] *See* I.N.S. v. Cardoza-Fonseca, 480 U.S. 421 (1987); Matter of Mogharrabi, 19 I. & N. Dec. 439 (BIA 1987); 8 C.F.R. §§ 208.139b)(2)(B).

[94] Cardoza-Fonseca, 480 U.S. at 430–431 (the well founded fear standard "obviously makes the eligibility determination turn to some extent on the subjective mental state of the alien" and an alien can "certainly have a well founded fear of an event happening when there is less than a 50% chance of the occurrence taking place").

[95] Matter of Mogharrabi, 19 I. &N. Dec. 439, 445 (BIA 1987).

[96] Matter of Acosta, 19 I. & N. Dec. 211, 222 (1985); *see also* Li v. Attorney General of the U.S., 400 F.3d 157, 164–68 (3d Cir. 2005) (reviewing legislative history of persecution).

[97] INS v. Elias-Zacarias, 502 U.S. 478 (1992).

[98] 8 C.F.R. § 208.13(b)(1).

[99] 8 C.F.R. § 1208.13(b)(1)(i).

[100] INA § 208(a)(2)(B).

[101] INA § 208(a)(2)(D).

[102] INA § 208(a)(3).

A grant of asylum entitles the applicant to remain in the country, authorizes him or her to work, and allows him or her to travel abroad with prior consent.[103] It also allows him or her to sponsor immediate relatives for immigrant petitions[104] and to acquire permanent residency.[105]

Withholding of removal is another remedy available to those whose life or freedom the immigration court determines would be threatened if removed to their home countries because of race, religion, nationality, membership in a particular social group, or political opinion.[106] It is a more narrow remedy that allows an applicant to stay in the United States to avoid removal to a country where the applicant will more likely than not face persecution. The same application for asylum covers a withholding of removal claim.[107] Withholding of removal corresponds to the concept of nonrefoulement in international law.[108] The concept of withholding first appeared in immigration law in 1950 in the context of deportation proceedings. At that time Congress prohibited deportation if a deportee would be subject to physical persecution.[109] The provision was made discretionary in 1952, and was changed to persecution on account of race, religion, or political opinion in 1965. In 1967 the United States agreed to abide by the 1967 U.N. Protocol Relating to the Status of Refugees, which itself incorporated the nonrefoulement provisions of the 1951 Convention Relating to the Status of Refugees.[110] The Convention provides the basis for the current withholding provision, at INA § 241. The statute states, in accord with the Convention, "The Attorney General may not remove an alien to a country if the Attorney General decides that the alien's life or freedom would be threatened in that country because of the alien's race, religion, nationality, membership in a particular social group, or political opinion."[111]

Withholding is a more limited remedy than asylum. Withholding is available only to the applicant. A noncitizen seeking withholding cannot include a spouse or children in his/her application. Withholding requires a showing of "clear probability of persecution," a higher standard than the "past persecution" or "well-founded fear of persecution" required of asylum applicants. Clear probability has been defined as a greater than 50% chance of persecution. On the other hand, withholding is mandatory once a "clear probability of persecution" has been

---

[103] INA 208(c)(1).

[104] INA § 208(b)(3).

[105] INA § 209.

[106] INA § 241(b)(3).

[107] 8 C.F.R. 208.1(a).

[108] Nonrefoulement is an international law principle, codified in various international conventions, that attempts to protect refugees from being repatriated back to countries where their lives or their freedom would be in jeopardy.

[109] Internal Security Act of 1950, 64 Stat. 987, 1010 (Sept. 23, 1950).

[110] Article 33 of the Convention states that "No Contracting State shall expel or return ("refouler") a refugee in any manner whatsoever to the frontiers of territories where his life or freedom would be threatened on account of his race, religion, nationality, membership of a particular social group or political opinion."

[111] INA § 241(b)(3).

proven, while a grant of asylum is discretionary.

In 2005, Congress passed the REAL ID Act, which modified the standard for determining both asylum and withholding. The Act requires that the applicant must "establish that race, religion, nationality, membership in a particular social group, or political opinion was or will be at least one central reason for persecuting the applicant."[112] Previous case law precedent only required a showing that the persecution would be "at least in part" on account of a protected ground.

The following categories of noncitizens are ineligible for withholding of removal: persons who have persecuted others or participated in their persecution; persons convicted of a serious crime and who are a danger to the community; persons who have committed a serious non-political crime outside the United States; and persons who can reasonably be regarded as security risks.[113]

d.   Convention Against Torture

An applicant who seeks asylum or withholding will typically also seek protection under the Convention Against Torture (CAT). The United States became a party to the United Nations Convention Against Torture and other Forms of Inhuman or Degrading Treatment or Punishment in 1994. Pursuant to the international agreement, Congress enacted legislation stating that "it will be the policy of the United States not to expel, extradite, or otherwise effect the involuntary return of any person to a country in which there are substantial grounds for believing the person would be in danger of being subjected to torture, regardless of whether the person is physically present in the United States."[114] INS promulgated rules to implement the legislation in 1999. CAT is not limited to protection for those who fit within the five protected grounds of asylum and withholding of removal.

There are two types of CAT protection.[115] The first is similar to withholding of removal and is referred to as Article 3 withholding. The second is called "deferral of removal" and is available to those who are barred from obtaining Article 3 withholding. The mandatory bars are the same as those for withholding under INA § 241(b)(3)(B). If even one of the bars exists, a judge must grant deferral of removal.

A CAT applicant must meet the definition of torture, which is defined as (1) an intentional act that (2) inflicts severe pain or suffering, mental or physical; (3) on a person or a third person who is in custody or control of the torturer; (4) with the consent, instigation, or acquiescence of a person acting in an official capacity; (5) with the purpose of coercing, intimidating or punishing the person or a third person, or obtaining a confession or information from the person or a third person. The applicant has the burden to show that it is "more likely than not" that s/he will

---

[112] REAL ID Act § 101(a)(30(B)(i), codified at INA § 208(b)(1)(B)(i).

[113] INA § 241(b)(3).

[114] PL 105–277, Title XXI Foreign Affairs and Restructuring Act of 1998, § 2242(a), 112 Stat. 2681–822, 105th Cong. 2d Sess. (1998); *see also* regulations relating to definition of torture at 8 C.F.R. § 208.16–18.

[115] 8 C.F.R. § 208.16(c)(2).

be tortured if removed to the proposed country.

In a CAT case, it may be difficult to determine government acquiescence. The regulations have defined it as prior awareness of the torture and a subsequent breach of a legal duty to intervene to prevent the torture.

CAT benefits are narrow. CAT relief does not lead to permanent residency. Nor does it provide for family members to join the applicant. It also does not prevent removal to a third country. A grant of deferral of removal under CAT is subject to termination. Withholding or deferral under CAT may be terminated if there is no longer a likelihood of torture in the person's country of origin.

e.   Registry (INA § 249; 8 U.S.C. 1259)

If a respondent in removal proceedings entered the United States before January 1, 1972 and has maintained continuous presence since then, that respondent may be eligible for a form of relief known as registry. The purpose of registry is to "create a legal record of entry for those who have none."[116] The registry provision allows those who have been in the United States illegally for a period of time to register and become lawful permanent residents. Originally, registry was a form of relief available to those who entered illegally and remained in the United States for at least five years. Consistent with this purpose, the dates of entry for registry eligibility were advanced every year until 1972. Since then, Congress has failed to update the cut-off date for registry eligibility. Thus, instead of providing relief to those who have resided in the United States for at least five years, the registry is now only available to those who can prove continuous residence for more than 7 times that long, rendering it progressively less useful.

In addition to continuous residence, a registry applicant must show that s/he is a person of good moral character, is not ineligible for citizenship, is not deportable as a terrorist or Nazi, and is not inadmissible as a criminal, subversive, violator of drug laws, smuggler, or immoral person under INA § 212(a). Moreover, noncitizens who entered the United States lawfully are ineligible for registry.

f.   Private Bills

Congressional legislators have the power to grant equitable relief from removal in the form of private legislation. Any member of Congress can introduce a bill to provide lawful permanent resident status for a private individual who cannot otherwise get relief. This is a very limited form of relief because very few private bills are introduced and passed each year. A stay of removal is not automatic with the introduction of private legislation, so an applicant must make a separate application for such a stay. Once a congressional committee seeks a report from DHS, a stay is usually granted.

The first step in obtaining this relief is to seek a Congressional sponsor to introduce a bill. The bill then goes to the immigration subcommittees of the Judiciary committees in each house of Congress. There are rules and protocols for

---

[116] Angulo-Dominguez v. Ashcroft, 290 F.3d 1147, 1149 (9th Cir. 2003).

granting such relief, which is usually predicated on extreme hardship.[117]

2.   Limited Relief

a.   Deferred Action

Deferred action is an administrative decision by the USCIS District Director, the Regional Commissioner, or their designees, not to prosecute or deport an individual who is otherwise removable. Deferred action may not be granted by an immigration judge. It does not confer any right to remain in the United States. Instead, it is considered an administrative decision to give a particular case or set of cases lower priority when setting priorities for removal. Among the factors that the agency considers in determining whether to grant deferred action are the likelihood of ultimately removing the noncitizen; the presence of favorable factors and whether those factors will generate adverse publicity; whether the person's continued presence is needed for an ongoing investigation or prosecution; and whether the individual is within a class of noncitizens targeted for high enforcement priority. The decision to grant deferred action is discretionary and cannot be judicially reviewed.[118]

b.   Voluntary Departure[119]

Voluntary departure is a form of relief that allows those who have received a notice to appear in removal proceedings to leave the United States on their own, rather than through a removal order. An immigration judge may grant voluntary departure at the beginning or at the end of removal proceedings as an alternative to issuing a removal order. Leaving the United States through voluntary departure avoids the ten year inadmissibility ground, which is triggered with a removal order.[120] It also avoids reinstatement of removal actions in the event the person returns to the United States illegally.

If a noncitizen seeks voluntary departure at the beginning of removal proceedings, s/he must be able to pay his/her own way out the country and must not be deportable as an aggravated felon or on terrorist grounds.[121] The respondent who seeks voluntary departure at the beginning of proceedings must concede removability, must make no other requests for relief from removal, and must waive all appeals. Because voluntary departure is discretionary relief, the respondent must show evidence of favorable factors and must explain away

---

[117] *See* Ryan Quinn and Stephen Yale-Loehr, *Private Immigration Bills: An Overview*, 9 BIB 1147 (Oct. 1, 2004) for an overview of the private bill process. *See* Robert Hopp and Juan P. Osuna, *Remedies of Last Resort: Private Bills and Deferred Action*, IMMIGRATION BRIEFINGS (June 1997) for an overview of criteria and procedures for private bills.

[118] Reno v. American-Arab Anti-Discrimination Comm., 525 U.S. 471 (1999).

[119] INA § 240B.

[120] INA § 212(a)(9)(A). Note that it does not avoid the separate 3- and 10-year bars that are a result of a noncitizen's unlawful presence within the United States for more than 180 days and one year, respectively.

[121] INA § 237(a)(2)(A)(ii) & § 237(a)(4)(B).

negative factors.[122] A judge may grant up to 120 days for voluntary departure if it is sought before the completion of proceedings.

Voluntary departure may also be sought at the conclusion of removal proceedings. The requirements at this stage of litigation are more stringent. The applicant must show that s/he has been physically present in the United States for at least one year prior to the initiation of removal proceedings, demonstrate good moral character for at least five years prior to the application, and s/he must not be deportable as an aggravated felon or terrorist.[123] The applicant must establish by clear and convincing evidence that s/he intends to, and has the means to, depart the United States.[124]

Voluntary departure at the conclusion of proceedings may be granted for no more than 60 days.[125] The applicant must post a departure bond within five days of the voluntary departure grant.

c.   Stays of Removal

A stay of removal is available for those who have been ordered removed and need more time in the United States. It is discretionary and is granted by U.S. Immigration and Customs Enforcement.[126] A stay is not automatically granted on appeal of an immigration judge's decision. Therefore, an applicant who appeals must also seek a stay of removal to avoid removal while an appeal is pending.

---

[122]   Matter of Arguelles, 22 I. & N. Dec. 811 (BIA 1999).

[123]   INA § 240B(b).

[124]   INA § 240B(b)(1)(D).

[125]   INA § 240B(b)(2).

[126]   8 C.F.R. § 1003.6(b).

Chapter 12

THE REMOVAL PROCESS

A. OVERVIEW OF THE REMOVAL PROCESS

The 1996 amendments to the INA established one administrative hearing system for noncitizens under INA § 240.[1] In a removal hearing an Immigration Judge decides issues relating to admissibility, deportability (removal after admission) and the grounds of relief from removal, including asylum. There are some key exceptions to the use of "ordinary" removal proceedings under INA § 240. These include: removal proceedings at federal, state and local prisons;[2] summary removal proceedings for aggravated felons;[3] summary procedures applied to crew members; and special terrorist removal court procedures.[4] Expedited removal, another exception to the ordinary removal procedure under INA § 240, applies to some applicants for admission into the U.S. and is covered in Chapter 10.[5]

This Chapter includes a review of these removal procedures as well as detention under the INA. The constitutional issues, including due process requirements, are covered in Chapter 3.B.

B. THE REMOVAL HEARING

1. Notice to Appear

Removal proceedings begin when DHS files a charging document with the Office of the Immigration Judge called a Notice to Appear [NTA].[6] The NTA is served on the noncitizen in person or by mail.[7] Under INA § 239, the NTA must provide notice about the nature of the proceeding, the specific alleged violations of law and information about the right to be represented by counsel at no expense to the government. The noncitizen also must be provided a list of free legal services.[8] The NTA requires the noncitizen immediately to provide an address and telephone number (if any) where she may be contacted by the Immigration Judge.[9] Issues

---

[1] Illegal Immigration Reform and Immigrant Responsibility Act of 1996, Pub. L. 104–208, 110 Stat. 3009 (IIRIRA), effective as of April 1, 1997. The term removable means, as defined in INA § 240(e)(2), that a noncitizen is either inadmissible under INA § 212(a) if she has not been admitted or that an noncitizen deportable under INA § 237 in she has been admitted to the U.S.

[2] INA § 238(a)(1).

[3] INA § 238(a)(2).

[4] INA § 236A (mandatory detention of suspected terrorists). Under INA § 236A(5) detention up to 7 days is permitted before an NTA or criminal arrest warrant must be issued.

[5] INA § 235.

[6] Form I-862, formerly referred to as an Order to Show Cause.

[7] Before IIRIRA, the charging document had to be served by certified mail. Under INA § 239(a)(1), (a)(2), personal service of any hearing notice is required if practicable, including changes of hearing dates and times. *See* In re M-D-, 23 I & N Dec. 540, 542 (BIA 2002).

[8] A hearing may not be scheduled until at least ten days after service of the NTA in order to provide the noncitizen the opportunity to obtain counsel.

[9] INA § 239(a)(1)(F)(i) & (ii) (Immediate notice also is required upon a change of address or telephone number.). Under INA § 239(c), service by mail on the noncitizen or his or her attorney is sufficient if sent to the address provided by the noncitizen when the NTA was initially issued.

relating to notice often arise in *in absentia* hearing (discussed in Section D.2. of this Chapter).

An NTA may be issued in a variety of circumstances. An NTA may be issued to a noncitizen after an arrest, to an arriving noncitizen, or to an individual who is already present in the United States, in order to begin removal proceedings. The INA distinguishes between those who have not been admitted deemed "arriving" noncitizens and other noncitizens who have not been admitted.[10] For example, those apprehended within the U.S. are not in the category of arriving noncitizens.

The INA covers both an arrest with a warrant (INA § 236) and an arrest without a warrant, upon reasonable suspicion, (INA § 287(a)). Arrest without a warrant, under INA § 287(a), may be made by an employee or officer authorized by the Secretary of Homeland Security.[11] If a noncitizen is arrested without a warrant, an NTA must be issued to begin removal proceedings within 48 hours of the arrest.[12] The decision whether to grant bond and release or continue detention also must be made within 48 hours. The subject of interior enforcement and the enforcement powers of DHS are covered in Chapter 13.G.

There is broad prosecutorial discretion to decide when and whether to issue an NTA.[13] An immigration officer may permit the noncitizen to depart the U.S. voluntarily rather than begin removal proceedings. Most noncitizens who are apprehended do not go through removal proceedings. In FY 2005, there were 965,538 voluntary departures and only 208,531 formal removals from the U.S.[14]

2.   Bond and Detention

The detention of noncitizens arriving at a border port of entry and seeking admission traditionally has been within the exclusive power of Congress and the Executive Branch implementing the INA.[15] Many provisions of the INA require or permit detention during the removal process of both arriving noncitizens seeking

---

[10] INA §§ 235(a)(1), 101(a)(13). A noncitizen is an arriving alien whether or not she arrives at a designated port of arrival and this includes aliens brought to the U.S. after having been interdicted in the international or U.S. waters.

[11] INA § 287 (a)(2) (The authority to arrest an individual without a warrant exists if the officer or employee has reason to believe a noncitizen is entering, attempting to enter or is present in the U.S. in violation of any law or regulation and the noncitizen is likely to escape before an arrest warrant can be obtained.).

[12] 8 C.F.R. § 287.3(d). The DHS regulations provide this procedural protection and in the case of emergency or extraordinary circumstances the removal hearing may begin with the issuance of the NTA after 48 hours. If a criminal arrest warrant is issued, in lieu of an NTA, it too must be issued within the 48 hours of the arrest of a noncitizen.

[13] Generally, an NTA will not be issued when a noncitizen is in some kind of deferred action program, if an immigrant visa is pending and, upon approval, the noncitizen will be eligible to adjust status, if a conviction is vacated or about to be vacated, if the noncitizen is a member of the armed forces, or if the noncitizen is an asylee.

[14] *See* 2005 DHS Yearbook of Immigration Statistics 95, Table 38.

[15] Wong Wing v. U.S., 163 U.S. 228 (1896); Schaughnessy v. United States ex rel. Mezei, 345 U.S. 206 (1953).

admission into the U.S. and noncitizens apprehended in the U.S.[16] Release from detention may occur by posting a bond under INA § 236(a) or by parole under INA § 212(d)(5). Each of these options is discussed below.

Detention has been expanded by the addition of mandatory detention provisions to the INA. Initially, this was an effort to ensure that noncitizens appear at their removal hearings and leave the U.S. if a removal order is issued. Detention while the removal proceedings are pending may last for months, and the noncitizen often is held in facilities far away from family and friends. The INA detention requirements, policies and administration have been the subject of significant and on-going criticism based on the conditions in facilities and broad use of these policies.[17] One concern has been detention in remote locations which can compromise an attorney's capacity to adequately represent clients because of the distance and lack of regular contact.[18]

Generally, noncitizens placed in removal proceedings are eligible for release in a bond hearing before an Immigration Judge under INA § 236(a) unless they have committed certain crimes or are suspected terrorists. Generally, noncitizens applying for admission are not eligible for release on bond. If a noncitizen has been arrested, a decision whether to continue detention pending removal or release on bond pending removal must be made within 48 hours of an arrest.[19] This time limit does not apply to noncitizens detained as certified suspected terrorists under INA § 236A.

If a noncitizen is eligible for bond and release from detention, then the statutory limits in INA 236(a) apply including a bond of at least § 1500.00.[20] The initial determination is made by the DHS District Director and the District Director may impose any other conditions of release in addition to the payment of security for the bond. The noncitizen has the burden to establish that she does not present a danger to persons or property, is not a threat to national security and does not pose a risk of flight under INA § 236(a).[21] The decision about whether to grant a bond usually is based on local family ties, prior arrests, convictions, appearances at

---

[16] INA §§ 235(a)(1), 101(a)(13). A noncitizen is an arriving alien whether or not she arrives at a designated port of arrival and this includes aliens brought to the U.S. after having been interdicted in the international or U.S. waters.

[17] *See* GAO Report, Alien Detention Standards (2007); M. Dow, American Gulag: Inside U.S. Immigration Prisons (2004); Pistone, *Justice Delayed Is Justice Denied: A Proposal for Ending the Unnecessary Detention of Asylum Seekers*, 12 Harv. Human Rights L.J. 197 (1999) (criticizing the detention of asylum seekers in the expedited removal process under INA § 235(a)).

[18] *See* Taylor, *Promoting Legal Representation for Detained Aliens: Litigation and Administrative Reform*, 29 Conn. L. Rev. 1647 (1997).

[19] 8 C.F.R. § 287.3(d) ("except in the even of an emergency or other extraordinary circumstance in which case a determination will be made within an additional reasonable period of time, whether the alien will be continued in custody or released on bond or recognizance").

[20] INA § 236(a)(2). The noncitizen's release on either bond or conditional parole is subject to revocation, resulting in rearrest under the original warrant and detention.

[21] 8 CFR § 1003.19(a)-(c). *See* Matter of D.J., 23 I&N Dec. 572 (A.G. 2003) (denial of bond premised on a general immigration policy issue represented a national security concern, i.e., the possibility of mass migration from Haiti and the Dominican Republic).

hearings, employment or lack of employment, membership in community organizations, manner of entry and length of time in the U.S., and financial ability to post bond.[22]

Mandatory detention during removal proceedings applies to noncitizens who are inadmissible or deportable for criminal offenses and terrorist activities under INA § 236(c). These noncitizens are ineligible for bond.[23] Mandatory detention under 236(c) applies to noncitizens: (1) inadmissible under any criminal ground or any security-related ground in § 212(a); (2) deportable under certain criminal grounds including multiple criminal convictions aggravated felonies, controlled substances, certain firearms offense and miscellaneous crimes; (3) deportable for a crime of moral turpitude if the sentence is to a term of imprisonment of at least one year; or (4) deportable for terrorist activities or association with terrorist organizations.[24] There are very limited grounds for release from custody under INA § 236(c)(2).[25] This statutory mandate has been upheld in by the Supreme Court.[26]

Bond is available to some noncitizens with criminal convictions under INA § 236(a). If the noncitizen has not committed a crime under INA § 236(c), then she is not subject to mandatory detention and is eligible for release on bond or conditional parole under INA § 236(a).

Detention pursuant to an arrest with or without a warrant is possible.[27] Under § 236(a), a noncitizen may be arrested and detained on a warrant issued by the Attorney General. An arrest without warrant is authorized under INA § 287(a).[28] Detention after an arrest is only permissible for 48 hours, at which point a decision must be made whether: (1) to begin removal proceedings by issuing an NTA; (2) to file criminal charges; or (3) to release the noncitizen from custody.[29] Detention up to seven days is permissible for certified suspected terrorists under INA § 236A. The procedures applied to certified terrorists under INA § 236A are discussed in Section C.5 of this Chapter.

---

[22] Matter of Patel, 15 I & N Dec. 666 (BIA 1976).

[23] INA §§ 236(c); 235(b)(1)(A); 235(b)(2); 235(b)(1)(B)(ii) (after a credible fear determination in expedited removal).

[24] INA § 236(c). Noncitizens subject to expedited removal under INA § 235(b) are also subject to mandatory detention.

[25] INA § 236(c)(2) permits release to assist in a major crime investigation, if release does not pose any risk to the safety of other persons or property, and if the noncitizen is likely to appear at any scheduled proceeding.

[26] Demore v. Kim, 538 U.S. 510 (2003) (upholding mandatory detention pending removal proceedings under INA § 236(c) of a lawful permanent resident who had conceded deportability based on a criminal conviction).

[27] INA § 287(a) permits interrogation and arrest by any officer or authorized employee of DHS if the noncitizen enters or attempts to enter unlawfully in view of the officer or if reasonable suspicion exists that the noncitizen is in the U.S. in violation of any law or regulation and is likely to escape before a warrant can be obtained.

[28] Under INA § 236(a), after a warrant has been issued, a noncitizen may be released from detention on a bond (minimum bond of § 1,500 and any other conditions imposed by the Attorney General) or released on conditional parole.

[29] 8 C.F.R § 287.3(d). See *supra* note 13.

Arriving noncitizens seeking admission into the U.S. must be detained under INA § 235(b)(2) and are not eligible for release on bond under INA § 236(a).[30] This includes lawful permanent residents who seek admission as defined in INA § 101(a)(13). Release on parole for very limited reasons is possible for arriving noncitizens.[31] Decisions about parole of an arriving noncitizen are made by District Directors and there is no review by an Immigration Judge of this determination even in the case of a lawful permanent resident.[32]

Noncitizens who are apprehended and detained under INA § 236 may seek review of the DHS detention decision before an Immigration Judge in a bond hearing. There is no review by an Immigration Judge of a DHS decision to deny bond and release if the noncitizen is detained under INA § 236(c) on criminal or terrorism grounds. All Immigration Judge decisions about bond or parole are discretionary judgments and are precluded from judicial review under INA § 236(e), which includes discretionary judgments regarding detention, release, and the grant or denial of parole or bond.[33] Arriving noncitizens who are detained by ICE under INA § 235 may not appeal a DHS custody decision to an Immigration Judge.[34]

3.   Legal Representation

At the removal hearing, the Immigration Judge must inform the noncitizen of the right to representation by counsel.[35] INA § 240(b)(4)(a) specifies that noncitizens "have the privilege of being represented, at no expense to the Government, by counsel of the alien's choosing who is authorized to practice in such proceedings."[36] The Immigration Judge must verify on the record whether or not the noncitizen wishes to be represented by counsel.[37] The noncitizen also must be informed by the Immigration Judge about the availability of free legal services, and the right to present evidence, cross examine witnesses, and appeal.[38]

---

[30] Under INA § 235(b)(2)(A) arriving noncitizens seeking admission, other than LPRs, must establish they are "clearly and beyond a doubt entitled to be admitted." An arriving noncitizen who is not clearly and beyond doubt entitled to admission "shall be detained" for a removal hearing under INA § 240. 8 C.F.R. § 236.1(c)(2). Kurzban's Immigration Law Sourcebook 136 (11th ed. 2008).

[31] INA § 212(d)(5). (Noncitizens applying for admission are eligible discretionary parole for on a case-by-case basis for "urgent humanitarian reasons or significant public benefit." Refugees are eligible only if there are "compelling reasons in the public interest."); 8 C.F.R. § 212.5 provides for the release on parole of an arriving noncitizen in the case of a serious medical condition; a pregnant woman; certain juveniles; and witnesses in government proceedings; and if detention is not in the public interest.

[32] See 8 C.F.R. § 236.1(c)(11). See also Matter of Collado-Munoz, 21 I&N Dec. 1061 (BIA 1997) (an LPR arriving at a border post of entry and seeking admission is not entitled to a bond hearing before an Immigration Judge).

[33] Judicial review is still available to raise constitutional or statutory challenges by habeas corpus.

[34] Arriving noncitizens are eligible for parole only and there is no renew by IJs of this discretionary decision. 8 C.F.R. §§ 236.1(c)(2), 212.5(b), 235.1(d).

[35] 8 C.F.R. § 1240.10(a)(1).

[36] See also INA § 292.

[37] 8 C.F.R. § 1240.10(a)(1).

[38] 8 C.F.R. § 1240.11(a)(2) refers to an Immigration Judge's obligation to inform of benefits for which the respondent has apparent eligibility if the record raises the reasonable possibility of eligibility. See,

There is no constitutional right to appointed counsel under the Sixth Amendment because deportation from the U.S. is not viewed as punishment akin to a criminal conviction.[39] Fifth Amendment procedural due process requirements must be met in deportation hearings. A right to the effective assistance of counsel exists under the Fifth Amendment, but a lack of representation does not violate due process.[40] In *Aguilera-Enriguez v. INS*, 516 F. 2d 565 (6th Cir. 1975), *cert. denied*, 423 U.S. 1050 (1976), the Sixth Circuit held that the "fundamental fairness" required under the Fifth Amendment is satisfied even when an indigent noncitizen, who requested appointed counsel, lacks any representation in a deportation hearing.

Noncitizens who are not represented by counsel are at a substantial disadvantage in removal proceedings, although lack of representation is not a denial *per se* of procedural due process.[41] A lack of representation, in some instances, can violate due process because of a lack of fundamental fairness. For example, in *Jacinto v. INS*, 208 F. 3d 735 (9th Cir. 2000), the court of appeals found that a noncitizen who was unrepresented was denied procedural due process because the Immigration Judge did not fully explain the right to representation by counsel or give her a full opportunity to present testimony.[42] In this case, the noncitizen requested asylum, withholding of deportation and voluntary departure. There was confusion because the noncitizen did not appear to understand she could be represented by counsel and also speak for herself and present testimony in support of her applications.

Ineffective assistance of counsel can violate principles of fundamental fairness and procedural due process guarantees. The due process right to representation includes a right to competent representation. The BIA has identified criteria for ineffective assistance of counsel claims to determine whether competent counsel would have acted otherwise and whether counsel's performance was so inadequate that it *may* have affected the outcome.[43] From 1988 to January 2009, under the BIA decision *Matter of Lozado*, an ineffective assistance of counsel claim must be supported by: (1) an affidavit setting forth the agreement that was entered into with former counsel with respect to the actions to be taken, as well as any representations made by counsel to the alien; (2) proof that the movant has informed former counsel of the allegations in writing as well as any response received; and (3) a statement detailing whether a complaint has been filed with appropriate disciplinary authorities and if not, why not.[44]

---

e.g., U.S. v. Arrieta, 224 F.3d 1076 (9th Cir. 2000) (apparent eligibility for INA § 212(h) relief).

[39] *See* Fong Yue Ting v. United States, 149 U.S. 698 (1893), discussed in Chapter 2.

[40] U.S. v. Gouveia, 467 U.S. 180 (1984).

[41] Fundamental fairness does not require that children are represented by counsel. *See, e.g.*, Machado v. Ashcroft, No CS-02-066-FVS (E.D.Wash. 2002), 79 Interp. Rel. 1044–45 (2003).

[42] *See also* Biwot v. Gonzales, 403 F.3d 1094, 1032–34 (9th Cir. 2004) (finding a violation of procedural due process when a noncitizen in detention was given only 5 days to find counsel).

[43] The Ninth Circuit has held that the BIA criteria should not be applied rigidly when other information sufficiently indicates the ineffective assistance of counsel may have affected the outcome of the case. Morales Apolinar v. Mukasey, 514 F.3d 893, 898 (9th Cir. 2008).

[44] Matter of Lozada, 19 I & N Dec. 637, 639 (BIA 1988).

In January 2009, shortly before the inauguration of President Obama, the Attorney General overruled *Matter of Lozado* by finding that only a statutory privilege to retain counsel exists, not a constitutional right under procedural due process guarantees of the Fifth Amendment. In *Matter of Compean*, a new set of criteria for deficient performance of counsel are identified. A person must show: (1) the lawyer's failing were egregious; and (2) prejudice resulted from the lawyer's errors.[45]

The lack of legal representation is a critical issue for noncitizens in removal proceedings who are often detained in remote locations and must rely on *pro bono* representation. A 2005 study by the Migration Policy Institute found that 24% of detainees represented by counsel in removal proceedings were successful in their claims for relief from removal compared to only 15% of unrepresented detainees.[46]

Legal assistance to noncitizens by federally funded Legal Services Corporation [LSC] agencies is very limited. LSC-funded organizations may only provide services to noncitizens who are permanent residents, immediate relatives of U.S. citizens who have applied for adjustment of status, noncitizens granted refugee status or asylum, or noncitizens granted withholding of removal under INA § 241(b)(3). There is an exception to the ban allows an entity to use non-LSC funds to serve victims of domestic abuse and for persons who have established a credible fear of persecution.[47]

Non-lawyers may represent noncitizens. Qualified organizations may practice before the Immigration Court and DHS if recognized by the Board of Immigration Appeals [BIA].[48] Law students and law graduates not yet admitted to practice also may represent noncitizens under the rules.[49]

Group rights presentations by lawyers now occur in many detainee facilities where noncitizens are detained pending removal. Detention pending removal is covered later in this Chapter. The need for adequate legal assistance is critical as the detainee population increases. These presentations inform noncitizens about the general process and issues in a removal hearing. These are conducted by lawyers and others who provide written materials, some counseling about individual cases, and, in some cases, pro bono legal representation.[50]

---

[45] Matter of Compean, 24 I & N Dec. 710 (A.G. 2009).

[46] *See* Kerwin, *Revisiting the Need for Appointed Counsel*, Migration Policy Institute Insight 6 (April 2005). The disparity has been particularly pronounced for asylum seekers. Non-detained applicants for asylum represented by counsel were granted relief in 39% of cases while unrepresented non-detained applicants were granted relief in only 14% of cases. *See* http://www.migrationpolicy.org/insight/Insight_Kerwin.pdf (last visited Nov. 6, 2008).

[47] 45 CFR §§ 1626.4, 1625.5.

[48] 8 C.F.R. § 292.2(a). Qualified organizations include any non-profit religious, charitable, social service or similar organization demonstrating it has at its disposal adequate knowledge, information and experience, and charges only nominal fees.

[49] The law student must be directly supervised by a faculty member, attorney or other accredited representative.

[50] *See EOIR Adds 12 new Legal Orientation Program Sites*, 85 Inter. Rel. 2781 (Oct. 20, 2008); Andrew I. Schoenholz, *The State of Asylum Representation: Ideas for Change*, 16 Geo. Imm. L.J. 739 (2002); Christopher Nugent, *Strengthening Access to Justice: Prehearing Rights Presentations for*

4.   Evidence, Burden of Proof and Hearing Procedures

This section covers how the removal hearing is conducted by the Immigration Judge. The hearing procedures used by an Immigration Judge can be challenged under procedural due process protections of the Fifth Amendment to U.S. Constitution if these violate fundamental fairness.[51] This section also covers evidence, the burden of proof and standard of proof in removal hearings.

a.   Hearing Procedures

The removal hearing is conducted by the Immigration Judge who administers oaths, receives evidence, and may interrogate, examine and cross-examine the noncitizen and any witnesses.[52] The noncitizen has a right to present evidence and cross-examine witnesses, including the right to present expert testimony. The noncitizen must receive a full and fair hearing, and if a noncitizen is prejudiced by the Immigration Judge's conduct of the hearing then there may be a violation of due process.[53] This requires the Immigration Judge to fully develop the record, and an Immigration Judge's refusal to allow the presentation of evidence may be a denial of procedural due process.[54] The Immigration Judge also must notify the noncitizen of her apparent eligibility for any forms of relief from removal. Relief from removal is covered in Chapter 11.

In *Jacinto v. INS*, a case involving an unrepresented person, the Immigration Judge did not clearly explain that the noncitizen had the right to testify and present evidence in support of her case, rather than give testimony only by examination of the DHS Trial Attorney. The Ninth Circuit found that the noncitizen was denied the opportunity to testify fully in her own behalf and suffered prejudice in her ability to present her asylum application. In *Sosnovskaia v. Gonzalez*, 421 F.3d 589, 592 (7th Cir. 2005), a decision denying asylum was reversed where the Immigration Judge refused to allow any evidence of one claim and ignored other evidence presented.[55]

A removal hearing may be held by video or telephone conference in some instances under INA § 240(b)(2). Telephone and video conference hearings also

---

Detained Respondents, 76 Int. Rel. 1077, 1078 (1999).

[51] *See* Goldberg v. Kelly, 397 U.S. 254 (1970); Matthews v. Eldridge, 424 U.S. 319 (1976).

[52] INA § 240(b)(1). The Immigration Judge has authority to issue subpoenas for witnesses and the presentation of evidence. The EOIR has adopted formal procedures for the timing, presentation and acceptance of evidence by IJs. *See* Immigration Court Practice Manual at www.usdoj.gov/eoir. There are separate guidelines for proceedings involving unaccompanied minors.

[53] *See* Jacinto v. INS, 208 F.3d 725 (9th Cir. 2000); United States v. Mendoza-Lopez, 481 U.S. 828, 837 (1987) (recognizing the possible defense against a criminal charge of illegal reentry after removal under INA § 276 of fundamentally unfair hearing procedures in the first removal hearing).

[54] The Ninth Circuit in *Jacinto* compared the removal hearing to social security hearings where there is an unfamiliar setting for the applicant, especially pro se applicants, who may not possess the legal knowledge to fully appreciate which facts are relevant, a lack of English language proficiency, the possibility of being removed to a situation where a noncitizen could face a threat to life, safety and well-being.

[55] 421 F.3d at 592 the procedure used by the Immigration Judge was an "affront to [the applicant's] right to be heard.").

present issues relating to the effectiveness of hearing procedures.[56] The Immigration Judge must evaluate the demeanor of a noncitizen to make a credibility determination, and this is difficult in a video or telephone conference hearing.

Noncitizens with limited English language ability will give testimony through a translator and they may only hear portions of the removal proceeding translated.[57] A full or simultaneous translation is not required by procedural due process.

b.   Evidence

The formal rules of evidence do not apply in removal hearings. Hearsay is admissible but only if it is probative and no fundamental unfairness will result from its' admission.[58] Unauthenticated documents also are admissible.[59] The leading case on the admission of hearsay is *Ezeagwuna v. Ashcroft*, 325 F.3d 396, 405–408 (3d Cir. 2003).[60]

In *Ezeagwuna*, the admission of "multiple" hearsay violated due process. The Immigration Judge relied almost entirely on a letter from the Vice Consul of a U.S. Embassy summarizing the results of an investigation of five documents and concluding that each document was fraudulent. The Immigration Judge did not have the investigative report, any information about the investigator, or the details about the investigation. The letter contained multiple hearsay, e.g., a summary of statements by three declarants who had stated to the investigator that certain aspects of the documents appeared to be fraudulent. The Third Circuit was concerned about the government's attempt to "use the prestige of the State Department letterhead to make its case and give credibility to the letter's contents."[61]

---

[56] *Rusu v. United States INS*, 296 F.3d 316, 322–23 (4th Cir. 2002) (rejecting the due process challenge; although "asylum hearing was conducted in a haphazard manner, we conclude that Rusu suffered no prejudice as a result"). *See also* Kalin, *Troubled Communications: Cross-Cultural Misunderstandings in the Asylum Hearings*, 20 Int'l MIGRATION REV. 230 (1986).

[57] *See* Amadou v. INS, 226 F.3d 724, 726–28 (6th Cir. 2000) (an incomplete or incorrect translation of a noncitizen's testimony can deny a full and fair hearing and due process if prejudice results). *See also* El Rescate Legal Services, Inc. v. EOIR, 959 F.2d 742, 752 (9th Cir. 1991) (no denial of due process if translation is limited to the questions directed to non-English speaking persons); United States v. Leon-Leon, 35 F.3d 1428, 1431 (9th Cir. 1994) (no denial of due process from failure to translate crucial parts of a hearing).

[58] 8 C.F.R. § 240.7(a). *Compare* Bustos-Torres v. INS, 898 F.2d 1053 (5th Cir. 1990) (admission of hearsay because unimpeachable).

[59] Rosendo-Ramirez v. INS, 32 F.3d 1085, 1087–89 (7th Cir. 1994) (no denial of due process where a form was admitted into evidence even after the Immigration Judge stated it was "obviously, carelessly drafted").

[60] *See also* Alexandrov v. Gonzales, 442 F. 3d 395, 404–07 (6th Cir. 2006) (denial of due process by relying on two highly unreliable hearsay memoranda from the U.S. Embassy in Sofia, Bulgaria to prove that the respondent's documents were fraudulent); Cunanan v. INS, 856 F.2d 1373, 1374–75 (9th Cir. 1988) reversing denial of voluntary departure because of the reliance on a hearsay declaration from the noncitizen's wife without providing the opportunity to cross-examine the wife.

[61] *Id.* at 407.

A noncitizen is entitled to "a reasonable opportunity" to present evidence, and examine and cross-exam witnesses under INA § 240(b)(4)(B). An Immigration Judge's reliance on undisclosed national security information can be a denial of due process. In *Kiareldeen v. Reno*, 71 F.Supp. 2d 402 (D.N.J. 1999), an Immigration Judge violated procedural due process by relying on classified evidence presented by the government, *ex parte* and *in camera*, to establish that the noncitizen was a suspected member of a terrorist organization and to oppose his request for adjustment of status.[62] The government had introduced unclassified summaries of the information and the federal court found these to be insufficient. Confidential information can be used in some cases. This is discussed below in Section D.5. of this Chapter.

c.   Burden of Proof and Standard of Proof

The burden of proof varies based on the nature of the charges and the position of the noncitizen in the removal proceeding. Since the 1996 IIRIRA amendments, removal hearings may address either inadmissibility under § 212(a) or deportability under INA § 237. The first issue in any removal proceeding, either for inadmissibility or deportability, is whether the respondent is a noncitizen or alien. The DHS bears the burden of proof to establish that the respondent is a noncitizen and that the Immigration Judge has jurisdiction.[63] In most cases, alienage is easily established and the issue before the Immigration Judge is eligibility for relief from removal. Relief from removal is covered in Chapter 11.

After alienage is established, the burden shifts to the noncitizen to prove by *"clear and convincing evidence"* that she is present in the U.S. based on a prior lawful admission.[64] The burden of proof is on the noncitizen to show the time, place, and manner of entry into the U.S.[65] If the noncitizen can not establish a prior lawful admission, then she is deemed an applicant for admission. An applicant for admission in removal proceedings bears the burden of establishing she is *"clearly and beyond doubt"* entitled to be admitted and is not inadmissible under INA § 212.[66]

Noncitizens have a due process right to refuse to answer questions if the answers would incriminate them in a criminal proceeding.[67] Unlawful entry is a crime under INA § 275. Silence alone is insufficient evidence for the government to

---

[62] 71 F. Supp. 2d at 413. The BIA procedures violated procedural due process, failing the constitutional requirement of *Matthews v. Eldrige*, 424 U.S. 319 (1976), because the private interest in physical liberty, the weighty national security interest of the government, and the risk of an erroneous decision due to the one-sided presentation of evidence was likely to result in erroneous deprivations.

[63] INA § 291. 8 C.F.R. § 1240.8(c) (the Service bears the burden to first establish alienage if a noncitizen charged with being in the U.S. without being admitted or paroled).

[64] INA § 240(c)(3)(A).

[65] *See also* INA § 291 (burden of proof is on the noncitizen in any application for any document required for entry or an application for admission and if she does not meet this burden, it is presumed the noncitizen is in the United States in violation of law).

[66] INA § 240(c)(2)(B).

[67] A noncitizen could refuse to testify about an unlawful entry into the U.S. since this is a criminal ground under INA § 275.

meet its evidentiary burden.[68] Adverse inferences can be drawn from silence when a noncitizen has failed to respond to evidence offered by the government. For example, if the government introduces evidence about alienage or the circumstances of entry into the U.S., then it is permissible to draw an inference from a noncitizen's silence.[69]

If the noncitizen can establish a prior lawful admission, she is no longer in the position of an applicant for admission. Under INA § 240(c)(3)(A), the government then has the burden of establishing by "clear and convincing evidence" that a noncitizens is deportable under one of the grounds in INA § 237.[70] The Immigration Judge's decision must be based on "reasonable, substantial, and probative evidence" under INA § 240(b)(3)(A).[71]

In many cases the noncitizen may concede deportability but request relief from deportation. In any application for relief from removal, the noncitizen bears the burden of proof to establish eligibility. Further, the various forms of relief from removal are discretionary, therefore the noncitizen also must present an argument that discretion should be exercised in her case.

In *Woodby v. INS*, 385 U.S. 276 (1966), the Supreme Court required a high standard of proof for deportation. The Court held that the government must establish by "clear, unequivocal and convincing evidence" that the facts alleged by the government as the grounds for deportation are true. The rationale for this heightened standard of proof was the severe burden and "drastic deprivations that may follow" upon deportation. Several courts of appeal have relied upon the *Woodby* clear, unequivocal and convincing evidence standard in the review of deportation decisions.[72] Other federal courts have relied on the clear and convincing evidence standard in INA § 240(c)(3)(A).[73]

The Immigration Judge is required to interpret the removal grounds in favor of the noncitizen, and thus construe these narrowly. This is referred to as the rule of lenity. In *Leocal v. Ashcroft*, 543 U.S. 1 (2004), the Supreme Court applied this rule of lenity and the presumption in favor of the noncitizen because of the longstanding principle of interpreting statutes in favor of noncitizens.[74]

---

[68] *See* Matter of Guevara, 20 I & N Dec. 238 (BIA 1991).

[69] *See, e.g.*, United States ex rel. Bilokumsky v. Tod, 263 U.S. 149, 153–54 (1923) (no rule prohibits immigration officers from drawing an inference from silence); *INS v. Lopez-Mendoza*, 468 U.S. 1032, 1044 (1984) (quoting/following *Bilokumsky*). *See* Daniel Kanstroom, *Hello Darkness: Involuntary Testimony and Silence in Deportation Proceedings*, 4 GEO. IMMIG. L.J. 599 (1990) (analyzing constitutional right against self-incrimination and the lack of fifth amendment protection in civil deportation proceedings).

[70] INA § 240(c)(3)(A).

[71] INA § 240(c)(3)(A). Woodby v. INS, 385 U.S. 276 (1966) (the government must establish by "clear, unequivocal and convincing evidence" that the facts alleged as grounds for deportation are true).

[72] Jaggernath v. U.S. Atty. General, 432 F.3d 1346, 1352–56 (6th Cir. 2006); Hernandez-Guadarrama v. Aschroft, 394 F.3d 674, 678–83 (9th Cir. 2005); Murphy v. INS, 54 F.3d 605 (9th Cir. 1995); Gameros-Hernandez v. INS, 883 F.2d 839 (9th Cir. 1995).

[73] Singh v. DHS, 517 F.3d 638, 643–46 (2d Cir. 2008); Bigler v. U.S. Att'y Gen., 451 F.3d 728, 732–33 (11th Cir. 2006).

[74] Leocal v. Ashcroft, 543 U.S. 1 (2004) (in a deportation premised on an aggravated felony, the

If the DHS establishes by clear and convincing evidence that a deportation ground applies to a noncitizen, then the burden of proof shifts to the noncitizen for relief from removal. The REAL ID Act of 2005 altered the burden of proof for applications for relief from removal filed as of May 11, 2005 by amending INA § 240(c). Under INA § 240(c)(4), the applicant for relief from removal has the burden to establish that she satisfies the applicable eligibility requirements; and that she merits a favorable exercise of discretion with respect to the relief requested. The REAL ID Act also permits an Immigration Judge to require corroborating evidence in some instances when making a credibility determination for an applicant for relief from removal.[75]

5.   Administrative Review

The Board of Immigration Appeals [BIA or the Board] receives appeals of the final decisions of Immigration Judges in most removal cases; both the government and noncitizen respondent can appeal the Immigration Judge's removal decision.[76] An appeal must be received by the Board within 30 calendar days of the Immigration Judge's decision with the specific reasons for appeal, including the findings of fact and conclusions of law being challenged.[77]

The ongoing problem of a backlog in BIA decisions led the BIA, in 1999, to adopt a streamlining mechanism to reduce it.[78] In 2002, the Attorney General further revised the streamlined procedure. As discussed in Chapter 5, a key feature of these reforms is the authority of one BIA member to review an appeal, and review by a single member occurs in a majority of cases.[79] One Board member may decide cases involving procedural or ministerial matters. Appeals decided by one member are handled in one of three ways: a case may be summarily dismissed,

---

underlying crime of violence must include the element of intent rather than a simple showing of negligence). *See also* INS v. St. Cyr, 533 U.S. 289 (2001) (1996 repeal of discretionary relief from deportation did not apply retroactively); Fong Haw Tan v. Phelan, 333 U.S. 6 (1948) (doubts resolved in favor of the noncitizen).

[75] INA § 240(c)(4)(B).

[76] *See* 8 C.F.R. § 1003.3. 8 C.F.R. 1003.1(b)(3) bars BIA appellate jurisdiction from some removal decisions including: (1) where the sole ground is the length of time of voluntary departure; (2) where there is an *in absentia* order of removal entered under either INA § 240(b)(5)(C) or former INA § 242B(c).

[77] 8 C.F.R. § 1003.3(b). *See also* Board of Immigration Practice Appeals Manual at http://www.usdoj.gov/eoir/vll/qapracmanual/apptmtn4.htm. Presently it is unclear whether the 30 day time limit is jurisdictional (may not be waived) or mandatory (waiver possible). *See* Eberhart v. U.S., 546 U.S. 12 (2005) (some mandatory time limits are not jurisdictional and can be waived) and Bowles v. Russell, 551 U.S. 205 (2007) (filing deadlines for cases in lower federal courts are jurisdictional and, therefore, can not be waived). As of 2008, most courts of appeal have found that the 30 day time limit in 8 C.F.R. § 1003.38(b) is not jurisdictional and can be waived. *See* Liadow v. Mukasey, 518 F.3d 1003 (8th Cir. 2008); Khan v. DOJ, 494 F.3d 255 (2d Cir. 2007); Huerta v. Gonzales, 443 F.3d 753 (10th Cir. 2006). *But see* Magtanong v. Gonzales, 494 F.3d 1190 (9th Cir. 2007).

[78] Single member review was permissible upon a finding "that the result reached in the decision under review was correct; that any errors in the decision under review were harmless or nonmaterial." 64 Fed. Reg. 56,135 (Oct. 18, 1999).

[79] 67 Fed. Reg. 54,878 (Aug. 26, 2002).

summarily affirmed without opinion [AWO], or decided using an abbreviated decision affirming, modifying or remanding back to the Immigration Judge.

A case will be referred to a three-member panel for a decision when: (1) there are inconsistencies among decisions, (2) a need to establish a precedent ruling exists; (3) a decision by an Immigration Judge or the DHS was made in violation of law; (4) a matter involves a national impact; or (5) a clearly erroneous factual determination was made by an Immigration Judge.[80]

A summary dismissal of an appeal by a single board member can occur if: (1) the notice does not state the specific reasons for appeal; (2) the appellee states it will file a brief and fails to do so without notice to the BIA; (3) the relief requests on appeal has been granted already; (4) if a finding of fact or conclusion of law has already been conceded by the appellee; (5) the Board lacks jurisdiction; (6) the appeal was filed late; or (7) the right to appeal was waived at the conclusion of the removal hearing.[81]

Affirmance without an opinion by a single Board member is permissible if three criteria are met: (1) the Immigration Judge's decision is correct; (2) any errors in the decision below are harmless or immaterial; and (3) the issue is either controlled by existing precedent or the factual or legal questions do not merit review by a three member panel.[82] AWO is authorized when a full and complete record, including specific findings of fact by the Immigration Judge, is available.[83]

These summary AWO decisions have quickened the pace of BIA adjudication. Federal court challenges to these summary proceedings as a denial of procedural due process have been unsuccessful.[84] As discussed in Chapter 5, criticism about immigration adjudications in 2005 and 2006 referred to the affirmance without opinion procedures as an example of the inconsistency in adjudication.[85] The 2006 Department of Justice 22-point reform plan dealing with immigration judges and other EOIR reforms included reform of the affirmance without opinion procedure. The plan noted the need to reduce the number of cases subject to this form of review. As of November 2008, many of these proposed reforms have not been implemented including new rules about affirmance without opinion.[86]

---

[80] 8 C.F.R. § 1003.1(e)(6).

[81] 8 C.F.R. § 1003.1(d)(2).

[82] 8 C.F.R. § 1003.1(e)(4).

[83] *In re S-H-*, 23 I&N Dec. 462, 465 (BIA 2002). *See also* Gallegher, *Practice and Procedure Before the Board of Immigration Appeals* 03-02 IMM. BRIEFINGS (Feb. 2003).

[84] Saodjede v. Ashcroft, 324 F. 3d 830, 831–32 (5th Cir. 2003); Gonzalez-Oropeza v. United States Attorney General, 321 F.3d 1331, 1333–34 (11th Cir. 2003); Albathani v. INS, 318 F.3d 365, 375–79 (1st Cir. 2003); Capital Area Immigrant's Rights Coalition v. U.S. Dept. of Justice, 264 F. Supp. 2d 14, 25–36 (D.D.C. 2003).

[85] *See, e.g.*, *Overwhelmed Circuit Courts Lashing Out at the BIA and Selected Immigration Judges: Is Streamlining to Blame*, 48 INTER. REL. 2005 (2005) (in the period ending March 2003 petitions for review for immigration cases filed in federal courts had increased 379%); Spencer S. Hsu and Carrie Johnson, *Effort on Immigration Courts Faulted*, WASHINGTON POST, Sept. 8, 2008, at A6.

[86] *See* Spencer S. Hsu and Carrie Johnson, *Effort on Immigration Courts Faulted*, WASHINGTON POST, Sept. 8, 2008, at A6.

Decisions of an Immigration Judge prior to the removal determination also may be appealed including determinations on bonds and detention pending removal, except for those detained as inadmissible or subject to mandatory detention. Immigration Judge decisions about requests for relief from removal such as cancellation of removal, adjustment of status, and asylum may be appealed to the BIA.

6.   Judicial Review

Before 1996 amendments by IIRIRA and AEDPA, the federal courts generally had the power to review BIA decisions. Federal circuit courts of appeal had jurisdiction to hear appeals of deportation decisions by the BIA. Appeals of exclusion (inadmissibility) decisions were heard by federal district courts.

The 1996 IIRIRA and AEDPA amendments and the more recent 2005 REAL ID Act changes to the INA have severely restricted judicial review. Currently, there is a limited judicial review in all removal proceedings initiated on or after April 1, 2007, under these amendments.[87]

A petition for review must be filed within 30 days of the date of the final order under INA § 242. A separate motion to stay of removal must be filed with the court. Before 1996, an appeal resulted in an automatic stay of removal. If the noncitizen is removed from the United States prior to a judicial decision, the court retains jurisdiction.

See Chapter 6 for in-depth coverage of judicial review.

C.   MOTIONS TO REOPEN OR RECONSIDER

Motions to reconsider and motions to reopen are permitted under INA §§ 240(c)(6) and (c)(7) and may be submitted to either the Immigration Judge or the BIA.[88] Most motions are filed directly with the BIA which usually has jurisdiction over a case after an appeal has been filed.[89] Motions to reopen to an *in absentia* order of removal are covered in INA § 240(b)(5)(c). *In absentia* orders of removal are discussed below in this Chapter.

Motions to reconsider a determination are based on errors in the underlying decisions, the availability of additional legal arguments, a change of law or further development of an aspect of the case that was overlooked. Motions to reopen are based on new factual information and must be supported by this new evidence. The

---

[87] In cases where the final order was entered prior to October 30, 1996, judicial review proceeds under pre-1996 law. The 1996 amendments included transition rules for cases involving a final order entered after October 30, 1996.

[88] 8 C.F.R. § 1003.23. The Immigration Judge may retain jurisdiction over a matter or the BIA may receive jurisdiction as a result of the appeal. The BIA will consider motions to reopen, motions to reconsider, motions to remand, motions to stay removal, as well as other motions permitted by the rules or Board of Immigration Practice Appeals Manual, *available at* http://www.usdoj.gov/eoir/vll/qapracmanual/apptmtn4.htm.

[89] 8 C.F.R. §§ 1003.2, 1003.23(b)(1).

new evidence must be material and must have been unavailable and undiscoverable at the time of the original hearing.[90]

Generally, only one motion to reconsider and one motion to reopen may be filed by a noncitizen with several exceptions. Motions are governed by statutory deadlines and jurisdictional requirements, regulations prescribing the form and timing of motions, as well as the Board of Appeals Practice Manual.[91] The deadline for filing a motion to reconsider is 90 days from the date of entry of a final administrative order of removal.[92] This filing deadline does not apply to a motion to reopen to apply for asylum based on a material change of circumstances.[93] Filing deadlines also do not apply to battered spouses, children or parents.[94] An Immigration Judge's decision to grant or deny a motion to reopen or reconsider is discretionary.[95] Motions filed with the Immigration Judge will not stay the execution of the decision to remove unless a stay of execution of the removal order is granted.[96] The BIA, as well as Immigration Judges and District Directors of the DHS have discretionary authority to stay removal pending a decision.

Motions to reopen claiming an ineffective assistance of counsel and a denial of Fifth Amendment due process must meet certain requirements. The 90 day filing deadline does not apply in some cases involving ineffective assistance of counsel claims. It is possible to file a motion to reopen for ineffective assistance of counsel after the filing deadline under an equitable tolling doctrine until a noncitizen learns of counsel's incompetence.

If the noncitizen leaves the U.S. while a motion to reopen or a motion to reconsider is pending before the BIA or Immigration Judge, she is deemed to have withdrawn the motion. The regulations also prohibit a noncitizen from filing a motion to reopen after leaving the United States while in removal proceedings.[97]

---

[90] 8 C.F.R. § 1003.2.

[91] INA §§ 240(c)(6), (c)(7); 8 C.F.R. 1003.

[92] INA § 240(c)(7)(C)(i). A different filing deadline applies to motions to reopen in absentia orders of removal under INA § 240(b)(5)(c).

[93] INA § 240(c)(7)(C)(ii) imposes no time limit on a motion to reopen to apply for asylum if: (1) it is based on changed country conditions arising in the country of nationality or the country to which removal has been order; and (2) such evidence is material and was not available or "would not have been discovered or presented at the previous proceeding."

[94] INA § 240(c)(7)(C)(iv).

[95] 8 C.F.R. § 1003.23(b)(1)(ii).

[96] 8 C.F.R. § 1003.23(b)(1)(v). A stay can be granted by the Immigration Judge, BIA, or ICE.

[97] 8 C.F.R. § 1003.23(b)(1). At least one court has held that the rule preventing a noncitizen from filing a new motion to reopen after leaving the U.S. only applies when a person leaves while still in removal proceedings. Lin v. Gonzales, 473 F.3d 979 (9th Cir. 2007).

D. SPECIAL REMOVAL PROCEDURES

1.   Criminal Cases

a.   Prison Hearings

In fiscal year 2005, noncitizens removed after a criminal conviction accounted for 43% of all removals.[98] The removal of noncitizens convicted of crimes has been a major focus of Congress over the last two decades. In 1988, Congress amended the INA and established a removal procedure for noncitizen criminals who commit aggravated felonies.[99] The 1990 Immigration Act amendments expanded the definition of aggravated felons and decreased the avenues of relief from deportation for noncitizen criminals.[100]

Removal hearings under INA § 238(a)(1) in prison occur when states send certified court records for noncitizens with state law convictions to DHS. The enhanced communication among local, state and federal agencies is coordinated by the Criminal Alien Tracking Center and the Law Enforcement Support Center. The DHS issues detainers using information from these agencies. Detainers are a request by DHS to local, state and federal prison officials to hold an noncitizen rather than release her from custody.[101]

Currently the special removal process for criminal noncitizens is designed to avoid any DHS detention after the completion of a prison sentence. Criminal convictions falling within INA § 238(a)(1), subject to the prison hearing process, include aggravated felonies, drug and firearm offenses, two crimes of moral turpitude committed within five years of entry, and the miscellaneous crimes under INA § 237(a)(2)(D).[102] These special prison removal hearings occur in federal, state and local correctional facilities. The hearings are initiated and completed, if possible, while the noncitizen is incarcerated. The right to counsel and access to counsel often is limited in prison removal hearings. The DHS is required to ensure that the right to counsel and access to counsel is not impaired during the process.[103]

Aggravated felony prison removal hearings are expedited proceedings conducted under INA § 238(a)(3). These aggravated felony prison hearings must be initiated and completed, to the extent possible, including any administrative

---

[98] *See* Alienikoff, Martin, Motomura & Fullerton 1092 (6th ed. 2008).

[99] INA § 101(a)(43). The Omnibus Anti-Drug Abuse Act of 1988, Pub. L. 100-690, 102 Stat. 4181 (Nov. 18, 1988), identified certain crimes as aggravated felonies, added new removal grounds for persons convicted of aggravated felonies, and established a special deportation procedure using prison hearings.

[100] Pub. L. 101-649, 104 Stat. 4978 (Nov. 29, 1990).

[101] 8 C.F.R. §§ 236.1, 287.7.

[102] INA § 238(a)(1) makes available special removal proceedings in federal, state and local correctional facilities for noncitizens convicted of any criminal offense covered in INA §§ 237(a)(2)(A)(iii), (B), (C) or (D), or any offense covered in INA § 237(a)(2)(A)(ii).

[103] INA § 238(a)(2).

appeals, before the aggravated felon's release from incarceration.[104] Aggravated felons in these special hearing procedures are subject to the conclusive presumption of deportability under INA § 238(c).

A noncitizen who is incarcerated may be eligible for early removal before the end of a criminal sentence in limited circumstances. This option is available under INA § 241(a)(4)(B), and permits early removal if the noncitizen was convicted of a nonviolent offense.[105]

b.   Administrative Removal

Administrative removal is available to remove aggravated felons who are not lawful permanent residents or who are not conditional permanent residents under INA § 216. Under INA § 238(b), these aggravated felons may be removed without a hearing before an immigration judge. The procedure must include reasonable notice to the noncitizen of the charges and an opportunity to inspect the evidence and rebut the charges.[106] The noncitizen may be represented by counsel. The INA further requires that the immigration official issuing the charges may not be the official who determines whether to issue a final order of removal.

In administrative removal proceedings there is a conclusive presumption of deportability under INA § 238(c). Noncitizens in administrative removal are not eligible for any discretionary relief.[107] A noncitizen subject to administrative removal may seek judicial review under INA § 242.[108] Review by the court of appeals is only available to consider constitutional questions and questions of law under INA § 242(a)(2)(D).

Federal courts have upheld the constitutionality of this administrative removal process finding that there is no violation of procedural due process. For example, *United States v. Benitez-Villafuerte*, 186 F.3d 651, 657 (5th Cir. 1999), *cert. denied* 528 U.S. 1097 (2000), involved a criminal prosecution for illegal reentry based on a prior administrative removal. The defendant claimed that the prior administrative removal violated procedural due process guarantees. The Fifth Circuit rejected the due process challenge and found that the administrative removal procedure provides a full and fair opportunity to be heard.

---

[104] INA § 238(a)(3).

[105] INA § 241(a)(4)(B). Early removal is available, and the Attorney General has discretion whether or not to grant a request. The INA specifically states there is no private right of action to compel early removal.

[106] INA § 238(b)(4).

[107] INA § 238(b)(5); relief under the Convention Against Torture is available. *See* Chapter 11.

[108] The DHS must wait at least 14 days following the removal order to allow judicial review.

c.   Judicial Removal

Federal courts have the power to enter an order of removal.[109] Judicial removal occurs when a U.S. District Court enters an order of removal at the time of sentencing in a federal criminal case. Under INA § 238(c)(1), a U.S. district court has jurisdiction to enter a judicial order of removal at the time of sentencing if the "order has been requested by the U.S. attorney with the concurrence of the Commissioner [DHS]." If the District Court denies the U.S. Attorney request for a judicial order of removal, the Attorney General may begin removal proceedings under INA § 240 based on the same ground of deportability or another ground of deportability.[110]

Under this judicial removal procedure, the U.S. Attorney must provide notice of the intent to seek judicial deportation and this must be served on DHS and the noncitizen criminal defendant. The U.S. District Court can decide whether to grant relief from removal after considering the DHS's recommendation and report about the noncitizen's eligibility for relief.[111] A person who is convicted of an aggravated felony is conclusively presumed to be deportable under INA § 238(c). The U.S. District Court has final authority whether to grant or deny relief. Both the noncitizen defendant and the government may appeal the decision of the District Court to the Court of Appeals.

2.   In Absentia Removal

The 1990 amendments to the INA included the possibility of *in absentia* orders of removal to address the problem of noncitizens failing to appear at their hearings.[112] If a noncitizen does not attend any hearing date during a removal proceeding, the INA permits an order of removal to be entered *in absentia* under INA § 240(b)(5). *In absentia* orders of removal are permissible only if the noncitizen has received proper written notice of the hearing date and any subsequent change in the date and/or time of a hearing.[113]

An *in absentia* order of removal can only be rescinded through a motion to reopen before the Immigration Judge.[114] The motion to rescind the removal order must establish either a lack of proper notice of the hearing, exceptional

---

[109] INA §§ 238(c)(2), (c)(5). A stipulated judicial order of removal under INA § 238(c)(5) permits the U.S. Attorney's may enter a plea agreement, if DHS agrees, and the noncitizen waives the right to notice and hearing on the issue of deportability and relief from removal.

[110] INA § 238(c)(4).

[111] INA § 238(c)(2)(C).

[112] In FY 2002 approximately 25% of Immigration Judge decisions involved noncitizens who failed to appear and for whom an *in absentia* order of removal was entered. In FY 2005 and FY 2006 *in absentia* orders of removal were 39% of the total Immigration Judge decisions. *See* Alienikoff, Martin, Motomura & Fullerton 1073 (6th ed. 2008) (citing EOIR, Department of Justice, FY 2006 Statistical Yearbook at H1-H2).

[113] INA §§ 239(a)(1), (a)(2). Personal service of any hearing notice is required if practicable, including changes of hearing dates and times. Service by mail on the noncitizen or his or her attorney is also sufficient if sent to the address provided by the noncitizen when the NTA was initially issued.

[114] INA § 240(c)(7)(C)(iii).

circumstances caused the failure to appear, or the noncitizen was in state or federal custody.[115] A motion based on failure to appear due to exceptional circumstances must be filed within 180 days after the date of the order. In the case where a noncitizen claims a lack of proper notice, a motion to reopen can be filed at any time.[116]

A lack of proper notice is established if there is a failure to provide notice and there is a failure to receive notice by the noncitizen. Recall that an NTA contains a notice of the obligation to immediately provide an address to the Immigration Court. Prior to April 1, 1997, the effective date of the IIRIRA amendments, the *in absentia* removal hearing process required notice by certified mail.[117] In this circumstance, a noncitizen could claim she had not received notice using the evidence provided by the certified mail process. Today, the noncitizen may not have evidence of the failure to receive notice because certified mail is not required.

A motion to reopen claiming exceptional circumstances must satisfy the statutory definition in INA § 240(e). Exceptional circumstances are beyond the control of the noncitizen such as battery or extreme cruelty to the noncitizen or the serious illness or death of a spouse, parent or child of the noncitizen. The INA further states that less compelling circumstances are not considered exceptional.[118] Exceptional circumstances can include ineffective assistance of counsel.[119] The Immigration Judge will evaluate the totality of the circumstances to decide whether exceptional circumstances exist.[120]

Equitable tolling of the 180 day statute of limitations for filing motion to reopen is possible under INA § 240(c)(7)(C)(iii). Equitable tolling is available if there is a claim of ineffective assistance of counsel. The rationale for equitable tolling is the view that the 180 day deadline is a statute of limitations rather than a jurisdictional requirement. In *Anin v. Reno*, 188 F.3d 1273 (11th Cir. 1999), the Court of Appeals rejected an ineffective assistance of counsel claim as an exceptional circumstance because the motion to reopen was filed after the 180 day deadline. The *Anin* court held that the deadline is mandatory and jurisdictional. Other circuits courts of appeal have found the 180 day deadline is subject to equitable tolling when there is

---

[115] INA § 240 (b)(5)(c).

[116] Under INA § 240(b)(5)(C), a motion to reopen also can be filed at any time if the noncitizen was in state or federal custody and the failure to appear was not the noncitizen's fault.

[117] Former INA § 242B added to the INA by the Immigration Act of 1990, Pub. L. 101-649, 104 Stat. 4978 (Nov. 29, 1990).

[118] Morales v. INS, 116 F.3d 145 (5th Cir. 1997) (exceptional circumstances did not exist when a noncitizen failed to appear because his car engine broke on the sixty mile drive to the hearing although the noncitizen began the drive one and one-half hours before the hearing, got a ride back home after leaving the car because he could not afford to repair it, and attempted to call the immigration court but could not find a telephone number in the phone book nor on the hearing notice).

[119] Matter of Grijalva, 21 I & N Dec. 472 (BIA 1996) (ineffective assistance of counsel established when noncitizen told by counsel not to attend proceeding, noncitizen filed complaint with state Bar, and noncitizen's claims corroborated by former counsel's affidavit).

[120] Herbert v. Ashcroft, 325 F.3d 68 (1st Cir. 2003) (totality of circumstances indicate exceptional circumstances when counsel filed emergency continuance request, noncitizen's relative arrived in court on time, and noncitizen's 30 minute delay resulted from a combination of ill child, bad weather, heavy traffic, and long line at courthouse security checkpoint).

an ineffective assistance of counsel challenge to an *in absentia* order of removal.[121] The Supreme Court's decision in *Bowles v. Russell*, 127 S.Ct. 2360 (2007) also adds to the confusion. In *Bowles*, the Supreme Court held that time limits for appealing judgments in civil cases to federal courts of appeal are jurisdictional and no equitable exceptions are permitted.

There is no appeal to the BIA of an *in absentia* order of removal.[122] The only vehicle for review is a motion to reopen. The denial of a motion to reopen an *in absentia* removal order can be appealed to the BIA. A BIA decision to grant or deny a motion to reopen or reconsider is discretionary. It is not an abuse of discretion to deny a motion even if the movant established a prima facie case for relief.[123] Judicial review of an *in absentia* removal order is limited to specific claims.[124] A motion to reopen to rescind an *in absentia* removal order based on exceptional circumstances or failure to obtain notice will result in an automatic stay of deportation.[125]

There are severe consequences stemming from an *in absentia* order of removal. A noncitizen against whom an *in absentia* removal order has been entered is ineligible for discretionary relief for ten years.[126] This includes voluntary departure, cancellation of removal, adjustment of status, change of nonimmigrant classification and registry. The noncitizen also is inadmissible for ten years as a person previously removed.[127]

3.   Reentry Cases — Reinstatement of Removal Orders

A summary removal procedure is used for noncitizens who reenter the U.S. unlawfully after an order of removal. The summary procedure, under INA § 241(a)(5), applies to those who have been physically removed or have voluntarily departed under an order of removal.

The summary removal procedure based on reinstatement of a prior removal order was established by the 1996 IIRIRA amendments. The summary removal process reinstates the prior removal order from its original date. This reinstatement of the prior removal order is performed solely by a DHS officer. The regulations for reinstatement of a prior removal order require that the DHS officer

---

[121] *See* Aris v. Mukasey, 517 F.3d 595 (2d Cir. 2008) (paralegal misinformed noncitizen about whether a hearing was scheduled, and, after he was deported *in absentia*, law firm failed to inform him of deportation); Pervais v. Gonzales, 405 F.3d 488 (7-05); Barges v. Gonzales, 402 F.3d 398 (3d 05). In *Saakian v. INS*, 252 F.2d 21 (1st Cir. 2001), the First Circuit held that a noncitizen was denied procedural due process when his appeal from denial of motion to reopen *in absentia* deportation order based on ineffective assistance of counsel was not heard on the merits.

[122] INA § 240(b)(7).

[123] Anin v. Reno, 188 F.3d 1273 (11th Cir. 1999) (relying on 8 C.F.R. § 3.2(a)(1999)).

[124] INA §§ 240(b)(5)(D), 242(b)(5). Judicial review of the order can address nationality claims, and the underlying elements of the *in absentia* order including validity of the notice, the reasons for not attending the hearing, and whether or not the noncitizen is removable.

[125] INA § 240(b)(5)(C).

[126] INA § 240(b)(7).

[127] INA § 212(a)(9)(A)(ii)(I). This applies to all removals.

determines: (1) the noncitizen is the person ordered removed using a fingerprint check if needed; (2) there was a final removal order; and (3) the noncitizen reentered the U.S. unlawfully.[128] DHS must give the noncitizen a written statement of the determination and give the noncitizen an opportunity to challenge the determination.

There is no right to a hearing before an Immigration Judge and no right to counsel. The noncitizen is not eligible for any relief from deportation, including adjustment of status. Further, the noncitizen may not file any motion to reopen or review the prior removal order. Only very limited relief from removal is available to the noncitizen subject to reinstatement.[129]

Judicial review of the summary removal based on reinstatement of a prior removal order is available in the Circuit Court of Appeal under the REAL ID Act amendments to the INA.[130] The REAL ID amendments added INA § 242(a)(2)(D) to permit judicial review of legal and constitutional challenges.[131]

Federal courts have upheld this summary removal procedure despite due process concerns. Recently, in *Morales-Izquierdo v. Gonzales*, 486 F.3d 484 (9th Cir. 2007) (*en banc*), the Court of Appeals upheld the reinstatement of an *in absentia* order of removal.[132] The Ninth Circuit confirmed that the regulation permitting reinstatement by an immigration officer, rather than an Immigration Judge, followed the intent of Congress to establish a summary procedure. Further, the Ninth Circuit determined that this decision by only an immigration officer satisfies Fifth Amendment procedural due process.[133] The court was satisfied with the procedural safeguards against an incorrect decision in reinstatement cases including the use of fingerprints and obtaining the prior order. Reinstatement does not violate due process, even in the case where the process afforded in the underlying removal order is challenged, because reinstatement does not change a noncitizen's rights or remedies. As a result, the only effect of the reinstatement order is to cause removal rather than any civil or criminal penalties or any additional obstacles to attacking the removal order.

The Supreme Court also has upheld the retroactive application of INA § 241(a)(5) to noncitizens who reentered the U.S. before the effective date of this

---

[128] 8 C.F.R. § 241.8.

[129] 8 C.F.R. §§ 208.31, 241.8(d). withholding of removal, claims under the Convention Against Torture and HRIFA or NACARA benefits.

[130] INA § 242(a)(2)(D).

[131] INA § 241(a)(5) states reinstatement of the prior removal order is not subject to being reopened or reviewed.

[132] The noncitizen challenged the DHS regulation permitting an immigration officer, rather than an immigration judge, to reinstate the order of removal as contrary to the statutory requirements for removal hearings under INA § 240. He argued that the INS explicitly exempts certain proceedings from this hearing requirement, such as expedited removal under INA § 235(b).

[133] The Ninth Circuit found that the regulation was a valid interpretation of the INA by applying both prongs of the test articulated in *Chevron USA Inc. v. Natural Res. Def. Council, Inc.*, 467 U.S. 837 (1984): (1) the regulation follows the intent of Congress to establish a summary proceeding; and (2) the DHS interpretation is a permissible construction.

IIRIRA amendment (April 1, 2007).[134] Applications for relief filed after April 1, 1997, the effective date of INA § 241(a)(5) also are barred. A noncitizen who reenters before IIRIRA but applies for relief after IIRIRA is subject to the ban on relief included in the reinstatement provision. This can occur if a noncitizen reentered and is apprehended after April 1, 1997 and applies for relief.

4.   Crew Members

Crewmembers are subject to a summary removal procedure under INA § 252(b). Crewmembers are noncitizens serving in good faith on board a vessel in a capacity required for normal operation and service of the vessel.[135] Crewmembers are permitted to "land temporarily" in the U.S. using a 29 day conditional landing permit under INA § 252(a), if the crewmember is admissible.[136]

Noncitizens who are not bona fide crewmembers or who do not intend to depart may have their conditional permit to land in the U.S. revoked by an immigration officer. If a conditional landing permit is revoked, then the crewman will be detained on board the vessel or aircraft and will be removed from the U.S. at the expense of the transportation line. This summary removal procedure applied to crewmembers is separate from the removal procedures under INA § 240. Accordingly, INA § 252 states that "nothing in this section [252] shall be construed to require the procedures prescribed in section 240 [8 U.S.C.A. § 1229a] to cases falling within the provisions of this subsection."[137]

5.   National Security

Suspected terrorists are subject to a summary removal procedure under INA § 501 or under INA § 235(c). These terrorist removal procedures operate independently from the removal procedure under INA § 240.

Suspected terrorists and noncitizens who threaten foreign policy or national security are subject to a distinct form of expedited removal under INA § 235(c).[138] If an immigration officer or an Immigration Judge suspects that an arriving noncitizen is inadmissible under terrorist or national security grounds, then a removal order will be issued and the immigration officer or Immigration Judge may "not conduct any further inquiry or hearing until ordered by the Attorney

---

[134] *See* Fernandez-Vargas v. Gonzales, 548 U.S. 30 (2006). This case applied reinstatement to a noncitizen who initially came to the U.S. in the 1970s, had been deported for immigration violations and made his last unlawful reentry in 1982. He had been in the U.S., on and off, for over 30 years and his last unlawful reentry occurred nearly 20 years before his adjustment of status application was filed based on an immediate relative petition after a marriage to a U.S. citizen in 2001. This case resolved a split in the circuits on this issue of retroactive application prior to the effective date of the IIRIRA amendments.

[135] INA § 101(a)(15)(D).

[136] Parole of the crew member into the U.S. under INA § 212(d)(5) is also possible.

[137] INA § 252(b).

[138] INA § 235(c) applies to those inadmissible under security grounds (espionage, sabotage, unlawful overthrow of the government), terrorist grounds, and foreign policy grounds under INA §§ 212(a)(3)(A) (other than clause (ii)), (B) or (C).

General."[139] The Attorney General is required to review these removal orders and is authorized to remove the noncitizen without further inquiry or hearing.[140] The Attorney General may rely on confidential information and consultation with "appropriate security agencies of the United States Government" to determine whether a terrorist or national security ground of inadmissibility applies. If the Attorney General does not order removal, then the A.G. must specify the type of further inquiry or hearing to be conducted.

The 1996 Anti-Terrorism and Effective Death Penalty Act [AEDPA] established the special terrorist removal court under INA § 501.[141] This only applies to noncitizens "certified" as terrorists and provides another option to the DHS in its use of classified information about a noncitizen.[142] Suspected terrorists are those who are removable under INA § 237(a)(4)(B).[143]

The Chief Justice of the Supreme Court must publicly designate five district court judges to serve on the terrorist court to conduct these removal proceedings.[144] Proceedings are initiated by the Attorney General who files an application with the terrorist court.[145]

There are some enhanced noncitizen procedural protections designed to counterbalance the summary process. Removal hearings by the terrorist removal court must be conducted in open court as expeditiously as practicable.[146] A noncitizen has a right to be present and to be represented by counsel at the hearing. A noncitizen who is financially unable to obtain counsel is entitled to have counsel assigned. Nevertheless, the process limits the noncitizens procedural protections. The Federal Rules of Evidence do not apply. There is no right to review any classified evidence presented or a right to suppress information, even if it is unlawfully obtained.[147] The government's burden of proof for deportation is

---

[139] INA § 235(c)(1)(C).

[140] A noncitizen may request consideration of a claim based on the Convention Against Torture under 8 C.F.R. § 208.18(d).

[141] Pub. L. 104-132, 110 Stat. 1214 (Apr. 24, 1996); Suspected terrorists are defined in INA § 237(a)(4)(B).

[142] DHS officers can rely on classified information in expedited removal based on natural security grounds of INA § 212(a)(3) or to oppose discretionary relief in ordinary INA § 240 removal proceedings. *See* above Section 4 (discussing *Kiareldeen v. Reno*, 71 F. Supp. 2d 402 (D.N.J. 1999).

[143] INA 237(a)(4)(B) is the deportation ground and refers only to noncitizens described in INA §§ 212(a)(3)(B) (terrorist activities) or (3)(F) (association with terrorist organizations).

[144] INA § 502(a). The same five judges may also be designated by the Chief Justice to serve under the Foreign Intelligence Surveillance Act (50 U.S.C. § 1803(a)).

[145] INA § 503(a)(1)(D). The application must include a statement of facts and circumstances with probable cause that the noncitizen is a terrorist, that the noncitizen is physically present in the U.S. and that the standard removal procedures would pose a risk to national security. The judge's decision to grant the application can include *ex parte, in camera* review of classified information system.

[146] INA § 504(a).

[147] INA §§ 504(e)(3)(A), (e)(1)(B). The government can introduce as evidence "the fruits of electronic surveillance and unconsented physical searches authorized under the Foreign Intelligence Surveillance Act."

reduced to a preponderance of the evidence rather than the burden of clear and convincing evidence standard in ordinary removal proceedings under INA § 240.[148]

Special procedures apply when an lawful permanent resident has a case in the terrorist removal court under INA § 504(e)(3)(F). A special attorney will be assigned to assist the permanent resident and this special attorney may review classified information on behalf of the noncitizen and challenge the veracity of the evidence contained in the classified information. It is a criminal offense for the special attorney receiving classified information to disclose any information to the noncitizen or any other attorney representing the noncitizen.[149]

Appeal of the decision of the terrorist removal court is available under an expedited procedure. The noncitizen must file a notice of appeal within 20 days and the D.C. Court of Appeals must render a decision within 60 days.[150]

E. DETENTION

Detention related to removal proceedings can occur during the removal hearing process, after a final removal order has been entered, and, when physical removal is unlikely although a final order of removal has been issued. Each of these types of detention is addressed below.

Some common aspects of all forms of detention include the obvious physical restraint on liberty; detention is authorized for arriving noncitizens who have never entered as well as long-term LPRs in certain circumstances. Generally, indefinite detention is not authorized. Long-term detention has come under much greater judicial scrutiny in recent years as discussed below.

DHS relies on detention to ensure appearance at hearings because nonappearance has been an ongoing concern, and to ensure physical removal upon the conclusion of proceedings. According to a 2007 Government Accounting Office report, the total number of noncitizens in removal proceedings who spend some time in detention per year increased from 95,214 in 2001 to 283,115 in 2006.[151] There are numerous criticisms about the nature of immigration detention.[152] Detention facility operations are similar to a prison setting and frequently are located in remote areas. There are national detention standards for ICE-operated facilities and contractor detention facilities.[153]

---

[148] INA § 504(g).

[149] INA § 504(e)(1)(F).

[150] INA §§ 505(a)(1), (c)(4)(B).

[151] *Alien Detention Standards: Telephone Access Problems Were Pervasive at Detention Facilities; Other Deficiencies Did Not Show a Pattern of Noncompliance*, GAO-07-875 (July 6, 2007) (In FY 2007, ICE received $953 million in funding for detention services).

[152] *House Judiciary Subcommittee Take Testimony of Medical Provided to ICE Detainees*, 85 Inter. Rel. 1737 (June 16, 2008); 85 Inter. Rel. 1477 (May 19, 2008).

[153] Detention Operations Manual, *available at* http://www.ice.gov/pi/dro/opsmanual/.

1.   Pending Removal

Many provisions of the INA require or permit detention of noncitizens who are arriving to request admission or who are apprehended in the U.S. Detention during the removal proceeding can occur after an application for admission into the U.S. at the border under INA § 235. Under INA § 235(b)(2), the inspection process for arriving noncitizens in the U.S. requires a determination by the DHS officer whether a noncitizen is "clearly and beyond a doubt entitled to be admitted." An arriving noncitizen who is not clearly and beyond doubt entitled to admission "shall be detained" for a removal hearing under INA § 240.[154] Under this provision, detention is required except in very limited circumstances.[155] Arriving noncitizens in expedited removal under INA § 235(b)(1), such as a credible fear determination, are subject to mandatory detention pending removal.

Detention can also occur upon apprehension inside the United States.[156] The detention requirements for these noncitizens are covered in INA § 236. If a noncitizen is arrested, the decision whether to issue an NTA to begin removal proceedings must be made within 48 hours of the arrest.[157] The decision whether to grant bond and release or continue detention also must be made within 48 hours. The special terrorist removal process permits detention up to seven days under USA PATRIOT Act amendments.[158]

Noncitizens who are *not arriving*, under INA § 236, may be released on bond. The noncitizen has the burden to show release on bond is warranted. Release on bond is a discretionary decision and there is no constitutional right to release on bond. Appeal of the DHS District Director's bond decision to an Immigration Judge and the BIA is available.[159] A noncitizen must establish that she does not present a danger to persons or property, is not a threat to national security and does not pose a risk of flight under INA § 236(a).[160]

Some noncitizens are ineligible for bond and release and are subject to mandatory detention pending removal under INA § 236(c). Those ineligible for

---

[154] INA § 235(b)(2)(A). Under INA § 235(b)(2)(C), Mexicans and Canadians requesting admission may be returned to Mexico or Canada pending removal proceedings under INA § 240.

[155] INA § 236. 8 C.F.R. § 212.5 permits release on parole of arriving noncitizens in the case of: (1) serious medical conditions; (2) pregnant women; (3) certain juveniles; (4) witnesses in government proceedings in the U.S.; and (5) if continued detention in not in the public interest.

[156] INA § 287(a) (providing authority to interrogate and arrest any person believed to be an alien).

[157] 8 C.F.R. § 287(3)(d). If a criminal arrest warrant is issued, it too must be issued within the 48 hours of the arrest of a noncitizen.

[158] INA § 236A(a) permits the A.G. to certify a noncitizen is a terrorist if there is reasonable grounds to believe the individual is excludable under INA §§ 212(a)(3)(A)(i) espionage/sabotage/export), (3)(A)(iii) (violent overthrow, opposition, control of government), (3)(B) (terrorist activities), 237(a)(4)(A)(i) (espionage or sabotage), 237(a)(4)(A)(iii) (violent overthrow, opposition, control of government), (4)(B) (terrorist activities) or is engaged in any other activity that endangers the national security.

[159] 8 C.F.R. §§ 236.1(d)(3), 1003.19(i).

[160] *See* Matter of Patel, 15 I & N Dec. 666 (BIA 1976) (factors in bond determinations include local family ties, prior arrests, convictions, appearances at hearings, employment or lack of employment, membership in community organizations, manner of entry and length of time in the U.S., and financial ability to post bond).

bond under INA § 236(c) include: (1) noncitizens who are inadmissible under any criminal ground; (2) noncitizens who are inadmissible under any terrorism grounds; (3) noncitizens deportable under certain criminal grounds including multiple criminal convictions, aggravated felonies, controlled substances, certain firearms offenses, and miscellaneous crimes; (4) deportable for a crime of moral turpitude if the sentence is to a term of imprisonment of one year or more; or (5) deportable for terrorist activities or association with terrorist organizations. Release from detention under INA § 236(c)(2) is only permitted for witness protection or cooperation, and only if there is no national security risk or risk of flight.

In *Demore v. Kim*, 538 U.S. 510 (2003) the Supreme Court rejected a due process challenge and upheld the constitutionality of INA § 236(c). In *Demore v. Kim*, an LPR had conceded deportability as an aggravated felon and did not request a hearing to challenge whether he was properly subject to INA § 236(c) mandatory detention. The constitutional issue was the lack of an individualized determination of whether Kim posed a flight risk and thus should be detained. The plurality relied on the nature of detention pending removal which usually is a relatively short period of time. Justice Kennedy's concurring opinion, creating the fifth vote, stated an LPR in mandatory detention could be entitled to an individualized hearing as to his risk of flight and dangerousness if the continued detention became unreasonable or unjustified.

The plight of unaccompanied minors who are placed in detention facilities raises serious concerns, although the detention of juveniles occurs under more protective procedures.[161] Juveniles, under the age of 18, who are arriving noncitizens are eligible for parole unlike most arriving noncitizens. Juveniles may be released to family members however a juvenile is not entitled to release from custody to non-family members. In *Reno v. Flores*, 507 U.S. 292 (1993), a constitutional challenge to the restraint on the liberty of noncitizen children upon a request for release to non-relatives was rejected by the Supreme Court.[162]

Juveniles may also be detained when a noncitizen parent is taken into custody by DHS. Prior to 2001, families were rarely detained because of the lack of bed space, and the INS had a policy of releasing families to avoid the detention of children.[163] After September 11, 2001, the INS began this detention policy, although alternatives exist to detention such as the Intensive Supervised Appearance Program (electronic monitoring). Concerns continue about the detention of children.[164] In 2007, a federal district court in a lawsuit filed against

---

[161] *See* Reno v. Flores, 507 U.S. 292 (1993). Juveniles are defined as noncitizens under the age of 18. 8 C.F.R. § 236.3.

[162] In *Reno v. Flores*, the Court rejected the assertion that noncitizen juveniles had a right to release from custody to non-family members. The juvenile detention regulations were upheld on procedural due process grounds as well.

[163] *A District Court Finds Conditions at Hutto Family Residential Center Substandard*, 84 INTER. REL. 936 (Apr. 23, 2007).

[164] *See House Judiciary Subcommittee Takes Testimony of Medical Care Provided to ICE Detainees*, 85 INTER. REL. 1737 (June 16, 2008); Office of the Inspector General, Dept. of Homeland Security, A Review of DHS' Responsibilities for Juvenile Aliens (2005); Amnesty International USA

DHS regarding the detention conditions for families with children at the Hutto detention facility in Taylor, Texas found that the conditions were substandard and the case was settled.[165]

2. After an Order of Removal

The statutory provision applying to the detention and removal of noncitizens after a removal order are set forth in INA § 241. Removal is required within 90 days of the order of removal.[166] This 90 day time period is referred to as the removal period. The removal period begins either: (1) when the order becomes administratively final; (2) when a court's final order is entered if a judicial appeal is sought and the administrative order was stayed; or (3) when a noncitizen is released from detention or confinement unrelated to the immigration process.[167]

Continued detention and suspension of the 90 day removal requirement is possible in three circumstances. First, continued detention is authorized if the noncitizen refuses or fails to obtain required documents for departure from the U.S.[168] The statute states that the noncitizen may "remain in detention during such extended period" while making travel arrangements. Second, noncitizens deemed inadmissible or deportable under any criminal or terrorist ground must be detained during the removal period.[169] "Under no circumstances" may the DHS release these noncitizens from custody during the removal period.[170] Third, continued detention is authorized for any noncitizen who is ordered removed and is inadmissible on any ground, and noncitizens who are found by DHS to be a risk to the community or unlikely to comply with the removal order.[171]

The INA specifies that after the 90-day removal period has ended, the noncitizen is "shall be subject" to DHS supervision.[172] The conditions that may be imposed for supervision are set forth in the INA and include: regularly appearing at an immigration office; submitting, if necessary, to medical and psychiatric exams; and providing information under oath about activities and any other information deemed appropriate. A bond may be required as part of an order of supervision.

Unaccompanied Children in Immigration Detention (2003), *available at* http://www.amnestyusa.org/refugee/pdfs/children_detention.pdf.

[165] Bunikyte v. Chertoff, 2007 WL 1074070 (W.D. Tex 2007).

[166] INA § 241(a)(1) (" . . . the Attorney General shall remove the alien from the United States within a period of 90 days. . . . ").

[167] INA § 241(a)(1)(B).

[168] INA § 241(a)(1)(C).

[169] INA § 241(a)(2).

[170] INA § 241(a)(2). Under no circumstances may a noncitizen be released if inadmissible or deportable under §§ 212(a)(2), (3)(B) or §§ 237(a)(2), (a)(4)(B), including all criminal grounds and terrorism grounds.

[171] INA § 241(a)(6) permits detention of those inadmissible under INA § 212(a) or removable under INA §§ 237(a)(1)(C), (a)(2), and (a)(4).

[172] INA § 241(a)(3).

The indefinite detention of a noncitizen after an order of removal because the noncitizen's home country will not accept her return has been challenged. The indefinite detention of inadmissible noncitizens has long been accepted in the U.S. immigration system.[173] Moreover, as discussed above, the continued detention after the 90 day removal period is also contemplated under INA § 241(a)(6). In *Zadvydas v. Davis*, 533 U.S. 678 (2001), the Supreme Court addressed the authority of the Attorney General when the removal period was extended indefinitely. The Court held there is a limit on continued detention under INA § 241(a)(6) when a noncitizen had been admitted to the U.S. in contrast to an applicant for admission. The 90 day removal period can be suspended and continued detention is authorized only in limited circumstances. The government had argued that indefinite detention was justified to prevent flight and protect the community from dangerous individuals.

In *Zadvydas*, the Court held there is an implicit limit on continued detention and the DHS is only authorized to detain a noncitizen after the removal period for a reasonable time period. A period of six months is the presumptive time limit for post-removal detention. An noncitizen for whom there is no significant likelihood of reasonably foreseeable removal must be released. The Court's decision was premised on the idea that "[f]reedom from imprisonment . . . lies at the heart of the liberty that [the due process] protects and indefinite detention for persons with final order who can not be removed to any country is impermissible."

After *Zadvydas* the Attorney General issued a memorandum to guide detention decisions. The Department of Justice published an interim regulation in November 2001 establishing procedures for the review of detention on a six months basis if removal was unlikely in the reasonably forseeable future.[174] Noncitizens have been released under these procedures, primarily noncitizens from Cuba, Laos, Vietnam and Cambodia.

A 2004 GAO report about detention after the *Zadvydas* decision concluded that ICE does not have readily available information to determine whether custody reviews are held in a timely manner.[175] The GAO report also concluded this lack of information made it difficult for ICE to ensure that custody determinations were consistent with the *Zadvydas* requirement of determining whether the likelihood of removal was reasonably forseeable.

In *Clark v. Martinez*, 543 U.S. 371 (2005), the Supreme Court addressed the issue of continued detention of noncitizens who are inadmissible under INA § 212 after the removal period. The Court held that the *Zadvydas* rule interpreting INA § 241(a)(6) to limit detention beyond the removal period applies to noncitizens who are inadmissible. As a matter of statutory interpretation, the detention authorized under INA § 241(a)(6) was applicable to noncitizens who were inadmissible and deportable. There was no distinction between the two groups included. The case

---

[173] *See* Schaughnessy v. United States ex rel. Mezei, 345 U.S. 206 (1953).

[174] 66 Fed. Reg. 56,967, Nov. 14, 2001.

[175] Immigration Enforcement: Better Data and Controls are Needed to Ensure Consistency with the Supreme Court Decision on Long-Term Detention, GAO 2004.

involved two Cubans who arrived in the U.S. in 1990 and had been paroled into the U.S. Their parole had been revoked in 2000 and 1993 and they were both inadmissible due to criminal convictions.

3.   Indefinite Detention

Continued detention of certified terrorists under INA § 236A after the removal period is permissible. Certified terrorists are not protected under the *Zadvydas* and *Clark* interpretations of INA § 241(a)(6) discussed above. Congress has expressly authorized mandatory, indefinite detention in INA § 236A.

A noncitizen detained as suspected terrorist under INA § 236A, who has not been removed and who is unlikely to be removed in the reasonably foreseeable future, may be detained for an additional six months if release will threaten national security of the U.S. or the safety of the community or any person.[176]

---

[176] INA § 236A(a)(6).

Chapter 13

IMMIGRATION ENFORCEMENT

A.　UNDOCUMENTED IMMIGRATION

The undocumented population in the United States grows by 300,000 to 500,000 individuals per year. In 2006, researchers at the Pew Hispanic Center estimated that twelve million undocumented immigrants resided in the United States.[1] Of that figure, 57 percent were from Mexico, 24 percent from other parts of Latin America, 9 percent from Asia, 6 percent from Europe and Canada, and 4 percent from Africa and other areas.[2] Almost two-thirds (68 percent) of the unauthorized population lives in eight states: California (24 percent), Texas (14 percent), Florida (9 percent), New York (7 percent), Arizona (5 percent), Illinois (4 percent), New Jersey (4

---

[1] Jeffrey Passell, Estimates of the Size and Characteristics of the Undocumented Population, Mar. 21, 2005, *available at* http://pewhispanic.org/reports/report.pho?ReportID=44.

[2] *Id.* at 4.

percent), and North Carolina (3 percent).[3] Almost a third of the undocumented population (32 percent) is spread throughout other parts of the country.[4] States such as Georgia, Colorado, Maryland, Massachusetts, Virginia, and Washington have more than 200,000 undocumented immigrants. Nevada, Oregon, Pennsylvania, Michigan, Ohio, Wisconsin, and Tennessee each have more than 100,000. Connecticut, Utah, Minnesota, Kansas, New Mexico, Indiana, Iowa, Oklahoma, and Missouri have more than 55,000 undocumented immigrants.[5]

Most undocumented immigrants are adults (8.8 million); 56 percent of these adults are men, and 44 percent are women.[6] About 1.5 million families have at least one parent who is undocumented along with children who are all U.S. citizens. Another 460,000 are mixed-status families in which some children are U.S. citizens and some are undocumented.[7]

Undocumented immigrants account for about 4.3 percent of the civilian labor force — about 6.3 million workers out of a labor force of 146 million. Although they can be found throughout the workforce, undocumented workers tend to be overrepresented in certain occupations and industries. They are much more likely to be in broad occupation groups that require little education or do not have licensing requirements. The share of undocumented immigrants who work in agricultural occupations and construction and extractive occupations is about three times the share of native workers in these types of jobs. In contrast, undocumented immigrants are conspicuously sparse in white collar occupations. Whereas management, business, professions, sales, and administrative support account for half of native workers (52 percent), fewer than one-fourth of the undocumented workers are in these areas (23 percent).

This Chapter is an overview of U.S. immigration enforcement. Throughout the country's history, the U.S. has become increasingly determined to keep people from entering the country without inspection and apprehend those who have entered and are undocumented.

B.   AT THE U.S./MEXICO BORDER

1.   Creation of the Border Patrol

By the 1960s the flow of undocumented Mexicans was rapidly increasing and straining the resources of the Border Patrol. In 1962, after a severe drought in northern and central Mexico leading to high unemployment, U.S. officials estimated that the number of aliens who crossed the border without inspection increased by 41 percent and reported a 2.9 percent increase in the number of deportable Mexicans apprehended by the Border Patrol. In addition, U.S. wage rates attracted Mexican laborers. In lower Texas, for instance, cotton pickers were

---

[3] *Id.* at 11.

[4] *Id.* at 11.

[5] *Id.* at 14.

[6] *Id.* at 18.

[7] *Id.* at 19.

paid $2.50 per hundred pounds, while cotton pickers in Mexico were paid 75 cents.[8] Within two years, 59 percent of the deportable aliens arrested were Mexican, a 13 percent increase over 1963, attributable to the termination of the Bracero program.[9]

During this era, the Border Patrol used airplanes to monitor the border and seek out concentrations of aliens in places such as ranch areas. These strategies helped to locate over 4,000 deportable aliens in 1963.[10] By 1964, over 56,000 aliens were transported back to Mexico using an airlift in order to return people closer to their homes in southern Mexico. Another 54,000 were transported back to Mexico via train to Chihuahua.[11]

Attempts to smuggle aliens also increased at the time. In 1966, for example, three small boats of smuggled aliens were found in Mission Bay near San Diego; a rental truck was parked nearby waiting to take people to interior points of California. The aliens had paid $125 to $150 each.[12] In 1967, more aliens were found, concealed in trucks, as well as in new cars being freighted across the Canadian border.[13] In 1977, the INS established an Office of Anti-Smuggling to reduce alien smuggling in hopes of "immobilizing criminal conspiracies responsible for bringing in and transporting undocumented aliens."[14] No one knows, of course, how many similar attempts succeeded.

During the last four months of fiscal year 1977, 100 extra Border Patrol agents were sent to Chula Vista to augment the permanent force. During that period, about 145,000 aliens were apprehended, compared to 96,ooo the previous year.[15]

Procedural restrictions on lawful residency disadvantaged Mexicans, thereby increasing the attraction of illicit entry. The ability to apply for lawful permanent resident status through adjustment of status without having to exit the United States was added by the 1965 amendments. Aliens, other than crewmen and natives of contiguous countries (i.e., Mexico and Canada) and islands, who had been admitted or paroled (i.e., entered with inspection), could apply for adjustment of status to permanent resident status without leaving the country to get an immigrant visa. The act specifically excluded any aliens born in any country of the Western Hemisphere.[16] In 1977, adjustment of status became available to Western Hemisphere immigrants if they qualified under an immigration category, but the provision does not apply to most undocumented Mexicans because the law requires that the person must have initially entered with inspection.[17] The procedural

---

[8] Immigration and Naturalization Service, 1963 Annual Report.

[9] Immigration and Naturalization Service, 1964 Annual Report.

[10] Immigration and Naturalization Service, 1963 Annual Report.

[11] Immigration and Naturalization Service, 1964 Annual Report.

[12] Immigration and Naturalization Service, 1966 Annual Report.

[13] Immigration and Naturalization Service, 1967 Annual Report.

[14] Immigration and Naturalization Service, 1977 Annual Report.

[15] Immigration and Naturalization Service, 1966 Annual Report.

[16] Immigration and Naturalization Service, 1977 Annual Report.

[17] Immigration and Naturalization Service, 1977 Annual Report.

challenges to obtaining lawful permanent residence status contributed to the decision on the part of many undocumented Mexicans to simply enter without inspection even though they may have been able to qualify under a lawful immigrant category.

A different procedural option became available for some Mexican citizens crossing the U.S. border in 1966. Despite the increased fears of smuggling, the United States started to issue border-crossing cards to alleviate travel difficulties. Border, passport, and visa requirements were waived for Mexican nationals with border-crossing cards. These allowed individuals to remain in the United States for up to six months. The Mexican government reciprocated with a card valid from thirty days to six months.[18]

Today, the Border Patrol (formerly part of INS) is the mobile and uniformed enforcement arm of the Bureau of Immigration and Custom Enforcement of the Department of Homeland Security, responsible for protecting more than 8,000 miles of international land and water boundary. The Border Patrol contains twenty-one sectors, including nine southwest border sectors, sectors on the northern border, and those in Livermore, California; Miami, Florida; New Orleans, Louisiana; and Mayaguez, Puerto Rico.

In spite of general problems with the federal budget in the 1990s, money for immigration enforcement steadily increased. While a general federal hiring freeze was experienced in 1992 and 1993, In 1994 the Border Patrol was able to hire 350 new officers (300 were added to San Diego and fifty to El Paso, where the need was regarded as greatest), and 700 new positions were added in 1995. Close to 1,000 more were added in 1996.

The Border Patrol is engaged in a variety of activities, including boat patrol operations, antismuggling operations, and employer sanctions. Even before the creation of the Homeland Security Department, the Border Patrol was involved in intelligence work. It also has desert-area rescue teams, emergency response teams, canine units, drug awareness programs for schools, and scouting activities for youth, and is involved in the detection of aliens with criminal backgrounds. Of course, the Border Patrol is best known for border surveillance (or "linewatching"), transportation and traffic checks, and interior enforcement.

Though the Border Patrol is involved in myriad functions, patrolling the southern border is its primary task and that is where resources have been constantly added since the 1970s. In the late 1980s, an estimated 11.3 to 3.9 million undocumented crossings along the southern border occurred annually; 1.2 to 3.2 million were Mexicans crossing the southwest border. By the mid-1990s, some 88 percent of the Border Patrol's agents were stationed along the Mexican border, and southern border apprehensions accounted for 98 percent of all border apprehensions. And while the Border Patrol has always believed that the simple, large presence of an organized force would serve as a deterrent to some Mexicans contemplating an illicit crossing, a substantial portion of linewatch time has been spent in the apprehension and deportation of undocumented Mexican immigrants.

---

[18] Immigration and Naturalization Service, 1966 Annual Report.

The apprehension aspect of linewatch operations continues to be a part of the Border Patrol routine. When deterrence does not work and persons suspected of surreptitious entry are observed, agents pursue and arrest. Although such agents usually work with partners, often pursuing individuals, sometimes four or five agents can effectuate the arrest of groups of up to seventy immigrants who have been detected in safe houses used by smuggling operations.

Once numerical limitations began being applied to Mexico in 1965 and in 1976, waiting lists developed and there was more pressure for Mexicans to enter surreptitiously in response to available seasonal work and recruitment efforts by U.S. growers. Much of the public and policy makers reacted negatively to 'the illicit entries by Mexicans, and the rise of anti-immigrant sentiment in the 1970s was conspicuous. Although INS officials acknowledged that Mexicans did not make up the majority of undocumented aliens in the country, Mexicans were targeted by INS sweeps. In the mid-1970s, as exclusionists advanced a labor displacement theory, Congress considered an employer sanction law that was referred to as the Rodino Bill, named after Congressman Peter Rodino, a powerful immigration policy figure in Congress. Exclusionists persistently complained about undocumented workers coming across the United States-Mexico border, and the commissioner of the INS routinely alleged that twelve million undocumented aliens were in the United States. In 1977, for example, of the deportable aliens arrested by the INS, more than 80 percent were Mexican. Mexicans also continued to be the targets of highly publicized INS raids in the interior of the country.

2.   Operation Gatekeeper

Beginning in 1994, the Clinton administration implemented Operation Gatekeeper, a strategy of "control through deterrence" that involved constructing fences and militarizing parts of the southern border that were most easily traversed. Instead of deterring migrants, their entry choices were shifted to treacherous terrain-the desert and the mountains. The number of entries and apprehensions were not at all decreased, and the number of deaths because of dehydration and sunstroke in the summer or freezing in the winter dramatically surged. In 1994, fewer than 30 migrants died along the border; by 1998, the number was 147; in 2001, 387 deaths were counted; and in 2007, 409 died.[19]

a.   Development of Operation Gatekeeper

The San Diego Sector of the DHS Border Patrol covers the section of the United States-Mexico border that historically has been the preferred site of entry for those entering the United States without inspection.[20] This sector contains sixty-six miles of international border.[21] Tijuana, Mexico's third largest city, lies

---

[19] California Rural Legal Assistance Foundation, Charts on page 191 of Defining America Through Immigration Policy; Frontera NorteSur, *2008 Migrant Death Count*, July 8, 2008, *available at* http://newspapertree.com/news/2630-2008-migrant-death-count.

[20] Gustavo De La Vinaa, U.S. Border Patrol San Diego Sector Strategic Planning Document, April 29, 1994, at I.

[21] *Id.* at 3.

directly south of San Diego, California, the sixth largest city in the United States.[22] A smaller Mexican city, Tecate, is situated in the eastern end of the sector.[23]

In 1994, over 450,000 apprehensions of illicit border crossings were made in the San Diego sector. This number far surpassed the sectors with the next highest apprehension: Tucson (139,473) and McAllen, Texas (124,251). In the period prior to the end of 1994, undocumented border crossers in the San Diego sector commonly entered in the western part of the sector near the city of San Diego. Often, many of these individuals traveled through private property, and some were even seen darting across busy freeways near the international border inspection station. Clearly, most of the illicit crossers entered along the fourteen-mile area from Imperial Beach (at the Pacific Ocean) to the base of the Otay Mountains.[24] Most of the stretch involves "easy terrain and gentle climbs," where the crossing lasts only ten or fifteen minutes to a pickup point.[25] Even individuals who were apprehended and turned back across the border were just as likely to attempt reentry in the westernmost part of the sector at that time.[26]

These highly visible border crossings resulted in tremendous public pressure on the INS to act. Residents of San Diego complained. Anti-immigrant groups demanded action. Politicians decried lack of border control. President Clinton came up with an answer and an approach to the question of "illegal immigration." In his State of the Union address on January 24, 1995, Clinton signaled a renewed get-tough policy against undocumenteds, including "mov[ing] aggressively to secure our borders by hiring a record number of border guards" and "cracking down on illegal hiring."[27] Knowing that Clinton faced reelection in 1996, administration officials hoped that renewed enforcement effort against undocumented aliens would shore up the president's support among voters in California, who overwhelmingly passed the anti-immigrant Proposition 187 in 1994.[28]

Operation Gatekeeper was one of several operations that resulted from the Clinton administration's commitment to a new aggressive enforcement strategy for the Border Patrol. In August 1994, the INS Commissioner Doris Meissner approved a new national strategy for the Border Patrol.[29] The heart of the plan relied on a vision of "prevention through deterrence," in which a "decisive number of enforcement resources [would be brought] to bear in each major entry corridor" and the Border Patrol would increase the number of agents on the line and make effective use of technology, raising the risk of apprehension high enough to be an

---

[22] *Id.*

[23] *Id.*

[24] Border Patrol, *Operation Gatekeeper: 3 Years of Results in a Glance* (1997).

[25] *Id.*

[26] INS Fact Sheet, *Frustrating Illegal Crossers at Imperial Beach and Moving the Traffic Eastward*, October 17, 1997.

[27] *72 Interpreter Releases* 169, January 30, 1995.

[28] *Clinton Will Seek Spending to Curb Aliens, Aides Say: Political Balancing Act*, N.Y. TIMES, January 22, 1995, at AI; Matthew Jardine, *Operation Gatekeeper*, 10 PEACE REV. 329, 333 (1998).

[29] U.S. Border Patrol, *Border Patrol Strategic Plan: 1994 and Beyond-National Strategy*, July 1994.

effective deterrent."[30] The specific regional enforcement operations that resulted included (1) Operation Blockade (later renamed Hold the Line), which commenced in September 1993 in the Greater El Paso, Texas areas; (2) Operation Gatekeeper, which commenced in October 1994, south of San Diego, California; (3) Operation Safeguard, which also commenced in October 1994 in Arizona; and (4) Operation Rio Grande, which commenced in August 1997 in Brownsville, Texas.[31] The idea was to block traditional entry and smuggling routes with border enforcement personnel and physical barriers.[32] By cutting off traditional crossing routes, the strategy sought to deter migrants or at least channel them into terrain less suited for crossing and more conducive to apprehensions.[33] To carry out the strategy, the Border Patrol was to concentrate personnel and resources in areas of highest undocumented alien crossings, increase the time agents spent on border-control activities, increase use of physical barriers, and carefully consider the mix of technology and personnel needed to control the border.[34]

In the San Diego sector, efforts would be concentrated on the popular fourteen-mile section of the border beginning from the Pacific Ocean (Imperial Beach) stretching eastward.[35] That stretch had been the focus of some resources before Gatekeeper. Steel fencing and bright lighting were already in place in sections of this corridor, erected in part with the assistance of the U.S. military.[36] Yet because of the persistent traffic of undocumented entrants along this corridor, phase I of Gatekeeper continued to concentrate on increased staffing and resources along the fourteen mile area.[37]

As the INS implemented its national border strategy, Congress supported these efforts; between 1993 and 1997, the INS budget for enforcement efforts along the southwest border doubled from $400 million to $800 million.[38] The number of Border Patrol agents along the southwest border increased from 3,389 in October 1993 to 7,357 by September 1998—an increase of 117 percent.[39] State-of-the-art technology, including new surveillance systems using electronic sensors linked with low-light video cameras, infrared night-vision devices, and forward-looking infrared systems for Border Patrol aircraft, were installed.[40]

Given these additional resources, Operation Gatekeeper buildup was impressive. Before Gatekeeper, the San Diego sector had 19 miles of fencing. By the end of

---

[30] *Id.* at 6.

[31] Petition on the Inter-American Commission on Human Rights of the Organization of American States (Feb. 9 1999), at 16, n.4.

[32] *National Strategy*, at 6–9.

[33] *Id.* at 7; U.S. General Accounting Office, *Illegal Immigration: Status of Southwest Border Strategy Implementation* 3 (May 1999).

[34] *Id.*

[35] *Id.* at 1, 4, 8.

[36] *Id.*

[37] *Id.* at 8.

[38] *Operation Gatekeeper: New Resources, Enhanced Results*, INS Fact Sheet, July 14th, 1998.

[39] 1999 GAO report, at 7.

[40] INS Fact Sheet, February 2, 1998.

1999, 52 miles were fenced. Half of this fencing runs from the Pacific Ocean to the base of the Otay Mountains. Fourteen miles contain primary fencing (a 10-foot wall of corrugated steel landing mats left over from the Vietnam War.) Two backup fences, each 115 feet tall, have been constructed. The first backup fence is made of concrete pillars. The second backup fence is made of wire mesh, with support beams. Both are topped with wire. Almost 12 miles of this stretch are illuminated by stadium lights. Some fencing has been erected on sections of the Otay Mountains, as well as around various East San Diego communities along the border.[41] The Department of Defense's Center for Low Intensity Conflicts as well as the Army Corps of Engineers provided guidance to INS on the development of Gatekeeper features.[42]

In contrast, in areas other than San Diego, the construction was not as significant. The El Centro sector covers 72 miles of the border and is sparsely populated on the U.S. side and has only 7 miles of fence — all of it between the contiguous border cities of Calexico and Mexicali. Arizona has 17 miles of fencing-6 in the Yuma sector and 9 in the Tucson sector. That fencing was erected exclusively in the towns and cities. Texas has the Rio Grande River and 7 miles of fencing from El Paso/Ciudad Juarez area-2 miles of primary and 5 of secondary. Thus, 73 miles of fencing was erected on the 2,000 mile and the 66-mile San Diego sector had 72 percent of it, as well as 54 percent of the illumination.[43] The 144-mile long San Diego and El Centro sectors have almost a third of the Border Patrol agents stationed on the 2,000 mile of southwest border.[44]

b.   Results of Operation Gatekeeper

In implementing its national strategy beginning in 1994, the INS made a key assumption about its "prevention through deterrence" approach: "alien apprehensions will decrease as [the] Border Patrol increases control of the border."[45] In other words, the INS anticipated that as the show of force escalated by increasing agents, lighting, and fencing, people would be discouraged from entering without inspection so that the number of apprehensions naturally would decline. In fact, the Border Patrol predicted that within five years, a substantial drop in apprehension rates border-wide would result.[46] The deterrence would be so great that "many will consider it futile to continue to attempt illegal entry."[47] These assumptions and predictions have not borne out.

Apprehension levels did not decline. The enforcement strategies began with Operation Gatekeeper in San Diego and Operation Blockade in El Paso in 1994. True, apprehension levels for those two sectors were considerably lower in 1998 than in 1993 (e.g., 531,689 apprehended in San Diego in 1993 compared to 248,092

---

[41] November 19,1999 letter to Mary Robinson.

[42] *Id.*, 1999 GAO Report, at 12.

[43] November 19, 1999 letter to Mary Robinson.

[44] October 6, 2000 letter to Gabriela Rodriguez Pizarro.

[45] *National Strategy*, at 4.

[46] September 30, 2000 letter to Mary Robinson.

[47] *National Strategy*, at 23.

in 1998). However, the apprehension levels surged in El Centro, Yuma, and Tucson during the same period (e.g., from 92,639 to 387,406 in Tucson; from 30,508 to 226,695 in El Centro; and from 23,548 to 76,195 in Yuma).[48] From 1994 to 1999, total apprehensions statistics along the southwest border actually increased by 57 percent![49] The increase continues. The number of apprehensions for all of the fiscal year 2000 was 1.64 million, which was an all-time high.[50] In sum, after Gatekeeper sealed the western most section of the border, apprehensions in San Diego declined, but crossers moved east and overall apprehensions actually increased substantially.

As Operation Gatekeeper closed the Imperial Beach corridor, the border-crossing traffic moved east. Frustrated crossers moved first to Brown Field and Chula Vista, and subsequently to the eastern sections of the San Diego sector.[51] Before Gatekeeper began in 1994, crossers were just as likely to make their second try at the westernmost part of the sector; but that changed very quickly. By January 1995, only 14 percent were making their second try near Imperial Beach. The illicit border traffic had moved into "unfamiliar and unattractive territory."[52] The tragedy of Operation Gatekeeper is the direct link of its prevention through deterrence strategy to an absolutely horrendous rise in the number of deaths among border-crossers who were forced to attempt entry over terrain that even the INS knew to present "mortal danger" due to extreme weather conditions and rugged terrain.

The death statistics are revealing. In 1994, 23 migrants died along the California-Mexico border. Of the 23, 2 died of hypothermia or heat stroke and 9 from drowning. By 1998, the annual total was 147 deaths — 71 from hypothermia or heat stroke and 52 from drowning. Figures for 1999 follow this unfortunate trend, and in 2000, 84 were heat stroke or hypothermia casualties. The total death count along the entire border for the year 2000 was 499. Of those, 100 died crossing the desert along the Sonora-Arizona border. Since 2001, Mexico's ministry of Foreign affairs has counted the deaths of 2,956 Mexican migrants crossing the border.[53] The federal agency has identified the main causes of death as dehydration (1062), drowning (583) and vehicle accidents (247).[54]

The INS thought that with the combination of fencing and increased spending on border patrols at the most frequently traveled routes, undocumented immigration would slow if not come to a complete halt altogether. But migrants were not deterred, and began looking for other areas to penetrate the border. However, the new areas of travel were risky; they were more dangerous and life

---

[48] *Id.* at 18–20.

[49] *Apprehension Statistics for the Southwest Border*, Oct. 7, 1999 (Chart prepared by California Rural Legal Assistance Foundation).

[50] 1999 GAO report, at 17–18, 20.

[51] *Id.* at 18–20.

[52] November 19, 1999 letter to Mary Robinson.

[53] Frontera NorteSur, *supra* note 19.

[54] *Id.*

threatening. Given the challenges, more migrants turned to costly smugglers to help them cross the border.

In spite of the aid of smugglers, the new routes were simply too dangerous for many border-crossers and death of migrants surged. The number of migrant deaths increased 600 times from 1994 to 2000; a number that could be attributed to Operation Gatekeeper's pushing surreptitious entries towards treacherous eastward routes.

3. The Secure Fence Act of 2006

The Secure Fence Act was signed by President Bush on October 26, 2006. The statute's main goals in regards to the U.S.-Mexico border were to "achieve operational control on the border" and "the construction of fencing and security improvements in the border area from the Pacific Ocean to the Gulf of Mexico."[55]

The Secure Fence Act defines "operational control" as the prevention of all unlawful U.S. entries, including entries by terrorists, other unlawful aliens, instruments of terrorism, narcotics, and other contraband.

The Secure Fence Act amends the Illegal Immigration Reform and Immigrant Responsibility Act of 1996 to direct the Secretary of Homeland Security to provide for at least 2 layers of reinforced fencing, the installation of additional physical barriers, roads, lighting, cameras, and sensors on over 700 miles of the U.S.-Mexico Border.[56] The surveillance measures were to be installed by May 30, 2007, and the fence construction was to be completed by May 30, 2008.[57]

C. HUMAN TRAFFICKING

Human trafficking is the world's fastest growing criminal activity.[58] It is a modern-day form of slavery. Measured by profitability, human trafficking ranks third only behind the arms and drug industries.[59] Human trafficking generates an estimated $9.5 billion in annual revenue and affects over 12.3 million people worldwide.[60]

Victims of human trafficking are subject to force, fraud or coercion for the purposes of sexual exploitation or forced labor. There are two major forms of human trafficking. As defined by the Trafficking Victims Protection Act of 2000

---

[55] The Secure Fence Act of 2006, Pub. L. 109-367, Oct. 26 2006, *available at* http://frwebgate.access.gpo.gov/cgi-bin/getdoc.cgi?dbname=109_cong_public_laws&docid=f:publ367.109.pdf.

[56] *Id.* at Sec. 3.

[57] *Id.*

[58] Office to Monitor and Combat Trafficking in Persons, U.S. Department of State, Trafficking in Persons Report 6 (June 3, 2005), *available at* http://www.state.gov/documents/organizatio/47255.pdf [hereinafter TIP Report 2005].

[59] Office to Monitor and Combat Trafficking in Persons, U.S. Department of State, Trafficking in Persons Report 13 (June 5, 2006), *available at* http://www.state.gov/documents/organization/66086.pdf. [hereinafter TIP Report 2006].

[60] *Id.* at 6.

(TVPA), "Severe Forms of Trafficking in Persons" involves either:

- Sex Trafficking: the recruitment, harboring, transportation, provision, or obtaining of a person for the purpose of a commercial sex act, in which a commercial sex act is induced by force, fraud, or coercion, or in which the person forced to perform such an act is under the age of 18 years; or
- Labor Trafficking: the recruitment, harboring, transportation, provision, or obtaining of a person for labor or services, through the use of force, fraud or coercion for the purpose of subjection to involuntary servitude, peonage, debt bondage or slavery.[61]

According to the Department of State, between 14,500 and 17,500 are trafficked into the United States annually.[62] Prior to 2000, no comprehensive federal law existed to protect victims of human trafficking or prosecute traffickers.[63] Punishment of human trafficking occurred through legislation aimed at specific components of the offense, such as immigration offenses or violations of involuntary servitude.[64] Prosecution of human trafficking using these means were minimal, and victims of human trafficking were frequently re-victimized because they were most often deported back to a country where they would be stigmatized and ostracized.[65]

Congress passed the Trafficking Victims Protection Act in October 2000 (TVPA), in the hopes of combating human trafficking more effectively and better protecting victims. TVPA allowed for easier prosecutions of human traffickers. Recent court decisions have interpreted the TVPA as expanding the Thirteenth Amendment anti-slavery provisions to apply to human traffickers.[66] In addition, the TVPA also revised the United States Code adding new crimes involving peonage and slavery, thereby expanding the definition of "involuntary servitude" to apply to human trafficking.[67]

The TVPA also increased maximum penalties for crimes relating to human trafficking. A life sentence is now allowed for death, kidnapping, an attempt to kidnap, aggravate sexual abuse, an attempt to commit aggravated sexual abuse, or an attempt to kill occurring in conjunction with a trafficking violation.[68] Sex trafficking is also made a crime punishable by life imprisonment when force, fraud or coercion is used to cause a person to engage in commercial sex acts.[69] The TVPA also augmented the penalties for kidnapping, inducing an individual into slavery, placing a person into peonage or selling someone into voluntary servitude from a

---

[61] Victims of Trafficking and Violence Prevention Act of 2000, Pub. L. 108-396, Oct. 28, 2000.

[62] U.S. Dep't of Health and Human Servs., Fact Sheet: Human Trafficking, *available at* http://www.acf.hhs.gov/trafficking/about/fact_humman.html.

[63] http://www.acf.hhs.gov/trafficking/about/fact_human.html.

[64] Angela D. Giampolo, *The Trafficking Victim's Reauthorization Act of 2005: The Latest Weapon in the Fight Against Human Trafficking*, 16 TEMP. POL. & CIV. RTS. L. REV. 195. at 197 (Fall 2006).

[65] *Id.*

[66] TIP Report 2005, *supra* note 1; and *see* Giampolo, *supra* note 64 at 200.

[67] TVPA § 7102(5).

[68] Giampolo, *supra* note 64, at 200.

[69] *Id.*

ten to twenty year maximum sentence, a fine, or both.[70] Moreover, the Act enhanced provisions safeguarding restitution to the victims for the full amount of the victim's losses and permitting victims to bring an action against their traffickers in federal district court.[71]

TVPA also allowed for better prosecution of human traffickers by adding provisions protecting their victims. The most important of these provisions was the creation of the "T" and "U" visas. Congress wanted to strengthen the ability of law enforcement agencies to detect, investigate and prosecute trafficking and crimes against immigrants. Congress recognized that in order to achieve this goal the victim's cooperation and assistance was necessary. Moreover, where the victims are undocumented immigrants, their status in the United States can directly affect their ability to cooperate and assist in investigation and prosecution efforts. The TVPA therefore provided specific avenues for victims of human trafficking and certain crimes to obtain lawful immigration status through the T and U Visas.

T visas grant legal status to victims of severe form of trafficking in persons.[72] The applicant must be on U.S. territory and must be willing to comply with reasonable requests for assistance in the investigation and prosecution of their traffickers.[73] The applicant must have a law enforcement official attest to their cooperation.[74] T visa holders are eligible to apply for permanent residency after three years if they can show that they would suffer "extreme hardship involving unusual and severe harm" if they were deported.[75]

The U Visa grants temporary legal status for a period of three years, after which an applicant can apply for adjustment of status to lawful permanent resident.[76] In order to qualify for a U Visa, applicants must demonstrate that they meet the requirements set forth in INA 101(a)(15)(U), 8 U.S.C. 1101(a)(15)(U). In order for an application to be successful, U Visa applicants must demonstrate that they 1) were a victim of a qualifying crime, such as assault, domestic violence, false imprisonment;[77] 2) and demonstrate that "the victim has been helpful, is being helpful, or is likely to be helpful" in the investigation or prosecution of the criminal activity.[78] In order to prove their cooperation, applicants must have a qualifying law enforcement official certify in writing that they were helpful in the investigation of the crime(s). U Visas are also available for qualifying relatives. A victim's spouse, child, or if the victim is a child, their parents and minor siblings may be granted U status.

---

[70] *Id.* at 201 and *see* TVPA § 7109(b)(2)(B).

[71] 18 U.S.C.A. § 1593, and *see* Giampolo, *supra* note 64, at 201.

[72] INA § 101(a)(15)(T)(i)(I), 8 U.S.C.A. § 1101 (a)(15)(T)(i)(I).

[73] *Id.*

[74] INA § 101(a)(15)(T)(i) (III), 8 U.S.C.A. § 1101(a)(15)(T).

[75] Giampolo, *supra* note 64, at 200.

[76] INA § 101(a)(15)(U), 8 U.S.C.A. § 1101(a)(15)(U).

[77] INA § 101(a)(15)(U)(iii), 8 U.S.C.A. § 1101(a)(15)(U)(iii).

[78] INA § 101(a)(15)(U)(i)(III), 8 U.S.C.A. § 1101(a)(15)(U)(i)(III).

D. LEGALIZATION

1.   Amnesty under IRCA (1986)

On November 6, 1986, President Reagan signed into law The Immigration Reform and Control Act of 1986 (IRCA).[79] IRCA was adopted after almost a decade of intensive, highly visible public debate punctuated by several bills that passed one or both houses by slim margins only to die without final approval. When the IRCA did pass, it did so only in the waning hours of the 99th Congress, after an exceedingly fragile compromise was stitched together, and then only by thin margins.[80]

This legislation contained two key provisions: employer sanctions and legalization, or amnesty, of undocumented aliens. This section focuses on the amnesty provisions of IRCA.

IRCA contained legalization programs for several groups. First, the general legalization provision granted amnesty to persons who had resided in the United States since before January 1, 1982. Second, the Special Agricultural Worker (SAW) program gave amnesty to agricultural workers, and lastly a program that gave Cubans and Haitians who had resided in the United States since before 1982 immediate permanent residence.

Before the 1970s, the United States government had never employed amnesty to address immigration problems.[81] The controversial nature of legalizing the status of millions of people illegally present in the country accounted for much of this reluctance.[82] Despite this controversy, Congress viewed an amnesty program as the least costly alternative, politically as well as financially and administratively.[83]

The debates over IRCA focused on three main questions.[84] The first question was whether to enact an immediate amnesty or a 'triggered' amnesty. A triggered amnesty would delay the legalization of aliens until a presidential commission had determined that adequate enforcement mechanism were in place.[85] The rational behind a 'triggered' amnesty was that without adequate enforcement, an amnesty would offer an invitation to thousands of aliens to cross the borders of the United States seeking legal status.[86] Some groups expressed support for a triggered amnesty, however widespread criticism quickly followed.[87] Many argued that the complexity of the provision would preclude its enactment and instead they

---

[79] Immigration Reform and Control Act of 1986, Pub. L. No. 99-603, codified as 8 U.S.C. § 1101.

[80] Juan P. Osuna, *Amnesty in the Immigration Reform and Control Act of 1986: Policy Rationale and Lessons from Canada*, 3 Am. U. J. Int'l. & Pol'y 145, at 148.

[81] *Id.*

[82] *Id.*

[83] *Id.*

[84] *Id.* at 162.

[85] *Id.*

[86] *Id.*

[87] *Id.*

advocated for a simplified administrative program.[88] Congress rejected a triggered amnesty in the final version of the bill in favor of a program beginning almost immediately.[89]

The cutoff date was the second major concern in the amnesty debates. Supporters of a restrictive amnesty wanted a date further in the past, whereas supporters of a liberal amnesty argued for a date closer to the date of enactment.[90] Ultimately, congress established a compromise between these two positions.[91] IRCA would grant amnesty to all undocumented immigrants present in the United States prior to January 1, 1982.[92]

The third issue discussed in the debates was whether to provide benefits and services to undocumented immigrants who were to receive amnesty.[93] The final version of the IRCA excluded aliens from receiving benefits for five years, except for a few selected programs such as disability benefits.[94]

a.   Amnesty for Persons Residing in the United States Since Before January 1, 1982

Title II of IRCA established an amnesty provision for undocumented aliens residing in the United States and directed the Attorney General to promulgate implementing regulations. Although Title II is divided into four sections, it is the first one, the legalization status sections, that is the most important for amnesty purposes.

IRCA established that the Attorney General shall adjust the undocumented status of "an alien to that of an alien lawfully admitted for temporary residence" if the alien meets certain requirements.[95] First, in order to be granted amnesty, undocumented immigrants had to have resided in the United States continuously since before January 1, 1982 in an unlawful status. According to INA § 245A(b)(1)(B)(ii), aliens are deemed to have 'resided continuously' if they were not absent from the United States for more than "brief, casual and innocent absences" since January 1, 1982.[96] In addition, the undocumented immigrant must have been maintaining a residence in the United States and their departure must not have been based on a deportation order.[97] This section was problematic because applicants had to provide tangible documentation that they had resided in the United States for more than five years.[98] According to the regulations, this

---

[88] *Id.*

[89] *Id.*

[90] *Id.*

[91] *Id.*

[92] *Id.*

[93] *Id.*

[94] *Id.*

[95] Immigration and Nationality Act, § 245A, 8 U.S.C.A. § 12255a.

[96] INA § 245A(3)(B).

[97] INA § 245A(g)(2)(B).

[98] INA § 245A(g)(2)(D).

documentation included such items as past employment records, such as paycheck stubs or tax forms; utility bills; school records; hospital or medical records; attestation by churches, unions or other organizations; or any other supporting documents, like money order receipts, bank books, social security cards, automobile registrations, deeds or contracts, or insurance policies. Many undocumented immigrants in the United States, however, avoided accumulating such documentation for fear of being discovered and deported.[99] Consequently, many applicants had a difficulty proving that they arrived before 1982.[100]

Another obstacle to proving continuous residence was that undocumented individuals who entered as nonimmigrants before January 1, 1982 had to establish that their periods of authorized stay expired before that date through the passage of time or that their unlawful status was known to the government as of that date.[101] The phrase 'known to the government' was a source of controversy.[102] The implementing regulations defined the phrase as meaning 'known to the INS,' despite considerable public opposition.[103] The regulations provided that an alien's unlawful status was known to the government in only four situations: 1) if the INS received information on the alien from another federal agency; 2) if the INS made an affirmative determination prior to January 1, 1982 that the alien was subject to deportation proceedings; 3) if the INS responded to an inquiry by another agency regarding the individual's status; 4) if the applicant produces documentation from a school stating that he or she had violated his or her nonimmigrant status.[104]

A lawsuit was filed to challenge the INS definition of the phrase "known to the Government." In *Farzad v. Chandler*, 670 F. Supp. 690 (N.D. Tex. 1987), the court held that the INS definition was inconsistent with IRCA and outside the scope of authority of the INS. In a different case, *Kalaw v. Ferro*, 651 F. Supp. 1163, 1170, the court endorsed the INS definition of the phrase. The decision in *Kalaw*, however, did express some concern that the INS interpretation of the phrase would make IRCA legalization difficult to administer.[105]

Second, applicants for amnesty under IRCA also had to show that they had not committed any felonies or more than two misdemeanors, and that they were otherwise admissible under INA § 212(a).[106]

Finally, in order to be granted amnesty, undocumented immigrants had to file an application for temporary residence between May 5, 1987 and May 4, 1988. Individuals granted amnesty under these provisions became temporary residents. They could only apply for permanent residence 18 months after they first applied for temporary residence. Moreover, in order not to lose their legal status,

---

[99] Wilentz, *Harvest of Confusion*, TIME, Nov. 3, 1986, at 28.

[100] *Id.*

[101] INA § 245A(a)(2)(B).

[102] Juan P. Osuna, *Amnesty in the Immigration Reform and Control Act of 1986: Policy Rationale and Lessons from Canada*, 3 AM. U. J. INT'L. & POL'Y 145, at 8.

[103] *Id.*

[104] *Id.* at footnote 140, and *see* 52 Fed. Reg. 43,845 (1987).

[105] *Id.*

[106] INA § 245A(a)(4).

temporary residents were required to adjust their status to permanent residents within twelve months of becoming eligible to file.[107] That deadline was extended twelve months for each applicant by the Immigration Act of 1990.

b.   Amnesty Program for Special Agricultural Workers (SAW)

The IRCA Amnesty Program for Special Agricultural Workers permitted aliens who had worked on perishable commodities for a specified period of time prior to May 1, 1986 to apply for temporary resident status. The SAW program's eligibility, benefit and application requirement provisions are somewhat more liberal than those in the general legalization program.

The SAW program was designed to maintain the availability of agricultural labor, while "protect[ing] workers to the fullest extent of all applicable federal, state, and local laws . . . to provide them with a status that insures their employment is fully governed by all relevant law without exception."[108] SAWs were not required to continue working in agriculture to gain permanent residency and could freely travel outside the United States in a manner similar to permanent resident aliens.[109]

In order to be eligible for amnesty under the SAW program, an applicant had to establish that: 1) they resided in the United States, and 2) had performed seasonal agricultural work for at least 90 man-days between May 1, 1985 and May 1, 1986.[110]

Under INA § 210(a)(1)(A), an applicant had to file for temporary residency during the eighteen-month period which began on June 1, 1987, and ended on November 30, 1988. Moreover, the agricultural worker had to be admissible under INA § 212(a). The provision that barred any individual convicted of a felony or more than two misdemeanors did not originally apply to SAWs, but it was added later.[111]

SAW contained a two-phase temporary residency provision. Applicants who had performed agricultural labor for 90 days during the prior three consecutive years fell into Group 1.[112] Group 1 had a cap at 350,000.[113] These SAWs became legalized for permanent residency on December 1, 1989.[114] Group 2 covered all other qualified applicants all those SAWs who would be eligible for Group 1 but for the cap, and all other agricultural workers with temporary residency status under INA

---

[107] INA § 245A(b)(1)(A).

[108] H.R. REP. NO. 682, 99th Cong., 2d Sess., pt. 1, at 46, *reprinted in* 1986 U.S.C.C.A.N. 5649, 5650.

[109] INA § 210(a)(4).

[110] INA § 210(a)(1)(B).

[111] *Id.*

[112] *Id.*

[113] *Id.*

[114] *Id.*

§ 210.[115] Group 2 SAWs obtained permanent residency status on December 1, 1990.[116] SAW temporary residents were adjusted automatically on that date and had to complete only a simple form to get their permanent resident cards.[117]

At the time that the application period had closed on November 30, 1988, more than 1.1 million undocumented immigrants had applied for amnesty under SAW, and more than half of them were in California.[118]

2.   Cubans and Haitians (1986)

For decades, Cubans and Haitians have been migrating to the United States seeking to flee the political turmoil and extreme poverty of their native countries. In the early months of 1980, declining economic conditions in Cuba cumulated in "a rising tide of dissatisfaction, particularly among those with relatives in the United States."[119] In response, Fidel Castro announced on April 4, 1980 that anyone who wished to leave Cuba could do so.[120] Thousands chose to do so through chartered flights to Costa Rica.[121] Yet due to the number of émigrés and their increasing publicity, Castro soon suspended air travel.[122] On April 20, 1980, he announced that anyone who wished to emigrate to the United States could, but only by boat and only through the port of Mariel.[123]

Within hours of this broadcast, fleets of boats left southern Florida to pick up relatives and others seeking to leave Cuba.[124] The Mariel boatlift began as a small boat exodus of several thousands of Cubans that were welcomed into the United States as refugees from the Castro government. After President Carter offered an "open arms" welcome to the initial group, however, these numbers swelled to over 125,000. All of the refugees were called "Marielitos" because of the port of Cuba from which they launched to sea.

The Carter administration had a hard time classifying this large group of Cubans, and declined to assign them refugee status.[125] The Cubans of the Mariel boatlift were already in the United States but the administration wanted to avoid setting a precedent that might encourage people from other countries to enter the United States without documents and claim to be refugees.[126] The Refugee Act of

---

[115] *Id.*

[116] *Id.*

[117] *Id.*

[118] Schuck, *supra* note 2, at 6.

[119] VERNON M. BRIGGS, JR., MASS IMMIGRATION AND THE NATIONAL INTEREST 143 (M.E Sharpe Publishers 2003).

[120] *Id.*

[121] *Id.*

[122] *Id.*

[123] *Id.*

[124] *Id.*

[125] *Id.* at 144.

[126] *Id.*

1980 allowed for asylee status to be granted to those already in the United States, but the status was meant for individual applicants and not large groups of people.[127]

Cubans were arriving from Mariel joined a number of boats crowded with Haitians émigrés. These Haitian boats had been arriving in southern Florida since the early 1970s, but the attention given to the Cuban refugees sparked public debate and controversy. Since Haiti and Cuba are neighboring islands that were both ruled by dictators (one leftist and anti-American, the other right-wing and pro-American),[128] the situation of their citizens fleeing to the United States had to be compared. Successive U.S. administrations had consistently contended that most Haitians were illegal immigrants while virtually all Cubans were refugees and asylees.[129] This disparate treatment of Haitians and Cubans had caused political and legal difficulties and evoked charges of racism because the Cubans tended to be white whereas Haitian immigrants were exclusively black.[130] Over the years, the INS had returned several hundred prospective immigrants to Haiti because they did not believe they were seeking protection from political persecution.[131]

As the number of Haitian immigrants increased during the Mariel Era, the Carter administration refused to exercise its authority to parole for Haitians as a group.[132] Instead, they were given the same status as Cubans who entered during this time. On June 20, 1980, the U.S. attorney general administratively established a new temporary status for the immigrants from both countries. They were designated as "Cuban-Haitian Entrants (Status Pending)" and were given a six-month parole into the United States.[133] This status was later extended to all those who entered as of October 10, 1980. In total, over 6,000 Haitians and 123,000 Cubans entered the United States during this six-month period and their immigration status remained uncertain.[134]

When Reagan replaced Carter in 1981, the Reagan administration began to take a strong stand against Haitians trying to enter the United States by sea.[135] The U.S. Coast Guard was ordered to interdict Haitians on the high seas and turn them back before they could enter U.S. territorial waters and claim asylum.[136] The U.S. government also simultaneously started placing all mass arrivals of people into detention centers rather than releasing them to sponsors, as had been the practice up to that time.[137] Lawsuits were filed to challenge this detention policy as racially

---

[127] *Id.*

[128] *Id.* at 145.

[129] *Id.*

[130] *Id.*

[131] *Id.*

[132] *Id.*

[133] *Id.* at 146.

[134] *Id.*

[135] *Id.*

[136] *Id.*

[137] *Id.*

discriminatory against Haitians, but the U.S. Supreme Court ultimately decided that detention policy was legal and not discriminatory.[138]

The Reagan administration continued to give Cubans preferential treatment and announced that all Cubans whose status was pending could adjust their status to become legal permanent residents under the Cuban Adjustment Act of 1966.[139] Efforts were also made by advocates to grant status to Haitians who had entered during the Mariel era, but these failed.[140]

IRCA was ultimately the legislation that concluded the controversy over the status of "Cuban-Haitian Entrants." Section 202 of the IRCA granted amnesty to Cubans and Haitians who had resided in the United States since before 1982.[141] The applicant had to : 1) have received an immigration designation as "Cuban/Haitian Entrant" or, 2) be a Cuban or Haitian national with respect to whom any record was established with the INS before January 1, 1982.[142]

In order to qualify, the Cuban or Haitian had to apply within a two year window, which ended on November 6, 1988.[143] Haitians and Cubans who applied and qualified became immediately eligible for permanent residence as of January 1, 1982, and were therefore immediately eligible for naturalization as well.[144]

3. Nicaraguans and Cubans (1997)

Several political groups sympathetic to the plight of undocumented immigrants after the passage of IIRIRA in 1996 petitioned Congress to enact reforms.[145] The establishment of IIRIRA posed a threat of mass deportation of immigrants throughout the United States.[146] In 1997, Central American advocates launched a new campaign to win legal permanent residency for Salvadorans and Guatemalans.[147] Salvadoran and Guatemalan authorities concerned with the destabilizing effects that would result from deportations also lobbied for a remedy.[148] Several months into the campaign, Salvadorans and Guatemalans joined forces with Nicaraguans who had fled the Sandinista government and were also victims of IIRIRA.[149] These lobbying efforts resulted in the passage of

---

[138] *Id.*

[139] *Id.*

[140] *Id.* at 147.

[141] IRCA, *supra* note 79, at section 202.

[142] *Id.*

[143] *Id.*

[144] *Id.*

[145] 14 CARDOZO J. INT'L & COMP. L. 177, at 191.

[146] *Id.*

[147] Susan Coutin, *The Odyssey of Salvadoran Asylum Seekers, North American Congress on Latin America Report on the Americas*, May 1, 2004, at 38 (noting that more than one million Salvadorans fled to the United States from 1980 to 1992 during El Salvador's civil war).

[148] *Id.*

[149] *Id.*

Nicaraguan Adjustment and Central American Relief Act of 1997 (NACARA).[150]

Congress passed NACARA to provide relief to select groups of immigrants and protect long-time residents from deportation. NACARA used separate provisions to address two statutorily distinct groups of immigrants. The first provision applies to Cubans and Nicaraguans, and the second applies to Guatemalans, Salvadorans and Eastern Europeans.

a.   NACARA provisions for Nicaraguans and Cubans

NACARA enables certain eligible non-citizens who are physically present in the United States to adjust to legal permanent residency status, regardless of whether they had been inspected and admitted or paroled.[151] In order to be eligible for adjustment of status under NACARA 202(a), an applicant must: 1) be a national of Nicaragua or Cuba; 2) have been physically present in the U.S. continuously from at least December 1, 2005 until the date the application is filed; 3) be otherwise admissible to the United States; and 4) have filed an application for adjustment of status before April 1, 2000.[152]

Pursuant to § 202, Cubans and Nicaraguans seeking permanent residency status under NACARA only had to complete an adjustment of status form. Applicants did have to show proof of continuous physical presence through reliable documentation. For the purposes of the statute, "continuous physical presence" meant physical presence in the United States with total absences not exceeding 180 days. Absences between November 19, 1997 and June 22, 1998, however, were not counted for continuous presence purposes.[153] Moreover, on March 17, 2000, the Department of Justice issued various final regulations that establish a more flexible standard for proving initial presence and continuous residence in the United States.[154]

Applicants for permanent residency under NACARA faced few bars to their adjustment. A Cuban or Nicaraguan applicant under NACARA was not subject to several inadmissibility requirements, such as public charge and labor certification provisions. Moreover, these applicants could be granted permanent residence even if they were in exclusion, deportation, or removal proceedings. If there had been a final administrative determination to deny their application, however, the applicant could not adjust their status under NACARA.

NACARA also allowed Nicaraguans and Cubans to file derivative claims for adjustment of status and obtain work authorization for their spouses and children.[155] In order to apply, the spouse or child had to be present in the United

---

[150] *Id.*

[151] Nicaraguan Adjustment and Central American Relief Act, Pub. L. No. 105-100, 111 Stat. 2160, Tit. II, Div. A (1997) [hereinafter NACARA].

[152] *Id.*

[153] *Id.*

[154] *See* 65 Fed. Reg. 15,846–15,925, reprinted in Interpreter Releases, March 24, 2000, Appendix II.

[155] *Id.* at § 202(d)(1)(B).

States.[156] If the individual was not in the United States, the primary applicant could file a parole application to request that their spouse or child be admitted into the country in order to apply for NACARA adjustment.[157]

4.   Haitians (1998)

NACARA allowed for the adjustment of status for certain Nicaraguan and Cuban national, and more limited immigration relief for immigrants from other countries. NACARA, however, failed to address the status of Haitian nationals who were in a similar position.[158] Advocates for Haitian immigrants made immediate calls for action.[159] President Bill Clinton responded by granting certain Haitian nationals Deferred Enforced Departure (DED) status pending congressional action to address their plight.[160] The Clinton Administration and a bipartisan coalition of members of Congress worked together to establish relief for at least some Haitian nationals who had entered the United States.[161] The Haitian Refugee Immigration Fairness Act of 1998 (HRIFA) was the result of these efforts. HRIFA was enacted as part of an omnibus bill for the fiscal year 1999.

HIFRA provides that certain Haitian nationals can adjust their status to permanent residence. HIFRA established that to be eligible for adjustment of status, a Haitian national must have been present in the United States on December 31, 1995, and 1) have filed for asylum before December 31, 1995, and 2) have been paroled in the United States prior to December 31, 1995, after having been identified as having a credible fear of persecution, or paroled "for emergent reasons deemed strictly in the public interest."[162] A Haitian could also be eligible for adjustment of status if they were a child, as defined by the INA, at the time of arrival and on December 31, 1995, who 1) arrived without parents and remained without parents in the United States since arrival; 2) became orphaned subsequent to arrival in the United States; or 3) was abandoned by parents or guardians prior to April 1, 1998, and had remained abandoned since that date.[163]

The statute also required that an eligible Haitian be physically present continuously from at least December 31, 1995 to the date the application was filed.[164] Again, aggregate absences of not more than 180 days did not affect the continuous physical presence required by the provision. Also, applicants were exempt from similar inadmissibility provisions as NACARA applicants. Haitians were still able to qualify for HRIFA if they were 1) considered a public charge; or 2) had labor certification or other special qualifications; 3) were present in the

---

[156] *Id.*

[157] *Id.*

[158] Austin T. Fragomen, IMMIGRATION FUNDAMENTALS: A GUIDE TO LAW AND PRACTICE 4-49 (Practicing Law Institute).

[159] *Id.*

[160] *Id.*

[161] *Id.*

[162] Haitian Refugee Immigration Fairness Act of 1998, Pub. L. 105-277 (Oct. 21, 1998).

[163] *Id.*

[164] *Id.*

United States without admission or parole; 4) were immigrants without proper documents; 4) had been unlawfully present in the United States.[165]

Derivate applications were also allowed. HRIFA allowed an applicant's spouse, child, or unmarried son or daughter to also be eligible for status under the act provided that the qualifying relative was: 1) a national of Haiti, 2) was otherwise admissible, and 3) applied for such adjustment and was physically present in the U.S. on the date the application was filed.[166] There was an exception to this last requirement for unmarried sons and daughters: they had to establish continuous physical presence from December 31, 1995 to the date of application. Spouses and children of the applicant only had to be physically present in the United States on the date the application was filed.[167]

Haitian HRIFA applicants faced certain obstacles to filing their applications. First, applications had to be filed between June 11, 1999 and April 1, 2000.[168] However, this limited application window only applied to principal applicants.[169] The period for eligible family members to apply remains open indefinitely.[170] A second obstacle applicants faced was dealing with the burdensome document requirements.[171] HRIFA applicants had to present a birth certificate.[172] They also needed documentary evidence that they had been present in the United States on December 31, 1995, and documents proving their residence for each 90 period since then.[173]

5.   The Proposed "Earned Legalization" Program

While President Bush's guestworker proposal was not introduced as independent legislation, his plan was incorporated into a bipartisan compromise in early April 2006 written largely by Senators Mel Martinez (R-Florida) and Chuck Hagel (R-Nebraska) (Hagel-Martinez bill). The compromise is best understood in the context of a number of other guest-worker proposals that have been proposed in Congress. Some, like the Hagel-Martinez bill, have included a separate path toward legalization (permanent residence and eventual citizenship) for undocumented workers. Others are limited to agricultural workers. Their approaches to wages vary. The most noteworthy are summarized in the following sections.

---

[165] *Id.*

[166] *Id.*

[167] *Id.*

[168] *Id.*

[169] *Id.*

[170] *Id.*

[171] *Id.*

[172] *Id.*

[173] *Id.*

a.   AgJOBS

In 2003, the Agricultural Jobs Opportunity, Benefits and Security (AgJOBS) Act was introduced in the House (H.R. 3142) and the Senate (S. 1645) after several years of bipartisan efforts and earlier iterations. The sponsors of the House Bill were Representatives Chris Cannon (R-Utah) and Howard Brennan (D-California). Senators Edward Kennedy (D-Massachusetts) and Larry Craig (R-Idaho) sponsored the Senate version. The bill would have granted lawful permanent residency to as many as 500,000 undocumented farmworkers and revised the current H-2A agricultural worker program. The bill represented a compromise between the farmworker advocates and their employers and contained several concessions on both sides.

After six years, a worker would be eligible for legalization. Under the legislation, temporary resident status would be granted to undocumented farmworkers who could establish proof of 575 hours of agricultural work or 100 workdays during the eighteen-month period preceding the introduction of the legislation. After the grant of temporary resident status, the farmworker would be required to complete an additional 2,060 hours of agricultural work or 360 workdays during the next six years to be eligible for lawful permanent residency.

The proposed changes to the current H-2A guestworker program by AgJOBS was significant. The legislation would replace the labor certification process of the present H-2A program (requiring that recruitment efforts of available U.S. workers have been attempted and failed) with the labor attestation found in the H-1B program (where the employer simply attests in a statement that U.S. workers are unavailable). This was a major concession by farmworker advocates who believe that the present labor certification process is more protective of farmworker wages than the proposed labor attestation process.

Changes to the wage structures were also contemplated by AgJOBS. The legislation would effectively freeze the Adverse Effect Wage Rate (AEWR) for three years. AEWR is used to determine the wages that farmworkers receive. Employers wanted to eliminate AEWR altogether. Currently, employers must pay workers the highest of three rates: the state or federal minimum wage, the AEWR, or the local prevailing wage. The AEWR was created under the Bracero program as a necessary protection against the depression in prevailing wages that results from guestworker programs.

The proposal also would expand the H-2A program by allowing temporary workers to enter the United States for a period of up to three years. After three years, these guestworkers would be obligated to return to their countries of origin. This provision sounded very familiar to the guestworker reform proposed by President Bush. However, AgJOBS' opportunity for legalization after six years was not part of the president's plan.

b.   Hagel-Daschle

Soon after President Bush announced his temporary worker proposal in January 2004, Senators Chuck Hagel (R-Nebraska) and Tom Daschle (D-South Dakota) unveiled their bipartisan immigration reform package that contained a temporary worker provision. [Note: Senator Daschle was not reelected to the Senate November 2004.]

A new H-2C category would be open to 250,000 nonimmigrant workers per year for five years and would not be limited to agricultural workers. Workers would be admitted for an initial period of two years, and employers would be allowed to petition for extensions for workers for an additional two years. Spouses and children of willing workers would be eligible for derivative status. Employers would be required to pay the prevailing wage, and H-2C employees would be allowed to maintain status and change employers after three months.

The legislation also contained a path to legalization ("earned adjustment of status") for undocumented immigrants who had resided in the United States for at least five years prior to the introduction of the legislation. They must also demonstrate aggregate employment in the United States for at least three of the five years immediately preceding the introduction of the legislation and for at least one year following the enactment. An alien who filed an application for earned adjustment of status would be required to pay a fine plus a $1,000 application fee.

An alien who was physically present in the United States on the date the legislation was introduced, but who did not satisfy the five-year physical presence requirements, would be able to apply for "transitional worker status." Transitional workers would be eligible for adjustment of status to permanent residence if they were lawfully employed in the United States for an aggregate of more than two but fewer than three of the five years immediately preceding the introduction of the legislation and are employed for at least two years following the enactment.

c.   Goodlatte-Chambliss

In November 2003, Congressman Bob Goodlatte (R-Virginia) introduced legislation that would substantially alter the H-2A agricultural worker program. The program's application process would be streamlined to become a labor attestation program, rather than the current labor certification program. Employers would simply promise to comply with requirements (e.g., temporary nature of the work, benefits, wages, recruitment of domestic workers). The Department of Labor would have seven days to review and approve the employer's petition for workers. The employer would still need to engage in "positive recruitment" (i.e., private market efforts) in areas of labor supply but would no longer be required to recruit U.S. workers through government job services efforts. The legislation would eliminate the AEWR. A special "prevailing wage" would apply that could be determined by the employers' own prevailing wage survey. Currently, H-2A employers must provide free housing to nonlocal U.S. and foreign workers, but under this legislation, employers could choose to provide a monetary housing allowance if the state's governor has certified that there is sufficient farmworker housing available in the area. With philosophical undertones similar to that of President Bush, Congressman Goodlatte felt that his legislation was a good way to address the problem of undocumented workers in the United States, by providing a streamlined temporary visa program through which farmworkers could be hired. Workers currently in the United States in undocumented status would be given a one-time chance to return home and apply for the program legally.

Senator Saxby Chambliss (R-Georgia) introduced a Senate bill in March 2004 that was almost identical to the Goodlatte bill. The Chambliss bill added a couple of noteworthy provisions. Currently, employers must reimburse workers for their transportation costs to and from their place of recruitment. This bill would allow employers to pay for travel costs to and from the place where the worker was approved to enter the United States, which could be the U.S. consulate hundreds of miles from the worker's home. The bill sought to overrule the decision in *Arriaga v. Florida Pacific Farms*,[174] regarding the Fair Labor Standards Act. It would essentially allow H-2A employers to reduce worker's wages below the federal minimum wage by imposing on the workers the obligation to absorb visa, transportation, and other costs related to entering the United States. Although the current H-2A program is intended to fill agricultural jobs that last fewer than eleven months, the Chambliss bill would distort the definition of "seasonal" employment by allowing an employer to file an unlimited number of applications for guestworkers during a twelve-month period.[175]

d.   SOLVE Act

In May 2004, congressional Democrats introduced the Safe, Orderly, Legal Visas and Enforcement Act of 2004 (SOLVE Act), sponsored by such legislators as Senator Edward Kennedy (D-Massachusetts) and Representatives Bob Menedez (D-New Jersey) and Luis Gutierres (D-Illinois). The comprehensive package proposed changes to facilitate family reunification in the immigrant visa categories and reductions in the waiting lists (backlog reduction) as well as adjustment to the income tests for sponsors and would have established a "future worker program." New programs would be established for workers in low skilled positions. H-1D visas would be available to 250,000 workers for a period of two years, and the visas would be renewable for two additional terms (six years total). H-2B visas would be available to 100,000 workers for a period of nine months and renewable for up to forty months. After three months with one employer, the workers in each category could change employers (job portability). The Department of Labor would have to agree through the "strengthened" attestation process that U.S. workers are not available and that the employment of foreign workers will not adversely affect the wages and working conditions of U.S. workers. H-2B and H-1D workers would be paid the prevailing wage, as determined by the shop's collective bargaining agreement or, in its absence, under federal labor laws.

The programs would include a path to permanent residency for undocumented immigrants. Immigrants who have been in the United States for five or more years as of the date the legislation was introduced are eligible, if they can demonstrate twenty-four months in aggregate employment in the United States and payment taxes. Applicants here fewer than five years are eligible for transitional status of five years, during which time they can work and travel abroad if necessary. After

---

[174] 305 F.3d 1228 (11th Cir. 2002).

[175] Farmworker Justice Fund, Inc. Policy Brief, September 2004.

twenty-four months, they too would be eligible for permanent residence.

e. Arizona Bill

Republican members of the Arizona congressional delegation came up with their own plan. H.R. 2899 was introduced by Congressmen Kolbe and Flake in the House and Senator McCain (S. 1461) in the Senate in July 2003. The legislation would have created a new nonimmigrant worker visa category, H-4A. Employers would have to provide the same benefits, wages, and working conditions provided to other employees similarly employed; the visa would be portable- employers could not prevent nonimmigrants from accepting work for a different employer. The employer would have to verify that the worker did not or would not displace a U.S. worker. The visa would be valid for an initial period of three years and could be extended once for another three years. The spouse and children of the worker would not be given a special visa to join the worker. A filing fee plus a $1,500 penalty would be required. Adjustment to legal permanent resident (LPR) status would be available to the H-4A nonimmigrant either by petition of employer or through self-petition, if the alien has maintained status for three years.

Critics of the McCain/Kolbe/Flake proposal included another Arizona Republican congressman, J.D. Hayworth. He claimed that the legislation was a "transparent path to amnesty" that would "only encourage a new wave of illegal aliens and make America's uncontrolled and unacceptable immigration debacle even worse than it is now." A local resident complained that the legislation was "not a solution because it does not address the true problem of uncontrolled borders with Mexico and Canada. It is a surrender because politicians from both parties are pandering to the Latino vote."[176]

f. McCain-Kennedy

With some fanfare and timed when the Migration Policy Institute announced the formation of an Immigration Task Force to analyze immigration policy, Senators McCain and Kennedy and Representatives Kolbe, Flake, and Gutierrez introduced sweeping immigration reform in May 2005 that included major guestworker components: H-5A and H-5B.

A new temporary worker visa (H-5A) would be created for nonagriculture or high skilled jobs. To qualify, the person must have a job offer. H-5A workers would have the same rights as U.S. workers under applicable federal, state, and local government and employment laws; they would not be treated as independent contractors. For the first year, at least 400,000 visas will be made available, with up to 80,000 more depending on demand. Available visas in subsequent years will follow similar formulas. After four years of work, H-5A visa holder may apply for lawful permanent resident status through an employer or through self-petition.

The H-5B program is for aliens (including undocumented) who are in the United States before the date of introduction of the legislation (May 2005). The person's spouse and children may also apply. The applicant must pay an initial $1,000 fine.

---

[176] John P. Hoeppner, *Border Proposal Is a Surrender*, Arizona Republic, Aug. 5, 2003, at 8B.

The initial period of authorized stay is for six (three plus three) years. After a period of time, the person eligible for adjustment to LPR status if still working, must pay an additional $1,000 fine, must submit to security checks, and must demonstrate knowledge of English and U.S. civics.

While Senator McCain went through great pains to make sure that the legislation is not viewed as an amnesty by emphasizing the penalties that undocumented workers would have to pay to participate in the program, Representative Tancredo immediately expressed opposition: "There might be a little more lipstick on this pig than there was before," he said, "but it is most certainly the same old pig. Time and time again, history has shown us that amnesty actually increases illegal immigration."[177] Similarly, Rosemary Jenks, director of government affairs for Numbers USA, which advocates reducing the undocumented immigrant population, said her group also opposed the McCain-Kennedy proposal and only "would support an exit amnesty, like a tax amnesty, that would allow illegal immigrants to leave and not apply a ban on future reentry."[178]

g.   Hagel-Martinez

For much of March 2006, the U.S. Senate wrangled over the issue of immigration. Although the McCain-Kennedy proposal sparked much of the debate that occurred first in the Judiciary Committee, Committee Chair Senator Arlen Specter (R-Pennsylvania) came up with his own legislation that attempted to balance McCain-Kennedy provisions with pressure from others to include strong enforcement provisions. For example, Republican Senate Majority Leader Bill Frist threatened to come up with his own Sensenbrenner-type bill if the Judiciary Committee failed to produce something. In fact, even though the committee did put forward a bill, Frist introduced his own bill (S. 2454) anyway, threatening to make his the central bill if an accord was not reached by Easter break. The Senate debate raged on.

Two days prior to the congressional break, a major breakthrough was made when a bipartisan compromise was cobbled together by Senators Hagel and Martinez. The Hagel-Martinez bill (S. 2611) was embraced by two-thirds of the senators, including Senators Frist, McCain, Kennedy, and Reid. The deal came after days of negotiations designed to persuade Republicans who had supported the more lenient measure that emerged from the Senate Judiciary Committee to shift their backing to a bill with more Republican ownership. The Democrats thought they still had enough votes to pass the Judiciary Committee version until two of the Judiciary Committee bill's primary sponsors, Senators McCain and Lindsey Graham (R-South Carolina), informed Kennedy that they were no longer with him and, instead, would back the Hagel-Martinez compromise. Able to secure a few changes in the compromise, Kennedy went to the Senate floor to urge Democrats to endorse the deal.

---

[177] Darryl Fears, *Immigration Measure Introduced*, WASHINGTON POST, May 13, 2005, at A8.

[178] *Id.*

The Hagel-Martinez compromise in early April addressed the issue of undocumented immigrants in a number of manners. For those who could prove that they had been in the country for five years or more (perhaps eight million), a renewable work visa would be granted after paying a $2,000 penalty, back taxes, and undergoing a criminal background check. After five years, those individuals could apply for legalization provided they remained employed, learned English, and did not commit crimes. For those undocumented who were in the country for more than two years but less than five (perhaps three million), a temporary work visa was available if they left the country and applied for the visa outside. The bill also provided for a Bush-type guestworker program for 325,000 visas annually.

The compromise immediately received criticism from the right and the left. Senator John Kyle (R-Arizona) dismissed the deal as "artificial and meaningless," and former House speaker Newt Gingrich (R-Georgia) called it "a cave-in" to the Democrats. Congressman Tancredo chimed in, "The Senate amnesty deal is miserable public policy."[179] On the other hand, the AFL-CIO President John Sweeney, desiring a broader legalization program, said the agreement "tears at the heart of true immigration reform."[180] Immigrant rights advocates were opposed because of provisions such as those that would preclude the participation of anyone who had used a false Social Security number to obtain employment in the past, permit indefinite and possibly permanent detention of deportable immigrants, expand the use of expedited removal proceedings, give local and state police the authority to assist the federal government in enforcing federal immigration laws, and permit the deportation of someone who has never committed a crime if the attorney general had reason to believe that the person is a member of a gang.

On April 7, 2006, the day before Congress took its break, the agreement on Hagel-Martinez appeared to fall apart. Republicans blamed the Democrats and vice versa. The disagreement was over whether amendments could be introduced to the bill floor of the Senate and what rules would be used in a Senate-House conference that would ultimately reconcile the Senate bill with the enforcement-only Sensenbrenner House bill. The Democratic leadership also was concerned about the rules that would govern the conference between the two bodies of Congress. They feared that without a bipartisan agreement on rules limiting concessions to the House, Congressman Sensenbrenner, who certainly would be one of the House conferees, would have his way and the legislation would come out of the negotiations intensely anti-immigrant. With no agreement over process, the Senate took its Easter break.

However, discussions continued. President Bush met with a bipartisan group in late April that included Senators Martinez, McCain, Kennedy, Reid, Specter, and Frist, signaling to many that the president was willing to endorse the legalization provisions of Hagel-Martinez. When the Senate reconvened on April 24, 2006, these senators were committed to bringing the legislation provisions of Hagel-Martinez. When the Senate reconvened on April 24, 2006, these senators were committed to bringing the legislation to the Senate floor by Memorial Day. They

---

[179] Jonathan Weisman, *Senate Offers Permits to Most Illegal Immigrants*, WASHINGTON POST, Apr. 7, 2006, at A1.

[180] *Id.*

worked tirelessly and considered countless amendments. On May 15, President Bush delivered a major primetime address to the nation on the immigration issue, reiterating his earlier message but acknowledging that undocumented immigrants with "roots in the country" deserve a path to citizenship. By May 25, Hagel-Martinez passed the Senate by a 62–63 margin.

The May 25 legislation differed somewhat from the early April bill. Undocumented immigrants who have been in the country five years or more can continue working and eventually become lawful permanent residents and citizens after paying at least $3,250 in fines, fees, and back taxes and learning English. Those here from two to five years would have to depart the country and apply to reenter under a guestworker program. Anyone convicted of a felony or three misdemeanors is barred from these programs. Those undocumented here less than two years would have to leave the United States. AgJOBS was incorporated, which would put a million undocumented farmworkers on the path to legalization. A guestworker program would be created for up to 200,000 workers per-year; visas would be good for three years with a possible three-year extension. An additional 370-mile, triple layer fence along the U.S.-Mexico border would be constructed. The president is authorized to send six thousand National Guardsmen to help at the border. Employers are subject to increased fines and criminal penalties for hiring unauthorized workers. The names of overstayed nonimmigrants would be added to a national crime database.

A Senate-House conference committee was formed to try to reconcile the enforcement-only Sensenbrenner House bill with the more comprehensive Hagel-Martinez Senate bill that contains a path to legalization for millions of undocumented, a compromise that would include legalization appeared doubtful. Certainly, Senator Frist's support remained important. Although he once supported the House version that would make illegal immigration a felony, he changed his position, remarking on how "a mature understanding" of the handling of undocumented immigration emerged in the Senate after weeks of debate. But Congressman Sensenbrenner, the chief negotiator for the House, stated that he would not accept any legislation that would put the undocumented immigrants on a path to citizenship, and his intransigence could prevail.

E. THE CRIMINALIZATION OF IMMIGRATION

1. Immigration Crimes

Immigrants who commit crimes are deported from the United States every day. They come from all over the world, including Mexico, Canada, Europe, Africa, and the Middle East. The U.S. Supreme Court even endorsed the removal of a Somalian refugee convicted of assault back to Somalia where no formal government exists.[181] In 2002, the United States began deporting Cambodian refugees convicted of crimes back to Communist-dominated Cambodia. So

---

[181] Jama v. Immigration and Custom Enforcement, 125 S. Ct. 694 (2005). Jama was convicted of third-degree assault, a moral turpitude crime, within three years of entering the United States. Jama v. INS, 329 F-3d 630, 631 (8th Cir. 2003).

although ICE may indeed be rounding up and removing hundreds of so-called illegal immigrants who have committed crimes, the agency also is engaged in deporting convicted lawful permanent resident aliens (those with "green cards") or refugees legally admitted under U.S. refugee provisions. And these deportees have served their sentences in the criminal justice system before being deported.

a. Deporting Immigrants Based on Criminal Convictions — "Aggravated Felony"

September 11, 2001, profoundly affected the immigrant community. The Department of justice and the U.S. Congress passed at least two dozen statutes and federal regulations in response. For example, immigrants with criminal convictions are now a primary concern for the Department of justice (DOJ) and DHS. Noncitizens, including lawful permanent residents, can be deported based on a criminal conviction. Lawful permanent residents are granted permission by the U.S. government to live and work in the United States for an indefinite period of time, establishing close relatives and ties. The Immigration and Nationality Act (INA) establishes three categories of crimes that place a lawful permanent resident at risk of deportation or prevent a noncitizen from ever becoming a lawful permanent resident: (1) aggravated felonies, (2) crimes involving moral turpitude, and (3) a variety of other-crimes involving firearms, domestic violence, or controlled substances.[182]

Under the INA's aggravated felony provision, neither the adverse effect on the family of a lawful permanent resident nor the exile of someone to a country he or she never knew is considered. Despite the unfairness of these laws, courts continue to sanction them under the plenary power doctrine.[183] Deportation is clearly more detrimental to the life of a noncitizen than the imposition of a criminal sentence. Yet courts continue to treat immigration proceedings as civil proceedings, failing to view deportation as a separate and additional punishment.[184]

A deported noncitizen faces the possibility of losing his or her family, friends, and livelihood forever. Many deported noncitizens are cast to countries with which they have virtually no ties. Surprisingly, courts continue to conclude that deportation is not an additional and unequal "punishment" for noncitizens. The aggravated felony provision subjects any noncitizen convicted of an aggravated felony to deportation from the United States.[185]

The courts no longer have authority to review an aggravated felony deportation, now termed "removal." According to the Ninth Circuit Court of Appeals, "few punishments are more drastic and final than expelling a person from his country

---

[182] Robin Bronen, *Immigration Consequences of Criminal Convictions*, Alaska justice Forum (2003), *available at* http://justice.uaa.alaska.edu/forum/2o/ispring2oo3/c-immigerim.html.

[183] David Cheng, *Emigres of the Killing Fields: The Deportation of Cambodian Refugees as a Violation of International Human Rights*, 25 B.C. THIRD WORLD L.J. 221,223 (2005).

[184] *Id.* at 224.

[185] Valerie Neal, *Slings and Arrows of Outrageous Fortune: The Deportation of "Aggravated Felons,"* 36 VAND. J. TRANSNAT'L L. 1619 (2003).

when their family members are residents."[186] The legislation mandating deportation of long-time, lawful residents with strong family ties in the United States when these noncitizens are convicted of an aggravated felony continues to be disguised as an exercise in good policy. Noncitizens convicted of serious crimes are then perceived as an intolerable threat to both U.S. citizens and resident noncitizens.[187]

People expect their government to protect them from dangerous foreign nationals, particularly in the wake of 9/11. However, a closer look at the sweeping mandatory deportation scheme governing criminal grounds for deportation reveals that the aggravated felony category is so broad that it includes many crimes that bear little relation to an actual threat to public safety.[188] Thus, the distorted effect of current deportation laws results in automatic deportation for convictions as minor as petty theft, urinating in public, or forgery of a check for less than $20.

b.   Deportation Provisions: Crimes Involving Moral Turpitude

Lawful permanent residents and refugees who have been convicted of certain crimes, or who have committed certain "bad acts" without being convicted, can be removed. Problems with drugs; crimes involving moral turpitude, prostitution, and firearms; sexual crimes; and a host of other offenses can cause problems. Even very minor offenses can lead to catastrophe.

An immigrant can be deported based on one or two convictions involving moral turpitude. Only one conviction of a crime involving moral turpitude is needed to render a lawful permanent resident deportable, if the crime was committed within five years after admission and if the offense had a potential sentence of one year. A noncitizen is deportable if convicted of two separate crimes involving moral turpitude at any time, regardless of the sentence and the time since admission.

Moral turpitude crimes include theft and robbery, crimes involving bodily harm, sex offenses, and acts involving recklessness or malice. Passing bad checks, credit card scams, burglary, and even perjury can involve moral turpitude. Assault with a deadly weapon, murder, rape, and arson involve moral turpitude because those offenses require an intent to do great bodily harm. Simple assault, simple battery, and simple driving under the influence generally do not involve moral turpitude. However, a conviction for driving under the influence while the person's license was suspended is a crime involving moral turpitude.[189]

Under a separate deportation provision, aliens who are convicted of any law relating to use or possession of a firearm (e.g., a gun) or "destructive device" (e.g., a bomb) are deportable.

---

[186] *Id.*

[187] *Id.*

[188] *Id.*

[189] *Matter Of Lopez-Meza*, Int. Dec. 3423 (BIA 1999). This holding, concerning an Arizona statute, was overturned by the Ninth Circuit, but just because the Arizona statute also included sitting in a parked vehicle while drunk. *Hemandez-Martinez v. Ashcroft*, 329 F.3d 1117 (9th Cir. 2003).

c.   Aggravated Felonies

Many offenses, including murder, certain drug offenses, alien' smuggling, and even theft (with a suspended sentence of one year), have been designated as aggravated felonies. These carry the most severe immigration consequences, with little hope of relief from deportation.

Under immigration laws, an alien convicted of an aggravated felony at any time after admission is deportable.[190] An aggravated felony is defined as murder, rape, sexual abuse of a minor, any illicit trafficking in any controlled substance (including drugs, firearms, or destructive devices), money laundering, or any crime of violence (except for purely political offenses) for which the term of imprisonment imposed is at least one year. The definition also includes offenses of theft, if the term of imprisonment imposed is at least one year; treason; child pornography; operation of a prostitution business; fraud or deceit in which the loss to the victim or victims exceeds $10,000; tax evasion in which the loss to the U.S. government exceeds $10,000; crimes relating to the Racketeer Influenced and Corrupt Organizations (RICO) Act, if the term of imprisonment imposed is at least one year; alien smuggling, except in the case of a first offense involving the assisting, abetting, or aiding of the alien's spouse, child, or parent and no other individual; document trafficking, if the term of imprisonment imposed is at least one year; failure to appear to serve a sentence, if the underlying offense is punishable by imprisonment for a term of five years; and bribery, counterfeiting, or forgery for which the term of imprisonment is at least one year. An attempt or conspiracy to commit any of the crimes just mentioned is also included.[191]

So what we might think of as minor crimes-for example, selling $10 worth of marijuana or "smuggling" one's baby sister across the border illegally-also are aggravated felonies. And being convicted of a misdemeanor as opposed to a felony does not automatically preclude aggravated felon status. For example, several offenses are classified as aggravated felonies once a one-year sentence is imposed. These include theft, burglary, perjury, and obstruction of justice, even though the criminal court may classify the crime as a misdemeanor.[192] A misdemeanor statutory rape (consensual sex where one person is under the age of eighteen) will

---

[190] 8 U.S.C. § 1227(a)(2)(A) (2004).

[191] The breadth of aggravated felonies has constantly expanded since the term was introduced in the immigration laws in 1988. *See* Anti Drug Abuse Act of 1988, Pub. L. No. 100-690, § 7344(a), 102 Stat. 4181, 4470–4471 (1988). The crimes treated as aggravated felonies prior to the 1996 changes in the law can be found at immigration and Naturalization Act, § 101(a)(43), 8 U.S.C. § 1101(a)(43) (2003). Prior to 1996, the aggravated felony ground for deportation was essentially similar to the other grounds for deportation. For example, drug convictions that constituted aggravated felonies were also independent grounds for deportation under a provision for deporting persons convicted of drug crimes. Similarly, any person who had two crimes involving moral turpitude was deportable, so it did not matter if the crimes were aggravated felonies. In some cases, however, the aggravated felony definition served to authorize deportation for a single crime, where the person would not otherwise have been deportable. For example, a person convicted of a murder committed more than five years after entering the country, who had no other criminal record, would have been deportable only as an aggravated felon. A noncitizen is only deportable by reason of an aggravated felony if the conviction occurred after 1988, which is the year in which the aggravated felony deportation ground was added.

[192] *See, e.g., United States v. Campbell,* 167 F.3d 94, 98 (2d Cir. 1999).

also be treated as an aggravated felony. And a misdemeanor conviction can be an aggravated felony under the "rape" or "sexual abuse of a minor" categories.[193]

Conviction of an aggravated felony results in harsh immigration consequences. For example, an aggravated felon is ineligible for release on bond, is ineligible for asylum (although the person might be eligible for.restriction of removal" or the protections of the Convention Against Torture), is ineligible for discretionary cancellation of removal (see Section 212(c) Waiver section), can be deported without a hearing before an immigration judge (if the person is not a permanent resident), and is not eligible for a waiver for moral turpitude offenses upon admission.

d.   Section 212(c) Waiver: Its Rise and Fall

Discretionary relief from deportation for long-time lawful permanent residents convicted of serious crimes, even those eventually classified as aggravated felonies, was available from 1976 to 1996. During that time, an immigration judge could consider issues of rehabilitation, remorse, family support in the United States, and employment opportunities for aggravated felons who had entered as refugees or as immigrants, if they had become lawful resident aliens and had resided in the country for at least seven years.

In 1976, the INA did not contain a provision that would provide relief to a lawful permanent resident convicted of a serious crime who had not departed from the United States. The language and application of INA § 212(c), however, provided the impetus for an interpretation that benefited many aliens:

> Aliens lawfully admitted for permanent residence who temporarily proceeded abroad voluntarily and not under an order of deportation, and who are returning to a lawful unrelinquished domicile of seven consecutive years, may be admitted in the discretion of the Attorney General without regard to the provisions of paragraphs (1) through (25) and paragraph (30) of subsection (a).[194]

Importantly, the "provisions of paragraphs (1) through (25) . . . of subsection (a)" included grounds of exclusion that barred the entry of aliens convicted of serious crimes involving moral turpitude and narcotics offenses.[195] Therefore, under INA § 212(C), a lawful permanent resident who had resided in the United States for seven years could proceed abroad voluntarily and be readmitted at the discretion of the attorney general, even if he or she had been convicted of a serious crime that rendered him or her excludable. In essence, INA § 212(c) provided a waiver of exclusion. In practice, the attorney general could grant the waiver in exclusion or deportation proceedings, as long as the person had proceeded abroad voluntarily at some point.[196]

---

[193] Matter of Small, 23 I. & N. Dec. 448 (BIA 2002).

[194] 8 U.S.C. § 1182 (c).

[195] *Id.* § 1182 (a)(2)(A)(i) (1976).

[196] *In re L*, 1 I. & N. Dec. 1 (BIA 1940).

That similar lawful permanent residents convicted of identical crimes would be treated differently only because one had never left the United States after immigrating and the other happened to leave and return after committing the deportable offense troubled the Second Circuit Court of Appeals in *Francis v. INS*.[197] The latter person would be eligible for the 212(c) waiver, while the former would not under the Board of Immigration Appeals' (Board) interpretation of the statute. The Second Circuit ruled that the Board's interpretation violated equal protection, and, therefore, held the waiver applicable to any lawful permanent resident who had resided in the country for at least seven years.[198] Soon thereafter, the Board adopted the *Francis* decision.[199] The result was that a lawful permanent resident who had resided in the United States for seven years could apply for and be granted a waiver under INA § 212(c) in deportation proceedings, thereby allowing the person to remain in the United States as a lawful permanent resident. To be granted the waiver, the person had to persuade an immigration judge to exercise favorable discretion.

In *In re Marin*,[200] the Board summarized the major factors for immigration judges to consider in Section 212(c) cases, although each case was to be judged "on its own merits."[201] In general, the immigration judge was required to balance the adverse factors evidencing an alien's undesirability as a permanent resident with the social and humane considerations presented on his or her behalf to determine whether granting of relief appeared "in the best interests of this country."[202] The alien had the burden of showing that the positive factors outweighed the negative ones. Favorable factors included such considerations as:

> family ties within the United States, residence of long duration in this country (particularly when the inception of residence occurred while the respondent was of young age), evidence of hardship to the respondent and family if deportation occurs, service in this country's Armed Forces, a history of employment, the existence of property or business ties, evidence of value and service to the community, proof of a genuine rehabilitation if a criminal record exists, and other evidence attesting to a respondent's good character [for example, affidavits from family, friends, and responsible community representatives].[203]

Factors deemed adverse to an alien included:

---

[197] *Francis v. INS*, 532 F.2d 268 (2d Cir. 1976).

[198] Id. at 273 (holding that "[r]eason and fairness would suggest that an alien whose ties with this country are so strong that he has never departed after his initial entry should receive at least as much consideration as an individual who may leave and return from time to time"). In fact, this ruling was consistent with the Board's own interpretation of a similar provision that was part of the statute decades earlier: In re A, 2 I. & N. Dec. 459 (BIA 1946), approved by the attorney general (1947) (holding that an alien had not reentered country following his conviction was not bar to exercise of discretionary relief in deportation proceeding).

[199] *In re Silva*, 16 I. & N. Dec. 26 (BIA 1976).

[200] *In re Marin*, 16 I. & N. Dec. 581 (BIA 1978).

[201] *Id.* at 584.

[202] *Id.*

[203] *Id.* at 584–585.

the nature and underlying circumstances of the exclusion [or deportation] ground at issue, the presence of additional significant violations of this country7s immigration laws, the existence of a criminal record and, if so, its nature, recency, and seriousness, and the presence of other evidence indicative of a respondent's bad character or undesirability as a permanent resident of this country.[204]

Section 212(c) relief was not automatic. For example, in *Ashby v. INS*, that the applicant was convicted of three crimes, committed over a six-year period, which involved the use of force and weapons, and was incarcerated for eight years were critical to the Board's denial, despite twenty-seven years of lawful permanent residence.[205] Also, in *Arango-Aradondo v. INS*, the Second Circuit upheld the denial of INA § 212(c) relief when the immigration judge carefully and thoroughly weighed the evidence in the alien's favor (including his drug and alcohol rehabilitation efforts, his long-time residency in the United States, his close family ties, and the hardship he would endure in Colombia given his HIV status and his lack of ties there) against the detrimental evidence (including his sporadic employment record, his failure to file taxes, and, most important, his "very lengthy and very severe" criminal record, together with his long involvement in the drug culture).[206]

As the number of negative factors grew in a Section 212(c) case, the respondent had to introduce offsetting favorable evidence, often labeled "unusual or outstanding equities." Courts required this heightened showing when an alien was convicted of a serious drug offense, particularly one relating to the trafficking or sale of drugs. For example, in *Varela-Blanco v. INS*,[207] a conviction of lascivious acts with a child (sexual abuse of an eight-year-old niece) was a serious crime requiring a demonstration of "unusual or outstanding equities" for Section 212(c) relief.[208] Although the applicant had resided in the United States for eighteen years, the first ten were in an unlawful status. Therefore, employment during his undocumented status was not considered.[209] Furthermore, the presence of family and considerable evidence of rehabilitation was insufficient.[210]

In *Paredes- Urrestarazu v. INS*,[211] the Ninth Circuit upheld a denial of Section 212(c) relief, even though the alien demonstrated unusual and outstanding equities. He entered the United States at age twelve, was married, and had a child and numerous relatives. However, very serious adverse factors, including gang-related armed robberies, general court-martial and dishonorable discharge from the military, false testimony concerning military service, past drug abuse, and an arrest for drug possession (despite completing a diversion program), outweighed the

---

[204] *Id.* at 584.

[205] *Ashby v. INS*, 961 F.2d 555, 557 (5th Cir. 1992).

[206] *Arango-Ardono v. INS*, 13 F.3d 610, 613 (2d Cir. 1994).

[207] *Valera-Blanco v. INS*, 18 F.3d 584 (8th Cir. 1994).

[208] *Id.* at 586.

[209] *Id.* at 587.

[210] *Id.* at 587–588.

[211] *Paredes-Urrestarazu v. INS*, 36 F.3d 801 (9th Cir. 1994).

equities.[212]

In *Diaz-Resendez v. INS*,[213] however, the Fifth Circuit found that an applicant who had been convicted of possession of twenty-one pounds of marijuana with intent to distribute met the rigorous standards for Section 212(c) relief. The applicant was fifty-four years old and had been a continuous lawful resident for thirty-seven years. He had been married to a U.S. citizen for twenty-nine years, had three children who were fully dependent on him, faced imminent breakup of his marriage if deported, and otherwise had a clean criminal record except for a drunk driving charge that ended his drinking.[214]

In contrast, in *In re Roberts*, the Board denied relief to an applicant convicted of a cocaine sale constituting drug trafficking, who was separated from his wife and four children, did not financially support any of them, had an irregular employment history, and had not paid income tax for some time.[215] Similarly, in *Nunez-Pena v. INS*, the Tenth Circuit found that the applicant's ten years of residence, family ties in the United States, progress toward rehabilitation, and record of steady employment did not meet the outstanding equities standard.[216] The applicant, who would be deported to Mexico, had been convicted of a serious heroin offense, had served two years in prison, and involved his brother and common-law wife in his drug activity. The court found it relevant that the applicant was fluent in Spanish and that a sibling and his father lived in Mexico. In *Vergara-Molina v. INS*, the Seventh Circuit approved the Board's finding of no unusual and outstanding equities in a case involving an applicant convicted of two controlled substance violations.[217] Evidence of his rehabilitation, steady employment, service to the community as a drug counselor, and good character were considered, but the court would not second-guess the Board.[218]

The necessity of demonstrating unusual or outstanding equities was not triggered exclusively by serious crimes involving controlled substances. A particularly grave offense also demanded such a showing.[219] Additionally, such a showing could be mandated because of a single serious crime, or because of a succession of criminal acts that, together, established a pattern of serious criminal misconduct. A respondent who demonstrated unusual or outstanding equities, as required, did not automatically obtain a favorable exercise of discretion, but absent such equities, relief would not be granted in the exercise of discretion.[220] There were cases in which the adverse considerations were so serious that a favorable exercise of

---

[212] *Id.* at 817–821.

[213] *Diaz-Resendez v. INS*, 960 F.2d 493 (5th Cir. 1992).

[214] *Id.* at 497.

[215] *In re Roberts*, 20 I. & N. Dec. 294 (BIA 1991).

[216] *Nunez-Pena v. INS*, 956 F.2d 223 (10th Cir. 1992).

[217] *Vergara-Molina v. INS*, 965 F.2d 682 (7th Cir. 1992).

[218] *Id.* at 685.

[219] *Cordoba-Chavez v. INS*, 946 F.2d 1244, 1249 (9th Cir. 1991); *In re Busceni*, 19 I. & N. Dec. 628, 633–634 (BIA 1988).

[220] *Akrap v. INS*, 966 F. 2d 267, 272–273 (7th Cir. 1992); *In re Roberts*, 20 I. & N. Dec. 294, 302–303 (BIA 1991).

discretion was not warranted even in the face of unusual or outstanding equities.[221] On the other -hand, Section 212(c) relief could not be categorically denied to drug offenders who served fewer than five years of incarceration.[222]

Rehabilitation of the respondent was a critical issue in Section 212(c) cases. The Board noted that an applicant with a criminal record "ordinarily" would be required to make a showing of rehabilitation before relief would be granted as a matter of discretion. Cases "involving convicted aliens [had to] be evaluated on a case-by-case basis, with rehabilitation a factor to be considered in the exercise of discretion."[223] In practice, the immigration judge would pay close attention to the testimony or statements from family members, friends, employers, parole or probation officers, counselors in or outside prison, and psychiatrists. The judge would want to discern whether the applicant would engage in criminal activity again and look for evidence that the person's life had changed to the point that such activity was a thing of the past.[224]

Thus, Section 212(c) cases permitted immigration judges to examine the respondent's crime, prison experience, current living situation, demeanor, attitude, job skills, employment status, family support, friends, social network, and efforts at rehabilitation in deciding whether to exercise favorable discretion. judges were even able to postpone the case to monitor the respondent's behavior before rendering a decision.[225]

In 1996, however, Congress enacted legislation that eliminated Section 212(c) relief as it had been applied for twenty years. In its place, a cancellation of removal provision was added that precluded even the possibility of relief for many who had been able to at least apply for discretionary relief from an immigration judge under the prior provision.[226] The new provision, INA § 240A(a), permits the attorney general to "cancel removal-for certain aliens who commit crimes if the alien (1) has been a lawful permanent resident for at least five years, (2) has resided in the United States continuously for seven years after having been admitted in any status, and (3) has not been convicted of any aggravated felony.[227] The no aggravated felony requirement thus eliminated relief for many lawful resident aliens who would have been eligible for Section 212(c) relief.

---

[221] *In re Busceni*, 19 I. & N. Dec. 628, 635–636 (BIA 1988).

[222] *Yepes-Prado v. INS*, 10 F.3d 1363, 1371 (9th Cir. 1993).

[223] *In re Edwards*, 20 I. & N. Dec. 191, 191 (BIA 1990).

[224] BILL ONG HING, HANDLING IMMIGRATION CASES 388 (1995).

[225] *See infra* note 242, *infra*, and accompanying text.

[226] *See* Katherine Brady, *Recent Developments in the Immigration Consequences of Crimes*, *in* OUR STATE OUR ISSUES: AN OVERVIEW OF IMMIGRATION LAW ISSUES 129 (Bill Ong Hing ed., 1996).

[227] 8 U.S.C. § 1229(a) (2004).

2.   Illegal Re-entry

It has been a federal criminal offense for a deported alien to illegally reenter the United States for over forty years. Congress enacted the original version of this offense as part of the Immigration and Nationality Act of 1952.[228] The United States prosecutes hundreds of individuals for this offense each year, and the number of illegal reentrants increased dramatically during the 1990s.[229] Despite the potentially severe penalties that can be imposed for an illegal reentry, many individuals who are deported each year attempt to reenter the United States.[230] The hope of reuniting with family and friends, securing employment, or returning to the home that they have lived in for the majority of their lives are some of the factors which lead people to take such a risk.[231]

An immigrant commits the crime of illegal reentry after deportation when he or she is deported and thereafter "enters, attempts to enter, or is at any time found in, the United States," without successfully having applied for readmission.[232] The statute applies to all individuals who have been denied admission, deported, excluded or removed, or who otherwise left the United States while an order of exclusion, deportation, or removal is outstanding.[233] To establish a defendant's guilt under this statute, the government therefore has to establish: 1) that the defendant is an undocumented immigrant; 2) that the defendant was deported; 3) that the defendant subsequently reentered or was found in the United States; 4) that the defendant has not received official permission to reenter; 5) and that the defendant reentered and was present in the United States voluntarily.

One of the worst effects of criminal offenses occurs when a person returns to the United States illegally. The statute carries varying criminal penalties for reentering undocumented immigrants. Immigrants without a prior criminal history are subject to a fine and/or a prison sentence of up to two years.[234] INA § 276(b) imposes harsher criminal punishments on individuals with certain prior criminal histories. Immigrants illegally reentering whose removal was subsequent to a conviction of three or more misdemeanors involving drugs, crimes against the person, or felony are subject to a fine and/or imprisonment of up to ten years.[235] Individuals who were inadmissible on security and related grounds under INA 235(c) are subject to a fine and imprisonment for 10 years.[236] An undocumented person who was previously removed because of an aggravated felony conviction can be fined and/or imprisoned for twenty years.[237] Illegal reentrants who were

---

[228] 8 U.S.C. § 276 (1952).

[229] James A. Fortosis, *Through the Funnel of Abstraction: Why Specific Intent Should be Required Mens Rea for Attempted Illegal Reentries*, 2007 U. CHI. LEGAL F. 503, 503.

[230] *Id.*

[231] *Id.*

[232] INA § 276, 8 U.S.C. § 1326.

[233] *Id.*

[234] INA § 276(a).

[235] INA § 276(b)(1).

[236] INA § 276(b)(3).

[237] INA § 276(b)(2).

removed under 241(a)(4)(B),meaning that they were nonviolent offenders who were removed prior to completing their sentence of imprisonment, shall be fined and/or imprisoned for up to ten years under INA § 276(b)(4).

If an illegal reentrant is prosecuted under this statute, they will be incarcerated for the remainder of their prison sentence which was pending at the time of their deportation, without any reduction for parole or supervised release, in addition to the other penalties imposed for their illegal reentry.[238]

The penalties for reentering can therefore be incredibly harsh. Moreover, defendants have few defenses against their prosecution for illegal reentry. According to the statute, a defendant can only challenge the validity of their deportation order if they demonstrate the following: first, that the defendant exhausted any administrative remedies that were available to seek relief against the order; second, that the deportation proceeding at which the order was issued improperly deprived the alien of the opportunity for judicial review; and third, the entry of the order was fundamentally unfair.[239]

F.   ENFORCEMENT AT PORTS OF ENTRY

1.   The Automated Entry-Exit System

Illegal Immigration Reform and Immigration Responsibility Act, § 110, 8 U.S.C.A. § 1221 was passed on September 30, 1996. Section 110 of IIRIRA required that within two years the Attorney General develop an "automated entry and exit control system" capable of (1) recording the departure of every alien from the United States and matching the record of departure with the record of the alien's arrival in the United States; and (2) enabling the Attorney General to identify, through on-line searching procedures, lawfully admitted nonimmigrants who remain in the United States beyond the period authorized by the Attorney General.[240]

There were many critics of Section 110 of IIRIRA who thought that Congress had not sufficiently considered a cost-benefit analysis when passing this provision. Opponents of the Automated Entry-Exit System worried that these controls would have detrimental effects on cross-border commerce and would be ineffective in controlling the drug trade or other criminal activities at the border. One opponent of Section 110, Bronwyn Lance, summarized the major concerns with regard to the automated entry-exit System, when he wrote:

> This new requirement, made with little forethought, will not prevent illegal immigration, but will be expensive to implement and cause inordinate delays at border crossings for both persons and transport. Additionally, the new law will not affect drug enforcement or terrorism prevention,

---

[238] INA § 276(c).

[239] INA § 276(d).

[240] IIRIRA, Pub. L. No. 104-208, § 110, 110 Stat. 3009.

and shows a willful disregard for America's diplomatic agreements with our neighbors.[241]

Another important issue raised by opponents of section 110 was that the automated entry-exit system failed in its other goal of helping to detect where visa overstayers. Critics explained that even if the Automated Entry- Exit System recorded information at the time of entry about a visitor's identity and expected place of stay in the United States, it could not be expected that six or more months later the alien would be at the same location.[242]

Following the passage of the IIRIRA, Congress extended the deadline for the automated entry-exit system to October 15, 1998.[243] In the Fiscal Year 1999 Omnibus Consolidated and Emergency Supplemental Appropriations Act, Congress further extended the deadline for implementation of the automated entry-exit system. The deadline for land border ports of entry and seaports was extended to March 30, 2001; however, the October 15, 1998, deadline for air ports of entry remained unchanged.[244] Congress also added language prohibiting significant disruption of trade, tourism, or other legitimate cross-border traffic once the entry-exit system was in place.[245]

In June 2000, Congress amended IIRIRA § 110 in by passing the Naturalization Service Data Management Improvement Act of 2000 (DMIA), which renamed the entry-exit system the "Integrated Entry and Exit Data System."[246] The new entry-exit system included provisions that: (1) rewrote § 110 to require the development of a system using data collected with no new documentary requirements; (2) set staggered deadlines for the implementation of the system at air, sea, and land border ports of entry; (3) established a task force to evaluate the implementation of the system and other measures to improve legitimate cross-border traffic; and (4) expressed the sense of Congress that federal departments charged with border management should consult with foreign governments to improve cooperation.[247]

Immediately following the terrorist attacks of September 11, Congress voted to allocate more funds for border and interior enforcement of the immigration laws by passage of the USA PATRIOT Act of 2001.[248] The entry-exit system was further

---

[241] Browyn Lance, *The Traffic Jam and Job Destruction Act: Why Congress Must Do Away With Border-Clogging Provision Slipped Into 1996 Law*, Issue Brief #171, June 1999, *available at* http://www.adti.net/imm/Section110.html.

[242] A June 1998 Senate Judiciary Committee Report (Senate Judiciary Report 105-197 on S. 1360, Border Improvement and Immigration Act of 1997, June 1, 1998).

[243] The "Extension of Date of Development of Automated Entry-Exit Control System" Act, Pub. L. No. 105-259, 112 Stat. 1918.

[244] Pub. L. No. 105-277, 112 Stat. 2681.

[245] Pub. L. No. 105-277, 112 Stat. 2681.

[246] Pub. L. No. 106-215, 114 Stat. 337.

[247] *Id.*

[248] The "Uniting and Strengthening America by Providing Appropriate Tools Required to Intercept and Obstruct Terrorism (USA PATRIOT) Act," Pub. L. No. 107-56, 115 Stat. 272, was signed into law on October 26, 2001.

developed through the implementation of the United States Visitor and Immigrant Status Indicator Technology program (U.S.-VISIT).

2.   U.S.-VISIT

The United States Visitor and Immigrant Status Indicator Technology program (U.S.-VISIT) was launched on January 5, 2004 and is intended to complement and reinforce the Automated Entry-Exit System first established under IIRIRA.[249] U.S. VISIT is meant to electronically record the entry of non-U.S. citizen visitors into the country and their exit from the United States, as well as verify each visitor's identity through the use of biometric identifiers encoded in their travel documents.[250] In theory, the system is also supposed to warn immigration officials when foreign visitors have failed to leave the country on the date they were expected to. U.S.-VISIT is currently in effect at 116 airports and 15 seaports, and the 154 land ports of entry.[251]

U.S.-VISIT requires the collection of personal data, photos and fingerprints at consular posts abroad and at ports-of-entry, as well as extensive database and information sharing.[252] Upon arrival in the United States, a foreign national who is subject to U.S.-VISIT is inspected by Customs and Border Protection (CBP) inspectors at a port-of-entry.[253] The individual's travel documents are scanned, and a digital photograph and inkless fingerprints of both index fingers are taken.[254] Depending on the results the CBP officer receives in the system, the officer either admits the visitor or requires the visitor to undergo more thorough examination.[255] DHS expected that U.S.-VISIT would assist in combating fraud and protecting the integrity of the U.S. visa.[256] However, questions remain regarding whether U.S.-VISIT can enhance the nation's security. Again concerns were raised regarding whether U.S.-VISIT really has anything to do with countering drug trafficking, halting the entry of terrorists into the United States, or with any other illegal activity near the borders.

There were also several other concerns about how the U.S.-VISIT program would meet the set deadlines for implementation, how the program would operate, and how the high costs of developing this system would be dealt with.

3.   NSEERS and Special Registration

The main goal of the National Security Entry-Exit Registration System (NSEERS), launched on September 11, 2002, is to subject a targeted minority of non-citizen visitors to a detailed registration process. NSEERS is designed to

---

[249] BERNARD P. WOLFSDORF, SECURE BORDERS, OPEN DOORS: CONSULAR PROCESSING ISSUES IN 2007.

[250] http://www.dhs.gov/xtrvlsec/programs/editorial_0527.shtm.

[251] http://www.dhs.gov/xtrvlsec/programs/editorial_0685.shtm.

[252] http://www.dhs.gov/xtrvlsec/programs/content_multi_image_0006.shtm.

[253] http://www.dhs.gov/xtrvlsec/programs/editorial_0525.shtm.

[254] Id.

[255] Id.

[256] http://www.dhs.gov/xtrvlsec/programs/content_multi_image_0006.shtm.

enable mass tracking of individual entries, departures, and domestic whereabouts. According to the Department of Justice memo authorizing the program, 'nonimmigrant aliens' are to be selected for registration according to four criteria: (1) all citizens or nationals of certain designated countries, (2) individual notification through a tracking database known as the "Interagency Border Inspection System" (IBIS), (3) pre-existing criteria defined by the Attorney General, and (4) officer discretion. Individuals registered under this program are to be questioned, fingerprinted, and provided with a special form complete with a "fingerprint identification number."

Questions asked during such registration go far beyond the routine and universal questions travelers answer while crossing international borders. Immigration officials have been instructed to ask individuals for e-mail addresses, personal details about parents and other family members, contact points in the United States, employers' addresses, school addresses, bank accounts, and credit card numbers. Before such visitors are allowed to enter the United States, officers are encouraged to provide extra comments and observations on the questioning form, while such travelers are instructed to sign a sworn statement verifying the accuracy of information provided.

Such monitoring does not end upon entry into the United States. Once individuals have been enrolled in this program, they are expected to report in person to an immigration office between day thirty and day forty of their visit, report to an immigration office again within ten days of the one-year anniversary of their arrival should they stay that long, notify the immigration authorities of every change of address while present in the United States within ten days of that change of address, and appear before an immigration inspecting officer at certain designated ports of departure prior to leaving. At each of these follow-up interviews, individuals are required to prove that they have done what they came to the United States to do, by showing hotel and gas station receipts, employment contracts, class schedules, and other documents. Any individual failing to comply fully with such instructions is to be classified as "out of status," and thus subject to potential, and sometimes immediate, deportation.

At all ports of entry, this "special registration" initiative has evolved in progressive stages since its public launching on the one-year anniversary of September 11, 2001. Initially, the only nationals subjected to such registration procedures were those of Iran, Iraq, Libya, Syria, and Sudan. In October 2002, Saudi Arabia, Yemen, and Pakistan were added to the list of designated countries.[257] At the same time, the IBIS system was implemented in consular offices throughout the world and the Attorney General's pre-existing criteria for "special registration" were specified. These criteria concentrate on what the United States government would consider security risks: unexplained trips to fifteen countries, including frequently visited United States allies such as Egypt, Saudi Arabia, and Pakistan; previous overstaying of non-immigrant visas; fitting current intelligence profiles; and demonstrating either suspicious behavior or

---

[257] *See* U.S. Department of State International Informational Program, Fact Sheet: National Security Entry-Exit Registration System (June 5, 2002), *available at* http://www.ice.gov/pi/specialregistration/archive.htm#what.

personal information upon arrival. Significantly, those considered dual nationals by the Immigration authorities — such as Syrian-born French citizens or Iraqi-born UK citizens — are also subject to such registration procedures despite the fact that the Attorney General's office has indicated that the nationality or citizenship used to enter the United States will be the one considered for special registration procedures.[258]

In November 2002, the NSEERS program was greatly expanded through implementation of what the immigration authority innocuously designated 'call-in registration' — ostensibly designed to track those admitted to the United States prior to implementation of the NSEERS 'special registration' program at all ports of entry. In this program, all 'nonimmigrant alien' adult male nationals — sixteen years and older — of the original five countries covered by the 'special registration' program (Iran, Iraq, Libya, Syria, and Sudan) were instructed to make a physical appearance at designated INS offices and register prior to December 16.

This initiative was internally justified as applying to "certain aliens, whose presence in the United States requires closer monitoring in the national security and/or law enforcement interests of the United States"[259] — initially defined only as all nationals of the five countries listed above. Individuals who failed to register, or registered late, were subject to deportation, and potentially vulnerable to criminal prosecution as well. Any information encountered during the registration process which might subject an interviewee to removal proceedings would cause the individual to be referred to the "investigations section" for "appropriate action" — meaning interrogation and potential detention or deportation.

In the very poorly distributed INS public announcement concerning these registration procedures, no mention was made of interrogation or deportation following compliance with "call-in" procedures. As a result, when thousands of male nationals from the five designated countries turned up at various INS offices, several hundred were detained nationwide — which resulted in an impromptu demonstration by nearly 1,000 relatives in Los Angeles, protest letters by several civil liberties, human rights, and ethnically-based advocacy organizations, and the assignment of volunteer escorts to record who was detained and for how long. Detentions, deportations, and personal abuses reportedly took place following referrals to "investigation sections."

In spite of widespread protest by affected communities, the Attorney General's office expanded the "call-in registration" program in the weeks following the December fiasco. Following the original five affected countries (Iran, Iraq, Libya, Syria, and Sudan), three more groups of countries were singled out for enforced "call-ins." The second group, whose nationals were obliged to visit INS offices prior to February 7, 2003 consisted of Afghanistan, Algeria, Bahrain, Eritrea, Lebanon, Morocco, North Korea, Oman, Qatar, Somalia, Tunisia, United Arab Emirates, and

---

[258] *See, e.g.,* Statement of Barbara Comstock, Director of Public Affairs, Regarding the National Security Entry-Exit Registration System, Department of Justice Press Release (Nov. 1, 2002), *available at* http://www.ice.gov/pi/specialregistration/archive.htm#what.

[259] *See* U.S. Department of State, Attorney General Ashcroft Announces Implementation of First Phase of the National Security Entry-Exit Registration System (Aug. 12, 2002), *available at* http://www.usdoj.gov/opa/pr/2002/August/02_ag_466.htm.

Yemen. The third group, instructed to visit INS offices by February 21, 2003 consisted of Pakistan and Saudi Arabia. Nationals of the fourth and final group — Bangladesh, Egypt, Indonesia, Jordan, and Kuwait — were instructed to visit the newly formed Department of Homeland Security offices by April 25, 2003.[260]

G.   INTERIOR ENFORCEMENT OF THE IMMIGRATION LAWS

1.   Employer Sanctions

Under IRCA, for the first time Congress prohibited employers from hiring workers who are not authorized to work in the United States, imposing civil and criminal penalties on violators. IRCA was the product of years of debate regarding the impact of undocumented immigrant workers on the United States. As part of the compromise that IRCA represented, amnesty (legalization) was granted to about three million undocumented aliens, and employers also became subject to penalties for new employment discrimination laws.

In response to intensive lobbying by civil rights advocates and concerned members of Congress who feared that employer sanctions would cause employment discrimination, protections were included in the law intended to safeguard against discrimination. In other words, IRCA contained provisions that attempted to ensure that employers would not use the new employer sanctions law as a pretext for discriminating against lawful immigrant workers. Prior to IRCA, private employers could require employees to be U.S. citizens, but after IRCA, employers had to hire a qualified immigrant job applicant, unless a citizen who was equally qualified applied for the job. Employers could be fined for such discriminatory hiring practices, as well as for requiring new immigrant employees to come up with more proof than necessary to establish eligibility to work.

IRCA's employer sanctions provisions placed great responsibilities upon the business community. Employers must verify that a new employee is authorized to work in the United States. The employer and the employee must complete an I-9 form. Employers who "knowingly hire" undocumented workers are subject to penalties, which can include fines ranging from $250 to $10,000 per unauthorized worker, as well as criminal penalties against the employer for pattern and practice violations.

IRCA mandated the General Accounting Office (GAO), the investigative arm of Congress, to conduct three annual studies from 1987 to 1989 to determine whether employer sanctions had resulted in "widespread discrimination." A "sunset" provision further stipulated that employer sanctions could be repealed if the GAO concluded that compliance caused employers to discriminate.

The first two status reports on employer sanctions by the GAO found that "one in every six employers in GAO's survey who were aware of the law may have begun or increased the practice of (1) asking only foreign looking persons for work

---

[260] Mae M. Cheng, *Final Day for INS Registry; Immigrant Advocates Continue to Criticize Program*, NEWSDAY, Apr. 25, 2003.

authorization documents or (2) hiring only U.S. citizens." In spite of the fact that almost 17 percent of employers admitted to practices that violated the discrimination provisions of IRCA, GAO concluded that the findings did not establish a pattern of "widespread discrimination," citing lack of conclusive evidence that the employer sanctions requirements were the cause of discrimination.

Upon the release of its second report, the GAO came under fire from both governmental and nongovernmental entities for using shoddy methodology in its evaluation of the possible discriminatory impacts of sanctions. The U.S. Commission on Civil Rights identified several problems inherent in both the methodology and the findings. For one thing, the commission argued that Congress needed to clarify the meaning of "widespread pattern of discrimination." Legal service providers and immigrant and refugee advocacy groups had been collecting evidence of IRCA–related discrimination since the law's inception. Organizations in New York, Chicago, San Francisco, Los Angeles, and Fresno established multilingual information and referral telephone hotlines upon the passage of IRCA to provide information to immigrants about the amnesty program and employer sanctions. Their experience revealed that employment discrimination as a result of employer sanctions was pervasive.

In 1989, a number of groups across the country began to compile information that they had received from individuals of mostly Asian, Latino, and Middle Eastern descent regarding discriminatory treatment they had experienced while seeking new employment or working in their current positions. Several civil rights organizations issued reports of the anecdotal evidence collected. While the reports documented disturbing accounts of discrimination, proponents of employer sanctions dismissed the data collected by advocacy groups as unreliable. Eventually, some of the independent research could not be ignored by the GAO. A methodological survey of 416 San Francisco employers was conducted in San Francisco, revealing that an overwhelming 97 percent of the firms regularly engaged in at least one employment practice that could be discriminatory under IRCA or other antidiscrimination laws. Another 53 percent reported that they engaged in three or more such practices. The research was submitted to the GAO in September 1989, and influenced the GAO's third report.[261] The GAO significantly improved the research methodology for its third and final report. Its staff used both direct contact with employers and teams of job search testers. Its new findings showed that as a direct result of IRCA, 461,000 employers nationwide (10 percent) discriminated on the basis of national origin, and 430,000 employers (9 percent) discriminated on the basis of citizenship status. These findings meant that an estimated 2.9 million employees were discriminated against based on national origin, and 3.9 million based on citizenship status. The research found that rates of discrimination were somewhat higher in cities with high Latino or Asian populations: "Our survey suggests that persons of Hispanic and Asian origins may have been harmed by employers' citizenship discrimination practices." As part of

---

[261] Lina M. Avidan, *Employment and Hiring Practices Under the Immigration Reform and Control Act of 1986; A Survey of San Francisco Businesses* (Coalition for Immigrant and Refugee Rights and Services, 1989).

the same report, the GAO contracted with Washington, D.C.– based Urban Institute to conduct a "hiring audit," by using a job applicant tester survey utilizing Latino and Anglo U.S. citizen college students to apply for a sample of 360 low skilled, entry-level jobs in Chicago and San Diego. The study found that the Anglo testers received 52 percent more job offers and 33 percent more interviews than the Latino testers, and that overall, the Latino testers were three times as likely as Anglo testers to encounter unfavorable treatment.

Despite the GAO's findings of "widespread" IRCA — related employment discrimination and similar evidence by independent researchers, Congress did not repeal employer sanctions. The findings were routinely dismissed by anti — immigrant groups, Senator Alan Simpson (a co-sponsor of IRCA), and the AFL — CIO as insignificant or unreliable. Several bills to repeal employer sanctions were introduced in Congress in 1990 and 1991, but none reached the floor of Congress (in spite of bipartisan support from Senators Kennedy and Hatch).

Although employer sanctions were not repealed, the Immigration Act of 1990 did strengthen IRCA's antidiscrimination provisions. The law increased employer and employee education, added special agricultural workers to the category of protected workers, changed the penalties for discrimination to conform with those for employer sanctions penalties, made document abuse an unfair immigration–related employment practice, prohibited retaliation against those who file charges, made it easier to prosecute for document abuse by adding civil as well as criminal penalties, and eliminated the requirement that a noncitizen who makes a discrimination charge must have filed an official "declaration of intent" to become a citizen.

By the early 1990s, many members of Congress, most notably Senator Simpson, contended that no further employer education was necessary to decrease employment discrimination. In fact, Simpson argued at a 1992 Senate judiciary Committee hearing that the employer sanctions provisions, both the documentation requirements and the antidiscrimination protections, were as familiar to employers as was the requirements to pay taxes.

While many politicians and business leaders claimed that compliance with employer sanctions had become a "regular part" of doing business in the United States, the experiences of immigrants and ethnic minorities suggested otherwise. Employer sanctions were often implemented and enforced selectively, discriminatorily, and as a means of intimidating undocumented workers who sought union representation or who complained about unfair labor practices, such as sexual harassment, wage and hour violations, and unsafe working conditions. Only a fraction of U.S. employers and workers have received education from the Office of Special Counsel (OSC). OSC's education program did not begin in earnest until 1990, when it initiated a grants program, contracting with local groups to conduct educational campaigns. The OSC is located in Washington, D.C., with no branch offices. Between 1987 and 1996, the OSC received 4,868 charges of discrimination from workers, but only 145 formal complaints were filed by the OSC against employers, 83 of who were fined for IRCA-related unfair employment practices. Distribution of INS's Handbook for Employers that explains the regulations and has pictures of acceptable documents also has been inadequate. Only two nationwide distributions of the handbook took place by 1996: one in 1987 and one in 1991.

Since 1990, no government-sponsored research examining the possibly discriminatory effects of employer sanctions has occurred. Lina Avidan's private survey of 422 employers in New York, Los Angeles, Chicago, and San Francisco conducted in 1992 revealed that 91 percent regularly engage in at least one employment practice prohibited under IRCA's antidiscrimination provisions, and 48 percent regularly engage in three or more. Half of the employers feel that the INS documentation requirements make it riskier to hire people who speak limited English, and more than a third (38 percent) feel it is riskier to hire Latinos, Asians, and people from the Caribbean.[262]

Although employer sanctions remain part of the immigration laws, by 2001, the concept had lost one of its ardent supporters. As organized labor, including the AFL–CIO, realized that its future viability rested solidly on the shoulders of immigrant workers, unions called for the repeal of employer sanctions and for the legalization of undocumented workers.

By the 1980s, contentious congressional debate over how to handle the problem of undocumented aliens, particularly Mexicans, took center stage. Clear support for employer sanctions was evident, but when IRCA was finally passed, support for legalization of undocumented immigrants was not as clear. The ambivalence over amnesty reflected the policy makers' desire to keep out undocumented Mexicans and not demonstrate any sign of approval for those already here.

Legalization applicants faced several challenges. Procedural hurdles discouraged many from even applying. The most difficult hurdle was obtaining documentation to approve the duration of time an applicant lived in the United States or worked in agriculture. Furthermore, each applicant was required to pay a filing fee as high as $420 per family-not an insignificant amount for many.

The implementation of legalization through INS and community agencies was inconsistent. Outreach efforts did not reach many eligible immigrants, the INS suffered from long–standing distrust in immigrant communities, and community service agencies miscalculated the needs of many applicants and suffered from bureaucratic problems themselves. Yet, important partnerships were formed, and the efforts INS officials finally implemented were impressive in many parts of the country. Most observers agree that the three million immigrants who benefited from legalization represent less than half of those who were actually eligible, and the ongoing employer sanctions provisions result in discrimination against lawful immigrants of color.

---

[262] Lina M. Avidan, *Employment and Hiring Practices Under the Immigration Reform and Control Act of 1986; A Survey of Businesses in Los Angeles, New York, Chicago and San Francisco* (Master's Thesis, Public Administration Department, 1992).

Congress and Employer Sanctions

Blame for continued migration might also be placed at the feet of Congress. Responding to public complaints about undocumented migration, Congress simply threw more border enforcement funds at the issue, while encouraging migration with weak employer sanction laws. Certainly many who support, as well as many who oppose, Gatekeeper claim that the failure to prosecute employers for hiring undocumented workers is a problem. Between 1992 and 1997, the number of INS fines levied against employers decreased from 2,000 to 888, and the amount of fines levied decreased from $17 million to $8 million.[263] Further, the Department of Labor had only 900 investigators to enforce workplace requirements such as minimum wage laws in 7 million U.S. workplaces in 1995.[264] Broadly speaking, however, criticism of weak employer sanction laws is misplaced. Enforcement of employer sanctions will not deter undocumented migration. U.S. employers' need for low-wage workers is too strong, and migrant motivations for entering are too great.

The conventional wisdom goes like this: if the country seriously enforces the laws that make it illegal for employers to knowingly hire undocumented workers, employers will stop hiring undocumented workers, undocumented migrants will get the message and stop migrating, and environmental deaths at the border will disappear. The Clinton administration argued that to control illegal immigration effectively, the federal government must "remove the magnet of illegal employment that draws illegal aliens" to the United States.[265] INS Commissioner Meissner said that border enforcement should be coupled with workplace disincentives."[266] The U.S. Commission on Immigration Reform (USCIR) similarly argued that since "employment opportunity is . . . the principal magnet which draws illegal aliens to the United States," the best thing to do is improve the system of employer sanctions enforcement, and labor standards enforcement should be enhanced as well.[267] USCIR's executive director observed that as a "nation we have a basic ambivalence about workplace enforcement."[268] Thus, Clinton's border czar Alan Bersin complained: "We have not been given the tools ñ a matter of deliberate policy ñ to have effective worksite enforcement. . . . Because people can show an employer phony documents, there's no reliable way to correctly identify [the immigration status of] people seeking work.[269] Similarly, although the *San Diego Union Tribune* applauded efforts that resulted in fewer crossings in urban areas, its editors were troubled by the environmental deaths, concluding that as "long as we continue to hire illegal

---

[263] Claudia E. Smith, *Operation Gatekeeper Report*, May 10, 2000, at 41 (unpublished paper on file with author).

[264] *Id.* at 43.

[265] *Id.* at 40.

[266] *Id.* at 42.

[267] U.S. Commission on Immigration Reforms, U.S. IMMIGRATION POLICY: RESTORING CREDIBILITY 50–53 (1994). The commission criticized the current verification process as "time-consuming and confusing," and urged a more efficient use of resources. *Id.* at 53.

[268] Smith, *Operation Gatekeeper Report*, at 14 (citing Susan Martin).

[269] Brae Canlen, *The Border Honcho*, 17 CALIFORNIA LAWYER 34, 37 (1997).

aliens, we will continue to have rampant illegal immigration."[270] Wayne Cornelius, a longtime' observer of the border, also notes that "work site enforcement is without doubt the weakest element of the current U.S. strategy for controlling illegal immigration."[271] In his view, "large numbers are still getting in, and because of low employer sanctions enforcement, they are just as employable today as they were before the current buildup of border enforcement capabilities began.[272] A binational body of experts chimed in, suggesting that the United States should assess the extent to which the demand of U.S. employers can be reduced through enhanced enforcement of labor standards, including wage and hour requirements, child labor prohibitions, and employer sanctions.[273] Even representatives of the California Rural Legal Assistance Foundation, ardent critics of Operation Gatekeeper, while not supporting employer sanctions, note the inconsistencies of U.S. policies: "During the last five years the INS has done virtually nothing to counteract the employer magnet that pulls migrants here - the undeniable hypocrisy of its immigration policy. For example, since the start of Gatekeeper, only a half - dozen employers of undocumented laborers have been prosecuted in either of California's border counties,"[274] and "the agency devotes only two percent of its enforcement man - hours to enforcing immigration laws at the work site.[275]

Could the employment of undocumented workers really be stopped? What would it take? Would the enforcement of employer sanctions really deter the employment of undocumented workers and their continued migration? It's doubtful. The fortitude, drive, and unbelievable desire to migrate north among border - crossers given the economic disparities, family ties, and tradition are factors that cannot be discounted lightly. And the labor market that relies on such workers is ingrained in our economy. In sum, assuming that employer sanctions will discourage further migration and the hiring of undocumented workers is unrealistic and simplistic. Employer sanctions enforcement, even with greater resources, faces insurmountable challenges.

Employer sanctions create additional problems as well. Many employers use employer sanctions as an excuse to discriminate. The General Accounting Office has reported that nearly one-fifth of employers discriminate against foreign-appearing or foreign-sounding job applicants because of employer sanctions. This is too much of a price to pay for a regime that has little incentive to discourage the hiring of undocumented workers anyway.

---

[270] *A Losing Battle: Border Patrol Scores Tactical Gains, Strategic Losses*, SAN DIEGO UNION TRIBUNE, November 5, 1999, B8. The editors noted: "Gatekeeper's physical measures have slowed the flow in San Diego County, replacing the chaos that once defined the border here [illegals] dashing across freeways or stampeding checkpoints." *Id.*

[271] Smith, *Operation Gatekeeper Report*, at 41.

[272] *Id.* at 22.

[273] Binational Study on Migration (1997), at 66.

[274] December 14, 1999. Letter to Gabriela Rodriguez Pizarro.

[275] CRLAF Fact Sheet.

2.   Detection Strategies

Immigration enforcement officials use various tactics to detect and apprehend people who are out-of-status. This section will discuss four main detection strategies: 1) how DHS uses immigration petitions to uncover undocumented individuals living in the country, 2) how ICE picks up people after criminal arrests, 3) how workplace sweeps are carried out to apprehend large groups of undocumented workers, and 4) how certain registration programs were intended to help detect individuals who are out-of-status.

a.   Petitions

Whenever an application for an immigration benefit is filed on behalf of an individual, an "alien registration file" is created for that person. Immigration petitions often involve disclosing a substantial amount of information about a person's identity, family and whereabouts. This information is then kept on file with DHS. It is an easy task for an ICE-Investigation officer to use this information to apprehend the applicant or their family members.

b.   Criminal Custody

Immigrants who are in criminal custody are particularly likely to be picked up by Immigration and Customs Enforcement. ICE often contacts local police to see if there are any immigrants being held on criminal charges.

ICE uses a system of "immigration holds" to facilitate their cooperation with local police. Immigration holds, or immigration detainers as they are sometimes called, are issued for people who are in criminal custody and who are suspected of being deportable or inadmissible. Once an immigration hold is issued to a person, the local police have the power to temporarily detain the immigrant beyond the time of their completed jail sentence in order for ICE to pick the person up.

According to 8 CFR § 287.7(d), immigration holds allow police to detain an immigrant who has completed their criminal sentence for 48 hours, excluding Saturdays, Sundays and holidays. After this period, the immigration hold expires and the immigrant can no longer be legally detained. The immigrant must be released whether or not ICE has had time to pick them up.

c.   Workplace Sweeps

Agriculture and other workplace sweeps for undocumented Mexican workers have been common immigration enforcement strategies since the mid twentieth century. Consider Operation Jobs, that occurred in April 1982. Five thousand people, primarily of Latin appearance, were arrested in nine metropolitan areas across the country. Critics of the raids charged that the operation was directed at Mexicans, whipped up anti-alien hysteria, and caused much fear in the Latino community, while providing no jobs for native–born citizens. Curiously, Operation Jobs was launched during the same week that restrictive legislation (the Simpson–Mazzoli Bill that contained employer sanctions provisions) was being marked up in the Senate subcommittee on immigration. The raids also coincided with Congress's consideration of additional funds for the old Immigration and Naturalization Service. Operation Jobs highlighted what had been going on for many years — focused sweeps by the INS at locations with large numbers of persons of Latin descent.

The constitutionality of the operation was challenged in northern California in *International Molders' and Allied Workers' Local Union No. 164 v. Nelson*,[276] the facts of which are representative of what happened nationwide. During the operation, the INS and Border Patrol conducted approximately fifty workplace raids in northern California as part of a nationwide campaign. During these raids, agents arrived at various workplaces, such as the Petaluma Poultry Processors, Mammoth Lakes Lodge, and Pacific Mushroom Farm. The agents carried with them "warrants of inspection" authorizing entry into the nonpublic areas of particular premises. Typically, the warrants named one or more individuals thought to be undocumented aliens who were working at a specified location, but then went on to allow the INS to seek and seize unspecified and unlimited "others" on the premises who might also be undocumented aliens. During Operation jobs, warrants were obtained for 8 of the approximately 50 raids. Although a warrant might list from 4 to 13 suspected undocumented aliens, as many as 70 people would be arrested, and few if any of these were the people named in the warrant. In the 8 warrants used for the raids described in the case, 192 individuals were arrested. Of these, 179 were "others" not identified in the warrants. Of the 51 persons named in the various warrants, only 13 were found on the premises.

The warrants said nothing about how the searches would be carried out, other than permissible hours of entry, or how INS agents would determine which persons were to be interrogated or seized as suspected "others." The warrants neither directed nor limited agents to the portions of the premises where the named suspects were likely to be found.

Officials admitted that they used the warrants to gain entry into workplaces for generalized searches for undocumented aliens. In many raids the INS agents made no particular effort to apprehend the suspects named in the warrants, but rather based their decisions as to which workers to question, detain, or seize solely on information or observation gained *after* they had entered.

Given these facts, the federal judge issued the following order against INS officials in northern California:

Good cause appearing therefor, the Court preliminarily enjoins defendants and their officers, agents, and employees in the San Francisco District of the United States Immigration and Naturalization Service and the Livermore Border Patrol Sector as follows:

1.   Each INS workplace entry, other than in public areas and open fields, must be based on at least one of the following: a valid warrant, a valid consent, or exigent circumstances not deliberately provoked by defendants' own conduct.

2.   Every INS warrant must particularly describe each suspect to be

---

[276] 643 F. Supp. 884 (N.D. Cal. 1986).

questioned or seized pursuant to the particularity requirement of the fourth amendment. There must be probable cause to believe each such person is an alien illegally present in the United States. A warrant need not in every case identify the suspect(s) by name, but the warrant and its supporting affidavits must contain enough specific identifying information to assure that the search for that person is reasonably likely to result in finding that person.

3.   A warrant may not provide that "others" may be searched and seized, if such "others" are unnamed or only conclusorily described by any supporting affidavits.

4.   When possible, each warrant must describe the particular area(s) of the workplace where the suspect(s) are likely to be found, in light of the information available to the defendants.

5.   Each warrant must provide that the agents executing the warrant, before searching any work area, must show the warrant to an authorized company representative, and ask that representative to produce the suspect(s) named or described in the warrant. Before the suspects are produced, agents may position themselves at exits and question or detain any workers attempting to flee. If the representative is. unwilling or unable to produce those suspects within a reasonable time, agents may then enter the work area to search for the suspects. Such searches must be directed at finding the named or described suspects as quickly as possible, rather than for general questioning of the entire workforce. This does not preclude agents from questioning or detaining workers who attempt to hide or flee.

6.   When agents have no warrant, but intend to obtain consent upon arrival at the worksite rather than ahead of time, they must not arrive or conduct themselves in a manner that would foreseeably provoke flight by workers, or that would leave a reasonable person with the belief that he had no choice but to consent to the raid. They must inform the representative of the nature and scope of the proposed survey. They may not expressly or impliedly suggest that the employer will face retaliation if he declines to consent.

7.   Agents may not deliberately provoke flight by workers in order to justify entries onto workplace premises.

8.   Absent a valid warrant or genuine exigent circumstances not deliberately precipitated by the agents themselves, agents may not detain workers without reasonable, articulable suspicion of illegal alienage. During non–detentive questioning, and before agents detain a worker, agents must give the worker a reasonable opportunity to produce his or her relevant documents, even if those documents are not on the worker's person but are in his constructive possession somewhere on the premises. Agents may accompany a worker who must retrieve his documentation.

9.   Absent a valid warrant or genuine exigent circumstances not deliberately precipitated by the agents' own conduct, agents may not arrest a worker except upon probable cause, based on articulable facts and reasonable inferences drawn therefrom, that the worker is an alien unlawfully present in the United States and is likely to escape before a warrant can be obtained for his arrest.

d. Other Workplace Strategies

Government workplace enforcement strategies were further emboldened by the Supreme Court in 1984. In *INS v. Delgado*,[277] INS officials, acting pursuant to warrants issued on a showing of probable cause that numerous unidentified undocumented aliens were employed at a garment factory, conducted two "factory surveys" of the workforce in search of undocumented aliens. A third factory survey was conducted with the employer's consent at another garment factory. During each survey, which lasted from one to two hours, INS agents positioned themselves near the factory exits, while other agents moved systematically through the factory, approaching most, but not all, employees at their work stations and, after identifying themselves, asking the employees one to three questions relating to their citizenship. The agents displayed badges, carried walkie-talkies, and were armed, although at no point during any of the surveys was a weapon ever drawn. If an employee gave a credible reply that he or she was a U.S. citizen or produced immigration papers, the agent moved on to another employee. During the survey, employees continued with their work and were free to walk around within the factory. Employees who were U.S. citizens or permanent resident aliens, and who had been questioned during the surveys and their union complained that the factory surveys violated their Fourth Amendment rights. They argued that the surveys constituted a seizure of the entire workforce, and that the INS could not question an individual employee unless its agents had a reasonable suspicion that the employee was an undocumented alien.

The Supreme Court disagreed with the plaintiffs, holding that the factory surveys did not result in the seizure of the entire workforce, and the individual questioning of the employees by INS agents concerning their citizenship did not amount to a detention or seizure under the Fourth Amendment. The Court ruled that interrogation relating to one's identity or a request for identification by the police does not, by itself, constitute a Fourth Amendment seizure. Unless the circumstances of the encounter are so intimidating as to demonstrate that a reasonable person would have believed he or she was not free to leave if he or she had not responded, such questioning does not result in a detention under the Fourth Amendment. In the Court's view, the entire workforce was not seized for the duration of the surveys, even though INS agents were stationed near the exits of the factory sites. The record indicated that the agents' conduct consisted simply of questioning employees and arresting those they had probable cause to believe were unlawfully present in the factory. This conduct should not have given employees any reason to believe that they would be detained if they gave truthful answers to the questions put to them or if they simply refused to answer. If mere questioning did not constitute a seizure when it occurred inside the factory, it was no more a seizure when it occurred at the exits.

The plaintiffs argued that the positioning of agents near the factory doors showed the INS's intent to prevent people from leaving. But the Court saw nothing in the record indicating that this is what the agents at the doors actually did. To the Court,

---

[277] 466 U.S. 210 (1984).

The obvious purpose of the agents' presence at the factory doors was to insure that all persons in the factories were questioned. The record indicates that the INS agents' conduct in this case consisted simply of questioning employees and arresting those they had probable cause to believe were unlawfully present in the factory. This conduct should have given respondents no reason to believe that they would be detained if they gave truthful answers to the questions put to them or if they simply refused to answer.

One worker described an incident that occurred during the October factory survey at Mr. Pleat, in which an INS agent stationed by an exit attempted to prevent a worker, presumably an undocumented alien, from leaving the premises after the survey started. The worker walked out the door and when an agent tried to stop him, the worker pushed the agent aside and ran away. But the Court felt that this was "an ambiguous, isolated incident" failing to provide any basis on which to support the plaintiffs.

Likewise, as to workers inside the buildings, the Court felt that the mere possibility that they would be questioned if they sought to leave the buildings should not have resulted in any reasonable apprehension by any of them that they would be seized or detained in any meaningful way. The INS conduct simply did not create a psychological environment that made employees reasonably afraid they were not free to leave.

Today, as the backlash against undocumented immigrants has heightened, raids and other internal enforcement efforts have been stepped up by ICE. The methods have included worksite operations, home invasions, and even monitoring of public schools. In the process, U.S. citizens and lawful permanent residents have been detained along with undocumented immigrants, resulting in a multitude of lawsuits against DHS. And while several thousand deportable aliens have been arrested as a result of these efforts, the totals are a far cry from the estimated 12 million undocumented immigrants living in the country. We really have to wonder whether such tactics are worth the effort. Consider some of the operations that have taken place.

Stillmore, Georgia

One ICE raid in Stillmore, Georgia, the Friday before Labor Day weekend in 2006, evoked outcry from local residents who labeled the ICE action as nothing short of "Gestapo tactics."[278] Nestled amid pine trees and cotton fields, undocumented Mexican immigrants supplied a stable workforce for a thriving poultry industry and for the onion fields in Vidalia a few miles away. Descending shortly before midnight, then over a three-day period, ICE agents swarmed throughout the area, arresting and deporting 125 undocumented workers.[279] Most of those rounded up were men, while their wives fled to woods to hide with their children in tow.[280]

---

[278] Dahleen Glanton, *Raid Exposes Ethnic Fault Lines; Town Grapples with Illegal Immigrant Crackdown*, CHICAGO TRIB., Dec. 11, 2006.

[279] *Id.*

[280] *Id.*

In the weeks after the raid, at least 200 more immigrants left town. Many of the women whose husbands were deported used their spouse's final paycheck purchase bus tickets to Mexico.[281] The impact was evident, underscoring just how vital the undocumented immigrants were to the local economy. Trailer parks lie abandoned. The poultry plant scrambled to replace more than half its workforce. Business dried up at stores where Mexican laborers once lined up to buy food, beer and cigarettes. The community of about a thousand people became little more than a ghost town. The raid included a trailer park operated by David Robinson, where immigrants were handcuffed and taken away. Robinson bought an American flag and posted it by the pond out front — upside down, in protest: "These people might not have American rights, but they've damn sure got human rights. There ain't no reason to treat them like animals."[282]

In May 2006, ICE launched Operation Return to Sender, an aggressive effort to rapidly increase deportation of undocumented immigrants violating removal orders. At this time ICE officials also began discussing enforcement issues with the Stillmore-based Crider poultry plant. Stillmore is a quiet community with few small businesses, a gas station and two convenience stores, intended to service local employees of the Crider plant, the largest employer of a community with roughly a thousand inhabitants. The plant employed slightly over 900 people, about 700 who had work documentation discrepancies when ICE began discussions with Crider's senior management in mid-2006.

On a state level the immigration debate in Georgia was intensifying. The state attracted attention after a federal report noted that Georgia had the fastest growing undocumented immigration population in the country.[283] In early 2006, the state legislature passed what many considered to be some of the most far-reaching immigration legislation in the nation, the Georgia Security and Immigration Compliance Act. The legislation has been likened to California's Proposition 187 and includes several strict requirements to curb immigration into the state and the hiring of undocumented workers. These provisions include requiring employers to use a federal database system (E-Verify) to verify employee documentation, requiring corrections officials to notify the state of any undocumented incarcerated persons, and requiring proof of citizenship for recipients of many medical and welfare benefits.[284]

In the summer months preceding the raid, the Crider plant began firing employees and pressuring others to resign upon suspecting improper work documentation. ICE officials swiftly cracked down at summer's end. The agency took the unusual approach of researching employee home address information and raided several homes shortly before midnight on Friday, September 1, the first day

---

[281] Dahleen Glanton *For Immigrants, Raid Dims Hope for a Better Life*, Chicago Trib., Dec. 11, 2006.

[282] Story cited in immigrationprof blog.

[283] Russ Bynum, *Immigration raids leave Georgia town bereft, stunned*, Seattle Times, Sept. 16, 2006, available at http://seattletimes.nwsource.com/html/nationworld/2003261371_immigaftermath16.html.

[284] Rick Lyman, *In Georgia Law, a Wide-Angle View of Immigration*, N.Y. Times, May 12, 2006, *available at* http://www.nytimes.com/2006/05/12/us/12georgia.html?_r=1&oref=login.

of Labor Day weekend. ICE's Labor Day weekend raid launched what became a series of raids lasting three weeks in the Stillmore area and the surrounding counties. The Stillmore raid focused mainly on male employees from the Crider plant, leaving many female and child family members stranded. Many remaining family members fled into the nearby woods in the hopes of avoiding detection. There was one report of a family hiding in a tree for two nights to avoid capture.[285]

Local residents witnessed the events, as ICE officials raided local homes and trailer parks, forcing many members of the community out of Stillmore. Officials were seen stopping motorists, breaking into homes and there were even reports of officials threatening people with tear gas.[286] Witnesses reported seeing ICE officials breaking windows and entering homes through floorboards.[287] Mayor Marilyn Slater commented, "This reminds me of what I read about Nazi Germany, the Gestapo coming in and yanking people up."[288]

The Crider Poultry plant was the primary employer in the town of a thousand. Other local businesses complained that they faced a severe drop in business in the weeks after the raids. One local caregiver in the community, a legal resident, took in a two-year old boy, a U.S. citizen born to undocumented Mexican parents, because his mother feared she could no longer sufficiently provide for him. The caregiver noted all her other customers disappeared after the raid, having been forced to leave Stillmore.[289]

San Rafael, California

On March 6, 2007, ICE officials raided the small communities of San Rafael and Novato in Marin County, arresting roughly 30 undocumented immigrants. This raid was also part of ICE's "Operation Return to Sender," the federal effort to crack down on immigrants who have stayed past their deportation orders. ICE officials parked several vans outside apartment complexes before dawn the Tuesday morning of the raids. Armed with warrants, many bearing dated and/or incorrect information, the police stormed homes and began arresting violators regardless of whether they were named in the original warrant. Many children were handcuffed along with their parents. The San Rafael raid drew criticism at the local and national level because of the nature and timing of the operation.

The San Rafael raid became a national symbol of the negative effects raids have on children. Juan Rodriguez, principal of Bahia Vista Elementary School, noted that on a typical day the school might have eight to ten children absent, but 77

---

[285] Patrick Jonsson, *Crackdown on Immigrants Empties a Town and Hardens Views*, CHRISTIAN SCIENCE MONITOR, Oct. 3, 2006, *available at* http://www.csmonitor.com/2006/1003/p01s01-ussc.html?s=hns.

[286] *SPLC Files Federal Lawsuit Challenging Constitutionality of Immigration Raids that terrorized Latino residents of Southeast Georgia Towns* PR NEWSWIRE, PUBLIC INTEREST SERVICES, Nov. 1, 2006, *available at* http://w3.lexis.com/lawschoolreg/researchlogin08.asp?t=y&fac=no.

[287] *Id.*; Jonsson, *supra* note 285.

[288] *Id.* Russ Bynum, *Immigration Raids Leave Georgia Town Bereft, Stunned*, SEATTLE TIMES, Sept. 16, 2006.

[289] *Id.*

children were absent the day of the raid.[290] Another local principal, Kathryn Gibney of San Pedro Elementary, testified before a congressional committee on the effect of ICE raids upon her school's children and their families. Stressing the level of fear the ICE raids placed on the community, Gibney noted that families kept kids at home and in hiding, describing an increased level of paranoia in the community. Gibney recounted instructions from the wife of man who had just been arrested to her daughter to pack a backpack and leave it by the door. If the child came home and found no one present she was to take the backpack to her aunt's house and stay with her in case her mother was also arrested and deported.[291] Gibney further lamented the long term effects of the raids, describing a frightened community with children asking teachers whether police would be coming to school, as well as "higher absenteeism, lower test scores and increased counseling for her students . . . '[ICE] left behind them a trail of fear.' "[292]

A young boy, Kebin Reyes, a U.S. citizen, symbolizes one of ICE's more egregious actions. Kebin, six-years-old the day of the raid, was seized along with his father, who did not have citizenship, and held at an ICE processing center in San Francisco. Kebin and his father, Noe Reyes, were held for over ten hours with only bread and water. Noe Reyes' requests to contact a family member to take Kebin home were repeatedly denied. Eventually, Kebin's uncle was able to pick up Kebin and remove him from the processing center. The American Civil Liberties Union has filed a lawsuit on Kebin's behalf.[293]

San Rafael's Mayor Alberto Boro criticized the raid's effect on the entire community. Boro was particularly disturbed by the broken relationship between local law enforcement and San Rafael's immigrant community. He criticized federal officials for identifying themselves simply as police, noting this caused confusion within the community that thought local law enforcement was responsible for the raids. He noticed that the raid resulted in a drop in calls to local law enforcement agencies and signaled a heightened level of mistrust of police within the community.[294]

New Bedford, Massachusetts

In March 2007, nearly 500 ICE officials descended upon the small southern New England community of New Bedford, Massachusetts. ICE officials targeted the local Michael Bianco, Inc. plant, a leather goods manufacturer that had manufac-

---

[290] Mark Prado, *30 Illegal immigrants targeted in Canal neighborhood raid*, MARIN INDEPENDENT JOURNAL, Mar. 7, 2007, *available at* http://www.marinij.com/marin/ci_5372749.

[291] *Id.*

[292] *Workforce Protections Subcom. Hearing: "ICE Workplace Raids: Their Impact on U.S. Children, Families and Communities*, 110th Cong., 2d Session, v. 154 Cong Rec D., No 83, May 20, 2008 (Statement of Kathryn Gibney, Principal, San Pedro Elementary School).

[293] Press Release, American Civil Liberties Union, Civil Rights Groups Sue Immigration Officials for Unlawfully Detaining Six-Year-Old U.S. Citizen (Apr. 26, 2007) (on file with Author) *available at* http://www.aclu.org/immigrants/detention/29526prs20070426.html.

[294] Jesse McKinley, *San Francisco Bay Area Reacts Angrily to Series of Immigration Raids.* N.Y. TIMES, Apr. 27, 2008, *available at* http://www.nytimes.com/2007/04/28/washington/28immig.html?n=Top/ Reference/Times%20Topics/People/M/McKinley,%20Jesse&pagewanted=all.

tured goods for brands such as Coach, Rockport and Timberland.[295] Recently, however, the factory had contracted with the government to produce goods for military operations in Iraq. Officials arrested 361 factory employees during the raid.

As with other larger raids, the event split families and underscored the negative effects the raids have on communities. Many of Bianco's employees were women, creating a crisis with caring for their children. Roughly 100 children were stranded with babysitters and other caregivers as their mothers were seized during the raid.[296] The majority of those arrested were moved to detention centers half-way across the country in Texas. Eventually, about 60 employees were released on humanitarian grounds, such as Rosa Herrara who was 8½ months pregnant at the time of her arrest.[297] Representatives from the Massachusetts State Department of Social Services went to Texas to lobby for the additional release of 21 detainees who were parents of children who had been left behind in New Bedford. Additional pleas from Governor Deval Patrick and two U.S. Senators had to be made before ICE released a handful of detainees back to Massachusetts so they could care for their children.[298] A seven-month-old infant who had been nursing became dehydrated after her mother's arrest; the baby lacked milk and needed urgent medical care.[299]

In communities across the country where raids occurred, local churches often provided safe haven and advocacy for the affected families. The National Council of La Raza released a report in late 2007, *Paying the Price: The Impact of Immigration Raids on America's Children*, documenting the affects of ICE raids, including community response, and used the events in New Bedford as part of their case study. The report noted a common theme throughout towns where raids had occurred — the use of local churches as a resource to affected communities. In New Bedford, St. James and Our Lady of Guadalupe became gathering places and refuge for those affected. The report pointed out that in the short term the Church provided a recognizable meeting point, central to the lives of members within the Latino community and was able to provide quick short term relieve without being slowed by bureaucratic gathering of information for statistical purposes or fear of offending partner organizations. In the long term however they were ill equipped and limited by small staff to meet the long term needs of immigrant communities.[300]

---

[295] Ken Maguire, *Factory Struggles After Immigration Raid*, WASHINGTON POST Mar. 28 2007, *available at* http://www.washingtonpost.com/wpdyn/content/article/2007/03/28/AR2007032801392.html.

[296] Ray Henry, *Children Stranded After Immigration Raid*, BOSTON GLOBE, Mar. 7, 2007, *available at* http://www.boston.com/news/local/massachusetts/articles/2007/03/07/children_stranded_after_immigration_raid/.

[297] Alexandra Marks, *After New Bedford Immigration Raid, Voices Call for Mercy and Justice*, CHRISTIAN SCIENCE MONITOR, Mar. 16, 2007, *available at* http://www.csmonitor.com/2007/0316/p01s02-ussc.html?page=1.

[298] NATIONAL COUNCIL OF LA RAZA, PAYING THE PRICE: THE IMPACT OF IMMIGRATION RAIDS ON AMERICA'S CHILDREN 28–29 (2007).

[299] Anahad O'Connor, *Immigration Agency Learns from '07 Raid*, N.Y. Times.com, March 6, 2006, *available at* http://thelede.blogs.nytimes.com/2008/03/06/a-year-later-debate-continues-about-raid/?scp=1-b&sq=%22New+Bedford%22+AND+Ice&st=nyt.

[300] NATIONAL COUNCIL OF LA RAZA, PAYING THE PRICE: THE IMPACT OF IMMIGRATION RAIDS ON AMERICA'S CHILDREN 36–37 (2007).

The La Raza study also analyzed the emotional and mental side effects upon children. While the long-term effects of the raids are still unraveling, psychologists have already observed and are concerned about long-term depression and other mental illness in family members. Psychologists have observed a level of fear among children resulting from separation from one or both parents. Children feared leaving the parent who was not seized and also questioned their parents' feelings for them. The report found that because younger children do not think in conceptual terms of citizen versus noncitizen, they translated the temporary parental absence as abandonment. Parents also noticed changes in behavior, such as children becoming more fearful and sometimes even more aggressive. One parent repeated that her child said "the parent 'love[es] money more than he loves me."[301]

Postville, Iowa

One of the largest immigration raids in U.S. history occurred in April 2008 in the small Midwestern town of Postville, Iowa. Postville represents the quintessential American melting pot in a community with a population of roughly 2,600 people. The community houses a mix of Hasidic Jews, who originally moved to Postville to open up a kosher meatpacking plant. They work alongside immigrant workers from Mexico and parts of Central American who staff the plant, along with other residents including descendants of German Lutheran migrants. The raid occurred at the kosher meat plant, Agriprocessors, Inc., the largest employer in town, and one of the largest in northeastern Iowa. ICE seized over 400 undocumented workers, including 18 juveniles.[302]

Agriprocessors employed approximately 970 workers, 80 percent of whom were believed to have fraudulent identification.[303] After the raid both Agriprocessor and the entire Postville community were in recovery mode. The company brought in a skeleton crew from New York to meet their staffing needs. Community residents observed the sudden drop in business and worried about the town's future. Postville is home to many Latino businesses, and in the days after the raids many storefronts posted signs in Spanish reading "closed".[304] Postville Mayor, Robert Penrod speculated on the effect of a possible Agriprocessor plant closure upon the town, estimating that "two-thirds of the homes here will sit empty [and] 95% of downtown business . . . will dry up."[305]

As in other communities the school system also felt the immediate impact of the raids. The local school district estimated that 150 of the 220 students from immigrant families were absent the day after the raid.[306] As in other communities,

---

[301] *Id.* at 50–51.

[302] Antonio Olivio, *Immigration raid roils Iowa Melting Pot*, CHICAGO TRIBUNE, May 18, 2008, *available*   *at*   http://www.chicagotribune.com/news/nationworld/chi-iowa-plant-raidmay19,0,3571577.story.

[303] *Id.*

[304] *Raids Could Make Postville a Ghost Town*, KAALTV.com, May 14, 2008 *available at* http://kaaltv.com/article/stories/S443938.shtml?cat=0.

[305] *Id.*

[306] Mary Ann Zehr, *Iowa School District Left Coping with Immigration Raid's Impact*, EDWEEK May   20,   2008,   *available*   *at*   http://www.edweek.org/

the Catholic Church became a refuge for the local immigrant population. One local nun, Sister Kathy Thrill, of nearby Waterloo where the detainees were being held at a local fairground, spoke out against the raids. She participated in an effort to collect donations for the affected families but noted the fear in the community. Many residents heard a story of someone who was stopped while shopping at a local Wal-Mart, and tales like these were scaring many families into hiding. Sister Thrill also spoke of her own apprehension as she got word of possible check points set up by ICE officials while she was en route to deliver donated items to families.[307]

This most recent raid also sparked criticism for the potential aftershocks on the American Jewish population who observes kosher dietary practice. Approximately one million American Jews follow kosher law. It is still too soon to tell how Agriprocessor's slowdown will affect the kosher meat market however there were reports of increased meat prices and hoarding of food in the days following the raid.[308]

One witness to the effects of the ICE raid in Postville labeled the government strategy "criminal," as the women were made to wear restrictive "humiliating GPS bracelets" while caring for their children, and hundreds of women and children were faced with the threat of being left "homeless and starving."[309]

The May raid was not the first sign of trouble for Agriproessors, Inc. The company had been under scrutiny for numerous violations of environmental laws, labor laws, and was on notice that there was an alleged methamphetamine lab being run from inside the plant. However, nothing has happened to management, and the ICE raid appears to have allowed Agriprocessors to avoid pending labor law investigations. David Strudthoff, the Postville Community Schools Superintendent commented, "They don't go after employers. They don't put CEOs in jail . . . it is like a natural disaster — only this one is manmade . . . In the end, it is the greater population that will suffer and the workforce that will be held accountable."[310]

---

login.html?source=http%3A%2F%2Fwww.google.com%2Fsearch%3Fhl%3Den%26client%3Dfirefox-a%26channel%3Ds%26rls%3Dorg.mozilla%253Aen-US%253Aofficial%26hs%3Di5G%26q%3DImmigration%2Braids%26btnG%3DSearch&destination=http%3A%2F%2Fwww.edweek.org%2Few%2Farticles%2F2008%2F05%2F21%2F38immig.h27.html&levelId=2100&baddebt=false.

[307] Jayne Norman, *Immigrants feel distress, shock, nun says*, DES MOINES REGISTER, May 21, 2008, *available at* http://www.desmoinesregister.com/apps/pbcs.dll/article?AID=/20080521/NEWS/805210358.

[308] Michelle Boorstein, *Raid on Slaughterhouse May Mean Shortage of Kosher Meat*, WASHINGTON POST, May 22, 2008, at A02, *available at* http://www.washingtonpost.com/wp-dyn/content/article/2008/05/21/AR2008052102471.html?hpid=sec-religion.

[309] Jonah Newman, Minneapolis, Letter to the Editor, NY TIMES, June 3, 2008.

[310] Spencer S Hsu, *Immigration Raid Jars a Small Town*, WASHINGTON POST, May 18, 2008, at A01, *available at* http://www.washingtonpost.com/wp-dyn/content/article/2008/05/17/AR2008051702474.html.

e.   National Security

i.   SEVIS and Other Student-Related Programs

The government has a history of monitoring and tracking foreign students in the United States under the pretext of protecting national security. As Susan Burgess describes, even though student visitors make up a small percentage of nonimmigrant admissions annually, the involvement of Eyad Ismoil in the World Trade Center bombing on February 26, 1993, sparked widespread concern about the INS's ability to track student whereabouts.[311] Ismoil, a Jordanian national, entered the U.S. on a student visa in 1989 but had dropped out of school and overstayed his visa.[312]

This incident and the public's response led to the passage of section 641 of IIRIRA in 1996.[313] This section of the statute provided that the Attorney General, in consultation with the Secretaries of State and Education, develop and conduct a program to collect certain information about F, J and M visa holders or applicants for such status who were nationals of five designated countries.[314] This information was collected from the approved schools and exchange programs, and was to be collected electronically when practicable.[315] The program was to be funded by fees of no more than $100 per student or exchange visitor.[316]

The Coordinated Interagency Partnership Regulating International Students (CIPRIS) was developed to implement section 641. CIPRIS is an internet based reporting system that was used cooperatively by the INS, the Department of State, the Department of Education, and members of the educational and exchange programs.[317] CIPRIS was a pilot project that began in June 1997 to test the concepts of electronic data collection and reporting methods.[318] This pilot project ended in October 1999.[319]

The Student and Exchange Visitor Program (SEVP) started developing in 2000 and was designed to incorporate the permanent version of CIPRIS. The terrorist attacks of September 11, 2001, however, led to renewed anxiety in regards to foreign students and let to a perceived need to accelerate a more thorough tracking and monitoring system.[320]

The USA PATRIOT Act of 2001 amended Section 641 of IIRIRA and it accelerated the earlier program by (1) requiring that it be fully implemented prior

---

[311] Susan N. Burguess, Sevis: Is it Academic?, 04-02 Immigr. Briefings 1, 1 (Feb. 2004).

[312] *Id.*

[313] *Id.*

[314] Pub. L. 104-208, 110 Stat. 3009, Sec. 641 (Sept. 30, 1996) codified at 8 U.S.C.A. § 1372.

[315] *Id.*

[316] *Id.*

[317] Burguess, *supra* note 311, at 4.

[318] *Id.*

[319] *Id.*

[320] *Id.* at 1.

to January 1, 2003, (2) authorizing funding to accommodate the accelerated implementation, and (3) imposing additional data collection requirements. In addition, the Enhanced Border Security and Visa Entry Reform Act of 2002 added to the requirements pertaining to data collection and reporting. Schools and exchange visitor programs were now required to report to ICE any student or exchange visitor who were supposed to enroll but failed to do so.

The Student and Exchange Visitor Information System (SEVIS) became an integral part of this new monitoring system. SEVIS is an internet-based program that is intended to enhance the government's ability to "manage and monitor" foreign students and exchange program visitors and their dependents. DHS monitors and tracks these individuals by requiring that, in order to accept foreign students or exchange visitors, the schools and exchange programs must be certified and enrolled in SEVIS and must adhere to its data collection requirements. SEVIS functions were given to the Immigration and Customs Enforcement (ICE) branch of DHS, as it is supposed to be a tool to protect national security.

SEVIS affects several nonimmigrant groups. In order to admit F-1, F-3, M-1 or M-3 students, schools are required to be enrolled in SEVIS. Similarly, in order to admit a J-1 exchange visitor, a program must register with SEVIS. Spouses and children of any of these nonimmigrants who enter the United States as dependents of the principal applicant are also subject to SEVIS reporting.

SEVIS imposed stringent reporting and record keeping requirements, which are codified in various laws and regulations. IIRIRA, The Patriot Act, the Enhanced Border Security and Visa Entry Reform Act, as well as DHS Regulations and Department of State Regulations all require the reporting of different types of information. For example, IIRIRA established that the identity and current U.S. address of the nonimmigrant had to be provided, as well as their nonimmigrant 1) classification and the date on which a visa was issued, extended, or approved; 2) the nonimmigrant's current academic status; and 3) any disciplinary action taken against the nonimmigrant as a result of his or her being convicted of a crime.[321] DHS regulations require an even longer list of information such as whether a student failed to maintain status or complete his or her program, or whether they graduated early.[322]

SEVIS also imposes a fee on each applicant, which is usually $100.[323] There is a lower fee of $35 for individuals applying for certain positions under the J Visa.[324]

SEVIS was established with the goals of improving national security, and as a way to modernizing the old paper system of tracking student visa recipients. It is unclear whether SEVIS has been able to achieve either of its main goals. In the conclusion of her article "SEVIS: Is It Academic," Burguess astutely notes that:

---

[321] 8 U.S.C.A. § 1372(c)(1)(A)-(D).

[322] 8 C.F.R. § 214.3(g)(3)(ii).

[323] 68 Fed. Reg. at 61, 151.

[324] Burguess, *supra* note 311, at 20.

Ultimately SEVIS cannot perform the DHS's function of investigation, follow-up and enforcement. Though it might serve to bring some status violators to ICE's attention, there seems to be little correlation between this massive compilation of data and preventing or deterring the criminal-minded from carrying out their evil deeds once they are inside the country. What SEVIS does do is effectively place schools and exchange programs at the front line of ICE enforcement responsibility with respect to these nonimmigrants.[325]

ii. The Penttbom Investigation

Immediately after the September 11 attacks, the FBI, in cooperation with several other law enforcement agencies, launched the Pentagon/Twin Towers Bombing Investigation (PENTTBOM).[326] Officials questioned and frequently detained individuals possibly involved in the September 11 attacks or other terrorist activities, as well as anyone who might have information of use to the investigation.[327] Undocumented immigrants were sometimes encountered fortuitously during the course of the investigation.[328] Even if they had no link to, or knowledge of, terrorist activities, they too were arrested, turned over to the former INS and detained.[329] Of the detainees held on immigration-related grounds (whether or not suspected of terrorism), the overwhelming majority were males, between ages twenty-six and forty, from Arab or Muslim countries.[330] About one-third were from Pakistan.[331]

To compound the controversy, the government has steadfastly refused to disclose to the public the names or whereabouts of the detainees, a policy that the D.C. Circuit has upheld.[332] In addition, a recent federal Bureau of Prisons regulation rooted in the PENTTBOM investigation authorized the monitoring of inmate-attorney conversations, sometimes with the inmate's knowledge and sometimes without it, in certain cases of suspected terrorism.[333]

The racial profiling used in this investigation, as well as the government tactics and secrecy were gravely concerning. Many individuals' constitutional and human rights seemed to be compromised. Widespread criticism of the PENTTBOM investigation developed. One of the most critical reports of post 9/11 anti-terrorism

---

[325] *Id.* at 25.

[326] Dan Eggen, *FBI's 9/11 Team Still Hard at Work; Dwindling Group Wants to See Probe Through to the End*, WASH. POST, June 14, 2004.

[327] *See* OFFICE OF THE INSPECTOR GENERAL, U.S. DEPARTMENT OF JUSTICE, THE SEPTEMBER 11 DETAINEES: A REVIEW OF THE TREATMENT OF ALIENS HELD ON IMMIGRATION CHARGES IN CONNECTION WITH THE INVESTIGATION OF THE SEPTEMBER 11 ATTACKS 69–70 (2003), *available at* http://www.usdoj.gov/oig/special/0306/full.pdf [hereinafter OIG REPORT].

[328] Stephen H. Legomsky, *The Ethnic and Religious Profiling of Noncitizens: National Security and International Human Rights*, 25 B.C. THIRD WORLD L.J. 161, 165 (2005).

[329] *Id.*

[330] *Id.*

[331] *Id.*

[332] *Id.*

[333] *Id.*

performance and its impact on immigrants, especially Muslim males, came from the Office of the Inspector General (OIG) of the Department of Justice (DOJ). The OIG testified before the Congress as to the plight of 9/11 detainees:

> Our review determined that 762 aliens were detained on immigration charges in connection with the PENTTBOM investigation in the first 11 months after the terrorist attacks. . . . Our review found that many September 11 detainees did not receive notice of the charges against them in a timely manner. . . . More than a quarter of the 762 detainees' clearance investigations took longer than 3 months. . . . Our review found serious problems in the treatment of the September 11 detainees housed at the MDC . . . the BOP imposed a total communications blackout for several weeks on the September 11 detainees held at the MDC. . . . Most of the September 11 detainees did not have legal representation prior to their detention at the MDC . . . detainees were placed in full restraints whenever they were moved, including handcuffs, leg irons, and heavy chains. . . . The detainees also were subjected to having two lights illuminated in their cells 24 hours a day. . . . We concluded that on occasion staff members used strip searches to intimidate and punish detainees.[334]

The government's high handed counter-terrorism measures and tactics were egregious enough to also attract the intervention of the courts.[335] In *United States v. Awadallah*, 202 F. Supp.2d 55, (S.D.N.Y. 2002), the Court opined:

> Having committed no crime — indeed, without any claim that there was probable cause to believe he had violated any law — [the witness] bore the full weight of the prison system designed to punish convicted criminals as well as incapacitate individuals arrested or indicted for criminal conduct . . . . [He was] repeatedly strip-searched, shackled whenever he [was] moved, denied food that complies with his religious needs . . . prohibited from seeing or even calling his family over the course of 20 days and then [pressured into] testifying while handcuffed to a chair.

The PENTTBOM investigation again exemplified that the U.S. government is willing to compromise immigrants' human rights and constitutional protections under the pretext of protecting national security. There is little connection between the government's detention and deportation of these immigrants and the investigation of terrorist activities. As the PENTTBOM investigation ensues, there is an ongoing threat that severe human rights violations are being committed by the U.S. government against many immigrants.

---

[334] Detainees: Hearing Before the Sen. Comm. on the Judiciary, 109th Cong. (2005) (statement of Glenn A. Fine, Inspector Gen. U.S. Dep't of Justice).

[335] Kam C. Wong, *The USA Patriot Act: A Policy of Alienation*, 12 MICH. J. RACE & L. 161, 168 (2006).

3.   The Scope of Enforcement Powers

There are certain provisions in our constitution that protect all individuals living in the United States, regardless of their immigration status. The following rights apply in the immigration enforcement context and are important to understand the scope of enforcement powers. First, under the Fourth Amendment of the Constitution, every person has the right not to be "unreasonably" searched or seized by the government. An arrest warrant can only be issued if there is a "probable cause" that a person has violated the law. Second, the Fifth Amendment established that no person can be deprived of life, liberty, or property without due process of law. Third, the Fourteenth Amendment guarantees "equal protection" under the law for any person affected by actions of local or state government. The Fourteenth Amendment ensures that people in similar situation are treated equally under the law. These constitutional provisions, along with certain sections of the INA and other statutes, grant immigrants certain rights and should limit the scope of the government's immigration enforcement power.

The rights and protections outlined in the Constitution, however, are dependent on court interpretation. Courts across the United States have differed in their interpretation of what these rights mean. Moreover, in general, courts have interpreted the Constitution and these laws to only narrowly protect immigrant rights and to give the government broad immigration enforcement power. The following sections of this Chapter will explore the scope of the government's immigration enforcement powers as defined by the courts in the context of stops and arrests, search and seizure, interrogations, and detention.

a.   Interrogations

The Immigration & Nationality Act (INA) provides that INS officers "shall have power without warrant . . . to interrogate any alien or person believed to be an alien as to his right to be or to remain in the United States . . . ." The Fourth Amendment, which the Supreme Court has applied to Border Patrol searches and seizures of all persons in the United States, circumscribes this power. An official can therefore only legally stop someone, for interrogation purposes, if they have good reason to believe that the individual is undocumented.

Courts use a balancing test to determine if a stop and interrogation is reasonable under the Fourteenth Amendment. Courts weigh how much an enforcement officer's conduct impedes a person's freedom against how strong a reason the officer has to suspect that the individual is undocumented. The more an enforcement officer's conduct interferes with a person's freedom, the greater the justification the officer needs to question that person.

This balancing test falls into three categories based on the intensity of the interrogation. An immigration enforcement officer can briefly question an individual if the officer has "articulable facts to justify a suspicion" that the individual is an "alien." This type of interrogation is referred to as "casual questioning." For this test to apply, the officer must question the individual without a show of force, and the person being questioned must be free to walk away.

When an immigration enforcement official stops an individual for longer than "brief questioning," it is a detentive stop. In most parts of the United States, the officer in this situation must have a "reasonable suspicion" that the person is an undocumented immigrant. Only a very short period of questioning is allowed during a detentive stop, however the person is not free to walk away. If during this questioning, the officer finds "probable cause" to believe the person is undocumented, the officer can arrest the person.

An agent can only legally arrest a person if they have "probable cause" to believe that the individual is undocumented. Because an individual's freedom is being curtailed, the officer needs strong evidence to meet this requirement. A person can be "under arrest" if they reasonably believe that they are not free to leave. A person does not have to be told they are under arrest or be hand-cuffed.

The difference between a "detentive stop" and an arrest is sometimes hard to recognize. Usually, if an immigration enforcement officer uses force against a person, displays weapons, questions the individual in a threatening manner, or uses coercive language, the courts will determine that a person has been arrested.

The Supreme Court, however, has found that use of coercive language or behavior by the police does not always constitute an arrest. In *California v. Hodari D*, 499 U.S. 621 (1991), the Supreme Court held that an arrest was not made until the coercion was complete — that is, until the person has completely submitted to the show of force or authority.

The scope of immigration enforcement power is subject to courts interpreting the Fourteenth amendment and other statutes. As we will see in the following sections, courts have usually used their powers to broaden the scope of enforcement power and limit the protections of individuals within the immigration context.

b.   Stops and Arrests

i.   Immigration Checkpoints

As the INS enforcement budget grew larger and larger, the Supreme Court, swayed by arguments that the undocumented alien problem was worsening, allowed more flexibility to INS enforcement strategies.

In 1973, the Supreme Court appeared to have put an end to the Border Patrol practice of "roving" near the United States–Mexico border to search vehicles, without a warrant or probable cause. In *Almeida–Sanchez v. United States*, INS officials unsuccessfully argued that as long as they were in the proximity of the border, their efforts in following and stopping cars located near the border was the "functional equivalent" of the border; on that theory, the Border Patrol felt that inhabitants of such vehicles were subject to the same intrusions as those at the border.[336] But within two years, the Supreme Court was overwhelmed by government claims of a crisis at the border opened the door to stops by roving patrols near the border under certain circumstances.

---

[336] Almeida-Sanchez v. United States, 413 U.S. 266 (1975).

In *United States v. Brignoni–Ponce* (1975), two Border Patrol officers were observing northbound traffic from a patrol car parked at the side of Interstate Highway 5 north of San Diego.[337] The road was dark, and they were using the patrol car's headlights to illuminate passing cars. They pursued Brignoni-Ponce's car and stopped it, saying later that their only reason for doing so was that its three occupants appeared to be of Mexican descent. The officers questioned the three occupants about their citizenship and learned that the passengers were aliens who had entered the country illegally. All three were then arrested, and Brignoni-Ponce was charged with two counts of knowingly transporting undocumented immigrants. At trial he moved to suppress the testimony of and about the two passengers, claiming that this evidence was the fruit of an illegal seizure because the officers did not have the authority to stop his car. The Court of Appeals agreed, holding that the Fourth Amendment, as interpreted in *Almeida-Sanchez*, forbids stopping a vehicle, even for the limited purpose of questioning its occupants, unless the officers have a founded suspicion that the occupants are aliens illegally in the country. The appellate court refused to find that Mexican ancestry alone supported such a founded suspicion and held that Brignoni-Ponce motion to suppress should have been granted.

The Supreme Court agreed that a roving patrol generally should not be allowed to stop a vehicle near the Mexican border and question its occupants about their citizenship and immigration status, when the only ground for suspicion is that the occupants appear to be of Mexican ancestry. But the Court carved an important exception: patrolling officers may stop vehicles if they are aware of specific articulable facts, together with rational inferences, reasonably warranting suspicion that the vehicles contain aliens who may be illegally in the country and the occupants can be questioned. Any number of factors may be taken into account in deciding whether there is reasonable suspicion to stop a car in the border area. Officers may consider the characteristics of the area in which they encounter a vehicle. Its proximity to the border, the usual patterns–of traffic on the particular road, and previous experience with alien traffic are all relevant. They also may consider information about recent illegal border crossings in the area. The driver's behavior may be relevant, as erratic driving or obvious attempts to evade officers can support a reasonable suspicion. Aspects of the vehicle itself may justify suspicion. For instance, officers say that certain station wagons, with large compartments for fold–down seats or spare tires, are frequently used for transporting concealed aliens. The vehicle may appear to be heavily loaded, it may have an extraordinary number of passengers, or the officers may observe persons trying to hide. The Court also acknowledged that trained officers can recognize the characteristic appearance of persons who live in Mexico, relying on such factors as the mode of dress and haircut.

The Court was willing to give more latitude to Border Patrol officers because of claims that undocumented Mexican migration was getting out of hand. The Court explained its reasoning, relying on figures provided by the government:

> The Government makes a convincing demonstration that the public
> interest demands effective measures to prevent the illegal entry of aliens at

---

[337] 422 U.S. 873 (1975).

the Mexican border. Estimates of the number of illegal immigrants in the United States vary widely. A conservative estimate in 1972 produced a figure of about one million, but the INS now suggests there may be as many as 10 or 12 million aliens illegally in the country. Whatever the number, these aliens create significant economic and social problems, competing with citizens and legal resident aliens for jobs, and generating extra demand for social services. The aliens themselves are vulnerable to exploitation because they cannot complain of substandard working conditions without risking deportation. . . .

The Government has estimated that 85% of the aliens illegally in the country are from Mexico. . . . The Mexican border is almost 2,000 miles long, and even a vastly reinforced Border Patrol would find it impossible to prevent illegal border crossings. Many aliens cross the Mexican border on foot, miles away from patrolled areas, and then purchase transportation from the border area to inland cities, where they find jobs and elude the immigration authorities. Others gain entry on valid temporary border--crossing permits, but then violate the conditions of their entry. Most of these aliens leave the border area in private vehicles, often assisted by professional "alien smugglers." The Border Patrol's traffic–checking operations are designed to prevent this inland movement. They succeed in apprehending some illegal entrants and smugglers, and they deter the movement of others by threatening apprehension and increasing the cost of illegal transportation.[338]

ii. Racial Profiling

A case in Illinois illustrates enforcement strategy by INS investigators that focuses on individuals with "Latin" appearance in both employment and nonemployment settings. In *Illinois Migrant Council v. Pilliod*,[339] the federal court of appeals upheld an order of a lower court critical of such INS tactics. The case involved six individuals and the Illinois Migrant Council (IMC), a nonprofit corporation, who brought a class action against officials of the INS. IMC was a community service agency that served as an advocate for illiterate migrant agricultural workers of Mexican heritage; the individual plaintiffs were U.S. citizens or permanent residents of Mexican descent. The plaintiffs alleged that INS officials were unconstitutionally stopping and questioning individuals simply on the basis of physical appearance, and without any basis for concluding that they were aliens.

One part of the case involved three street encounters between INS agents and four individuals. On September 18, 1974, plaintiffs Sandoval and Montanez were driving in Sandoval's car to the IMC office in Rochelle, Illinois. As they parked outside the office and were leaving the car, an INS car pulled alongside and the agents got out of their car. When Montanez was asked where he was born, he replied, "Mexico." He was asked for his identification and produced a satisfactory

---

[338] United States v. Brignoni-Ponce, 413 U.S. 873, 879 (1975).

[339] 540 F.2d 1062 (7th Cir. 1976).

permanent resident alien card after being threatened otherwise with jail in Chicago. When Sandoval, a U.S. citizen of Mexican descent, was asked to produce identification, and refused to do so, the agents said they would have to take him to Chicago and forced him into the back seat of their car. He again refused to produce identification, but was ordered out of the car when he implied that he was a U.S. citizen.

During the first week of October 1974, plaintiff Lopez was walking to his office at 19 West Jackson Boulevard in Chicago when he was asked by two strangers if he lived in the area. He responded "No" but said that he worked around there. Then he was asked where he was born. When he inquired why he was being interrogated, the agent said he was from the INS and flashed his identification. Lopez then said that he was born in New Mexico. He is an American–born citizen of Mexican descent. At the time, he was attired in boots made in New Mexico, Levis jeans, an Illinois shirt, and a Mexican jacket.

Jose Ortiz, a member of the plaintiff class, stated that when he was walking with a friend on September 18, 1974, in Rochelle, Illinois, two INS agents stopped them and asked for Ortiz's papers. He was allowed to leave upon complying.

Other incidents involved "area control operations" conducted by agents without search or arrest warrants. At 4:30 A.M. on September 18, 1974, defendant Theodore Glorgetti, an INS employee, and thirty–two armed INS agents began simultaneous operations on preselected targets in Rochelle, Illinois. First, they knocked on the unlocked doors and entered two La Hacienda buildings where fifty–five female employees of the Del Monte Food Company were sleeping. The agents proceeded from bedroom to bedroom, demanding that the women occupants produce their papers. Afterward they left the buildings without making any arrests.

The agents also searched the Del Monte cottages where male immigrant employees resided. The INS agents used essentially the same method of operation in those cottages. When one of the residents, the same Jose Ortiz mentioned before, was unable to produce his green card evidencing legal residency, he was forced to accompany the INS agents on their search and was released only when another Del Monte employee assured them that Ortiz's papers were in order.

At the same time, an INS agent repeatedly kicked on the door of a small farmhouse near Rochelle occupied by Alonzo Solis, a U.S. citizen migrant worker. The agent tried to force his way into the house but desisted only when the Solis's child cried and Solis ordered him out. Solis dressed and showed the agent his "certificate" outside the house, whereupon the agent left.

At 5:00 A.M., INS agents also conducted similar operations at Del Monte plants 109 and 110. They questioned everyone who appeared to be of Latino heritage. Two Del Monte supervisors offered no resistance because they believed they had to allow the agents to search the plants.

In Mendota, Illinois, at 8:00 A.M. on September 26, 1974, defendant Giorgetti and thirty agents first went to the Motor Wheel plant. Nineteen employees were interviewed by Giorgetti, ten were arrested, and five of the ten were subsequently permitted to return to work. The agents then proceeded to several other industrial targets in Mendota and to hotels, boardinghouses, and private dwellings, resulting in the apprehension of 108 undocumented aliens, 104 of whom were still in detention at the time of the hearing below.

The court ruled that these INS enforcement strategies were improper, because a person should not be stopped by an INS agent unless the agent reasonably suspects that he or she is an alien illegally in the country, or at least that the person is an alien. Latin appearance alone is not sufficient basis for INS agents to stop and question.

While the rules outlined in the *International Molders' Union and Illinois Migrant Council* cases are still to be followed by ICE officials, agents remain vigilant in their efforts to focus on Mexicans. One example of brazen government strategies involved the sweep of an entire downtown area of a California town in conjunction with local law enforcement officials. On September 8, 1984, a raid of bars in the central valley town of Sanger, California, resulted in the deportation Of 255 undocumented aliens. Five law enforcement agencies blockaded the main street downtown, swept through bars, and arrested forty people on criminal charges. Officers from the Fresno County Sheriffs Department, Sanger Police Department, Fresno Police, Department, state Department of Alcoholic Beverage Control (ABC), and Border Patrol closed off downtown Sanger streets and entered sixteen bars. For the next two hours, they served thirty–five warrants and made forty arrests, mostly for misdemeanor offenses, while. Border Patrol agents asked bar patrons for identification and arrested 255 undocumented aliens. Officers entered bars and ordered that no one leave. An agent from ABC searched for liquor law violations and police officers attempted to serve individual arrest warrants on charges of B–girl activities, receiving stolen property, prostitution, gambling, and narcotics.

Meanwhile, a Border Patrol agent asked in English who had citizenship or legal residency documents. Those with documents were detained in another room for about forty minutes, while other patrons were searched and questioned. Of the hundred patrons in the bar, forty–seven were undocumented. One was arrested for having a concealed weapon. The other fifty–two patrons were detained although they were U.S. citizens or legal residents and were accused of no crime.

One bar owner (who was not cited for any wrongdoing) was appalled by what he saw: "Officers came in like Hitler's police or the police in South Africa. [Those suspected by the INS] were herded like cattle. I can't believe this can happen in the United States." What happened was clear to William Kennedy, an attorney with California–Rural Legal Assistance, who investigated: "These are *racist raids*. There's no way to characterize them any other way. They're looking for *brown–skinned people*, not any others."[340]

Antonio Martinez fell prey to one of the more unusual INS enforcement, strategies also directed primarily at Mexicans in southern California in 1993. Martinez received a letter from the INS and read it several times, getting, an uneasy feeling each time. After two years of battling the INS to legalize his status

---

[340] Julie Charlip, *Sanger Sweep Stirs Questions on Civil Rights Violations*, THE FRESNO BEE, October 14, 1984, at A1 (emphasis added).

so he could remain here with his American wife and daughter, the offer seemed too good to be true. Come to the Federal Building, bring some identification, and we'll give you a work permit good for a year, the letter said. How could the letter not be authentic? asked Martinez's wife, Ariel, a California native. It was written on INS stationery and said Martinez qualified under the "Immigration and Nationality Act of 1993."

In the end, Ariel's optimism and belief in the INS's credibility won out. On July 20, Martinez, his wife, and the couple's eighteen–month–old daughter drove to the INS office in downtown San Diego to pick up his permit. But instead of being welcomed by their adopted country, Martinez and dozens of others were promptly arrested and deported. The sting letter was sent to Martinez and more than 600 others, resulting in sixty apprehensions, though eighteen immigrants were released for a variety of technical reasons. Attorneys who saw the letter quickly determined that it was an INS sting because the law referred to in the letter does not exist. INS officials in San Diego said the operation targeted people who were under judges' orders of deportation, though several who received letters disputed this. After promising a work permit, the letter said: "Since this is a one–time event, failure to report to this office at this time will render you ineligible to receive your employment authorization."

Immigration officials avoided sending copies of the letters to immigrants' attorneys because they feared that the lawyers would alert their clients to the sting. They also said that two of the immigrants apprehended but later released were freed because they had pending appeals to their deportation orders. In addition, two others were released because they had become permanent residents. Four immigrants who received the letter were also released because they were "the right names but wrong persons."[341]

In border cities and areas, the former INS also engaged in some rather devious enforcement "sting" strategies. In the late 1980s in El Paso, Texas, the INS used a phony letterhead from "Argim" Ford. Argim is *migra* spelled backward, a Spanish word used by Mexicans to describe the INS. The bogus letters were sent to Spanish–surnamed individuals indicating that they might win a Ford Bronco if they showed up for a drawing. When letter recipients showed up, their immigration documentation was checked. Fifty–five of those who showed up turned out to be undocumented immigrants, and were deported.[342] There have even been reports of Border Patrol agents disguised as saguaro cacti waiting at the border to catch illicit border crossers.

c.   Search and Seizure

In 1976, the Court articulated a major exception to the Fourth Amendment's protection against search and seizure to accommodate the Border Patrol even further. The case, *United States v. Martinez–Fuerte*, involved the legality of a fixed checkpoint located on Interstate 5 near San Clemente, California, the

---

[341] H.G. Reza, *Immigrants Deported in INS Sting Operation*, L.A. TIMES, July 31, 1993, at A1.

[342] Id. J. Michael Kennedy, *Aliens Fear Massive Deportations; at El Paso Border, Rumor Mill is the Biggest Worry*, L.A. TIMES, March 14, 1987, at I-1.

principal highway between San Diego and Los Angeles.[343] The checkpoint is sixty-six road miles north of the Mexican border. Approximately one mile south of the checkpoint is a large black-on-yellow sign with flashing yellow lights over the highway stating "ALL VEHICLES, STOP AHEAD, 1 MILE." Three-quarters of a mile farther north are two black-on-yellow signs suspended over the highway with flashing lights stating "WATCH FOR BRAKE LIGHTS." At the checkpoint, which is also the location of a State of California weighing station, are two large signs with flashing red lights suspended over the highway. These signs each state "STOP HERE-U.S. OFFICERS." Placed on the highway are a number of orange traffic cones funneling traffic into two lanes where a Border Patrol agent in full uniform, standing behind a white on red "STOP" sign, checks traffic. Blocking traffic in the unused lanes are official U.S. Border Patrol vehicles with flashing red lights. In addition, there is a permanent building that houses the Border Patrol office and temporary detention facilities. There are also floodlights for nighttime operations.

The "point" agent standing between the two lanes of traffic visually screens all northbound vehicles, which the checkpoint brings to a virtual, if not a complete, halt. Most motorists are allowed to resume their progress without any oral inquiry or close visual examination. In a relatively small number of cases the "point" agent will conclude that further inquiry is in order. He directs these cars to a secondary inspection area, where their occupants are asked about their citizenship and immigration status. The average length of an investigation in the secondary inspection area is three to five minutes. A direction to stop in the secondary inspection area could be based on something suspicious about a particular car passing through the checkpoint, but in the three situations that were challenged in *Martinez–Fuerte*, the government conceded that none of the three stops was based on any articulable suspicion.

In the first situation, Amado Martinez–Fuerte approached the checkpoint driving a vehicle containing two female passengers. The women were undocumented Mexican aliens who had entered the United States at the San Ysidro port of entry by using false papers. They rendezvoused with Martinez–Fuerte in San Diego to be transported northward. At the checkpoint their car was directed to the secondary inspection area. Martinez–Fuerte produced documents showing him to be a lawful resident alien, but his passengers admitted being present in the country unlawfully. He was criminally charged with two counts of illegally transporting aliens.

The second situation involved Jose Jimenez–Garcia, who attempted to pass through the checkpoint while driving a car with one passenger. He had picked up the passenger by prearrangement in San Ysidro after the latter had been smuggled across the border. Questioning at the secondary inspection area revealed the illegal status of the passenger, and Jiminez–Garcia was charged with two counts of illegally transporting an alien.

The third case involved Raymond Guillen and Fernando Medrano–Barragan. They approached the checkpoint with Guillen driving and Medrano–Barragan and

---

[343] 428 U.S. 543 (1976).

his wife as passengers. Questioning at the secondary inspection area revealed that Medrano–Barragan and his wife were undocumented aliens. A subsequent search of the car uncovered three other undocumented aliens in the trunk. Medrano–Barragan had led the other aliens across the border at the beach near Tijuana, Mexico, where they rendezvoused with Guillen, a U.S. citizen. Guillen and Medrano–Barragan were jointly indicted on four counts of illegally transporting aliens and four counts of inducing the illegal entry of aliens.

The defendants argued that the routine stopping of vehicles at a checkpoint was invalid because *Brignoni–Ponce* must be read as prohibiting any stops in the absence of reasonable suspicion. However, the Court recognized that maintenance of a traffic–checking program in the interior is necessary because "the flow of illegal aliens cannot be controlled effectively at the border." The Court noted the "substantiality of the public interest in the practice of routine stops for inquiry at permanent checkpoints, a practice which the Government identifies as the most important of the traffic–checking operations." The checkpoints (a similar one was in Texas) were located on important highways; in their absence such highways would offer undocumented aliens a quick and safe route into the interior. Routine checkpoint inquiries apprehend many smugglers and undocumented aliens who succumb to the lure of such highways. And the prospect of such inquiries forces others onto less efficient roads that are less heavily traveled, slowing their movement and making them more vulnerable to detection by roving patrols. Therefore, the Court held:

> A requirement that stops on major routes inland always be based on reasonable suspicion would be impractical because the flow of traffic tends to be too heavy to allow the particularized study of a given car that would enable it to be identified as a possible carrier of illegal aliens. In particular, such a requirement would largely eliminate any deterrent to the conduct of well–disguised smuggling operations, even though smugglers are known to use these highways regularly.

Thus, fixed checkpoints, even though more than fifty miles away from the border, were constitutional. Again, the Court cited the importance of supporting the Border Patrol's efforts in enforcing immigration laws that were being violated by Mexicans.

> It has been national policy for many years to limit immigration into the United States. Since July 1, 1968, the annual quota for immigrants from all independent countries of the Western Hemisphere, including Mexico, has been 120,000 persons. Act Of Oct. 3, 1965, § 21(e), 79 Stat. 921. Many more aliens than can be accommodated under the quota want to live and work in the United States. Consequently, large numbers of aliens seek illegally to enter or to remain in the United States. We noted last Term that "[e]stimates of the number of illegal immigrants [already] in the United States vary widely. A conservative estimate in 1972 produced a figure of about one million, but the Immigration and Naturalization Service now suggests there may be as many as 10 or 12 million aliens illegally in the country." *United States v. Brignoni–Ponce*, 422 U.S. 873, 878 (1975) (footnote omitted). It is estimated that 85% of the illegal immigrants are from Mexico, drawn by the fact that economic opportunities are signifi-

cantly greater in the United States than they are in Mexico.

Interdicting the flow of illegal entrants from Mexico poses formidable law enforcement problems. The principal problem arises from surreptitious entries. . . . The United States shares a border with Mexico that is almost 2,000 miles long, and much of the border area is uninhabited desert or thinly populated and land. Although the Border Patrol maintains personnel, electronic equipment, and fences along portions of the border, it remains relatively easy for individuals to enter the United States without detection. It also is possible for an alien to enter unlawfully at a port of entry by the use of falsified papers or to enter lawfully but violate restrictions of entry in an effort to remain in the country unlawfully. Once within the country, the aliens seek to travel inland to areas where employment is believed to be available, frequently meeting by prearrangement with friends or professional smugglers who transport them in private vehicles.

In fiscal year 1973, 175,511 deportable aliens were apprehended throughout the nation by linewatch agents stationed at the border itself. Traffic–checking operations in the interior apprehended approximately 55,300 more deportable aliens. Most of the traffic–checking apprehensions were at checkpoints.

The Supreme Court majority was not concerned with the racial overtones of its decision even though the Border Patrol essentially was picking out those who looked Mexican for secondary inspection. A dissenting opinion by justice William Brennan warned: "Every American citizen of Mexican ancestry and every Mexican alien lawfully in this country must know after today's decision that he travels the fixed checkpoint highways at [his] risk." But the majority indicated that it would encourage lower courts to act against the Border Patrol if there was evidence of "the misuse of checkpoints to harass those of Mexican ancestry."

Less than a decade later, in 1984, the Supreme Court made it quite clear that the Fourth Amendment's protection against illegal search and seizure was not available to aliens fighting deportation, even if INS officials acted illegally. In *INS v. Lopez-Mendoza*, Adam Lopez–Mendoza was arrested by INS agents at his place of employment, a transmission repair shop.[344] Responding to a tip, INS investigators arrived at the shop shortly before 8:00 A.M. The agents had not sought a warrant to search the premises or to arrest any of its occupants. The proprietor of the shop firmly refused to allow the agents to interview his employees during working hours. Nevertheless, while one agent engaged the proprietor in conversation, another entered the shop and approached Lopez-Mendoza. In response to the agent's questioning, Lopez-Mendoza gave his name and indicated that he was from Mexico with no close family ties in the United States. The agent then placed him under arrest. Lopez-Mendoza underwent further questioning at INS offices, where he admitted he was born in Mexico, was still a citizen of Mexico, and had entered this country without inspection by immigration authorities. While the arrest was illegal, the Supreme Court refused to exclude Lopez-Mendoza's admission that he was not a legal resident. It was important to the Court that deportation proceedings were civil rather than criminal proceedings, and the Court also felt that applying the Fourth Amendment exclusionary rule would have little deterrent effect on illegal

---

[344] 468 U.S. 1032 (1984).

police activity. In fact, the Court felt that excluding evidence after an illegal arrest by INS officials would have great societal costs.

The first cost is one that is unique to continuing violations of the law. Applying the exclusionary rule in proceedings that are intended not to punish past transgressions but to prevent their continuance or renewal would require the courts to close their eyes to ongoing violations of the law. This Court has never before accepted costs of this character in applying the exclusionary rule.

Presumably no one would argue that the exclusionary rule should be invoked to prevent an agency from ordering corrective action at a leaking hazardous waste dump if the evidence underlying the order had been improperly obtained, or to compel police to return contraband explosives or drugs to their owner if the contraband had been unlawfully seized.

Once again, the Court was also influenced by the perceived need to support INS activities to combat the problem of undocumented aliens.

Immigration officers apprehend over one million deportable aliens in this country every year . . . A single agent may arrest many illegal aliens every day. Although the investigatory burden does not justify the commission of constitutional violations, the officers cannot be expected to compile elaborate, contemporaneous, written reports detailing the circumstances of every arrest. At present an officer simply completes a "Record of Deportable Alien" that is introduced to prove the INS's case at the deportation hearing; the officer rarely must attend the hearing. Fourth Amendment suppression hearings would undoubtedly require considerably more, and the likely burden on the administration of the immigration laws would be correspondingly severe.

As the Court said, "There comes a point at which courts, consistent with their duty to administer the law, cannot continue to create barriers to law enforcement in the pursuit of a supervisory role that is properly the duty of the Executive and Legislative Branches." Effectively, the Court implied that point is reached when the issue of controlling the perceived problem of undocumented Mexicans is before the Court.

Thus, when it comes to the southwest border, the Border Patrol conducts three kinds of inland traffic–checking operations in an effort to minimize undocumented immigration. Permanent checkpoints, such as the one at San Clemente, are maintained at or near intersections of important roads leading away from the border. They operate on a coordinated basis designed to avoid circumvention by smugglers and others who transport the undocumented aliens. Temporary check-points, which operate like permanent ones, occasionally are established in other strategic locations. Finally, roving patrols are maintained to supplement the checkpoint system.

d.   Detention

ICE detains more than 280,000 adults and children every year: immigrants, refugees, and newcomers.[345] They are detained because they are in removal proceedings, because a final order of removal has been entered against them, or because they are suspected of being involved in terrorist related activities. Without the right to government-appointed counsel, an estimated ninety percent of these immigration detainees go unrepresented in their cases before the Immigration Court-often due to poverty and the limited pro bono resources available to this population. Detainees, often with limited English skills and limited education, have to face a trained immigration prosecutor in adversarial administrative proceedings before an Immigration Judge without any help.

While this detention is considered civil for these administrative immigration proceedings, detainees are held at hundreds of facilities nationwide- the majority of which are local and county jails under DHS contract.[346] Immigration detainees, including innocent asylum seekers, may be commingled with criminal convicts.[347] Since DHS has a significant annual budget for detention and removal, immigration detention has become a significant profit-making enterprise for the private and public incarceration industry alike.[348]

The conditions in these detention facilities are often abhorrent.[349] Since detention is contracted out contracts out and the system is decentralized, detention, ICE is unable to ensure access to counsel and uniform and fair treatment of detainees.[350] In November 2000, after numerous lawsuits attempting to force the government to change and years of advocacy by concerned organization, a more comprehensive set of "Detention Standards" was issued that became effective in 2001.[351] These "Detention Standards" apply to DHS detention facilities and contract centers, such as local or county jails.[352] Despite these new standards, however, detention facilities continue to provide inadequate food and medical treatment to their detainees, and many detainees suffer severe human rights abuses in these facilities.[353]

---

[345] Detention Watch, About the U.S. Detention and Deportation System, *available at* http://www.detentionwatchnetwork.org/aboutdetention.

[346] *Id.*

[347] *Id.*

[348] *Id.*

[349] *Id.*

[350] *See* Steven Neeley, *Immigration Detention: The Inaction of the Bureau for Immigration and Customs Enforcement,* 60 ADMIN. L. REV. 729, 730 (2008).

[351] *Id.*

[352] *Id.*

[353] *Id.* at 731–32.

e. Mandatory Detention during Removal Proceedings

Courts have long held that detention incidental to removal proceedings is allowed. Courts have justified broad detention provisions as necessary to protect the public safety and ensure that immigrants ordered removed actually leave the country.

In 1996, during a period of rampant anti-immigrant sentiment, Congress enacted several draconian immigration laws, and along with other harsh enforcement provisions, Congress imposed mandatory detention on several groups of non-citizens. Mandatory detention means that an individual is not entitled to bond and must remain in detention while their removal proceedings are under way. These detention provisions, which went into effect in 1998, imposed mandatory detention on many individuals because of their criminal history. INA § 236A(c) requires mandatory detention of individuals if they are deportable under INA § 237(a)(2)(A) because: 1) they have committed two crimes of moral turpitude after admission; 2) are aggravated felons; 3) have committed drug crimes, firearms offenses, or miscellaneous crimes; 4) have committed a crime involving moral turpitude for which the sentence is at least one year; 5) or are deportable on terrorist grounds. INA § 236A(c) also imposes mandatory detention on any individual who is inadmissible under INA § 212(a)(2). Mandatory detention is therefore imposed on a large number of individuals who are in removal proceedings for being inadmissible as INA § 212(a) includes any person who has been convicted of a CIMT as well as a slew of other crimes.

The 1996 laws also imposed mandatory detention on persons in expedited removal who are applying for asylum but who have not established that they have a credible fear of persecution.

Immigration advocates voiced their concerns regarding these broad mandatory detention provisions. Once an individual is in immigration detention, it becomes incredibly difficult to find representation, or communicate with their attorney if they do manage to find someone to take their case. Moreover, once in detention, hearings are expedited. These barriers made it difficult for individuals to raise any valid immigration claim they might have in court.

Unfortunately, in 2003, the Supreme Court reviewed these mandatory detention provisions under INA§ 236(c) and upheld them as constitutional, even when applied to lawful permanent residents. In *Demore v. Kim*, the majority asserted that "Congress was justifiably concerned that deportable criminal aliens, who are not detained continue to engage in crime and fail to appear for their removal hearings in large numbers, may require that they be detained for the brief period necessary for their removal proceedings."[354]

---

[354] 538 U.S. 510, 513 (2003).

f.   Mandatory Detention after a Final Order of Removal

Once a final order of removal has been entered, removal of that individual must be carried out within a 90 day period.[355] INA § 241(a)(2) established that persons subject to final removal orders may be detained during this removal period. Moreover, the statute requires that persons who have been found inadmissible or removable for criminal or security grounds be mandatorily detained during this time.[356]

Many non-citizens who have final orders of removal against them are placed in detention. However, for various reasons, some of these individuals cannot be removed within the 90 day window. For example, countries such as Laos and Cuba do not take people after they have been ordered removed, and so natives of those countries have a hard time finding a country that will accept them. Many immigrants therefore found themselves in indefinite detention, with no hope of leaving the United States or of being released from immigration detention.

In 2001, the Supreme Court addressed the issue of indefinite detention of non-citizens ordered removed. In *Zadvydas v. Davis*, the Supreme Court reaffirmed that at least in regards to aliens living inside the United States, substantive due process applies to immigration detention.[357] Moreover, INA 241(a)(6) did not authorize indefinite detention.[358] The Court determined that detention is only permissible for a period reasonably necessary to secure the noncitizen's removal.[359] The Court read the statute as having a presumptive six-month limit on detention, and also held that when there is no reasonable likelihood of removal, there cannot be a basis for continued detention.[360]

This was one of the few decisions by the Court in recent years that has limited the scope of enforcement powers with regards to immigration detention.

g.   Mandatory Detention for Suspected Terrorists

In the wake of the terrorist attacks of September 11, 2001, Congress passed the USA-PATRIOT Act. The PATRIOT Act allowed the Attorney General (AG) and the Deputy Attorney General (DAG) to detain any suspected terrorists, regardless of the provision discussed above.

Under INA § 236A(a)(3), the AG and the DAG can certify an individual them if there are reasonable grounds to believe that the person falls within one of the terrorism grounds of inadmissibility or deportability. The AG and the DAG can also certify an individual when there are reasonable grounds to believe that the person is engaged in any other activity that will endanger the national security of

---

[355] INA § 241(a)(2).

[356] INA § 241(a)(2).

[357] 533 U.S. 678 (2001).

[358] *Id.*

[359] *Id.*

[360] *Id.*

the United States.[361]

Once the AG or DAG certifies someone, that person is subject to special detention provisions. Under these special provisions, the AG must place the person in removal proceedings, or charge the person with a criminal offense within seven days of commencement of detention, or the person must be released.

While proceedings are pending, the person must remain in custody, even if they are eligible for, or granted, relief from removal. The only way a person can be released from detention under these provisions is if the AG determines that the individual no longer falls within one of the specified grounds of terrorist related activity.

Moreover, even if an individual is ordered removed, they can still be detained if the person's release will threaten the national security of the United States, or the safety of the community, or any person. Their detention needs to be reevaluated every six months.[362]

---

[361] INA § 236A(a)(3).

[362] INA § 236A(a)(7).

Chapter 14

THE RIGHTS OF IMMIGRANTS

A. PUBLIC BENEFITS

With the implementation of recent sweeping welfare reform legislation, the Personal Responsibility and Work Opportunity Reconciliation Act of 1996, federal public assistance programs became unavailable to permanent resident and undocumented aliens alike. The law authorized state and local governments to deny locally-funded benefits to legal immigrants, transgressing the long-standing tradition of treating citizens and legal immigrants alike in terms of public benefits eligibility.[1] Although a budget compromise in 1997 allowed refugees and lawful immigrants who were in the United States prior to the 1996 reform to continue receiving benefits, new immigrants and refugees would be severely affected.

New legal immigrants are barred from participation in two federal benefits programs: Supplemental Security Income (SSI) and Food Stamps. SSI provides monthly cash grants to low-income persons who are aged, blind, or disabled. Food Stamps are vouchers, redeemable for food at participating vendors. The only classes of immigrants exempted from these restrictions are (1) refugees, asylees, and individuals granted withholding of deportation, but only for the first five years after being granted that status; (2) active duty service members, veterans, and their direct family members; and (3) lawful permanent residents who can prove that they have worked at least forty qualifying quarters (ten years) for social security purposes.

Since welfare reform legislation authorizes states to exercise the option to pass legislation denying legal immigrants access to state-administered federal pro-

---

[1] *See* Graham v. Richardson, 403 U.S. 365 (1971).

grams, a range of benefits can be affected: non-emergency Medicaid, Title XX social services block grants, and Temporary Assistance to Needy Families (TANF), the state block grant program that replaced Aid to Families with Dependent Children (AFDC). States use Title XX social services block grants for a variety of purposes, including child care, programs to combat family violence, and in-home care for disabled persons. As the costs of social welfare programs shift to the states, states will face increasing temptations to exercise their option to deny legal immigrants assistance under these programs. The same classes of legal immigrants exempt from federal SSI and Food Stamps restrictions are shielded from state-adopted restrictions.

Undocumented immigrants are barred from receiving any of the chief federal public benefit programs: TANF, Food Stamps, Medicaid, SSI, unemployment compensation, school loans and grants, and subsidized housing. Many of these programs have been historically closed to undocumented immigrants. However, under former law, immigrants were eligible to receive Medicaid, SSI, and AFDC if they were considered to be "permanently residing in the United States under color of law,[2] a category eliminated by welfare reform's blanket bar against unqualified immigrants. Prior law also enabled immigrants to qualify for social security benefits and unemployment compensation if they had employment authorization and a valid social security number. These programs are not completely foreclosed to all unqualified immigrants.

Many states have worked to fill in some of the gaps in non-citizen coverage mandated by the 1996 laws. In fact, over half of the states spend their own money to cover at least some of the immigrants who are ineligible for federally funded services. A growing number of states or counties provide health coverage to children and/or pregnant women, regardless of their immigration status. State-funded programs are often temporary or at risk of being cut or eliminated, in state budget battles. In determining an immigrant's eligibility for benefits, it is important to understand the federal rules as well as the rules of the state in which an immigrant resides.[3]

The 1996 welfare law created two categories of immigrants for benefits eligibility purposes: "qualified" and "not qualified." Contrary to what these names suggest, the law excluded most people in *both* groups from *eligibility* for many benefits, with a few exceptions. The qualified immigrant category includes:

- Lawful permanent residents, or LPRs (persons with green cards).
- Refugees, persons granted asylum or withholding of deportation/removal, and conditional entrants.
- Persons granted parole by the Department of Homeland Security (DHS) for a period of at least one year.
- Cuban and Haitian entrants.

---

[2] *See* Holley v. Lavine, 553 F.2d 845 (2d Cir. 1977). *See generally* Bill Ong Hing, *Don't Give Me Your Tired, Your Poor: Conflicted Immigrant Stories and Welfare Reform*, 33 HARV. C.R.-C.L. L. REV. 159 (1998).

[3] Updates on federal and state rules are available at the website of the National Immigration Legal Center, www.nilc.org.

- Certain abused immigrants, their children, and/or their parents.[4]

All other immigrants, ranging from undocumented immigrants to many persons lawfully present in the United States, are considered "not qualified."[5]

In 2000, Congress established a new category of non–U.S. citizens, *victims of trafficking*, who, while not listed among the qualified immigrants, are eligible for federal public benefits to the same extent as refugees.[6] In 2003, Congress clarified that "derivative beneficiaries" listed on trafficking victims' visa applications (spouses and children of adult trafficking victims; spouses, children, parents, and minor siblings of child victims) also may secure federal benefits.[7]

With some important exceptions detailed below, the law prohibits not-qualified immigrants from enrolling in most federal public benefit programs.[8] Federal public benefits include a variety of safety-net services paid for by federal funds.[9] But the welfare law's definition does not specify which particular programs are covered by the term, leaving that clarification to each federal benefit-granting agency. In 1998, the U.S. Department of Health and Human Services (HHS) published a notice

---

[4] In order for an immigrant to considered to be a "qualified alien" under the battered spouse or child category, the immigrant must have an approved visa petition filed by a spouse or parent, a self-petition under the Violence Against Women Act (VAWA) that sets forth a prima facie case for relief, or an application for cancellation of removal under the VAWA. The spouse or child must have been battered or subjected to extreme cruelty in the United States by a family member with whom the immigrant resided, or the immigrant's parent or child must have been subjected to such treatment. The immigrant must demonstrate a "substantial connection" between the domestic violence and the need for the benefit being sought. And the battered immigrant, parent, or child must have moved out of the household of the abuser.

[5] Before 1996, some of these immigrants were served by benefit programs under an eligibility category called "permanently residing in the U.S. under color of law" (PRUCOL). PRUCOL is not an immigration status, but a benefit eligibility category that has been interpreted differently depending on the benefit program and the region. Generally, it means that DHS is aware of a person's presence in the United States but has no plans to deport or remove him or her from the country. Some states continue to provide services to these immigrants using state or local funds.

[6] The Victims of Trafficking and Violence Protection Act of 2000, Pub. L. No. 106-386 § 107 (October 28, 2000). Federal agencies are required to provide benefits and services to individuals who have been subjected to a "severe form of trafficking in persons," without regard to their immigration status. To receive these benefits, the victim must be either under 18 years of age or certified by the U.S. Department of Health and Human Services (HHS) as willing to assist in the investigation and prosecution of severe forms of trafficking in persons. In the certification, HHS confirms that the person either (a) has made a bona fide application for a T visa that has not been denied, or (b) is a person whose continued presence in the United States is being ensured by the attorney general in order to prosecute traffickers in persons.

[7] Trafficking Victims Protection Reauthorization Act of 2003, Pub. L. No. 108-193, § 4(a)(2) (December 19, 2003).

[8] Welfare law § 401 (8 U.S.C. § 1611).

[9] "Federal public benefit" is described in the 1996 federal welfare law as (a) any grant, contract, loan, professional license, or commercial license provided by an agency of the United States or by appropriated funds of the United States, and (b) any retirement, welfare, health, disability, public or assisted housing, postsecondary education, food assistance, unemployment, benefit, or any other similar benefit for which payments or assistance are provided to an individual, household, or family eligibility unit by an agency of the United States or appropriated funds of the United States.

clarifying which of its programs fall under the definition.[10] The list of 31 HHS programs includes Medicaid, the State Children's Health Insurance Program (SCHIP), Medicare, Temporary Assistance for Needy Families (TANF), Foster Care, Adoption Assistance, the Child Care and Development Fund, and the Low-Income Home Energy Assistance Program.

The welfare law also attempted to force states to enact new laws, after August 22, 1996, if they choose to provide state or local public benefits to not-qualified immigrants.[11] Such micromanagement of state affairs by the federal government is potentially unconstitutional under the Tenth Amendment.

The law includes important exceptions for certain types of services. Regardless of their status, "not qualified" immigrants remained eligible for emergency Medicaid,[12] if they are otherwise eligible for their state's Medicaid program.[13] The law did not restrict access to public health programs providing immunizations and/or treatment of communicable disease symptoms (whether or not those symptoms are caused by such a disease). School breakfast and lunch programs remain open to all children regardless of immigration status, and every state has opted to provide access to the Special Supplemental Nutrition Program for Women, Infants and Children (WIC).[14] Also exempted from the restrictions are in-kind services necessary to protect life or safety, as long as no individual or household income qualification is required. In January 2001, the attorney general published a final order specifying the types of benefits that meet these criteria. The attorney general's list includes child and adult protective services; programs addressing weather emergencies and homelessness; shelters, soup kitchens, and meals-on-wheels; medical, public health, and mental health services necessary to protect life or safety; disability or substance abuse services necessary to protect life or safety; and programs to protect the life or safety of workers, children and youths, or community residents.[15]

States can receive federal funding for TANF, Medicaid, and SCHIP to serve qualified immigrants who have completed the federal five-year bar.[16] "Humanitar-

---

[10] HHS, Personal Responsibility and Work Opportunity Reconciliation Act of 1996 (PRWORA), "Interpretation of 'Federal Public Benefit,'" 63 FR 41658–61 (August 4, 1998). The HHS notice clarifies that not every benefit or service provided within these programs is a federal public benefit.

[11] Welfare law § 411 (8 U.S.C. § 1621).

[12] Emergency Medicaid cover the treatment of an emergency medical conditions, which is defined as: " a medical condition (including emergency labor and delivery) manifesting itself by acute symptoms of sufficient severity (including severe pain) such that the absence of immediate medical attention could reasonably be expected to result in: (A) placing the patient's health in serious jeopardy, (B) serious impairment to bodily functions: or (C) serious dysfunction of any bodily organ or part. 42 U.S.C. § 1396b(v).

[13] Welfare law § 401(b)(1)(A) (8 U.S.C. § 1611(b)(1)(A)).

[14] Welfare law § 742 (8 U.S.C. § 1615).

[15] U.S. Dept. of Justice (DOJ), "Final Specification of Community Programs Necessary for Protection of Life or Safety under Welfare Reform Legislation," A.G. Order No. 2353-2001, published in 66 FR 3613–16 (January 16, 2001).

[16] States were also given an option to provide or deny federal TANF and Medicaid to most qualified immigrants who were in the United States before August 22, 1996, and to those who enter the United States on or after that date, once they have completed the federal five-year bar. Welfare law § 402 (8

ian immigrants," refugees, persons granted asylum or withholding of deportation/ removal, Cuban/Haitian entrants, certain Amerasian immigrants (described below), and victims of trafficking — are exempt from the five-year bar, as are "qualified" immigrant veterans, active duty military, and their spouses and children.

Approximately half of the states use state funds to provide TANF, Medicaid, and/or SCHIP to some or all of the immigrants who are subject to the five-year bar on federally funded services, or to a broader group of immigrants.[17]

Congress restricted eligibility even for many qualified immigrants by arbitrarily distinguishing between those who entered the United States before or "on or after" the date the law was enacted, August 22, 1996. The law barred most immigrants who entered the United States on or after that date from "federal means-tested public benefits" during the five years after they secure qualified immigrant status.[18] Federal agencies clarified that "federal means-tested public benefits" are Medicaid (except for emergency care), SCHIP, TANF, Food Stamps, and Supplemental Security Income (SSI).[19] No other programs are subject to a five-year bar.

Although the 1996 law severely restricted immigrant eligibility for food stamps, subsequent legislation restored access for many of these immigrants. Qualified immigrant children, the humanitarian immigrant and veterans groups described above, lawful permanent residents with 40 quarters of work history, certain Native Americans, lawfully residing Hmong and Laotian tribe members, and immigrants receiving disability-related assistance[20] are now eligible regardless of their date of entry into the United States. Qualified immigrant seniors who were born before August 22, 1931, may be eligible if they were lawfully residing in the United States on August 22, 1996. Other qualified immigrant adults, however, must wait until they

---

U.S.C. § 1612). Only one state, Wyoming, denies Medicaid to immigrants who were in the country when the welfare law passed. Colorado's proposed termination of Medicaid to these immigrants was reversed by the state legislature in 2005 and never took effect. In addition to Wyoming, six states (Alabama, Mississippi, North Dakota, Ohio, Texas, and Virginia) do not provide Medicaid to all qualified immigrants who complete the federal five-year ban. Five states (Indiana, Mississippi, South Carolina, Texas, and Wyoming) fail to provide TANF to all qualified immigrants who complete the federal five-year ban.

[17] See Guide to Immigrant Eligibility for Federal Programs, 4th ed. (Los Angeles: National Immigrant Law Center, 2002), and updated tables at www.nilc.org/pubs/Guide_update.htm. See also Shawn Fremstad and Laura Cox, Covering New Americans: A Review of Federal and State Policies Related to Immigrants' Eligibility and Access to Publicly Funded Health Insurance (Washington, DC: Kaiser Commission on Medicaid and the Uninsured, November, 2004), retrieved from www.kff.org/ medicaid/7214.cfm[0].

[18] Welfare law § 403 (8 U.S.C. § 1613).

[19] HHS, Personal Responsibility and Work Opportunity Reconciliation Act of 1996 (PRWORA), Interpretation of "Federal Means-Tested Public Benefit," 62 Fed. Reg. 45,256 (August 26, 1997); U.S. Dept. of Agriculture (USDA), Federal Means-Tested Public Benefits, 63 Fed. Reg. 36,653 (July 7, 1998). The SCHIP program, created after the passage of the 1996 welfare law, was later designated as a federal means-tested public benefit program. See Health Care Financing Administration, The Administration's Response to Questions about the State Child Health Insurance Program, Question 19(a) (September 11, 1997).

[20] For this purpose, disability-related programs include: SSI, Social Security disability, state disability or retirement pension, railroad retirement disability, veteran's disability, disability-based Medicaid, and disability-related General Assistance, if the disability determination uses criteria as stringent as those used for SSI.

have been in qualified status for five years before their eligibility for food stamps can be considered.

Several states provide state-funded food stamps to some or all of the immigrants who were rendered ineligible for the federal program.[21]

Congress imposed its most harsh restrictions on immigrant seniors and immigrants with disabilities who seek assistance under the SSI program.[22] Although advocacy efforts in the two years following the welfare law's passage achieved a partial restoration of these benefits, significant gaps in eligibility remained. SSI, for example, continues to exclude not-qualified immigrants who were not already receiving the benefits, as well as most qualified immigrants who entered the country after the welfare law passed[23] and seniors without disabilities who were in the United States before that date.

"Humanitarian" immigrants (refugees, persons granted asylum or withholding of deportation/removal, certain Amerasian immigrants, or Cuban and Haitian entrants) can receive SSI, but only during the first seven years after having obtained the relevant status. The main rationale for the seven-year time-limit is that it was supposed to provide a sufficient opportunity for humanitarian immigrant seniors and those with disabilities to naturalize and retain their eligibility for SSI as U.S. citizens. However, a combination of factors, including immigration backlogs, processing delays, former statutory caps on the number of asylees who can adjust their status, language barriers, and other obstacles have made it impossible for most of these individuals to naturalize within seven years. During the 2007–2008 Congressional term, the House and Senate passed different bills providing a two-year extension of SSI eligibility to humanitarian immigrants who are approaching or were terminated from assistance due to the seven- year time limit, but as of this writing no new law had been enacted.[24]

A few states provide cash assistance to immigrant seniors and persons with disabilities who were rendered ineligible for SSI; some others provide much smaller general assistance grants to these immigrants.[25]

B. GENERAL EMPLOYMENT-RELATED RIGHTS AND BENEFITS

Except for certain areas when making U.S. citizenship a prerequisite to employment is considered proper (e.g., federal civil service jobs or state public functions jobs), for the most part, aliens have the same employment-related rights as those enjoyed by U.S. citizens. For example, federal minimum wage laws apply

---

[21] *See* NILC's updated tables on state-funded services, at www.nilc.org/pubs/Guide_update.htm.

[22] Welfare law § 402(a) (8 U.S.C. § 1612(a)).

[23] Most new entrants cannot receive SSI until they become citizens or secure credit for 40 quarters of work history (including work performed by a spouse during marriage, persons "holding out to the community" as spouses, and by parents before the immigrant was 18 years old).

[24] The SSI Extension for Elderly and Disabled Refugees Act (H.R. 2608 and S. 821).

[25] *See* Guide to Immigrant Eligibility for Federal Programs, 4th ed. (Los Angeles: NILC, 2002), and updated tables, *available at* www.nilc.org/pubs/Guide_update.htm.

to employers who hire documented as well as undocumented workers.[26] Similarly the federal Occupational Safety and health Act does not differentiate between documented and undocumented workers in its requirement that employers provide a safe place of employment.[27]

Undocumented as well as documented workers are also covered by the National Labor Relations Act. In *Sure-Tan, Inc. v. NLRB*,[28] the Supreme Court held that it was an unfair labor practice to constructively discharge undocumented alien workers by reporting them to INS in retaliation for participating in union activities. In accordance with *Sure-Tan*, the NLRB placed the burden of proof on employers to show that unlawfully fired alien workers were not entitled to be in the United States or eligible to work, and the only acceptable evidence was a final INS ruling to that effect.[29] The Supreme Court has added a wrinkle here, however. In *Hoffman Plastics Compounds, Inc., v. National Labor Relations Board*,[30] the Court held that undocumented workers discharged during a union organizing drive cannot sue for back pay for wrongful terminations under the National Labor Relations Act, at least under the fact circumstances of the case, in which the worker had given the employer false documents to get work and the employer did not discover that they were false until the time of the National Labor Relations Board proceedings. Nevertheless, back pay was awarded up to the time the employer discovered the employee's status. The court held that a back pay award was an appropriate remedy so long as the awarded reflected the employee's actual losses. Although IRCA would have prevented the employer from hiring the employee, the National Labor Relations Board could reasonably award back pay to him for compensation for lost work up until his status as an undocumented immigrant was discovered.

Usually all workers, whether citizens or aliens, are entitled to worker's compensation benefits for work-related injuries. In determining eligibility, most state statues are concerned with residence rather than immigration status. For example, in Florida, the definition of "employee" for worker's compensation purposes includes aliens, whether lawfully or unlawfully employed.[31] Alaska is one state that limits worker's compensation benefits to citizens, permanent residents, or aliens in the United States under "color of law."[32]

Unemployment insurance benefits are made available to workers who have quit work with good cause or who have been discharged without good cause. Benefits are drawn from a fund financed by state and federal taxes. The federal statue restricts these benefits to aliens who are lawful permanent residents, authorized to work, or who are in the United States under "color of law."[33] Furthermore, the unemploy-

---

[26] 29 U.S.C. § 201–219.

[27] 29 U.S.C. § 651–678.

[28] 467 U.S. 216 (1984).

[29] *See NLRB Reverses Position on Labor Remedies for Undocumented Aliens*, 65 INTERPRETER RELEASES 989 (1988).

[30] 237 F.3d 639 (D.C. Cir. 2001).

[31] Fla. Stat. 440.02.

[32] Alaska Stat. 23.20.381(b).

[33] 26 U.S.C. § 3304(a)(14)(A).

ment insurance programs usually require that the person be "able and available for work," a requirement that undocumented workers who do not have DHS permission to work cannot meet. In contrast, unemployment disability benefits may be available even to undocumented workers because for disability purposes, the claimant does not have to be able and available for work.[34]

Social Security benefits are usually available to all former workers as long as they have contributed their share to the Social Security program and are aged, blind, or disabled.[35] Therefore, Social Security disability and old age retirement benefits are generally available to eligible citizens, permanent residents, and aliens permanent residing in the United States under color of law. Visitors and students, for example, would not qualify. Benefits also are payable to surviving widows and widowers who are undocumented or who did not even reside in the United States with the wage-earner spouse. However, the removal of an otherwise qualified alien can operate to terminate benefits under these Social Security programs.[36] Furthermore, Medicare benefits for retired wage earners are conditioned on five years of permanent residency in the United States.[37]

One of the difficulties in becoming eligible for Social Security insurance benefits today, however, is that the issuance of a Social Security number is forbidden to an alien who is not a permanent resident or refugee, or who has not been gratned employment authorization from DHS. Note, however, that employers cannot avoid paying their FICA and FUTA contributions for employees on the grounds that the employees are undocumented and do not have Social Security numbers.[38]

C.   EMPLOYMENT AND LICENSES

Most employment and licensing restrictions imposed by the federal government, state governments, and private employers have come in the form of limiting certain occupations to U.S. citizens. Whether such restrictions are proper usually depends on which entity has imposed the restriction and/or what the occupation entails.

1.   State Restrictions

As a general rule, state restrictions limiting state jobs and the issuance of licenses to U.S. citizens have been subjected to strict equal protection scrutiny by the U.S. Supreme Court. For example, in *In re Griffiths*,[39] the exclusion of lawful permanent residents from the practice of law in Connecticut was invalidated, and in *Sugarman v. Dougall*,[40] a New York law providing that only U.S. citizens could hold permanent state civil service positions was struck down.

---

[34]   Ayala v. California Unemployment Ins. Appeals Bd., 54 Cal. App. 3d 676 (1976).

[35]   42 U.S.C. § 401–431.

[36]   *Id.* 402(n).

[37]   *Id.* 1395o; *see* Mathews v. Diaz, 426 U.S. 67 (1976).

[38]   Rev. Rul. 82-116, 1982-1 C.B. 152.

[39]   413 U.S. 717 (1973).

[40]   413 U.S. 634 (1973).

However, in the state employment area, beginning with *Folie v. Connelie*,[41] the Supreme Court has deferred to the state requirement of U.S. citizenship when the position entails a public function, or involves the "formulation, execution, or review of broad public policy." Thus, in *Folie*, the Court held that New York could bar aliens from holding state law enforcement positions. In *Ambach v. Norwick*,[42] the court ruled that public school teaching fell within the public functions exception as well. Similarly, in *Cabell v. Chavez-Salido*,[43] the Supreme Court indicated that probation officer positions in California could be limited th U.S. citizens. Note that some citizen-only statues, such as the one in *Ambach*, provide that lawful permanent residents who file declarations of intent to become citizens under INA § 334(f) can also qualify for the employment.

Without the showing of the involvement with a public function or broad public policy, however, the state cannot require U.S. citizenship as a condition of state employment.

State laws that attempt to limit the issuance of certain licenses to U.S. citizens have followed the fate of the Griffiths case and have been struck down. In *Bernal v. Fainter*,[44] for example, the Supreme Court ruled that it was unconstitutional for Texas to require citizenship of notary publics in the state. In *Examining Board of Engineers v. Flores de Otero*,[45] Puerto Rico's citizenship requirement for engineer and architect licenses was also ruled invalid. Similarly, it has been held that state liquor and dental licenses cannot be conditioned on U.S. citizenship.[46]

2.   Federal Restrictions

Unlike the strict scrutiny the courts give to state employment and licensing restrictions, similar federal restrictions are usually given great deference when it comes to noncitizen rights to federal employment or licenses. For example, an executive order limiting federal civil service jobs to U.S. citizens has been upheld.[47] A federal statute limiting all federal employment to citizens and aliens who have applied for naturalization has similarly been held constitutional,[48] although nationals of the People's Republic of China who were protected by an April 1990 executive order were granted special permission to apply for federal civil service jobs.[49] In addition, the limitation of FCC broadcasting licenses to U.S. citizens has also been upheld.[50]

---

[41] 435 U.S. 291 (1978).

[42] 441 U.S. 68 (1979).

[43] 454 U.S. 432 (1982).

[44] 467 U.S. 216 (1984).

[45] 426 U.S. 572 (1976).

[46] Kalra v. Minnesota, 590 F. Supp. 971 (D. Minn. 1983); Szeto v. Louisiana State Bd. Of Dentistry, 508 F. Supp. 268 (E.D. La. 1981).

[47] Mow Sun Wong v. Campbell, 626 F.2d 739 (9th Cir. 1980), cert denied, 450 U.S. 959 (1981).

[48] Yuen v. Internal Revenue Serv., 649 F.2d 163 (2d Cir.), cert denied, 454 U.S. 1053 (1981).

[49] *See OPM Clarifies Government Work Restrictions of PRC Nationals*, 69 Interprter Releases 508 (Apr. 27, 1992).

[50] Campos v. FCC, 650 F.2d 890 (7th Cir. 1981).

D. EMPLOYMENT DISCRIMINATION

Prior to 1986, private employers could require job applicants to be United States citizens. However, as part of the political compromise that led to the passage of the Immigration Reform and Control Act of 1986 (IRCA), private employers can no longer limit job openings to U.S. citizens.

It is an unfair immigration-related employment practice for an employer to discriminate against a person authorized to work with respect to hiring the individual for employment or discharging the individual from employment on the basis of:

- The individual's national origin; or
- The individual's citizenship status, as long as the person is a *protected* citizen or alien.[51]

An employment discrimination provision was made part of IRCA for two basic reasons:

- Concern that some unsavory employers will use the law against hiring unauthorized workers (employer sanctions) as an excuse to not hire individuals "who look like aliens;" and
- Concern that some employers will not bother to learn the employer sanctions rules carefully and simply "take the easy way out" by not hiring someone who "looks" foreign or who does not present a particular document.

The term *protected* individual includes the following:

1. Citizens or nationals of the United States;
2. Lawful permanent resident aliens;
3. Aliens lawfully admitted for temporary residence;
4. Refugees; and
5. Asylees.

An alien ceases being a *protected* individual if

- He or she fails to apply for naturalization within six months of the date of becoming eligible to apply for naturalization (usually after being a lawful permanent resident for five years); or
- He or she has filed for naturalization in a timely fashion but has not become naturalized as a citizen within two years of the application. This essentially covers applicants who fail to pursue their application after being called in for the naturalization exam or interview. Processing time utilized by INS in handling the application does not count toward the two-year period.[52]

Although *national origin* is not defined in the immigration laws, in the Title VII employment discrimination context, the term refers both to "the country where a person was born" and to "the country from which her ancestors came."[53] Thus,

---

[51] 8 U.S.C. § 1324b(a)(1).

[52] 8 U.S.C. § 1324b(a)(3).

[53] Espinoza v. Farah Mfg., 414 U.S. 86, 88–89 (1973).

employers cannot favor one nationality group over another in their work force.

The IRCA immigration-related employment discrimination law does not apply to every employer. Exceptions include:

1.   Employers with less than four employees;
2.   Where the discrimination based on national origin is covered by Title VII of the Civil Rights Act of 1964, 42 U.S.C. § 2000e-2; or
3.   Where the discrimination based on citizenship status is required or essential for an employer to do business with an agency of the federal, state, or local government.[54]

It is not an unfair immigration-related employment practice for an employer to hire a citizen or national of the United States over another individual who is an alien if the two individuals are equally qualified.[55]

Thus, an employer cannot limit job openings to U.S. citizens, but if two applicants — one a citizen, one a lawful permanent resident — are equally qualified, the law permits (but does not require) the employer to hire the citizen over the alien. The employer must be prepared to show that he or she has specifically evaluated the qualifications of the two job applicants.

An unfair immigration-related employment practice does occur, however, if the lawful permanent resident is better qualified than the citizen, and the employer hires the citizen.

Employers who try to interfere with the rights of an employee or job applicant under the IRCA employment discrimination rules face penalties for that interference. An employer who fears that an employee is going to file a complaint against the employer risks making things worse if he or she tries to dissuade the employee from complaining. The law provides that an unfair immigration-related employment practice occurs when an employer intimidates, threatens, coerces, or retaliates against any individual for the purpose of interfering with any right or privilege under the general rule.

This interference is prohibited whether it occurs in response to an individuals intent to file or actual filing of charges under the law, or simply if the individual is helping someone else who is complaining by testifying or assisting in the investigation. An individual who has been intimidated, threatened or retaliated against also can claim discrimination under the law.[56] Retaliation by employers against employees for availing themselves of state and federal labor rights is always a bad idea — even when the employee is undocumented.[57]

An employer can also be accused of an unfair immigration-related employment practice if he or she:

---

[54] 8 U.S.C. § 1324b(a)(2).

[55] 8 U.S.C. § 1324b(a)(4).

[56] 8 U.S.C. § 1324b(a)(5).

[57] *See* Contreras v. Corinthian Vigor Ins. Brokerage Inc., 103 F. Supp. 2d 1180 (N.D. Cal. 2000).

- Requests more or different documents than are required for purposes of the I-9 process (see chapter 2); or
- Refuses to honor documents offered by the employee that on their face appear reasonably genuine.[58]

In order for an employer to actually be found liable for an unfair immigration-related practice in one of these situations, the government must show that the employer intended to discriminate.

Citizenship discrimination occurs when an employer disfavors a person because of the individual's citizenship or immigration status. One blatant form of citizenship discrimination that is a clear violation occurs when a private employer requires that all job applicants be U.S. citizens while none of the statutory exceptions apply to the employer's situation.

To consider whether citizenship discrimination has occurred, these questions should be considered:

1. Is the employer treating an applicant or worker differently than other workers because of the person's citizenship or immigration status?
2. Is the person eligible to work?
3. Is the person a protected individual — U.S. citizen, national, lawful permanent resident, lawful temporary resident, refugee, or asylee?

    Citizenship discrimination has occurred if the answer to all three inquiries is affirmative.

Thus, in addition to a "citizens-only-need-apply" rule, the employer can be liable for citizenship discrimination if

1. The employer says that only citizens and "green-card holders" can work for the employer.
2. The employer has a policy of not hiring refugees.
3. The person does not hire an applicant because the EAD has an expiration date, and the person is a protected individual.

Illegal citizenship discrimination by the employer is a prohibited activity that occurs in the context of hiring, firing, recruiting, or referring the person to work for someone else for a fee. The citizenship discrimination provision does not apply to other work issues that relate to the "terms and conditions" of employment, such as:

1. Promotions,
2. Salary increases,
3. Vacations, or
4. Work assignments.

If a worker is treated badly because of her citizenship or immigration status and that person resigns due to the mistreatment, the employer also may be liable for citizenship discrimination. Thus, an employer who hires a worker but then proceeds to not provide equal pay, or demotes the worker in terms of seniority, may be liable. If the employer's actions are so extreme that the worker has no choice but to quit,

---

[58] 8 U.S.C. § 1324b(a)(6).

this may be the equivalent of firing someone based on citizenship status. This is called constructive discharge. Workers also are protected from retaliation by employers if the workers have filed a charge against the employer, or if they support the charges of another worker.

IRCA employment discrimination provisions cover only hiring, firing, recruitment or referral for a fee, and retaliation. However, changes in a person's working conditions also can be so bad that they would be considered a constructive discharge.

E. NATIONAL ORIGIN DISCRIMINATION

A person's national origin refers to the person's place of origin (or that of the person's ancestors) as well as those things (physical features, dress, language) that are identified specifically with the people of that place of origin. Thus, the Equal Employment Opportunity Commission (EEOC), which handles discrimination claims under Title VII of the Civil Rights Act of 1964, finds national origin discrimination when an individual is treated differently from others because of the "individual's, or his or her ancestor's, place of origin; or because an individual has the physical, cultural or linguistic characteristics of a national origin group." If a person is discriminated against because he or she is associated by marriage or in other ways with a particular national origin group, that discrimination is also considered to be national-origin based.

An employer who is guilty of discrimination based on national origin may be subject to a claim under the IRCA employment discrimination laws or Title VII of the Civil Rights Act of 1964. The injured party must elect only one of these routes. The main difference in the protections afforded by these two laws is that the immigration-related provision covers smaller employers while Title VII covers mainly larger employers.

Specifically, Title VII covers employers with 15 or more full or part-time workers, who work for at least 20 out of 52 weeks during the year. In contrast, the IRCA employment discrimination provision covers employers employing four to 14 part or full-time workers, and larger employers not covered by Title VII. For example, seasonal employers who have more than 14 workers, but do not employ them for at least 20 weeks a year are covered by the IRCA provision. Note that most states also have laws that protect against discrimination based on national origin.

The most common example of national origin discrimination is when an employer refuses to hire someone who is from a particular country. Thus if an employer does not want to hire people from Japan, or Mexico, or France, or Iran, that would constitute national origin discrimination. Similarly, if an employer does not want to hire a person who was born in the United States because that person's parents are from Iran, that too would be national origin discrimination.

An employer would also be in violation of the law if the job applicant in a sense represents a particular national origin. For example, if an applicant's spouse is from Mexico, many of the applicant's friends are of Mexican origin, and the employer refuses to hire the applicant due to those reasons, that would be problematic.

Similarly, if one spouse has adopted the Japanese surname of the other spouse and the employer refuses employment because of the surname, discrimination has occurred.

Some jobs require a higher level of English proficiency than others. If an employer requires a certain level of English proficiency for a particular position, the employer must be able to provide justification for the particular level of proficiency required. A secretary is generally required to know more English than a janitor. If an employer requires more English than is reasonably required for a particular job, national origin discrimination may have occurred. Such a practice is discrimination if the effect of the requirement is that some qualified workers are treated differently than other qualified workers solely on the basis of their ability to speak English. The goal of the law is to ferret out those employers who are simply using English proficiency as a pretext for not hiring applicants of particular national origins.

Discriminating against an applicant because of what is perceived as an "accent," can also be problematic. Generally, an accent should only be taken into account only if it interferes with the worker's ability to do the job. The employer cannot use an applicant's purported accent simply as a pretext for not hiring applicants from a particular country or region of the world.

An employer may be guilty of committing unlawful discrimination if he or she imposes a rule that requires workers to speak only English at certain times. Some courts allow English-only rules if the employer can show that the rule is required by a legitimate business necessity. For example, there may not be a legitimate business necessity for imposing a rule that workers cannot speak Spanish to each other during their breaks or at any time during work hours. But requiring that everyone helping on a surgical team in a hospital speak only English during surgery might be legitimate.

Some courts do not require employers to justify English-only rules by showing a business necessity unless

- The persons to whom the rule is applied have difficulty speaking English, or
- The rule is applied in such a way as to create a work environment that is hostile to workers from minority national origin or language groups.

F. INCOME TAX CONSIDERATIONS

For federal income tax purposes, if aliens are considered a resident, their entire worldwide income is taxable, but nonresidents are subject to tax on income earned in the United States.[59] The determination of whether an alien is considered a resident or nonresident for federal income tax purposes is not, however, controlled by immigrant or nonimmigrant status.

The Tax Reform Act of 1984[60] provides a definition of resident alien for U.S. income tax purpose. Under § 7701(b) of the Internal Revenue Code, aliens will be

---

[59]   IRC § 871; 26 C.F.R. § 1.1; Di Portanova v. United States, 690 F.2d 169 (Ct. Cl. 1982).

[60]   Pub. L. No. 98-369, 98 Stat. 494 (1984).

considered residents if they have either (1) been a lawful permanent resident of the United States during the calendar year, or (2) meet the requirements of a substantial preference test.

In general, the substantial preference test is met if the alien has been present in the United States for 31 days or more during the current calendar year and for 183 days within the last three years, as computed under a formula that counts each day present in the country in the current calendar year as a full day, each day in the first preceding year as one-third of a day, and each day in the second preceding year as one-sixth of a day.

If an individual is present in the United State for fewer than 183 days during the calendar year and establishes that he or she has a closer connection with a foreign country than with the United States and a tax home in that country for the year, the individual will usually not be subject to tax as a resident on account of the substantial preference test. Maintenance of a U.S. abode will not automatically prevent an individual from establishing a tax home in a foreign country.[61] But if an individual is present for as many as 183 days during a year, this closer connections/tax-home exception will not be available.

The closer-connections/tax-home exception is also not available if the alien has an application for lawful permanent residence pending, or has taken steps to apply for lawful permanent residence. Filing preliminary forms is considered an affirmative step toward seeking permanent residence status.

The closer-connections/tax-home exception does apply to an alien who could not physically leave the Untied States because of a medical condition that arouse during the person's presence, even if the person was present for more than 182 days during the year.

Time spent in the United States on a valid F-1, J-1, or diplomatic visa is not counted for purposes of the substantial preference test. However, this exemption does not apply if the alien was exempted on this basis for any part of two of the six preceding calendar years.

Resident and nonresident aliens are also subject to state income tax, depending on the state residence.

Provisions in 26 C.F.R. §§ 301 *et seq.* provide an additional gloss on the definition of resident alien for tax purposes. For example, generally, aliens are deemed to be resident aliens with respect to a calendar year if they are lawful permanent residents of the United States at any time during that year.

Aliens who do not qualify for a Social Security number cannot claim the earned income tax credit (EIC). The EIC is a federal tax credit for working families who have moderately low incomes. To qualify for the tax credit, the family unit must contain at least one child, who must have resided in the taxpayer's home for at least half the year.

Until 1993, aliens who did not have a Social Security number were able to file a tax return and claim the EIC by writing in the words "applied for" or "section

---

[61] IRC §§ 162(a)(2), 911(d)(3).

503(c)" in lieu of providing a Social Security number. Beginning with the 1994 tax year, the IRS required each taxpayer, spouse, dependent, and EIC-qualifying child to provide a valid number, or be subject to delays and penalties. The practice varied, however, depending upon the particular IRS office processing the claim.

Only aliens who have DHS-issued employment authorization may obtain a Social Security number that allows them to post earnings and qualifying quarters to their Social Security account. Aliens who are residing lawfully in the United States, such as nonimmigrants, but who do not have employment authorization, may obtain a non-work Social Security number for certain limited purposes. But this non-work card will not be acceptable proof of employment eligibility for purposes of satisfying the I-9 employment verification requirements, posting earnings to a Social Security account, or claiming the EIC. Only persons who include their taxpayer identification number (defined as the Social Security number) and that of their spouse may claim the EIC.[62]

G.   EDUCATION BENEFITS

Children in the United States, citizens, permanent residents, refugees, and undocumented alien children have a right to attend elementary public schools. *Plyler v. Doe.*[63] The importance of such education is too great to deny to children as a class on the basis of immigration status. Similarly, in institutions of higher education, it is unconstitutional for a state to require lawful permanent residents or refugees who have met all other residency requirements to pay additional nonresident tuition.[64]

Nonimmigrants who enter the United States to attend school, such as with F-1 visas, are usually charged a higher nonresident tuition fee in state colleges and universities because by virtue of their status they do not hold the requisite intent to establish domicile.[65] However, there is support for the proposition that loan, scholarship, and financial aid programs for colleges and universities cannot be limited solely to U.S. citizens.[66]

---

[62]   IRC § 32(c)(1)(F).

[63]   457 U.S. 202 (1982).

[64]   Jagnandan v. Giles, 379 F. Supp. 1178 (N.D. Miss. 1974).

[65]   *Cf.* Toll v. Moreno, 458 U.S. 1 (1982).

[66]   Nyquist v. Mauclet, 432 US. 1 (1977); Chapman v. Gerard, 456 F.2d 577 (3d Cir. 1972).

Chapter 15

CITIZENSHIP

A. THE MEANING OF CITIZENSHIP

Citizenship is more than simply a formal legal status. Citizenship characterizes modes of participation and governance, embodies identities and commitments, and confers rights and duties.[1] Defined this broadly, citizenship also is not confined to any single nation; and within nations, to any single governmental unit, as it includes states, provinces, and other localities.[2] Nevertheless, the possession of formal legal citizenship in the United States, while it does not guarantee equality under the law or belonging,[3] remains fundamentally important and may even function as a precondition to rights and membership, particularly in a post 9/11 context.[4] This Chapter focuses on the types of formal citizenship available in the United States and examines how its acquisition, legal standing, and loss has been intimately tied to U.S. national identity struggles, including the ebbs and flows of racialized, exclusionary politics in times of heightened national security.[5]

---

[1] Linda Bosniak, *Citizenship Denationalized*, 7 IND. J. GLOBAL LEGAL STUD. 447, 450 (2000). *See also generally* Kitty Calavita, *Law, Citizenship, and the Construction of (Some) Immigrant "Others,"* 30 LAW & Soc. INQUIRY 401 (surveying the literature on the various dimensions of citizenship); ROGERS M. SMITH, CIVIC IDEALS: CONFLICTING VISIONS OF CITIZENSHIP IN U.S. HISTORY 30 (1997) (describing citizenship laws as designating the criteria for membership in a political community and the key prerogatives that constitute membership); GERALD L. NEUMAN, STRANGERS TO THE CONSTITUTION: IMMIGRANTS, BORDERS AND FUNDAMENTAL LAW 3 (1996) (concluding that membership questions in the U.S. define the "domain of constitutionalism."); Stephen H. Legomsky, *Why Citizenship?*, 35 VA. J. INT'L. L. 279,287–300 (1994) (analyzing the functions of citizenship in terms of political participation, rights and disabilities, symbolism and community, allegiance, sovereignty, and the world order).

[2] Linda Bosniask, *Multiple Nationality and Postnational Transformation of Citizenship*, 42 VA. J. INT'L L. 979, 1000 (2002). *See also* Yishai Blank, *Spheres of Citizenship*, 8 THEORETICAL INQUIRIES L. 411 (2007) (arguing that, contrary to its state-centered conception, citizenship is determined, managed and controlled in three distinct yet intertwined territorial spheres: the local, the national, and the global).

[3] *See, e.g.*, S. David Mitchell, *Undermining Individual and Collective Citizenship: The Impact of Exclusion Laws on the African-American Community*, 34 FORDHAM URB. L.J. 833 (2007) (documenting especially the exclusionary effect of felon exclusion laws on African-Americans) and Rebecca Tsosie, *The Challenge of "Differentiated Citizenship": Can State Constitutions Protect Tribal Rights*, 64 MONT. L. REV. 199, 200 (2003) (discussing the challenge of differentiated citizenship for Native Americans). *See also generally* William E. Forbath, *Caste, Class, and Unequal Citizenship*, 98 MICH. L. REV. 1 (1999) (critiquing the limited view of equal citizenship among modern liberal constitutional scholars which leave out social and economic rights and documenting the rise and loss of a conception of a broader conception of social citizenship in U.S. history). *See also generally* Goodwin Liu, *Education, Equality, and National Citizenship*, 116 YALE L.J. 330 (2006) (proposing to address educational inequality among states by advancing a constitutional right to equal national citizenship).

[4] *See* Catherine Dauvergne, *Citizenship with a Vengeance*, 8 THEORETICAL INQUIRIES L. 489, 490 (asserting that citizenship as a formal status is enjoying resurgence of authority at present that is directly linked to a worldwide crackdown on undocumented migration). *See also generally* Audrey Macklin, *Who is the citizen's Other? Considering the Heft of Citizenship*, 8 THEORETICAL INQUIRIES L 333 (2007) (noting the strong link between legal and social citizenship); Linda Bosniak, *Constitutional Citizenship Through the Prism of Alienage*, 63 OHIO ST. L.J. 1285 (2002) (arguing that while " 'alien citizen' is not an entirely incoherent notion within the terms of conventional constitutional thought . . . the citizenship that noncitizens can aspire to remains limited in scope . . . because the constitutional ideal of equal citizenship is committed not only to universal rights . . . but also to an ethnic and national solidarity and to a practice of bounded national membership") and Earl M. Maltz, *Citizenship and the Constitution: A History and Critique of the Supreme Court's Alienage Jurisprudence*, 28 ARIZ. ST. L.J. 1135 (1996) (examining the role that citizenship has played to constitutional lawmaking in the U.S.).

[5] *See, e.g.*, Mae M. Ngai, BIRTHRIGHT CITIZENSHIP AND THE ALIEN CITIZEN, 75 FORDHAM L. REV. 2521

B. ACQUIRING CITIZENSHIP

The United States recognizes three types of citizenship: (1) by birth in the country, or *jus solis;* (2) by descent or being the child of at least one U.S. citizen parent, also known as *jus sanguinis,* or (3) through naturalization. Every year, about half a million people are naturalized as citizens, while about four million or so, are born as citizens either here in the U.S. or by having U.S. citizen parents.[6]

1.   Jus Solis

a.   Its Origins

The United States is among a few nations, mostly in the Western Hemisphere, that assign citizenship on the circumstance of birth within the territorial boundaries of the nation, regardless of the parents' citizenship.[7] The United States adopted the doctrine of birthright citizenship directly from the British common law, which itself was derived from England's medieval past.[8] The Calvin Case, decided in 1608,[9] became the earliest, most influential theoretical expression of what became the common law birthright citizenship.[10] Sir Edward Coke, along with fourteen other leading members of the English bench, conferred birthright citizenship on Robert Calvin, a child born in Scotland after James I of England acceded to the Scottish throne as James VI.[11] In doing so, Sir Coke held that all persons born within any territory ruled by the King of England were subjects of the King and owed their allegiance to him and were therefore entitled to all the benefits of English law.[12] Sir Coke further rooted his decision in the devine law of nature,[13] giving his theory of birthright citizenship the strongest possible foundation.[14]

Remarkably, birthright citizenship in the United States remained a status conferred by the common law for centuries, as opposed to through statutory or constitutional law.[15] The 1787 Constitution references birth citizenship but does not define it or confer it as a right. Even the Act of 1790,[16] the first law to address

---

(2007) (documenting the nullification of birth citizenship for the " 'unassimillable' Chinese, 'enemy-race' Japanese, Mexican 'illegal aliens,' and Muslim 'terrorists' ").

[6] Office of Immigration Statistics, Dept. of Homeland Security, www.dhs.gov/ximgtn/statistics/.

[7] Polly J. Price, *Natural Law and Birthright Citizenship in Calvin's Case* (1608), 9 YALE J. L. & HUMAN. 73, 74, 77 (1997).

[8] *Id. See also* Note, Lisa Maria Perez, *Citizenship Denied: The Insular Cases and the Fourteenth Amendment,* 94 VA. L. REV. 1029 (2008).

[9] Calvin v. Smith, 77 Engl. Rep. 377 (K.B. 1608).

[10] Price, *supra* note 7, at 74.

[11] Calvin, 77 Eng. Rep. at 379.

[12] *Id.* at 409.

[13] *Id.* at 392.

[14] JAMES H. KETTNER, THE DEVELOPMENT OF AMERICAN CITIZENSHIP 1608–1870, at 17 (1978).

[15] Price, *supra* note 7, at 74.

[16] An Act to Establish a Uniform Rule of Naturalization, 1 Stat. 103 (Mar. 26, 1790), repealed by Act. Of Jan. 29, 1795, 1 Stat. 414.

citizenship by descent and through naturalization, did not codify it as a right.[17] In 1830, thus, the U.S. Supreme Court affirmed that "[n]othing is better settled at the common law than the doctrine that the children even of aliens born in a country, while the parents are resident there under the protection of the government, and owing temporary allegiance thereto, are subjects by birth."[18] It was not until the aftermath of the U.S. Civil War, a struggle in part over slavery, that three constitutional amendments were adopted to foster racial equality: the Thirteenth Amendment, which abolished slavery; the Fifteenth, which prohibited race-based voting restrictions, and the Fourteenth, which, in addition to conferring citizenship rights, included a due process and equal protection clause. The Fourteenth Amendment, ratified in 1868, overturned *Scott v. Sandford*, which had declared that Black slaves and free Blacks were not "citizens," even if born in U.S. territory.[19] The pertinent parts of the Fourteenth Amendment read: "All persons born or naturalized in the United States and subject to the jurisdiction thereof, are citizens of the United States and of the State wherein they reside."[20]

b.   Birthright Citizenship for Undocumented Children

In recent years, citizenship by birth of children born in the U.S. to undocumented parents has come under attack by scholars and members of Congress alike. Some uphold the constitutional standing of birthright citizenship and are, therefore, proposing a constitutional amendment to abolish birthright citizenship to children born to the undocumented in order to eliminate incentives for unauthorized immigration.[21] Others, however, argue that the phrase "subject to the jurisdiction thereof" understood historically and in light of the Fourteenth's Amendment's legislative history, rejects a classical *jus solis* understanding of birthright citizenship under English common law.[22] Rather, they argue, the phrase "subject to the jurisdiction" imposed an additional connection to the nation requirement, measured in terms not of the child at birth but through his or her parent.[23] To some, this requires that the child's parent/s be citizens or lawful permanent residents to claim a meaningful affiliation with the nation on the basis of consent and reciprocity, in contrast to the undocumented parents who usurped their way into the nation.[24]

Critiques to the revisionist interpretation of the Fourteenth Amendment include the textual meaning of jurisdiction, since the word does not usually mean allegiance or consent of the subject but refers instead to the power of a sovereign

---

[17] *See infra* notes 87–93 and 119–24 and accompanying text (discussing the jus sanguinis and naturalization provisions of the 1790 Act respectively).

[18] Inglis v. Trustees of the Sailor's Snug Harbor, 28 U.S. (3 Pet.) 99, 164 (1830).

[19] 60 U.S. 393 (1856).

[20] U.S. Constitution, 14th Amendment, § 1.

[21] Price, *supra* note 7, at 78–79 (discussing H.R.J. Res. 56, 104th Cong. (1995).

[22] William Ty. Mayton, *Birthright Citizenship and the Civic Minimum*, 22 GEO. IMMIGR. L.J. 221, 224–225 (2008).

[23] *Id.* at 242–47.

[24] *Id.* at 223 and 257–58. *See also* PETER SHUCK AND ROGERS SMITH, CITIZENSHIP WITHOUT CONSENT: ILLEGAL ALIENS IN THE AMERICAN POLITY (1985).

over the subject.[25] Also, the historical fact that undocumented persons were here, namely illegally smuggled slaves, who were nonetheless conferred citizenship under the Fourteenth Amendment, also casts doubt on the reciprocal allegiance theory.[26] The proposed re-interpretation of the Fourteenth Amendment must also contend with evidence of a strong precedential value of the Calvin case in the U.S. colonies.[27] Prior to 1868, for example, the U.S. Supreme Court referenced the Calvin *jus solis* doctrine on five occasions,[28] as did also federal courts.[29] State courts especially transformed the doctrine from a medieval concept of kings and subjects to a doctrine of citizenship by birth in the U.S.[30]

A different counter-argument to the re-interpretation of the constitutional birthright provision rests on the historical and textual context surrounding the Fourteenth Amendment's adoption, including the co-terminus debates of the adoption of the Civil Rights Act of 1866 and the Amendment itself.[31] The birthright citizenship provision was adopted first in the 1866 Act, and the debates there turned on whether Native American should gain birthright citizenship.[32] Then the consensus became that only those Native American who lived outside tribal jurisdiction, and not those who lived within tribes and under tribal government should gain birthright citizenship through the Act.[33] To achieve that, the text of the Act became: "All persons born in the United States and not subject to any foreign power, excluding Indians not taxed, are hereby declared to be citizens in the United States."[34] The argument here becomes that "Indians not taxed" meant to

---

[25] Gerard N. Magliocca, *Indians and Invaders: The Citizenship Clause and Illegal Aliens*, 10 U. Pa. J. Const. L. 499, 512–13(2008). Critiques to the revisionist argument also suggest normative reasons against it, including protecting egalitarian and equality principles, the nation's commitment to political justice, the desirability of governmental responsiveness to the interests of all over whom it exerts general jurisdiction. *See, e.g.*, Chistopher L. Eisgruber, *Birthright Citizenship and the Constitution*, 72 N.Y.U. L. Rev. 54, 72–96 (1997) and Jonathan C. Drimmer, *The Nephews of Uncle Sam: The History, Evolution, and Applicaton of Birthright Citizenship in the United States*, 9 Geo. Immigr. L.J. 667,671 (1995).

[26] Magliocca, *supra* note 25, at 513–14.

[27] *See* Price, *supra* note 7, at 141.

[28] *Id.* at 139 (citing to Inglish, 28 U.S. 99; The Venus, 12 U.S. (14 Cranch) 253 (1814); Dawson's Lessee v. Godfrey, 8 U.S. (8 Cranch) 321 (1808); Lambert's Lessee v. Paine, 7 U.S. 97 (1805); M'Ilvaine v. Coxe's Lessee, 6 U.S. (5 Cranch) 280 (1805)). *But see* Mayton, *supra* note 22, at 235–238 (arguing that two Supreme Court cases decided in the 1830's, Shanks v. Dupont, 28 U.S. 242, and Inglis v. Sailors' Snug Harbour, 28 U.S. at 99, departed from the jus soli doctrine to approve instead an "election" doctrine by which, in the wake of the Revolutionary War, persons might of their own will choose either British or U.S. citizenship).

[29] Price, *supra* note 7, at 139 (citing to U.S. v. Rhodes, 27 F. Cas. 785 (C.C. Ky. 1866) (No. 16, 151); Case of Williams, 29 F. Cas. 1330 (C.C. Conn. 1799) (No. 17, 708). *See also* Bernadette Meyler, *The Gestation of Birthright Citizenship, 1868–1898, State's Rights, The Law of Nations, and Mutual Consent*, 15 Geo. Immigr. L.J. 519, 528–32 (2001) (discussing numerous federal and state cases that adopted the Calvin case jus solis doctrine, despite claims by certain revisions scholars of a single decision in 1844 of *Lynch v. Clarke*).

[30] Price, *supra* note 7, at 139–44.

[31] Mayton, *supra* note 22, at 241–47.

[32] *Id.* at 243.

[33] *Id.*

[34] Civil Rights Act of 1866, Ch. 31, § 1, 14 Stat. 27 (1866) (Sen. Trumbull).

exclude Native Americans born under tribal jurisdiction, while "subject to any foreign power," included, according to the debates, "children born on our soil to temporary sojourners."[35] Some would interpret this latter phrase to mean "any child born on U.S. soil to parents who were temporary visitors to this country and who, as a result of foreign citizenship of the child's parents, remained a citizen or subject of the parent's home country."[36] This interpretation ignores the fact, however, that during the debate common law precedent was cited to reject the claim that birthright citizenship would impose additional political or allegiance requirements on parents.[37] Read in this light, the phrase "subject to any foreign power" referred to the traditional exception under common law, which referred to children of ambassadors and enemy aliens in hostile occupation.[38]

As to the Fourteenth Amendment, Sen. Howard proposed from the beginning what would become the text of the amendment, including the wording "subject to the jurisdiction thereof."[39] There does not exist an explanation for the change in wording from the 1866 Act, but some argue that the single phrase was intended to capture both the "Indians not taxed" and the "not subject to any foreign power" of the Civil Rights law.[40] Some debate as to the meaning of the term does exist, but that evidence is far from conclusive, despite statements to the contrary.[41] Sen. Howard explained when introducing the phrase that it meant to exclude "persons born in the United States who are foreigners, aliens, who belong to the families of embassadors or foreign ministers accredited to the Government of the United States."[42] Prof. William Ty Mayton reads this explanation to deny birthright citizenship to aliens generally,[43] but that is far from clear as a better explanation is that the final qualifier means that only children of ambassadors or foreign ministers born in the U.S. would be excluded. Indeed, this is consistent with Sen. Howard's own understanding when he introduced the Amendment, as he explained: "This Amendment which I have offered is simply declaratory of what I regard as the law of the land already. . . . "[44]

On the floor debate of the Fourteenth Amendment, when the question turned again to Native Americans, Sen. Howard provided the same distinction that was made during the 1866 Civil Rights Act debate, and it was in this context that Sen. Howard explained that "subject to the jurisdiction" "ought to be construed so as to imply a full and complete jurisdiction . . . that is to say, the same jurisdiction in

---

[35] Mayton, *supra* note 22, at 244 (citing to CONG. GLOBE, 39th Cong., 1st Sess. 2896 at 1117(1866)).

[36] John C. Eastman, *Politics and the Court: Did the Supreme Court Really Move Left Because of Embarrasment Over Bush v. Gore?*, 94 GEO. L.J. 1475, 1486 (2006).

[37] CONG. GLOBE, 39th Cong., 1st Sess. 2896 at 1832 (1866)) (Rep. Lawrence) ("In the great case of Lynch v. Clarke1 Sand [Ch. 583 (N.Y. Ch. 1844)], it was conclusively shown . . . that all 'children born here are citizens without any regard to the political condition or allegiance of their parents.").

[38] Magilocca, *supra* note 25, at 507.

[39] Mayton, *supra* note 22, at 244–45.

[40] *Id.*

[41] *See id.* at 245–47.

[42] CONG. GLOBE, *supra* note 37, at 2890.

[43] Mayton, *supra* note 22, at 245.

[44] CONG. GLOBE, *supra* note 37, at 2890.

extent and quality as applies to every citizens of the United States now."[45] Those who would read a "connection" or "consent" requirement to the Fourteenth Amendment birthright citizenship suggest that this explanation of the "subject to the jurisdiction" phrase denotes a reciprocal relationship between the sovereign and subject at the time of birth or contributive responsibilities between them, such as to limit birthright citizenship to children of lawful permanent residents and perhaps citizens.[46] Prof. Gerard N. Magliocca, however, challenges this reliance on the Native American citizenship debate to limit citizenship to undocumented children in that the framers of the Fourteenth Amendment intended the "subject to the jurisdiction" clause "as a way of enhancing trial autonomy, not as a tool for limiting citizenship.[47] Native American tribes, Magliocca, explains, were differently situated than slaves because, while they lived within the U.S., most Native Americans retained their tribal identity and considered themselves as co-equal sovereigns; that is, they were on the same legal plane as foreign ambassadors with respect to citizenship.[48]

Perhaps more importantly, the U.S. Supreme Court has affirmed the conventional view that the Civil Rights Act of 1866 and the Fourteenth Amendment sought to affirm the common law approach to birthright citizenship and extend the rule to newly freed slaves.[49] In 1898, the Court upheld the birthright citizenship of children born to Chinese immigrants with permanent lawful status but no eligibility for naturalization.[50] Then, the Court observed that birthright citizenship for aliens had not been "contested or doubted until more than fifty years after the adoption of the Constitution." The Supreme Court resolved that "subject to the jurisdiction thereof" meant to exclude only Native Americans, children of diplomatic representatives in a foreign state, and children born of "alien enemies in hostile occupation" in the U.S.[51] *Wong Kim Ark* remains the Court's final pronouncement on the issue of birthright citizenship for children of "aliens" born in the U.S., and lower courts citing to it continue to affirm it,[52] even when the

---

[45] *Id.* at 2895.

[46] Mayton, *supra* note 22, at 246 and SHUCK AND SMITH, *supra* note 24, at 5. *See also* John C. Eastman, *Born in the U.S.A.? Rethinking Birthright Citizenship in the Wake of 9/11*, 42 U. RICH. L. REV. 955, 960–61 (2008).

[47] Magliocca, *supra* note 25, at 501–02.

[48] *Id.* at 505–06.

[49] For an interesting historical discussion of the crucial thirty-year period that elapsed between the ratification of the Fourteenth Amendment and the Supreme Court's justification of jus solis in Wong Kim Ark, *see generally* Meyler, *supra* note 29.

[50] United States v. Wong Kim Ark, 169 U.S. 649 (1898).

[51] *Id.* at 682. Some suggest that it might be possible to equate undocumented immigrants to the "enemy alien" in hostile occupation exception to *jus solis* that already existed under common law. *See* Magliocca, *supra* note 25, at 522–26.

[52] The early cases between 1898 through the early 1900's citing to Wong Kim Ark concern Chinese individuals born in the U.S. *See, e.g.*, Lee Sing Far v. U.S., 94 F. 834 (9th Cir. 1899) (affirming citizenship of child born in the U.S. of Chinese parents who had permanent domicile and residence in the U.S.); and In re Giovanna, 93 F. 659 (D.C. N.Y. 1899) (children of Chinese nationals born in the U.S. are citizens and not subject to exclusion under the immigration laws on their return when their parents return from a temporary visit abroad).

U.S. born child has grown up outside the U.S.,[53] and, implicitly, in cases defining the scope of rights of U.S. citizenship children born to undocumented parents.[54]

c.   Native Americans and their Birthright Citizenship

As to Native Americans, their birthright citizenship today is recognized only through statute.[55] Even prior to *Wong Kim Ark*, in *Elk v. Wilkins*, a case involving a Native American born in a reservation, the Supreme Court held that an "Indian" born in the U.S. but within tribal authority was not born "subject to the jurisdiction" of the U.S. and thus did not acquire U.S. citizenship at birth.[56] Congressional conferral of birthright citizenship to Native Americans, moreover, was a gradual process that occurred over a considerable period of time.[57] Congress first granted citizenship to certain tribal nations through treaties as an incentive to remove them from the West,[58] or even as part of U.S. territorial acquisition of Mexico.[59] Congress also granted citizenship through legislation to certain tribes, and through the passage of the General Allotment Act in 1887, which codified for most American Indians the idea of dividing Indian lands into individual holdings to promote assimilation and destroy tribal relations.[60] The 1924 Indian American Citizenship Act[61] granted concurrent U.S. citizenship with their respective tribes on all Native Americans.

---

[53] *See, e.g.*, Dos Reis ex rel. Camara v. Nicolls, 161 F.2d 860 (1st Cir. 1947) (child born in the U.S. of a Portuguese father and a Brazilian mother, who was taken by them as a child to a Portuguese island remained a U.S. citizen and did not lose citizenship through involuntary service in the Portuguese military); Perkins v. Elg., 99 F.2d 408 (C.A.D.C. 1938) (minor child born in U.S. of a naturalized U.S. citizen who took on his father's foreign citizenship as a child when his father abandoned U.S. residence and returned to his country of birth could elect to restore his birthright citizenship).

[54] These case concern, for example, the entitlement of U.S.-born citizen children to stay deportation proceedings of their parents or to confer immigration benefits to "immediate relatives." *See, e.g.*, Coleman v. U.S., 454 F. Supp. 2d 757 (N.D. Ill. 2006) (holding that a removal order for the mother would nto impinge on the child's Fourteenth Amendment right because he would remain free to live in the U.S.); Acosta v. Gaffney, 558 F.2d 1153 (C.A. N.J. 1977) (holding that parent's deportation order did not deny U.S. citizen child the right to live in the U.S. because her return to Colombia would merely postpone, but not bar, her residence in the U.S. were she to choose to return); Perdido v. INS, 420 F.2d 1179, 1181 (5th Cir. 1969) (deportation order against parents of a citizen child did not deprive child of a constitutional right); and Lopez v. Franklin, 417 F. Supp. 345 (D.C. Mich.) (holding that not giving native-born citizens under the age of 21 the privilege to confer the "immediate relative" immigration benefit on their parents did not violate their rights as citizens). Other cases involve the citizen child's eligibility for social service benefits, despite their parents undocumented status. *See, e.g.*, Intermountain Health Care, Inv. v. Board of Com'rs of Blaine County, 707 P.2d 1051 (Idaho 1985).

[55] INA § 301(b). For a thoughtful treatment on the exclusion of Native American from the Fourteenth Amendment, *see* Early M. Maltz, *The Fourteenth Amendment and Native American Citizenship*, 17 CONST. COMMENT. 555 (2000).

[56] 112 U.S. 94 (1884).

[57] Ediberto Roman, *The Citizenship Dialectic*, 20 GEO. IMMIGR. L.J. 557, 583 (2006).

[58] *Id.*

[59] The Pueblo Indians became citizens through the Treaty of Guadalupe Hidalgo. *Id.*

[60] *See id.*

[61] 43 U.S. Stats at Large, Ch. 233, at 253 (1924).

d. Birthright Citizenship and the Territories

Birthright citizenship is also only statutorily recognized with regard to persons born in the U.S. unincorporated territories," as such places do not form part of the U.S. within the meaning of "born in the United States" under the Fourteenth Amendment.[62] Today, these places include Puerto Rico,[63] American Samoa, Guam, the Northern Mariana Islands, and the United States Virgin Islands.[64] In a series of cases that became known as the Insular Cases, the U.S. Supreme Court adopted the doctrine of territorial incorporation, and thus sanctioned the exclusion of residents of unincorporated territories from Fourteenth Amendment birthright citizenship.[65] Combined, the Insular Cases hold that the term "United States" as used in the Constitution, excludes all territories which Congress has opted under its powers not to incorporate as part of the United States.[66] Professor Gerald Neuman has critiqued the Insular Cases for creating a "geographically restrictive social compact approach" which limits the applicability of constitutional provisions to a territorially defined class of beneficiaries while excluding any peoples whom Congress is not prepared to regard as equals.[67] Others have questioned the constitutional validity of the Insular Cases, arguing that the common law codification of *jus solis* rule by the Fourteenth Amendment would confer citizenship on any person born in a place where the United States has actual exercise of power.[68]

e. The Meaning of "Natural Born"

A separate question has been whether the term "natural born Citizen" as used in Article II of the U.S. Constitution to describe who is eligible for the office of President[69] requires birth in U.S. territory.[70] The meaning of "natural-born

---

[62] Perez, *supra* note 8, at 1029.

[63] At the time of U.S. acquisition of Puerto Rico from Spain, the U.S. insisted upon ratification of the Treaty of Paris in 1898 that the citizenship status of Puerto Rican people was subject to the will of Congress. Treaty of Peace Between the United States of America and the Kingdom of Spain, U.S.-Spain, Dec. 10, 1898, 30 Stat. 1754. In 1990, Congress passed the Foraker Act, Ch. 191, 31 Stat. 77, and declared that Puerto Ricans were "citizens of Porto Rico," a meaningless citizenship given that Puerto Rico did not retain any sovereignty. Perez, *supra* note 8, at 1036–37. It was not until 1917 with the Jones Act, Ch. 145, 39 Stat. 951, 953 (1917) that Puerto Ricans were declared citizens of the United States, although the grant was only derivative as the acquisition of future U.S. citizenship depends on the Puerto Rican parentage and not mere birth in the island. Perez, *supra* note 8, at 1037.

[64] Roman, *supra* note 57, at 586–88. Congress granted citizenship to the residents of the Virgin Islands in 1927, to the residents of Guam in 1950, and to the residents to the Northern Mariana Islands in 1976. The residents of American Samoa are treated as nationals, rather than citizens. *Id. See also* Guam Organic Act of 1950, 48 U.S.C. § 1421et seq.

[65] Downes v. Bidwell, 182 U.S. 244, 287 (1901); Dorr v. U.S., 195 U.S. 138 (1904); Balzac v. Porto Rico, 528 U.S. 298 (1922).

[66] For a discussion of the Insular Cases, *see* Perez, *supra* note 8, at 1036–46.

[67] Neuman, *supra* note 1, at 83–85. *See also* Roman, *supra* note 57, at 586–89.

[68] Perez, *supra* note 8, at 1055–57.

[69] U.S. Const. art. II, § 1, cl. 5.

[70] *See* Lawrence Friedman, *An Idea Whose Time Has Come – the Curious History, Uncertain Effect, and Need for Amendment of the "Natural Born Citizen" Requirement for the Presidency*, 52 St.

Citizen" has never been definitively interpreted by the courts and is unlikely to be taken up given its political character, despite that many candidates to the U.S. presidency have been born abroad to U.S. citizen parents.[71] Most scholars agree, however, that it includes any person who was a citizen at the time of his or her birth, under then-current law, whether by birth in the United States within the meaning of the Fourteenth Amendment or through statutory conferral.[72] This interpretation is based on the history of the adoption of Article II's "natural born Citizen" at the Constitutional Convention of 1787, as well as an examination of British common law in effect at the time of its adoption.[73] Evidence on the meaning of "natural born Citizen" clause is scant in the 1787 Convention's debates,[74] but it appears to have been introduced to prevent the erection of a monarchy headed by a foreign ruler.[75] As well, the conferral of *jus sanguinis* citizenship through statute by the British well before the U.S. Revolution also suggests that the Framers understood the term "natural born" to include both a *jus solis* and *jus sanguinis* conception of citizenry.[76] Included in the "natural born Citizen," then, are children born in the United States within the meaning of the Fourteenth Amendment, as well as children who are born citizens under the then-existing statute conferring citizenship at birth,[77] which today includes Puerto Ricans born in Puerto Rico,[78]

Louis U. L.J. 137, 143 (2007) (qualification of foreign-born U.S. citizen as "natural born Citizen" "is an open question").

[71] J. Rebekka S. Bonner, *Who May Be President? Constitutional Reinterpretation of Article II's "Natural Born" Presidential Eligibility Clause, available at* http://ssrn.com/abstract+1133663. Such presidential candidates have included Lowell Weiker, born in Paris to a US father and English mother; Barry Goldwater, born in the territory of Arizona before it became a state, George Romney, born in a Mormon colony to U.S. parents in Chihuahua, Mexico; Christian Herter, born to U.S. parents in France; Franklin D. Roosevelt, Jr., born in Canada to U.S. parents; and most recently John McCain, who was born to U.S. parents in the Panama Canal. *Id.*

[72] *See* Stephen E. Sachs, *John McCain's Citizenship: A Tentative Defense* (unnumbered manuscript), *available at* http://ssrn.com/abstract=1236882; Sarah Helen Duggin & Mary Beth Collins, *"Natural Born" in the USA: The Striking Unfairness and Dangerous Ambiguity of the Constitution's Presidential Qualifications Clause and Why we Need to Fix it*, 85 B. U. L. Rev. 53, 83 (2005); Jill A. Pryor, *The Natural-Born Citizen Clause and Presidential Eligibility: An Approach for Resolving Two Hundred years of Uncertainty*, 97 Yale L.J. 881, 896 (1988); and Charles A. Gordon, *Who can be President of the United States: The Unresolved Enigma*, 28 Md. L. Rev. 1, 31 (1968).

[73] Bonner, *supra* note 71 (unnumbered manuscript).

[74] The records that exist include the proposed text introduced by Alexander Hamilton on June 18, 1787, which read "[n]o person shall be eligible to the office of President of the United States unless he is now a Citizen of one of the States, or hereafter be born a Citizen of the United States. Second, notes prepared by Pierce Butler on August 31, 1787 provide a similar construction: "No person shall be eligible to the Office of President . . . who shall not be a natural born Citizen of the United States, excepting those who now or at the time of the Adoption of This Constitution shall be a citizen of the said States of whom may be President." Third, the phrase also appears in a letter from John Jay to George Washington (and possibly others attending the Convention) urging Washington that "it would be wise and seasonable to provide a strong check to the admission of Foreigners into the administration of our National Government; and to declare expressly that the Command in Chief of the American Army shall not be given to nor devolve on, any but a natural born Citizen." Finally, there were at least two proposed revisions, including the imposition of residency requirements on top of the "natural born" provision that were not adopted. *See* Bonner, *supra* note 71 (unnumbered manuscript).

[75] *See* Gordon, *supra* note 72, at 5.

[76] Bonner, *supra* note 71 (unnumbered manuscript).

[77] In fact, the debate over whether Senator John McCain is a "natural-born" citizen has principally

Native American born in a U.S. reservation,[79] and certain children of U.S. citizen parent/s born abroad.[80] It does not, however, include naturalized citizens because they are not citizens at birth.[81]

2.   Citizenship by Descent for Children Born Abroad

a.   Its Origins

Jus sanguinis citizenship has been available under U.S. law from the beginning, and today more than three-and-a-half million U.S. citizens are derivative citizens born abroad to at least one-U.S. citizen parent.[82] Even so, there is disagreement on whether its conferral has been solely through statute, rather than through constitutional or common law.[83] There is agreement that at common law the British recognized that children born abroad to subjects serving in the military were citizens at birth.[84] In addition, beginning in 1350, England enacted a series of statutes that provided that persons born abroad to British parents would have the same rights of inheritance available only to natural born children.[85] Scholars have since disagreed on whether these statutes codified the common law or augmented it.[86]

Despite British history, the U.S. Constitution was silent on citizenship by descent. Congress first conferred a right to derivative citizenship in 1790 when it declared that "the children of citizens . . . that may be born beyond the seas . . . shall be considered as natural born citizens," except for those "persons whose fathers have never been resident in the United States."[87] This act by Congress could suggest that *jus sanguinis* was not part of the fundamental law in the U.S. on citizenship, although, here too, others argue that Congress merely codified what had already existed as law.[88] This is at least consistent with an 1863

---

been about the meaning of the statute in effect at the time of his birth. For different views on the topic contrast Grabiel J. Chin, *Why Senator John McCain Cannot Be President: Eleven Months and a Hundred Yards Short of Citizenship*, ARIZONA LEGAL STUDIES, DISCUSSION PAPER No. 08-14 (July 2008) *with* Stephen E. Sachs, *John McCain's Citizenship: A Tentative Defense*, Manuscript, *available at* http://ssrn.com/abstract=1236882.

[78]   INA § 302.

[79]   INA § 301(b).

[80]   INA § 301 (c)-(h) (jus sanguinis citizenship generally) and INA § 303 (jus sanguinis citizenship for persons born in the Panama Canal).

[81]   Merlinda L. Seymore, *The Presidency and the Meaning of Citizenship*, 2005 B.Y.U. L. REV. 927, 930 (2005).

[82]   United States Census Bureau, *Profile of Selected Demographic and Social Characteristics for the Native Population*: 2000, Table FBP-1 (2000), *available at* http://www.census.gov/population/cen2000/stp-159/native.pdf.

[83]   *Id.* at 77–78l.

[84]   Sachs, *supra* note 72, at 6–10.

[85]   Id. at 7. *See also* Bonner, *supra* note 71 (unnumbered manuscript).

[86]   *Id.*

[87]   1 Stat. 103 (1790).

[88]   Mayton, *supra* note 22, at 233.

ruling by the New York Court of Appeals, which declared *jus sanguinis* to be an organic rule of U.S. citizenship[89] and conferred such right on children who, perhaps inadvertently, had been left out of the definition in the 1802 reenactment of the 1790 Act.[90] However, at various times, as early as 1898, the U.S. Supreme Court has chosen to interpret the Naturalization Clause to include the conferral of citizenship by descent, although not without strong dissents.[91] Scholars have also questioned this interpretation because it would require that derivative citizenship be considered a form of naturalized or elective citizenship after birth,[92] as opposed to an automatic birth citizenship that would be covered under the "natural born Citizen" clause of Art. II of the U.S. Constitution.[93]

Despite the Court's prevailing view that Congress' power to confer derivative citizenship rests with the Naturalization Clause, the Court, has not equally granted derivative citizens Fourteenth-Amendment status as naturalized citizens. Instead, it has read the Fourteenth Amendment as requiring that the naturalization occur inside U.S. territory.[94] In 1971, in *Roger v. Bellei*, the Court declined to recognize Bellei's Fourteenth Amendment citizenship right as a foreign-born man who had one citizen-parent but who failed to meet the post-birth statutory residency requirement for derivative citizenship, thus relinquishing the right.[95] If Bellei could establish a Fourteenth Amendment right to derivative citizenship at birth, then his failure to meet the residency requirement would have been immaterial. The Court, however, considered Bellei neither born in nor naturalized in the U.S., nor subject to its jurisdiction and concluded that "[h]e is simply not a Fourteenth-Amendment-first-sentence-citizen." By focusing on Bellei's location outside the U.S., the Court avoided the question of whether derivative citizenship was a form of naturalization. In his dissent, Justice Black argued for a broader interpretation of the word "in" to include being "naturalized into it," based on his understanding of the legislative history of the Citizenship Clause:[96]

---

[89] Ludlam v. Ludlam, 26 N.Y. 356 (1863).

[90] The 1802 Act declared that "children of persons who are not, or have been citizens of the United States, shall, though born out of the limits and jurisdiction of the United States, be considered as citizens of the United States," which meant that children born abroad to persons who became citizens after 1802 could not gain citizenship. Mayton, *supra* note 22, at 235.

[91] In dictum, the Court held in *Wong Kim Ark* that "[the Fourteenth Amendment] had not touched the acquisition of citizenship by being born abroad of American parents; and has left that subject to be regulated, as it had always been, by Congress, in the exercise of the power conferred by the Constitution to establish an uniform rule of naturalization." 169 U.S. at 701–02. The Court has adopted this same interpretation, not without objection, in the more recent cases of Miller v. Albright, 523 U.S. 420, 426 (1998), and Nguyen v. INS, 533 U.S. 53, 61(2000). *See infra* notes 109–116 and accompanying text.

[92] The INA defines the term naturalization as the "conferring of nationality of a state upon a person after birth, by any means whatsoever." INA § 101(a)(23).

[93] *See infra* notes 69–81 and accompanying text (discussing the meaning of "natural born").

[94] The Clause provides: "All persons born or *naturalized* in the United States."

[95] 401 U.S. 815 (1971).

[96] *Id.* at 843. That clause was added in the Senate rather late in the debates of the Fourteenth Amendment and as originally introduced its reference was to all those "born in the United States or naturalized by the laws thereof." The final version of the Citizenship Clause was undoubtedly intended to have this same scope") (citations omitted).

Thus, Congress has the power to grant derivative citizenship, although the source of this power is not entirely settled. The prevailing view continues to be that such power rests with the Naturalization Clause, which would grant Congress plenary power to define the terms of derivative citizenship.[97] And while derivative citizenship does not fall within the meaning of the Fourteenth Amendment's naturalization citizenship clause, its plausible treatment as part of the fundamental meaning of citizenship at the time of the Constitution's adoption would argue for greater judicial intervention.[98] Determining whether and how much this power is subject to judicial review is important, especially when such statutes have traditionally included provisions that discriminate on the basis of gender.[99] The 1790 statute, for example, created the first distinction between citizen-fathers and citizen-mothers, and citizen-mothers were not able to pass citizenship to their foreign-born children when they married a foreign national, for instance.[100] Then in 1855, the amended statute precluded mothers altogether from passing citizenship to their foreign-born children, a provision that was not rescinded until 1934.[101] Gender-based distinctions exist also under current law; this time, however, to burden certain U.S. citizen fathers, not mothers, in their conferral of derivative citizenship to their children.[102]

b.   The Statute

The statute in effect at the time of the child's birth determines the requirement for derivative citizenship.[103] The statutory conferral of *jus sanguinis* citizenship depends on several factors, the marital status of the child's citizen parent, and the length of time the citizen parents have resided in the U.S. Under current U.S. law, adopted since 1952 and supplemented by later amendments, citizenship by descent is provided for primarily in sections 301(c), 301(g), 309(a), and 309(c) of INA.[104] Sections 301(c) and 301(g) of the INA list universally applicable conditions for acquisition of citizenship by descent, and sections 309(a) and 309(c) provide overriding rules for persons born out of wedlock.

Citizenship by descent for children born to a married couple requires that at least one parent be a U.S. citizen at the time of the child's birth abroad. Citizenship by descent may also be conferred on a child who is adopted internationally and subsequently admitted as a child of a U.S. citizen[105] The Child Citizenship Act of 2000 grants automatic citizenship to a child born abroad who (1) was fully and

---

[97] *See infra* notes 127–134 and accompanying text.

[98] *Id.*

[99] *See* Notes, Michael G. McFarland, *Derivative Citizenship: Its History, Constitutional Foundation, and Constitutional Limitations*, 63 N.Y.U. ANN. SURV. AM. L. 467, 478 (2008).

[100] It read: [T]he right of citizenship shall not descend to persons whose fathers have never been resident in the United States."Act of March. 26, 1790, ch. 3, § 1, 1 stat. 103, 104.

[101] McFarland, *supra* note 99, at 480–81.

[102] *See infra* notes 109 and accompanying text.

[103] For a good historical discussion of U.S. derivative citizenship statutes, *see* McFarland, *supra* note 99, at 477–82.

[104] *Id.* at 482.

[105] INA § 320.

finally adopted; (2) is under eighteen years of age; (3) was admitted to the U.S. as an LPR; and (4) is in the legal and physical custody of at least one parent who is a U.S. citizen.[106]

In addition, laws require residency or physical presence in the U.S. by the citizen parent(s). The laws differ depending on whether the child was born to two U.S. citizen parents or to one U.S. citizen parent and a foreign national. If the child is born abroad to two U.S. citizen parents, then at least one of them must have resided in the U.S. or its outlying possessions prior to the birth of the child at any time and for however long.[107] If the child is born to only one U.S. citizen parent, the U.S. citizen parent must have been physically present in the U.S. or its outlying possessions for cumulative periods totaling not less than five years, at least two of which were before the U.S. citizen parent was fourteen years old.[108] The logic behind the physical presence requirement is that a citizen parent who spends enough time in the U.S. will absorb U.S. customs and values, which will then be transmitted to the child.

The INA definition imposes additional requirements for U.S. citizen fathers when the child is born outside the context of a traditional marriage. If the child is born out of wedlock, the father (though not the mother) must demonstrate a bona-fide parent-child relationship with the mother.[109] Before a child born abroad can gain U.S. citizenship, INA § 309(a) requires the unwed U.S. citizen father to establish that: (1) clear and convincing evidence proves a blood relationship between father and child; (2) the father had U.S. nationality at the time of child's birth; (3) the father (unless deceased) agrees in writing to provide financial support until the child reaches the age of eighteen; and (4) the father legitimated, recognized, or had a court declare parentage with the child. For children born out of wedlock to a U.S.-citizen mother, INA section 309(c) does not provide conditions for the application of sections 301(c) and 301(g), but rather, supersedes them. According to section 309(c), "[n]otwithstanding the provision of subsection [309](a)," an out-of-wedlock child will be a citizen if its mother was a U.S. citizen at the time of its birth and "the mother had previously been physically present in the United States or one of its outlying possessions for a continuous period of one year."

---

[106] Pub. L. 1-06-395, 8 U.S.C. §§ 1431–33. For an insightful discussion and critique of the Child Citizenship Act, *see* Victor C. Romero, *The Child Citizenship Act and the Family Reunification Act: Valuing the Citizen Child as well as the Citizen Parent*, 55 FLA. L. REV. 489 (2003).

[107] INA § 301(c). The term "the United States" as used here also includes the U.S. territories of Puerto Rico, Guam, and the U.S. Virgin Islands, as well as the Commonwealth of the Northern Mariana Islands. INA § 101(a)(38). The term outlying possessions means Samoa and Swains Islands. INA § 101(a)(29).

[108] INA § 301(g). Physical presence includes time in the military or employment in the U.S. foreign service. INA § 301(g).

[109] INA § 101(b)(D).

c.   Gender Discrimination

U.S. citizen plaintiffs have recently raised equal protection challenges to the current derivate citizenship laws but have been unsuccessful. First in 1998, in *Miller v. Albright*, a U.S. citizen father challenged the additional requirements relating to children born out of wedlock to citizen-fathers, but the Court's plurality opinion held that the statute could easily satisfy even heightened scrutiny.[110] Interestingly, Justice Scalia's concurrence, joined by Justice Thomas, concluded, without citing authority, that Congress' exclusive authority to confer derivative citizenship rests in the Naturalization Clause.[111] In his dissent, Justice Breyer vehemently disagreed with the inclusion of derivative citizenship in the Naturalization Clause; instead, Justice Breyer viewed derivative citizenship as part of the original understanding of citizenship at the time of adoption of the U.S. Constitution, and, as such, subject to greater constitutional scrutiny.[112] Two years later, in *Nguyen v. INS*, a case that involved the same legal challenge, this time raised the child claiming derivative citizenship, a divided Supreme Court (5-4) upheld the law as constitutional, and to do so applied intermediate scrutiny standard to the law without actually deciding what standard of review would apply in such cases.[113] Rather, the Court concluded that since INA's differing treatment of them under equal protection "serves important governmental objectives and . . . the discriminatory means employed are substantially related to the achievement of those objectives," it was unnecessary to decide whether only a rational-basis of review should apply. The holding was particularly jarring as applied to the facts in the case because Nguyen had been abandoned by his mother at birth and raised by his U.S. citizen father in the U.S. from the age of six.[114] Here, it was Justice O'Connor, joined by Justices Souter, Ginsberg, and Breyer, who dissented, no doubt concerned over the watering down of equal protection review as applied to gender-based discrimination.[115] Justice O'Connor also, moreover, disagreed that derivative citizenship means the same thing as "naturalization," where Congress has enjoyed plenary power.[116] Rather, Justice O'Connor urged the Court to consider and resolve the question of whether Congress should have the same deference in cases involving derivative citizen cases as they have in cases involving aliens where the underlying question is whether the person is a citizen in the first place.[117]

---

[110] 523 U.S. 420, 426 (1998).

[111] *Id.* at 453.

[112] *Miller*, 523 U.S. at 481.

[113] 533 U.S. 53, 61 (2000).

[114] *Id.* at 70.

[115] *Id.* at 73 ("In a long line of cases spanning nearly three decades, this Court has applied heightened scrutiny to legislative classifications based on sex. The Court today confronts another statute that classifies individuals on the basis of their sex. While the Court invokes heightened scrutiny, the manner in which it explains and applies this standard is a stranger to our precedents.").

[116] *Id.* at 95.

[117] *Id.* at 96–97.

3.   Citizenship Through Naturalization

a.   Its Origins

Congress is authorized by the U.S. Constitution to establish a "uniform Rule of Naturalization"[118] In the exercise of this power, in 1790 Congress established that "any alien, being a free white person . . . may be admitted to become a citizen,"[119] The "white person" requirement remained in effect through 1952,[120] although Congress amended the Act in 1873 to allow naturalization to "aliens of African nativity and to persons of African descent."[121] During this period, and at least until the 1920s when immigration national quotas severely restricted immigration from southern and eastern Europe and barred immigration from Asia,[122] courts entertained requests for a finding of whiteness from a number of naturalization claimants. In the absence of a Congressional meaning of the term "free white persons" in the 1790 Act, courts struggled to come up with standards to assess "whiteness."[123] These cases reveal a desire to achieve white hegemony, including through the assimilation of certain groups (i.e., Mexicans), as well as racial exclusion altogether for other groups (i.e., the Japanese).[124] Racial ineligibility for naturalization, moreover, affected women beyond those who were racially barred from naturalization. In 1907, Congress stripped of citizenship any woman who married a foreign national, since that wife would take the nationality of her husband.[125] Congress partially repealed this law in 1922, but the law continued to apply to women who married men ineligible to naturalize, usually those who married Asian men, until 1931.[126]

---

[118] U.S. Const. art. 1, § 8, cl. 4.

[119] The 1790 Act, *supra* note 16, at Ch. 3, § 1, 1 Stat. 103 (repealed 1952).

[120] Congress selectively lifted naturalization's racial restrictions in the twentieth century. First, for foreign policy reasons, Congress allowed the Chinese to naturalize in 1943. Next were Filipinos and Indians who were allowed to naturalize in 1946, followed by persons from Guan in 1950. In 1952, Congress removed all racial barriers to naturalization. Leti Volpp, *"Obnoxious to their very Nature":* *Asian American and Constitutional Citizenship*, 8 ASIAN L.J. 71, 74 (2001).

[121] *Id.* at 386.

[122] The Immigration Act of 1924, restructured the criteria for admission and limited immigration from any particular country to 2 percent of their nationality in 1890. the law struck most deeply at Jews, Italians, Slavs, and Greeks who immigrated particularly after 1890. The 1924 Act also provided for the permanent exclusion of any "alien ineligible for citizenship," which again meant non-whites, and primarily Asians. BILL ONG HING, DEFINING AMERICA THROUGH IMMIGRATION POLICY 46–47 (2004).

[123] J. Allen Douglas, *The "Priceless Possession" of Citizenship: Race, Nation, and Naturalization in American Law, 1880–1930*, 43 DUQ. L. REV. 369, 394–41 (2005) (discussing the range of legal reasons employed by courts to define "whiteness," from physical identification based on appearance to the ethnography of family lineage, and from geographic origin to community sentiment).

[124] *Id. See also generally* George A. Martinez, *Immigration and the Meaning of United States Citizenship: Whiteness and Assimilation*, 46 WASHBURN L.J. 335, 336–43 (2007) and Note, John Tehranian, *Performing Whiteness: Naturalization Litigation and the Construction of Racial Identify in America*, 109 YALE L.J. 817 (2000) and IAN F. HANEY LOPEZ, WHITE BY LAW: THE LEGAL CONSTRUCTION OF RACE (1996).

[125] Expatriation Act, ch. 2534, § 3, 34 Stat. 1228, 1228–29 (1907).

[126] Leti Volpp, *Divesting Citizenshp: On Asian American History and The Loss of Citizenship Through Marriage*, 53 UCLA L. REV. 405, 407–410 (2005). *See also* Deenesh Sohoni, *Unsuitable Suitors:*

Congress enjoys broad discretion to legislate the requirements for naturalization, as Court's have treated its conferral as a privilege, not a right. The constitutionality of the racial and gender bars to naturalization were never directly challenged in court. In 1923, however, the U.S. Supreme Court, at least *in dicta*, upheld the validity of the "white persons" requirement in a case involving a challenge by a Japanese national ineligible to Naturalize to Washington's Constitution, which prohibited the ownership of land by "aliens other than those who in good faith have declared intention to become citizens.[127] The Court declared that "Congress is not trammeled" by the Naturalization Clause and "may grant or withhold the privilege of naturalization upon any grounds or without any reason, as it sees fit."[128] Subsequent direct challenges to the unqualified oath requirement promising to bear arms in defense of the United States failed because "[n]aturalization is a privilege, to be given, qualified, or withheld as Congress may determine."[129] Citizenship through naturalization, once conferred, however, becomes a constitutional right in the same standing as birthright citizenship.[130] The U.S. Supreme Court defines naturalization as the "act of adopting a foreigner, and clothing him with the privileges of a native citizen."[131] Naturalized citizens, however, cannot become President,[132] and, moreover, face different challenges from the Native born on such issues as loss of citizenship[133] or dual nationality.[134]

b.   The Statute

Over the course of the 19th Century, Congress amended the naturalization laws several times to attach certain requirements, including lawful entry, enumerated years of continuous residence, intention to reside in the U.S. permanently, ability to write his or her name, ability to speak English, good moral character, and attachment to the principles of the U.S. Constitution.[135] These naturalization requirements are intended to promote and maintain cohesion within the national community, as well as to promote the political assimilation of foreign nationals into

---

Anti-Miscegenation Laws, Naturalization Laws, and the Construction of Asian Identities, 41 Law & Soc'y Rev. 587 (2007); Kevin R. Johnson, *Racial Restrictions on Naturalization: The Recurring Intersection of Race and Gender Immigration and Citizenship Law*, 11 Berkeley Women's L.J. 142 (1996).

[127] Terrace v. Thompson, 263 U.S. 197 (1923).

[128] *Id.* at 220.

[129] U.S. v. Macintosh, 283 U.S. 605, 615, (1931) reversed on statutory grounds Girouard v. U.S., 328 U. S. 61 (1946) (petitioners found not to be attached to the principles of the Constitution when he would not promise in advance to bear arms in defense of the United States unless he believed the war to be morally justified). *See also* U.S. v. Schwimmer, 279 U.S. 644, 649 (same), reversed on statutory grounds Girouard v. U.S., 328 U.S. 61 (1946).

[130] Schneider v. Rusk, 377 U.S. 163, 165. *See also* Knauer v. U.S., 328 U.S. 654, 657; 66 S. Ct. 1304, 1306 (1946) (declaring that "naturalization is not second-class citizenship").

[131] Boyd v. State of Nebraska, 143 U.S. 135, 162 (1892).

[132] Seymore, *supra* note 81, at 932 (arguing that the Natural-Born Citizen Clause perpetuates second-class citizenship status for naturalized citizens).

[133] *See infra* notes 219–308 and accompanying text.

[134] *See infra* notes 197–218 and accompanying text.

[135] Douglas, *supra* note 123, at 385.

U.S. democracy.[136] The English Language and Civics requirement, as well as the requirement of attachment to constitutional principles especially have been questioned, even if national cohesion and assimilation are deemed legitimate objectives, for failing to meet their objectives, for conflicting with U.S. liberal traditions, or for serving, instead, an exclusionary agenda.[137]

Currently, there are eight basic statutory requirements to naturalization:

1. Lawful Permanent Residence

Only persons lawfully admitted as LPRs are eligible for naturalization.[138] INA § 318 also specifies that naturalization may not be conferred while removal proceedings are pending or while a final finding of removability is outstanding. If a person has honorably served in time of war or declared hostility, LPR status as a precondition is unnecessary.[139]

2. Residence and Physical Presence

The durational residency requirement has been around since the passing of the first Citizenship Act in 1790.[140] Under current law, the applicant must have "resided continuously" after being admitted as an LPR in the United States for either (1) a five-year period immediately preceding the filing of the application[141]; or (2) a three-year period immediately preceding the filing of the application when the applicant became an LPR through marriage to a U.S. citizen and has been living in that marital union during that three-year period.[142] The INA defines residence as a "person's principal, actual dwelling place in fact, without regard to intent."[143] However, because residence must also be continuous, long absences, even if the person meets the principal residence requirements, can disqualify the person from citizenship. Generally, "continuous residence" means the applicant cannot have traveled outside the U.S. for more than six months, unless the applicant can establish that he did not intend to abandon his residence in the U.S. for such period.[144] Absences for longer than a year break the continuity

---

[136] *See* Peter J. Spiro, *Questioning Barriers to Naturalization*, 13 GEO. IMMIGR. L.J. 479, 480 (1999).

[137] *Id. See also generally* Gerald L. Neuman, *Justifying U.S. Naturalization Policies*, 35 VA. J. INT'L L. 237 (1994).

[138] INA § 318.

[139] INA § 329.

[140] Spiro, *Questioning Barriers to Naturalization*, *supra* note 136, at 509. The period was first five years, then extended to five, and for a brief period was increased to fourteen under the Alien and Sedition Acts of 1798. *Id.*

[141] INA § 316(a).

[142] INA § 319(a).

[143] INA § 101(a)(33).

[144] INA § 316 (b). The regulations at 8 C.F.R. 316.5(c)(1)(i) provide examples which would support a claim that residence had not been interrupted even with an absence of between six and twelve months: (a) the applicant did not terminate her employment in the U.S.; (b) the applicant's immediate family remained in the U.S.; (c) the applicant retained full access to her U.S. abode; or (d) the applicant did not obtain employment while abroad.

automatically, and the clock must begin anew.[145] In addition, the applicant must be physically present in the U.S. for at least half of the five- or three-year residency requirement.[146] There are more flexible requirements for children of U.S. citizens or for applicants who have served in the U.S. military.[147] The durational residency requirement, along with lawful entry, are among the least controversial, and is usually justified in that societal integration requires time and presence in a country, even when globalization is making the world smaller and U.S. culture transnational.[148]

3.   Good Moral Character

The applicant must demonstrate that he is of good moral character, at minimum for the periods for which residence and physical presence are required.[149] Congress imposed the "good moral character requirement" as early as 1790,[150] but did not define it.[151] Instead, the term was judicially defined and assessed character, i.e., conduct, as well as reputation; i.e., perceptions of conduct by the community.[152] Under current law, INA § 101(f) defines what acts would preclude a finding of good moral character, although the list is not exhaustive. These categories include alcoholism, the commission of specified crimes, being a professional gambler, the commission of fraud to obtain immigration benefits, and having been incarcerated for an aggregate period of 180 days or more. Some categorized activities, such as the commission of an aggravated felony as the term is defined in INA § 101(a)(43), preclude a permanent finding of "good moral character." The character qualification seems grounded in the protection of the political process, although felony disenfranchising laws are able to quite well fulfill that objective.[153] The real purpose of the requirement, thus, appears to be ensuring the country's ability to remove the foreign national from U.S. soil, as citizens cannot be deported. The character deportation rationale, however, especially for U.S. long-term residents, is questionable, since it is difficult to allocate responsibility to the criminal's original national community, as opposed to other factors, including perhaps the place where the person grew up.[154] Further, the nature of transnational crime today does not at all guarantee that removal is safer to U.S. communities.[155]

---

[145] INA § 316(c).

[146] INA § 316 (c).

[147] INA §§ 322 and 328.

[148] Spiro, *Questioning Barriers to Naturalization, supra* note 136, at 511–12.

[149] INA § 316(a)(3).

[150] Spiro, *Questioning Barriers to Naturalization, supra* note 136, at 509.

[151] Douglas, *supra* note 123, at 391.

[152] *Id.* at 392–94.

[153] *See* Spiro, *Questioning Barriers to Naturalization, supra* note 136, at 516.

[154] *Id.* at 512.

[155] *Id.*

4.   Age

The applicant must be at least eighteen years old to apply for naturalization.[156] However, under the Child Citizenship Act of 2000, any child who (a) has a U.S. citizen parent; (b) is under age eighteen; and (c) resides in the U.S. as an LPR, in the legal and physical custody of the citizen parent, automatically becomes a citizen when the naturalization petition is approved for the parent.[157] This provision applies to both biological and adopted children, although to qualify as a child under immigration laws, the child must have been adopted prior to reaching the age of 16.[158] For children who do not qualify for automatic citizenship, INA § 322 allows parents to file on their behalf for naturalization, as long as (1) the children have a U.S. citizen parent who files the application; (2) either the citizen parent or the children's citizen grandparent (parent of the citizen parent) has been physically present in the U.S. for five years, at least two of which were before either the parent or grandparent reached the age of fourteen; (3) the children are under the age of eighteen; and (4) the children reside outside the U.S. in the legal and physical custody of the citizen parent but are temporarily present in the U.S. after a lawful admission.

5.   English Language

Congress first adopted the ability to speak the English language requirement in 1906, and subsequently added in 1950, a literacy component, which remains to today.[159] Under current law, the petitioner must demonstrate during an interview with an immigration officer "an understanding of the English language, including an ability to read, write, and speak words in ordinary usage."[160] Generally, this involves conversing and responding in English to questions on the civics test, described below. There are a few exceptions to the English language requirement based on physical or mental disability, which must be substantiated through a medical examination.[161] The exception also applies to a person who is over fifty years of age and has been living in the U.S. for at least twenty years as an LPR, or a person who is over fifty-five years of age and has been living in the U.S. for at least fifteen years as an LPR.[162] Even with these exceptions, the English language requirement represents the most formidable obstacle to naturalization. Some defend the requirement as consistent with encouraging immigrant's broad and political assimilation, the former insofar as a common language is constitutive of the community and provides and important bond among its members, and the latter insofar as language is important for responsible political participation.[163]

---

[156] INA § 334(b).

[157] INA § 320.

[158] INA § 101(b)(E)(i).

[159] Spiro, *Questioning Barriers to Naturalization, supra* note 136, at 489–91.

[160] INA § 312(a)(1).

[161] INA § 312(b)(1).

[162] INA § 312((b)(2).

[163] *See* Neuman, *Justifying U.S. Naturalization Policies, supra* note 137, at 263–68. *See also* Spiro, *Questioning Barriers to Naturalization, supra* note 136, at 492–95.

Those who oppose it question not only the premise that the English language has defined or unified the U.S. community but also because its fails to achieve its unifying purpose for the substantial numbers of those who learn it for purposes of naturalization but still do not make English their primary language.[164]

6.   Knowledge of Civics

This requirement grew out of the early naturalization requirement that an applicant show an attachment to constitutional principles, and it was ultimately codified in 1950, as part of the anti-Commnunist Internal Security Act.[165] The current statute requires the applicant to demonstrate "knowledge and understanding of the fundamentals of the history, and of the principles and the form of government, of the United States.[166] Persons with a medically demonstrated physical or developmental condition can be exempted from this requirement,[167] as can, at the discretion of the interviewing immigration officer, persons over sixty-five years old who have lived in the U.S. for more than twenty years.[168] Even those applicants who have been exempted from the language requirement must pass the civics portion of the test in their own language, however. An official naturalization test was first implemented in 1986, and remained unchanged until 2006.[169] In September 20007, CIS unveiled the final one hundred questions to the new citizenship test, created to be "more standardized, fair, and meaningful."[170] The new test, implemented nationwide as of October 2008, includes one hundred revised questions, from which ten are randomly selected.[171] The English reading and writing portions of the examination will remain the same but it will contain more civic-based questions.[172] CIS has described this new test as emphasizing "the fundamental concepts of American democracy and the rights and responsibilities of citizenship."[173] CIS stated goal is to "inspire immigrants to learn about the civil values of this nation so that after they take the oath of citizenship they will participate fully in our great democracy."[174] The test has pleased some groups who perceive the new test as a better tool to encourage civic participation

---

[164] Spiro, *Questioning Barriers to Naturalization, supra* note 136, at 494–95.

[165] Internal Security Act of 1950, ch. 1024, § 30, 64 Stat. 984, 1013. *See also* Spiro, *Questioning Barriers to Naturalization, supra* note 136, at 497–98.

[166] INA § 312.

[167] INA § 312(b)(1).

[168] INA § 312(b)(3).

[169] Keun Dong Kim, *Citizenship Exam Redesigned to Focus on Concepts Rather than Trivia*, 21 GEO. IMMIGR. L.J. 155, 155 (2006).

[170] USCIS, *Redesigned Naturalization Test*, http://www.uscis.gov/natzpilot.

[171] The test is available at http://www.uscis.gov/files/nativedocumetns/100q.pdf.

[172] The vocabulary lists for the reading and writing components are *available at* http://www.uscis.gov/files/nativedocumetns/reading_vocab.pdf and http://www.uscis.gov/files/nativedocuments/writing_vocab.pdf.

[173] Press Briefing, USCIS, Pen and Pad: New Naturalization Test 30–33 (Sept. 27, 2007), *available at* http://www.uscis.gov/files/pressrelease/natzndtbl_72sep07.pdf.

[174] Press Release, *USCIS Issues Questions and Answers for New Pilot Naturalization Exam* (Nov. 30, 2006), *available at* http://www.uscis.gov/files/pressrelease/NatzTestQs113006.pdf.

among immigrants.[175] Others, however, view the new test either as a meaningless barrier to naturalization,[176] while other critique it for its perpetuation of a bounded construction of citizenship that, by its nature, promotes a universalist citizenship ideology that particularly disfavors minority groups.[177]

7.   Political or Ideological Requirements

The history of ideological exclusion from naturalization began in 1906, when Congress adopted what became know as an anti-anarchist provision [i.e., those opposed to organized government] following the assassination of President Mckinley.[178] That provision was applied broadly to deny naturalization to members of the Industrial Workers of the World, a global workers' union.[179] Then it was expanded in 1940 to include those who believed in the overthrow of the U.S government, or belonged to an organization advocating such action, which was applied broadly to members of the Communist Party.[180] Under current law, applicants who, either during the ten-year period immediately preceding the filing of the application or during the interval between the filing and the taking of the final oath of citizenship, have been affiliated with communist, totalitarian, or terrorist groups or have advocated their ideals, including through speeches and publications" are disqualified from naturalization.[181] The requirement is controversial especially because it relies on proxies, most notably membership in the Communist Party, as conclusive evidence that a person, if granted citizenship, would undermine U.S. polity.[182] As well, ideological qualifications conflict with bedrock principles of U.S. liberal tradition, including freedom of thought, speech, and association.[183] They may be justified, however, insofar as the applicant's acceptance of the republican framework is a pre-requisite to the person's political incorporation, of if the ideological criteria are compatible with U.S. national identity.[184]

8.   Attachment of the Principles of the U.S. Constitution

An applicant must demonstrate an attachment to the principles of the U.S. Constitution and allegiance to the U.S. government by taking an oath both in writing on the application and during the induction ceremony. The oath is a promise that the applicant supports the Constitution, renounces all foreign

---

[175] Kim, *supra* note 169, at 157.

[176] *Id.* at 156.

[177] Julian Wonjung Park, *A More Meaningful Citizenship Test? Unmasking the Construction of a Universalist, Principled-Based Citizenship Ideology*, 96 CAL. L. REV. 999, 1002 (2008).

[178] Spiro, *Questioning Barriers to Naturalization, supra* note 136, at 501–02.

[179] *Id.* at 502.

[180] *Id.*

[181] INA § 313.

[182] Spiro, *Questioning Barriers to Naturalization, supra* note 136, at 503–04.

[183] *See* Neuman, *Justifying U.S. Naturalization Policies, supra* note 137, at 256–60.

[184] *Id.* at 260–63.

allegiances, is willing to defend all federal laws against all enemies, will bear true allegiance to those laws, and will bear arms for the U.S. if required by law.[185] The oath was first introduced as part of the naturalization act of 1795[186] and evidences a strong norm against dual citizenship[187] as discussed below.

Beyond these eight statutory requirements for naturalization, DHS has imposed a few additional requirements. Non-statutory criteria that may be considered include: non-support of dependents; adultery; and failure to register with the Selective Service between eighteen and twenty-six years of age, but only if the applicant knowingly and willfully failed to register during the period for which the applicant must establish a history of good moral character. A person who fails to file taxes or to pay back-taxes prior to filing an application for naturalization could also be denied, especially since the failure to do so could be considered a crime.

c.   Adjudication and Judicial Review

Finally is the question of adjudication. Congress also has broad discretion to allocate by statute the functions of administrative agencies and courts in the adjudication of Naturalization petitions. For more than a century, courts had an exclusive role in granting or denying citizenship. In 1906, however, responding to concerns over the absence of a uniform naturalization process, including the intermittent acceptance by courts of non-white immigrants as citizens, Congress for the first time established an administrative agency, the Bureau of Immigration and Naturalization, in order to "provide for a uniform rule for the naturalization of aliens throughout the United States."[188] Overtime and especially under the current statute, the adjudicatory function by administrative agencies over Naturalization petitions has increased. The current statutory scheme was put in place in 1990, when Congress transferred the authority to grant naturalization to the Attorney General (now the Secretary of Homeland Security through the Department of Homeland Security). This was the first time that Congress provided an executive agency the formal power to award citizenship without court intervention.[189] Courts, however, continue to possess robust powers to ensure the speedy resolution of citizenship cases, as well as to review denials. First, the statute provides that courts have jurisdiction over matters in which the agency has failed to adjudicate within 120 days, in which case the court "may either determine the matter or remand the matter, with appropriate instructions."[190] Second, when a person has been denied naturalization following an administrative appeal,[191] courts retain jurisdiction to conduct *de novo* review, and the court "shall make its own

---

[185] INA § 337(a).

[186] Act of Jan. 29, 1795, ch. 20, § 1, 1 Stat. 414. For a discussion of the original oath requirement, *see* Neuman, *Justifying U.S. Naturalization Policies, supra* note 137, at 253–54.

[187] Spiro, *Questioning Barriers to Naturalization, supra* note 136, at 504.

[188] Law of June 29, 1906. *See* Douglas, *supra* note 123, at 389–90. *See also* Nancy Morawetz, *Citizenship and the Courts,* 2007 U. Chi. Legal F. 447, 451–54 (2007).

[189] *Id.* at 454.

[190] INA § 336(b).

[191] The 1990 Acts introduced an administrative appellate review process for the first time. Morawetz, *supra* note 188, at 455.

findings of fact and conclusions of law and shall, at the request of the petitioner, conduct a hearing de novo on the application."[192] Both the express authority in a statute for courts to take jurisdiction before the administrative process is completed and the de novo review standard are unusual in administrative law, and especially in immigration law.[193] Congress views citizenship, including its acquisition through naturalization, an important right such that enhanced procedures should protect those seeking citizenship.[194] The current judicial review process, however, has not consistently achieved its intended results. One problem has been that the current statute permits judicial intervention only when delays occur between an initial examination and a decision, but it says nothing about delays during other stages of the proceedings.[195] Thus, courts have not always remedied administrative delays in the adjudication of naturalization. Second, courts have taken different approaches to their fact-finding role, with some courts reviewing cases solely on the agency record while others conduct their own fact-finding.[196]

C. DUAL NATIONALITY

Dual nationality, defined simply as the formal possession of citizenship in at least one more nation, has long been disfavored in the United States.[197] More recently, U.S. laws have evolved to accommodate dual nationals in most instances, even as distaste for its possession or retention remains.[198]

Initially, dual nationality resulted when the birth countries of immigrants who naturalized in the United States refused to release them from the perpetual allegiance doctrine that then attached to common law *jus solis* citizenship.[199] In the early nineteenth century, the United States recognized the prerogative of other states to restrict expatriation, and, in effect refused request for diplomatic intervention from dual nationals against their birth country, even from those who might find themselves drafted into the military after a temporary visit abroad.[200] By the mid-nineteenth century, however, as U.S. immigration grew, U.S. authorities found themselves having to more firmly protect naturalized U.S. citizens from military service obligations.[201] The issue intensified in 1868 when Britain arrested several naturalized U.S. citizens and tried them for treason in connection with an Irish uprising.[202] Congress moved quickly to enact legislation affirming expatria-

---

[192] INA §§ 310 (b, c).

[193] Morawetz, *supra* note 188, at 451.

[194] *Id.*

[195] *Id.* at 457.

[196] *Id.* at 459–60.

[197] Peter J. Spiro, *Dual Nationality and the Meaning of Citizenship*, 46 EMORY L.J. 1411, 1415 (1997).

[198] *Id.*

[199] *Id.* at 1418–25.

[200] *Id.* at 1425–26.

[201] *Id.* at 1427.

[202] *Id.*

tion as "a natural and inherent right of all people, indispensable to the enjoyment of the rights of life, liberty, and the pursuit of happiness,"[203] and directed the President to employ all means short of war to secure the release of U.S. citizens.[204] This act marked the beginning of the decline of the perpetual allegiance doctrine for birth citizens also in much of Europe.[205]

Compelled dual nationality, thus, was largely resolved by the late nineteenth century, but dual nationality by choice remained, even as they faced little toleration and were perceived as threats to the community.[206] These dual nationals included not only naturalized citizens but also an increasing number of children born to immigrant parents yet to naturalize as well as children born abroad to U.S. citizen parents.[207] U.S. laws responded to each of these in turn. By 1907, for example, Congress codified the existing administrative practice of requiring a renunciation oath upon naturalization, with the intended effect of triggering denationalization by the birth country.[208] In practice, however, the oath requirement has not resulted in denationalization and many naturalized citizens retain their dual nationality despite taking the oath.[209] For dual nationals born abroad or living abroad, the U.S. imposed a type of informal election requirement by requiring residence in the U.S.[210] As well, Congress passed a series of lax expatriation laws, such that the payment of taxes or the holding of agricultural land or the participation of politics abroad, and even the return of naturalized citizens to their homeland past a certain period, could result in the loss of nationality.[211] The enforcement of some of these laws intensified, of course, during the Cold War, during which time any active political identification with a foreign state provided grounds for expatriation.[212] Courts, including the U.S. Supreme Court upheld much of these practices against constitutional attack.[213] Eventually, the U.S. Supreme Court reined in these laws by imposing substantive restrictions on what acts could result in a loss of nationality, but also by imposing a requirement that the act be done with the specific intent of relinquishing citizenship.[214] Thus, the United States has softened significantly in its legal attitudes against dual nationality, even as it remains

---

[203] Act of July 27, 1868, sh. 249, 15 Stat. 223 (codified at 22 U.S.C. § 1732 (1976)).

[204] Spiro, *Dual Nationality*, *supra* note 197, at 1428.

[205] *Id.* at 1429–30.

[206] *Id.* at 1431–32.

[207] *Id.* at 1435–36.

[208] *Id.* at 1435.

[209] *Id.* at 1457–60.

[210] *Id.* at 1437–38.

[211] *Id.* at 1440–41.

[212] *Id.* at 1443–44.

[213] *Id.* at 1445–46 (discussing MacKenzie v. Hare, 239 U.S. 299 (1915) (upholding the expatriation of a U.S. born woman citizen by virtue of her marriage to a foreign national) and Perez v. Brownell, 356 U.S. 44 (1958) (upholding the expatriation of a naturalized citizen who voted in a foreign political election).

[214] *See infra* notes 219–308 and accompanying text on Loss of Citizenship.

unpopular.[215] Mexico's adoption in 1998 of a constitutional grant of dual nationality at the heels of similar changes by other countries (such as El Salvador) that have traditionally sent large numbers of immigrants to the United States, has provoked renewed fervor against dual nationality.[216] Some political scientists, for example, have argued that the dual nationality of naturalized citizens, especially Latinos, disconnects immigrants from the U.S. political system.[217] Moreover, some post 9/11 practices suggest increased intolerance for the perceived divided loyalties that attach to dual nationality.[218]

D. EXPATRIATION OR LOSS OF CITIZENSHIP

Citizenship acquired through birth or naturalization may be lost through a process formerly known as expatriation and now simply called loss of citizenship.[219] The U.S. Supreme Court considers relinquishment of U.S. citizenship a right.[220] Loss of citizenship can also occur through statutory revocation, although the Fourteenth Amendment protects individuals from governmental abridgment of a right to citizenship.[221]

1.   The History of Expatriation Laws

Congress has legislated to denationalize only sparingly.[222] Expatriation laws have existed since 1865, when Congress declared deserters as having abandoned their U.S. citizenship.[223] In 1868, Congress passed the Expatriation Act and to declare expatriation a natural and inherent right, though its purpose was primarily to protect naturalized U.S. citizens with dual nationality who returned to their countries of origin.[224] In 1907, Congress set out the actions that would effect this

---

[215] Spiro, *Dual Nationality, supra* note 197, at 1456 (discussing State Department policies disfavoring dual nationality).

[216] *See e.g.*, David A. Martin, *New Rules on Dual Nationality for a Democratizing Glove: Between Rejection and Embrace*, 14 GEO. IMMIGR. L.J. 1 (1999) and Notes and Comments, Chris Dangaran, *The Duel Over Dual Nationality Amendments*, 7 SW. J. L. & TRADE AM. 47 (2000).

[217] Jeffrey K. Staton, et al., *Costly Citizenship? Dual Nationality Institutions, Naturalization, and Political Connectedness* (June 19,2007), *available at* SSRN: http://ssrn.com/abstracts=995569. *See also* Jeffrey K. Staton, et al., *Dual Nationality Among Latinos: What are the Implications for Political Connectedness?*, 69 J. OF POLITICS 470 (2007).

[218] The issue comes up frequently with regard to the availability to U.S. jobs that require a security clearance, for example U.S. Department of State Policies on Security Clearance state that "[d]dual nationality is a relevant element in some cases." And while DOS does not adopted a blanket rule against dual citizens in making security clearances, the issue is considered on a case by case basis. U.S. Department of State, *Dual Citizenship: Security Implications*, (June 2007), *available at* http://careers.state.gov/docs/DualCitizenship.pdf.

[219] In 1994, Congress amended the Immigration and Nationality Act to replace the reference to expatriation with the phrase loss of citizenship. INTCA § 105.

[220] *See* Afroyim v. Rusk, 387 U.S. 253, 263–66, 87 S. Ct. 1660, 1665–67 (1967).

[221] *Id.*

[222] T. Alenxander Aleinikoff, *Theories of Loss of Citizenship*, 84 MICH. L. REV. 1471, 1476–78 (1986).

[223] Sec. 21, Act of March 3, 1865, 13 Stat. 487.

[224] *See supra* notes 198–204 and accompanying text.

expatriation.[225] 1907 Expatriation Act was also aimed at solving problems occasioned by dual nationality, although this time the aim was to restrict the right of persons to retain their original nationality upon naturalizing as U.S. citizens.[226] Between 1907 and 1922, women who married U.S. citizens who naturalized in another country lost their citizenship because women acquired the nationality of their husbands.[227] In 1940, Congress added several new grounds for loss of nationality, such that citizenship could be lost by voting in a political election of a foreign sate, or accepting the duties of an office or employment under the government of a foreign state for which only nationals of the state were eligible, desertion in a time of war, and for conviction of treason or attempting to overthrow the U.S. government.[228] In 1944, Congress also moved to denationalize a person for departing the United States in time of war in order to avoid military service. Congress also made minor changes in 1952, including amending the provision relating to employment in a foreign government to read as the provision reads under current law.[229] Also in 1954, Congress authorized denationalization for certain convictions under the Smith Act.[230] Generally, all statutes repealing a prior expatriation law have provided that citizenship lost under the former statute is not restored by its repeal, unless that prior statute would be unconstitutional under current constitutional doctrine; as such, the law in effect at the time of the person committed the expatriating act could apply, unless it is declared unconstitutional.[231]

Post 9/11, some members of Congress attempted but failed to pass legislation that would have stripped of citizenship persons broadly to anyone becoming members or providing material support to a terrorist organization.[232] Despite its failure, Hamdi, at least renounced his citizenship as part of his settlement agreement upon his release as an "enemy combatant."[233] Saad Gul has argued that Hamdi's renunciation clause would be unconstitutional under current Supreme

---

[225] Act of March 2, 1907, Pub. L. 59-193, 34 Stat. 1228.

[226] *See supra* notes 207–209 and accompanying text.

[227] DANIEL LEVY, U.S. CITIZENSHIP AND NATURALIZATION HANDBOOK, § 15:6 (2008).

[228] Ch. 876, 54 Stat. 1137 (1940).

[229] Aleinikoff, *supra* note 222, at note 28. The Smith Act or the Alien Registration Act of 1940, 8 U.S.C. § 2385, makes it a crime to "knowingly or willfully advocate, abet, advise or teach the duty, necessity, desirability or propriety of overthrowing the Government of the United States or of any State by force or violence, or for anyone to organize any association which teaches, advises or encourages such an overthrow, or for anyone to become a member of or to affiliate with any such association."

[230] Ch. 1256, § 2, 68 Stat. 1146 (1954).

[231] LEVY, *supra* note 227, at §§ 15:1 and 15:3.

[232] Comment, Charles H. Hooker, *The Past as Prologue: Schneiderman v. United States and Contemporary Questions of Citizenship and Denationalization*, 19 EMORY INT'L L. REV. 305, 310–17 (2005). Similar legislation was introduced but never passed to denationalize U.S. citizens of Japanese ancestry indicating loyalty to the Emperor of Japan. *See, e.g., Expatriation of Certain Nationals of the United States: Hearings before the House Committee on Immigration and Naturalization*, 78th Cong., 2d Sess. (1944).

[233] Saad Gul, *Return of the Native? An Assessment of the Citizenship Renunciation Clause in Hamdi's Settlement Agreement in the Light of Citizenship Jurisprudence*, 27 N. ILL. U. L. REV. 131, 155–57 (2007).

Court doctrine, which requires that expatriation be voluntary, as explained below.[234]

2. Constitutional Scrutiny of Expatriation Statutes

After the Cold War, Congress' expatriation laws met fierce judicial hostility. In 1967, the Court held that the Constitution did not confer on Congress an affirmative power to expatriate any citizen and affirmed that persons cannot lose their citizenship unless they relinquished it voluntarily.[235] To the contrary, the Fourteenth Amendment protected persons from any governmental abridgment of his or her citizenship rights.[236] Then in 1980, the Court clarified its earlier holdings to affirm that expatriation also requires an independent showing of intentionality to relinquish U.S. citizenship by the person who commits the expatriating act.[237] In addition, since the 1950's, the Court has disallowed certain acts, even when committed voluntarily, to become the sole basis for expatriation.[238] These include deserting armed forces during wartime,[239] departing or remaining outside the United States to avoid military service,[240] voting in a foreign political election,[241] and possessing dual nationality.[242] In 1986, Congress revised the expatriation sections of the Immigration and Nationality Act to comport with Constitutional requirements. Congress made the 1986 amendments retroactive so that current determinations of whether a person expatriated himself by acts committed before 1986 must be based on the current statute.[243]

3. The Current Law

Currently, the INA has seven grounds that, if performed voluntarily and "with the intention of relinquishing United States nationality,"[244] results in a loss of nationality. In general terms, these are (1) obtaining naturalization in another country; (2) taking an oath of allegiance for a foreign sovereign; (3) serving in the armed forces of a foreign state as an officer or in any capacity when those forces are engaged in hostilities against the U.S.; (4) accepting a government post with another state after acquiring the nationality of that state or when the post requires

---

[234] *Id.* at 134–163.

[235] *Afroyim*, 387 U.S. at 253. Earlier cases had also required voluntariness. *See, e.g.*, Nishikawa v. Dulles, 356 U.S. 129, 133.

[236] *Afroyim*, 387 U.S. at 261–62.

[237] Vance v. Terrazas, 444 U.S. 252, 261.

[238] In contrast, in 1915, the Court upheld a statute that stripped a woman of her birthright citizenship solely by virtue of her marriage to a foreign national. Mackenzie v. Hare, 239 U.S. 299 (1915). Marriage-based expatriation has not existed since 1931 because Congress repealed it outright. Sec. 3(a) Act of March 3, 1931, Pub. L. No. 71-829, 46 Stat. 1511.

[239] Trop v. Dulles, 356 U.S. 86, 86.

[240] Kennedy v. Mendoza-Martinez, 372 U.S. 144 (1963).

[241] Afroyim, 387 U.S. at 253.

[242] Kawakita v. U.S., 343 U.S. 717, 724.

[243] Immigration and Nationality Act, Amendment of 1986, Pub. L. 99-653, 100 Stat. 3655, at § 23(g).

[244] INA § 349(a).

an oath of allegiance to that foreign country; (5) making a formal renunciation of nationality; (6) making a written renunciation of nationality; or (7) committing of treason or attempting to overthrow the U.S. government.[245] When citizenship is lost under the statute, it also divests in the same sense that U.S. citizenship vests upon a child when both parents naturalize.[246] Thus, a child who acquired or would have acquired citizenship through the parent also loses his or her citizenship with the parent who is expatriated. In addition, because voluntary expatriation could have tax advantages, Congress passed a law in 1996 to penalize persons who voluntarily relinquished citizenship to obtain tax advances by barring them from seeking admission to the U.S. in the future.[247]

Congress also created more flexible evidentiary requirements for establishing the voluntariness and intentionality that appeared to modify the burden of proof standard required in earlier Court cases. In 1961, the INA established an evidentiary presumption that a person who has performed any expatriating act has done so voluntarily, which can be rebutted upon showing by the preponderance of the evidence that the acts were not undertaken voluntarily.[248] In 1980, the Court upheld this evidentiary presumption and expressly rejected that the Government must prove voluntariness with clear and convincing evidence,[249] a standard the Court had required in earlier rulings.[250] In other words, under current law, proving with a preponderance of the evidence that the person has committed one of the expatriating acts in the INA is sufficient, and it is the citizen who must prove with a preponderance of the evidence that he or she committed the act under duress.[251]

With regard to intentionality, the Court also affirmed the statutory requirement that intent is proved with the preponderance of the evidence rather than higher burden of proof.[252] The Court explained, moreover, that any of the specified acts for expatriation could be highly persuasive evidence of a purpose to abandon citizenship.[253] The Court did not, however, define what conduct would support a finding that a citizen who performed a statutory imperative act intended to terminate citizenship. As a result, lower court decisions on loss of citizenship cases have tended to be fact-specific, and there is no simple certainty when it comes to

---

[245] *Id.* Except for six and seven, the person must have taken up residence outside the United States and its outlying possessions before expatriation can take effect. INA § 351(a).

[246] Levy, *supra* note 227, at § 15:1.

[247] Illegal Reform and Immigrant Responsibility Act, Pub. L. 104-208, 110 Stat. 3009-546, § 352(b). In addition, under current tax laws, persons who renounced their citizenship to avoid tax liability face serious adverse consequences. IRS Notice 97-19, Guidance for Expatriates Under §§ 877, 2501, 2107, and 6039F (March 10, 1997) reproduced in 74 Interpreter Releases (May 23, 1997).

[248] Vance v. Terrazas, 444 U.S. 252, 254–55 (1980) (citing to then Section 349(a)(2) of the INA, 66 Stat. 267, as amended, 75 Stat. 656).

[249] *Terrazas*, 444 U.S. at 254.

[250] *See, e.g.*, Nishikawa, 356 U.S. at 133 and Kawakita, 343 U.S. at 724.

[251] *Terrazas*, 444 U.S. at 268–70.

[252] *Id.* at 267.

[253] *Id.* at 261.

assessing the issue of intent to relinquish citizenship.[254] Then in 1990, the Department of State made a policy decision to presume that the U.S. citizen does not intend to relinquish citizenship when obtaining naturalization in a foreign state, subscribing to routine declaration of allegiance to a foreign state, or accepting non-level employment with a foreign government.[255] This standard in effect has allowed certain U.S. citizens not only to vote in foreign elections but even to assume a high political post without risking denationalization.[256]

E. DENATURALIZATION

In addition to loss of citizenship through expatriation, naturalized citizens may have their naturalization revoked. Denaturalization statutes have also encountered judicial resistance because a liberty interest that accrues as soon as naturalization is conferred[257] and consequently the Court has held that "it should not be lightly revoked."[258] As well, First Amendment values have influenced the Court's rulings to interpret or apply statutes to favor the person facing a loss of citizenship.[259] This has been the result of the Court's concern over denaturalization proceedings being employed as part of a broader campaign to stamp out perceived disloyalty during times of heightened national security periods in the United States. Such was the case, for instance, when the government targeted alleged communists or pro-Nazi sympathizers for denaturalization.[260]

Denaturalization rulings, however, also reveal deep disagreement among the Justices about how much individual rights considerations should trump Congressional intent to denaturalize,[261] at least insofar as denaturalization retains a relationship to Congress' powers to grant naturalization in the first place.[262] Denaturalization generally can occur at any time post-naturalization[263] whenever

---

[254] Alan G. James, *Expatriation in the United States: Precept and Practice Today and Yesterday*, 27 San Diego L. Rev. 853, 893–94 (1990).

[255] *Id.* at 895–96.

[256] Spiro, *Dual Nationality*, *supra* note 197, at 1454–55.

[257] *Schneiderman*, 320 U.S. at 1337. *See also* Chaunt v. U.S., 364 U.S. 350, 354 (1960).

[258] *Schneiderman*, 320 U.S. at 1337.

[259] *See e.g.*, *Schneiderman*, 320 U.S. at 1341 and 1343.

[260] *See, e.g.*, Charles H. Hooker, *The Past as Prologue: Schneiderman v. United States and Contemporary Questions of Citizenship and Denationalization*, 19 Emory Int'l L. Rev. 305, 319–46 (Discussing the historical context of the *Scneiderman*, 320 U.S. at 134, case, which involved the denaturalization of Schneiderman because of his affiliation with the Workers Party of the America and the Young Workers League of America, and the Baumgartner v. U.S., 322 U.S. 665 (1944), and Knauer v. U.S., 328 U.S. 654 (1946) cases, which involved the denaturalization of a German nationals essentially for their support of the Nazi regime).

[261] *See, e.g.*, *Schneiderman*, 320 U.S. at 1369 (three dissenting justices stating that the Court cannot change or modify the will of Congress by reading a freedom of thought prescription to statutory interpretation) and Klapprott v. U.S., 333 U.S. 601 at 625 (1949) (three justices disagreeing that Court can disallow default judgments in denaturalization proceedings where Congress has not expressly invalidated them in the statute).

[262] *See, e.g.*, Johannessen v. U.S., 225 U.S. 227, 238 (1912).

[263] Costello v. U.S., 365 U.S. 265, 282 (1961) (disallowing a challenge to denaturalization proceedings

the recipient of the privilege procured it invalidly. The Court has long affirmed Congress' power to strip a person of his citizenship by naturalization when it has been unlawfully or fraudulently procured.[264] In contrast, statutes that would impose substantive restrictions on the acts of naturalized citizens post-naturalization are invalid.[265] Currently the Immigration and Nationality Act permits "setting aside the order admitting [a] person to citizenship and canceling the certificate of naturalization on the ground that such order and such certificate were illegally procured or were procured by concealment of a material fact or by willful misrepresentation.[266] "Illegally procured" and "concealment of a material fact or by willful misrepresentation" constitute two separate grounds for denaturalization.[267] Thus, the government has generally relied on applicants' omissions or misrepresentations to start denaturalization, which were also the circumstances of denaturalization proceedings that targeted alleged communists or Nazi supporters. These are also the circumstances, in fact, in denaturalization cases today against alleged terrorists who may have failed to disclose all of their associations with any group that could be perceived as supporting terrorism or misrepresented any fact, including biographical ones, that could have led the government to discover damning facts.[268]

Congress responded to the Courts' limitations on denaturalization based on omitting or misrepresenting past membership in communist organizations by enacting the Internal Security Act of 1950.[269] This Act, which remains law,[270] creates a presumption of lack of attachment to the U.S. Constitution if within five years after a person naturalizes, he or she becomes "members of or affiliated with organization, membership in or affiliation with which at the time of naturalization would have been precluded . . . " This provision, which has not been invoked, is likely unconstitutional, insofar as it creates post-Naturalization conditions found unconstitutional in *Scheiderman*.[271] A separate denaturalization ground that

---

twenty-seven years after the conferral of naturalization).

[264] *See, e.g., Johannessen*, 225 U.S. at 238; U.S. v. Ginsberg, 243 U.S. 472 (1917); and Knauer v. U.S., 328 U.S. at 1336.

[265] *Schneider*, 377 U.S. at 163 (striking down a 1952 statute that denaturalized citizens shown to have had continuous residence for thee years in the territory of the foreign state in which they were formerly a national after becoming citizens).

[266] INA § 340(a). The INA also allows revocation of admission to citizenship when there has been a criminal conviction for procuring naturalization by fraud. INA § 340(e). Person who claimed U.S. citizenship as the spouse or child of the denaturalized person will also automatically lose their citizenship as of the time of the order setting aside the principal's citizenship. INA § 340(d).

[267] Under all prior statutes from 1906 to 1952, the basis of denaturalization was fraud or illegality. LEVY, *supra* note 227, at § 14:3. The Court, however, has not drawn a distinction between fraud and the new terms under the statute. *Costello*, 365 U.S. at 287.

[268] *See, e.g.*, Lety Volp, *Citizenship Undone*, 75 FORDHAM L. REV. 2579, 2583 (2007) (noting several cases involving denaturalization proceedings against Muslim-Americans for their alleged association with terrorists organizations).

[269] Ch. 1024, 64 Stat. 987, amended by Immigration and Nationality Act, ch. 477, 66 Stat. 163 (1953).

[270] Current version INA § 340(c).

[271] *See supra* note 265 and accompanying text. *See also* Comment, Charles H. Hooker, *The Past as Prologue:* Schneiderman v. United States *and Contemporary Questions of Citizenship and Denationalization*, 19 EMORY INT'L L. REV. 305, 340–44 (2005).

creates post-Naturalization conditions applies to person who received their naturalization based on their service in the U.S. armed forces. Such persons are subject to denaturalization proceedings if at any time subsequent to naturalization the person is separated from the military under other than honorable conditions.[272] The constitutionality of this provision is also uncertain.

In order to balance individual rights concerns against Congress' naturalization powers, the Court has at times imposed strict procedural safeguards in favor of persons facing denaturalization on the bases of alleged fraud. The Court has required the Government to prove by "clear, unequivocal, and convincing" evidence that the applicant sought to obtain naturalization illegally or fraudulently.[273] This standard of proof is very strict and has required that facts be construed in favor of the citizen, in so far as it is reasonably possible.[274] Moreover, more often than not, on appeal the Court will not accept the concurrent findings of fact of two lower courts, but will examine the facts de novo.[275] When the Government proves either ground for denaturalization, the Court, however, has rejected the application of equitable discretion to consider mitigating factors in favor of the denaturalizing the defendant.[276] Such factors could include the circumstances surrounding the omitted or misrepresented facts, such as whether the association with a particular group was with knowledge or compelled or mitigating factors in cases involving the commission of crimes.[277]

The U.S. Supreme Court has not distinguished doctrinally between willful misrepresentation and concealment, even though the statute speaks of both "concealment of material fact" and "willful misrepresentation." Instead, the Court holds that misrepresentation must also be of a material fact and that concealment must also be willful.[278] Following this approach, the Government must prove four separate factors: (1) that the naturalized citizen concealed or misrepresented a fact; (2) that the misrepresentation or concealment was willful; (3) that the fact was material; and (4) that the naturalized citizen procured citizenship as a result of the misrepresentation or concealment.[279] Concealment means that the petitioner for naturalization has sworn under oath that the person lacks a record of misconduct or has never done certain actions, usually by failure to list these in the naturalization application.[280] Misrepresentation refers to lies or false answers to questions in the naturalization application that generally require the disclosure of certain facts or

---

[272] INA § 329(c).

[273] The Court first declared the rule in *Schneiderman*, 320 U.S. at 1335. *See also* Fedorenko v. U.S. 449 U.S. 490, 505, 101 S. Ct. 737, 746–47 (1981) and Knauer v. U.S., 328 U.S. at 657–58.

[274] *Schneiderman*, 320 U.S. at 1335.

[275] *See, e.g., Knauer*, 328 U.S. at 657. *But cf.* Berenyt v. INS, 385 U.S. at 635.

[276] Fedorenko v. U.S., 449 U.S. 490, 517 (1981). For a critique of the preclusion of equitable discretion in denaturalization cases *see* Amy D. Ronner, *Denaturalizatin and Death: What it Means to Preclude the Exercise of Judicial Discretion*, 20 GEO. IMMIGR. L.J. 101 (2005).

[277] Ronner, *supra* note 276, at 111–115.

[278] Fedorenko, 449 U.S. at 507.

[279] Kungys v. U.S., 485 U.S. 759, 767 (1988).

[280] *See* U.S. v. Oddo, 314 F.2d 115, 116 (2d Cir. 1963), *cert. denied*, 375 U.S. 833 (1963).

conduct.[281] When questions in the naturalization application are ambiguous, however, the alleged concealment or misrepresentation cannot be the basis for denaturalization. For example, in several cases where petitioners belonged to communist organizations but answered no in a question pertaining to belief in or affiliation to anarchism, the Court rejected the finding of denaturalization.[282] Willful means simply that the applicant must have purposefully concealed or misrepresented a material fact. It is sufficient that the applicant knowingly concealed or misrepresented material facts in the naturalization process, without actual proof of intent to deceive.[283]

The Supreme Court's holdings regarding the requirement that the omission or misrepresentation must also be material have created confusion. In *Chaunt v. U.S.*, the Court concluded that the Government proved the elements of concealment and willful misrepresentation when the applicant did not disclose his criminal record.[284] Nevertheless, the Court reversed the lower courts to deny denaturalization on the bases that the criminal record was immaterial to the determination of denaturalization given that the offenses charged were of extremely light consequence.[285] The Court's early holdings on the meaning of material concealment or misrepresentation, however, created confusion among the lower courts, and in 1988, the Court decided *Kungys v. US* in order to clarify its definition.[286] Many scholars have noted *Kungy's* failure to do so.[287] In part, the problem resides in that the *Kungy's* Court produced five different written opinions, in addition to Justice Scalia's plurality holding.[288] Justice Scalia interpreted material fact to parallel the same requirement in criminal fraud statutes,[289] and treated it as a question of law to be determined by judges.[290] To be material, the statement needs only to "be predictably capable of affecting" or have a "natural tendency to influence" the agency's determinations.[291] A finding of material concealment or misrepresentation, converts the procurement prong (4) into a rebuttable presumption against the petitioner of disqualification for naturalization.[292] To overcome the presumption, the petitioner must establish with a preponderance of the evidence that he or she in fact met the requirement affected

---

[281] *Costello*, 365 U.S. at 272; (representing that person was a real estate agent when in fact he was a bootlegger). In *Costello*, the Court treated the misrepresentation as concealment, despite finding that the real estate business was no more than a cover up for his real occupation. *Id.* at 276, 540.

[282] *See* Maisenberger v. U.S. 356 U.S. 670, at 672 (1958) and Nowak v. US., 356 U.S. 265, 276, (1961).

[283] *Chaunt*, 364 U.S. at 355. *See also* LEVY, *supra* note 227, at § 14.3 (citing to lower court holdings).

[284] *Chaunt*, 364 U.S. at 352.

[285] *Id.*

[286] 485 U.S. at 768–69 (Justice Scalia discussing the confusion created by the Court's earlier decision in *Chaunt* and *Costello*).

[287] *See* LEVY, *supra* note 227, at § 14:7.

[288] Only Justice Brennan and Chief Justice Rhenquist fully joined Justice Scalia's opinion. In addition, Justice Brennan, Justice O'Connor, and together Justices Marshall, Stevens, and Blackmun wrote separate concurring opinions, while Justice White dissented.

[289] *Kungys*, 485 U.S. at 769–70.

[290] *Id.* at 771.

[291] *Id.*

[292] *Id.* at 777.

by the misrepresentation or concealment.[293] Justice Brennan's concurrence held that the burden-shifting presumption should only arise when the Government produces "evidence sufficient to raise a fair inference [and not merely a possibility] that a statutory disqualifying fact actually existed," coupled with the fact that the concealment or misrepresentation necessarily frustrated the Government's investigative efforts.[294] Justice Brennan, therefore, would impose a stricter evidentiary burden on the government, which is more consistent with the Court's stricter application of the materiality test.[295] As applied to the facts, the Court still reversed the Court of Appeals and affirmed the district court to disallow denaturalization.[296] Kungys made false statements about his date and place of birth in his visa and naturalization applications. The Court did not consider that the government proved with clear, unequivocal and convincing evidence "that had petitioner disclosed the information, it would have likely produced either outright denial or an investigation regarding the discrepancy in the original visa application."[297] "Even a high probability," the Court held, is not enough."[298]

Beyond concealment or misrepresentation, *"illegally procured"* can also include unwitting ineligibility for naturalization.[299] The Supreme Court has allowed denaturalization proceedings when the applicant did not strictly comply with all the conditions precedent to naturalization, on the basis that the certificate was *"illegally procured."*[300] Probably the single most important basis for "illegally procured" naturalization is when the applicant committed fraud in the original petition for permanent residence.[301] In *Fedorenko*, the Court held that fraudulently procured visas are not valid and would render illegal any subsequent naturalization derived from those visas.[302] In *Kungys*, however, the Court rejected this rationale,[303] considering instead, whether providing "false testimony" during the visa procurement stage would bar the person from establishing good moral character, which would have made naturalization "illegally procured."[304] Good moral character is a statutory prerequisite to naturalization and disqualifies, *inter alia*, any person who within the required permanent residence period (usually five years) "has given false testimony for the purpose of obtaining any benefits under the [INA § 101(f)(6)]." As applied, Kungys was not disqualified because his misrepresentation at the time of applying for his visa had occurred beyond the statutory period

---

[293] *Id.*

[294] *Id.* at 783.

[295] LEVY, *supra* note 227, at §§ 14.10 and 14.11.

[296] *Kungys*, 485 U.S. at 759.

[297] *Id.* at 774.

[298] *Id.*

[299] LEVY, *supra* note 227, at § 14.16.

[300] *Fedorenko*, 449 U.S. at 506.

[301] LEVY, *supra* note 227, at § 14.17.

[302] *Fedorenko*, 449 at 515.

[303] *Kungys*, 485 U.S. at 779.

[304] *Id.* at 773–74.

required under the good moral character provision.[305] In addition, only oral testimony triggers the good moral character bar.[306] *Kungys* did not require the misrepresentation, however, to have to be material for purposes of establishing good moral character.[307] Some lower courts, however, are not reading *Kungys* as replacing the holding in *Fedorenko*, but as supplementary. Therefore, post-Kungys, some lower courts have continued to denaturalize relying on *Fedorenko* based upon material misrepresentations in the original visa process.[308]

---

[305] *Id.*

[306] *Id.*

[307] *Id.* at 839 (J. Stevens concurring in judgment).

[308] *See, e.g.*, U.S. v. Demjanjuk, 367 F.3d 623 (6th Cir. 2004).

Chapter 16

THE FUTURE OF U.S. IMMIGRATION LAW[1]

In 1952, Congress passed the comprehensive federal immigration statute, the Immigration Nationality Act (INA)[2] the provisions of which have been discussed extensively in this book. The INA has been amended almost annually since 1952, sometimes in minor ways and other times with major overhauls. *See* Chapter 2. The last several years have seen many calls for major immigration reform in the United States, but to this point, significant — denominated by many as "comprehensive" — immigration reform efforts have failed.[3] At least as this book

---

[1] Parts of this Chapter are adapted from Kevin R. Johnson, *Protecting National Security Through More Liberal Admission of Immigrants*, 2007 U. Chi. Legal F. 157 and Kevin R. Johnson, Opening the Floodgates: Why America Needs to Rethink Its Borders and Immigration Laws 200–11 (2007).

[2] Pub. L. No. 82-414, 66 Stat. 163 (1952) (codified as amended in scattered sections of Titles 8, 18 and 22 U.S.C.).

[3] For different perspectives on "comprehensive" immigration reform, *see* Sheila Jackson Lee, *Why*

goes to press, Congress has been unable to pass a major overhaul of the immigration laws. Much may change, however, with the election of President Barack Obama and new Congress in November 2008.

The politics of immigration are almost as complex as the body of law that regulates it. Importantly, as a political matter, immigration is not a liberal/conservative, Red State/Blue State, Democratic/Republican issue. Immigration often results in odd political bedfellows, with there often not being a clear and clean divide between the Republican and Democratic parties. Labor unions at times have supported immigration restrictions in hopes of protecting domestic workers while the *Wall Street Journal* has championed liberal admissions of labor. *Both* popular political parties have restrictionist and expansionist immigration wings. *Both* parties have contributed significantly to the immigration regime in which we live.

After much delay, the nation in 2005–07 engaged in a fractious national debate over reform of the immigration laws, with a particular focus on undocumented immigration from Mexico. In December 2005, the House of Representatives passed the Sensenbrenner bill[4] named after its sponsor Representative James Sensenbrenner (R-Wisconsin), which was so one-sided in enforcement direction that it provoked protests of thousands of people on the streets of cities across the United States — something unprecedented in the country.[5] The Senate passed a more moderate reform proposal, which included legalization and guest worker components in addition to less extreme enforcement measures.[6]

One complicating factor for immigration reform is that the events of September 11, 2001 have seriously distorted the immigration debate. Discussion of ordinary immigration reform was hijacked by the "war on terror," and any proposal that did not focus on border enforcement and removals, faced claims that it would help to

---

Immigration Reform Requires a Comprehensive Approach That Includes Both Legalization Programs and Provisions to Secure the Border, 43 Harv. J. Legis 267 (2006); Christopher J. Walker, *Border Vigilantism and Comprehensive Immigration Reform*, 10 Harv. Latino L. Rev. 135 (2007); Marc R. Rosenblum, *"Comprehensive" Legislation vs. Fundamental Reform: The Limits of Current Immigration Proposals*, Migration Policy Brief, Jan. 2006; Margaret E. Dorsy & Miguel Diaz-Borriga, *Senator Barack Obama and Immigration Reform*, 38 J. Black Studies 90 (Sept 2007); *see also* Judith Golub, *Immigration Reform Post-9/11*, 13 U.S.-Mex. L.J. 9, 9 (2005) ("[D]espite the current uncertainty and the changed environment, immigration reform is inevitable.").

[4] *See* Border Protection, Antiterrorism, and Illegal Immigration Control Act of 2005, H. Rep. 4437, 109th Cong. 1st Sess. (2005). The Sensenbrenner bill among other things, would have made the mere status of being an undocumented immigrant a felony subject to imprisonment as well as deportation from the United States, and would have imposed criminal sanctions on persons who provided any sort of humanitarian assistance to undocumented immigrants. *See id.* §§ 203, 205, 109th Cong., 1st Sess.

[5] *See* Teresa Watanabe & Hector Becerra, *500,000 Pack Streets to Protest Immigration Bills*, L.A. Times, Mar. 26, 2005, at A1 (Los Angeles); Mark Johnson & Linda Spice, *Thousands March for Immigrants*, Milwaukee J. Sentinel, Mar. 24, 2006, at A1 (Milwaukee); Nathaniel Hoffman, *Protest Supports Illegal Workers*, Contra Costa Times, Mar. 22, 2006 (San Francisco); Oscar Avila & Antonio Olivo, *A Show of Strength: Thousands March to Loop for Immigrants' Rights*, Chi Trib, Mar. 11, 2006, at A1 (Chicago). For analysis of the meaning and impact of the spring 2006 immigrant rights marches, *see* Bill Ong Hing & Kevin R. Johnson, *The Immigrant Rights Marches of 2006 and the Prospects for a New Civil Rights Movement*, 42 Harv. C.R.-C.L. L. Rev. 99 (2007); Sylvia R. Lazos Vargas, *Emerging Latina/o Nation and Anti-Immigrant Backlash*, 7 Nev. L.J. 685 (2007).

[6] *See* Comprehensive Immigration Reform Act of 2006, S. 2611, 109th Cong, 2d Sess (2006).

create serious — and unacceptable — national security risks.[7]

From 2005 to 2007, Congress struggled mightily with immigration reform. The nation experienced a divisive debate of programs for legalization of undocumented immigrants, guest worker programs, and a myriad of enforcement measures.[8] In the end, Congress grappled with an immigration reform bill — known as "comprehensive immigration reform" — that included enforcement measures, a guest worker program[9] and a form of legalization for undocumented workers. The granting of "amnesty" to undocumented immigrants became a charged political word[10] and contributed to a political backlash against the reform proposal.

Ultimately, the controversy ended with Congress failing to enact any immigration reform proposal but agreeing only to authorize extension of a fence along the United States's southern border with Mexico.[11] Congress did so even though there is no evidence that this — or any other border enforcement only measure — will decrease the flow of undocumented immigrants to the United States.[12]

Whatever the causes, serious discussions of immigration reform failed in the second term of George W. Bush's presidency. The future of U.S. immigration law reform is far from certain. The nation most likely will see in the near future reform

---

[7] See BILL ONG HING, DEPORTING OUR SOULS: VALUES, MORALITY, AND IMMIGRATION POLICY 140–63 (2006); Jennifer M. Chacón, *Unsecured Borders: Immigration Restrictions, Crime Control and National Sovereignty*, 39 CONN. L. REV. 1827 (2007); Kevin R. Johnson & Bernard Trujillo, *Immigration Reform, National Security After September 11, and the Future of North American Integration*, 91 MINN. L. REV. 1369 (2007); *see also* Donald Kerwin & Margaret D. Stock, *The Role of Immigration in a Coordinated National Security Policy*, 21 GEO. IMMIGR. L.J. 383 (2007) (analyzing how immigration law can serve national security ends).

[8] *See supra* note 3 (citing authorities). Many commissions, groups, and other entities issued reports and recommendations on immigration reform. *See, e.g.*, REPORT OF THE INDEPENDENT TASK FORCE ON IMMIGRATION AND AMERICA'S FUTURE IMMIGRATION AND AMERICA'S FUTURE: A NEW CHAPTER IMMIGRATION POLICY INSTITUTE (2006).

[9] For critical analysis of guest worker programs, *see* Cristina M. Rodriguez, *Guest Workers and Integration: Toward a Theory of What Immigrants and Americans Owe One Another*, 2007 U. CHI. LEGAL F. 219; Karla M. Campbell, *Guest Worker Programs and the Convergence of U.S. Immigration and Development Policies: A Two-Factor Economic Model*, 21 GEO. IMMIGR. L.J. 663 (2007); Andrew J. Elmore, *Egalitarianism and Exclusion: U.S. Guest Worker Programs and a Non-Subordination Approach to the Labor-Based Admission of Nonprofessional Foreign Nationals*, 21 GEO. IMMIGR. L.J. 521 (2007); Merav Lichtenstein, Note, *An Examination of Guest Worker Immigration Reform Policies in the United States*, 5 CARDOZO PUB. L. POL'Y & ETHICS J. 689 (2007). For a partial defense of such programs, *see* Howard F. Chang, *Liberal Ideals and Political Feasibility: Guest-Worker Programs as Second-Best Policies*, 27 N.C. J. INT'L L. & COM. REG. 465 (2002).

[10] For a defense of amnesty, *see* Bill Ong Hing, *The Case for Amnesty*, 3 STAN. J. C.R. & C.L. 233 (2007); *see also* Bryn Siegel, Note, *The Political Discourse of Amnesty in Immigration Policy*, 41 AKRON L. REV. 291 (2008); Monica Gomez, Note, *Immigration by Adverse Possession: Common Law Amnesty for Long-Residing Illegal Immigrants in the United States*, 22 GEO. IMMIGR. L.J. 105 (2007). The term "amnesty" now alone generates political opposition in the United States. Spain, which faced similar issues in addressing a large undocumented population, referred to the regularization of their immigration status as a "normalization." *See* Maria Pabón López, *Immigration Law Spanish Style: A Study of Spain's Normalización of Undocumented Workers*, 21 GEO. IMMIGR. L.J. 571 (2007).

[11] *See* Secure Fence Act of 2006, Pub. L. No. 109-367, 120 Stat. 2638 (2006).

[12] *See* JOHNSON, *supra* note 1, at 114–15.

proposals that include a guest worker program, legalization of undocumented immigrants, and increased enforcement measures, similar to those seen in the most recent comprehensive immigration reform proposal. However, there have been some immigration legislation surprises in the past, with the Immigration Act of 1990 a striking example. *See* Chapter 2.

A full range of possible immigration reform measures runs the gamut. Immigration reform could be incremental, with "comprehensive" immigration reform of some sort.[13] Such reform might be more sensitive to human rights concerns than current U.S. immigration laws.[14] Or it might include greater involvement of state and local governments, which, as we saw in Chapter 4, is controversial.[15]

There are related possibilities for change in the treatment of immigrants in the United States. Issuing driver's licenses to undocumented immigrants, which has proven to be hotly contested[16] and better tracking systems of immigrants and nonimmigrants,[17] which had proven to be difficult to implement, are just a few of the other measures that have been proposed to improve our immigration laws.

In debate over immigration reform, policy-makers in seeking to limit undocumented immigration frequently neglect strategies that might improve the integration of legal, as well as undocumented, immigrants into U.S. society. This is so even though a frequent complaint about immigrants is their so-called "failure to assimilate." *See* Chapters 1 and 2. Facilitating naturalization of immigrants is one way to smooth formal legal integration of immigrants, but the U.S. government has been inconsistent with naturalization law (with current lengthy backlogs), as well as other programs, such as access to public benefits, which might facilitate immigrant integration.[18] See Chapter 15 for discussion of naturalization. Some

---

[13] *See, e.g.*, Symposium, *Immigration Reform and Policy in the Current Politically Polarized Climate*, 16 TEMP. POL. & CIV. RTS. L. REV. 309 (2007); Muzaffar Chishti, *A Redesigned Immigration Selection System*, 41 CORNELL INTL L.J. 115 (2008); Asa Hutchinson, *Keynote Address: Holes in the Fence: Immigration Reform and Border Security in the United States Symposium*, 59 ADMIN. L. REV. 533, 537–38 (2007); Katherine L. Vaughns, *Restoring the Rule of Law: Reflections on Fixing the Immigration System and Exploring Failed Policy Choices*, 5 U. MD. L.J. RACE, REL., GENDER & CLASS 151 (2005). For a form of comprehensive reforms including interior enforcement, a guest worker program, legalization, and foreign development, based on Catholic social thought, *see* Michael A. Scaperlanda, *Reflections on Immigration Reform, the Workplace and the Family*, 4 U. ST. THOMAS L.J. 508, 523–28 (2007).

[14] *See* Lesley Wexler, *Human Rights Impact Statements: An Immigration Case Study*, 22 GEO. IMMIGR. L.J. 285 (2008); Elazabeth M. Bruch, *Open or Closed: Balancing Border Policy with Human Rights*, 96 KY. L.J. 197 (2007/08).

[15] *See* Cristina M. Rodriguez, *The Significance of the Local in Immigration Regulation*, 106 MICH. L. REV. 567 (2008).

[16] *See* Kevin R. Johnson, *Driver's Licenses and Undocumented Immigrants: The Future of Civil Rights Law?*, 5 NEV. L.J. 213 (2004); María Pabón Lopez, *More Than A License to Drive: State Restrictions on the Use of Driver's Licenses by Noncitizens*, 29 S. ILL. U. L.J. 91 (2004/05); *see also* Sylvia R. Lazos Vargas, *Missouri, the "War on Terrorism," and Immigrants: Legal Challenges Post 9/11*, 67 MO. L. REV. 775, 798–807 (2002) (analyzing controversy in Missouri over driver's license eligibility for undocumented immigrants).

[17] *See infra* note 52 (citing authorities).

[18] *See* Judith Bernstein-Baker, *Citizenship in a Restrictionist Era: The Mixed Messages of Federal*

states, such as Illinois, North Carolina, and Iowa, have embraced policies attempting to facilitate integration of immigrants.[19] A number of states have passed laws allowing undocumented high school graduates to pay in-state fees at public universities.[20] Additional English as a Second Language classes, which are chronically over-enrolled[21] and increased bilingual education, which has been cut back in recent years,[22] also would facilitate English language acquisition.

At bottom, the United States needs immigration laws that are enforceable and are perceived as legitimate and respected. Policies that facilitate integration of immigrants into U.S. society are a possibility that unfortunately also warrant consideration.[23]

One informed observer has stated that

> [a] thoughtful and responsible reform package must accomplish a few things. First, it must address the dilemma of the existing undocumented immigrant population in our country. Second, it must regulate future flows of immigrants consistent with our labor market needs and economic interests in an increasingly inter-dependent world. Third, it must advance the protection of both U.S. and foreign workers. Finally, it must reflect the deeply engrained American value of fairness.[24]

These are important guideposts to consider in evaluating changes to the U.S. immigration laws. This Chapter attempts to sketch out some possible arguments for true — and lasting — immigration reform. It builds on some of the issues identified in Chapter 1 as fueling global migration. As one of the co-authors of this book has argued, economic, moral, and policy arguments militate in favor of more liberal admissions of immigrants to the United States.[25] Another far-reaching possibility analyzed later in this Chapter is the economic integration of the United States,

---

Policies, 16 TEMP. POL. & CIV. RTS. L. REV. 367, 381–84 (2007).

[19] *See* Rodriguez, *supra* note 15, at 582–90.

[20] *See* Rodriguez, *supra* note 15, at 605–09; Michael A. Olivas, *IIRIRA, the DREAM Act, and Undocumented College Student Residency*, 30 J.C. & U.L. 435 (2005).

[21] *See* James Thomas Tucker, *The ESL Logjam: Waiting Times for ESL classes and the Impact on English Learners; English as a Second Language*, NATIONAL CIVIC REV., March 22, 2007, vol. 96, No. 1. Increasingly, the private sector has promoted immigrant assimilation with employers, among other policies, promoting English language acquisition. *See* Pamela Constable & N.C. Aizenman, *Companies Take Lead in Assimilation Efforts*, WASH. POST, Aug. 9, 2008, at B1. *See generally* AMERICAS SOCIETY AND COUNCIL OF THE AMERICAS, U.S. BUSINESS AND HISPANIC INTEGRATION: EXPANDING THE ECONOMIC CONTRIBUTIONS OF IMMIGRANTS (2008).

[22] *See* Kevin Johnson & George Martinez, *Discrimination by Proxy: The Case of Proposition 227 and the Ban on Bilingual Education*, 33 U.C. DAVIS L. REV. 1227 (2000) (analyzing elimination of bilingual education in California).

[23] *See, e.g.*, SECURING THE FUTURE: U.S. IMMIGRANT INTEGRATION POLICY: A READER (Migration Policy Institute, Michael Fix ed., 2007). State and local governments can play important roles in the integration of immigrants into U.S. society. *See* Rodriguez, *supra* note 15, at 581–609.

[24] Chishti, *supra* note 13, at 116.

[25] Some of these arguments are fleshed out in greater detail in JOHNSON, *supra* note 1. For a review of the book, *see* Karen E. Bravo & Maria Pabón López, *Crisis Meets Reality: A Bold Proposal for Immigration Reform*, 61 SMU L. REV. 191 (2008).

Canada, and Mexico modeled after the successful European Union.[26]

A. THE STATUS QUO

To appropriately evaluate potential immigration reforms, one must consider the current political and legal terrain of modern U.S. immigration law and policy.

1. The "War on Terror"

In the twenty-first century, immigration has taken on the specter of terrorism. Commentators and pundits have repeated like a mantra that "September 11th changed everything." One cannot deny that that fateful day, with the tragic loss of human life, unquestionably transformed U.S. society. Outside the United States, in addition to wars in Afghanistan and Iraq, the U.S. government engaged in detentions and, at times, the abuse of prisoners.[27] The President declared that persons that he designated as "enemy combatants" had precious few rights under the law.[28] In addition, in the name of national security, the U.S. government arguably compromised the privacy rights of citizens and immigrants.[29]

---

[26] Considerable attention has been paid to the growing economic integration of North America. *See, e.g.*, Emily Gilbert, *The Inevitability of Integration? Neoliberal Discourse and the Proposals for a New North American Economic Space After September 11*, ANNALS OF THE ASSOCIATION OF AMERICAN GEOGRAPHERS, vol. 95, at 202 (2005); Axel Huelsemeyer, *Toward Deeper North American Integration: A Customs Union?*, CANADIAN-AMERICAN PUB. POL'Y, Oct. 2004, at 2; THE FUTURE OF NORTH AMERICAN INTEGRATION: BEYOND NAFTA (Peter Hakim & Robert E. Litan eds., 2002); *see also* ERIC HELLEINER, TOWARDS NORTH AMERICAN MONETARY UNION? (2006); Emily Gilbert, *Money, Citizenship, Territoriality and the Proposals for a North American Monetary Union*, POL. GEOGRAPHY, vol. 26, at 141 (2006). Of course, opposition, including claims that integration surrenders national sovereignty, to any such a union would be strong. *See, e.g.*, Jonah Goldberg, *Villains and the Immigration Debate*, USA TODAY, June 5, 2007 at 11A:

> Did you hear the real reason President Bush is so gung-ho to cram his immigration "amnesty" bill through Congress? Its first step toward creating the North American Union, where the United States, Canada and Mexico become one giant country and the dollar is replaced by the Amero. Just ask Lou Dobbs and Pat Buchanan about it.

See generally JEROME R. CORSI, THE LATE GREAT USA: THE COMING MERGER WITH MEXICO AND CANADA, (2007); COLIN D. STANDISH & RUSSELL R. STANDISH, THE EUROPEAN UNION, THE NORTH AMERICAN UNION, THE PAPACY, & GLOBALISM (2007).

[27] *See, e.g.*, Symposium, *Torture and the War on Terror*, 37 CASE W. RES. J. INT'L L. 145 (2006); Diane Marie Amann, *Abu Ghraib*, 153 U. PA. L. REV. 2085 (2005); Diane Marie Amann, *Guantánamo*, 42 COLUM. J. TRANSNAT'L L. 263 (2004); Sanford Levinson, *In Quest of a "Common Conscience": Reflections on the Current Debate About Torture*, 1 J. NAT'L SEC. L. & POL'Y 231 (2005); Marcy Strauss, *The Lessons of Abu Ghraib*, 66 OHIO ST. L.J. 1269 (2005).

[28] *See, e.g.*, Hamdan v. Rumsfeld, 548 U.S. 557 (2006) (holding that military tribunals created by Bush administration violated the law); Hamdi v. Rumsfeld, 542 U.S. 507 (2004) (ruling that U.S. citizen held as "enemy combatant" had right to judicial determination of the propriety of that classification); *see also* Boumediene v. Bush, 128 S. Ct. 2229 (2008) (holding that Guantanamo detainee had right to challenge his designation as "enemy combatants" by habeas corpus); Rumsfeld v. Padilla, 542 U.S. 426 (2004) (finding that court in which action was filed lacked jurisdiction over U.S. citizen defendant to entertain challenge to indefinite detention of U.S. citizen classified as "enemy combatant").

[29] *See, e.g.*, Uniting and Strengthening America by Providing Appropriate Tools Required to Intercept and Obstruct Terrorism Act (USA PATRIOT Act), Pub. L. No. 107-56, 115 Stat 272 (2001). For criticism of the USA PATRIOT Act, *see*, for example, David Cole, *Enemy Aliens*, 54 STAN. L. REV 953,

When it comes to immigration law and policy, the events of September 11, 2001 had especially dramatic impacts. Fears of terrorism led to tighter immigration restrictions in many areas, from stricter monitoring of foreign scholars and students seeking to enter the United States on nonimmigrant (temporary) visa[30] to new immigration requirements and procedures. Many measures targeted Arab and Muslim noncitizens, including registration requirements, mass detentions, and targeted deportation operations.[31] Later, all noncitizens felt the impacts of the various security measures.[32]

Incendiary arguments continue to be made about the need to close the borders to immigrants in the fight against terrorism.[33] Even though not one of the September 11 terrorists entered without inspection (much less from Mexico), it has been claimed that the entry of undocumented immigrants from Mexico into the United States is a substantial security risk.[34] As Professor Enid Trucios-Haynes aptly observed,

---

966–74 (2002); Natsu Taylor Saito, *Whose Liberty? Whose Security? The USA PATRIOT Act in the Context of COINTELPRO and the Unlawful Repression of Political Dissent*, 81 OR. L. REV. 1051, 1111–28 (2002). Due to political pressures based on civil liberties concerns, Congress amended the law to reduce certain governmental powers before its reauthorization. *See* USA PATRIOT Improvement and Reauthorization Act, Pub. L. No. 109-177, 120 Stat. 192 (2006).

[30] *See* Michael A. Olivas, *The War on Terrorism Touches the Ivory Tower — Colleges and Universities After September 11: An Introduction*, 30 J. C. & U. L. 233 (2004); Victor C. Romero, *Noncitizen Students and Immigration Policy Post-9/11*, 17 GEO. IMMIGR. L.J. 357 (2003); Eugene McCormack, *Total Graduate Enrollments Rise; Number of Foreign Students Drops*, CHRON. HIGHER ED., Nov. 11, 2005, at 38; *see also* CONGRESSIONAL RESEARCH SERVICE, FOREIGN STUDENTS IN THE UNITED STATES: POLICIES AND LEGISLATION (2006) (outlining various legal issues facing foreign students seeking admission into the United States).

[31] For a sampling of criticism of the various measures, *see* Raquel Aldana-Pindell, *The 9/11 "National Security" Cases: Three Principles Guiding Judges' Decision-Making*, 81 OR. L. REV. 985 (2002); Sameer M. Ashar, *Immigration Enforcement and Subordination: The Consequences of Racial Profiling After September 11*, 34 CONN. L. REV. 1185 (2002); Cole, *supra* note 24; Bill Ong Hing, *Vigilante Racism: The De-Americanization of Immigrant America*, 7 MICH. J. RACE & L. 441 (2002); Thomas W. Joo, *Presumed Disloyal: Executive Power, Judicial Deference, and the Construction of Race Before and After September 11*, 34 COLUM. HUM. RTS. L. REV. 1 (2002); Victor C. Romero, *Decoupling "Terrorist" From "Immigrant": An Enhanced Role for the Federal Courts Post 9/11*, 7 J. GENDER, RACE, & JUST. 201 (2003); Leti Volpp, *The Citizen and the Terrorist*, 49 UCLA L. REV. 1575 (2002). A plethora of reports have documented the civil and human rights abuses in the "war on terror." *See, e.g.*, MIGRATION POLICY INSTITUTE, AMERICA'S CHALLENGE: DOMESTIC SECURITY, CIVIL LIBERTIES, AND NATIONAL UNITY AFTER SEPTEMBER 11 (2003); U.S. DEP'T OF JUSTICE, SUPPLEMENTAL REPORT ON SEPTEMBER 11 DETAINEES: A REVIEW OF THE TREATMENT OF ALIENS HELD ON IMMIGRATION CHARGES IN CONNECTION WITH THE INVESTIGATION OF THE SEPTEMBER 11 ATTACKS (2003); U.S. OFFICE OF THE INSPECTOR GENERAL, THE SEPTEMBER 11 DETAINEES: A REVIEW OF THE TREATMENT OF ALIENS HELD ON IMMIGRATION CHARGES IN CONNECTION WITH THE INVESTIGATION OF THE SEPTEMBER 11 ATTACKS (2003); U.S. OFFICE OF THE INSPECTOR GENERAL, REPORT TO CONGRESS ON IMPLEMENTATION OF SECTION 1001 OF THE USA PATRIOT ACT (2003).

[32] *See* Kevin R. Johnson, *September 11 and Mexican Immigrants: Collateral Damage Comes Home*, 52 DEPAUL L. REV. 849, 866–67 (2003).

[33] *See, e.g.*, PATRICK J. BUCHANAN, STATE OF EMERGENCY: THE THIRD WORLD INVASION AND CONQUEST OF AMERICA (2006); Michelle Malkin, *Invasion: How America Still Welcomes Terrorists, Criminals, and Other Foreign Menaces To Our Shores* (2002); *see also* Jan C. Ting, *Unobjectionable but Insufficient — Federal Initiatives in Response to the September 11 Terrorist Attacks*, 34 CONN. L. REV. 1145 (2002) (questioning, in a more balanced fashion, whether the United States had done enough in the "war on terrorism").

[34] *See, e.g.*, Kris W. Kobach, *The Quintessential Force Multiplier: The Inherent Authority of Local*

[i]mmigration dominates policy discussions in the post-September 11, 2001 world in a manner that has distorted traditional issues and concerns relating to noncitizens. To some, the perception or reality of porous U.S. borders requires the most strenuous methods of border enforcement. *In the eyes of many, immigration reform proposals since 2001 have focused exclusively on enforcement without sufficient acknowledgment of the human consequences on the noncitizens, both authorized and unauthorized, throughout our community.*[35]

Fear over September 11 has served as a convenient excuse for more punitive immigration law and enforcement proposals and pursuit of a restrictionist immigration agenda. Proposals for increased border enforcement along the U.S. southern border with Mexico have been claimed to be necessary to improve national security. However, there is little evidence suggesting that there is a realistic threat of terror from Mexico. One study found that "[n]ot one terrorist has entered the United States from Mexico.[36] There has not been nearly as much of a focus on the U.S. border with Canada despite the fact that a bona fide terrorist, the "Millennium bomber," was apprehended seeking to cross the U.S. border from the North.[37]

2.   Undocumented Immigration

Despite the current myopic focus on terrorism, unrealistic immigration laws in place for decades have forced millions of migrants to evade the law to enter or remain in the United States and, once here, live in the shadows of American social life. As President George W. Bush correctly observed in calling for immigration reform in 2006, "*illegal immigrants live in the shadows of our society. . . . [T]he vast majority . . . are decent people who work hard, support their families, practice their faith, and lead responsible lives.* They are part of American life, but they are beyond the reach and protection of American law."[38]

It is critical to understand that, as outlined in Chapter 1, many unskilled and medium-skilled workers have no line to wait in to immigrate legally to the United States. *See also* Chapter 7. This encourages migration in violation of the law. The

---

Police to Make Immigration Arrests, 69 ALB. L. REV. 179, 179 (2005). In a comment consistent with the tenor of the current debate, Senator John Cornyn emphasized that the debate over immigration reform "is . . . and I would say first and foremost about our Nation's security. *In a post-9/11 world, border security is national security.*" 152 CONG. REC. S2551 (Mar. 30, 2006) (Cornyn, Sen.) (emphasis added).

[35] Enid Trucios-Haynes, *Civil Rights, Latinos, and Immigration: Cybercascades and Other Distortions in the Immigration Reform Debate*, 44 BRANDEIS L.J. 637, 638 (2006) (emphasis added).

[36] Peter Beinart, *The Wrong Place to Stop Terrorists*, WASH. POST, May 4, 2006, at A25 (discussing study making this finding); *see* ROBERT S. LEIKEN, THE QUANTITATIVE ANALYSIS OF TERRORISM AND IMMIGRATION: AN INITIAL EXPLORATION 2 (2006) ("Despite media alarms about terrorists concealed in the illegal traffic crossing the Mexican border, not a single [person charged or convicted of terrorist acts, or killed in such acts] entered from Mexico.") (footnote omitted).

[37] *See* Sam Howe Verhovek, *2nd Man Sought for Questioning in Bomb Plot*, N.Y. TIMES, Dec. 19, 1999, at § 1, p. 42; Scott Sunde & Elaine Porterfield, *Wider Bomb Plot Possible*, SEATTLE POST-INTELLIGENCER, Dec. 18, 1999, at A1.

[38] ADDRESS TO THE NATION ON IMMIGRATION REFORM, PRESIDENTIAL PAPERS OF THE PRESIDENTS (May 22, 2006) (emphasis added).

flow of undocumented immigrants is directly related to legal avenues available to come to the United States.

The conundrum facing immigration reform today is that more liberal admissions to avoid the incentive for undocumented immigrants often is characterized as sacrificing national security. However, an open society need not be a country whose national security is more at risk than one with nominally closed borders. Commentators have proposed more flexible immigration admission systems that would better ensure national security than the current regime.[39] In modern times, to improve the security of the nation, as well as to pursue other legitimate goals, the United States needs to dramatically revamp its immigration admissions system. A scheme that better matches the political, social, and economic factors contributing to the demand for immigration — while minimizing the incentive for undocumented immigration and thus limiting the creation and maintenance of a shadow population of millions of people — would better ensure the security of the nation.[40]

A carefully-crafted, and more liberal, admissions scheme also could allow for a more secure and safer United States. The current system of tracking lawful immigrants and temporary visitors, which is woefully inadequate, needs to be vastly improved. The nation requires an immigration system that ensures that the United States government has the basic information, such as name and address, about as many immigrants in the United States as is feasible. Such information is necessary for effective law — criminal as well as immigration — enforcement that will allow the nation to better protect national security and public safety.[41]

Somewhere in the neighborhood of 12 million undocumented immigrants currently live in the United States.[42] Rather than engaging in futile efforts to close the border, the U.S. government needs to address the modern political, economic, and social realities currently fueling undocumented immigration to the country and

---

[39] *See, e.g.*, Bill Ong Hing, *Misusing Immigration Policies in the Name of Homeland Security*, 6 NEW CENTENNIAL REV. 195, 207–16 (2006) (suggesting, among other things, that national security may have improved by adoption of better intelligence strategies and the legalization of undocumented immigrants in the United States); Jan Ting, *Immigration Law Reform After 9/11: What Has Been and What Still Needs to Be Done*, 17 TEMPLE INT'L & COMP. L.J. 503, 512–15 (2003) (contending that current immigration formulas for admission are too rigid in light of the developments since September 11 and that the U.S. government needs greater flexibility to deal with changing social, political, and economics circumstances).

[40] *See* JOHNSON, *supra* note 1, at 189; Jeffrey Manns, *Private Monitoring of Gatekeepers: The Case of Immigration Enforcement*, 2006 U. ILL. L. REV. 887, 930–72.

[41] *See* Stephen H. Legomsky, *The New Path of Immigration Law: Asymmetric Incorporation of Criminal Justice Norms*, 64 WASH. & LEE L. REV. 469 (2007); Kevin R. Johnson, *Protecting National Security Through More Liberal Admission of Immigrants*, 2007 U. CHI. LEGAL F. 157, 176–186 (2007).

[42] JEFFREY S. PASSEL, THE SIZE AND CHARACTERISTICS OF THE UNAUTHORIZED MIGRANT POPULATION IN THE U.S. (Pew Hispanic Center 2006), *available at* http://pewhispanic.org/files/reports/61.pdf, estimates that, as of March 2006, the undocumented immigrant population in the United States amounted to between 11.5 and 12 million. The U.S. government, whose estimates generally have been lower than those of non-governmental groups, estimated that, in January 2005, 10.5 million undocumented immigrants lived in the United States compared to 8.5 million in January 2000. *See* U.S. DEP'T OF HOMELAND SECURITY, ESTIMATES OF THE UNAUTHORIZED POPULATION RESIDING IN THE UNITED STATES: JANUARY 2005, at 214 (Aug. 2006).

contributing to the millions of people who live and work in our communities in contravention of the U.S. immigration laws. Generations of migrants from Mexico have made their way to the United States.[43] Absent dramatic economic and social changes (and the recent economic downturn appears to have dampened immigration to the United States), immigrants will continue to come lawfully and unlawfully to the United States for jobs and to reunite with family members. In modern times, migrants literally risk life and limb to come to this land of freedom and opportunity.[44]

Recent years have seen increasingly harsh efforts in the United States to close the borders, almost exclusively focused on the southern border with Mexico. Nevertheless, a large, and until recently, undocumented population lives in the United States. Over the last decade or so, *increased* border enforcement efforts, to the surprise of many, have been accompanied by an *increase* in the size of the undocumented population. Stricter borders have discouraged return migration by migrants to their homelands so that undocumented immigrants are more likely to come and stay in the United States rather than come and go. One study concluded that "[t]here is *no* evidence that the border enforcement build-up . . . has substantially reduced unauthorized border crossings" and that "[d]espite large increases in spending and Border Patrol resources . . . , the number of unauthorized immigrants increased to levels higher than those" before 1986.[45] The bottom line is that the undocumented population has doubled since the mid-1990s.[46]

The fact that there are so many undocumented immigrants in the United States confirms what most Americans well know — that the immigration laws are routinely violated and, at least as currently configured, are effectively unenforceable. Undocumented workers know that if they are able to make the

---

[43] *See* Gerald P. Lopez, *Undocumented Mexican Migration: In Search of a Just Immigration Law and Policy*, 28 UCLA L. Rev. 615, 641–72 (1981); Joanne D. Spotts, *U.S. Immigration Policy on the Southwest Border from Reagan Through Clinton, 1981–2001*, 16 Geo. Immigr L.J. 601 (2002).

[44] For a sampling of literature analyzing the deadly impacts of increased border enforcement measures, *see* Timothy J. Dunn, The Militarization of the U.S.-Mexican Border, 1978–1992: Low Intensity Conflict Doctrine Comes Home (University of Texas 1996); Karl Eschbach, Jacqueline Hagan, & Nestor Rodriguez, Causes and Trends in Migrant Deaths Along the U.S./Mexico Border, 1985–1998 (2001); Joseph Nevins, Operation Gatekeeper (2002); Wayne A. Cornelius, *Death at the Border: Efficacy and Unintended Consequences of US Immigration Control Policy*, 27 Population & Dev. Rev. 661 (2001); Karl Eschbach et al., *Death at the Border*, 33 Int'l Migration Rev. 430 (1999); Bill Ong Hing, *The Dark Side of Operation Gatekeeper*, 7 UC Davis J. Int'l L. & Pol'y 121, 123 (2001); Jorge A. Vargas, *U.S. Border Patrol Abuses, Undocumented Mexican Workers, and International Human Rights*, 2 San Diego Int'l L.J. 1 (2001). Much popular literature focuses on the travails of immigrants seeking to unlawfully enter the United States from Mexico. *See, e.g.*, Sonia Nazario, Enrique's Journey (2006); Ken Ellingwood, Hard Line: Life and Death on the U.S.-Mexico Border (2004); Luis Alberto Urrea, The Devil's Highway: A True Story (2004).

[45] Belinda I. Reyes et al., Holding the Line? The Effect of the Recent Border Build-Up on Unauthorized Immigration, at viii, xii (2002) (emphasis added).

[46] *See* Jeffrey S. Passel, Estimates of the Size and Characteristics of the Undocumented Population (Pew Hispanic Center Mar. 2005), *available at* http://pewhispanic.org/reports/report.php?reportIP=44; Department of Homeland Security, *Illegal Alien Resident Population* (undated), *available at* http://www.dhs.gov/xlibrary/assets/statistics/illegal.pdf.

often-arduous journey to the United States, they can obtain work[47] and that the job will pay more than most of them would have been able to earn in their native countries. Employers willingly hire undocumented workers and cherish this relatively inexpensive supply of labor. A short drive to a day laborer pick up point in many American cities demonstrates both undocumented immigrants' ready ability to obtain work and employers' enthusiasm in hiring them.[48]

Given that the efforts to seal the borders have proven to be little more than a futile gesture, it makes no sense from an immigration or security standpoint to simply continue to throw resources at fortifying the borders, increasing border enforcement, and engaging in the futile attempt to keep all undocumented immigrants out of the country. As it turns out, incremental enforcement measures have had a limited impact on undocumented immigration from Mexico.[49]

Put simply, the United States needs a more realistic immigration scheme that does not result in massive violations of the law and the creation and maintenance of a population of millions of people who are unknown and unprotected by law. The current immigration laws in many respects resemble the failed Prohibition-era anti-alcohol laws.[50] In both instances, enforcement of the law failed dramatically and, to make matters worse, resulted in widespread negative collateral consequences, including widespread violation of the law, criminal activity, and diminished legitimacy of the law.

Ultimately, U.S. border enforcement has proven to be the equivalent of tilting at windmills.[51] The U.S. government simply has been unable to keep migrants — who are so determined that they are willing to risk their lives — from unlawfully entering the country. In addition, the current computer systems in place are woefully incomplete and poorly track legal immigrants who have entered and reside in the United States.[52] Thus, even for noncitizens that enter through legal

---

[47] For analysis of the failure of employer sanctions to deter the employment of undocumented immigrants, see Michael J. Wishnie, *Prohibiting the Employment of Unauthorized Immigrants: The Experiment Fails*, 2007 U. Chi. Legal F. 193; Cecelia M. Espenoza, *The Illusory Provisions of Sanctions: The Immigration Reform and Control Act of 1986*, 8 Geo. Immigr. L.J. 343 (1994).

[48] For studies of day laborers, see Abel Valenzuela, Jr., et al., On the Corner: Day Labor in the United States (2006); Abel Valenzuela, Jr. & Edwin Melendez, Day Labor in New York: Findings From the NYDL Survey (2003).

[49] See Belinda I. Reyes, *U.S. Immigration Policy and Unauthorized Mexican Immigration*, 2007 U. Chi. Legal F. 131.

[50] See Kevin R. Johnson, *Open Borders?*, 51 UCLA L. Rev. 193, 245–52 (2003).

[51] See Peter Andreas, Border Games: Policing the U.S.-Mexico Divide (2001) (analyzing the difficulties of border enforcement reducing undocumented immigration while offering concrete benefits to politicians in pursuing border enforcement strategies).

[52] See Statement by Margaret D. Stock Before U.S. House Committee on International Relations, Subcommittee on Oversight and Investigations, Cong. Q. Cong. Testimony (May 11, 2006) (listing U.S. General Accountability Office studies noting various deficiencies in computerized immigrant tracking systems used by the Department of Homeland Security); *Think All Illegal Immigrants Are Sneaking In? Think Again: Years After 9/11, Government Still Can't Track All Who Overstay Visas*, USA Today, May 2, 2006, at 12A (discussing flaws in current tracking system); Nicole Gaouette, *U.S. Installs Visitor Tracking Stations*, L.A. Times, Dec. 31, 2005, at A17 (to the same effect).

channels, the U.S. government lacks reliable systems and data about who is here, who is not, when they entered, and when they left.

Moreover, the U.S. government has made few efforts to remove noncitizens that lawfully entered the country on temporary visas, such as students and tourists, but overstayed their terms. Visa overstays likely constitute somewhere between 25 and 40 percent of the undocumented population.[53] Early on the Bush administration made workplace enforcement one of its lowest priorities.[54] Increased monitoring after September 11 does not appear to have had much of an impact. Increasing — and controversial — raids and more interior enforcement in recent years also have had little overall impact on the undocumented population in the United States.[55]

The political resistance to interior enforcement from employers, as well as immigrant rights advocates, makes such enforcement politically difficult.[56] However, increased border enforcement without any effort to regulate the availability of jobs to undocumented immigrants, will ultimately do little to change the status quo. Jobs and superior economic opportunity in the United States are the primary magnets bringing immigrants to this country. Their continued availability will continue to fuel migration to this country.

3. Collateral Impacts — Including Meaningful Immigration Reform — of the "War on Terror"

While the war on terror has dominated the national and international consciousness, constructive immigration reform efforts have fallen by the wayside. Serious discussions of a bilateral agreement regularizing migration between the United States and Mexico, such as will be discussed later in this Chapter, ended

---

[53] *See* PASSEL, *supra* note 42 at 16.

[54] In 1999, 240 full time employees in the entire United States were devoted to workplace enforcement of the immigration laws; by fiscal year 2003, the number had dropped precipitously to 90. *See* U.S. GEN. ACCOUNTABILITY OFFICE, IMMIGRATION ENFORCEMENT: PRELIMINARY OBSERVATIONS ON EMPLOYMENT VERIFICATION AND WORKSITE ENFORCEMENT EFFORTS 3 (2005). The number of employers prosecuted for employing undocumented immigrants dropped from 182 in 1999 to 4 in 2002; in 1999, the U.S. government imposed fines against 417 companies but only three in 2004. *See* Spencer S. Hsu & Kari Lydersen, *Illegal Hiring is Rarely Penalized; Politics, 9/11 Cited in Lax Enforcement*, WASH. POST, June 19, 2006, at A1.

[55] *See* Raquel Aldana, *Of Katz and "Aliens": Privacy Expectations and the Immigration Raids*, 41 U.C. DAVIS L. REV. 1081, 1092–96 (2008) (discussing raids of meatpacking plants in December 2006); Sandra Guerra Thompson, *Immigration Law and Long-Term Residents: A Missing Chapter in American Criminal Law*, 5 OHIO ST. J. CRIM. L. 645, 655 (2008) (mentioning raids); Anil Kalhan, *The Fourth Amendment and Privacy Implications of Interior Immigration Enforcement*, 41 U.C. DAVIS L. REV. 1137 (2008) (analyzing legal impacts of raids and other forms of interior immigration enforcement); Shoba Sivaprasad Wadhia, *Under Arrest: Immigrants' Rights and the Rule of Law*, 38 U. MEM. L. REV. 853, 862–88 (2008) (same); David B. Thronson, *Immigration Raids and the Destabilization of Immigrant Families*, 43 WAKE FOREST L. REV. 391 (2008) (identifying negative impacts on families of immigration raids); *see also* Huyen Pham, *The Private Enforcement of the Immigration Laws*, 96 GEO. L.J. 777 (2008) (studying various modes of private enforcement of the immigration laws).

[56] *See* Manns, *supra* note 40, at 935–44; Lori Nessel, *Undocumented Immigrants in the Workplace: The Fallacy of Labor Protection and the Need for Reform*, 36 HARV C.R.-C.L. L. REV. 345, 359–61 (2001); Michael J. Wishnie, *Emerging Issues for Undocumented Workers*, 6 U. PA. J. LAB. & EMP. L. 497, 516–21 (2004).

abruptly on September 11.[57] Efforts to remove the harshest provisions of 1996 immigration reform laws, see Chapter 2, — thought by some observers at the time to be as draconian as any in U.S. history[58] — also evaporated on that day; the political climate made liberalization of the immigration laws next to impossible, at least for the short run.[59] Over the last few years, President Bush's efforts to recommence discussion of immigration reform, and his advocacy of a guest worker program, faced vociferous resistance from the restrictionist wing of the Republican Party.[60] In the end, the Mexican government could not move the U.S. government forward in jointly addressing migration between the two nations.[61]

B.   THE PROVERBIAL "FLOODGATES"

The intuitive reaction to any suggestion that the United States liberalize immigration admissions is that we cannot open the "floodgates" to people from all over the world.[62] The nation, so the argument goes, would be overwhelmed by hordes of foreigners. Fears have been exacerbated by the public security concerns given the terrorist acts of September 11 discussed earlier in this Chapter. If we opened the door an inch more, the nation, it is feared, would be overrun and terrorists would come with the masses.

The floodgates concerns are greatly overstated. Most people the world over would prefer to stay put in their native lands.[63] Most Mexicans, for example, prefer to — and in fact do — stay in Mexico. The fears of mass migration in the expanding European Union, which generally permits labor migration between member

---

[57] See Johnson, *supra* note 32, at 866–67.

[58] See, e.g., PETER H. SCHUCK, CITIZENS, STRANGERS, AND IN-BETWEENS 143 (1998) (characterizing the 1996 reforms as "the most radical reform of immigration law in decades — or perhaps ever").

[59] See Johnson, *supra* note 32, at 866–67.

[60] See Barbara Hines, *So Near Yet So Far Away: The Effect of September 11th on Mexican Immigrants in the United States*, 8 TEX. HISP. J. L. & POL'Y 37 (2002); Johnson, *supra* note 27, at 866–67.

[61] See Johnson, *supra* note 32, at 866–67.

[62] See JOHNSON, *supra* note 1, at 26–31.

[63] As one knowledgeable commentator observed:

> Most people have no inclination to leave their native soil, no matter how onerous conditions become. Would-be emigrants must fight off the ties of family, the comfort of familiar surroundings, the rootedness in one's culture, the security of being among "one's own," and the power of plain inertia. Conversely, being uprooted carries daunting prospects: adjusting to alien ways, learning a new language, the absence of kith and kin, the sheer uncertainty of it all.

ALAN DOWTY, CLOSED BORDERS: THE CONTEMPORARY ASSAULT ON FREEDOM OF MOVEMENT 223 (1987); see MICHAEL WALZER, SPHERES OF JUSTICE 38 (1983); Joseph H. Carens, *Aliens and Citizens: The Case for Open Borders*, 49 REV. POL. 251, 270 (1987). Similarly, Professor Rubén G. Rumbaut observes that

> [i]t never ceases to surprise me that, in a world of 6.5 billion people, 98 percent are "stayers," living in the country of their birth; that the remaining two percent, international migrants of a bewildering variety of origins, migration motives, and modes of adaptation to their new environments, are at heart ambitious, determined, and intrepid souls, which is what makes migration the "selective" process that it is; and that, all things considered, so little focused attention is paid to either of those two facts.

Migration Policy Institute, Migration Information Source, http://www.migrationinformation.org/ USfocus/print.cfm?ID=361, last visited on Aug. 17, 2008.

nations, have not come to pass.[64] The ease of travel between the states of the United States (and the territory of Puerto Rico), despite various economic disparities, have not led to a mass migration from poorer states, such as Mississippi and West Virginia, to more affluent states, such as New York and California. Exceptions to this rule periodically result from catastrophic events, such as Hurricane Katrina in New Orleans in 2005.

Even if they might encourage somewhat greater rates of migration, realistic immigration laws that are efficiently enforced might improve, not undermine, the security of the nation. Immigration laws that better fulfill the nation's labor needs would eliminate a powerful magnet to circumvent the law by employers. Serious reform of the immigration laws to liberalize immigration thus would improve compliance with the law. Increased compliance in turn would add to the legitimacy of the law, one of the perennial problems with the immigration laws today.

Moreover, border controls are much more focused on national security and public safety than those found in the current U.S. immigration laws, might well improve our security. Efforts could be made to bar hardened criminals and those reasonably suspected of terrorist activities from entering the United States while admitting other immigrants more liberally. Immigration authorities thus would focus on barring from entry into the country true threats to the national security and public safety.

Contrary to intuition, liberal admissions of immigrant workers that better fulfill the demand for labor in the United States[65] are entirely consistent with efforts to protect the nation from terrorism. More liberal migration with fewer time-consuming bureaucratic paperwork requirements would allow the U.S. government to pay full attention to, and focus its enforcement efforts on, the true dangers to public safety and national security.[66] Rather than routine checks on mundane matters such as income and assets, see Chapter 10, U.S. immigration authorities could focus on terrorists, dangerous criminals, drugs and other contraband, and public health risks. There no longer would be a need to engage in the endless search to come up with a — or any — reason to keep every noncitizen out of the United States. Enforcement efforts could move beyond the morass of complex visa requirements, exclusion grounds, per country caps, and the many technicalities of the Immigration and Nationality Act that have made its enforcement cumbersome as well as ineffective and unfair.[67]

---

[64] *See* World Bank EU 8, Quarterly Economic Report: Special Topic September 2006 — Labor Migration From the New EU Member States (2006).

[65] *See generally* Special Feature, *Working Features: Linking Debates About Insourcing and Outsourcing of Capital and Labor*, 40 Tex. Int'l L.J. 691 (2005) (roundtable discussion on the interrelationship of immigration and labor); Jennifer Gordon, *We Make the Road by Walking: Immigrant Workers, the Workplace Project, and the Struggle for Social Change*, 30 Harv. C.R.-C.L. L. Rev. 407 (1995) (discussing "growth of underground economy"); Jennifer Gordon, *Transnational Labor Citizenship*, 80 S. Cal. L. Rev. 503 (2007) (analyzing devices to address cross-border migration).

[66] *See* Golub, *supra* note 3, at 14.

[67] *See* Johnson, *supra* note 1, at 200–11.

C. THE PROBLEMS ENDEMIC OF CURRENT IMMIGRATION LAW AND ENFORCEMENT

The current U.S. immigration laws have many negative consequences, including those discussed below. In addition, the fairness and impartiality of the immigration bureaucracy has been consistently questioned.

1. Labor Exploitation

The current operation of the immigration laws has negative labor market consequences. Indeed, the large undocumented population harkens back to the days following the abolition of slavery in the United States, with a racial caste of workers in the secondary labor market. Indeed, there have been increasing reports of outright slavery and involuntary servitude of immigrants in the modern United States.[68] The new "Jim Crow" has undocumented immigrants working for low wages in poor conditions — and virtually unprotected by law — in one labor market with all others in a superior labor market.[69]

There are many other adverse consequences associated with the current immigration laws. Undocumented workers are exploited in the workplace[70] and lack basic legal rights.[71] Because many are people of color, the nation effectively has in place an exploitable racial caste labor market. This labor market operates outside of the confines of law, with undocumented workers receiving few legal protections and often working for low wages in poor conditions. More realistic immigration law and policy that allow labor migration could help dry up this secondary labor market and its exploitation of undocumented workers.

---

[68] *See* HUMAN RIGHTS CENTER (UNIVERSITY OF CALIFORNIA, BERKELEY), FREEDOM DENIED: FORCED LABOR IN CALIFORNIA 1 (2005); Free the Slaves & Human Rights Center of the University of California, *Hidden Slaves: Forced Labor in the United States*, 23 BERKELEY J. INT'L L. 47 (2005); Ellen L. Buckwalter, Maria Perinetti, Susan L. Pollet & Meredith S. Salvaggio, *Modern Day Slavery in Our Own Backyard*, 12 WM. & MARY WOMEN & L. 403 (2006).

[69] Leticia Saucedo has written on the "brown collar" workplace. *See* Leticia M. Saucedo, *Addressing Segregation in the Brown Collar Workplace: Toward a Solution for the Inexorable 100%*, 41 U. MICH. J.L. REF. 447 (2008); Leticia M. Saucedo, *The Browning of the American Workplace: Protecting Workers in Increasingly Latino-ized Occupations*, 80 NOTRE DAME L. REV. 303 (2004); Leticia Saucedo, *The Employer Preference for the Subservient Worker and the Making of the Brown Collar Workplace*, 67 OHIO ST. L.J. 961 (2006).

[70] *See* Maria L. Ontiveros, *To Help Those Most in Need: Undocumented Workers' Rights and Remedies Under Title VII*, 20 N.Y.U. REV. L. & SOC. CHANGE 607 (1993–94); Donna E. Young, *Working Across Borders: Global Restructuring and Women's Work*, 2001 UTAH L. REV. 1.

[71] *See, e.g.*, Hoffman Plastic Compounds, Inc v. NLRB, 535 U.S. 137 (2002) (holding that undocumented immigrant lacked full legal rights under federal labor law and was not entitled to reinstatement despite being unlawfully terminated for union organizing activities). For analysis and critique of *Hoffman Plastic, see*, for example, Christopher David Ruiz Cameron, *Borderline Decisions:* Hoffman Plastic Compounds, *the New Bracero Program, and the Supreme Court's Role in Making Federal Labor Policy*, 51 UCLA L. REV. 1 (2003); Robert I. Correales, *Did* Hoffman Plastic Compounds, Inc. *Produce Disposable Workers?*, 14 BERKELEY LA RAZA L.J. 10 (2003); Ruben J. Garcia, *Ghost Workers in an Interconnected World: Going Beyond the Dichotomies of Domestic Immigration and Labor Laws*, 36 U. MICH. J.L. REF. 737 (2003); Maria Pabón Lopez, *The Place of the Undocumented Worker in the United States Legal System After* Hoffman Plastics: *A Comparative Analysis*, 15 IND. INT'L & COMP. L. REV. 301 (2005); *Developments in the Law — Jobs and Borders*, 118 HARV. L. REV. 2171, 2224–47 (2005).

2.   Human Trafficking and Death on the Border

Evasion of the law by millions of undocumented immigrants has created highly organized networks.[72] In no small part due to tighter immigration enforcement, the trafficking of human beings today is big business and a growth industry, with its tentacles reaching across the entire United States. International criminal syndicates, which dominate the trafficking market, profit handsomely.

Human misery and death often directly result from human trafficking. Besides risking life and limb, some immigrants are effectively enslaved to pay off smuggling fees, with thousands of immigrant women forced into the sex industry and other exploitative labor relationships.[73] The trafficking of human beings — with its devastating impacts — flows immediately from heightened immigration enforcement. Recognizing these collateral impacts, Congress has passed laws in response to human trafficking. Nonetheless, the problem remains.[74]

3.   A Non-Responsive Immigration Bureaucracy

The immigration bureaucracy has long failed to respond to the needs of immigrants and frequently accused of being unfair and biased. The nation needs an immigration bureaucracy that effectively and efficiently enforces the law and commands the respect and confidence of the public. As discussed in Chapter 6, many currently lack respect and confidence in the agencies that enforce the immigration laws. The Immigration and Naturalization Service (INS), which until the spring of 2003 had primary responsibility for enforcing the immigration laws, had long been criticized as inefficient, arbitrary, and incompetent. The agency had a reputation among advocates as focusing almost exclusively on enforcement, not service.[75] Criticism of the incompetence of the INS understandably hit a fever pitch when the agency mailed visa renewals to two of the September 11 hijackers months after their deaths. This inexplicable administrative error contributed

---

[72] *See generally* Jennifer M. Chacón, *Misery and Myopia: Understanding the Failures of U.S. Efforts to Stop Human Trafficking*, 74 FORDHAM L. REV. 2977 (2006) (analyzing generally modern problem of trafficking of immigrants into the United States); Jayashri Srikianth, *Perfect Victims and Real Survivors: The Iconic Victim in Domestic Human Trafficking Law*, 87 B.U. L. REV. 157 (2007) (same).

[73] *See* Rosy Kandiathil, *Global Sex Trafficking Victims Protection Act of 2000: Legislative Responses to the Problem of Modern Slavery*, 12 MICH. J. GENDER & L. 87 (2005); Susan W. Tiefenbrun, *Sex Slavery in the United States and the Law Enacted to Stop it Here and Abroad*, 11 WM. & MARY J. WOMEN & L. 317 (2005); Susan W. Tiefenbrun, *The Domestic and International Impact of the U.S. Victims of Trafficking Protection Act of 2000: Does Law Deter Crime?*, 2 LOY. U. CHI. INT'L L. REV. 193 (2005).

[74] *See* Trafficking Victims Protection Act of 2000, Pub. L. No. 106-386, 114 Stat. 1464, 1466 (codified as amended at 22 U.S.C.§§ 7101–7110 (2000)); Trafficking Victims Protection Reauthorization Act of 2003, Pub. L. No. 108-93, 117 Stat. 2875 (2003).

[75] *See* Nancy Morawetz, *Understanding the Impact of the 1996 Deportation Laws and the Limited Scope of Proposed Reforms*, 113 HARV. L. REV. 1936, 1948–50 (2000); Margaret H. Taylor, *Promoting Legal Representation for Detained Aliens: Litigation and Administrative Reform*, 29 CONN. L. REV. 1647, 1698–1700 (1997). Because of the chronic problems in the administration of the immigration laws, the blue ribbon U.S. Commission for Immigration Reform, chaired by former Congresswoman Barbara Jordan, recommended major structural reforms to the U.S. immigration bureaucracy. *See* U.S. COMM'N FOR IMMIGRATION REFORM, BECOMING AN AMERICAN: IMMIGRATION AND IMMIGRANT POLICY 147–203 (1997).

significantly to the quick and successful congressional push to reorganize the immigration bureaucracy and for the creation of the Department of Homeland Security (DHS), which has assumed most of the U.S. government's immigration functions.[76]

The DHS, to this point, appears as enforcement-oriented as the old INS. This is not altogether surprising because the agency was created with the primary purpose to better protect "homeland security." Nor has there been any dramatic improvement in the efficiency of administrative operations with the dismantling of the INS.[77] Unless the DHS better balances its enforcement and service functions, pouring more and more resources into a dysfunctional agency is hardly likely to improve things. Specifically, increasing funding to add Border Patrol officers without significantly improving training is likely to make matters worse, not better.[78]

4.   The Need to Deregulate U.S. Immigration Law

A system that allows for easier migration of labor to the United States would likely decrease the incentive for circumventing the immigration laws. More liberal admissions grounds allowing workers and migrants who lack family members in

---

[76] *See Sensenbrenner Leading the Charge for Immediate INS Overhaul: Belated Visa Approval Notification for Sept. 11 Terrorists Has Congress Clamoring for Control of the Immigration Agency*, 60 CONG. Q. WEEKLY, Mar. 16, 2002, at 705.

[77] For criticism of the Department of Homeland Security's handling of immigration matters, *see* M. Isabel Medina, *Immigrants and the Government's War on Terrorism*, CENTENNIAL, 225, 230–32 (2006); *see also* Victor Romero, *Race, Immigration, and the Department of Homeland Security*, 19 ST. JOHN'S J. LEGAL COMM. 51, 52 (2004) (observing "that to the extent that the nation's immigration powers will be placed under the Department of Homeland Security suggests to me that any existing racial stereotypes regarding immigrants will be perpetuated rather than diminished. Put simply, post-9/11, the age-old stereotype of the foreign, Arab terrorist has been rekindled, and placing our immigration functions under the auspices of an executive department charged with 'homeland security' reinforces the stereotype of the 'immigrant as terrorist.' "); Thomas W. Donovan, *The American Immigration System: A Structural Change With a Different Emphasis*, 17 INT'L. J. REFUGEE L. 574 (2005) (recognizing added complaints of inefficiency arising from shift of immigration authority from Immigration & Naturalization Service (INS) to Department of Homeland Security); Noel L. Griswold, Note, *Forgetting the Melting Pot: An Analysis of the Department of Homeland Security Takeover of the INS*, 39 SUFFOLK U.L. REV. 207, 227–28 (2005) (arguing that shift from INS to Department of Homeland Security transformed immigration matters into national security issues); Jeffrey Manns, Legislation Comment, *Reorganization as a Substitute for Reform: The Abolition of INS*, 112 YALE L.J. 145 (2002) (asserting that reallocation of power from INS to DHS will refocus immigration priorities to national security concerns); *see also* Chacón, *supra* note 7, at 1884–88 (contending that current immigration and removal policies are counterproductive to making nation safer); Johnson & Trujillo, *supra* note 7, at 1396–1403 (arguing that the "war on terror" unfortunately came to dominate the much-needed national discussion of immigration reform).

[78] *See* Gabriela A. Gallegos, Comment, *Border Matters: Redefining the National Interest in U.S. Matters*, 92 CAL. L. REV. 1729, 1757–58 (2004) (stating that 1996 immigration reform law failed to ensure adequate training in light of "the Border Patrol's checkered history of abuse in the Southwest") (footnote omitted); Ruchir Patel, *Immigration Legislation Pursuant to Threats to US National Security*, 32 DENV. J. INT'L L. & POL'Y 83, 97 (2003) (criticizing USA PATRIOT Act for increasing Border Patrol agents but failing to ensure better training). The Border Patrol frequently has been accused of physically and otherwise abusing immigrants. *See* Johnson, *supra* note 50, at 222 nn.165–67 (citing authorities). *See generally* ALFREDO MIRANDÉ, GRINGO JUSTICE (1990 ed.) (analyzing how law, including immigration law, has been employed to subordinate persons of Mexican ancestry in the United States).

the United States, would be a good first step. With a more liberal immigration admission scheme, complex inquiries into migrants' family histories, incomes, and purposes for entering the country, could be made for the most part irrelevant to the U.S. government. Such inquiries today are the bread-and-butter of border enforcement officers' jobs and the bane of lengthy visa applications, consular officer interviews, immigration stops, and document checks.[79] More liberal admissions would allow for savings of time and effort in the vast majority of immigrant admissions, with finite resources better devoted to the relatively few cases involving serious criminal and terrorist activities — the very cases that deserve careful attention by a government seeking to protect the safety of its citizens in this troubled world.

Narrower exclusion grounds in the U.S. immigration laws would be more realistic than the current blanket exclusions that, for example, bar the immigration of poor and working people from the developing world, for no other reason than that they are poor and working people.[80] With relaxation of the exclusion grounds, the nation could devote scarce enforcement resources to efforts to bar the entry into the United States of criminals, terrorists, and other dangers to society. Such a true security and public safety emphasis would likely make the United States safer than the current unfocused enforcement emphasis that has pervaded U.S. border controls and their enforcement since the early twentieth century. *See* Chapter 2.

As seen in other areas of law enforcement, more focused immigration law enforcement has a greater likelihood of rooting out unlawful conduct than scattershot efforts that infringe on the civil rights of large numbers of people.[81] Racial profiling by police has done little to make the nation's streets safer and has alienated, angered, and injured the very communities whose cooperation is needed to effectively fight crime.[82] Racial profiling also has long been a problem of immigration enforcement.[83]

Immigration enforcement that is carefully crafted is less likely to frighten immigrant communities — the very communities whose assistance is essential if

---

[79] *See* STEPHEN H. LEGOMSKY, IMMIGRATION AND REFUGEE LAW AND POLICY 444–95 (4th ed. 2005) (summarizing immigration admission procedures).

[80] *See* Immigration & Nationality Act § 212(a)(4), 8 U.S.C. § 1182(a)(4) (providing that "[a]ny alien . . . likely at any time to become a public charge is inadmissible"). *See generally* KEVIN R. JOHNSON, THE "HUDDLED MASSES" MYTH: IMMIGRATION AND CIVIL RIGHTS 91–108 (2004) (analyzing history of excluding poor and working noncitizens from the United States). For statistics for fiscal year 2002 showing that the public charge exclusion was a substantive ground (as opposed to procedural grounds, such as an incomplete application, for example) frequently relied upon in denial of an immigrant visa by the State Department, *see* DEPARTMENT OF STATE, REPORT OF THE VISA OFFICE 2007 (2007), *available at* http://travel.state.gov/visa/frvi/statistics/statistics_4179.html.

[81] *See* Kevin R. Johnson, *U.S. Border Enforcement: Drugs, Migrants, and the Rule of Law*, 47 VILL. L. REV. 897, 912–15 (2002) (reviewing experience of U.S. Customs Service and its adoption of a policy limiting searches resulting in fewer searches and increased rate of searches finding contraband).

[82] *See* David A. Harris, *The Stories, the Statistics, and the Law: Why "Driving While Black" Matters*, 84 MINN. L. REV. 265, 298–300 (1999).

[83] *See, e.g.*, U.S. v. Lara-Garcia, 478 F.3d 1231 (10th Cir. 2007); Mancha v. Immigration and Customs Enforcement, 2007 U.S. Dist. LEXIS 89414 (N.D. Ga. Dec. 5, 2007); Commonwealth v. Lora, 451 Mass. 425 (2008). *See generally* Kevin R. Johnson, *The Case Against Race Profiling in Immigration Enforcement*, 78 WASH. U. L.Q. 675 (2000).

the United States truly seeks to successfully fight global terrorism. Unfortunately, the war on terror has almost undoubtedly chilled Arabs and Muslims living in the United States from cooperating with the government in counter-terrorism efforts.[84]

Most importantly, a system in which illegal migration is reduced would allow for improved tracking of all noncitizens entering and living in the United States. Currently, millions of undocumented immigrants live and work in this country, with little governmental knowledge about them. It is difficult to see how the existence of this huge "shadow population" could in any way be in the national interest. Nor is there any evidence that the U.S. government as a practical matter could end undocumented immigration under the current laws and remove all of the undocumented immigrants from the country.[85]

Reduction of the undocumented immigrant population in a meaningful way through enforcement of the immigration laws within the United States through removal seems highly unlikely. Despite record levels of deportations in the years since September 11, 2001.[86] officials at the highest levels of the U.S. government recognize that removal of all undocumented immigrants from the country is simply not possible. In 2004, Undersecretary of the Department of Homeland Security Asa Hutchinson candidly admitted that "it is 'not realistic' to think that law-enforcement authorities can arrest or deport the millions of illegal aliens now in the United States." He further stated that he "did not think that the American public has the 'will . . . to uproot' those aliens."[87] In 2006, President George W. Bush himself acknowledged that "[m]assive deportation of the people here is unrealistic. It's just not going to work."[88] The increased raids during the waning years of the Bush administration have not done much to reduce the undocumented population.

The costs of the massive deportation campaign needed to remove all undocumented immigrants from the United States would be astronomical. A 2005 study estimated that it would cost $41 billion a year for five years to fund a serious effort to remove all undocumented immigrants from the country. It further concluded that

> *While the net benefits of adopting such a policy are largely speculative,* we do know that spending $41 billion annually over five years ($206 billion in total) would:

---

[84] *See* Susan M. Akram & Kevin R. Johnson, *Race, Civil Rights, and Immigration Law After September 11, 2001: The Targeting of Arabs and Muslims*, 58 N.Y.U. ANN. SURV. AM. L. 295, 327–55 (2002).

[85] *See* JOHNSON, *supra* note 50, at 245–52.

[86] *See, e.g., Michael Chertoff Holds a Briefing on the Secure Border Initiative*, CQ TRANSCRIPTIONS (Aug. 23, 2006) (offering estimate that the U.S. government would engage in a record number of removals in the fiscal year).

[87] Jerry Seper, *Rounding Up All Illegals "Not Realistic,"* WASH. TIMES, Sept. 10, 2004, at A1 (quoting Hutchinson).

[88] Elisabeth Bumiller, *In Immigration Remarks, Bush Hints He Favors Senate Plan*, N.Y. TIMES, Apr. 25, 2006, at A22 (quoting President Bush) (emphasis added).

- Exceed the *entire* budget of the Department of Homeland Security for FY 2006 ($34.2 billion);
- Approach the *total* amount of money required by the 33 federal agencies responsible for homeland security activities for FY 2006 ($49.9 billion);
- *More than double* annual spending on border and transportation security ($19.3 billion);
- Comprise half the annual cost of the Iraq War ($74 billion); and
- *More than double* the annual cost of military operations in Afghanistan ($16.8 billion).[89]

In fashioning responses to the current immigration situation, it is important to keep in mind that only true comprehensive reform — not the incremental reform floated about in Congress — will likely minimize the tragic human costs resulting from immigration restrictions in the U.S. immigration laws and address the long term pressures for migration to the United States.

Some contend that incremental reform will not work and that bolder initiatives are necessary to cure the ills of U.S. immigration law. In that vein, more open borders have been analyzed.[90] In this era of globalization and an increasingly integrated world economy, the United States requires a system of immigration admissions that better comports with social, political, and economic factors contributing to immigration than the current broken system.[91] At a most fundamental level, the nation needs immigration laws that avoid the creation and re-creation of a large undocumented immigrant population. The history of failed border enforcement suggests that just adding more, and more, border enforcement simply will not work. Nor is it likely to improve the security of the nation.

One co-author has advocated a system in which prospective immigrants are presumed admissible unless they are found to pose a danger to national security and public safety.[92] This represents a reversal of the presumption in the current U.S. immigration laws that one cannot enter unless he or she shows that they fall into one of the categories for admission.[93]

---

[89] RAJEEV GOYLE & DAVID A. JAEGER, DEPORTING THE UNDOCUMENTED: A COST ASSESSMENT 2 (July 2005) (some emphasis in original) (some emphasis added).

[90] *See* JOHNSON, *supra* note 1; JASON RILEY, LET THEM IN: THE CASE FOR OPEN BORDERS (2008). SATVINDER JUSS, INTERNATIONAL MIGRATION AND GLOBAL JUSTICE (2006); TERESA HAYTER, OPEN BORDERS: THE CASE AGAINST IMMIGRATION CONTROLS (2d ed. 2004).

[91] *See* Walter A. Ewing, *From Denial to Acceptance: Effectively Regulating Immigration to the United States*, 16 STAN. L. & POL'Y REV. 445, 445 (2005) ("U.S. immigration policy is based on denial. Most lawmakers in the United States have largely embraced the process of economic 'globalization,' yet stubbornly refuse to acknowledge that migration, especially from developing nations to developed nations, is an integral and inevitable part of this process.").

[92] *See* JOHNSON, *supra* note 1, at 36–38.

[93] *See* Immigration & Nationality Act § 214(b), 8 U.S.C. § 1184(b) (presuming that every alien seeking admission to the Untied States is an immigrant, *i.e.*, a noncitizen who seeks to remain indefinitely); JOHNSON, *supra* note 1, at 54.

D.   A NORTH AMERICAN UNION? INCREASED ECONOMIC INTEGRATION OF CANADA, MEXICO, AND THE UNITED STATES

When the appropriate time comes, this nation hopefully will study the important issue of regularizing the flow of labor from Mexico into the United States. The North American Free Trade Agreement might be expanded to permit labor migration to mirror the free trade of goods and services among the member nations. One possibility — although it undoubtedly would be highly controversial — is a North American Union modeled on the European Union permitting labor migration among Canada, Mexico, and the United States.[94]

Some preliminary steps might need to be taken before the implementation of any kind of regional migration arrangement. One observer notes that the European Union invested billions of dollars in the infrastructure of new members, and argues that the United States must consider an economic adjustment strategy for Mexico to decrease migration pressures and allow for the possibility of more manageable, freer movement into the United States.[95] This is a possibility although foreign investment is not always popular in the United States.

It goes without saying that, in the modern world, free trade is much more prevalent than free migration.[96] At the tail end of the twentieth century, regional common markets gained popularity. Most nations perceived the economic benefits of more integrated economies but were reluctant to move from a restricted to a fully open scheme immediately. In several important instances, including the European

---

[94] *See* T. Alexander Aleinikoff, *Legal Immigration Reform: Toward Rationality and Equity, in* BLUEPRINTS FOR AN IDEAL LEGAL IMMIGRATION POLICY 5, 5–6 (Richard D. Lamm & Alan Simpson eds., 2001). For greater exploration of possible integration of the United States, Mexico, and Canada into a North American Union, *see* BILL ONG HING, ETHICAL BORDER: NAFTA, GLOBALIZATION, AND MEXICAN MIGRATION (forthcoming 2009); Robert A. Pastor, *The Future of North America: Replacing a Bad Neighbor Policy,* 87 FOR. AFF. 84 (2008); Stephen Zamora, *A Proposed North American Development Fund: The Next Phase of North American Integration Under NAFTA,* 40 LOY. U. CHI. L.J. 93 (2008); Naomi Gal-Or, *Labor Mobility Under NAFTA: Regulatory Policy Spearheading the Social Supplement to the International Trade Regime,* 15 ARIZ. J. INT'L & COMP. L. 365 (1998); Elizabeth L. Gunn, Note, *Regionalizing Labor Policy Through NAFTA: Beyond President Bush's Temporary Worker Proposal,* 28 B.C. INT'L & COMP. L. REV. 353 (2005); *see also* Jennifer Gordon, *Transnational Labor Citizenship,* 80 S. CAL. L. REV. 503 (2007) (envisioning freer labor migration between nations and more liberal notions of citizenship); M. Isabel Medina, *At the Border: What Tres Mujures Tell Us About Walls and Fences,* 10 J. GENDER, RACE & JUST. 245 (2007) (analyzing critically concept of discrete border between United States and Mexico); Ernesto Hernandez-Lopez, *Sovereignty Migrates in U.S. and Mexican Law: Transnational Influences in Plenary Power and Non-Intervention,* 40 VAND. J. TRANSNAT'L L. 1345 (2007) (noting that the United States and Mexico have been acting in increasingly transnational ways with respect to migration); Katie E. Chachere, *Keeping America Competitive: A Multilateral Approach to Illegal Immigration Reform,* 49 S. TEX. L. REV. 659 (2008) (contending that United States must work with other nations on immigration). *See generally* L. RONALD SCHEMAN, GREATER AMERICA: A NEW PARTNERSHIP FOR THE AMERICAS IN THE TWENTY-FIRST CENTURY (2003) (advocating generally greater cooperation between nations in the Americas); THE FUTURE OF NORTH AMERICAN INTEGRATION: BEYOND NAFTA (Peter Hakim & Robert E. Litan eds., 2002) (analyzing integration of North America).

[95] *See* Timothy A. Canova, *Closing the Border and Opening the Door: Mobility, Adjustment, and the Sequencing of Reform,* 5 GEO. J. L. PUB. POL'Y 341 (2007).

[96] *See* PAUL R. KRUGMAN & MAURICE OBSTFELD, INTERNATIONAL ECONOMICS: THEORY AND POLICY 177–78 (3d ed. 1994).

Union, labor migration between the member nations evolved out of increased trade of goods and services.

1.   The European Union

The most well-known example of a regional migration system exists in Europe, which shares certain historical, cultural, political, and social commonalities with North America. After gaining experience with the free trade of goods and services, the member nations of the European Union (EU) concluded that the economic benefits of easy labor migration would, as a whole, also benefit the member states.[97] Today, labor migration is generally permitted within the EU nations. Although much-feared, the elimination of border controls between the member nations proved to be relatively pain-free. Indeed, the great success of the European Union has contributed to its potential expansion — other nations want in on a good thing. Compare the relative value of the Euro with the American dollar to see the economic benefits experienced by the EU. Consequently, in the future, the EU may be joined by as many as ten new members.[98]

As a testament to its success, the European Union model is being imitated. Several regions of Northern Europe, South America, and Africa have allowed, or are considering allowing, relatively freer migration between member states.[99] In certain regions, racial, ethnic, class, and cultural differences between citizens of different nations — even neighbors — may make such arrangements difficult. However, the fact that such arrangements are even being floated for consideration shows that globalization is beginning to triumph over a world of insular nations and closed borders.

2.   The Political Feasibility of a Regional Arrangement

At least initially, regional migration arrangements, such as the one that exists in much of Europe, represent a more politically viable alternative — at least in the first instance — to completely open borders.[100] Under such an arrangement, free trade of goods and services would be accompanied by labor migration between nations within a designated region. Because regional arrangements only develop with the consent of sovereign nation-states, national sovereignty is respected. As a purely practical matter, it is far easier to obtain popular consent for (or acquiescence to) regional arrangements because the people in the region are more likely to share important cultural and racial commonalities and have experience interacting with each other. For similar reasons, regional arrangements have been advocated as a politically viable alternative to the current system for admitting

---

[97] *See* Randall Hansen, *Migration to Europe Since 1945: Its History and Its Lessons*, Pol. Q., 2005, at 25.

[98] *See* Keith B. Richburg, *The EU and the Power of the People*, Wash. Post, Nov. 8, 2002, at A27.

[99] *See* Larry Rohter, *South American Trading Bloc Frees Movement of Its People*, N.Y. Times, Nov. 24, 2002, at § 1, p. 6.

[100] *See* Roger Nett, *The Civil Right We Are Not Ready For: The Right of Free Movement of People on the Face of the Earth*, 81 Ethics 212, 227 (1971).

refugees to the United States, with nations allowing for the resettlement of refugees facing persecution in nearby nations.[101]

Under a regional arrangement, nations allow the resettlement of refugees facing persecution in nearby nations. Allowing for regional migration tends to ameliorate fears of opening the "floodgates" to immigrants discussed earlier in this Chapter. Because a regional arrangement only provides entry to more "local" immigrants, it offers the appearance of more control over the numbers of migrants coming into a nation. In addition, greater racial and cultural homogeneity among populations in a region would tend to moderate opposition to a regional refugee resettlement plan.

Less controversial than open borders, a regional migration pact may be the most feasible solution to the United States's perceived immigration woes. Even so, such an agreement would not come easily.[102] The U.S. government adamantly opposed even discussing the issue of immigration between the United States, Canada, and Mexico while forming the North American Free Trade Agreement in the early 1990s. Although concern with Mexican migration continues to flourish in the United States, over the long haul, the tripartite trading relationship holds the potential for evolving into a European Union-like labor migration relationship.[103]

The nations of North America have increasingly worked together on migration-related issues in recent years. Canada and the United States have increasingly cooperated with respect to migration controls in recent years.[104] The United States and Canada, in 2002, entered into an agreement involving refugees and cooperation on a variety of immigration measures designed to tighten security after September 11, 2001. This shows the willingness on the part of two North American nations to work together on immigration issues.[105]

Similarly, over the course of the twentieth century, the United States and Mexico developed an increasingly closer economic and political relationship.[106] In fact, the U.S. government has even enlisted Mexico to aid on this nation's border

---

[101] See James C. Hathaway, *A Reconsideration of the Underlying Premise of Refugee Law*, 31 HARV. INT'L L.J. 129 (1990).

[102] See supra note 26 (citing authorities).

[103] See JASON ACKLESON, ACHIEVING "SECURITY AND PROSPERITY"; MIGRATION AND NORTH AMERICAN ECONOMIC INTEGRATION (Immigration Policy Center, Feb. 2006) Aleinikoff, *supra* note 94, at 5–6; Kevin R. Johnson, *Free Trade and Closed Borders: NAFTA and Mexican Immigration to the United States*, 27 U.C. DAVIS L. REV. 937 (1994); John A. Scanlan, *A View From the United States-Social, Economic, and Legal Change, the Persistence of the State, and Immigration Policy in the Coming Century*, 2 IND. J. GLOBAL LEGAL STUD. 79, 123–25 (1994); Gallegos, *supra* note 78; Gunn, *supra* note 94.

[104] See Johnson & Trujillo, *supra* note 7, at 1391–92.

[105] See Agreement for Cooperation in the Examination of Refugee Status Claims from Nationals of Third Countries, Aug. 30, 2002, U.S.-Canada at http://www.cic.gc.ca/english/policy/safe-third.html, last visited Aug. 22, 2006; Audrey Macklin, *Disappointing Refugees: Reflections on the Canada-U.S. Safe Third Country Agreement*, 36 COLUM. HUM. RTS. L. REV. 365 (2005); *see also* Special ABA Committee Report on the Canada-U.S. Border: Balancing Trade, Security, and Migrant Rights in the Post-9/11 Era: ABA Immigration and Nationality Committee, International Law Section, 19 GEO. IMMIGR. L.J. 199 (2004) (discussing increased cooperation between the United States and Canada on migration issues).

[106] See Johnson & Trujillo, *supra* note 7, at 1391–92.

enforcement efforts.[107] To this end, the Mexican government, at the behest of the U.S. government, has taken steps to limit Central Americans from traveling through Mexico in route to this country.[108] The burgeoning relationship between the two neighboring nations creates the potential for future cooperation on migration issues well beyond simply fighting crime and drug trafficking in the border region.[109]

In recent years, the highest levels of the U.S. and Mexican governments have discussed possible bilateral measures addressing migration between the two states. This represents a sharp turnaround from the early 1990s, when NAFTA's approval hinged on *not* addressing immigration.[110] Only days before September 11, 2001, an agreement to regularize migration between the United States and Mexico appeared to be on the immediate horizon. Unfortunately, the migration pact under discussion never came to fruition. Serious consideration of this option ceased on September 11, 2001.[111]

In 2005, after a hiatus of several years following the events of September 11, the United States and Mexico again began to discuss migration between the two nations.[112] However, serious barriers remain in the United States. The antipathy for immigrants — especially those from Mexico, *see* Chapter 2 — in the United States, and concern with "opening the floodgates" to mass migration, remain major stumbling blocks. The diversity of peoples in North America and economic disparities between the United States and Mexico militate against a regional migration pact.[113] To make matters worse, Congress has consistently increased border enforcement along the United States's southern frontier.[114]

In 2005, the United States, Canada, and Mexico embarked on the Security and Prosperity Partnership of North America to work on common economic and

---

[107] *See* CONGRESSIONAL RESEARCH SERVICE, MEXICO-UNITED STATES DIALOGUE ON MIGRATION AND BORDER ISSUES, 2001–2005 (UPDATED JUNE 2, 2005); CONGRESSIONAL RESEARCH SERVICE, MEXICO'S IMPORTANCE AND MULTIPLE RELATIONSHIPS WITH THE UNITED STATES (Jan. 18, 2006); Elizabeth A. Whitaker, *U.S. Governments Efforts With Mexico to Address Immigration Issues*, Testimony before the House International Relations Committee, *available at* http://www.state.gov/p/wha/rls/rm/2006/69604.htm.

[108] *See* Steven W. Bender, *Sight, Sound, and Stereotype: The War on Terrorism and Its Consequences for Latinas/os*, 81 OR. L. REV. 1153, 1161–64 (2002); Bruce Zagaris, *International Criminal and Enforcement Cooperation in the Americas in the Wake of Integration: A Post-NAFTA Transition Period Analysis with Special Attention to Investigating in Mexico*, 3 SW. J.L. & TRADE AM. 1, 51–54 (1996).

[109] *See* Alan D. Bersin, *El Tercer Pais: Reinventing the U.S./Mexico Border*, 48 STAN. L. REV. 1413 (1996).

[110] *See* JOHNSON, *supra* note 1, at 957–59; *see* Kevin R. Johnson, *An Essay on Immigration, Citizenship, and U.S./Mexico Relations: The Tale of Two Treaties*, 5 SW. J. L. & TRADE AM. 121, 130–34 (1998) (discussing "NAFTA's Avoidance of Immigration").

[111] *See* Johnson, *supra* note 32, at 866–67.

[112] *See* David Stout, *Bush and Neighbors Promise to Cooperate*, INT'L HERALD TRIB., Mar. 24, 2005, at 5.

[113] One could in an optimistic vein, point to the fact that the EU has allowed member nations to join that are as relatively poor as Mexico is to the United States. *See* JOHNSON, *supra* note 1, at 28–30.

[114] *See* CONGRESSIONAL RESEARCH SERV., MEXICO-U.S. RELATIONS: ISSUES FOR THE 109TH CONGRESS 8–13 (updated June 2, 2005).

security issues.[115] This increased cooperation may help facilitate collaboration on economic matters including labor and migration issues common to the three nations.

3. The Costs of a Regional Migration Arrangement

Despite their political advantages, regional regimes are not cost-free. Regional blocs almost necessarily lead to border fortifications at the outer perimeter of the community of nations. The problems inherent in any system of border controls are therefore shifted from national to regional boundaries. With internal controls between the EU member nations eased, border controls were erected around the EU's outer perimeter to keep noncitizens from outside the Union from entering.[116] The result was the creation of the so-called "Fortress Europe."[117] The border controls were designed in no small part to thwart a mass migration from Northern Africa into France and Germany. As a condition of EU membership, Spain created its first comprehensive immigration law and greatly limited migration from North Africa.[118]

Fortress Europe's external border controls have led to problems similar to those resulting from the United State's system of closed borders. Due to the borders at its external frontier that are designed to bar the entry of migrants from the developing world, the EU has experienced problems with racial discrimination and sporadic nativist outbursts.[119] It has also seen increased undocumented immigration.[120]

With aggressive enforcement of the borders at the perimeter of the common market, EU border enforcement has human costs that are strikingly similar to

---

[115] *See* Johnson & Trujillo, *supra* note 7, at 1391–92; Jason Ackelson & Justin Kastner, Routinizing Cooperation and Changing Narratives: The Security and Prosperity Partnership of North America (June 2006); Jason Ackleson & Justin Kastner, The Security and Prosperity Partnership of North America (Dec. 2005); Greg Anderson & Christopher Sands, Negotiating North American: The Security and Prosperity Partnership (Hudson Institute White Paper 2007); Alexander Moens with Michael Cost, Saving the North American Security and Prosperity Partnership: The Case for a North American Standards and Regulatory Area C. Frasier Inst., 2008); Emily Gilbert, *Leaky Borders and Solid Citizens: Governing Security, Prosperity and Quality of Life in a North American Partnership*, Antipode, at 77 (2007).

[116] *See* Kevin R. Johnson, *Regional Integration in North America and Europe: Lessons About Civil Rights and Equal Citizenship*, 9 U. Miami Int'l & Comp. L. Rev. 33, 40–43 (2000–01); *see also* López, *supra* note 10, at 586–89.

[117] *See* Johnson, *supra* note 1, at 162–63.

[118] *See* Kitty Calavita, *Immigration, Law, and Marginalization in a Global Economy: Notes From Spain*, 32 Law & Soc'y Rev. 529, 542–48 (1998). *See generally* Kitty Cavalita, Immigrants at the Margins: Law, Race, and Exclusion in Southern Europe (2005).

[119] *See* Bob Hepple, *Race and Law in Fortress Europe*, 67 Mod. L. Rev. 1 (2004); Lydia Esteve Gonzalez & Richard MacBride, *Fortress Europe: Fear of Immigration? Present and Future of Immigration Law and Policy in Spain*, 6 U.C. Davis J. Int'l L. & Pol'y 153 (2000). *See generally* Christian Joppke, Selecting by Origin: Ethnic Migration in the Liberal State (2005).

[120] *See* Michael A. Becker, Note, *Managing Diversity in the European Union: Inclusive European Citizenship and Third-Country Nationals*, 7 Yale Hum. Rts. & Dev. L.J. 132 (2004); Aristides Diaz-Pedrosa, Note, *A Tale of Competing Policies: The Creation of Havens for Illegal Immigrants and the Black Market Economy*, 37 Cornell Int'l L.J. 431 (2004).

those seen in the United States. Migrants to Europe face similar perils as those facing undocumented Mexican immigrants attempting to enter the United States. Like Mexican migrants, undocumented migrants to Europe seek to evade border fortifications by making a hazardous journey across the Mediterranean Sea. Migrants from North Africa who successfully migrate, encounter increased discrimination, at times, even violence, for example.[121]

The problems experienced with the emergence of Fortress Europe demonstrates why regional arrangements are a second-best alternative to more generally open and liberal immigration admissions systems. With its regional arrangement, the costs of closed borders do not completely disappear but are shifted to the outer boundaries of the regional arrangement. As a political matter, however, it is far easier to build popular support for smaller scale migration plans than for an immediate move to a comprehensive system of liberal admissions.

4.   A Possible North American Union?

In the end, the signals are decidedly mixed as to whether there will be any kind of U.S./Mexico migration agreement in the near future. Indeed, as the discussion of a possible agreement with Mexico fell by the wayside after September 11, Congress has moved in the opposite direction. In 2005, Congress bolstered border enforcement with the REAL ID Act.[122] It then considered much more enforcement-oriented proposals. Congress, and the public, continues to fear opening the floodgates to Mexican migration and wants to do everything it can to shut the door. As discussed previously, terrorism added fuel to the fire, and the U.S. government has used the "war on terror" to justify efforts to bolster the U.S./ Mexico border.

Nonetheless, there are signs that, in the long run, some kind of migration accord will be reached between the United States and Mexico. Both Mexico and the United States have much at stake in continued labor migration between the two nations. The Mexican economy annually receives billions of dollars in remittances from Mexican nationals living and working in the United States.[123] It needs these

---

[121] *See* Johnson, *supra* note 116, at 42–43; Manuel Caro, *Tying Racism in El Ejido To Spanish and European Politics*, 54 Rutgers L. Rev. 893, 897–902 (2002); Jane E. Larson, *Class, Economics, and Social Rights*, 54 Rutgers L. Rev. 831, 833–37 (2002); Maria Pabón López, *Immigration Law Spanish-Style: A Study of Spain's Normalización of Undocumented Workers*, 21 Geo. Immigr. L.J. 571, 591–93 (2007).

[122] *See* REAL ID Act of 2005, Title B of the Emergency Supplemental Appropriations Act for Defense, the Global War on Terror, and Tsunami Relief, 2005, 109 Pub. L. No. 12, 119 Stat. 231 (2005).

[123] *See* Jorge A. Vargas, *U.S. Border Patrol Abuses, Undocumented Mexican Workers, and International Human Rights*, 2 San Diego Int'l L.J. 1, 80 (2001) (mentioning the importance of billions of dollars of remittances to Mexico from immigrants in the United States); *see also* Matthew C. Wilson, *The Economic Causes and Consequences of Mexican Immigration to the United States*, 84 Denv. U.L. Rev. 1099, 1118–20 (2007) (discussing the consequences of remittances from the United States to Mexico); Alexander C. O'Neill, Note, *Emigrant Remittances: Policies to Increase Inflows and Maximize Benefits*, 9 Ind. J. Global Legal Stud. 345 (2001) (analyzing the importance of remittances from migrants to developing countries to fund economic development); Victoria Lehrfeld, Comment, *Patterns of Migration: The Revolving Door From Western Mexico to California and Back Again*, 8 La Raza L.J. 209, 245–50 (1995) (studying the flow of money from United States to Mexico).

resources to subsidize economic growth and dampen political unrest. Mexico thus has much to gain by ensuring that its citizens have access to jobs, that the risk of labor exploitation is reduced, and that migrants are able to secure a more durable immigration status than that held by undocumented immigrants.[124]

At the same time, the U.S. economy benefits handsomely from immigrant labor, particularly in the service, agriculture, and other low skill, labor-intensive industries.[125] Many sectors of the U.S. economy, such as the agricultural, construction, and service industries rely heavily on undocumented labor. This reliance has been built over generations and is unlikely to end with mere changes to the law.[126] Absent a radical restructuring of the U.S. economy, immigration policy must take the reliance of certain sectors on immigrant labor into account.

Ultimately, the key ingredient to significantly reducing migration from Mexico is economic growth in Mexico.[127] Policies that foster this growth are likely to diminish migration pressures. However, economic growth is a painfully slow process. Moreover, it is not clear if there is political will in the United States to invest in Mexico.

Free migration among the North American Free Trade Agreement nations would be in keeping with certain existing political, economic, and social realities. Labor integration between the United States and Mexico is occurring. Market forces have driven U.S. employers and Mexican workers in this direction for years. Immigration law has been a minor hindrance to immigrants and employers but has not been an effective deterrent to unlawful conduct. Efforts to bar the employment of undocumented workers have been largely ineffective. Employer sanctions have not been consistently and effectively enforced.[128] Certain industries in the United States, such as those in the agriculture, construction, and many service industries rely on the type of low wage labor provided by immigrants. Unlike other industries, which have increasingly moved operations overseas to exploit low wage labor, jobs in these industries cannot be exported. Low wage immigrant labor therefore will likely remain essential to the American economy.

---

[124] The Mexican government's interest in protecting migrant labor in the United States thus is not solely humanitarian; increasing wages and benefits for Mexican migrants also increases remittances to Mexico. *See* Richard Griswold del Castillo, *Mexican Intellectuals' Perception of Mexican Americans and Chicanos, 1920-Present*, 27 AZTLÁN 33, 49 (2002); Xinying Chi, Note, *Challenging Managed Temporary Labor Migration as a Model for Rights and Development for Labor-Sending Countries*, 40 N.Y.U. J. INT'L L. & POL. 497, 505–06 (2008); Deanna Ford, *Tapping the Development Potential of Migration Through MFIs*, 12 GEO. PUB. POL'Y REV. 11, 11–14 (2006); Lehrfeld, *supra* note 123, at 245–250.

[125] *See* JOHNSON, *supra* note 1, at 131–67.

[126] *See* Cornelius, *supra* note 44, at 668–69.

[127] *See* U.S. COMM'N FOR THE STUDY OF INT'L MIGRATION AND COOPERATIVE ECON. DEV., UNAUTHORIZED MIGRATION: AN ECONOMIC DEVELOPMENT RESPONSE (1990); Philip L. Martin, *Economic Integration and Migration: The Case of NAFTA*, 3 UCLA J. INT'L L. & FOREIGN AFF. 419 (1998).

[128] *See supra* note 47 (citing authorities).

E.   CONCLUSION: THE FUTURE OF U.S. IMMIGRATION LAW

The future of U.S. immigration law is difficult to predict. Incremental reform appears most likely in the short run, with some kind of legalization, guest worker, and enforcement programs possible. A regional arrangement appears more likely to be a mid to long-term possibility in North America.

TABLE OF CASES

[References are to pages]

[References are to pages]

[References are to pages]

[References are to pages]

[References are to pages]

[References are to pages]

TABLE OF CASES

[References are to pages]

INDEX

[References are to pages.]

A

[References are to pages.]

[References are to pages.]

[References are to pages.]

[References are to pages.]

[References are to pages.]

[References are to pages.]

[References are to pages.]

[References are to pages.]

[References are to pages.]

[References are to pages.]

[References are to pages.]

[References are to pages.]

[References are to pages.]

[References are to pages.]

[References are to pages.]